INSIDERS

MW01046322

INSIDERS' GUIDE® TO
NEW ORLEANS

THIRD EDITION

BECKY RETZ AND JAMES GAFFNEY

INSIDERS' GUIDE®

GUILFORD, CONNECTICUT
AN IMPRINT OF THE GLOBE PEQUOT PRESS

The prices and rates in this guidebook were confirmed
at press time. We recommend, however, that you call
establishments before traveling to obtain current information.

To buy books in quantity for corporate use
or incentives, call **(800) 962–0973, ext. 4551**,
or e-mail **premiums@GlobePequot.com**.

INSIDERS' GUIDE®

Text design by LeAnna Weller Smith
Maps by XNR Productions, Inc © The Globe
Pequot Press

ISSN: 1543-8686
ISBN: 0-7627-3456-6

Manufactured in the United States of America
Third Edition/First Printing

Cities of the Dead. NEW ORLEANS METROPOLITAN CONVEN-
TION & VISITORS BUREAU, INC./ANN PURCELL

St. Louis Cathedral. NEW ORLEANS METROPOLITAN CONVENTION & VISITORS BUREAU, INC./CARL PURCELL

Audubon Park Fountain. NEW ORLEANS METROPOLITAN CONVENTION & VISITORS BUREAU, INC./RICHARD NOWITZ

[Top] *Mardi Gras.* NEW ORLEANS METROPOLITAN CONVENTION & VISITORS BUREAU, INC./JEFF STROUT
[Bottom] *Mardi Gras.* NEW ORLEANS METROPOLITAN CONVENTION & VISITORS BUREAU, INC./ROMNEY CARUSO

Jazz Fest. NEW ORLEANS METROPOLITAN CONVENTION & VISITORS BUREAU, INC./CARL PURCELL

New Orleans Museum of Art. NEW ORLEANS METROPOLITAN CONVENTION & VISITORS BUREAU, INC./CARL PURCELL

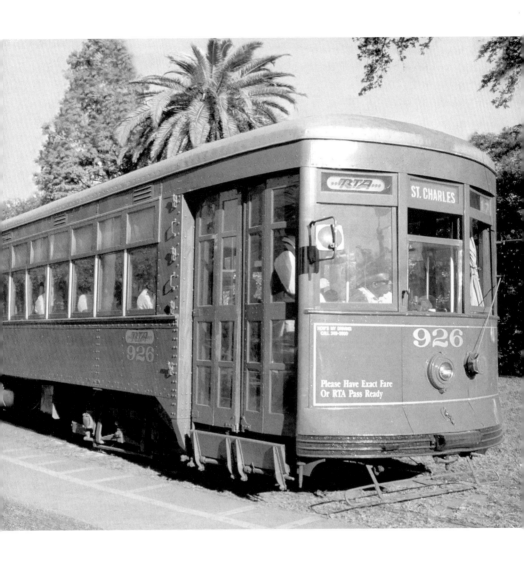

St. Charles Avenue Streetcar. NEW ORLEANS METROPOLITAN CONVENTION & VISITORS BUREAU, INC./HARRY COSTNER

Royal Cafe. NEW ORLEANS METROPOLITAN CONVENTION & VISITORS BUREAU, INC./CARL PURCELL

French Quarter. NEW ORLEANS METROPOLITAN CONVENTION & VISITORS BUREAU, INC./RICHARD NOWITZ

[Top] *Nottoway Plantation Home.* NEW ORLEANS METROPOLITAN CONVENTION & VISITORS BUREAU, INC./RICHARD NOWITZ
[Bottom] *Oak Alley Plantation.* NEW ORLEANS METROPOLITAN CONVENTION & VISITORS BUREAU, INC./RICHARD NOWITZ

Cornstalk Hotel. NEW ORLEANS METROPOLITAN CONVENTION & VISITORS BUREAU, INC./RICHARD NOWITZ

[Top] *Acme Oyster House.* NEW ORLEANS METROPOLITAN CONVENTION & VISITORS BUREAU, INC./RICHARD NOWITZ
[Bottom] *Commander's Palace.* NEW ORLEANS METROPOLITAN CONVENTION & VISITORS BUREAU, INC./RICHARD NOWITZ

French market seafood vendor. NEW ORLEANS METROPOLITAN CONVENTION & VISITORS BUREAU, INC./CARL PURCELL

Desire. NEW ORLEANS METROPOLITAN CONVENTION & VISITORS BUREAU, INC./RICHARD NOWITZ

CONTENTS

CONTENTS

Directory of Maps

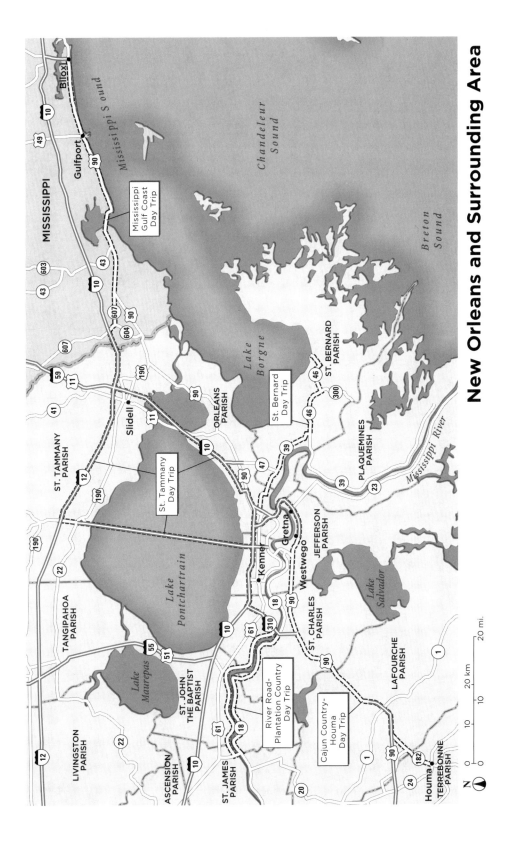

New Orleans and Surrounding Area

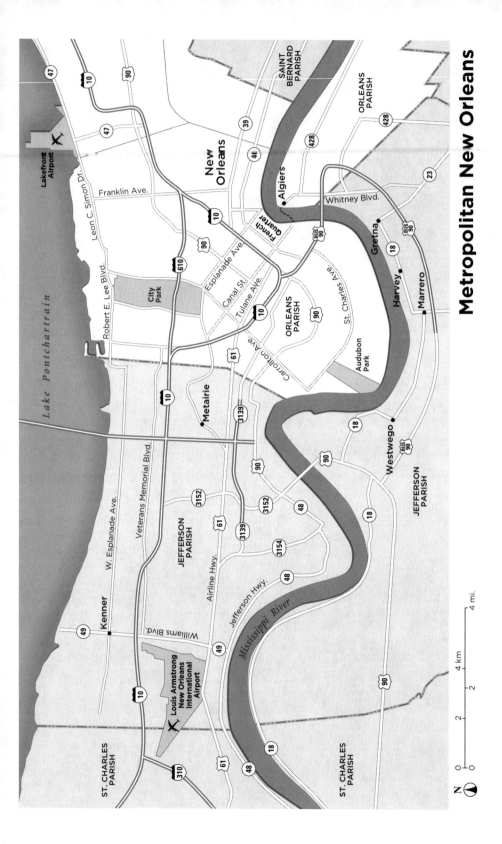

Metropolitan New Orleans

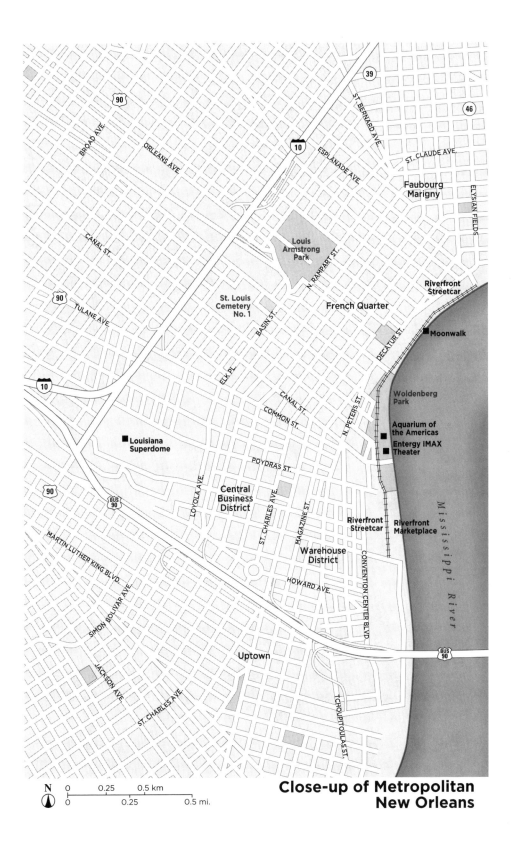

Close-up of Metropolitan New Orleans

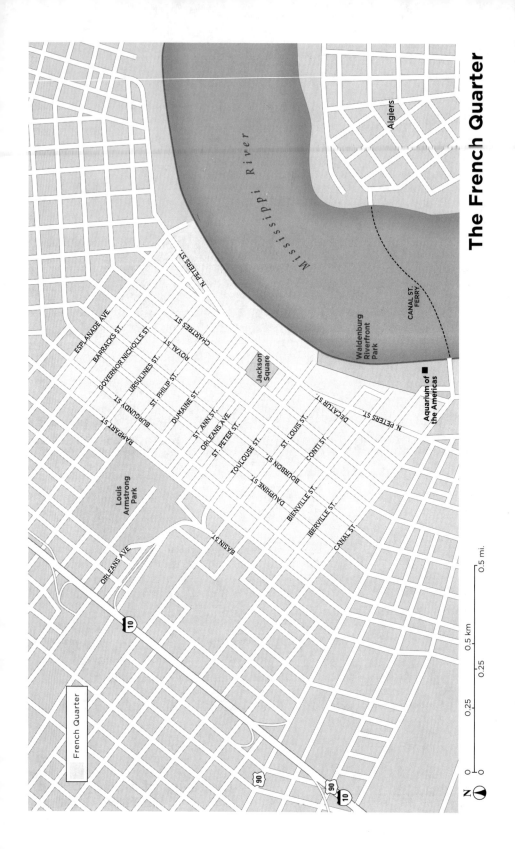

The French Quarter

Algiers

Mississippi River

CANAL ST. FERRY

N. PETERS ST.

ESPLANADE AVE.

BARRACKS ST.

GOVERNOR NICHOLLS ST.

URSULINES ST.

ST. PHILIP ST.

DUMAINE ST.

ST. ANN ST.

ORLEANS AVE.

ST. PETER ST.

TOULOUSE ST.

ST. LOUIS ST.

CONTI ST.

BIENVILLE ST.

IBERVILLE ST.

CANAL ST.

ROYAL ST.

CHARTRES ST.

DAUPHINE ST.

BOURBON ST.

DECATUR ST.

N. PETERS ST.

RAMPART ST.

BURGUNDY ST.

BASIN ST.

ORLEANS AVE.

Jackson Square

Waldenburg Riverfront Park

Aquarium of the Americas

Louis Armstrong Park

French Quarter

10

90

90

10

N

0   0.25   0.5 km
⊢———┴———┴———⊣
        0.25   0.5 mi.
0 ⊢———┴———⊣

PREFACE

New Orleans is a fiercely independent riverport and cultural island of good-natured people, rumbling streetcars, midnight mystery, courtyard romance, and simple pleasures. In fact, a city with this much color, historic architecture, oak-framed greenspaces, and renowned dining might be expected to be five times its size. But it's exactly this small-town compactness mixed with big-city possibilities that makes exploring this one-of-a-kind destination a pleasure—and a wise choice—for visitors.

Welcome to New Orleans.

Natives and transplants alike say New Orleans is hard to shake once it gets into your blood—which helps explain why most locals never leave and why so many who do wind up coming back. Compared with most other cities, coming to the Big Easy is like arriving at Oz—everything changes from humdrum sepia tones to vivid living color. Novice and seasoned globe-trotters alike agree that New Orleans is among the most exciting and unique places in the world. It's hard to disagree after seeing this remarkably diverse city through the eyes of a visitor while pulling duty as informal tour guide for out-of-town friends and family. They marvel at the genuine warmth of the people, the aromas of its restaurant kitchens, and the richness of its multicultural heritage. This is not a city to be taken for granted.

Perhaps movies, TV, and other media have shaped your impressions of New Orleans. If so, you might have been led to think of this crown jewel of the Mississippi River as barely more than a nonstop party town in which Mardi Gras thrives 365 days a year and everyone speaks with Cajun accents. This couldn't be further from the truth. More so than ever, New Orleans is a sophisticated, cosmopolitan city rolling into the 21st century firmly rooted in its multiethnic tradition of devotion to family, religion, education, community, and hard work. And this 300-year-old child of the swamps has governed itself this way far longer than many places in the United States. If anything, the city's renowned joie de vivre is the result of our appreciation for the fragility of life, having weathered over the centuries numerous cataclysmic disasters, not the least of which are hurricanes, yellow fever epidemics, and the Saints losing a Super Bowl play-off slot.

No matter how you slice the French bread, America should consider itself fortunate to count New Orleans as one of the top honeymoon hot spots and international tourism destinations in the world. As a convention town the Big Easy is second to none. If the city seems to bring a bounty of blessings to the national table, it's due largely to the effortless charm and indefatigable spirit of centuries-old Creole pride still evident in the people who call it home.

As for the nuts and bolts: The introduction in each chapter is designed to give readers a lay of the land, while Insider's tips—look for the **i**—will help visitors better navigate behind the scenes. Close-ups highlight aspects of the city that merit special attention. If you're a newcomer, the back chapters of the book deal with specific relocation concerns, such as real estate, child care, education, health care, media, and worship. If you have comments or questions about anything you read in *Insiders' Guide to New Orleans,* please feel free to write the publisher at: The Globe Pequot Press, P.O. Box 480, Guilford, CT 06437-0480. Or visit the Web site at www.GlobePequot .com. Happy reading!

ACKNOWLEDGMENTS

There are a number of people without whose help this book would never have been written. I'd like to thank Beverly Gianna with the New Orleans Metropolitan Convention and Visitors Bureau, who provided many good leads and even more good photos; the folks at the Louisiana Office of Tourism; and Victor Andrews, without whose technical assistance there would be no authors' photos in this book. I'd also like to express my gratitude to my mentors, Will Peneguy and Ed Tunstall, without whose encouragement writing may have simply become something I always wished I had done; to my co-author, Jim Gaffney, for his talent in both writing and editing, and for the times he made my work read better than I wrote it; and to Globe Pequot editor Julie Gribbins for making the editing process such a pleasure.

Personally, I'd like to thank Chris, Roslyn, Mike, Robbie, Lisa, Danny, Suzi, Janet, Greg, Michael, David, Melissa, Maggie, Maddie, Jessica, Brandon, Kyle, Diane, Alice, Sally, Michael, Eddie, and Ben for being the kind of family that I feel blessed to be a part of. I am also eternally grateful to my sister and friend Roslyn Milligan for her words of wisdom and her ability to make me laugh when I start taking things too seriously. Finally, I want to thank Chris "Stockpile" Fremin for being the kind of person any mother would be proud to call her son and for allowing me to be a part of his inspiring artistic evolution.
—Becky Retz

A flame of eternal gratitude flickers in this author's window for his wife, Cathy Jacob Gaffney, a tireless proofreader, critic, and, ultimately, one-person cheering section throughout the research and writing phases of this update. Thank you for being a blessing in my life and for your unflinching faith in my ability to reach a goal.

Another individual instrumental in this endeavor is my coauthor and colleague Becky Retz, to whom I owe a world of thanks for recommending me for this project all those years ago. Others include historian William de Marigny Hyland, for teaching me the stories of the Islenos of lower St. Bernard Parish; Beverly Gianna of the New Orleans Metropolitan Convention and Visitors Bureau, for always being there to help; Leonard J. Hansen, my mentor and colleague, for his support, encouragement, and guidance through the years; and the editors at Globe Pequot Press, for an excellent job editing the chapters.

Finally, I would like to thank the spirit of travel discovery that lives within us all.
—James Gaffney

HOW TO USE THIS BOOK

First, here's how *not* to use this book. A couple of years ago during Carnival, a woman was observed walking down Bourbon Street, which, at the time, was crowded with thousands of masked revelers—many dancing, others unabashedly trading flashes of flesh for trinkets thrown from balconies. There she strode, this woman, oblivious to the human sea of color and laughter surrounding her because she never once glanced up from her guidebook.

Don't do that.

HOW THIS BOOK IS ORGANIZED

Insiders' Guide to New Orleans follows a simple format. There's a Preface just to say "Where y'at?" (New Orleans-ese for "How do you do?") and a series of chapters designed to help you get acquainted with the city in order to make that upcoming visit the exceptional experience it should be. The Getting Here, Getting Around chapter offers the nuts and bolts of transportation—except, of course, what time your plane leaves. (Although we do tell you whom to call to find out.)

Like all unflinchingly peerless destinations, New Orleans has a long history peppered with fascinating people and their memorable stories. Read all about it as the History and Overview chapters unfold the tales of where we've been and where we are, respectively.

Need a place to stay? New Orleans has everything from swank chrome-and-glass high-rise hotels to charming antebellum inns decorated with antiques, the best of which can be found arranged alphabetically in Hotels and Bed-and-Breakfast Inns.

(If you're looking for a campground, check Parks and Recreation.)

Now that we've got you settled in, the first thing you'll want to do is eat. Trust us. It's hard to find a bad meal in the Big Easy, but for the best locales check out Restaurants, listed alphabetically by area, to find out where New Orleanians go for the city's best jambalaya, gumbo, oyster po-boys, barbecue shrimp, and bread pudding, to name but a few indigenous delicacies.

For visitors with the right attitude, New Orleans is synonymous with fun. And if this city stands to teach you anything about what makes good cheer flow, we recommend memorizing the Nightlife text and working your way slowly to the head of the class. The next morning when you come to—er, wake up—check out the Attractions chapter, listed by categories, to discover exactly where we've got a whole lotta shakin' going on during daylight hours. If traveling to New Orleans with youngsters, God love 'ya, you'll be in need of Kidstuff. For convenience, Kidstuff activities are also listed in Attractions—except, of course, those that no rational adult would opt for without rug rats in tow.

Feeling the need for a little soul cleansing? The chapter on Worship has everything a visitor needs to know about local denominations but was afraid to ask. The Arts, Parks and Recreation, Spectator Sports, and Day Trips are designed to help visitors sample some of the city's best fun as well as cultural and outdoor offerings.

Those planning to call New Orleans home, meantime, can get their compass bearings by checking out the chapters on Relocation, Retirement, Health Care and Wellness, Education, and Media.

OTHER USES
FOR THE BOOK

Other practical ways to use this book include: as gift wrapping for two plane tickets tucked between the pages (this idea has more meaning if the tickets are to New Orleans); giving a separate copy to each friend that you missed while you were away with circles around the places that reminded you of them; or sticking it underneath a table leg to stop an annoying wobble. Just remember, the important first stop in all of these plans is: Buy the book and buy often.

AREA OVERVIEW

Grace, it might be said, is one of those elusive conventions of human existence created to explain that odd composure of the soul when it encounters a moment of near perfection. New Orleans, it might also be said, is a city of such grace. Eccentric. Serene. Self-possessed. Quixotic. Irrepressible. All the while it is easy on the eyes, has a good heart and a sense of humor, roots for the underdog, never forgets to ask how your mama's doing, and loves you just the way you are. Sounds like the perfect date.

This riverport checkerboard of working-class neighborhoods, middle-class enclaves, and Uptown society tumbles through life with the motto "Let the good times roll" and enjoys itself with more exuberance than just about any other place on Earth. While this is a predominately Catholic city steeped in religious tradition, it's also liberally mixed with a history of equal devotion to carefree pleasures best exemplified by the world's greatest free show on earth—Mardi Gras. For proof just hang out with festivalgoers on oak-lined St. Charles Avenue during a nighttime Carnival parade, as colorfully costumed float riders toss doubloons, panties, and plastic beads to a jubilant crowd shouting, "Throw me something, mister!" You'll get the picture.

For this and other reasons, the unsavory parallels of the outside real world, such as abstinence (except during Lent) and dispatch (unless we're hosting a World's Fair or major national convention), hold little interest. Instead, the newspaper obits are scanned daily so as not to miss paying last respects at a wake for even a distant relative or acquaintance. We trundle the kiddies off to City Park for a ride on the historic carousel's flying horses or to Bayou St. John to feed the ducks—just because we did the same thing when we were youngsters. And because this loosen-the-tie town has never cottoned to stuffy

formalities, kids are taught early on to respect grown-ups by addressing them as, say, Miss Judy or Mister George. Last names are reserved for strangers.

This is a city of neighborhoods—and what neighborhoods. Uptown, for example, has its old money, stately oaks, Greek Revival and Italianate homes, streetcars, Tulane and Loyola Universities, Audubon Park and Zoo—not to mention the quasi-bohemian ambience of Magazine Street and its vintage clothing stores, antiques shops, art galleries, and restaurants. For proof just take an Uptown streetcar downtown past St. Charles Avenue's Garden District of drop-dead gorgeous mansions built by no-nonsense Americans arriving in the 19th century who wanted little to do with their freewheeling Creole counterparts in the French Quarter. You'll get the picture.

Meantime, the French Quarter bordering the Mississippi River is anchored by Jackson Square's sidewalk artists and palm readers, St. Louis Cathedral, paddle wheelers, Lucky Dog vendors, Royal Street antiques shops, the buzz of Bourbon Street, the French Market, and, of course, Cafe du Monde. Step inside one of the Quarter's historic, candlelit courtyards crumbling with history and lush with banana palms and fiery-red bougainvillea to discover why 19th-century aristocratic Creoles couldn't care less about the standoffish American newcomers Uptown.

Over the centuries the world's great rivers have given birth to great cities, and this Mississippi River offspring—a wondrous amalgam born of French, Spanish, African, and Caribbean cultures—is certainly no exception. Simply put, it's nearly impossible to pigeonhole this spirited, offbeat city. Just look at the nicknames given to New Orleans over the years: the Crescent City, the City that Care Forgot, the Big Easy, the Cradle of Jazz, America's

 **AREA OVERVIEW**

New Orleans Vital Statistics

Nickname: Big Easy, Crescent City

Mayor/Governor: New Orleans: Mayor Ray Nagin
Louisiana: Governor Kathleen Blanco

Major cities: Baton Rouge (State Capital), New Orleans, Lafayette, Shreveport

Population: Orleans Parish: 476,492
Jefferson Parish: 451,459
St. Bernard Parish: 66,486

Area (sq. miles): 365

Average temperatures (hi/lo): July, 81/72°F

Average temperatures (hi/lo): January, 63/44°F

Average days of sunshine: 216

New Orleans founded: 1718

Louisiana founded: U.S. purchased Louisiana Territory in 1803; Louisiana statehood April 1812.

Major universities: Tulane, Loyola, Xavier, University of New Orleans, Dillard, Southern University of New Orleans.

Important dates in history:
1682—French explorer La Salle erects a cross at the mouth of Mississippi River and names the territory Louisiana after the King of France.
1718—Jean Baptiste Lemoyne and other Frenchmen lay out the streets and found La Nouvelle Orleans (New Orleans).
1762—New Orleans becomes a Spanish colony by the signing of the Treaty of Fontainebleau.
1788—The Great Fire destroys 856 houses, including the cathedral where the St. Louis Cathedral stands today.
1794—St. Louis Cathedral construction begins.
1801—After the death of one Spanish governor and the rapid succession of two more, Louisiana is ceded back to the French in the Secret Treaty of St. Illdefonso.
1803—Napoleon I cedes Louisiana to the United States for the sum of $8 million francs. This sale becomes known as the Louisiana Purchase. William C. C. Claiborne and General James Wilkinson take possession of the Louisiana Territory at New Orleans in the name of the United States.
1812—Louisiana admitted to the Union as the 18th state.
1814–1815—British forces place New Orleans under siege. General Andrew Jackson defeats the British in the final action at the Battle of New Orleans, effectively ending the War of 1812.
1831—Cholera epidemic strikes New Orleans, killing 6,000 people in just 20 days.
1831—The United States Mint is built in New Orleans. It will make money from 1838 to 1862 and 1879 to 1910.
1838—The first Mardi Gras parade in New Orleans.
1850—Place d'Armes officially renamed Jackson Square.

1861—The state of Louisiana secedes from the Union as the Civil War gets under way.

1865—Louisiana returns to the Union as the Civil War comes to a close.

1967—The city buys an NFL expansion franchise: the New Orleans Saints.

1975—The Superdome is completed and opened for its first game in August, to the tune of $161 million and seating for up to 87,000 fans.

1984—The Louisiana world exposition.

1988—New Orleans hosts the Republican National Convention.

Major area employers: Oil and gas, health care, education, convention/tourism.

Famous locals: Jean Baptiste le Moyne, Sieur de Bienville/Jean Lafitte, Louis Armstrong, Truman Capote, Antoine "Fats" Domino, Anne Rice, Paul Prudhomme, Emeril Lagasse, Harry Connick Jr., Mahalia Jackson, the Neville Brothers (Aaron, Art, Charles, and Cyril), Wynton and Branford Marsalis, Bryant and Greg Gumbel, Dr. John (Malcom John Reben-nack Jr.), Buddy Bolden, "Jelly Roll" Morton, and Andrew Young.

City holidays: Mardi Gras, All Saints' Day

Toll roads: Crescent City Connection and Causeway Bridge

Major interstates: Interstate 10

Major airports: Louis Armstrong New Orleans International Airport

Public transportation: Regional Transit Authority (for buses and streetcars)

Military bases: Belle Chasse Naval Station

Alcohol laws: 21; can buy on Sunday; no closing law on how late bars are open; alcohol is available in supermarkets.

Daily newspapers: *The Times Picayune*

Sales tax: 9 percent

Room tax: 13 percent (+$1.00–$3.00, depending on size of hotel)

most European city, Banana Republic, and the northernmost island in the Caribbean. New Orleans is also the birthplace of Creole cuisine and home to one of professional football's losingest teams. For the record, this colorful city also has green streetcars and red beans and rice.

Ties that bind in this overgrown small town include where you went to high school, potholed streets, Christmastime's Mr. Bingle, cafe au lait, and the sweat-defining summertime humidity. New Orleans cherishes its homegrown chefs much the same way Boston embraces its MIT math geniuses and L.A. its celluloid heroes. Writers ranging from William Faulkner and Tennessee Williams to John Kennedy Toole and Anne Rice have trawled the city's secret soul to hold up a mirror of words as poignant as anything Pablo Neruda ever wrote about his Chilean homeland. As Williams's character Blanche DuBois observes in *A Streetcar Named Desire:* "Don't you just love these long rainy afternoons in New Orleans when an hour isn't just an hour—but a little piece of eternity dropped into your hands . . . and who knows what to do with it?"

TUNE TOWN

In New Orleans music is everywhere there's a crowd, from Mardi Gras parades and seasonal festivals to nightclubs, jazz funerals, and Bourbon Street sidewalks.

Take your pick—zydeco, gospel, rhythm and blues, rock, salsa. Traditional jazz also is alive and well, thanks largely to the ranks of both older and younger musicians following the improvisational spirit of local pioneers Buddy Bolden, Sidney Bechet, Louis Armstrong, Joseph "King" Oliver, and Jelly Roll Morton, to name but a few. A host of avant-garde and modern jazz masters, including Alvin Batiste, Earl Turbinton, and Edward "Kid" Jordan, continue to push the musical envelope. One of New Orleans's premier musical families is headed by pianist Ellis Marsalis and includes sons Wynton (who won two Grammys for best jazz and classical recordings in 1984), former *Tonight Show* bandleader Branford, and younger brothers Delfeayo and Jason. Listen to the Neville Brothers perform live and experience firsthand how four of the city's best-known ambassadors of the distinctive New Orleans sound fuse funk, soul, and rhythm and blues into an irresistible match made in heaven. The Big Easy can also brag that it was the home of Mahalia Jackson, Al Hirt, Pete Fountain, Louis Prima, the Dixie Cups, and Harry Connick Jr.

Rhythm and blues, too, found a spiritual home in New Orleans when native-born Antoine "Fats" Domino (who still lives here) topped the charts in the 1950s. And if artists such as Irma Thomas, Clarence "Frogman" Henry, Allen Toussaint, Dr. John, and Marcia Ball ring a bell, it's because these award-winning native Louisianians can still be found gracing popular local venues like Tipitina's, Snug Harbor, Cafe Brasil, House of Blues, Jimmy's, and Howlin' Wolf. Gospel tips the heavenly scales with such nationally celebrated groups as the Zion Harmonizers and the 60-member Gospel Soul Children. Zydeco and Cajun bands offer up two-stepping music at Mulate's, Michaul's, and the Maple Leaf Bar. Rafter-shaking home-grown rock bands such as the Radiators and Cowboy Mouth also make the local rounds when not on national tours. Add to this mix the city's pulsating Latin music scene headed by the likes of Los Babies

del Merengue, Ruben "Mr. Salsa" Gonzales, and the Iguanas. As New Orleans rhythm and blues artist Ernie K-Doe once mused, "I'm not sure, but I'm almost positive that all music came from New Orleans." Either way, the city's legendary musicians past and present have lavished the Big Easy with a hip soul and a rhythmic heart that beats in time with the angels. Amen.

FOOD NATION

It's a safe bet you will roux the day you first tasted a perfectly seasoned crawfish étouffée in New Orleans. Dining in this self-styled Food Nation has always been, at its best, a social occasion and at its worst, an obsession. Jealous outsiders, including researchers at the Centers for Disease Control, have suggested that our love affair with food has resulted in waistlines with more spare tires than a junkyard and the life expectancy of a chicken at an Ozzy concert. To which we respond: "Shaddup and pass da' Tabasco."

Sure, many locals lean on the fat and sassy side. But, if the truth be told, New Orleanians are hardly the craven clutch of artery-clogged, gumbo-lapping night-crawlers many nutritionists make us out to be. Still, where else in the world do people gather for a meal and rhapsodize about what they last ate (and where) and what they plan to eat next (and where)? Pull up a chair with locals at a Friday-night seafood blowout during Lent and marvel as hands blur while the pile of empty crawfish tails assumes Mt. McKinley heights. Initiate yourself with the tradition of dunking freshly baked French bread in the spicy melted buttah that bathes a dozen jumbo barbecued shrimp. See what we mean?

We compare notes and swap tales of dining lore with a thirst for detail that makes many locals walking food encyclopedias. New Orleans can't help it if the city is flavored by more than its share of nationally acclaimed culinary wizards—for example, Paul Prudhomme, Leah Chase, Emeril Lagasse, and Susan Spicer. Plus, it's impossible not to be seduced by the city's multicultural menu of French, African, Cajun, Caribbean, and Spanish cooking traditions (with flourishes added by German, Irish, and Italian immigrants). At the drop of a hat, we pull up our socks to head to one of the city's old-line Creole institutions like Galatoire's or go as we are for a megaburger chowfest at a neighborhood eatery like Port of Call. We're blessed with lots of both.

Signature recipes range from andouille gumbo, sausage and chicken jambalaya, and crawfish bisque to sauce piquante, oysters Rockefeller and oysters Bienville, red beans and rice, courtbouillon, and muffuletta sandwiches. And we've barely warmed up the cast-iron skillet. To turn salivary glands into water slides just add deep-fried shrimp po-boys, oysters on the half shell, soft-shell crab, and fresh fish from local waters served more ways than you can shake a net at. The Ferdie sandwich at Mother's and hamburgers and mocha shakes from Camellia Grill are among our favorites. And no adult worth his or her culinary chops would be caught dead without at least a passing familiarity with menus at some of the city's heralded fine-dining establishments like Commander's Palace, Antoine's, Galatoire's, the Grill Room, and the Pelican Club.

BEWITCHED AND BETWEEN

The "Isle d'Orleans" (as Napoleon called it) is strangely different than other U.S. and Southern cities. "You don't sound like a Southerner" is one of the most overheard comments made by newcomers to locals. That is because the only people here who have Southern accents are usually visitors from other Southern states. New Orleans speech inflections, especially in working-class neighborhoods, are more Brooklynese. Still, the city possesses its own vocabulary: "Lagniappe" (LAN-yap), for example, is "a little something extra", while a praline (PRAW-leen) is a bonbon of

pecans browned in sugar. Order your po-boy (a huge French-loaf sandwich split down the middle and filled with meat or seafood) "dressed" if you want lettuce, tomato, and mayonnaise. Sidewalks are often called "banquettes," and "neutral grounds" are called medians everywhere else in the country. Grocery shopping is referred to as "making groceries," balconies are called galleries, gris-gris (GREE-GREE) is a voodoo charm, a cold drink is a soda, the Vieux Carre is the French Quarter, and Mardi Gras organizations are called krewes (pronounced just like "crews"). Red beans and rice is a popular Monday dish dating back to when homemakers slow-cooked this simple food on wash day. Snow cones are called snowballs and come in a gadzillion flavors (in New Orleans you can order yours topped with ice cream or, better yet, condensed milk).

The first thing you'll notice when you fly into New Orleans is how the town is built on a crescent—hence the moniker Crescent City—of the 2,350-mile Mississippi River, referred to as "the lawless stream" by Mark Twain in his book *Life on the Mississippi*. Second, swamps surround the city. In fact, an estimated 20 percent of the city's 365 square miles is unreclaimed swamp. If you find it odd that this "port city" is 102 miles from the Gulf of Mexico, so be it. New Orleans sits about 6 feet below sea level and, as a result of the high water table, is the only U.S. city to bury its dead in aboveground tombs. One of our "cities of the dead" is a former horse race track, and the tombs are arranged in the elliptical pattern of the original track. The late historian Mel Levitt, dean of New Orleans's TV news commentators, once estimated that New Orleans had roughly 3,000 bars, 41 cemeteries, and 700 churches of various denominations. Because New Orleans didn't have a zoning law until 1930, some visitors are shocked to see all three—saloon, church, and restaurant—on the same block. Locals find a certain efficiency to the arrangement, though. Another by-product of the city's low elevation and high water table are the numerous (and inescapable) pot-holes. City workers seem to have a devil of a time keeping up with repairs.

What else makes New Orleans unique? Insomniacs, nightcrawlers, conventioneers, all-purpose partygoers, and would-be vampires alike love this city partly because it's the only one in the country besides Las Vegas without a closing law. Many bars and some restaurants are open round the clock. How much of this is due to the fact that Louisiana was once a French colony and governed as a foreign province for almost 100 years under French and Span-ish rule—or the fact that this is the only state that still bases its civil law on Roman (rather than Anglo-Saxon) law, practicing the Napoleonic Code? Not much.

WEATHER OR NOT YOU COME

Bring an umbrella, especially if you plan to visit this city of one million residents dur-ing the hottest, most humid, and stickiest time of the year, which usually runs from May to September. Summer months in particular can torment even the most stalwart visitor accustomed to Central American jungles. And consider yourself forewarned: Hell hath no fury like New Orleans in August, so if you plan to visit during this unbearable month—good luck. Just walk outdoors and wait for the nanosecond it takes for your eyeglasses to steam over. Fortunately, the occasionally heavy afternoon thunderstorms during peak summer months sometimes help cool things down; at other times they make New Orleans feel like a megasauna. Visi-tors soon come to understand why New Orleanians move a little slower (it's a life-saving strategy) and usually toward the nearest air conditioner. Winter months are mild, if not a little damp, compared with the rest of the country, but it's not uncom-mon for Santa to show up in Bermuda shorts and a tank top. Mid- to late-October and early spring—when temperatures are extremely pleasant—consistently draw rave reviews from locals and visitors alike.

In many ways the city is like a big family—tight-knit, full of warmth, occa-sionally given to infighting, and often leery of outsiders. New Orleanians are among the most genuine and friendly persons encountered anywhere in the world. We are generous to a fault. After all, the word "lagniappe," meaning a little something extra, is part of the city's vocabulary. And like any family we bristle when misguided souls "from not here" mouth off about one of our foibles or idiosyncrasies. We're well aware of our shortcomings, thank you very much.

Once a lag-behind city, the Big Easy today has big dreams for the future. Evi-dence can be found in Six Flags New Orleans theme park, Harrah's casino, the 300,000-square-foot phase III addition to the Ernest N. Morial Convention Center, plus the 18,500-seat New Orleans Arena (adjacent to the Louisiana Superdome) for basketball and hockey games, Zephyr Field for AAA baseball (see Spectator Sports), and the Ogden Museum of Southern Art. Other additions include the D Day Museum, the Maya-themed Jaguar Jungle exhibit at Audubon Zoo, the interactive Pacific Coast Adventures exhibit at the Aquarium of the Americas ("feel the spray from an orca's blowhole"), plus new river barge excursions. Plans currently under way include the Audubon Institute's 30,000-square-foot insectarium, the Warehouse District's Art-Works showcase for Louisiana visual artists, and new hotel construction.

Year-round Old Testament-like plagues of cockroaches, termites, and mosquitoes still drive us crazy. But this is a city with a streak of kindness a mile wide. Simply put, New Orleans takes care of its own and gossips about them later. It understands the sliding-trombone poetry of a jazz funeral on a drizzly afternoon, as well as the long-gone echo of raucous ragtime and lusty laughter from a palm-flanked Storyville courtyard. Say what you will about New Orleans. This will always be a city where wild dreams slow-dance in the moon shadows till the sun comes up and the red azaleas look red once more.

GETTING HERE, GETTING AROUND

etting around a city like New Orleans—where the West Bank just across the Mississippi River is actually south of the city, and South Carrollton and South Claiborne Avenues meet—can be a challenge for anyone with a logical mind.

First, never expect a local to give directions in terms of north, south, east, and west. The city just doesn't work that way. New Orleans follows a bend in the Mississippi River (thus its Crescent City moniker), and so, too, do its streets. Directions are generally given in terms of Uptown, Downtown, the river, and the lake. It's confusing, but you'll get the hang of it—in about five years.

This chapter should help. Plus, New Orleanians are generally very friendly and happy to help visitors find their way. Just ask.

GETTING TO NEW ORLEANS

The Airport

Louis Armstrong New Orleans International Airport (www.flymsy.com) is located about 12 miles outside the city in Kenner.

AIRLINES

Passenger airlines serving New Orleans include:

Air Canada
(888) 247-2262
www.aircanada.ca

AirTran
(800) 247-8726
www.airtran.com

America West Airlines
(800) 235-9292
www.americawest.com

American Airlines
(800) 433-7300
www.aa.com

Continental Airlines
(800) 523-3273
www.continental.com

Delta Airlines
(800) 221-1212
ww.delta.com

Frontier Airlines
(800) 432-1359
www.frontierairlines.com

JetBlue Airways
(800) 538-2583
www.jetblue.com

Northwest/KLM
(800) 225-2525
www.nwa.com

Southwest Airlines
(800) 435-9792
www.iflyswa.com

Flying your own plane into town? Then you'll be headed for New Orleans Lakefront Airport. The airport, in New Orleans on the shore of Lake Pontchartrain, offers full maintenance service for both jet and propeller aircraft and helicopters, aircraft parking, and flight training. Call Aviaport customer service at (504) 242-9496.

The Louis Armstrong New Orleans International Airport was originally named after aviator John Moisant, who died here. While competing in a 1910 contest, Moisant hit turbulence, crashing in a stockyard. Today, the only reminder of Moisant is the airport code "MSY" on baggage tickets. "M" is for Moisant, and although nobody's certain, some believe "SY" is for "stockyard."

Taca
(800) 535-8780
www.grupotaca.com

United Airlines
(800) 241-6522
www.ual.com

US Airways
(800) 428-4322
www.usairways.com

From the Airport

TAXIS

The set rate for a ride from Louis Armstrong New Orleans International Airport to downtown New Orleans is $28 for up to two people or $12 per person for three or more. Pickup is on the lower level outside baggage claim.

AIRPORT SHUTTLE SERVICE

A one-way ticket downtown costs $13 (as does the return trip), with a three-bag-per-person limit. Pickup and ticket purchases are made on the lower level outside baggage claim. Call (504) 522-3500 or toll-free (866) 596-2699.

JEFFERSON TRANSIT (PUBLIC BUS)

This is by far the best deal. Only $1.50 gets you from the airport to Elk Place in the middle of the downtown Central Business District. Look for the Airline Drive bus outside Entrance #7 at the airport's upper level. It leaves every 15 to 20 minutes on weekdays and every 30 minutes on weekends. The trip may take up to an hour.

GREYHOUND

You can pick up a Greyhound bus on the upper level outside Entrance #7. Tickets are purchased from the driver. For fares and schedules call (800) 231-2222 or (504) 525-9371.

CAR RENTAL

A number of car rental agencies are located on the airport terminal's lower level, with several more nearby. They are:

Alamo
(504) 469-0532
www.alamo.com

Avis
(504) 464-9511
www.avis.com

Budget
(504) 467-2277, (800) 527-7000
rent.drivebudget.com

Enterprise
(800) 261-7331
www.enterprise.com

Hertz
(504) 469-0532
www.hertz.com

National
(504) 466-4335
www.nationalcar.com

Thrifty
(504) 463-0800
www.thrifty.com

PARKING

The airport has 3,000 short-term and 2,500 long-term parking spaces. Rates are $2.00 for the first hour, $2.00 each additional half hour, and $10.00 to $15.00 per day; $17.00 per day for valet parking. All cars entering the parking area are subject to search.

Trains and Interstate Buses

It's easy to catch a train or bus in New Orleans because there's only one place to do it—the downtown Union Passenger Terminal (at the end of Loyola Avenue near the Superdome), home to Amtrak and Greyhound.

Amtrak
Union Passenger Terminal
1001 Loyola Avenue, New Orleans
(800) 872-7245
www.amtrak.com
Amtrak offers three major lines through New Orleans: The City of New Orleans runs between the Big Easy and Chicago; the daily Crescent heads east, chugging all the way to New York via Washington, D.C.; and the Sunset Limited passes through New Orleans on its way from Los Angeles to Orlando, Florida.

Greyhound
Union Passenger Terminal
1001 Loyola Avenue, New Orleans
(504) 524-7571, (800) 231-2222
www.greyhound.com
If you want to leave the driving to Greyhound, also make your way to Union Passenger Terminal. The ticket office is open 24 hours. Call for schedules.

GETTING AROUND

OK, so now you're in the city. Have no fear, New Orleans is a pretty easy city to get around in once you learn the lay of the land. For traveling purposes, you will mostly be concerned with a few main areas of the city: Downtown, Uptown, and, to a lesser extent, the Lakefront. (There

are a few outlying areas you may want to visit, and directions are provided with those individual listings.)

Parts of Town

Downtown covers the Central Business District, the Warehouse District, the French Quarter, and Faubourg Marigny. Uptown encompasses the Garden District, with all those beautiful St. Charles Avenue mansions, the University area, and the Riverbend. The Lakefront is the northern-most part of the city, located on Lake Pontchartrain. It is also where you'll find City Park.

The best part is that you can get to and from these areas without getting on the expressway (I-10), which has a tendency to back up at any given hour.

FRENCH QUARTER

What is now known as the French Quarter was the original city of New Orleans. It is a relatively small area on the Mississippi River. The French Quarter is 7 blocks "wide" from the Mississippi River to Rampart Street (so named for the wall, or "rampart," built to protect the fledgling city from Indian attacks) and 15 blocks "front to back" from Canal Street to Esplanade Avenue. This is one of the few parts of the city where the streets are laid out in a proper grid, with loads of interesting shops, restaurants, and art galleries and wonderful street performers. When walking around, stay on the beaten path, especially at night. Although New Orleans has seen a decrease in crime during recent years, it's still one of our biggest

When setting off on a French Quarter stroll, take along a pocket full of dollar bills with which to tip street performers. They are a major part of the French Quarter's charm, and you'll definitely get your money's worth.

You may call it a highway or freeway where you come from, but here people say "expressway"—and it always refers to Interstate 10.

headaches. Just stick with the (sober) crowds and you should be fine.

FAUBOURG MARIGNY

Right "behind" the French Quarter (just downriver) is Faubourg Marigny, a funky little bohemian neighborhood that is almost an extension of the Quarter. There are good places to hear live music there.

CENTRAL BUSINESS DISTRICT (CBD)

At the "front" (just upriver) of the French Quarter is Canal Street, which marks the edge of the Central Business District. Though Canal is still considered the city's main street, most of the bigger businesses moved to Poydras Street long ago. The three biggest streets to know for getting around downtown are Canal and Poydras Streets and Tulane Avenue. All three run parallel to one another and perpendicular to the Mississippi River. Also note that street names change at Canal Street. For example, after Carondelet Street crosses Canal Street, it becomes Bourbon Street in the French Quarter.

THE WAREHOUSE DISTRICT

The Warehouse District is adjacent to the Central Business District and is basically indistinguishable from it, save for all those art galleries, New York designer stores,

Although lovable in many respects, New Orleanians are notoriously bad drivers. Watch out for people running red lights, turning or changing lanes without signaling, and exhibiting particularly slow reaction time.

and chichi digs in converted textile mills, replete with doorpersons and valet parking, overlooking the Mississippi River. This is the newest hip place to live for the young professional with a penchant for dressing in black and smoking gold-tipped Russian cigarettes.

UPTOWN

Uptown is upriver from Downtown. Got that? Its main and by far most beautiful street is St. Charles Avenue, which runs from noisy Canal Street through the congested Central Business District and Warehouse District, all the way down the lap of luxury known as the Garden District, to the Riverbend. All roads Uptown lead to St. Charles Avenue. Confused as to which one is St. Charles? Just follow the streetcar. Or, better yet, ride it.

It's hard to miss St. Charles Avenue's Garden District mansions and university area, the latter so named because it is home to both Loyola and Tulane Universities, around the 6000 block. Directly across The Avenue (as St. Charles is often referred to because it really is all that) from the universities is Audubon Park, nearby the must-see Audubon Zoo. Don't walk through the park after dark.

A few blocks past the universities, St. Charles Avenue ends at the Riverbend. As the street, like the river, bends (hence the Riverbend name) it becomes Carrollton Avenue. If you like, you can drive down Carrollton all the way to City Park; the St. Charles streetcar line, however, ends before it.

THE LAKEFRONT

You may want to visit the Lakefront. Its West End boasts good, mostly down-home seafood restaurants, while the nearby shore of Lake Pontchartrain is a quiet, uncrowded area in which to relax. To get to the Lakefront from Downtown, take Canal Street away (northwest) from the Mississippi River. The street dead-ends, as it were, at Greenwood Cemetery. (The cemetery was built in an early attempt at urban planning to keep the city from growing any larger. Don't ask.) Take the dogleg—a right and immediate left—around the cemetery. You are now on Canal Boulevard, which can be taken all the way to the lake. To get to West End, take Canal Boulevard to Robert E. Lee Boulevard. Turn left and then right at the next stop light—Pontchartrain Boulevard.

That should basically get you around the city. There are a couple of outlying areas you may want to visit. You may have noticed that rather than counties, Louisiana is divided into parishes. Orleans Parish is made up of the City of New Orleans and a small area on the west bank of the Mississippi River called Algiers. On either side of Orleans Parish—on both the east and west banks—is Jefferson Parish.

EAST JEFFERSON

East Jefferson, which includes Metairie (where the Zephyrs play) and Kenner (where the airport is), is best accessed by taking I-10 west. Yes, you take I-10 west to get to East Jefferson. Go figure. If traveling during peak traffic hours, it may be easier to take Airline Drive, which may well qualify as the least scenic route in America. Before I-10 was built, Airline Highway was the main road to Baton Rouge.

After the interstate was built, Airline Highway fell to pot. Local government recently tried to polish up the highway's tarnished image by changing a stretch of its name to Airline Drive, though they might have done better by first ridding this depressing thoroughfare of its tumbledown motels, hookers, biker bars, hubcap shops, and tattoo parlors. *C'est la vie.* What's important to know is that Airline—highway, drive, *whatever*—takes you on a straight shot from Downtown to New Orleans International Airport in Kenner. This is where Jimmy Swaggart got in trouble. Just remember: Friends don't let friends solicit prostitutes.

International visitors who want to take advantage of the state's tax-free shopping program can turn in their refund paperwork (obtained from participating merchants at the checkout counter) before they leave town at the Tax Free Shopping office in Louis Armstrong New Orleans International Airport.

WEST JEFFERSON

There are two ways to get to West Jefferson, better known as the West Bank. There is a ferry landing where Canal Street meets the Mississippi River. The ferry goes to Algiers Point. The Canal Street Ferry costs $1.00 per car and is free for pedestrians. This is a really nice ride at night and offers a great view of the city. It's also a good way to get to any Algiers destination, such as Blaine Kern's Mardi Gras World, where Carnival floats are built and stored. Do not take the ferry if you're headed to any other parts of the West Bank (you do not want to drive through the neighborhood you'll have to negotiate to get out of Algiers).

To get to other parts of the West Bank, take the Mississippi River Bridge (its official name is the Crescent City Connection, but nobody calls it that). This will connect you to the West Bank Expressway, which will get you anywhere else you want to go on the West Bank.

On the Move

Regional Transit Authority
www.regionaltransit.org
Use Regional Transit Authority buses, which have citywide routes, for tooling around the city. Regular fare costs $1.25; $1.50 for express. Schedules are available from the RTA office, 2817 Canal Street, or by calling (504) 242-2600. The RTA also

Streetcar

"They told me to take a streetcar named Desire, and then transfer to one called Cemeteries and ride six blocks and get off at—Elysian Fields!"

—Blanche DuBois, in Tennessee Williams's *A Streetcar Named Desire*

Say what you will, but as far as we're concerned you can never say enough about the poetry in motion that is a New Orleans streetcar. Even Tennessee Williams can be forgiven for futzing with the facts when he has Blanche DuBois get off the streetcar on Elysian Fields at the beginning of his famous play *A Streetcar Named Desire.* Truth is the streetcar never ran down Elysian Fields. Never. Anyone else who tried such a literary maneuver would have been hog-tied to the tracks of the City Park kiddie railroad. But Tennessee? Well, he's always been a different story.

The city's national historic landmark, which can trace its roots back to 1831, is the oldest continuously operated street railway system in the United States. But don't let that fact impress you any more than it did the city back in 1963 when it stopped running the streetcar down Canal Street in a regrettable move to save money by relying on public buses fueled by—then—cheap gas.

Today visitors can ride the clanging streetcars the 13.1 miles from Canal and Carondelet (pronounced ca-ron-de-LET) Streets, across from Bourbon Street in the French Quarter, all the way down St. Charles Avenue to the Riverbend, and then along Carrollton Avenue to Claiborne Avenue and Palmer Park and Playground—or vice versa. Cost is $1.25 per person for the 90-minute round-trip (exact change required).

Riding the streetcar is one of the best ways to leisurely soak up the oozing charm of St. Charles Avenue, not the least of which are the famous thoroughfare's canopies of moss-draped oak trees, Garden District mansions, Audubon Park, and Tulane and Loyola Universities.

The city's 35 streetcars were built from 1923–1924, and each carries 52 passengers. Sometimes it seems like more, though, during the after-school and after-work crush, as well as during peak tourist times, including Mardi Gras and Jazzfest. The best times to ride include late morning and early afternoon.

Whether picking up the streetcar at Canal Street or anywhere along St. Charles Avenue, passengers can get off at the Riverbend area (where the streetcar turns northeast from St. Charles Avenue and continues down Carrollton Avenue) and walk across the street and up onto the levee for a view of the Mississippi River. Others prefer to browse Riverbend's newsstands, boutiques, and eateries. Either way, the Riverbend is an important juncture: The original streetcar line, founded in 1935, was built to connect New Orleans with the city of Carrollton.

Not to be outdone are the seven red-with-gold-trim vintage streetcars unveiled in 1988, which run the 1.9-mile line along the city's riverfront between the French Quarter and river view at the foot of Poydras Street. Truth is there is not a whole lot to see except the back of Jax Brewery and some less than photogenic wharfs. All that may change under a $14-million expansion project making a 0.5 mile addition to the line with new two-directional tracks and shelters. Until then the riverfront streetcars earn their keep in part by providing tired French Quarter sightseers with easy transportation to the Aquarium of the Americas.

Undoubtedly the biggest news on the line in 2004 was the long-awaited return of streetcars to Canal Street after an absence of 40 years. Just as it did originally, the 4.1-mile line runs the length of Canal Street, which separates the French Quarter and downtown, from the Mississippi River to the cemeteries. An additional mile-long branch runs along Carrollton Avenue to City Park, home of the New Orleans Museum of Art.

Yet the most ironic development was the recently announced (and now indefinitely shelved) proposal to add a new

Palm tree, streetcar, and azaleas. COURTESY OF LOUISIANA OFFICE OF TOURSIM

3-mile streetcar extension from the existing line on Canal Street to the Industrial Canal. Officials had planned to call the route the Desire Line after the Tennessee Williams play. If so, perhaps there is the chance the streetcar, whose route would follow North Rampart Street and St. Claude Avenue, will at long last stop at Elysian Fields.

Take the new Canal Streetcar line all the way down Carrollton Avenue to City Park and the New Orleans Museum of Art, located at the end of the line. And before you ride back, also explore the surrounding historic Esplanade Ridge neighborhood—full of beautiful homes, charming restaurants, and the winding Bayou St. John.

offers VisiTour Passes good for unlimited rides. Cost: $5.00 per day or $12.00 for three days; available at hotels and shopping areas.

STREETCARS

The St. Charles Streetcar is a terrific way to see Uptown and one of the city's most enjoyable forms of transportation. Cost: $1.25. The Riverfront Streetcar doesn't offer much of a view, but if you're in the French Quarter and don't feel like walking all the way to the Aquarium of the Americas, climb aboard for $1.50.

There are two streetcars on the new Canal Streetcar line: cemeteries and City Park/Museum. Check the top front of the car to find out which one you're boarding. The Cemeteries car isn't as scary as it sounds. It simply runs the entire length of Canal Street, which ends at City Park Avenue, where a number of the city's cemeteries are located. As a visitor, you will be much more likely to want to ride the City Park/Museum car, which also follows Canal Street but turns right at Carrollton Avenue. This line ends at beautiful City Park, home to the New Orleans Museum of Art. Cost: $1.25.

TAXIS

New Orleans is really not a cab-hailing town. If you need a taxi, most of the major downtown hotels have cab stands, or call for pickup. United Cab is the biggest taxi company. Call (504) 522-9771.

DRIVING

The two most important things to remember when driving around New Orleans are watch out for the potholes and don't break the law. The city is built below sea level atop a swamp, so everything sinks. Potholes are everywhere and there's no way to avoid them. Consequently, negotiating New Orleans streets is not unlike driving in a Third World country. Just relax and, most important, slow down.

Do not speed in New Orleans. Generally, the speed limit is 25 mph on undivided streets and 35 mph on divided streets. If you get pulled over for speeding, not only will it cost you an astronomical amount of money, but also an out-of-towner is much more likely than a local to be taken directly to jail to pay the fine.

Here are some other laws and safety tips to keep in mind:

• No open containers are allowed in vehicles.
• The police are really cracking down on drunk driving. Don't drink and drive or you'll find yourself in jail faster than you can say, "We'll have one for the road."
• Front-seat passengers and children under age 13 are required to wear safety belts.
• Emergency vehicles use red and blue lights. Do not pull over for a car with only flashing white lights. The Louisiana Office of Tourism recommends that anyone stopped by an unmarked "police" car should pull to a well-lighted, populated area. Ask to see official identification, or ask that a marked car be dispatched.

PARKING

Parking is another hassle. Do not park illegally in the city. Always read the signs, especially during Mardi Gras and other special events. *NOTE:* If you are parking at the end of a block, a NO PARKING sign at the other end may include the entire block. So check before you park. The most worry-free solution is put the car in a parking lot. They're everywhere.

If you do park on the street and your car is not there when you return, it may have been towed to the auto pound at 400 Claiborne Avenue. To find out, call (504) 565-7450. Be prepared to identify your car by license plate number, make, color, and location it was parked.

If you plan to use public transportation while in town, consider buying a pay-one-price VisiTour pass good for unlimited rides on city streetcars and buses. (See write-up in this chapter for details.)

HISTORY 🏛

Since the beginning, New Orleans has been a city that has survived, sometimes, it seems, despite the best efforts of man and God. It all started in 1682 when Robert Cavelier de LaSalle, while exploring the mostly unknown North American continent, entered the Mississippi River from the Illinois River, eventually making his way to the Gulf of Mexico. Along the route, he claimed this brave new world for the glory of France and named the region for King Louis XIV.

He then raced back to France, where the king's fledgling territory ran into its first obstacle. It seems Louis was not too crazy about LaSalle's idea of building a colonial empire for France by establishing a city on the river. All could have been lost then and there. But the king noticed that the land was adjacent to the Spanish claim of what would eventually become Texas—which just so happened to be owned by his brother-in-law and which Louie planned to get his hands on once his ailing kin kicked the bucket. It looked like smooth sailing for LaSalle—that is, until he got back to the New World and was unable to locate the mouth of the river again. Eventually he landed his crew in the pre-Texas region with the bright idea of hiking all the way back to Canada and retracing his steps. His crew, understandably, killed him. All of which goes to show how much people hate it when you give them bad directions.

It was another decade before anybody else in France had the guts to go near Louisiana, and it may have been even longer had the King of Spain not announced that all land bordering the Gulf of Mexico was his. So in 1698 Louis sent the Le Moyne brothers—Pierre Le Moyne, Sieur d'Iberville, and Jean-Baptiste Le Moyne, Sieur de Bienville (commonly referred to as Iberville and Bienville) to defend France's land claim. Of course, they had problems of their own, mostly in the form of a hurricane (which wiped out the first settlement in its second year) and fires. (In fact, the city's history is full of devastating fires, which is ironic considering that it is surrounded by water.) The first order of business was setting up a base of operations along the modern-day Mississippi Gulf Coast and naming Biloxi the capitol of the Louisiana Territory. It was now time to find the Mississippi River. But rather than risk mutiny and death as LaSalle had, the brothers enlisted the help of local Indians in their search.

Now the Indians, the Choctaws, were an interesting bunch. They were not the stereotypical proud warriors of old Western movies or even the spiritual peace-loving tribes of new Western movies. As the late historian John Chase put it, "Their outstanding characteristic was laziness; in truth it is doubtful that the world ever knew a class of people of whom it can more correctly be said that they didn't give a damn." Chase goes on to point out that although the region basically required an amphibious way of life, the Choctaws never learned to swim or even bathe. And whereas most Native Americans wore feathers at their head, the Choctaws attached them at the waist so that they stuck out in back like a tail.

This was a motley crew.

That bit of trivia concerning the Choctaw character is worth mentioning because it has some relevance to modern New Orleans. The city's population has long been known for its laissez-faire attitude toward just about every aspect of life, which most observers have attributed to the city's European roots (we even use French words to describe it). However, in light of what we now know about the Choctaws, it could be surmised that the City That Care Forgot started forgetting to care long before the Europeans arrived.

FIRE ON THE BAYOU

Back to the Le Moyne boys' search for the Mississippi River. The Choctaws were understandably a shy bunch and therefore difficult to make contact with. (Besides, what did they care?) The Frenchmen solved this problem by capturing an old brave who was too slow to get away and then planted him on the beach (where they knew his tribesmen could see him), presented him with gifts, and built a shelter and fire for his comfort. Unfortunately, as Chase writes in his book *Frenchmen, Desire, Good Children:* "[T]he roaring fire ignited the grass and burned the old man to a crisp."

This did not help their cause.

Almost unbelievably though, Bienville was eventually able to make friends with a group of Choctaws (maybe they hadn't heard about the other incident) who agreed to show him the way to the river when they finished hunting. Though he probably should have known better, Bienville marked the rendezvous point by lighting a fire—which, of course, raged out of control and burned down miles of forest. At this point, the French were forced to find the river on their own, which they eventually did.

During their journey up the river, about 100 miles inland the explorers came upon a tract of land at a bend in the river. To the north was what we know as Lake Pontchartrain. There was also a small stream (later called Bayou St. John) that led to the lake. Eighteen-year-old Bienville saw this as a perfect spot to establish a riverfront city. His older brother disagreed and went back to France. However, Bienville, with his youthful dream of a great river city, stayed behind and became commanding officer of the territory. But he had to wait nearly two decades to make his dream come true.

In 1717 a Scotsman named John Law persuaded the King of France that there was money to be made in Louisiana. The following year Bienville was promoted to territorial governor and instructed to establish a city on the river from which to protect France's New World empire. Of course, he knew just the spot. The City of New Orleans was promptly established and declared the new capital because of its strategic location and because, according to historian Chase, a French sergeant had fallen asleep with a pipe in his mouth and burned down Biloxi.

Back in France, Philip II (the former Duke of Chartres and the country's Regent during the infancy of Louis XV) was the inside man whose influence had assured royal approval of John Law's economic plan—a plan so sound that many called Law the inventor of inflation. Philip was also a despicable human being. When royal heirs began suspiciously dying near the end of Louis XIV's reign, it was Philip and his daughter (with whom he was accused of having an extremely close relationship) who were accused. However, the charges were never proven, and in his will the dying king named Philip France's Regent. By this time, Philip, a man of such objectionable character that his own mother's writings basically branded him a loser, had inherited the title of Duke of Orleans. He is the man for whom John Law named the new city.

And to think, all Bienville got named after him was a street.

A CITY OF CRIMINALS AND IRON LACE

Engineer Adrian de Pauger laid out the original city, which consisted of a central square with streets forming a grid around it. Today this area is known as the French Quarter with Jackson Square still at its center. As fate would have it, though, the building of the city was not easy going. Much of the land was swamp—perfect breeding ground for mosquitoes, snakes, and alligators. The Mississippi River often overflowed its banks, hurricanes visited from the Gulf and, of course, there were fires.

Then there were the people. In order to populate the new colony, John Law succeeded in getting two laws passed. One stated that anyone in a French prison, no matter what the crime, would be freed provided that he or she moved to Louisiana. Likewise, anyone who was out of work for three days was sent to a New World home. Therefore, much of the city's early population was made up of criminals and ne'er-do-wells. Amazingly, the city not only survived, it thrived—perhaps because the land and these early settlers were made for each other.

New Orleans remained under French rule until 1762, when Louis XV ceded the territory to Spain. New Orleanians were enraged when the first Spanish governor, Don Antonio de Ulloa, arrived. In response, a mob of angry locals ran him out of town. The New Orleans Rebellion of 1768 marks the first American revolution against a European crown. King Carlos squelched the rebellion by sending in Don Alexander "Bloody" O'Reilly, who promptly executed the rebel leaders. Frenchmen Street in Faubourg Marigny (the neighborhood just downriver of the French Quarter) was named for these original American revolutionaries.

Although the city was never to adopt the Spanish language or culture, it did inherit the Spaniards' architecture. Two fires (wouldn't you know it), in 1788 and 1794, destroyed most of the original French buildings. These wooden structures were replaced while the Spanish were running the city with sturdier brick buildings constructed in the Spanish style—flush against the street with arched walkways, interior courtyards, and iron lace balconies. Many of these introductions remain, giving the French Quarter its decidedly Spanish look.

UH-OH, AMERICANS

Meanwhile, elsewhere on the continent, the big happening was the settling of the Ohio River Valley following the American Revolution. This was important to the development of the Crescent City

because those frontiersmen from Tennessee and Kentucky soon found that the most practical way to get their goods to world markets was down the Mississippi River to the port town of New Orleans. The first river traffic consisted of rafts and flatboats. These crude crafts could not make the trip back up river, so after the boats were unloaded, they were broken apart and sold as lumber. Many of the wooden houses built in New Orleans at that time were made from these flatboats. The frontiersmen would then spend the next few weeks walking home.

It wasn't until the arrival of the second wave of river traffic—the keelboats—that the trouble really started. The Creoles, as early New Orleanians called themselves, had become quite a sophisticated bunch, and, generally speaking, life in New Orleans was rather genteel—especially when contrasted with the rowdy behavior of the keelboatmen. Unlike their predecessors, the keelboatmen (whose vessels could make the return trip upriver) were professional boatmen and, by all accounts, never in the mood to pass up trouble. They were known for brawling—and winning. Understandably, this did not go over well with locals, and there were constant run-ins with the authorities. Hostilities grew, and in 1798 the Spanish government ruled the New Orleans port off-limits to the keelboatmen.

The boatmen were mostly from Tennessee and Kentucky, both of which had recently been granted statehood. They went to the American government and threatened that if something were not done they would either take the port by force or secede from the Union. Meanwhile, Napoleon was now running France and had taken back Louisiana from Spain. (He did things like that.)

Back in Washington, President Thomas Jefferson decided that the best solution to the port problem was to buy New Orleans, which he had wanted to do since he took office two years earlier. Off went statesmen Robert Livingston and James Monroe to broker the deal with Napoleon, who was busy trying to conquer Europe and had little interest in his American territory—except as a source of income. (Taking over a continent is expensive.) So, in walk Livingston and Monroe authorized to pay up to $10 million for New Orleans but only if the French emperor will throw in Florida. Napoleon promptly turns around and offers the entire Louisiana Territory (nearly 900,000 square miles) for $15 million—a price that works out to about 4 cents an acre. Livingston and Monroe had no authority to make such a agreement, no time to consult the president, and were pretty sure it was unconstitutional (which it turns out it was). However, they inked the deal, thus doubling the size of the United States and establishing the American tradition of never passing up a great sale.

The Louisiana Purchase was signed in 1803, and the next several years were pretty good ones for New Orleans. Americans and their money flooded into the city; New Orleans received both statehood and the steamboat in 1812; and along with the lifting of long-standing French-Spanish trade restrictions, the city became a boomtown.

AN "ECLECTIC" VICTORY

But another major battle lay ahead for New Orleans. By the second decade of the 19th century, the city's population had become quite eclectic. There were the Creoles of both French and Spanish extraction, the newly arrived Americans, a sizable black population made up of both slaves and free people of color (New Orleans had by far the largest population of pre–Civil War free people of color), a handful of Choctaws and brutish keelboatmen, and a small band of pirates led by Jean Lafitte. Actually, Lafitte was more of a smuggler than a pirate, and many affluent New Orleanians were regular customers for his duty-free booty. Lafitte and his Baratarians were headquartered downriver of the city at Barataria Bay and

LaSalle originally named the newly discovered territory "Louisiane" after the French King Louis XIV. The Spanish name was "Luisiana." The surviving "Louisiana" is a mingling of the two.

were quite familiar with this swampy region—a fact the English would later bemoan.

America had been at war with England (once again) since, well, 1812. In 1814 British forces had employed the visually impressive Congreve rocket at the Battle of Bladensburg, which successfully scared away 5,000 raw American recruits. As a result, the British were able to take and burn Washington, inspiring Francis Scott Key to write about "the rockets' red glare, the bombs bursting in air." The British were figuring on a similar victory in New Orleans, where the troops, made up of the aforementioned eclectic group, were no more seasoned.

It was now early 1815, two weeks *after* the Americans and British had signed a peace treaty ending the War of 1812. Unfortunately, neither army was aware of this bit of trivia when they met in the swamps a few miles south of New Orleans in present-day Chalmette. General Sir Edward Michael Pakenham led 14,000 veteran British soldiers. Meanwhile, General Andrew Jackson commanded an estimated 2,800 irregulars, many of whom would not even have spoken to one another before this. Luckily Jackson's troops found they had one thing in common: They all hated the British.

When the smoke cleared, the score was unmistakable: 3,000 British soldiers killed, wounded, or captured; 7 Americans killed, 6 wounded. No one is exactly sure why the completely unexpected defeat was so decisive. It has been suggested that in this particular battle, not knowing the rules of the game helped the Americans. The experienced British wore bright-red uniforms, marched in lines, and had bagpipers announcing their presence.

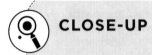

Cemeteries

Laissez les bon temps rouler, let the good times roll, is an oft-heard phrase in New Orleans. And why wouldn't it be in a city that has, virtually since its emergence from the swamp, experienced almost nonstop reminders of how short life really is? The Big Easy has a long history of floods, fires, and epidemics (in 1853 alone 12,000 people died of yellow fever) that have inspired in locals the wisdom never to take life too seriously as well as the burning question: What do you do with all those bodies?

Actually, burying the dearly departed was a problem from the beginning. Because New Orleans lies below sea level, the only high ground was the natural silt levee created by the Mississippi River's annual overflow. Locals began burying the dead there until it occurred to them that the digging was weakening the city's only flood protection. In 1721 New Orleans' first city engineer, Adrien de Pauger, designed a cemetery to be built on the outskirts of town. The St. Peter's Street Cemetery was situated between what are now Burgundy and Rampart Streets in the French Quarter.

This worked for a while, until the city began to grow toward and around the cemetery and folks decided that they did not like looking at graves while sitting on their front stoops. Officials responded by building a 5-foot brick wall around the cemetery. The wall was dedicated with much fanfare on All Saints' Day 1743. Participants arrived for the ceremony, also bearing flowers to commemorate the dead

(as was the custom throughout Europe). All Saints' Day has been an important holiday in New Orleans ever since.

Residents made do with St. Peter's until 1788, a big year for natural disasters. First, the banks of the Mississippi overflowed, flooding the entire city; then, on Good Friday, 865 homes burned to the ground in a fire that destroyed most of New Orleans; and somewhere in the mix a variety of epidemics did what they do best, killing a large portion of the population. (Some people even consider this a worse year than 1979, when Mardi Gras was canceled because of a police strike.) As a result, the filled-to-overflowing cemetery had to be closed and covered with lime to avoid more pestilence.

New Orleans' oldest surviving "city of the dead," St. Louis No. 1, was built by royal decree the following year. However, mourners still faced the problem of burying their dead in, literally, watery graves. The decision was made to erect aboveground tombs, and because swamp-based New Orleans has no natural stone, they were constructed of brick. Unfortunately, in the city's subtropical climate, the bricks seemed to be competing with the bodies to see which would deteriorate first. To keep the tombs from falling apart, plaster was added to the outside and eventually painted white—a symbol of purity. (Although the idea that many of those passionate, good-time-loving Creoles made it to their graves pure, in practically any respect, seems naively optimistic.)

With the influx of Americans to the city following the 1803 signing of the Louisiana Purchase, accommodations had to be made for their dead, as well. The class system, which still exists in New Orleans culture to some degree, was reflected in the solution. The new Protestants would be buried at the back of the cemetery, behind the Catholic Creoles, with black people at the very end. (Sometimes, a person can't catch a break even when they're dead.)

These houses of the dead have changed little over the centuries. Generally the aboveground tomb is about 10 feet long with a 7-foot-long interior slab on which the coffin rests; the last 3 feet at the back of the structure are open from top to bottom. The tomb was not allowed to be opened for a year and a day after a body was placed inside to make certain that the "inhabitant" was past the point of spreading disease. Here, the burning sun of New Orleans' long, hot summers combines with the enclosed tomb to virtually cremate the body, leaving little behind by the next year. The remains that, well, remain are then pushed to the back, falling into that 3-foot hollow area, or *caveau,* before the next coffin is placed inside.

OK, so what if Uncle Herd kicks off just six months after MawMaw? Well, that's where the waiting wall comes in. That's right, the body would be placed in a sort of limbo lobby located within the outer walls of the cemetery until proper internment could safely take place. It may sound morbid, but it's a system that's worked for 200 years, and most of the city's families still own tombs.

In fact, some interesting notables have made their permanent homes in St. Louis Cemetery No. 1, including Etienne de Bore, the city's first appointed mayor and the first man to granulate sugar; Paul Morphy, North America's premiere world-class chess champion, whose former home is now a quaint little restaurant called Brennan's; and famed voodoo queen Marie Laveau. (The other tomb bearing the name Marie Laveau is in St. Louis No. 2 and is believed to belong to her daughter).

And sometimes a resting place is considered interesting on the basis of who doesn't show up. The plot of William C. C. Claiborne, Louisiana's first governor, is also located in St. Louis No. 1. It contains the bodies of both his first and second wives, with his brother-in-law buried in the middle. Nobody's quite sure how or why the body of the governor himself ended up somewhere else.

On the edge of the city, Metairie Cemetery, full of grand and unusual monuments, represents a virtual who's who of dead New Orleanians. The long list of blue bloods includes nine Louisiana governors, eight mayors, and more than 50 kings of Carnival. There's also Mel Ott, New Orleans greatest contribution to the game of baseball. In his 22-year career with the New York Giants, Ott scored 1,859 runs (including 511 homers), tallied 1,860 RBIs, and maintained a lifetime average of .304. His lustrous career is in direct contrast to his tomb, which is one of the cemetery's more modest.

Legendary steamboat captain LeVerrier Cooley obviously decided that he could, in fact, take it with him. When he

Because New Orleans is situated below sea level, most of the city's cemeteries are filled with above-ground tombs, some of which are very ornately adorned. GAFFNEY/RETZ

died in 1931, the ship's bell from Cooley's *Ouachita* became the centerpiece of his tomb.

In his book *Proud, Peculiar New Orleans: The Inside Story,* Buddy Stall tells the tale of one of Metairie Cemetery's most interesting monuments and the man who built it. Daniel Moriarty, an Irish immigrant and successful business-man, was known as an inattentive and some say harsh husband to his wife, a woman several years his senior. Upon Mrs. Moriarty's death in 1887, his con-science apparently kicked in and he decided to build her the largest monu-ment Metairie Cemetery had ever known. This was also a way for the Hibernian to thumb his nose at those members of New Orleans society who had snubbed him because his blood never managed to be the correct shade of blue.

The 85-foot monument featured a huge granite shaft topped with a cross and life-size statues of "the four graces." (When Moriarty put in his request for the statues and was told that there were, in fact, only three graces—Faith, Hope, and Charity—Moriarty said he didn't care and wanted four anyway.) The circular walk around the base was made of stones from various places around the country, each weighing 11 tons. The final cost for this 19th-century tomb was $185,000. However, Moriarty never finished paying for it.

Supposedly, Mrs. Moriarty was sensi-tive about anyone knowing exactly how much older she was than her husband and stipulated in her will that only the date of her death should appear on her tomb. Moriarty gave the information to the stonecutter who, after completing the work, realized that the information was off by a day. The cutter approached Moriarty and explained that an under-standable mistake had been made by the widower in his time of grief but that it could be corrected for a paltry $2.50. Moriarty replied, "The hell with it, I've spent enough already."

Josie Arlington, the famed Storyville madam, is another interesting resident of Metairie Cemetery. Around the turn of the 20th century, a canal that ran past the cemetery featured red lights as mark-ers, one of which ironically shone down on Arlington's tomb. Locals joked that Josie was working late.

It's hard to tell how big a role these very visible cities of the dead have played in the development of the New Orleans psyche. At the very least, their presence (there are more than 40 ceme-teries within the city limits) seems to have instilled a certain cultural accept-ance of the inevitability of death not found in communities where graveyards are kept as far away from the living as possible.

Laissez les bon temps rouler.

These traditional practices were meant to intimidate opponents. However, the uninitiated Americans didn't know that. They simply found that the bright colors, straight lines, and noise made the British easier to pick off. It also often has been mistakenly observed that the battle was nothing more than a waste of time and lives, as it took place after the treaty was signed. However, the British parliament had not yet ratified the treaty, and many historians believe that had that country's soldiers won the Battle of New Orleans, England may have rethought its peace agreement.

NEW ORLEANS'S DEATH-DEFYING DEVELOPER

As for General Jackson, the battle made him a national hero who went on to become the seventh president of the United States—and a prominent statue in Jackson Square, which brings us to Micaela Leonard Almonester Baroness de Pontalba, one of the city's most interesting redheads. She was born in 1795, the daughter of 70-year-old Don Andres Almonester, a wealthy landowner. When she was 16, Micaela entered into an arranged marriage with her 20-year-old cousin Joseph Xavier Celestin Delfau de Pontalba of Paris, whom everyone apparently called Tin-Tin and whom Micaela had never met until the day of the wedding. Besides three children and intertwining lineages, the couple had nothing in common. And talk about in-law troubles—her father-in-law so disliked her that one day he shot her four times in the chest. (It would have been six times, but he missed twice.) Thinking her dead, he then fatally shot himself in the heart twice, although nobody's really sure how he got off that second shot. Miraculously, the baroness survived. Eventually, she left Paris, where the scandalous incident had taken place, and returned to New Orleans.

In 1848 she began building her legacy—two luxurious row houses flanking either side of Jackson Square. The identical three-story buildings would each accommodate 16 shops on the ground floor, with the second and third floors housing residences. She insisted that the initials AP (for Almonester-Pontalba) be designed into the balcony ironwork. The latter of the buildings was completed in 1851. Today, they are considered the oldest apartment houses in America. An interesting footnote: Local legend has it that although she and her husband did not get along, the baroness had a real thing for Andy Jackson.

Unfortunately, her affections were unrequited. However, she apparently had the last laugh. It seems that the building of her apartment houses sparked the city to make improvements to Jackson Square. This included finally completing the statue of General Andrew Jackson for which the cornerstone had been laid more than a decade earlier. To this day, the spurned baroness, wherever she may be, has the satisfaction of General Jackson forever tipping his hat in the direction of her house.

FORTUNES AND FEVERS

As a result of the Battle of New Orleans, the general got his statue and the baroness got her gesture. As for the city, the battle had finally done what peaceful coexistence never could: It united the various ethnic factions long enough for people to start making some real money. The port was jammed with business, cotton was king, and by 1850 New Orleans was the fourth largest city in the United States. Everything was coming up magnolias and crepe myrtles for the Crescent City. So, of course, it was time for another disaster.

Along came the yellow fever epidemic of 1853. Actually, mostly because it was built on a swamp, New Orleans was visited by yellow fever pretty much every

Besides being the birthplace of jazz, New Orleans was home to another noteworthy American first. In 1859, on the corner of Bourbon and Toulouse Streets, the French Opera House was built. It was the residence of the continent's first permanent opera company.

year. But 1853 was the worst. More than 10,000 people died that summer—an average of more than 100 people a day. The worst was August 20, when 269 people perished. Homes were turned into hospitals and wagons were driven down the street with the drivers calling, "Bring out your dead." Piles of corpses lay rotting in cemeteries. Yellow fever outbreaks continued, but after the horrible summer of '53, God seemed to show mercy and the epidemics decreased in occasion and severity until they ended altogether in 1905.

Almost unbelievably, the local economy was doing so well that the dead were quickly replaced by newcomers eager to cash in on the city's prosperity. Of course, the only reason cotton (not to mention sugarcane) was king was because there were non-wage-earning slaves picking it. During this time New Orleans was one of the country's biggest slave markets. And the backs on which the city's prosperity had been built would eventually lead to its downfall. New Orleans' glory days abruptly came to an end in 1861 with Louisiana's secession from the Union and the beginning of the Civil War, known on this side of the Mason-Dixon line as the War Between the States.

THE BUTLER DID IT

In 1862 Union troops occupied New Orleans and liked the place so much they stayed 15 years. The most prominent figure during this period was General Benjamin "Spoons" Butler, commander of the federal forces in New Orleans. He was much hated among the locals because of his liberal interpreta-

tion of the Confiscation Act of 1862. Butler seized at will a goodly amount of private property from homes, including many a family's silver service (thus his nickname).

The city's women, openly hostile toward occupying soldiers, would immediately get off a streetcar if soldiers boarded and sometimes literally spit in their faces. (Remember, the Creoles were an independent and spirited bunch.) In response, Butler passed an ordinance that any woman insulting or showing contempt for a soldier "shall be regarded and held liable to be treated as a woman of the town plying her avocation." Even Butler's closest advisors thought it a bit harsh to basically make it legal to punish a snubbing with rape. Needless to say, there was no more spitting and there is no record of the order ever being carried out.

However inhumane Butler was seen to be, New Orleans fared rather well compared with other occupied Southern cities. For the most part, citizens were allowed to go about their daily lives, and it was Butler who ordered the city scrubbed from top to bottom, which is credited with eliminating yellow fever outbreaks during the war. Also, as authors Joan B. Garvey and Mary Lou Widmer write in *Beautiful Crescent: A History of New Orleans,* unlike Atlanta, New Orleans was never bombarded. "It was governed efficiently," write the authors, "and the physical comfort of the citizens was better during the federal administration than it had been under the Confederacy."

HOUSE OF THE RISING FUN

After the war, New Orleans went through the difficult period of Reconstruction and faced the challenge of rebuilding its economy without the help of free slave labor. Never having learned to type, the Big Easy fell back on what it was best at: fun. Vice was the name of the game in late 19th century New Orleans. Saloons and gambling establishments abounded and, by some counts, there was a house of ill repute on every city block. In 1898, in response to pleas from the police and the church community, city leaders decided that something had to be done to rein in this never-ending party.

New Orleans businessman and alderman Sidney Story came up with a plan to create a regulated prostitution district. He left the wording of the ordinance to attorney Thomas McCaleb Hyman, whose challenge was to write a law legalizing prostitution that would stand up in court. The ingenious result was simple: The law said it was illegal for prostitutes to work *outside* the area bounded by North Robertson and North Basin Streets, from the Customs House to St. Louis Street. The ordinance made no mention of the legality of prostitution inside this area. The ordinance passed, and a church group soon filed suit. The case went all the way to the U.S. Supreme Court, which upheld the law's constitutionality. Of course, the respectable Mr. Story was appalled when he read local newspaper accounts of this new sin sub-city, which had been dubbed Storyville.

Storyville's pleasure palaces thrived and were credited with not only satisfying the city's carnal cravings but also providing the incubator for an emerging new music—jazz. Although America's only original art form was actually born a few blocks away, it was in the ground-floor gambling and entertainment areas of Storyville's brothels (working girls were allowed to ply their trade upstairs only) that jazz received its first mainstream audience. In the early part of the 20th century, jazz pioneers such as Jelly Roll Morton and Louis Armstrong first played in Storyville.

The prostitutes' biggest business had always come during Mardi Gras, and before the creation of Storyville, an annual prostitutes' costume party was established known as "The Ball of the Two Well Known Gentlemen." The event was a huge success and grew larger each year until the curiosity of even the city's "proper ladies" got the best of them and they began

wrangling invitations. The idea was that behind a mask, one could anonymously see firsthand the torrid behavior one could so self-righteously disapprove of later. In 1906 Josie Arlington, one of Storyville's most prominent madams, came up with a plan to deal with these unwanted high-brow guests. After everyone had arrived at the ball, Arlington had the place raided by some of her police buddies, who carted off to jail any woman who could not prove she was a prostitute. This highly embarrassing moment for those society women may be the only case in history in which a brothel was raided and women were arrested for not working there. Needless to say, there were no further intrusions at the prostitutes' ball.

Of course, all good things must come to an end. In 1917 Storyville was finally closed under pressure from the U.S. Secretary of War, who quoted a ban on open prostitution within 5 miles of a military installation. Within a year, writes local historian Buddy Stall in Buddy Stall's New Orleans, "venereal diseases were back because prostitutes were no longer required to obtain regular medical checkups, crimes against nature jumped up, unwed mothers were on the rise, and houses of ill repute sprang up all over town—including in the French Quarter and the elaborate Garden District."

HOOKED ON THE KINGFISH

During the first half of the 20th century, New Orleans saw its port become one

---

Visitors are often surprised that New Orleanians do not have a traditional Southern accent. In fact, it is much more akin to that heard in the boroughs of New York. This is because as American port cities, the Big Easy and the Big Apple had much the same mixture of influences as a variety of immigrants made their way to both "shores."

of the world's busiest. River-flooding problems were finally stabilized with U.S. Corps of Engineers–built levees, and the Vieux Carré Commission was established to undertake preservation of the French Quarter. The most interesting and controversial figure in the state during this time was Huey P. Long. The Kingfish (a nickname he gave himself) was a political powerhouse. Elected governor in 1928, he came to represent the kind of savior people were looking for to rescue them from the ravages of the Depression. His book *Every Man a King* outlined his plan to end this bleak chapter in the nation's history. "A chicken in every pot" was the slogan of his Share the Wealth campaign, through which he declared that no one in America should be allowed to make more than $1 million a year and that any amount over that should be put into a fund for the poor. His popularity rose so fast and so wide that he was elected to the U.S. Senate just two years after becoming governor.

Long's biggest driving force seemed to be his ego. His second book was a slightly premature *My First Days in the White House.* And his best known accomplishment in the Senate was leading a weeklong filibuster against a bill backed by President Franklin Roosevelt. Long himself spoke for more than 15 hours, during which time he supposedly complained that the bill circumvented Mosaic Law by violating the book of Leviticus, chapters 15 and 16. According to the book *Beautiful Crescent,* he also read the U.S. Constitution and Declaration of Independence, parts of Victor Hugo's *The Laughing Man,* other Bible chapters, a monologue on Greek mythology, and a recipe for fried oysters. Alas, the filibuster failed. But soon afterward those in the know began taking his presidential ambitions seriously. Long's political career was ended by an assassin's bullet as he walked through the state capitol in Baton Rouge on September 8, 1935.

To this day, there is much speculation that his bodyguards killed him. However controversial his life and death, the city owes Long a debt of gratitude for the original New Orleans airport, the Huey P. Long Bridge over the Mississippi River, Louisiana State University Medical Center, and free textbooks in public schools.

WAR AND PEACE

In the 1940s New Orleans, like the rest of the country, entered World War II. Along with men donning uniforms and women collecting rubber, the city's major contribution to the war effort took place on City Park Avenue at Higgins Industries. Here, boatbuilder Andrew Jackson Higgins designed and built his ramped landing craft used to ferry soldiers and equipment to shore during the decisive D-day invasion. President Eisenhower later told biographer Stephen Ambrose that the Higgins landing crafts, the production of which marked the first major influx of women into the New Orleans job market, were the reason the Allies won the war.

After the war, as in most cities, the New Orleans population spread out, creating new suburbs and returning its attention to the place its heart had always been—home. Perhaps in no other town its size do people have less interest in what goes on beyond the city limits. In most parts of the United States, people are commonly asked where they were when they heard President Kennedy had been shot. In New Orleans the question is much more likely to be, "Where were you when Betsy hit?" referring to Hurricane Betsy, whose 145 mph winds and torrential rain devastated the city in 1965 and set a standard by which all future storms would be measured. Why does the city seem to purposely separate itself from its own country and, to a large extent, the rest of the state? Maybe it's because New Orleans has had such a different (and often much richer) history than the rest of the country. Maybe it's an attitude left over from the time of the Creoles, when Americans were seen as outsiders. Or maybe, living in, hands down, the nation's culinary capital, people are just too busy eating to care.

For more information on other aspects of New Orleans history, check out the Close-ups on the New Orleans Voodoo Museum and New Orleans Cemeteries as well as the chapters on Mardi Gras, Annual Events and Festivals, Attractions, and Spectator Sports.

New Orleans is big on remembering war heroes in statuary. Do you know the secret code? If the right leg of the hero's steed is raised, the soldier lived through battle. If the left leg is up, the soldier died in battle. If both front legs are raised, the rider went on to greater glory (as in the case of the statue of General Andrew Jackson in Jackson Square, who became the seventh president of the United Stated). If all four legs are up, it means the horse died in battle. Just kidding.

HOTELS

The disarmingly seductive charm of this rollicking port city's historic lusty digs has lit the love lamp of more than a few river kings and steel magnolias over the years. Step into the past inside a 19th-century Greek Revival mansion and former home to generations of Creole gentry. Pass a stormy night on a mahogany four-poster bed, sharing secrets while listening to the hypnotic rain dance on the French double windows. Awaken slowly to the morning light caught in the lace curtains and find that croissants and cafe au lait have been left by room service outside the door along with a spray of flaming-red bougainvillea. Push open the double doors and step out onto a private wrought-iron balcony overlooking a tropical, gas lamp-dotted courtyard garden of Japanese magnolias and sweet olive, with a lovely triple-tiered fountain. The thrum of city life seems worlds away from this Elysian of Creole quietude.

For generations of New Orleanians, the city's hotels have been where the action is—from high society chow-downs and brimmed-hat afternoon teas to romantic in-town weekends and after-six elbow bending at a favorite watering hole. Any town can have hotels, but the Big Easy is among the Western Hemisphere's best examples of what it means to be a bona fide hotel city—and to acknowledge it with uncommon grace. Ultra-posh European-style hotels with chandelier-lit marble lobbies and multimillion-dollar artwork collections can boast guest books signed by Hollywood's hottest flavors of the month and European jet-setters who couldn't care less. The lap of nouveau luxury can be found inside the city's towering glass-and-brass high-rises, with rooftop fitness centers and sweeping panoramas of the mighty Mississippi and crumbly French Quarter. Boutique hotels offer elegant alternatives to megahotels

with conventioneer-jammed lobbies, as well as dainty inns long on history but short on amenities. Many properties have undertaken expensive and lengthy renovations and modernizations—after all, many of the hotels are 100 years old or more. Of course, an accommodating city like New Orleans can be counted on to rescue travel budgets from the brink of disaster by offering a range of midpriced and family-friendly chain hotels and motels as well. Granted, they may not offer tea and scones or four-star dining, but there are plenty of such accommodations scattered throughout the city (check the Yellow Pages), plus they'll save you enough money to go out and enjoy afternoon tea on your own.

Guests with special needs will find they have not been forgotten. A growing number of hotels both large and quaint offer, for example, nonsmoking and/or allergen-free rooms (even floors) and are partially or wholly wheelchair accessible. To be on the safe side, it's strongly recommended that you call ahead to check. Those traveling with pets or very small children should also check ahead. Unless otherwise noted, the hotels in this chapter accept most major credit cards and offer rooms with color TV (most with remote control; many with pay-per-view channels), telephones, private baths, and air-conditioning. Other amenities are listed by individual hotel. The front desk invariably has tour brochures or is staffed by someone who can tell you where to find them.

Preferred and convenient locations include Uptown, the Central Business District/Warehouse Arts District, and, of course, the French Quarter. We will focus on accommodations in these areas. Of course, budget chain motels can be found in town as well as in the adjacent Jefferson Parish suburbs of Metairie and Kenner on the east bank of the Mississippi River and in Gretna on the west bank—15 to 20 minutes from New Orleans.

The most expensive times of the year to visit New Orleans include Mardi Gras, the French Quarter Festival, the New Orleans Jazz and Heritage Festival (see Annual Events and Festivals chapter), conventions, and holidays. Expect to pay more—sometimes *much* more—during these times. Many if not most properties require a two- to five-night minimum stay during these high-traffic times. Peak season is during spring and fall, but summertime (and early December) guests can expect widely varying discounts. Hotels also offer specially discounted travel packages throughout the year. Check these out. Also call ahead to find out the reservation and cancellation policy, as this varies depending on hotel and time of year. Now lay your head on a goosedown pillow and think about exciting Big Easy explorations still to come. Sweet dreams.

PRICE CODE

The price in all cases reflects the average rate for high-season, double-occupancy accommodations. Many if not most hotels have a range of price codes as rooms and suites vary in size, amenities, and desirability. Price codes do not include special services provided by the hotel such as babysitting, valet laundry, parking (if charges apply), telephone calls, room service, hotel-motel tax (11 percent if applicable), and per-head room-night taxes ($1.00 to $3.00).

$	Less than $85
$$	$85 to $125
$$$	$126 to $175
$$$$	$176 to $225
$$$$$	$226+

FRENCH QUARTER

Bienville House Hotel　　　**$$–$$$$**
320 Decatur Street, New Orleans
(504) 529–2345, (800) 535–7836
The white canopy below the iron-trellis

balconies and quartet of colorful flags provides shade for guests strolling through the Creole double doors into this French Quarter–style manor. Murals and gracious furnishings offer a taste of Old World charm. A multimillion-dollar lobby-to-rooftop renovation has created new interior and exterior appointments—for example, an elegantly furnished lobby, four sundecks, 83 guest rooms, and a tropical flagstone courtyard and pool. Triple-sheeted beds provide a sumptuous nightly welcome, while a new state-of-the-art "life safety" and sprinkler system lets guests sleep with confidence. A coffeemaker is on hand to brew that first jolt of java in the morning before heading down to the lobby for a day-starting complimentary continental breakfast. Some rooms have balconies overlooking the courtyard and pool; others have nice views of the Mississippi River.

Indoor valet parking and guest access to a nearby fitness center are two perks of this intimate boutique property and one-time riverfront warehouse. A Decatur Street address means only a short walk to antiques shop-studded Royal and Chartres Streets, the IMAX theater, and Jax Brewery shopping center. The Monteleone family, who also run the 600-room hotel on Royal Street that bears their name, purchased this property in 1972. New restaurants, bistros, and other signs of life are cropping up everywhere on this once sleepy street, now enjoying a resurgence.

Bourbon Orleans　　　**$$–$$$$$**
717 Orleans Street, New Orleans
(504) 523–2222, (800) 521–5338
www.bourbonorleans.com
Step into the legendary Orleans Ballroom (if it's unoccupied) and try to imagine the 19th-century quadroon balls, where Creole dandies wooed the city's famously bewitching quadroons—women of mixed races. Today the fully restored ballroom built by entrepreneur John Davis is the centerpiece of this hotel accented by a white-columned lobby of crystal

chandeliers and Oriental rugs. Step out onto a quiet balcony and listen to the jazz echoing from nearby Bourbon Street. Or sip a Sazerac in the courtyard where pirate Jean Lafitte once strolled and smell the soft jasmine on the warm evening breeze. More than 200 custom-designed guest rooms, including 50 townhouse suites, offer views of French Quarter street life, picturesque rooftop skylines, or the tranquil inner courtyard overlooking the pool. The property is 2 blocks from Jackson Square in the heart of the French Quarter.

Rooms feature Chippendale and Queen Anne furnishings accented by two-poster canopied king beds, marble-topped wetbars, and antique writing desks. Marble-finished bathrooms feature the modern touch of a second telephone. Other amenities include a morning newspaper, oversize towels, nightly shoe shine, coffeemakers, bedroom and bathroom TVs, concierge, valet parking, and voice mail. All the favorite tastes of New Orleans are served during breakfast, lunch, and dinner inside the Cafe Rue Orleans. Nightly cocktail hour (with complimentary hors d'oeuvres) is held in the elegant lobby bar. Business needs are met by the hotel's secretarial, multilingual translation, photocopying, fax, telex, daily stock market report, and national and international courier services. Cribs and rollaway beds are available at no extra charge. A $14 million renovation projected to be completed in 2004 promises to restore the property "to its former glory."

Chateau Sonesta Hotel
New Orleans $$$-$$$$$
**800 Iberville Street, New Orleans
(504) 586-0800, (800) 766-3782
www.sonesta.com**
During a triple-digit meltdown day several summers ago, the hotel lobby won Best Air-Conditioning honors hands-down. Crystal chandeliers sparkle from ornate European-style ceilings; the polished marble floors are accented by faux marble columns, jardinieres, and a serene foliage-lush entryway fountain. Demi-chandelier

sconces styled after the beautiful chandeliers illuminating the lobby corridor accentuate the dusty rose-colored wallcoverings and carpets. The fanlight-crowned beveled-glass double doors near the front of the lobby open to The Clock Bar, a popular lounge hangout. Or exit the front doors of this former (and forever beloved) D. H. Holmes department store, turn right, walk a few blocks, and you're on Bourbon Street. La Chatelaine Restaurant is open daily. Also located at the hotel is The Red Fish Grill (see Restaurants), owned and operated by Ralph Brennan of the famous restaurateur family.

More than 251 traditionally furnished guest rooms and suites feature 12-foot ceilings, armoires, double, queen, or king beds, minibars, coffeemakers, and dataport telephones. Many rooms have double French doors that open to balconies overlooking Bourbon Street (book early if you want this ringside view for Mardi Gras), Dauphine Street, or the interior pool and courtyard areas. The third-floor poolside patio and bar offers views of the lush ground-level courtyard with huge hibiscus trees. The drinks are good and the guests always look as though they're happy to be here.

The Claiborne Mansion $$$-$$$$$
**2111 Dauphine Street, New Orleans
(504) 949-7327
www.claibornemansion.com**
Cleo Pelleteri, the congenial owner who bought and renovated this architectural masterpiece in 1993, had no idea that one day her registry would be among the most valuable in the entire city. But, then, who could have fathomed that renowned artist LeRoy Neiman would sign the guest book with a hand-drawn caricature of himself complete with hat, moustache, and dangling cigarette? Pelleteri, however, is mum as to the other luminaries (and there are plenty) who've graced this three-story Greek Revival mansion, built in 1859 by W. C. C. Claiborne II, son of Louisiana's first American governor. Discretion is alive and well at this understated oasis of Creole luxury tucked in the

Faubourg Marigny neighborhood 4 blocks from the French Quarter. This three-story mansion with exterior yellow walls is across the street from Washington Square Park, next door to the popular Santa Fe restaurant, and within easy walking distance of the Marigny's funky bookstores, bric-a-brac shops, and cafes.

Neutral tones, 14-foot ceilings, original pinewood floors, and minimally decorated off-white walls throughout the house provide European-style sophistication for the discerning traveler. Exquisite finishing detail includes a lovely sitting nook at the end of the second-floor hallway and original artwork and framed photography by Julia Sims. Individually decorated rooms and suites feature fresh flowers, oversize marble bathrooms, queen-size beds, telephones with voice mail, and sumptuous breakfasts prepared in the original open-hearth kitchen in the service wing out back. Some rooms have four-poster canopied beds draped with patterned fabric. Modern flourishes include sleek black-metal curving pedestals for the color TV sets and, in some suites, contemporary iron poster beds with white linens. (Another personal touch includes the crystal chandelier Pelleteri had spray-painted white that hangs in the ultraspacious second-floor hallway.)

Splurge on the Creole-style double-parlor suite (No. 11) just off the foyer, featuring original medallion ceilings and a separate living area with marble mantel, a 19th-century-style writing desk, and a Rohler & Campbell grand piano. The bedroom has two iron-post double beds and a palatial bath complete with dressing area, a bronze chandelier, and plush terry robes. The two-story service wing has additional rooms on the ground and second floors that overlook what is perhaps one of the loveliest courtyards in the city. Two towering oak trees provide shade for a tropical garden overflowing with angel trumpets, magnolias, ginger, witch hazel, palms, and ferns. A breezy cabana with ceiling fans fronts a Romanesque pool and, beyond, Pelleteri's personal veggie garden. Complimentary evening wine, cocktails, and hors d'oeuvres are served in the courtyard. Artfully arranged "moon-lighting" in the towering oaks turns the courtyard into a magical place when the sun goes down. Other amenities include complimentary continental breakfast and off-street parking.

Cornstalk Hotel $-$$$
915 Royal Street, New Orleans
(504) 523-1515, (800) 759-6112
www.cornstalkhotel.com

A famous . . . *fence?* As they say, only in New Orleans. But look closely at this beautifully ornate, iron-lace handicraft (if you can take your eyes off the four-columned Greek Revival home in the background). Notice how the intricate pumpkin vines and morning glories entwine the large iron columns topped by ripe ears of corn shucked on their stalks. Carriage drivers often stop in front of this two-story mansion with their out-of-town passengers. They tell the story of Dr. Joseph Biamenti, who brought his young bride to live here from her native Iowa in 1850. She grew homesick for her Midwestern fields of waving corn, so the young groom had the iron treasure built "to soften her loneliness." Judge Francis-Xavier Martin, first Chief Justice of the state supreme court and author of the first history of Louisiana, lived here in the early 1800s. Harriet Beecher Stowe stayed here and was reportedly inspired to pen *Uncle Tom's Cabin* from her visits to nearby slave markets.

Open the beveled-glass front door of this Victorian charmer and step into the chandelier-lit lobby of antique mirrors and dark-green carpet. The hotel's 14 rooms have been furnished with stained-glass windows, fireplaces, and Oriental rugs; some have canopied beds and chandeliers. Vaulted ceilings feature rosettes, scrolls, cherubs, and medallions—relics of the craftsmanship seen in Louisiana sugar plantation homes. Complimentary continental breakfast and morning newspaper can be enjoyed in your room, on the front gallery, or on the breeze-swept balcony overlooking Royal Street (the last being the choice of honeymooners). There's no restaurant or lounge (or pool), but the hotel's convenient Royal Street address puts guests a stone's throw from Bourbon Street and numerous nearby up- and downscale bars and eateries.

Dauphine Orleans $$$$
415 Dauphine Street, New Orleans
(504) 586-1800, (800) 521-7111
www.dauphineorleans.com

Back in the 1850s, May Bailey's girls practiced the world's oldest profession in what is now the hotel bar; Audubon painted his birds in the studio cottage, which today is a meeting room named in his honor. To show off some real New Orleans smarts, though, it won't hurt to know that the romantic Dauphine Patio was once part of the historic Hermann-Grima estate. French double doors open to a tropical palm-filled courtyard accented by the 111-room hotel's exterior yellow walls and lush hanging ferns. The 14 Dauphine Patio rooms of this motor hotel feature exposed brick walls, cherry-wood armoires, bronze chandeliers, and other elegant refinements such as fabrics in rich textures and subdued patterns. Baths have marble-finished sunken tubs. Goosedown pillows in the smoke-free Evergreen rooms should help guests sleep like a baby before rising to a complimentary continental breakfast served with the daily newspaper at your door. Noteworthy freebies include afternoon tea, hors d'oeuvres at cocktail time, and French Quarter transportation. Extra amenities include welcome cocktails, a fitness center, courtyard pool, cable TV, and secured on-site parking.

The Frenchmen $-$$$$
417 Frenchmen Street, New Orleans
(504) 948-2166, (888) 365-2775
www.frenchquarterquartet.com

Each of this hotel's 27 spacious rooms, some with private balconies, has been refurbished and individually decorated with period furnishing reminiscent of the swank Creole homes of the mid-19th century. High ceilings and ceiling fans complete the look. First- and second-floor rooms of this 1850s town house open to a swimming pool and heated spa nestled in a tropical New Orleans courtyard garden. A 24-hour concierge is available to help point guests in the right direction, while the riverfront trolley less than a block away provides a convenient and fun way to get there. Complimentary continental breakfast and limited off-street parking are available. This Faubourg Marigny hotel is a half block from the French Quarter across Esplanade Avenue.

The Historic French
Market Inn $$-$$$$
501 Decatur Street, New Orleans
(504) 561-5621, (888) 538-5651
www.frenchmarketinn.com

Cozy and historic best describe this restored two-story 19th-century inn, built for Baron Joseph Xavier de Pontalba. Today 68 comfortable rooms with original exposed-brick walls and antique furnishings are situated 2 blocks from Jackson Square and 1 block from the Jax Brewery shopping complex. Complimentary cocktails and continental breakfast are part of the package. A pool and hot tub offer relaxation amid the brick courtyard of potted plants, lounge chairs, and table sets.

Hotel Maison deVille $$$$-$$$$$
727 Toulouse Street, New Orleans
(504) 561-5858, (800) 634-1600
www.maisondeville.com

John James Audubon lived with his family in cottage No. 2 in 1821 while he produced a portion of his wildlife masterpieces for *Birds of America*. The apothecary Antoine Amede Peychaud, another early resident, is remembered for serving a potent drink he created of brandy and bitters in a coquetier, or egg cup. More than a century later, Tennessee Williams lived in No. 9 and quaffed Sazeracs in the courtyard garden while working on *A Streetcar Named Desire*. (The lion's share of Dick Cavett's 1974 interview with the legendary playwright was filmed in the courtyard.) Elizabeth Taylor and Robert Redford are among the notable guests. But you don't have to be a famous artist or writer to hear the whisper of Southern grace inside this historic urban getaway.

Sections of this hotel date back to the mid-1700s though much was rebuilt around 1800 after a fire destroyed most of the French Quarter. The main building at 727 Toulouse Street includes the reception room, parlor, concierge, and nine guest rooms. Across the tranquil courtyard and its three-tiered iron fountain are four 1780s slave quarters, later used as *garçonnieres*—bachelors' quarters for the single adult males of Creole families. Each has been painstakingly restored and converted into luxury guest accommodations. The seven Audubon Cottages on nearby Dauphine Street are where the naturalist created some of his oil portraits. The cottages reflect a Creole version of the half-timbered houses of Europe. The old carriage house adjacent to the courtyard is now a two-story suite.

High ceilings, original brick walls, and fireplaces set the historic mood in each of the 16 rooms and 7 cottages; antiques, four-poster beds, and marble bathrooms add romantic overtones. Complimentary amenities include continental breakfast, afternoon tea, or sherry in the parlor (designed for quiet readers), pillow pralines at turndown, and free shoe shine if you park your loafers outside your door before going to bed. The hotel's award-winning Bistro (see Restaurants), decorated with red-leather banquettes, beveled-glass mirrors, and French impressionist–style paintings, has garnered its share of culinary accolades over the years.

Hotel Monteleone $$$–$$$$$
214 Royal Street, New Orleans
(504) 523–3341, (800) 535–9595
www.hotelmonteleone.com
In 1886 Antonio Monteleone, a shoemaker from Contessa, Italy, put his name on this hotel across the street from his cobbler shop. More than a century and five major

additions later, this opulent and (still) family-owned landmark inspires some people to say, "The French Quarter begins in the lobby of the Monteleone." Just push past the gleaming brass front doors and step into the sparkling lobby. European elegance never enjoyed a better nouveau interpretation, accented by a quartet of gleaming teardrop-shaped crystal chandeliers, polished marble floors, and, of course, the hotel's gorgeous grandfather clock carved in mahogany by Antonio Puccio in 1909, which towers 12 feet and chimes at the quarter hour. The renovated Queen Anne ballroom provides a richly woven flashback to 18th-century drawing rooms with its mix of Wedgwood and Arabesque art forms, Italian chandeliers, and European tapestries.

This is the kind of place where guests can expect to find the longtime bellman affectionately nicknamed "Hotel" Al. He started work here in the 1950s. One of the bartenders began his first shift in the early 1970s when the revolving Carousel Bar, which opened in 1944, was already famous among locals and visitors alike. But barstools, not flying horses, are the mode of transportation within the lounge's cobalt-blue walls. Artwork lighting includes wall-mounted lamps clutched by plaster clown fists. Nightclub-style, high-backed booths and a starlight ceiling in the adjoining room set the stage for nightly entertainment at the grand piano.

Today this landmark is one of the oldest continuously operated hotels in the city. People from Tennessee Williams and Truman Capote to political kingpins and movie stars have called it home. The hotel's 600 guest rooms and suites are elegantly furnished with armoires and king- and queen-size beds; some suites have four-poster canopied beds, separate vanity and dressings areas, and views of the French Quarter. Head rooftop to freshen your tan line, to take a dip in the heated pool, or walk a few miles on one of the fitness center's treadmills. The hotel's two lounges and three restaurants include the fine-dining Hunt Room Grill. Valet parking is available in the hotel's 350-car garage; complimentary coffee in the morning should help start off the day's activities.

An ongoing $60 million renovation ~~scheduled for completion in 2004 will cre~~ ate 20 new minisuites and one grand suite.

Hotel St. Marie $$–$$$
**827 Toulouse Street, New Orleans
(504) 561-8951, (800) 366-2743
www.hotelstmarie.com**
This elegantly restored property owned by New Orleans' Valentino family (which also owns the Place d'Armes and Prince Conti Hotels; see below) offers the easy comfort and subtle grace of an authentic European guesthouse. Brick walls with traditional gaslights frame the modest palm- and fern-lined courtyard and pool of this 94-room hotel, a half block from Bourbon Street. Many rooms offer balcony views of the French Quarter. Guests can dine out or opt for the hotel's 827½ Restaurant, which serves breakfast, lunch, and dinner Tuesday through Friday. The open-air, street-side Bistro serves breakfast and lunch daily. Valet parking and complimentary continental breakfast and daily newspaper are included in the tariff.

Hotel Villa Convento $$–$$$
**616 Ursulines Street, New Orleans
(504) 522-1793
www.villaconvento.com**
More than one carriage driver has told wide-eyed visitors the story of the legendary House of the Rising Sun. Some people speculate that it might have been this place once upon a time. No one is sure. What is known is that this four-story Creole town house was built around 1833 on land purchased from the Ursuline nuns (whose convent is nearby; hence the name). The property passed to a succession of owners and even served time as a rooming house. The most famous tenant, Jimmy Buffett, came back with a video crew to film a documentary on his early life in New Orleans. The modern-day owners, the Campo family, bought this historic building in 1981. The family comes with a little history of its own—they are Isleños, descendents of Canary Islanders who immigrated to New Orleans from Spain in the early 1800s. Today 25 rooms located 2 blocks from the French Market are individually decorated; some have high ceilings, four-poster beds, and balconies overlooking Ursulines Street. Two courtyard rooms feature original brick walls; two fourth-floor suites offer panoramic views of the Mississippi River and Vieux Carré rooftops. Complimentary coffee, tea, and croissants are served each morning.

Le Richelieu $$–$$$$$
**1234 Chartres Street, New Orleans
(504) 529-2492, (800) 535-9653
www.lerichelieuhotel.com**
All things being equal, an "affordable class" hotel such as this—with its history, charm, service, and discretion—should cost a whole lot more. Maybe that's why ex-Beatle Paul McCartney (for whom money is certainly no object) hunkered down here with his brood for two months back in 1975 while recording his Wings album *Venus and Mars* at Sea-Saint Studio during Mardi Gras. McCartney, his wife, Linda, and three children booked an entire floor. When fans asked if the cute former Mop Top was registered at the hotel, they were told "no." It was the truth (the registration was in the name of his company). But how did the Mac avoid being mobbed on the streets while he mingled with revelers? He did what a lot of Carnivalites do—

he masked as a clown/jester. On Ash Wednesday, the day after Mardi Gras when things get back to normal, Sir Paul reportedly composed a song called "My Carnival" at the hotel. The tune never made it onto the album. Does it matter? (Guests can stay in the Paul McCartney Suite for $225 and up per night.)

This motor hotel is named for the Armand-Jean du Plessis, Duke and Cardinal de Richelieu, the powerful Prime Minister of Louis XIII and the acknowledged architect of France's 17th-century grandeur. A portrait of Cardinal Richelieu, painted by local artist Carl Cramer, hangs in the lobby. The site was originally part of a 1745 land grant from Louis XV of France to the Ursuline nuns so that they could care for sick French soldiers and establish a school for "young ladies." As a result, a caserbes, or lodging, and hospital were built at this location, which housed French, Spanish, and American soldiers for more than a century. A rebellion led by French patriot Nicholas Chauvin de La Freniere broke out when outraged colonists learned that the cash-strapped Louis XV had secretly given Louisiana to his cousin, Charles III of Spain. La Freniere and four of his compatriots were executed by firing squad in the barracks courtyard of what is now the hotel's parking lot. Interestingly, the La Freniere–led "October Rebellion" of 1766 was the first revolution against a foreign power on soil of the Continental United States. The land was divided into lots and sold to citizens in 1824.

This quiet and historic Greek Revival row house and former macaroni factory located on the edge of the French Quarter near Faubourg Marigny has long attracted luminaries. Signed photographs of guests including Mickey Rooney and Barry Manilow hang on the manager's office walls. Longtime owner Frank Rochefort and manager Joanne Kirkpatrick oversee 86 individually decorated Victorian rooms and suites with quality reproduction furnishings, armoires, brass ceiling fans, desks, hair dryers, ironing boards, and refrigerators. Other amenities

include percale sheets and free local calls. Some rooms have balconies overlooking the courtyard and pool or Chartres Street. Additional creature comforts include valet laundry, babysitting, cafe, bar/lounge, room service, and private self-park-and-lock lot (one of the few hotels in the city where guests can park their own cars and keep their keys). The hotel is nearby the Old U.S. Mint and French Market and within walking distance of Jackson Square and Bourbon Street.

Maison Dupuy Hotel $$$–$$$$$
1001 Toulouse Street, New Orleans
(504) 586-8000, (800) 535–9177
www.maisondupuy.com
Historic footnotes have never failed to lend charm and nuance to the 300-year-old French Quarter—and this address is no exception. John Pitot, the first elected mayor of New Orleans, built the first U.S. cotton press at this site in the 18th century. During the 19th and 20th centuries, this corner site was home to everything from a blacksmith shop to a sheet metal company. It wasn't until 1973 that Clarence and Milton Dupuy built and opened their hotel (the last allowed in the French Quarter before a moratorium was enacted in 1975). The brothers sold the property in 1996 to the Thayer Lodging Group, which undertook an extensive $5 million renovation one year later.

Today guests at this residential neighborhood hotel, 2 blocks from Bourbon Street, can count on peace and quiet—a commodity worth its weight in gold to anyone visiting during Mardi Gras or other special events. Two hundred remodeled and redecorated spacious guest rooms each feature imported draperies, signature local art, 19th-century furnishings (including armoires and writing desks), and marble bathrooms. Balconies overlook the French Quarter or the hotel's lush fountain courtyard accented with gas lamps and potted palms—a best-kept secret perfect for romantic evening dinners. Other amenities include a fitness center and an on-site restaurant, Dominique's, presided

HOTELS

Have more questions than answers? For visitors and in-town weekenders staying at the city's hotels, the concierge is a font of information and the inside track on everything from the best nights to dine at a particular restaurant to advice on where to locate that hard-to-find voodoo gris-gris. These savvy professionals of the hotel industry are worth their weight in gold (or at least a good tip).

over by acclaimed chef Dominique Macquet, a native of Mauritius and a graduate of the South African Culinary School.

Olivier House Hotel $$$–$$$$$
**828 Toulouse Street, New Orleans
(504) 525-8456
www.olivierhouse.com**
Original exposed brick walls, hanging ferns, huge banana trees, and a caged pair of curious macaws make the gas lamp–dotted garden courtyard an appealing place in which to savor the hotel's complimentary morning coffee. This trio of town houses was built in 1839 for wealthy plantation owner Marianne Bienvenue Olivier. In 1970 Jim and Kathryn Danner bought and renovated the property, 1 block from Bourbon Street, and still operate it as a 42-room hotel. To the right of the lobby is a spacious chandelier-lit parlor with original brass lighting fixtures and a marble-mantel fireplace.

No two guest rooms or suites are alike. The Lobby Suite fronts Toulouse Street and features a queen bed, mahogany headboard, plush scarlet carpet, marble fireplace mantel, and 16-foot ceilings. The Garden Suite is tucked away at the far back end of the courtyard. Lush foliage bathed by sun rays streaming through a skylight and arched windows adorn a gurgling fountain in the airy, well-lit living area; a circular wrought-iron staircase leads to the loft bedroom and private bath. The Honeymoon Suite has

romance written all over it. This quaint Creole cottage dates to the 1700s and features antique furnishings and rugs, armoires, marble-mantel fireplace, separate dining and living areas, full kitchen, and wet bar. The large sunken bath off the bedroom looks nearly as inviting as the cottage's private brick courtyard with privacy wall and a pair of Adirondack chairs.

Omni Royal Orleans $$$$–$$$$$
**621 St. Louis Street, New Orleans
(504) 529-5333, (800) 843-6664
www.omnihotels.com**
If it's views you're after, this 346-room luxury hotel has plenty. For starters there's the seventh-floor pool lounge, La Riviera, open April through October, which offers a limited lunchtime menu of sandwiches and salads but serves up one of the best rooftop views of the French Quarter skyline in the city. Head up the concrete steps to the breeze-cooled observation deck for a terrific panorama of St. Louis Cathedral, the Mississippi River, and the Crescent City Connection twin span. Where's the beef? It's downstairs at the ground-level Old English–style Rib Room, an award-winning eatery best known for its mesquite-grill rotisserie. Just as savory are the window-table views of passersby on Royal Street. The Touche Bar meantime is a sidewalk cafe that comes alive when the after-work crowd of French Quarter antiques and art dealers drops by.

Rooms decorated in 19th-century style for the "casual voyager" looking for grace and comfort offer romantic views of lush tropical courtyards, Jackson Square, the Mississippi River, or the rooftops of the Vieux Carré. Amenities include hair dryers, goosedown pillows, minibars, original artwork, complimentary high-sped wireless Internet access and computer modem hookups and dataports, 24-hour room service, same-day valet and laundry services, babysitting, fitness center, and (perhaps most important considering the city's unpredictable weather) umbrellas. The present-day hotel sits on the historic site of the original St. Louis Exchange Hotel, built in the 1830s when this French-turned-American colony was growing by leaps and bounds, flush with cash and visitors from upriver cities. After the 1841 fire it was rebuilt into the St. Louis Hotel. Guests were charged $2.50 a day, and dinner was served to gentlemen from three until five o'clock; ladies at five o'clock. The "free lunch" was born at the main bar thanks to management, who figured all those noontime drinkers needed some nourishment.

Many of those same drinkers included young Creole gents who ordered their refreshments by the name of the container in which it was served—coquetier (egg cup), which sounds like "cocktail" when said in French. A hurricane destroyed the hotel in 1915; 45 years later this hotel was built and opened its doors.

Spanish wrought-iron balconies, a French facade, and interior combination of 19th-century English, French, Spanish, and American antiques and artifacts pay homage to the past. So, too, does the impressive marble stairway guarded by a pair of priceless Venetian Moors, which leads to the brightly lit lobby of gilt mirrors, freshly cut flowers, polished brass appointments, and crystal chandeliers. Just off the lobby is the elegant drawing room–like atmosphere of the Esplanade Lounge and its selection of flaming coffees and French pastries. All of which have made this place a favorite among Europeans.

Place d'Armes $$-$$$
625 St. Ann Street, New Orleans
(504) 524-4531, (800) 366-2743
www.placedarmes.com
Sometimes there's a lot to be said for simplicity. And if you want to get far from the madding crowd of megahotels but still be close to the action, this small, casual property with classic old New Orleans architecture may hold the key. Near Jackson Square, this hotel, located between Chartres and Royal Streets, is only a few

magic yards from St. Louis Cathedral, Cafe du Monde, the Mississippi River, and many other French Quarter attractions. Or walk 2 blocks in the opposite direction and you're on Bourbon Street. Nine adjoining, beautifully restored 18th-century row houses with 83 guest rooms (warning—some don't have windows) surround a lushly landscaped pool courtyard of magnolia and banana trees, perfect for relaxing at the end of the day before heading out to dinner at one of the nearby seafood or Creole dining establishments. Complimentary continental breakfast and valet parking make up the short list of amenities (there is no restaurant or lounge) at this comfortable charmer.

Prince Conti Hotel $$$
830 Conti Street, New Orleans
(504) 529-4172, (800) 366-2743
www.princecontihotel.com
Discreetly tucked away near the heart of the French Quarter, ½ block off Bourbon Street, is this European-style pension hotel with 71 refurbished guest rooms, many with period antiques. Guests can start off the day with complimentary homemade biscuits and New Orleans coffee and chicory at the new breakfast cafe. Other amenities include secured drive-in parking and valet laundry. Located in the carriageway is The Bombay Club, a sophisticated lounge featuring nearly 100 different types of martinis.

The Saint Louis $$-$$$$
730 Bienville Street, New Orleans
(504) 581-7300, (800) 535-9706
www.stlouishotel.com
This site was the 19th-century home of a Spanish family and, later, a brewing company before the present-day hotel was built in 1971. Two of the best features of this gem, a mix of French colonial and Creole architecture, are its quiet brick courtyard and central location in the French Quarter, ½ block from Bourbon and Royal Streets. Secluded privacy in elegant surroundings close to the Quarter's

nerve center may seem like a tall order, but this courtly retreat of Creole gentility pulls it off without breaking a sweat. Many of the 83 spacious rooms and suites, each decorated with French Provincial antiques or reproductions, have wrought-iron balconies overlooking the hotel's lush Mediterranean courtyard and stone fountain (except during inclement weather, when it's covered by rain flaps). All rooms feature separate vanity areas, concierge service, complimentary newspaper, and minibars; some have beautifully decorated parlors and walk-in closets.

The hotel's award-winning Louis XVI Restaurant (see Restaurants chapter) offers top-shelf white-linen service and Creole-Continental cuisine at its best. But the weekend brunches may be the best way to enjoy the courtyard. Order the eggs Sardou or Benedict to get the morning off right, teamed with a side of steaming grits and an eye-opening Bloody Mary. On Fat Tuesday this courtyard venue earns its stripes as an ideal place for breakfast (reservations are a must) because you will be only yards away from Mardi Gras and all of its Carnival madness.

Soniat House $$$-$$$$$
1133 Chartres Street, New Orleans
(504) 522-0570, (800) 544-8808
www.soniathouse.com

Talk about grand introductions. We're referring, of course, to the fabulous carriageway entrance to this quintessential romantic hotel, especially at night, when a multitude of candles light the shadowy, lush courtyard. From the open galleries framed by lace ironwork to the lovely peach walls accented by white double French doors with romantic fanlights, this scene has been known to breathe the fire of pure Creole passion into more than one couple on their umpteenth "honeymoon." Originally built in 1829 by prosperous plantation owner Joseph Soniat Dufossat as a double town house for his large family's city visits, this brick-walled time capsule has played host to such modern-day guests as Brad Pitt, Jessica Lange, and

Robert Duvall. And if they enjoyed the privacy and discreet service, you probably will, too. This place is as peaceful as a country inn (it's next to an 18th-century Ursuline convent) and as intimate as a private home (you'd never know it was 2 blocks from looney-bin Bourbon Street). Of course, a meticulous restoration prior to its opening in 1983 didn't hurt.

Proprietor Rodney Smith has furnished each room and suite with all the comforts of a luxury hotel without disturbing the architectural integrity of the house. Rooms feature the English, French, and Louisiana antiques Smith and his wife, Frances (who owns an antiques business), have collected during their quarter century of world travel. Their attention to detail at this 33-room-and-suite "best small hotel in New Orleans" makes guests and travel cognoscenti alike nearly pass out with praise. (On a wall of framed testimonials is this one: "These people will spoil you rotten.") Consider: Custom fabrics, antique Oriental rugs, four-poster beds draped with a canopy of linen or century-old crewel embroidery, silk curtains, polished hardwood floors, woodcut prints, and paintings by contemporary New Orleans artists. The more down-to-earth amenities include bathside telephones, Frette Egyptian cotton bed linens, goosedown pillows, and spa baths in several of the rooms.

Enjoy breakfast (the only meal served) at one of the white-linen tables around the lily pond in the lush garden courtyard of sweet olive trees, Japanese magnolias, pineapple guava, and ferns. Steaming freshly baked biscuits are accompanied by strawberry preserves (homemade in Smith's hometown of Pontchatoula, 90 minutes away), sweet butter, fresh-squeezed orange juice, and rich Creole coffee. Cocktail hour is whenever you like at the courtyard honor bar, where guests get to play bartender. And, if that isn't enough, the hotel's private car can be booked for airport transfer. A three-night minimum stay is required on weekends year-round.

Ursuline Guest House **$$**
708 Ursulines Street, New Orleans
(504) 525-8509, (800) 654-2351
www.ursulineguesthouse.com
Complimentary wine is served at five
o'clock each evening in the rectangular
palm-framed courtyard of this 18th-
century hotel. This adults-only budget
accommodation, tucked several blocks
away from the noise of Bourbon Street
in a quiet residential neighborhood, has
been a favorite among gay and lesbian
travelers for years. Of course, everyone is
welcome. Half the 14 rooms are on ground
level and open onto the breezy courtyard,
which features a Jacuzzi; many of the
second-floor rooms open onto a gallery.
Guest rooms are clean, pleasant, and sim-
ply furnished with double or queen beds,
ceiling fans, and brick fireplaces. (Some
guests may find the rooms with window-
unit air conditioners a bit noisy.) Compli-
mentary breakfast is served each morning.
Reserve one of the three available off-
street parking spaces early (cost is $12
per night).

W New Orleans
French Quarter **$$$-$$$$$**
316 Chartres Street, New Orleans
(504) 581-1200, (800) 448-4927
www.whotels.com
The echo of a nearby paddle wheeler's
calliope welcomes fans of small European
hotels to this intimate property. Many of
the 98 deluxe, newly remodeled, and traditionally furnished rooms and carriage
house suites have balconies overlooking
the lushly landscaped and flower-filled
fountain courtyard and pool; others overlook French Quarter streets. Oversize
rooms have double, queen, or king beds
with 250 thread count sheets, down comforters and pillows, oversize desks, 27-inch
TVs with high-speed Internet access, coffeemakers, minibars, and dual-line telephones with voice mail. Room service for
breakfast, lunch, and dinner is available
from Bacco (see Restaurants chapter).
But it would be a shame not to experience
in person this highly acclaimed on-site

restaurant owned by the Brennan family
of Brennan's and Commander's Palace
fame. So take a lint brush to the sports
coat or slip into that cute little number
you bought on Royal Street yesterday
afternoon, and head downstairs for dinner.
One block from Royal Street's art galleries
and antique shops, 2 blocks from bustling
Bourbon Street, and 4 blocks from Jackson Square, this hotel offers valet parking,
complimentary newspaper, and 24-hour
coffee and tea service.

CBD/DOWNTOWN AND WAREHOUSE DISTRICT

The Ambassador **$$-$$$$**
535 Tchoupitoulas Street, New Orleans
(504) 527-5271, (888) 527-5271
www.ahno.com
Many of the city's hotels possess the req-
uisite charm and elegance to woo visitors
"from the moment they enter the lobby
doors." And this facility, with its sparkling
white porcelain floors, certainly deserves
to be in that number. But it's while head-
ing in the opposite direction that guests
will come to appreciate one of this hotel's
finest attributes—its location, smack in the
middle of the Warehouse Arts District.
The trendy district is chock-a-block with
renovated warehouses now serving as art
galleries and studios, restaurants, condos,
nightclubs, and even the Louisiana Chil-
dren's Museum. The district is an imagina-
tive, fun, and leisurely place to stroll,
especially after the bustling French Quar-
ter crowds only 3 blocks away have
started to work your last good nerve.
Three 19th-century coffee warehouses
were renovated to create this property—
an intermingling of old and new set
against the city's thriving riverfront dis-
trict. Each of the 165 guest rooms come
with four-poster wrought-iron beds, hard-
wood floors, and 18th-century-style desks;
51 guest rooms also have 13-foot ceilings,
nightly turndown, and wrought iron bal-
conies. Amenities include complimentary
continental breakfast and 24-hour lounge,

in-room safe, coffeemakers, and hair dryers. Telephones with voice mail and
fax/modems will help captains of commerce get down to business. A tropical
courtyard features a flowing fountain and
oversize swimming pool.

Courtyard by Marriott $$$–$$$$
124 St. Charles Avenue, New Orleans
(504) 581-9005, (800) 321-2211
This 140-room hotel in the Central Business District is only a 10-minute walk to
the French Quarter's famed Pat
O'Brien's—and, most likely, a 30-minute
walk back. (In New Orleans the shortest
distance between any two bars is a
zigzag.) Spacious, moderately priced
lodgings offer guests at this six-story
hotel a chance to explore the past: Courtyard worked with a local historical society
to re-create the Verandah hotel, which
stood on the site from 1839 to 1855.
Ornate iron-trellis balconies overlook St.
Charles Avenue and provide views of
downtown New Orleans; a dramatic
atrium inside incorporates original Verandah columns. Attention to the comfort of
present-day business and leisure guests
can be seen in such amenities as large
work desks, complimentary newspaper,
"reach-anywhere phones," indoor
whirlpool, and exercise room. The hotel is
on the St. Charles Avenue streetcar line,
which provides easy access to nearby
attractions.

Fairmont Hotel $$$–$$$$$
123 Baronne Street, New Orleans
(504) 529-7111
www.fairmont.com
Huey P. Long used this well-loved landmark as his campaign headquarters. Eight
U.S. presidents from Coolidge to Clinton
have stayed under its roof. Haile Selassie
and General Charles DeGaulle once
enjoyed its Victorian extravagance (but
not together). It was the model for Arthur
Hailey's best-selling novel *Hotel* (staff
remembers him taking "copious" notes
and can even identify some of the charac-

ters in the book). In 1932 radio station
WWL–AM set up shop here and has
broadcast performances nationwide live
from the Blue Room for nearly two
decades. And if that's not enough, the
Sazerac Bar & Grill is the home of the
famous bourbon-and-bitters drink of the
same name, invented here more than 140
years ago. The hotel was sold to the Fairmont's family of luxury hotels in 1965.

Walk under this building's gray canopy
and past the bronze front doors into the
opulent block-long lobby. Gilded columns,
green potted palms, red Oriental rugs, and
sparkling crystal chandeliers show the
way. If by-the-book European refinement
has a name, it's this Big Easy institution—
one of the oldest grand hotels in the
country. This property has been near to
the hearts of generations of New Orleanians since it opened in 1893 as the six-
story Grunewald "in full readiness for the
Carnival of 1894." An adjacent 400-room,
14-story annex was added and opened in
1908. In 1923 the hotel was renamed the
Roosevelt (in honor of Teddy, who had
died five years earlier) after the original
Grunewald was demolished and the
annex's public rooms were refurbished at
a cost of $500,000. A 16-story edifice, the
same height as the annex, was completed.

A five-year, $5-million renovation has
restored the original grandeur while
adding state-of-the-art services and
amenities demanded by sophisticated
travelers. A good example is the rooftop
resort with a view of the city, heated pool,
tennis courts, and glass-enclosed fitness
center. The Fairmont Court offers freshly
baked pastries in the morning, desserts in
the afternoon, and hors d'oeuvres in the
evening accompanied by traditional New
Orleans jazz. The Sazerac Bar & Grille is
now open.

All rooms (including 85 luxury suites)
have been tastefully redefined in contemporary residential style with guests' comfort in mind. Most feature king or queen
beds with extra-length mattresses, 200-
thread-count linens, down pillows, billowy

comforters, and, for nights out on the town, electric shoe polishers. New tile floors, hand-milled soaps, and oversize towels add a personal touch to the marble bathrooms. Other amenities include a business center, in-room fax machines, and 24-hour room service. During the holidays the lobby is transformed into a "winter wonderland" decorated with Christmas trees, a manger, and thousands of lights.

Holiday Inn Downtown
Superdome $$–$$$$$
330 Loyola Avenue, New Orleans
(504) 581-1600, (800) 535-7830
www.holiday-inn.com
It's hard to miss the 150-foot mural of the early 1900s Selmer clarinet painted by local artist Robert Dafford on the Poydras Street exterior side of this downtown hotel. The mural is how this franchise property tips its horn to the birthplace of jazz and the legendary New Orleans musicians like Buddy Bolden and Louis Armstrong who made it all possible. Dafford and Louisiana artists Shirley Messina, Stig Marcussen, and Daniel Breaux were commissioned to create the original series of art seen throughout the property's public areas and guest room floors.

Check out the murals of Carnival parades in the Mardi Gras Lounge as well as those of famous jazz musicians in the lobby. Particularly noteworthy is the depiction of First Man of Jazz Buddy Bolden performing at the Union Sons Hall (nicknamed "Funky Butt Hall") in 1905. Bolden is the cornet player in the middle. Nearly 300 rooms and suites, 2 blocks from the Superdome and 3 blocks from the French Quarter, include telephones with voice mail, hair dryers, irons/ironing boards, and minisafes. Guest rooms on the key-access club level floor also have honor bars and coffeemakers; a club room serves continental breakfast and afternoon hors d'oeuvres. Other amenities include a rooftop pool, ATM service, complimentary morning coffee and evening ice cream in the lobby, and a restaurant, lounge, and gift shop.

Hotel de L'Eau Vive $$–$$$$$
315 Tchoupitoulas Street, New Orleans
(504) 592-0300
www.hoteldeleauvive.com
The hotel name means house of the living waters, a fitting and serene moniker for this four-story all-suite hotel located in a historical landmark on a quiet, tree-lined stretch of the Central Business District. The elegantly furnished lobby tells only part of the story of this 34-suite property, opened in 1988. The rest is to be found in the one-bedrooms suites, each with spacious living room outfitted with private phone, TV, and sofa sleeper; full kitchen (with dishes and small appliances); plush bedroom with armoire; and glistening-tile bathroom featuring whirlpool and shower. Rates include double occupancy up to four persons, making this property a bargain for traveling families looking to splurge a tad on luxury. (Two- and three-bedroom suites are also available.) A pool surrounded by a lush tropical courtyard adds a nice touch of New Orleans–style leisure. Other amenities include complimentary coffee daily and free croissants and Danish Saturday through Monday.

Hotel Inter-Continental
New Orleans $$–$$$
444 St. Charles Avenue, New Orleans
(504) 525-5566, (800) 455-6563
http://neworleans.intercontinental.com
Longtime New Orleans chef Willy Cohn's Veranda restaurant menu isn't the only reason to stay at this 500-room modern luxury hotel. Although many people who have sampled the Creole-Continental fare prepared by the Cologne, Germany, native (and officer of the Confriere de la Chaine des Rotisseurs) say it's one of the best reasons. This stylish hotel, part of a London-based joint venture by Pan American Life Insurance Co. and Inter-Continental Hotels and Resorts, is on the St. Charles Avenue streetcar line; the Superdome, Convention Center, and the Warehouse Arts District are within easy walking distance.

Comfortably furnished rooms in this 15-story, glass-and-granite downtown

It's been said that the Sunday brunch was invented in New Orleans. Not surprisingly, many of the best hotels offer Sunday (and even Saturday) brunches. Some offer buffets, others feature courtyard dining and live jazz, while still others tout "bottomless" champagne. A few offer all of the above. Reservations are often required.

high-rise include such amenities as mini-bars and separate dressing areas; the bath area has a hair dryer, telephone, and mini-TV. Six "environmental" rooms are equipped with special water- and air-filtration systems. Nearly 40 deluxe guest rooms and suites on the Governor's Floor include six executive suites named after some of Louisiana's historic heads of state. Each suite is decorated in the furnishings and paintings of its statesman's time period. Extra amenities include large marble baths, plush bathrobes, Jacuzzis, full kitchens, dual-line dataport telephones, and a lounge offering complimentary cocktails and continental breakfast. A landscaped garden courtyard with original musical sculpture is on the fifth floor; the pool and fitness center (equipped with Lifecycles, treadmills, a Universal weight machine, and free weights) are rooftop. Four restaurants and lounges, including the Veranda, offer breakfast, lunch buffet, dinner, and a Sunday champagne jazz brunch.

Hotel LeCirque $-$$
2 Lee Circle, New Orleans
(504) 962-0900, (800) 684-9525
www.hotellecirque.com
Travel and Leisure magazine has already given a thumbs-up to this hip new 137-room boutique hotel, centrally located on the St. Charles Avenue streetcar line between Uptown and downtown's Central Business and Warehouse Arts Districts. Step inside and see why. Lobby decor is minimalist Asian fusion with an emphasis on clean lines augmented by Art Deco accents, bamboo half-walls, original art-

work, and retro chairs in the sunken public sitting area. Guest rooms continue the theme with framed black-and-white art photographs, muted colors, and sconces. Amenities include walk-in showers (but no tubs), hair dryers, iron/ironing boards, coffeemakers, TV, and dataports. A full gym and indoor pool are on-site.

Hotel Monaco $$-$$$$
333 St. Charles Avenue, New Orleans
(504) 561-0010
www.monaco-neworleans.com
If "Rick" had owned a hotel instead of a bar in the movie *Casablanca,* it might have looked like the Hotel Monaco. "Savvy," "urbane," and "hot" are just a few of the words that have been used to describe the ambience. From the exterior Art Deco signage to the lobby's irresistibly well-traveled, eclectic decor, this 19-story, $34-million restoration, opened in summer 2001, is a sensualist's dream hotel. Built in 1926, the one-time Masonic Temple features a mostly original Art Deco lobby of black and cream marble walls and potted palms. The front desk looks like a row of stacked steamer trunks; the hotel's garment bags are zebra-striped. The artfully decorated public sitting area features Caribbean and African flourishes, a nod to this city's cultural ties to the West Indies and West Africa, and floor-to-ceiling gauze curtains that create an intimate, cozy environment for the hotel's complimentary wine hour, held daily from 5:00 to 6:00 P.M.

The 250 guest rooms (including 22 suites) feature faux mink throws, leopard-print terry robes, partial mosquito netting over the beds, down comforters, armoires, and cordless telephones. Sliding pocket doors open to pistachio-colored bathrooms decked out with palm-tree wallpaper, Aveda bath products, and Starbucks coffee. Other amenities include computer dataports, complimentary high-speed Internet access, a safe large enough for a laptop computer, stereo, minibar, voice mail, complimentary shoe shines, daily *USA Today,* coffee (and even water for runners), and hair dryer. This pet-friendly property also offers guests 24-hour room service, valet laundry, and complimentary goldfish to keep you company. The popular Cobalt restaurant (see Restaurant chapter) and a 22,500-square-foot fitness center are located here.

Hyatt Regency New Orleans $$$–$$$$$
**500 Poydras Plaza, New Orleans
(504) 561-1234, (800) 233-1234
www.hyatt.com**

Sleep in, enjoy a late breakfast, and still be among the first customers through the doors at Macy's during one of its daylong sales. Then go see the nation's largest domed stadium and home to the New Orleans Saints and the Sugar Bowl. It's a snap when you're a guest at this 32-story atrium hotel, which is connected to the New Orleans Centre shopping complex and the Louisiana Superdome. Grab your camera and credit cards and take the hotel's free shuttle down to the Riverfront and French Quarter for a day of sightseeing. When night falls, head back for dinner and take the glass elevator up to the casual Top of the Dome steak house (order the prime rib), the city's only revolving rooftop restaurant. Stop by the Atrium Mint Julep lounge for an after-dinner cognac. Public areas in the modern lobby feature contemporary furnishings, such as marble-and-bronze tables. The 1,184 guest rooms and suites located in the heart of Downtown are traditionally furnished. Many rooms have terraces or patio views. Other amenities include a business center, outdoor pool, whirlpool, and fitness center.

International House $$$–$$$$$
**221 Camp Street, New Orleans
(504) 553-9550, (800) 633-5770
www.ihhotel.com**

The gas lamps gracing the Camp Street entrance of this 12-story elegant boutique hotel were designed by Drew Bevelo, a third-generation New Orleans lantern maker whose family's shop is still located in the French Quarter. Bevolo based his design on a hazy 1918 photograph that he found crumpled in an archive. Inside the 1906 beaux-arts building, the forged-steel front desk inspired by a windblown field of Louisiana wild irises is not the only striking feature found in the stylish, contemporary lobby. The handsome hand-made chandeliers by local furniture designer Guy Martin feature silk shades and nickel-plated chili peppers hanging from 25-foot ceilings above a floor of marble and indigenous oak. Decor changes with the seasons, a tradition upheld by generations of New Orleanians, who alter their homes for summer and winter in response to climatic conditions. Here, for example, as winter gives way to summer, wool gives way to sisal rugs and cotton slipcovers, which allow furnishings to breathe as well as to keep perspiration off the fine upholstery.

The hotel bar, Loa, named for the divine spirits of voodoo, sets a deliciously sensual mood for casting a love spell thanks to its sumptuous seating, sculpted bar, and candlelight-only illumination. (Order the Flambeau, an equally intoxicating mix of spiced rum, Grand Marnier, and Chambord.)

All 119 "minimalist" rooms are furnished with eclectic touches ranging from mineral water–bottle vases with fresh local wildflowers to armoires inspired by Dutreuil Barjon Jr., a free man of color who distinguished himself as one of Louisiana's finest 19th-century craftsmen. Other accents include crinkle sheers, plush duvets, and original black-and-white photographs of New Orleans jazz greats. Bathrooms feature terry-cloth robes, Aveda bath products, and double-headed glass showers or oversize tubs. Guests looking for the ultimate discreet touch will appreciate the private telephone number direct to each room. Nonsmoking floors are available. For an extra fee and 30 days' advance notice, honeymoon couples in search of something off the beaten path can opt for the Sanctuary of Love voodoo package: A voodoo priestess builds an altar in your room and leads you through a ceremony of love spells to bless your union. The ritual is not legally binding. The International House established the first World Trade Center in the United States in 1949, becoming an international gathering place and New Orleans icon for presidents, ambassadors, and other dignitaries of the day. Its founding principle, "peace through trade," was a cornerstone of political thought following World War II.

The Lafayette Hotel $$$–$$$$$
**600 St. Charles Avenue, New Orleans
(504) 524-4441, (800) 733-4754
www.neworleansfinehotels.com**
The dignified Old World charm of the polished French mahogany front desk complements a foyer of Italian marble floors, wood moldings, and English carpets. When the Wirth family built this five-story brick hotel in 1918 on fashionable St. Charles Avenue, it was intended to spur the transformation of the neighborhood "from a sleepy line of boardinghouses into a hum of activity," according to a September 3, 1916, article in the *New Orleans Item*. During World War II, however, the property was used by the Navy as barracks for Waves (Women Accepted for Volunteer Emergency Service) and afterwards fell into disrepair. The hotel reopened for the 1984 World's Fair but closed two years later until 1991, when developers Mickey Palmer and Patrick Quinn pumped $6 million into a major renovation effort.

This historic hotel adjacent to the Warehouse Arts District and 5 blocks from the French Quarter was worth the wait. It has been restored to its former splendor with original French doors and wrought-iron balconies (a perfect spot for catching beads from Mardi Gras parades that roll down The Avenue). Each of the 44 rooms and suites upstairs is individually decorated and furnished with designer fabrics, gilt mirrors, and English botanical prints; the lavish marble baths with elegant brass fittings are matched by such thoughtful touches as thick terry bathrobes and French-milled soaps. Other amenities include minibars, hair dryers, and umbrellas. (Suites feature a wet bar, refrigerator, and VCR; some have four-poster beds and a whirlpool.) Attentive yet unobtrusive service is the name of the game here. Two new restaurants have opened—the casual Lafayette Sports Club and the city's first Russian fine-dining venue, Rasputin.

Le Meridien $$$–$$$$$
**614 Canal Street, New Orleans
(504) 525-6500
www.meridienneworleans.com**
Traditional French luxury mixed with contemporary elegance is the hallmark of this downtown ultraluxury property staffed by multilingual employees. The 494-room hotel is on the border of the French Quarter and within easy walking distance of the Mississippi River attractions, streetcar lines, and Jackson Square. Its 30-story tower is set back from the facade of its Canal Street entrance so as not to detract from the architecture of adjacent historic buildings, one of which dates to 1840.

This worldwide chain of luxury hotels completed a $6 million renovation of its New Orleans property, which opened in 1984. Rooms have been spruced up with new bedspreads, drapes, wall coverings, and carpets as well as armoires, credenzas, lamps, and artwork. Another aspect of the renovation was innovation: Each room is wired with a state-of-the-art telephone system, which includes two separate phone lines, both equipped with modem access, dataports, and voice mail (even the cable TV sets are computer-compatible). Other amenities include 24-hour room service, same-day valet service, babysitting, heated outdoor pool, sauna, whirlpool, massage and fitness center, aerobic room, and Nautilus equipment. More than half the rooms are smoke-free.

Murals adapted from a 1940 Commedia dell'Arte fabric from Milan adorn the rotunda that separates the elegant lobby from the Jazz Meridien, a club-style lounge with a three-story atrium. The lounge is decorated with marble floors and tables, oak-paneled pillars, and brass railings, ideal for an evening of live jazz entertainment. Nearby is the casually elegant Midi restaurant, offering country French cuisine from Provence and the wines of Côte du Rhône. Authentic French collectibles, from elegant china and glassware to decorative accessories and artifacts, create a cozy, homelike atmosphere. French window boxes filled with lavender, dried wheat, and bright-green grass evoke the charming French countryside. Chef Emmanuel Bernard is the mastermind behind the menu.

Le Pavillon Hotel $$–$$$$$
833 Poydras Street, New Orleans
(504) 581–3111, (800) 535–9095
www.lepavillon.com
It's surprising this hotel one of the city's grandest—doesn't cause traffic accidents. Drive past the white-columned facade of this chip-off-the-Old-World-block property and see if you can resist staring at the antique Czech crystal chandeliers visible in the lobby behind the glass double front doors. Marble railings from the Grand Hotel in Paris and faux marble columns also accent this 1907 hotel's sparkling lobby. This downtown property on the corner of Baronne Street comes with plenty of history. It was built on the site of one of the city's earliest sugarcane plantation homes. The original owners, the Jesuits, purchased it directly from New Orleans founder Sieur de Bienville. By the turn of the 19th century, the area was a forbidding fringe of cypress thickets and cemeteries, described by a writer of the day as a place of "foul deeds and midnight murders (where) no ordinary courage was required to venture alone." Later it served as the main depot for the New Orleans and Carrollton railroad. In the 1860s it was transformed into the National Theater, often called Werlein Hall after owner Philip Werlein, founder of the famous music store. When construction of the present-day hotel (then called the New Hotel Denechaud) was completed, it featured the first hydraulic elevators in the city.

In 1991 the hotel was placed on the National Register of Historic Places. Today graciousness is the byword of the 226 masterfully appointed guest rooms and suites furnished in European and American antiques. Some of the seven suites feature European-style mahogany canopies, marble bathrooms, and many other elegant touches. Valet parking, 24-hour room service, and complimentary shoe shine are just some of the extra personal services guests can expect. Work up a sweat at the executive fitness center, relax with a cocktail at Le Gallery Lounge, or take a swim and enjoy the sweeping city views from the rooftop heated pool. Massive gilt columns, ornate woodwork, and a marble fireplace augment the Crystal Room, known for sumptuous dining.

Maison Pierre Lafitte $$
108 University Place, New Orleans
(504) 527–5800, (800) 726–5800
The seven suites with the lofts, exposed ceiling beams, original brick walls, and circular metal staircases are certainly among the most interesting on this block. Ongoing renovation of this compact property with 17 suites only 2 blocks from the French Quarter is giving the rooms a real dressing up. In addition to armoires and Tiffany-style lamps, each room features ceiling fans, double beds, kitchenettes with microwave ovens, and Victorian draperies. Exposed-brick hallways add a historic touch to this three-story building, adjacent to the legendary Fairmont Hotel. No pool or on-site restaurant, though. Just a small lobby with a brick archway, offering complimentary coffee and rolls. The Orpheum Theater is across the street.

Omni Royal Crescent $$$–$$$$$
535 Gravier Street, New Orleans
(504) 527–0006
www.omnihotels.com
In recent years the city's boutique hotels such as this one have offered travelers a cozy and elegant alternative to the

tug-of-war between large convention properties and charming little inns. One of the best things about this century-old refurbished building, only a block from Bourbon Street, is the 24-hour room service. Since the first was erected in 1862 during the Civil War, buildings at this site have served as a Junior Achievement office, a drug company warehouse, a local AFL–CIO headquarters and a frozen yogurt store. But the present incarnation, located in the heart of the Financial District, is hard to beat. A European-style jewel-box lobby features cozy sitting areas decorated with Oriental rugs, 19th-century paintings, and objets d'art. (Libraries on each floor provide quiet reading sanctuaries.) Ninety-eight rooms are simply but tastefully decorated and feature marble baths and bathroom floors, Egyptian cotton linens, tropical-weight cotton bathrobes and slippers, bedside cassette players with classical music selections, fax machines, and dual-line phones with computer ports. Other features include a 24-hour fitness center with sauna and whirlpool, rooftop sundeck with Roman-style pool, and French Quarter skyline views.

The Pelham $$$–$$$$$
444 Common Street, New Orleans
(504) 522–4444, (800) 272–4583
www.neworleansfinehotels.com
Several years ago a $3-million conversion of this 1850s Financial District property on the site of the Bienville Plantation gave rise to this 60-room boutique hotel decorated with chandeliers, Oriental rugs, and iron Corinthian support columns. Two blocks from the French Quarter, each of the 60 guest rooms is luxuriously appointed and features 10-foot windows overlooking Canal Street, exposed-brick walls, four-poster beds, 14-foot ceilings, crown molding, European and antique furnishings, and marble baths. Amenities include plush terry robes, complimentary newspaper (delivered to your room) and shoe shine, hair dryer, and fine English soaps and lotion. The recently opened

Huey's Diner is open 24/7 and serves American and New Orleans-style breakfast, lunch, and dinner.

Renaissance Pere Marquette $$–$$$$$
817 Common Street, New Orleans
(504) 525–1111
www.renaissancehotels.com
Marriot International Inc. gave the historic Pere Marquette building a new lease on life when it reopened in October 2001 as the 280-room hotel of the same name. Joining a growing list of new hotels in the Big Easy keeping a keen eye on cutting-edge decor is this property, located 2 blocks from the French Quarter, with its ultrasleek lobby of forward-thinking architecture design. Regional artistic influences and different time periods weigh in vis-a-vis furnishings, decorative treatments, and artwork. Guest rooms feature two-line telephones, voice mail, dataport, cordless phones, and large workspaces with reading lamps. Amenities include down-filled comforters and duvets on premium mattresses, bathrobes, minibar, in-room coffee and tea, safe, hair dryer, iron, and ironing board. Added touches include an outdoor pool, complimentary health club, valet laundry, 24-hour in-room dining, and concierge services.

The Ritz-Carlton $$$$–$$$$$
921 Canal Street, New Orleans
(504) 524–1331, (800) 241–3333
www.ritzcarlton.com
How flattering that the world's preeminent ultraluxury hotel chain didn't forget the City that Care Forgot. This warmly welcomed $200-million new kid on the block opened in the late summer of 2000 in Maison Blanche, the former Canal Street shopping legend and beloved landmark. Restoration preserved the historic 12-story Art Nouveau building's glazed terra-cotta exterior, prismatic glass, and other turn-of-the-20th-century design elements. It seems only fitting that some of the 452 rooms, including club rooms and deluxe suites, decorated in timeless Southern luxury, offer an

ideal vantage point from which to view the Carnival parades that roll down Canal Street. Amenities include twice-daily maid service, 24-hour room service, minibar, in-room safe, and marble bath with terry robes. Other features of the property, steps away from the French Quarter, include a lush courtyard, ground-level gallery of boutiques, and an award-winning day spa with 16 treatment rooms. The hotel's French Quarter Bar Restaurant serves traditional New Orleans fare, complemented by terrific local music.

Sleep Inn $$–$$$
334 O'Keefe Avenue, New Orleans
(504) 524-5400, (888) 524-8586
An ATM in the lobby *and* direct-dial no-charge local calls? You betcha. Welcome to the new world of modern family-friendly accommodations. And this nicely landscaped property offers a choice of 129 newly constructed, spacious, and attractively furnished guest rooms tucked in the heart of Downtown only 3 blocks from the French Quarter. Perks include outdoor pool, exercise room, guest laundry room, complimentary continental breakfast and newspaper, on-premises parking, and a business center with computer, fax, copier, and printer. Rooms also feature electronic entry, oversize walk-in showers, phones with dataport and voice mail, and 25-inch remote-control cable TVs. Nonsmoking rooms are available.

Windsor Court $$$$–$$$$$
300 Gravier Street, New Orleans
(504) 523-6000, (888) 596-0955
www.windsorcourthotel.com
Bill Gates (who rented the ultralavish 10-room penthouse) and Princess Anne are on the honor roll of luminaries who have unpacked their bags inside this Southern testimony to impeccable British refinement. Pull into the circular brick drive-in courtyard and see for yourself. Inside this 23-story rose-colored granite facade of roof-level terraces, balconies, and bay windows is a marble-and-jardinieres lobby of Old World elegance and contemporary

design. A $6 million collection of 17th-through 20th-century furnishings and art-work includes paintings by Reynolds and Gainsborough; many lean heavily on depictions of (the real) Windsor Court and the life of the Royal Family.

Of the 324 sumptuous guest accommodations, all of which enjoy a private balcony or bay window overlooking the city or the Mississippi River, 266 are suites with separate living areas, minikitchen or wet bar, in-room safe, three telephones (each with two incoming lines and data-ports), and dressing room with marble vanity adjoining the bedroom and spacious Italian marble bathroom. Baby grand pianos and four-poster beds with Oriental canopies accent the 22nd floor's 2,000-square-foot penthouses—pinnacles of the city's hotel establishment.

Relax in the English-style Polo Lounge for a double martini before adjourning to the Grill Room. This award-winning and internationally acclaimed restaurant (see Restaurants chapter) is open for breakfast, lunch, and dinner as well as weekend brunch. Other hotel amenities include a sundeck with pool, Jacuzzi, and fitness center with sauna, steam room, massage facilities, and showers. This ultraposh hotel in the heart of the financial district, 2 blocks from the French Quarter and the Aquarium of the Americas, is a member of the elite international family of Orient-Express Hotels.

W New Orleans $$$–$$$$$
333 Poydras Street, New Orleans
(504) 525-9444
www.whotels.com
A $20 million renovation gave a face-lift to this towering glass high-rise, built for the 1984 World's Fair, with 423 stylishly furnished rooms and suites with standard and king beds, as well as views of the Mississippi River (suites have Jacuzzis). Rooms are fully stocked with Aveda bath products, plush down comforters, 250 thread-count sheets, and 27-inch TVs with high-speed Internet access. This 23-story Financial District property is conveniently

situated at the corner of Tchoupitoulas Street 2 blocks from the Mississippi River and 4 blocks from Canal Street and the French Quarter immediately beyond. The Convention Center, Superdome, and Warehouse Arts District are within easy walking distance. For exercise check out the health club and outdoor pool.

Wyndham New Orleans $$$$-$$$$$
100 Iberville Street, New Orleans
(504) 566-7006
www.wyndam.com
Oh, the luxuries—and views—you'll encounter here, starting with the Carrera marble lobby full of antiques and jardinieres, on the 11th floor of the Canal Place Shopping Centre. Tea is served in the lobby every afternoon—along with round-the-clock panoramic views of the city, Mississippi River, and French Quarter courtesy of the arched two-story windows. The 30th-floor rooftop pool offers similar views for those wishing to swim off the previous night's meal. Head downstairs to the multi-screen cinema at The Shops at Canal Place, or browse the complex's Gucci, Williams-Sonoma, and other upscale stores.

A major $20-million renovation has framed 438 spacious guest rooms and suites with pastel decors, large marble baths, dataport/voice-mail phones, stocked minibar, coffeemakers, in-room safes, hair dryers, and irons/ironing boards. A complimentary health club is available as well as 24-hour room service from the award-winning Riverbend Grill, which offers breakfast, lunch, and dinner daily and a Sunday jazz brunch. The megaluxury hotel is only steps away from the city's riverfront trolley and the Aquarium of the Americas.

Wyndham Riverfront
Hotel $$$$-$$$$$
701 Convention Center Boulevard
New Orleans
(504) 524-8200
www.wyndham.com
Maybe it's the lovely fountain that makes the multicolumned drive-in entrance to

this hotel look smart enough to be in the French Quarter. Instead, this luxury 202-room property is conveniently situated on the edge of the Warehouse Arts District, across the street from the Riverwalk shopping and restaurant complex, the Convention Center, and within easy walking distance of Harrah's casino, the French Quarter, and Aquarium of the Americas. A rice mill once occupied the site of the present-day lobby, home to a cozy bar and E's Cafe, which serves breakfast, lunch, dinner, and brunch. Weekend guests are treated to the sight of New Orleans–based cruise ships that dock at nearby Julia Street Wharf in between voyages to the western Caribbean.

Globe-trotters familiar with this international chain's reputation for service as well as comfortable, pleasantly furnished accommodations will not be disappointed. Rooms come with irons/ironing boards, coffeemakers, hair dryers, and telephones with voice mail and dataports. Traveling dealmakers will appreciate the oversize desks, phones with extralong cords, 100-watt "work-friendly lighting," and business services. Valet parking, complimentary newspaper, valet laundry, and a fully equipped exercise room are among the other amenities. Also complimentary is the New Orleans–style hospitality.

MID CITY

Best Western Patio Motel $-$$$
2820 Tulane Avenue, New Orleans
(504) 822-0200, (800) 270-6955
www.bestwestern.com
Budget-conscious travelers who don't mind staying 10 to 15 minutes from either the French Quarter or Uptown will find this chain accommodation a bargain. Perks include free Downtown and French Quarter shuttle service, double-, queen-, and king-size beds, complimentary coffee, secured enclosed parking, a large glass-enclosed spa, on-site laundry facilities, and a restaurant next door. The 75 spa-

cious rooms are clean and simply furnished. Those traveling with youngsters will be glad to know the property has two large outdoor pools. Pets allowed at no charge.

UPTOWN

The Columns   **$$–$$$$**
3811 St. Charles Avenue, New Orleans
(504) 899–9308, (800) 445–9308
www.thecolumns.com
Imagine a stretch of The Avenue so lush with oak trees that you might actually miss this hotel's four massive white columns. But this three-story Victorian mansion, listed in the National Registry of Historic Places, has earned the allegiance of many a local who has sipped a sunset cocktail on its spacious front porch as the day slip-slides away like the St. Charles Avenue streetcar passing in front. The view is simply unsurpassed. Open the beveled-glass double front doors and step inside. *Pretty Baby* was filmed here, and framed pictures of Brooke Shields—then and now—hang in the Victorian Bar to the right of the lobby. On weekend nights this dimly lighted British-style watering hole hosts a regular Uptown crowd. Make yourself at home by slipping into one of the dark-wood booths (one especially cozy nook is in back) and order a favorite drink while music plays and the TV behind the bar broadcasts sports. Part of the enduring charm of this hotel is how little it has changed over the years. Owners Claire and Jacques Creppel have decorated the high-ceiling rooms with small armoires and comfortable double beds. Twenty guest rooms and suites on the second and third floors have private baths and other modern touches. The large second-floor wooden balcony of white wicker chairs offers a wonderful view of St. Charles Avenue. Breakfast is served in a quiet dining area located off the lobby.

The Pontchartrain   **$$$–$$$$$**
2031 St. Charles Avenue, New Orleans
(504) 524–0581, (800) 777–6193
www.pontchartrainhotel.com
Ol' Blue Eyes and Frankie Laine used to hold court in the Bayou Bar, the site of the Saints' NFL agreement inking and humpday Martini Night, with live piano music set against murals of Louisiana bayous, birds, and aquatic flowers. Old World elegance runs a dead heat with Southern hospitality at this blue-canopied grande dame built in 1927 by Lyle Aschaffenburg in a Moorish architectural style. Today this venerated structure is as much a part of the neighborhood as the century-old oaks extending over the streetcar tracks in the center of St. Charles Avenue—just outside the front door. It was named in honor of Count de Pontchartrain, from the Court of Louis XVI, and the five gaslight standards lining the sidewalk are duplicates of the ones in the Place Vendome. A glass-enclosed garden courtyard is encased by 18th-century gates from London; the faux marble columns in the barrel-vaulted lobby continue an age-old tradition imported from Italy. The elevator is adorned with Elizabeth Hadden–handpainted floral decorations, and the canvas murals in the Caribbean Room, Patio Room, and Bayou Bar are the creations of the late New Orleans artist Charles Reinike. The lobby, corridors, and guest rooms are furnished with antiques and artworks, many left as estate pieces by permanent residents

---

Looking to Mardi Gras mambo? Don't wait until the last minute to reserve a room unless you relish the prospect of driving into the city each day from, say, Mississippi. Book your hotel early—a year in advance isn't a bad idea. During Carnival most, if not all, hotels have minimum-stay requirements (usually two to five nights). Guests can expect room rates to be at yearly highs.

HOTELS

throughout the years. The hotel continued to house permanent residents until 1990.

All 118 rooms and suites have 12-foot ceilings and white-tile bathrooms and are elegantly furnished with antiques and king- or queen-size beds. Suites (which also have full kitchens or kitchenettes, coffeemakers, and separate living room and entertainment/dining areas) are named after well-known guests who have graced the hotel's portals over the years—Rita Hayworth, Walt Disney, Truman Capote, Yul Brenner, and Lillian Hellman, to name a few. Other amenities at this posh Garden District hotel, five minutes from the French Quarter and only blocks from trendy Magazine Street, include 24-hour room service, complimentary shoe shine, French Quarter shuttle service, hair dryers, valet parking, valet and laundry service, and morning newspaper delivery.

Prytania Park Hotel   **$$**
1525 Prytania Street, New Orleans
(504) 524-0427, (888) 498-7591
www.prytaniaparkhotel.com
Budget-bound travelers won't have to scrimp on luxury at this renovated 1850s

Greek Revival hotel situated in a quiet section of the historic Garden District. Nor will they have to worry that this value hotel is off the beaten path—it's only 1 block from the St. Charles Avenue streetcar line and minutes from the French Quarter and Audubon Zoo. Original fine millwork, tiled baths, spacious marble-and-mirrored dressing areas, and plush carpeting add to the value of staying at this cozy replica of a small European hotel. Guests can enjoy their complimentary breakfast and morning paper in their rooms or head out to the courtyard. Another convenience is the free (and unlimited) use of the hotel's secured and well-lit parking area. Hand-carved period English pine furnishings fill 62 spacious historic and contemporary rooms (13 are located in a Victorian townhome), all of which have high ceilings, ceiling fans, refrigerators, and microwave ovens. Some of the pastel-colored rooms have armoires as well as airy lofts reached by a circular metal staircase; others feature linen-draped four-poster beds.

BED-AND-BREAKFAST INNS 🛏️🍴

Nobody does a better job showcasing New Orleans's timeless charm than the city's bed-and-breakfast inns. Stroll along a romantic flagstone walkway in the shade of ancient oaks and sycamores. Unwind in a Jacuzzi while listening to the hypnotic rustle of banana tree leaves on a secluded tropical courtyard. Enjoy a breakfast of buttery croissants, fresh berries, and strong, hot café au lait while watching the city come alive from a private balcony trimmed in wrought-iron lace.

Take your pick of mostly 150-year-old Victorian, Italianate, or Greek Revival homes adorned with 19th-century antiques. Many inns have four-poster beds, footed cast-iron tubs, marble mantels, 13-foot ceilings, and original pine floors. Even a value-oriented, European pensione-style accommodation features a 1,000-book library and a lush pool and patio area. New Orleans has always been a city full of interesting people, and these inns are where many of them lived. One was the lavish home of a wealthy West Indies sugar planter forced to take refuge in the city following an inconvenient insurrection in Santo Domingo. Another belonged to a free man of color who lived there 20 years before the Civil War. Yet another is a former orphanage built by nuns while New Orleans was being occupied by Union soldiers. These inns represent more than simply a place to stay; they give visitors the opportunity to touch the past—to sleep in its bed, sit at its table, and walk in its gardens.

PRICE CODE

All inns accept all major credit cards. Rates are based on double occupancy, high season.

$	less than $85
$$	$85–$125
$$$	$126–$175
$$$$	$176–$225
$$$$$	$226 +

HOW THE CHAPTER IS ORGANIZED

As every inn is located within 10 or 15 minutes of the French Quarter, they are simply listed in alphabetical order. Several are in the French Quarter, some are in Faubourg Marigny (the neighborhood adjacent to the Quarter to the east), and the rest are Uptown. All Uptown inns, except one, are located in the Garden District area; therefore in this chapter "Garden District" and "Uptown" are used interchangeably. Some entries mention the Lower Garden District, which is that part closest to Downtown and the French Quarter. Marigny inns are within walking distance of the Vieux Carré, and Uptown accommodations are all close to either the streetcar or Magazine Street bus, both of which get folks Downtown in short order.

Officially, a bed-and-breakfast is supposed to be an owner-occupied home renting out one or more rooms and a guesthouse or inn is not owner-occupied and offers fewer than 15 rooms. In reality, proprietors tend to play rather fast with these rules, so we've simply lumped them all together.

B&W Courtyards
Bed & Breakfast $$$–$$$$
2425 Chartres Street, New Orleans
(504) 945-9418, (800) 585-5731
bandwcourtyards.com
The Courtyards is located in the neighborhood adjacent to the French Quarter, in

BED-AND-BREAKFAST INNS

Remember, the Garden District and the Lower Garden District are both part of Uptown, the area settled by the Americans when they began arriving in the city in the 19th century following the 1803 Louisiana Purchase. The French Quarter and Faubourg Marigny are both Downtown, most of which was built by the French and Spanish Creoles.

Faubourg Marigny. It offers a taste of old New Orleans with a Caribbean twist in a collection of three 19th-century buildings connected by courtyards. All rooms are meticulously decorated and feature private baths, cable TV, phones, central air and heat, and fresh flowers. Most rooms open onto a courtyard. The inn was the first-place winner of the 1997 Mayor's Golden Hammer Award for restoration. Rates include an expanded continental breakfast served 8:30 to 10:00 A.M. Adults only.

Beau Sejour   **$$–$$$$**
1930 Napolean Avenue, New Orleans
(504) 897-3746, (888) 897-9398
beausejourbandb.com
In 1906 Beau Sejour was built to be the grandest home on Uptown's Napolean Avenue by the Cahn family. Painstakingly renovated and restored by Gilles and Kim Gagnon in 1992, this elegant New Orleans bed-and-breakfast features six bright, spacious guest rooms with private baths and stately yet comfortable living areas including queen- or king-size beds. The home is decorated in the traditional New Orleans style, blending country and European antiques with Louisiana touches. Breakfast can be enjoyed in the sunny dining room or on the tropical patio. Even more important, Beau Sejour is on the parade route. More than a dozen Mardi Gras parades pass directly in front of the house and can be viewed comfortably from Beau Sejour's balconies and porches. All rooms have

cable television and phones. Rates include continental breakfast.

The Benachi House   **$$**
2257 Bayou Road, New Orleans
(504) 525-7040, (800) 308-7040
www.nolabb.com
This Greek Revival house was constructed in 1858 by Nicolas M. Benachi, Consul of Greece and founder of New Orleans' Greek Orthodox Congregation. Join owner Jim Derbes, a university instructor with an extensive background in historic preservation, on a tour of this authentically restored home and its spacious grounds, just minutes from City Park.

See the display of 18th- and 19th-century artifacts unearthed by the Louisiana Archeological Society from the Benachi backyard. The house, declared a landmark by the Orleans Parish Landmark Commission, is located on Bayou Road, also known as the Historic New Orleans Trace. The trace, located on the Esplanade Ridge (a national historic district), originally connected the Mississippi River with area bayous. As the city grew, the trace became a country road and, eventually, the redbrick street it is today. From this *rendezvous des chasseurs,* or meeting place of the hunters, Benachi and his friends would hunt the nearby swamps.

The Benachi House retains much of its original detail, including 14-foot ceilings fitted with decorative medallions and banded cornices; carved European black-marble mantles; Rococo revival chandeliers by Cornelius & Baker; Greek key doorways; and heart-of-pine floors. Elegant 19th-century antique furnishings complete the Gothic and Classical Revival, American Empire, and Victorian picture of mahogany and rosewood, crafted by local cabinet-makers Mallard, Seignouret, and Barjon. Four guest rooms, each named for one of Benachi's children, feature private or shared baths, and adjoining sitting rooms, and may be reserved as a suite. Guests are invited to relax in the parlors and library or stroll the oak- and sycamore-shaded grounds landscaped to include romantic walkways and terraces constructed of pink Belgian flagstones found on the site.

Secure, free parking is provided, and smoking is allowed outdoors only. Rates include a complete breakfast in the grand dining room as well as an evening beverage.

Bonne Chance $$$
621 Opelousas Avenue, Algiers Point
(504) 367-0798
www.bonne-chance.com
Shaded by a huge live oak tree, this grand Eastlake Victorian home dating back to the 1880s features gingerbread moldings and four spacious porches wrapped in delicate hues of pink, green, and lavender. The interior is elegantly furnished with period antiques as well as Oriental rosewood furniture. The two-room guest suites feature a sitting room/library, bedroom with a queen-size bed, porch, private bath, ceiling fans, two cable TVs, a VCR, and minirefrigerator. Bonne Chance, meaning good luck, is located a short ferry ride across the Mississippi River from the French Quarter in Algiers Point. Rates include continental breakfast served in the dining room or on the porch. Owner Dolores Watson offered the proprietor's quote of the day: "We are very flexible on our rates and readily offer discounts—even during special events." Now that is bonne chance.

A Creole House $-$$$
1013 St. Ann Street, New Orleans
(504) 524-8076, (888) 251-0090
www.acreolehouse.com
A Creole House is located in the heart of the French Quarter with easy access to Bourbon Street, antiques shops, riverboats, and restaurants. The lifestyle of patrician antebellum Creoles is reflected in this preserved 1830s home. Thirty-one guest rooms are tastefully and individually decorated in period style and receive daily maid service. Guests are invited to relax in the home's courtyard or take a guided

tour of the area with pickups at the front door three times each day. Rates include a continental breakfast.

Degas House $$-$$$
2306 Esplanade Avenue, New Orleans
(504) 821-5009, (800) 755-6730
www.degashouse.com
Built circa 1852, the Degas House offers a gateway to the personal side of a legendary painter. Drawn to the city by his two brothers and a host of maternal relatives, French Impressionist Edgar Degas made New Orleans the only American city in which he lived and worked. Though his stay was relatively short, Degas began 22 works while here. A large collection of prints of his paintings adorn the mansion, located in the Esplanade Ridge Historical District. The common spaces of the house are open to guests, including the rooms believed to be Degas's studio. Breakfast is served in this sun-lit space that brings in the beauty of a tropical New Orleans patio. Each guest room is named for a member of the Degas family. The color selections of the rooms were guided by Degas's letters home and by some of his paintings set in the house. All rooms feature period furnishings, cable TV, phones, and private baths; one has a whirlpool.

Guests who stay in the bridal suite enjoy exclusive use of the upper balcony that stretches across the entire front of the house, providing a "tree house view" of Esplanade Avenue. The third-floor garret rooms, like the Parisian garrets of bohemian artists, are built into the original

Degas House was the temporary home of French Impressionist Edgar Degas. Today it serves as a bed-and-breakfast inn as well as a tribute to the artist. One-hour guided tours, which include viewing of the award-winning documentary Degas in New Orleans, a Creole Sojourn, *are available to the public by appointment. (See write-up in this chapter.)*

attic space of the house, creating large yet intimate rooms with queen or double beds. Guided tours of the home can be arranged for up to 40 people. They cover various aspects of Degas's work in New Orleans, Impressionism, architecture, preservation, and the history of the development of New Orleans and Esplanade Ridge. Rates include an extended continental breakfast weekdays and Creole breakfast on weekends. Discount rates are available Tuesday through Thursday and during summer months.

Many inns and hotels offer discounted rates and special package deals during July and August, generally the city's slowest period for tourism. There are great deals to be had, but be forewarned—average daily temperatures in the high 90s are common during that time of year.

Depot House at Madame Julia's Boardinghouse $
748 O'Keefe Avenue, New Orleans
(504) 529-2952

The Depot House is a unique enterprise—a bed-and-breakfast situated in an old railroad-style boardinghouse. The 15 rooms located in a building dating back to 1830 are intimate and homey, sort of like staying at grandma's house. There are no phones or televisions, but there is a queen-size bed; some rooms have an extra daybed. Shared baths are a short walk down the hall, and visitors get to pass some pretty nifty antiques along the way. The inn is run by Dennis and Joanne Hilton, who have been hosting visitors at the St. Charles Guest House for more than 25 years. Parking is free and secure in a locked lot, and rates include a continental breakfast served in the colorful, tented "urban garden."

Esplanade Villa $$-$$$
2216 Esplanade Avenue, New Orleans
(504) 525-7040, (800) 308-7040
www.nolabb.com

Built in 1880, Esplanade Villa evokes the charm and elegance of New Orleans during its 19th-century renaissance. This Italianate, two-family dwelling was part of a local architectural tradition that connected successive family generations. In 1995 the building was restored, decorated, and furnished. Thirteen-foot ceilings, breezes and sunlight pouring through generous windows, a palette of rich Victorian colors, and 19th-century antiques take visitors back to an unhurried time in old New Orleans.

Each of the home's three larger guest suites overlook Esplanade Avenue from a small private porch and feature a second bed in the sitting room. Two slightly smaller suites at the rear of the house accommodate one or two guests. All suites have a sitting room and a private tiled bath featuring a footed cast-iron Victorian tub and a pedestal sink. In the larger suites the sink is located in the bedroom, European style, for convenience.

The Garden District Bed & Breakfast $-$$$
2418 Magazine Street, New Orleans
(504) 895-4302

This 1890 Victorian town house recently restored to its original splendor, from its 12-foot ceilings to its Southern pine floors, is located in the historic Garden District on Magazine Street, not far from quaint antiques shops and musty used-book stores. The house's five double-room suites feature antique furniture, private baths, balconies, air-conditioning, ceiling fans, open fireplaces, and private phones. If you must, there's cable TV and a fax available. Guests should also take time to enjoy the tropical garden patio.

The House on Bayou Road $$$-$$$$$
2275 Bayou Road, New Orleans
(504) 945-0992, (800) 882-2968
www.houseonbayouroad.com

This luxury bed-and-breakfast is nestled on two acres of gardens ponds and patios just blocks from the French Quarter. The main house was built in 1798 for physician-diplomat Domingo Fleitas. Originally a Canary Islander, Fleitas had the home constructed in the West Indies Creole style of the day, with wide galleries and an abundance of French doors opening onto flowering patios. Eight rooms and suites feature private baths, period antiques, and wet bars. The swimming pool and hot tub are available for guest use. There is no smoking indoors. Children 12 and older are welcome.

Rates include secured off-street parking as well as full plantation breakfast and champagne brunch on weekends.

The inn also offers guests two- and five-day classes in traditional Louisiana cooking in conjunction with the Cuisine Eclairee cooking school. Classes include cooking and visits to local restaurants for demonstrations, dinners, and wine tastings.

The Josephine $$$
1450 Josephine Street, New Orleans
(504) 524-6361, (800) 779-6361
The Josephine was built in 1870 in the Italianate style with fluted Doric and Corinthian columns. This graceful home is decorated with French antiques, gilt mirrors, and silver sideboards. Each of the six spacious guest rooms has a private bath and opens onto a balcony or gallery overlooking the surrounding lawns and a hidden courtyard garden. The house received the Historic District Landmark Commission's restoration award in 1990. Rates include a light Creole breakfast of café au lait and fresh breads served on a tray.

Lafitte Guest House $$$-$$$$
1003 Bourbon Street, New Orleans
(504) 581-2678, (800) 331-7971
Laffitteguesthouse.com
In 1849 Paul Joseph Geleises moved to Bourbon Street and raised everybody's property values by building his family a four-story, 14-bedroom mansion at the then-exorbitant price of $11,700. Today

The House on Bayou Road B&B also offers guests two- and five-day New Orleans cooking classes. Learn tips on making a perfect "roux" as well as other local "secrets." At the end of the program, students put their new knowledge to the test by preparing a meal. Bon appetit! (See write-up in this chapter.)

guests can sit on one of the home's wrought-iron balconies and toast his foresight with their café au lait while enjoying delicate breakfast pastries and watching French Quarter artists on the street below make their way to Jackson Square to set up shop for the day. Not a bad way to start the morning. All 14 rooms of this meticulously restored guest house are carpeted and have private bath and a queen- or king-size bed and are furnished with antiques and reproductions authentic to the period. Most have fireplaces, and some have private balconies.

Each room is luxuriously decorated and distinctly different from the next. A spacious room off the grand parlor, features a queen-size bed with crown canopy and a marble fireplace, while the next room has a draped Victorian half-tester bed and a wet bar. Open a door and the two rooms become an elegant suite, which through French doors opens onto the lush courtyard. Rates include continental breakfast as well as wine and hors d'oeuvres in the parlor at cocktail hour.

Lamothe House $-$$$
621 Esplanade Avenue, New Orleans
(504) 947-1161, (888) 696-9575
www.www.lamothehouse.com
As a wealthy sugar planter in the West Indies, Jean Lamothe developed a taste for the finer things in life. And thanks to a late-18th-century revolution in San Dominque that brought the planter north to New Orleans, modern travelers to New Orleans can also develop a taste for the finer things in life—at the Lamothe House.

Looking for an unusual B&B experience? Many plantations offer accommodations in addition to tours. Check out the "Plantations" section of the Day Trips chapter.

Located at the eastern edge of the French Quarter, this Victorian mansion was one of New Orleans' earliest brick-built double town houses. As was the practice at the time, the house was built with a *porte cochere*—a carriageway running through the center of the house to a courtyard paved with flagstones. Originally decorated to suit a family of very good fortune, the home retains the ambience of a bygone era with high formal ceilings, authentic furnishings, cypress floorboards, and original hand-wrought iron fastenings on the doors and windows.

One suite features a pair of canopied four-poster beds, an ornate armoire, marble-top dressers, and decorative plasterwork. All 20 rooms have private baths. Amenities include a continental breakfast featuring coffee served from a 200-year-old Sheffield urn as well as afternoon wine served in the comfortable parlor.

Le Chateau de Claudine $$$
**2127 Esplanade Avenue, New Orleans
(504) 943-8418, (866) 515-7378
www.lechateaudeclaudine.com**
As lovely as its name, this Edwardian-style home was owned by Paul Cheval, a free man of color, nearly 20 years before the Civil War. Located in the historic Esplanade Ridge District, the three-story house sits on lushly landscaped, parklike acreage, surrounded by a pond, two private decks, and ample gardens. All one- and two-bedroom suites feature private baths and are richly appointed with period furniture and authentic decorations. Le Chateau also offers secluded areas for private parties and complimentary local phone service. Rates include a full gourmet breakfast as well as shuttle service to and from New

Orleans International Airport with a three-night stay.

The Little Yellow House $$
**1820 Dauphine Street, New Orleans
(504) 947-6575**
Located right off Esplanade Avenue in the historic Faubourg Marigny, this traditional New Orleans shotgun house that sleeps up to four offers total privacy with one bedroom (and full bath) upstairs, a futon and half bath down. The charming tropical courtyard is scented by a sweet olive tree. But the most impressive aspect of this conveniently located B&B are affable hosts Angela and Russ Carll. These native New Orleanians, who live right next door in a twin little yellow house, have welcomed travelers from all over the world. They know just about everything that's going on and can give insider advice on where to eat, shop, and play.

The McKendrick-Breaux House $$$-$$$$
**1474 Magazine Street, New Orleans
(504) 586-1700, (888) 570-1700
www.mckendrick-breaux.com**
Resident owner Eddie Breaux spent three years painstakingly restoring this house before opening it as a bed-and-breakfast in 1994. Located in the Lower Garden District, the McKendrick-Breaux House consists of two Greek Revival–style structures: a three-story masonry building and two-story frame town house connected by a courtyard and patio. The buildings, constructed in 1865 and 1857, respectively, feature most of the original plasterwork, woodwork, and flooring. Seven guest rooms—with private baths, telephone, voice mail, modem line, and cable TV—are furnished with antiques and decorated with fresh flowers as well as the works of local artists. Some rooms open onto the courtyard and patio outfitted with garden furniture and tropical plants. Rates include a breakfast of homemade muffins and breads, cereal, fruit, juice, coffee, and tea. Off-season rates are available mid-July through late August.

Park View Guest House   **$-$$**
7004 St. Charles Avenue, New Orleans
(504) 861-7564, (888) 533-0746
www.parkviewguesthouse.com
Location, location, location—the three top
things this 22-room antiques-filled guesthouse has going for it. Butter a croissant
during your complimentary continental
breakfast in the black-and-white-tiled
Audubon Room while savoring the be-
still-my-heart view of Audubon Park just
beyond the wall of tall windows. Or kick
back in the funky-chic public area off the
lobby and watch the St. Charles Avenue
streetcar rumbling past the front window
under one of the loveliest tunnels of live
oaks in the city. Tulane and Loyola Universities are a diploma's throw away; the Big
Easy's wild side is found at the zoo in
Audubon Park across the street. Catch the
streetcar outside the front door and within
minutes you're strolling the French Quarter. The foyer has two admirably stocked
bookcases (fancier hotels would call theirs
a "library"), and some of the rooms have
four-poster beds and English armoires.
Fifteen rooms have private baths. The
three-story pink Victorian mansion, listed
on the National Register of Historic Places,
also represents an excellent value.

Rathbone Inn   **$-$$$$**
1227 Esplanade Avenue, New Orleans
(504) 947-2100, (800) 947-2101
Located 2 blocks from the French Quarter,
this elegant mansion was built as a home
for the Rathbone family in 1850. Accom-
modations range from more economical
rooms with a queen- or king-size bed to
large architecturally detailed two- and
three-room suites. Most rooms have high
ceilings and a distinctive character, com-
plete with antique reproductions from the
antebellum period. All have private baths
and kitchenettes. The parlor is reminiscent
of an 1850s plantation ballroom. In the
afternoons and evenings, guests are
invited to unwind in the outdoor Jacuzzi
beneath banana trees in the secluded
tropical patio area. Rates include conti-
nental breakfast of coffee, juice, and

If you have a chance, pass by the statue
of Margaret Haughery (see the listing
for St. Vincent's Guest House) at Camp
and Prytania Streets. The first statue
ever erected to honor a woman in this
country is quite memorable.

pastries. Reduced rates for summer;
weekly and monthly stays are available.

Rosewalk House   **$$**
320 Verret Street, Algiers Point
(504) 368-1500, (888) 368-1500
Located a short ferry ride across the Mississippi River in historic Algiers Point, Rosewalk House gives visitors a unique
perspective. It's the only bed-and-breakfast
boasting a romantic nighttime view of
New Orleans's city lights. Though officially
a part of New Orleans, Algiers Point on the
west bank of the Mississippi River has a
character all its own. In 1719 Jean-Baptiste
Lemoyne, sieur de Bienville, founder of the
City of New Orleans, was granted the
west bank tract. Much of the original
architecture eventually developed in the
1800s remains.
　　Rosewalk House is a converted two-
family dwelling offering four guest rooms
with private baths. Upon entering the
home, visitors find a stately formal parlor
decorated with antiques and a sentimen-
tal collection of World War II memorabilia.
The Pirates of the Caribbean room features
an antique four-poster bed with feather
mattress, fireplace with cypress mantel,
private bath with a ball-and-claw-foot tub,
and a rear-second-floor location with a
view of the historic Algiers bell tower.
Outside, as might be expected, is a
secluded courtyard surrounded by a fragrant rose garden.
　　Rates include a full Creole breakfast
served in the formal dining room, on the
upstairs balcony overlooking the city, or
on the garden patio as well as morning
paper, cable TV/VCR, and full use of the
glass-enclosed den overlooking the patio.

St. Charles Guest House $-$$
1748 Prytania Street, New Orleans
(504) 523-6556
www.stcharlesguesthouse.com

Located in the Garden District, the St. Charles Guest House may be as close as one can get to finding European pensione-style accommodations in the States. As its owners aptly describe this small hotel, which offers everything from "back-packer" rooms for $40 to queen-bed rooms with private baths for $95, the St. Charles is simple, cozy, and affordable. Thirty-six rooms are situated in four adjacent buildings constructed between 1890 and 1910.

Owners Dennis and Joanne Hilton (no relation to the megahotel) have hosted visitors for more than 25 years, and their approach is definitely low-tech. There are no room phones or TVs, though guests are encouraged to choose a book from the inn's library and enjoy it in the shade of the lush banana trees that decorate the secluded pool and patio area. When visitors are ready to venture out, the Hiltons have developed a special guide book to their favorite spots. Guests are invited to make themselves afternoon tea or coffee, and rates include a continental breakfast served in a sunny poolside breakfast room. You can't beat this with a stick.

St. Peter House Hotel $-$$
1005 St. Peter Street, New Orleans
(504) 524-9232, (888) 604-6226
www.crescent-city.org

Located on "the quiet side" of the French Quarter, this intimate hotel was built as a private residence in the early 1800s. Charming courtyards and broad balconies trimmed in wrought-iron lace welcome visitors who wish to stay near—but not in—the fray of New Orleans nightlife. Rooms, some of which are furnished with antiques, feature private baths, direct-dial telephones, and cable TV. One- and two-bedroom suites are also available. Rates include a continental breakfast and a 24-hour front desk maintained for guests' convenience.

St. Vincent's Guest House $-$$
1507 Magazine Street, New Orleans
(504) 566-1515, (504) 523-3411
www.stvincentsguesthouse.com

In the mid-19th century there was an acute need for orphanages as yellow fever epidemics decimated the population, leaving numerous children homeless. In 1861, while the city was under Union occupation, the imposing structure of St. Vincent's was built by the Daughters of Charity, an order of Catholic nuns known for social service.

Financial backing for the project chiefly came from Margaret Haughery, an illiterate Irish immigrant who became a successful businesswoman. Orphaned herself and having lost both a husband and baby to disease, Haughery, a baker, vowed to spend her life alleviating the suffering of children. Before her death in 1882, Haughery donated large sums of money generated by her steam-operated bakery to several orphanages without regard to the children's gender, religion, or race.

On the day of her funeral, all New Orleans closed down as scores followed her coffin to St. Louis Cemetery No. 2, where she rests today. A statue of this generous woman, which simply bears the name "Margaret," still stands at Camp and Prytania Streets. It is the first statue ever erected to commemorate a woman in the United States and the only statue built in honor of a baker.

Today the orphanage is a 73-room European-style guesthouse furnished to reflect "Victorian New Orleans"—ceiling fans, wicker furniture, and a large court-yard. The carriage house clock was a gift to the sisters from Haughery upon completion of St. Vincent's. All rooms have private baths, and most of the staff speak more than one language. A breakfast buffet is served 8:00 to 10:30 A.M. daily for an additional $5.00. Lunch and traditional English tea are served afternoons in the tearoom.

RESERVATION SERVICES

Bed & Breakfast Inc.
1021 Moss Street, New Orleans
(504) 488–4640, (800) 729–4640
www.historiclodging.com
B&B Inc. reserves accommodations in
French Quarter and Uptown classic
suites, private cottages, and historic
homes in all price ranges. This local company, founded in 1981, also offers free
property descriptions.

HOSTELS

Marquette House   **$**
2249 Carondelet Street, New Orleans
(504) 523–3014
hometown.aol.com/nineworlns/myhome
page/index.html

New Orleans's only official AYH youth hos-
tel is located Uptown in a 100-year-old
Greek Revival home a block off the St.
Charles Avenue streetcar line. Men and
women are accommodated in separate
dormitories. A kitchen, showers, dining
area, lounge, patio-garden, and picnic tables
are provided. Day use is permitted and
there is no curfew. Visitors are expected to
clean up after themselves. There is no age
limit. Everyone, including families and senior citizens, is welcome. Sheets are available for rent for $2.00 and towels are 50
cents. Private apartments with a bath and
kitchen are also available for around $50.
Grocery, laundry, and restaurants are
nearby at the Amazing Igors.

RESTAURANTS

The Big Easy is an embarrassment of dishes. From world-class culinary art to down-home bayou cookery, the city has curried the favor of global gourmets and local epicures, as well as the food lover merely passing through town. For more than 150 years local kitchens have been tantalizing palates with culinary pleasures worthy of opium dreams. A mere short list of New Orlean's famous indigenous foods prompts even the seasoned restaurantgoer to marvel at the melange of local culinary riches: jambalaya, gumbo, pommes soufflé, oysters Bienville and Rockefeller, po-boy and muffuletta sandwiches, courtbouillon, crawfish étouffée, trout amandine, soft-shell crab meunière, shrimp remoulade, blackened redfish (or blackened anything, for that matter), barbecue shrimp, spicy andouille, boudin sausages, and red beans and rice. The City that Care Forgot never forgets dessert, from classic crème brûlée and bread pudding with whiskey sauce to flaming bananas Foster and chocolate pudding–filled, seven-layer doberge cakes. Just for the record, all of the above were invented here. And many of them are washed down with traditional cafe brûlot, a local potation of coffee flamed with cinnamon sticks, cloves, orange, and lemon rind with brandy and Grand Marnier. Can there be any doubt that in New Orleans, dining is no mere pastime but rather a way of life?

A multiethnic melting pot, the city's dining joie de vivre owes a gustatory debt to the time-honored cooking traditions of its early Native American, French, West African, Spanish, West Indian, and Acadian inhabitants. Almost from the moment the ramparts were built around the colonial swampland settlement, New Orleans seemed destined for great culinary possibilities. Early on, pots full of tasty sustenance simmered with the bounteous harvest of indigenous foodstuffs culled from nearby bayous and rivers—crawfish, oysters, shrimp, crab, finfish, and other southeast Louisiana delicacies. Gumbo, or "gombo," is the West African word for okra—a signature ingredient in one of the region's mainstays. Jambalaya can trace part of its roots to the French and Spanish words for ham, "jambon" and "jamon," respectively. And the legendary trapping and fishing skills of resourceful bayou Cajuns, exiled from Nova Scotia in the 1700s, moved "one-pot" cooking to the front burner with andouille sausage jambalaya and chicken macque choux.

The 19th and early 20th centuries saw the arrival of Americans from the colonies as well as Irish, German, and Italian immigrants. One of the city's oldest grocery stores, Central Grocery Co. (established in 1906) is owned and operated by descendents of the original Italian family that founded this French Quarter landmark. Here visitors sit elbow-to-elbow munching on the New Orleans–born Italian bread feast called the muffuletta, stuffed with provolone cheese and deli meats and topped with tangy olive salad. Further spicing up the local dining scene of this cosmopolitan city has been the arrival in recent decades of people from Cuba, Central America, Vietnam, the Caribbean, and other regions of the world. Bennachin, on Carrollton Avenue, tempts taste buds with the rich flavors of Cameroon and Gambia found in such dishes as *nsouki ioppa,* the traditional West African gumbo with sausage and smoked turkey. Scandinavian cuisine may, in fact, be the only thing missing from New Orleans menus. OK, so maybe it is impossible to find *kochanina* (pork gelatin) or *aggost* (egg custard with herring). But stay tuned.

The Big Easy is a hedonist's Valhalla. As such, it seems only fitting that the city should lay claim to a grand choice of places to eat, ranging from sparkling lairs of world-class cuisine to dimly lit nooks serving up down-home grub. Many cities can boast of having "something for everyone in every price range." But competition among Big Easy restaurants for diners' dollars is so fierce that it seems the bad spots are usually forced to shut their doors in about 15 minutes. The best of the bunch meantime enjoy the awards and accolades that pour in with astonishing regularity. In fact, literary pageants of devotion flow from the pens of the nation's food cognoscenti.

Meanwhile, the culinary wizards who keep faithful locals chanting the mantra "there's no place like home" have become national household names—Paul Prudhomme, Emeril Lagasse, Susan Spicer, and Frank Brigtsen, to name but a few. Just as L.A. celebrates its celluloid heroes and Boston its math geniuses, so too does the Big Easy hold its purveyors of the bouffage in high esteem. Lift a spoonful of deftly torched crème brûlée to your mouth and let the caramelized top and creamy flanlike center loll on your palate like the heaven on earth it is. Discover the smoky secrets of meunière sauce on a soft-shell crab so large the spindly legs straddle the edges of your plate. Venture into the murky roux of a gumbo simmering with Cajun kitchen pride.

Not surprisingly, choosing a restaurant in this city can be as difficult as picking which azure-water Caribbean beach to snorkel or which Paris museum to browse. Should you celebrate your anniversary at Commander's Palace or the Grill Room, two highly acclaimed dining venues? Better to grab an afternoon delight at Port of Call, home to one of the city's premier megaburgers, or stop by Mother's, where the roast beef "debris" po-boy is the stuff of rich legend? Remember, too, that in New Orleans the ambience can be as pleasurable to the senses as the food. Hit one of the old-line Creole dens and find yourself surrounded by antique gilt mirrors, sparkling Bohemian crystal chandeliers, ornate ironwork balconies, marble columns, and

other accoutrements of elegant dining. Huddle around a white-linen table under a lush, gas-lamp courtyard for vintage romance served with pan-seared pork loin. Slide into a bistro banquette under lazily spinning ceiling fans for a blended taste of New Orleans magic called courtbouillon. Or dive headlong into a lively neighborhood joint hopping with friendly locals, but don't get offended if your waitress calls you "dawlin'"—it's just a longtime local way of breaking the ice.

The choices of dining spots in this chapter have been restricted to those that have stood the test of time. With few exceptions, each has been on the local scene at least a year or longer, while many can point to long histories inextricably entwined in the cultural fabric of the city. If you dine in the courtyard at the Bistro at Maison deVille Hotel, for example, you may well imagine hearing the clinking of ice in Tennessee Williams's Sazerac glass. The playwright lived in No. 9 and enjoyed the New Orleans–born cocktail as he sat in the courtyard working on *A Streetcar Named Desire*. Antoine's, the city's oldest restaurant, opened in 1840 and since that time has hosted everyone from Mark Twain and Enrico Caruso to five U.S. presidents.

New Orleans is home to its share of nationally franchised restaurant chains, but unless they originated here don't look for them in this chapter. Some of those which do call New Orleans home include the pasta house Semolina, Copeland's Cheescake Bistro, Copeland's Cajun Creole Cafe, and the now-international Ruth's Chris Steak House. You'll find an easy-to-follow "Price Code" with detailed information on the first page of this chapter.

Many restaurants in the city post their menus in the window or elsewhere, such as on the Internet, giving patrons the chance to check prices before sitting down to eat. This diner-friendly gesture is also an excellent way for potential guests to get the complete menu picture—take advantage of it.

Unless otherwise noted, the restaurants in this chapter accept most major credit cards. Those that accept cash only are so designated. Most, if not all, restaurants have nonsmoking rooms and/or tables available, and a growing number have banned smoking altogether. Accessibility for the physically challenged diner is a growing concern among the city's restaurants, and many of them have taken steps in recent years to ensure that they are wheelchair accessible. However, as many restaurants are housed in older buildings, some of the restrooms, for instance, may not as yet be retrofitted to accommodate wheelchairs. Other concerns among many diners today include whether a restaurant prepares vegetarian dishes or meatless alternatives to traditional beef and poultry dishes. To be on the safe side, and to ensure the most enjoyable possible dining experience, it's always a good idea to call ahead to check on where the restaurant stands on such issues as smoking/nonsmoking, wheelchair accessibility, and meatless meal preparation.

For convenience this chapter is divided by the following neighborhoods: Esplanade, Faubourg Marigny, French Quarter, CBD/Downtown, Warehouse District, Uptown, Carrollton/Riverbend, Mid City, and Lakefront/Bucktown/Lakeview. Restaurants are listed alphabetically under each neighborhood. Keep in mind that virtually everything in the city, including its restaurants, is at most no more than a 15-minute drive or cab ride from where you're staying. So don't let distance be a hindrance to adventurous dining.

Like most cities in subtropical climates, New Orleans tends to run on the casual side in both attitude and dress. Even nighttime attire, weather permitting, is usually no more than jeans, T-shirts, shorts, short-sleeve shirts and blouses, sundresses, walking shoes, and so on. Still, as this is the South, some women wouldn't be caught dead transgressing the unwritten fashion law of no white shoes between Labor Day and Easter. But if you're not from the South, really, don't sweat it. Travelers will want to dress

accordingly for the special occasion of breaking bread at some of the city's finer establishments. Jackets and ties for the gents and evening dresses for the ladies will usually suffice. If hitting one of the chic bistros downtown or in the Warehouse District, dress in black (if you want to blend in with the waitstaff), or slip into the stylish threads you packed for such an occasion. But what you'll find in New Orleans, even in some of the better restaurants, is a mostly relaxed and laid-back dress code. As always, if in doubt call ahead.

PRICE CODE

Our price code is based on dinner for two, without appetizers, dessert, alcoholic beverages, tax, or tip. Your own bill at any given restaurant will be higher or lower, depending on what you order and fluctuating restaurant prices. Prices are for dinner; those establishments that offer lunch typically have reduced-price menus.

$	Less than $20
$$	$21 to $35
$$$	$36 to $50
$$$$	More than $50

FRENCH QUARTER

Acme Oyster House $
724 Iberville Street, New Orleans
(504) 522-5973
www.acmeoyster.com
Though it sounds like the place Wyle E. Coyote goes when he's got a hankering for seafood, he's probably about the only one you won't find sucking down raw oysters in this French Quarter landmark. This relaxed, classic oyster bar is the kind of place where you're just as likely to run into locals, foreign visitors, or celebrities such as Matt Dillon, Deion Sanders, and Ellen Degeneres while Fats Domino and the Neville Brothers blare over the noisy crowd from the jukebox. The folks here must be doing something right—they've been in business since 1910. Originally

located around the corner on Royal Street, the Acme Cafe sat next to the infamous old Cosmopolitan Hotel, described by the *New Orleans Item* as "the scene of the making and breaking of Louisiana politicians." No doubt many of them celebrated their victories as well as drowned their sorrows at Acme. In 1924 a fire destroyed the building and the Acme Oyster House was reestablished at its present location. At the bar or at a table, the raw oysters are always a best bet and are routinely ranked as the city's most popular in local surveys. However, for those who insist on having their food cooked, the oysters are just as good on a po-boy or as part of a seafood platter. Also recommended are the red bean Poopa, and gumbo Poopa consisting of a French bread "bowl" filled with either red beans and rice or sausage-and-shrimp gumbo. And there's a good stock of local beers to wash it all down. Lunch and dinner are served daily.

Alex Patout's
Louisiana Restaurant $$$
720 St. Louis Street, New Orleans
(504) 525-7788
www.patout.com
"Sophisticated down-home cooking" is a phrase oft-overheard when talk turns to Alex Patout's menu of Cajun-inspired southwestern Louisiana seafood classics. "Every dish, no matter how long it's been done, can be changed to make it better," says the proprietor-chef and cookbook author. "We can never afford to sit back and say, 'There's nothing better than this.' Sometimes it takes common sense and sometimes it takes slow development, but what I tell chefs is this: Take every dish and keep it in your mind that you can do something to make it better." Thus is the philosophy behind this casual fine-dining establishment, which may help explain why *Esquire* dubbed Patout "a tyrant, genius chef." The New Iberia native comes from a Cajun family whose cooking traditions date to 1828—the year the first Patout arrived in Louisiana from France.

Time waits for no one except Chef Alex. His specialty is roasting—very slowly—his favorite Cajun classics, which are served in a subdued, softly lit decor of dark-green carpets, wainscoting, and paintings of Louisiana bayou birds and other wildlife. Pleasant introductions include the roast duck (served on a bed of oyster dressing with sweet potato praline casserole) and classic *cochon du lait* (succulent slices of pork from a pig roasted over the restaurant's own pit and served with home-style pork gravy). Patout's country-style "pot cooking" sensibilities are famous and well represented by his rabbit sauce piquant (fresh Louisiana rabbit cooked slowly in sauce piquant) and fried soft-shell crab. Dinner is served daily, and reservations are suggested.

So, you're in a hurry? Better not be when you pull up a chair at many neighborhood eateries. In the Big Easy virtually everything save for the New Orleans Hornets moves at a slower pace that reflects the city's laid-back approach to life.

Antoine's $$$$
713-717 St. Louis Street, New Orleans
(504) 581-4422
www.antoines.com
"I didn't have to go around the world," Numa Vinet, the now-retired 53-year veteran waiter once said, "the whole world came here to me at Antoine's." And what a world. This is the city's first restaurant and the sign hanging outside announces modestly, SINCE 1840. Inside, the guest list of notables who have dined at this venerable haute Creole dining institution reads like a who's who. Mark Twain, Groucho Marx, and Enrico Caruso have enjoyed this restaurant's classic ambience, as have Tennessee Williams, five U.S. presidents (including both Roosevelts), Henry Kissinger, Admiral Richard Byrd, and scads of royalty such as

the Duke and Duchess of Windsor. And that's just the tip of the iceberg—of the A-list. The library—you heard right—contains more than 400 volumes on cooking and wine, some of which are more than 250 years old (one cookbook published in Paris dates to 1659). Many members of the waitstaff have worked here for decades, including several who have punched the clock for nearly half a century. Daytime maitre d' Cliff Lachney has been with the restaurant 45 years.

Some menu items come with a history every bit as rich as the sauces prepared under the watchful eye of fifth-generation proprietor Bernard Guste. The pompano en papillote was created to honor a French balloonist who entertained here, the paper bag used to retain the flavor of the fish being fashioned to resemble his inflated balloon. And since 1899 more than three million orders of oysters Rockefeller, named for the nation's then-richest family and perhaps the restaurant's most famous original dish, have been served. Buddy Ebsen once observed, "You haven't lived until you've burned your tongue on oysters Rockefeller at Antoine's. Long may you wave."

Founder Alciatore Antoine was only 27 when he opened the restaurant that bears his name. The ageless restaurant has been in his family ever since. Among the two-story gallery of dining dens is the famed Rex Room established in 1942 and home to the only complete collection of Carnival medals issued by the Rex organization (in New Orleans that's a very big deal) including the first one issued in 1872 to honor the visit of the Russian Grand Duke Alexis. The terrazzo floor and vaulted ceiling aren't half bad either.

Unfortunately, "mixed" is the oft-repeated word used by locals when critiquing their forays into this French Quarter legend. The exhaustive menu in French may be overwhelming to the uninitiated, but that's what the gentle waitstaff is for. If fish floats your boat, the menu's 28 fish preparations will put you in good

company. Recommendations include the original filet de truite a la Marguery (speckled trout poached in a white wine sauce with fresh shrimp, mushrooms, and herbs) and the pompano Pontchartrain (grilled pompano filet with sautéed lump crabmeat). Other well-known house signatures include the puffed potatoes and noisettes d'agneau Alciatore—medallions of lamb wrapped in bacon, broiled, and served with a tangy béarnaise sauce on top of a grilled pineapple slice. Save room for dessert, especially the peche melba (a candied peach half, vanilla ice cream, raspberry sauce, and chopped toasted almonds) and the fraises au kirsch (fresh strawberries and kirsch liqueur).

Arnaud's $$$$
813 Bienville Street, New Orleans
(504) 523-5433
www.arnauds.com

"Count" Leon Bertrand Arnaud Cazenave, a French-born wine salesman, raconteur, and gastronome, opened this restaurant in 1918. The quintessential New Orleanian, Count Arnaud was given to starting his day with a split of champagne before moving onto his cherished half-and-half bourbon and coffee elixirs. By the time of his death in 1948 at age 76, this establishment was already regarded as a grand purveyor of haute-Creole cuisine and one of the country's fine-dining legends. Presidents, princes, movie stars, and other celebs have dined here, and the international award–winning menu still includes favorite dishes created by the founder. Today native-born executive chef Tommy DiGiovanni oversees such menu traditions as smoked pompano Bourgeás, oysters Bienville (baked with shrimp, mushrooms, and bread crumbs and topped with glacage), and shrimp Arnaud (chilled, boiled shrimp marinated in the restaurant's famous homemade remoulade sauce). The trout meunière is still crisply fried and bathed in a velvety sauce of veal stock, lemon, and butter and served with crunchy brabant potatoes. The café brûlot (coffee flamed with cinnamon sticks, cloves, orange, and lemon rind with brandy and Grand Marnier) is a New Orleans tradition not to be missed. Dinner is served daily and lunch is served Monday through Friday. A Sunday brunch menu includes pain perdu (Creole-style French toast), eggs Fauteux with house-smoked fresh Gulf pompano, and eye-openers such as Absinthe Suissesse, milk punch, and gin fizz. Reservations are suggested.

This massive restaurant is composed of six public and 10 private dining rooms in a block-long rambling structure of restored 18th- and 19th-century French Quarter buildings connected by hallways. When upscale hotelier-turned-restaurateur Archie Casbarian took over Arnaud's in 1978, he spent $1.6 million to restore what had become a decaying relic to its former glory. To help finance his dream, he "sold" 20 tables for $10,000 each for three years, which included $4,000 worth of food and drink each year as part of the deal. Today a dozen sparkling chandeliers, classic ceiling fans, original mosaic tile floors, and etched-glass windows create a warm and well-dressed environment. Silverware and china patterns resemble the restaurant's original setting. The special entrance at 813 Bienville Street at Bourbon Street opens to the Jazz Bistro, known for live jazz. Two vintage bars, one on either side of the main dining room, offer postprandial pleasures as well as the clubby Arnaud's Cigar Bar, with its massive freestanding humidor organized by brand, size, and rating. Carnival queen Germaine Cazenave Wells' Mardi Gras Museum (she's Arnaud Cazenave's daughter) on the second floor is open to the public during restaurant hours. The museum offers a behind-the-scenes peek at more than two dozen family Carnival gowns and costumes dating from 1941, 70 vintage photographs, and oodles of memorabilia. "Vintage Champagne," the gown chosen as the introduction to the exhibit, is from the 1954 Krewe of Sparta, when the theme was "Royal Repast."

Bacco $$$
310 Chartres Street, New Orleans
(504) 522–2426
www.bacco.com

A neoclassical decor of Venetian chandeliers, antique French iron gates, and Gothic arches from an old Tuscan church set the mood for a romantic escape into Italian cuisine. From dining booths inscribed with Italian love poems, to the 18th-century French compass-point wood carvings, to the murals handpainted by Jacques Lame, to the hand-blown Venetian glass grapes, this is one of the city's most visually stunning, award-winning restaurants. Kudos from national magazines such as *Bon Appetit, Esquire,* and *Food & Wine* keep pouring in. In a city where Creole cuisine reigns supreme, this Italian trattoria offers a refreshing departure. Homemade pastas, wood-fired pizzas, and fresh regional seafood are artfully prepared by executive chef Haley Gabel, featured in the TV series *Great Chefs of the New Guard,* who broke new ground in 1993 as the first woman to hold the reins of a Brennan family kitchen.

Mouthwatering signature dishes include foie gras pizza (with caramelized Chianti onions, roasted Portobello mushrooms, mozzarella, and seared Hudson Valley foie gras drizzled with white truffle oil); mussels steamed in vermouth; hickory-grilled pork tenderloin (with a sweet and sour prune sauce); roasted shrimp and pasta salad; and chicken cacciatore. Haley's best-known creation, crawfish ravioli with sundried-tomato pesto butter sauce, is a seasonal favorite. Each tabletop is adorned with a bottle of olive oil and roasted garlic for the wonderfully chewy breads.

Owner Ralph Brennan—a member of the Brennan restaurant family of Commander's Palace fame, and one of eight third-generation cousins involved in the New Orleans restaurant industry—opened the restaurant in 1991. (Besides being a former president of the National Restaurant Association, Brennan is owner and operator of the French Quarter's Red Fish

Grill and a co-owner of Mr. B's Bistro.) Bacco is open for lunch and dinner (and Sunday brunch). Reservations are recommended but not required.

Bayona $$$$
430 Dauphine Street, New Orleans
(504) 525-4455

Many out-of-towners recognize proprietor-chef Susan Spicer by her trademark bandana. Few however know that the New Orleans native's career is as remarkable as her eggplant caviar and olive tapenade appetizer, cream of garlic soup, and mustard-glazed lamb loin. Spicer began her cooking career in New Orleans in 1979 as an apprentice to chef Daniel Bonnot at the St. Louis Hotel's Louis XVI Restaurant. Three years later she opened the Savoir Faire bistro at the St. Charles Hotel as chef de cuisine. In 1985 she traveled extensively and returned to work as the opening chef at the Bistro at Maison deVille in the Maison deVille Hotel. In 1990 she launched Bayona, offering her "New World cuisine" in a romantic, 200-year-old Creole cottage in the heart of the French Quarter. The three-room main dining area downstairs offers a warm, European-style ambience, with terra-cotta–colored walls, dark green faux-marble accents, and huge hand-colored photographs of Italian gardens and trompe l'oeil Mediterranean landscapes. The intimate upstairs dining room is ideal for parties of ten or more; in fall and spring the lush fountain courtyard is the place to be. Signature starters include the eggplant caviar and tapenade with herb croutons and layered crawfish and spinach crepe. For entrees try the sautéed salmon with Choueroute and Gewürztraminer sauce and pecan-crusted rabbit with Creole mustard–tasso cream sauce.

Like many of the city's best chefs, this 1996 Ivy award winner has garnered her share of national acclaim. Spicer has also served as guest chef aboard Cunard's *Sea Goddess* and at the famed Oriental Hotel in Bangkok. For Spicer there seem to be no limits. Today she is a role model for a generation of young trailblazing chefs. Bayona is open for lunch Monday through Friday and dinner Monday through Saturday. Reservations are encouraged.

Bella Luna $$$
914 North Peters Street, New Orleans
(504) 529-1583
www.bellalunarestaurant.com

If you're looking for a romantic spot to pop the question, you simply can't do much better than table No. 1, tucked away in a cozy corner with its own private balcony, no less. The sweeping view of the Mississippi River and French Quarter at night is pure magic. The window-lined dining room, located on the second floor of the French Market, is a magnet for marriage proposal dinners. And if anyone knows a good place to leave his heart, it's Tony Bennett. He's eaten here, as have other celebs ranging from Quincy Jones to Don Johnson and Montel Williams. Of course, the panorama is breathtaking from any of the tables as well as the three semicircular booths facing the windows. If you do have to wait for a table, the bistro-style dining room's stylish mahogany bar is another good place to drink up the candlelit ambience. Owner and executive chef Horst Pfeifer opened this establishment in 1991 and his eclectic menu of flavorful Creole, Continental, and Southwestern creations keeps local restaurantgoers coming back for more. The lobster bisque with roasted corn and homegrown sweet basil is a must; likewise the paneed baby white veal (topped with fresh steamed asparagus and jumbo lump crabmeat sauce). Smart fish, veal, and lamb dishes include the steamed Maine lobster tossed with calamari ink pasta, roma tomatoes, basil chiffonade, carmelized onions, and asiago cheese; the sautéed veal liver in a caper tomato jus with roasted onions and garlic; and the herb-crusted lamb loin with au gratin potatoes. Try the fudge brownie cappuccino pie for dessert. (If all goes well, we'll see you at the wedding.) Dinner only is served daily.

Bennachin $
1212 Royal Street, New Orleans
(504) 486–1313

The exciting, traditional tastes of West Africa aren't the only thing awaiting adventurous diners to this casual neighborhood cafe. A linguistics lesson is provided by the menu written in the languages of the Basso people of Cameroon and the Mandinka people of Gambia—native homes of co-owners Alyse Njenge and Fanta Tambajang, respectively. (Don't fret, the English names and descriptions of each dish are also provided.) Lively music from the African continent plays amid a pleasantly Spartan dining room of large colorful paintings of village life. This may be one of the best places in town to appreciate the significant culinary role the African diaspora has played in local cooking traditions during the past 275 years. The nsouki ioppa, for example, is the traditional (and original) West African version of gumbo and comes with beef sausage and tasty strips of smoked turkey. Dohdoh (fried ripe plantains) and akara (black-eyed pea fritters) are other hearty appetizers to consider before getting down to the serious business of entree selection: poultry, fish, and lamb dishes, prepared as spicy as guests request. Meals are simple and usually accompanied by a combination of makdowa (fried ripe plantains), mbondo cone (coconut-rice), couscous, steamed mandowa (broccoli), cassava, and jama-jama (sautéed spinach), depending on the dish. The kembel-ioppa (sautéed lamb strips and bell peppers in a curry-accented ginger sauce) and the sisay singho (spiced baked chicken leg and thigh) are popular. Several of the dishes can be ordered vegetarian style. Lunch and dinner are served daily.

The Bistro at Maison deVille $$$$
727 Toulouse Street, New Orleans
(504) 528–9206
www.maisondeville.com

In New Orleans there are numerous versions of the Parisian-style bistro. Loyalists insist this spot may come the closest to capturing the heart and soul of the real thing, with its sophisticatedly understated decor of red-leather banquettes, ceiling fans, beveled-glass mirrors, Impressionist-style paintings, natural wood floor, and white table linens. But don't discount the courtyard; weather permitting, it is a must for romantics who want to dine where Tennessee Williams worked on *A Streetcar Named Desire* while staying here at the Maison deVille Hotel, whose guest register has also included Mick Jagger and Elizabeth Taylor. A seasonal nouvelle-Creole menu that incorporates local seafood and produce has earned executive chef Greg Picolo a loyal following. The grilled filet of venison is wrapped in apple-smoked bacon; the roasted pavé of salmon arrives stuffed with crab, shrimp, and scallops, alongside a grilled vegetable polenta cake. Other favorites include the citrus-grilled shrimp. Your just desserts should include the almond and sundried cranberry bread pudding. The dress is smart, and lunch and dinner are served daily. Reservations are strongly recommended.

Brennan's $$$$
417 Royal Street, New Orleans
(504) 525–9711
www.brennansneworleans.com

NBC-TV's Garrick Utley once said, "You haven't eaten breakfast until you've eaten breakfast at Brennan's." No question, breakfast at this world-famous restaurant is still a hands-down favorite among those eager for a taste of New Orleans history. The unforgettable signature triad of this institution, whose first location opened in 1946, includes the hearty turtle soup, eggs Benedict or Sardou, and, of course, the flaming bananas Foster invented at Brennan's. But breakfast is by no means the only time to partake of this culinary legend. Romance and intimate elegance are also timeless signatures of this landmark founded by Owen E. Brennan Sr. and located in the historic pink-stucco Morphy Mansion. Today Brennan's three sons—Owen Jr. ("Pip"), Jimmy, and Ted—oversee the restaurant's dozen graceful dining rooms, plus a tropically lush courtyard, as well as a 50,000-bottle wine cellar rated by *Wine Spectator* as one of the best in the world. Among the numerous entrees that have stood the test of time are the original redfish Jaime, topped with lump crabmeat in a fresh mushroom and red wine sauce. Breakfast, lunch, and dinner are served daily, and reservations are highly recommended.

Broussard's $$$$
819 Conti Street, New Orleans
(504) 581-3866
www.broussards.com

Oh, no. Yet *another* Creole-French grande dame restaurant? This is New Orleans—best get used to it. Over the years, writers from *Travel Holiday, Esquire, National Geographic Traveler,* and other magazines certainly have while dining at this venerable establishment. The smartly appointed dining room of gilt mirrors, bent-wood chairs, and 19th-century furnishings competes for your dining options with a romantic, century-old candlelit fountain courtyard of wisteria and night-blooming jasmine. Even the entryway of this original 1824 family home signals that you're someplace special. Bronze chandeliers with porcelain tulips hang from exposed cypress-beam ceilings above the imported Italian floors and walls of hand-painted tiles festooned with cherubs.

Evangeline Parish native Joseph Broussard came to New Orleans in 1907, married a local girl named Rosalie, and 13 years later purchased the old Borrello home, where he set to work combining local Creole flavors with his formal chef's training in Paris. Many of the original dishes created by Broussard, who had worked at Antoine's just 2 blocks away, are still served in this establishment purchased by Evelyn and Berlin-born chef Gunter Preuss in 1993.

Most locals agree that Broussard's is better than it has been in ages. Today the Acadian-French menu is highlighted by crabmeat ravigote (with lemon, onions,

capers, and avocado slices), shrimp with two remoulades, hearts of palm and asparagus salad, and oysters anyway you like them (try the creamy Bienville with tasso, mushroom, bell pepper, onion, and shrimp). Also popular are the pompano Napoleon (with shrimp and scallops in a puff pastry daubed in mustard-caper cream), roasted duck (in a marinated apples currant bourbon demi-glace), and pork rib chop in a garlic, caraway, and mustard crust). Best bets include the Louisiana-style bouillabaisse (with oysters, shrimp, and Gulf fish in a saffron-flavored tomato broth topped with crabmeat and rouille croutons) and grilled wild game—quail breast, boar sausage, and venison chop on apple red cabbage with a Grand Veneur pepper corn sauce).

Cafe du Monde $
800 Decatur Street, New Orleans
(504) 525-4544
www.cafedumonde.com

Whether it's for a light breakfast or simply an afternoon respite, no trip to New Orleans would be complete without a stop at Cafe du Monde where locals have indulged in hot, creamy café au lait (coffee and chicory with steamed milk) and the sweet perfection of beignets (square holeless doughnuts topped with powdered sugar) since 1862. In fact, this French Quarter spot seems to have been destined for that purpose. Even before Cafe du Monde was built, there was a coffee stand here run by a free woman of color who sold coffee to the French Creoles after St. Louis Cathedral Mass. Sitting beneath the open-air canopy, sipping a cup of heaven and listening to the street musicians who play for cafe patrons most of the day and sometimes into the evening, will be the best $3.00 you ever spent. (But have a heart and throw a couple of bucks into that open instrument case as you leave, OK?) Also, on the way out walk around the back of the cafe where a picture window allows visitors to watch the beignets being made. Open 24 hours a day; many people find themselves beginning *and* ending their day here. In a city where the drinking never stops, coffee is often the best nightcap. No alcohol is served, and no credit cards are accepted.

Cafe Maspero's $
601 Decatur Street, New Orleans
(504) 523-6250

For locals the biggest challenge here has always been how to beat the lines of people waiting to get in, which can wrap around the corner during peak season. No problem. According to restaurant staff, your best bet for beating the sidewalk blues is to come after 2:00 P.M. weekdays and 3:00 P.M. weekends. Even if your timing is bad, it's worth getting in the queue for a chance to sample the famous pastrami sandwich served inside this 1820s building of redbrick archways, across the street from the Jax Brewery shopping complex. The mouthwatering sandwich includes a generous portion of thinly sliced New York–style peppery pastrami, oven-warmed and served (with melted cheese if you're smart) on freshly baked French bread with fries. A quick check of nearby tables reveals the popularity of the seafood plates and sandwiches (with oysters, shrimp, or catfish) as well as the chicken sandwich served with two—count 'em—grilled chicken breasts sautéed in Greek spices. Forget about leaving home without it, though, as credit cards are not accepted at this casual joint, which opened in 1971.

Cafe Sbisa $$
1011 Decatur Street, New Orleans
(504) 522-5565
www.cafesbisa.com

Set in a French-style 1820s structure that once housed a ship's chandler, this renovated dining den has offered traditional Creole and Continental dishes since the Sbisa family opened their restaurant here at the turn of the 20th century. A handful of tables on the second floor "balcony" overlook the first-floor dining room. The bistro-style first floor has a 1903 mahogany bar that runs the length of one wall, with

a huge painting by acclaimed New Orleans artist George Dureau, and wood-paneled walls with original exposed brick. Guests can also dine on the picturesque patio and veranda out back (weather permitting) or on the balcony overlooking the French Market across the street. The Sunday jazz brunch is popular for its New Orleans breakfast staples—turtle soup and gumbo, poached eggs on crabcakes with hollandaise, and eggs Benedict. Creole omelettes feature crawfish and spicy andouille sausage topped with hollandaise. Other brunch favorites include grillades and grits, and trout amandine. Local flavors also dominate the daily dinner menu, from bouillabaisse to roasted duck and blackened redfish. Reservations are recommended.

Clover Grill $
900 Bourbon Street, New Orleans
(504) 598-1010
www.clovergrill.com

Eager to earn your tourist wings? Tumble into this street-corner legend between midnight and 4:00 A.M. for a post-bar hopping chow-down and plop into one of the window booths. "We may not be pretty but we think we are" is the motto of this lively, campy grill open 24-7, which became part of the French Quarter scene in 1950. Food is served with an attitude and house rules include "Please keep your date seated to avoid accidents" and "We don't eat in your bed, so please don't sleep at our tables." Though fun 'round the clock, the witching hours are the best times to soak up this colorful, offbeat, and marvelously funky venue. Characters abound. Triple-egg works of diner art include omelettes "first concocted in a trailer in Chalmette, Louisiana," prepared to order and served with hash browns, grits, or fries. Transform your plain-jane Geaux Girl waffles into luscious vamps with the optional banana, pecans, and ice cream. Burgers made to order, club and deli sandwiches, as well as chicken-fried steak and grilled chicken breast platters are served. The Clover Grill's "pretty sister" restaurant, Poppy's Grill, is at 717 St. Peter Street, (504) 524-3287. The restaurant, across the street from Pat O'Brien's bar, is open 24-7 and offers a similar menu.

The Court of Two Sisters $$
613 Royal Street, New Orleans
(504) 522-7261
www.courtoftwosisters.com
A romantic courtyard of white-linen table-cloths, quietly flowing fountains, flowering plants, and flickering gaslights, all set under a canopy of wisteria and sycamores, has been luring locals and visitors alike for years to this establishment's daily jazz brunches. Airy, well-lit indoor dining is always available in the Terrace Room. But it would be a shame not to enjoy the open-air ambience of one of the city's famous courtyards, tucked in the back of one of the most historic structures in the French Quarter. (By the way, when Charlie Fradella's Sensational Jazz Band strolls by your table, ask them to play "St. James Infirmary"—you won't be disappointed).

A favorite among locals entertaining out-of-town guests, this restaurant is located on the site of the original residence of Sieur Etienne de Perier, royal governor of colonial Louisiana between 1726 and 1733. The present-day structure, built in the 1830s, was reportedly the home of the "outrageous" Marquis de Vaudreil, the colonial royal governor who helped transform New Orleans from a marshland village into a "petit Paris." The Court is named for the two aristocratic Creole sisters, Emma and Bertha Camors, who ran a post–Civil War European-style boutique and millinery shop of imported Parisian finery for a good part of the 19th century. (They died within two months of each other in 1944 and lie side by side in St. Louis Cemetery No. 3.)

As for the buffet? Best loosen your girdles and belts. Owners Jerome and Joe Fein III have concocted an impressive roster of more than 60 freshly prepared items: for example, eggs Benedict, waffles, and omelettes (all made while you wait), hot boiled shrimp and crawfish, roast beef, grillades and grits, shrimp and oyster pasta, quiches, ceviche, jambalaya, gumbo, steaming Creole seafood creations, imported cheeses, and desserts—not the least of which are the crepes Suzette and bread pudding in whiskey sauce. Reservations are always suggested for brunches (especially weekends), served daily 9:00 A.M. to 3:00 P.M. Dinner is served daily.

Crescent City Brewhouse $$
527 Decatur Street, New Orleans
(504) 522-0571
www.crescentcitybrewhouse.com
Sit at one of the second-floor balcony tables overlooking bustling Decatur Street and rediscover the German heritage of microbrewed fine beers in a city better known for its café au lait. This always lively dining venue is popular with tourists and locals alike and offers an ample menu of New Orleans–style appetizers, po-boys, wraps, pastas, and grilled and fried seafood entrees, plus some German specials. A selection of acclaimed, house-brewed natural premium beers is a major draw. The full-bodied, dark mahogany Black Forest brewed in the traditional Munich style offers a strong and sparsely hopped introduction; Red Stallion is a malty and aromatic Vienna-style beer with a nice copper color. Those who like to stick closer to home will find a classic Pilsner, light in both color and taste with a flowery bouquet, which bears the closest resemblance to domestic beers. Can't make up your mind? Choose one of the beer samplers for a tour de hops. Or ask about the special lagers that brewmaster and proprietor Wolfram Koehler has prepared for the month. New Orleans native and executive chef Mark Latino oversees the kitchen's eclectic menu. His oyster club gives the classic oyster po-boy an imaginative twist. Fresh-shucked Louisiana oysters are rolled in raw oats, deep-fried, and layered with fresh spinach leaves,

avocado, tomatoes, sauerkraut, and grilled Canadian bacon, then served on fresh rye bread with herbsaint aioli. Wiebelt's traditional German-style pork sausage sandwich comes with sauerkraut and homestyle potatoes. A Brewhouse specialty every bit as hearty as its Black Forest beer is the Louisiana quail, stuffed with tart apples, walnuts, and tasso and coated with an orange-balsamic glaze on warm spinach. Nightly live jazz keeps the joint jumping weekdays till 9:00 P.M. and weekends till midnight. Lunch and dinner are served daily.

Felix's Restaurant and Oyster Bar $$
739 Iberville Street, New Orleans
(504) 522–4440
www.felixs.com

The sign over the bar of this half-century-old L-shaped restaurant, which opens onto both Iberville and Bourbon Streets, says it all: OYSTERS R IN SEASON. This crowded, informal eatery is where you can smell the crawfish boiling starting at 8:00 every morning. It's also the setting for many visitors' introduction to the fine art of eating raw oysters. Similar to, but pricier and more touristy than its neighbor Acme Oyster House across the street, Felix's offers an abundance of oyster offerings. There's raw, Bienville, Rockefeller, en brochette, stewed, fried, broiled, or in an omelette created by chef Isria Washington, who has run the kitchen for more than 20 years. Other good choices include gumbo, crawfish po-boy, seafood platter, and fried or grilled fish of the day. The full bar features more than a dozen varieties of beer. Breakfast omelettes are hearty and come in such varieties as Western, Spanish, Italian sausage, cheese, and shrimp. Although the eating is good, the wait can be long in this 220-seat restaurant that, especially when big conventions are in town, often has lines coming out both the Iberville and Bourbon Street entrances. Breakfast, lunch, and dinner are served daily. Open till 1:30 A.M. on Friday and Saturday, Felix's is also a popular late-night eating spot.

Galatoire's $$$$
209 Bourbon Street, New Orleans
(504) 525–2021
www.galatoires.com

As longtime customers often said, once you opened the door to Galatoire's, you were in Galatoire's—and that was only after a sometimes long wait in line on the sidewalk if you came on a Friday afternoon. Fortunately, a recent renovation of the venerable Creole dining den has added not only second-floor seating but also a waiting area for customers, as well as an overall fresh look. What hasn't changed is the fact that Galatoire's is the place to see and be seen on Friday afternoons when the restaurant is filled with fresh-scrubbed debutantes, lawyers in Brooks Brothers suits, politicians, dowagers sporting broad-brimmed hats, and the like. If the walls could talk . . . A longtime regular tells of the time he hosted a reporter who got so inebriated that he had to be poured onto the upstairs couch to sleep it off. When the reporter roused, still thoroughly in his cups, he was spotted by the host's eagle-eyed waiter crawling on his hands and knees across the dining room. The waiter, concerned for the guest's safety, called to the host: "Look, he's trying to escape!"

Even if you don't have your own waiter (another Galatoire's tradition), the chatty dining room of this family-owned restaurant, founded in 1905 by French Pyrennes–born Jean Galatoire, has the culinary cure for what ails you: Crabmeat Maison, grilled pompano, escargot bordelaise, oysters en brochette, trout meunière or amandine, crabmeat canape Lorenzo, and filet béarnaise, for starters. Marion Atkinson, a cousin of the late General George S. Patton, has dined at Galatoire's since 1916. For more than 20 years she has come to Galatoire's almost nightly, sitting at the same table and exchanging greetings with fellow patrons. Martinis are served with separate glass bowls overflowing with olives and onions. No reservations are accepted at this establishment, which is open for lunch and dinner Tues-

Glossary of New Orleans Food Terms

Andouille—A plump, smoked Cajun sausage made primarily with pork and often used as an ingredient in red beans and rice.

Beignet—A soft, square-shaped doughnut minus the hole sprinkled with powdered sugar and often enjoyed with café au lait.

Bisque—Crawfish heads stuffed with crawfish meat are found in the heartier versions of this time-honored thick Cajun soup served over rice.

Boudin—A hotly spiced Cajun sausage of cooked rice and pork.

Bouillabaisse—The New Orleans version of this traditional tomato-based French fish chowder features shellfish and finfish found in local waters.

Café au lait—Dark-roasted New Orleans–style chicory coffee and hot milk traditionally mixed in equal measures.

Café brûlot—An after-dinner hot coffee drink mixed with spices, orange peel, and liqueurs, mixed in a chafing dish, flamed, and served in special cups.

Chicory—A dried, ground, and roasted herb root used to flavor coffee.

Courtbouillon (*coo-BEE-yon*)—A roux-based fish soup or stew mixed with rice.

Crawfish—A red, shrimp-size "minilobster" found in local fresh waters.

En papillote—A fish baked in a paper bag to seal in the natural flavors.

Étouffée (*ay-too-FAY*)—a rouxless sauce (made up of butter and/or natural shellfish fats) used to smother Cajun seafood dishes. Good examples include crawfish or shrimp étouffée.

Filé (*FEE-lay*)—Powdered dried root bark of the sassafras tree used mostly to flavor and/or thicken gumbos—as in filé gumbo.

day through Sunday (jackets are required after 5:00 P.M. and all day Sunday).

Gumbo Shop $
630 St. Peter Street, New Orleans
(504) 525-1486
www.gumboshop.com
Part of the fun of sampling longtime New Orleans staples is learning how they got their name. Most New Orleans chefs will tell you that two of the most important ingredients to any successfully prepared traditional gumbo are filé and okra. "Kombo" is the Indian word for filé and "gombo" is the West African word for okra. Hence the name. As for jambalaya, two stories are passed about. One has it that the dish was named for the French and Spanish words for ham—"jambon"

and "jamon," respectively. The story we like best though has a more romantic spin: A long-ago famished traveler arriving late at night at a local inn was prepared a rice-based dish created by a cook called Jean who was nicknamed "Balayez," which means "mix good things together." The traveler was so impressed with the result that he called the meal "Jean Balayez," which eventually became "jambalaya." Either way, guests at this establishment, located in a building that dates to 1795, can count on consistently prepared and hearty portions. Start off with an appetizer of blackened fish nuggets or grilled boudin with Creole mustard, and then dive into the signature seafood okra gumbo, mixed with sautéed onions, bell peppers, and celery and blended with

Gumbo—A roux-thickened soup prepared any number of ways but typically with one or more of the following: seafood (oysters, shrimp, and/or crab), sausage (such as andouille), chicken, okra, and *z'herbes* (mustard greens).

Grillades (*GREE-yads*)—A tomato and gravy-based dish of thinly cut and browned veal or beef round. Grillades and grits is a popular New Orleans breakfast dish.

Jambalaya—A seasoned rice-and-tomato based "sweep-up-the-kitchen" dish prepared with virtually endless combinations of beef, chicken, crawfish, pork, sausage, and shrimp.

Meunière—A New Orleans seafood butter sauce framed by freshly ground black pepper, lemon juice, and finely minced fresh parsley.

Mirliton—A locally popular green squash, called chayote or vegetable pear elsewhere, used both as an accent veg-

etable and an edible container for stuffing with ham or shrimp.

Po-boy—The classic New Orleans fresh French bread sandwich, which can be found stuffed with virtually everything under the sun—from fried shrimp, oysters, soft-shell crabs, and catfish to roast beef, meatballs, deli meats, rib-eye, pork chops, and even french fries.

Red beans and rice—A New Orleans staple of kidney beans mixed with rice, seasonings, spices, and typically thick slices of sausage.

Remoulade—A tangy, salmon-colored sauce with Creole (and sometimes Dijon) mustard, horseradish, vinegar, and other flavorings, first served in New Orleans with shrimp.

Roux—A reddish-brown base of flour and fat (butter, lard, or oil), plus the so-called holy trinity of chopped onions, bell peppers, and celery, for many New Orleans sauces and food preparations.

shrimp and crab into a thick roux and served over rice. Heartier appetites might want to opt for the chicken andouille gumbo or the jambalaya, which is served with spicy smoked Cajun sausage and chicken seasoned and simmered in chicken stock. Other rib-sticking traditions include shrimp Creole, red beans and rice, and crawfish étouffée (peeled crawfish tails simmered in a spicy sauce of onion, bell peppers, celery, garlic, and cayenne pepper and served over rice). Open daily for lunch and dinner, the place can get noisy during weekends when conventioneers are in town. But the lively ambience is what makes this eatery a fun place to recharge batteries during long romps in the French Quarter. As testimony to its popularity among international tourists,

menus are available in Japanese, Spanish, French, and Italian.

Jean Lafitte $$$
240 Bourbon Street, New Orleans
(504) 524-0114
It's good to rise above the crowd from time to time. And the ironwork balcony of this traditional Cajun-Creole restaurant provides a splendid view of Bourbon and Bienville Streets—and the haggard tourists who weren't as clever as you were to find this little escape. Executive chef Michel Clavelin oversees a kitchen where the stocks, bases, and sauces are made fresh from scratch daily (as proof, the kitchen doesn't have a freezer). Vegetarians, carnivores, and those with dietary restrictions can ask to have any dish customized.

Clavelin puts his unique stamp on the frog legs (served with citrus marinade and mango salsa), crusted potato salmon, and crawfish pesto pasta. Dinner is served daily. Reservations are suggested.

K-Paul's Louisiana Kitchen $$$$
416 Chartres Street, New Orleans
(504) 524-7394
www.chefpaul.com

Chef Paul Prudhomme, who was born and raised in Louisiana's Cajun country, began cooking with his mother when he was only 7 years old. With no electricity and a family of 13 children to feed, Prudhomme learned early the art of using fresh, seasonal ingredients to cook for a crowd. That tradition was carried over to this world-famous chef's French Quarter restaurant, which, he boasts, has no freezer on the premises. The original K-Paul's, which Prudhomme opened in 1979, was a modest 62-seat facility whose biggest feature, besides blackened redfish, was the long line of people who waited hours to get in. A few years ago, however, the building was extensively renovated based on the original designs of the 1834 structure, adding a second-floor dining room, a balcony, and a courtyard, bringing the seating capacity to 200. Each dining room features an open kitchen for customers' entertainment. The restaurant also now takes reservations for meals of such signature dishes as blackened Louisiana drum; blackened pork chops stuffed with ricotta, asiago, mozzarella, and cacio-cavello cheeses and fresh basil and served with mushroom-Zinfandel sauce; and the sumptuous sweet potato pecan pie served with chantilly cream. Like any of the city's more expensive restaurants, lunchtime at K-Paul's provides the best value for your buck. The intimate yet casual first-floor dining room features exposed brick walls. Seating is on a first-come, first-served basis. The second-floor dining room, open only for dinner by reservation, features booths and a more elegant ambience. Coats are not required, but "dressy casual"

attire is recommended. Lunch and dinner are served Monday through Saturday.

La Marquise Pastry Shop $
625 Chartres Street, New Orleans
(504) 524-0420

Some call it cozy, others claustrophobic. Either way, tourists as well as French Quarter residents on their way to work have been stopping by this petite den of sweet-tooth delectables located near Jackson Square since it opened in 1972. From freshly baked Napoleons and petits fours to tiramisu and cheesecake, it's hard not to find something to satisfy that constant craving. Cappuccino, espresso, and mocha, as well as a selection of French croissants, tortes, pies, and cookies (from the mothership Croissant d'Or at 617 Ursulines Street) are served. The place is open for breakfast and lunch; credit cards are not accepted.

Louis XVI $$$
730 Bienville Street, New Orleans
(504) 581-7000
www.louisxvi.com

Tourists and locals have long seen eye to eye when it comes to the classic French cuisine of this candlelit epicurean oasis tucked inside the St. Louis Hotel. Plush European-style decor in cream colors reminiscent of Paris in the 1920s is accented by white table linens, crystal lighting, and black lacquer–framed mirrors. Numerous framed awards hang on the wall leading to the main dinner room. The room overlooks the hotel's Mediterranean-style fountain courtyard of lush foliage and wrought-iron balconies—one of the prettiest in the French Quarter. Executive chef Agnes Bellet does not believe in veering far from the French classics in either preparation or presentation. Creamy sauces, red meats, and flaming desserts are menu standards. Signature dishes include the beef filet marinated venison-style in a sweet and spicy sauce, a fish of the day (topped with sautéed banana, red bell pepper, tomato parsley, and beurre meunière) and feuilleté de crustace (puff pastry filled with shrimp, oysters, crabmeat, and crawfish in a light cream sauce). Both the beef Wellington (fortified with a perigueux sauce) and the French mustard–encrusted rack of spring lamb are served tableside from a gueridon. Breakfast in the courtyard is another local tradition, and the retractable canopy makes it suitable for dining virtually year-round. Start off with a brandy milk punch. This will help relax you while waiting for your New Orleans–style eggs Sardou (poached eggs served on creamed spinach and artichoke bottoms topped with hollandaise sauce) or eggs Lafayette (served on an English muffin topped with nantua sauce and crawfish). Traditional breakfast offerings include Belgian waffles plus a handful of heart-healthy alternatives. Breakfast and dinner are served daily and reservations are recommended.

Maximo's Italian Grill $$
1117 Decatur Street, New Orleans
(504) 586–8883
www.maximositaliangrill.com

This Italian grill has at long last come into its own, say longtime restaurant-goers. Jazz music and a collection of Herman Leonard jazz photographs set the mood in this 1829 building, which bustles on weekends. The wine selection never fails to reap kudos (it's one of the city's few recipients of *Wine Spectator*'s prestigious "Best of Award of Excellence"), and this chic bistro is probably one of the best places in town to sample vintages by the glass. Opt for balcony seating or a place at the lively grill-bar overlooking the open kitchen, which prepares a slew of fire-roasted shrimp and fish, pan-roasted veal T-bones, gourmet antipasto, and grilled portobello mushrooms, as well as lamb and steak dishes. It's hard to go wrong ordering the fire-roasted chicken and sausage with prosciutto, Fontina cheese, mushrooms, and cream. Dinner only is served nightly.

Mike Anderson's Seafood $$
215 Bourbon Street, New Orleans
(504) 524–3884
www.mikeandersons.com

It seems only fitting that Mike Anderson, former All-American football player at LSU, opened his first seafood restaurant near the gates of his alma mater in Baton Rouge. In the 1980s he opened this Bourbon Street eatery which was followed by a quick-service food court location in a downtown mall—Riverwalk, 1 Poydras Street, (504) 522-7727. The French Quarter location, housed in a 200-year-old building with ceiling fans and exposed original brick walls, offers relaxed dining and a 60-item menu full of gumbos, étouffées, bisques, fried and broiled seafood platters and dinners, po-boys, and much more. The raw oyster special Monday through Thursday 2:00 to 6:00 P.M. is popular. Skeptics might have reservations about an ex-football player opening a restaurant, but these are put to rest by the signature dishes that have made Anderson's popular: jumbo shrimp broiled in sherry, butter, and spices; the Norman (butterfly shrimp or fried fish filet topped with crab étouffée); and Joliet Rouge (fresh broiled snapper topped with sautéed lump crabmeat and fresh mushrooms). Portions are generous. Appetizers, soups, salads, and steaks are served. The restaurant is open for lunch and dinner daily.

Mr. B's Bistro $$$$
201 Royal Street, New Orleans
(504) 523–2078
www.mrbsbistro.com

Gourmet magazine editor Gail Zweighental, whose dining experiences span the globe, rated this restaurant's New Orleans–style barbecue shrimp as one of her favorite dishes of 1997. In an episode of the NBC-TV sitcom *Naked Truth,* Holland (Camilla) Taylor tells Tom (Jake) Verica: "I just think it is a shame for you to come all this way and yet still not be anywhere at all. It's sort of like making a pilgrimage to Mr. B's in New Orleans and then leaving without ever tasting their gumbo ya ya." Jake replies: "It is legendary!" These are only two examples of how the Creole cuisine created by executive chef Michelle McCraney, a former sous chef at Emeril Lagasse's Nola, has put this restaurant on the map. Located across the street from the graceful Monteleone Hotel, Mr. B's Bistro is part of the Brennan family restaurant dynasty (hence the "B" in Mr. B's) and run by the brother-and-sister team of Ralph and Cindy Brennan. This establishment opened in 1979 and has culled raves from patrons who have dined amid its softly lit, club-meets-bistro decor accented by a wall-long dark-wood bar that bustles with the after-work crowd. But the dark-roux gumbo ya ya (with chicken and smoky andouille sausage) and barbecue shrimp (served with French bread for dipping into the peppery butter sauce) aren't the only home runs. So too are the duck spring rolls, braised Mississippi rabbit, pasta jambalaya (with Gulf shrimp, andouille sausage, duck, and chicken morsels tossed with spinach fettuccine), and hickory-grilled fish. Lunch is served Monday through Saturday; dinner daily; jazz brunch Sunday.

Nola $$$
534 St. Louis Street, New Orleans
(504) 522-6652
www.emerils.com

Superstar chef Emeril Lagasse's second restaurant, opened in 1992, is found inside a two-story exposed-brick structure, built in 1827 and a former warehouse that evokes a sort of New York Soho funky-chic. The vogue digs host a hip, upscale clientele of movers and shakers from the business, media, and art communities for lunch and dinner daily. Locals nod to one another over distinctive menu items that lean heavily on Louisiana's acclaimed cooking roots; they are created by Lagasse, the energetic Food Channel staple.

Try the fresh Louisiana crabcake with fire-roasted beurre blanc sauce or the sautéed shrimp with warm remoulade over homemade angel hair pasta. Imagi-

native salads include fried oysters with fresh spinach, creamy herbsaint dressing, crispy bacon, and chowchow-pickled fennel and mirliton runs a close second. For the main course Lagasse kicks out the culinary jams with his slow-roasted duck au jus (prepared in a sweet and spicy glaze and served with buttermilk-cornbread pudding and fire-roasted corn salad). Fancy fish? Try the cedar plank–roasted citrus and horseradish-crusted fresh fish (in a lemon-butter sauce with a Vietnamese seafood salad with fresh watercress and ginger-lime scented veal glaze). Reservations are recommended.

Old Coffee Pot $
714 St. Peter Street, New Orleans
(504) 524–3500

Next door to the world-famous Pat O'Brien's bar is this less well-known spot popular with local folk on the prowl for a stick-to-your-ribs Creole breakfast. Established in 1894, this courtyard restaurant (indoor dining is available, too) has long been a secret pleasure of New Orleanians. House specials include lost bread (the Creole version of French toast) and award-winning callas (Creole rice cakes served with grits and Vermont maple syrup). Many opt for one of the egg or omelette dishes. The Benedict-style eggs Jonathan, for instance, arrives at the table stuffed with ham, tomatoes, and oysters, topped with hollandaise sauce and served with grits or home-style potatoes and flaky buttermilk biscuits. The eggs Conti are poached in a white wine sauce with green onions and fresh chicken livers, served over fresh homemade biscuits. For an irresistible taste of local flavors, plunge your fork into the Rockefeller omelette stuffed with fresh creamed spinach, oysters, herbs, spices, and cheese topped with a light cream sauce. For breakfast, a host of wake-up-little-snoozy drinks range from traditional Bloody Marys to meet-me-in-the-70s Harvey Wallbangers, Singapore Slings, and Tequila Sunrises. The menu also includes a dozen local seafood dishes and platters, daily specials, po-boys, and salads. Breakfast (till 3:00 P.M.), lunch, and dinner are served daily.

The Pelican Club $$$
615 Bienville Street
(on Exchange Alley), New Orleans
(504) 523-1504

On Friday and Saturday nights, live music greets guests as they enter this bistro-style restaurant's bar and reception area. The mahogany bar against the wall dates to 1919 and provides a courtly spot for cocktails while waiting to be seated. In fact, if the restaurant is overcrowded, you might have to enjoy your memorable meal at one of the four window tables over-looking Exchange Alley. (Yes, the floor is imported hand-painted Italian tile, but you'll just have to manage.) Chances are, though, your reservations included a request for seating in the middle dining room—bright and airy with white walls, leather banquettes, black-wood chairs, and slowly spinning ceiling fans. (As this place can get a tad noisy on weekend nights, the Club Room, with its noise-absorbing dark carpets and oak-paneled walls, would be a good choice if you're looking for a more quiet spot.) But regardless of where guests sit in this vibrant dining establishment, popular with both the blue-jeans and dress-up crowds, the contemporary menu with Louisiana traditions and Asian flair makes for memorable meals. Executive chef Richard Hughes Jr. and chef de cuisine Chin Ling have concocted some gratifying palate pleasers including such starters as duck and shiitake mushroom spring rolls and scallop-stuffed artichoke with roasted garlic beurre blanc. But the Pelican Club's dynamic duo really take flight when it comes to their sensational paella-style jambalaya and Louisiana cioppino. Ditto for the pecan-and-coconut-crusted tilapia and the panéed Gulf fish (with crawfish and topped with a roasted jalapeño hollandaise). Dinner is served daily and reservations are recommended.

Peristyle $$$
1041 Dumaine Street, New Orleans
(504) 593-9535

Chef-proprietor Anne Kearney's Provençal-inspired, bistro-style menu changes by design according to seasonal fresh ingredients. But one thing locals have come to count on from one of America's hottest young chefs (so named by *Wine Spectator*) are the creative ways in which she prepares regional fish, game, fowl, and shellfish. Part of the fuss over Kearney's intimate, consistently top-rated establishment can be traced to such creations as the Parisian-style ham and fennel slaw, the pan-roasted veal sweetbreads with prosciutto and roasted garlic, and the grilled filet with mushroom-orzo croquette and braised leek-stuffed tomato in sauce Lyonnaise. The Ohio native spent three years under the tutelage of another local culinary icon, Emeril Lagasse (see Emeril's and Nola), researching and writing scripts for his *Essence of Emeril* TV series on the Food Channel, testing recipes for Lagasse's cookbook, *Louisiana: Real and Rustic,* and working in his restaurant kitchen. Fortunately, the restaurant, on the ground floor of a two-story, 19th-century structure, retains the charm it once reflected through antique frame mirrors and a row of small theater lights above the wooden banquette seating. The restaurant takes its name from the Peristyle at City Park. Two 13-foot murals painted in the 1920s by Alonzo Lansford depict New Orleans's City Park shortly after the Peristyle's construction in 1905. Complimentary valet parking is available. Dinner is served Tuesday through Saturday; lunch Friday only (with limited seating).

Port of Call $
838 Esplanade Avenue, New Orleans
(504) 523-0120
www.portofcallneworleans.com

For as long as anyone can remember, this lively, dimly lit corner restaurant has been the place to drop anchor for one of the biggest and juiciest hamburgers in town. These plump, half-pound treasures, ground fresh daily, arrive hot on a toasted sesame seed bun. By the time you've added the lettuce, pickles, and thick slices of onion and tomato served on the side, using a knife and fork makes pretty good sense. The baked potato that comes with the burgers is almost a meal in itself, especially if you order it with the works. Steaks, pizzas, and specialty house drinks such as the Windjammer, a blend of tropical juices mixed with two kinds of rum, and the Bahamian-style Goombay Punch round out the menu. During weekends the bar near the front door is usually crowded with people waiting for tables. The rope fishing nets hanging from the ceiling and an oldies-playing jukebox add to the entertaining atmosphere of this popular eatery. Open daily for lunch and dinner.

Quarter Scene $
900 Dumaine Street
(504) 522-6533

Tourists looking to get off the beaten path of Bourbon Street will find the relaxed mood of this friendly best-kept secret a refreshing change of scenery—and not just because of the unique artwork by local artists, which includes two large murals painted by Marc Marino. Nowadays this one-time 24-hour restaurant still bustles with a local clientele especially during breakfast and after-hours. This being New Orleans, the fact that this establishment doesn't serve alcohol but draws local musicians, bohemians, bon vivants, and the bar crowd can only mean one thing: Patrons are allowed to bring in their own (mixers are sold). As a result, weekend brunch proceeds smoothly, particularly when enhanced by the homemade Louisiana-seasoned corned beef hash or the eggs Beauregard flavored with tasso and tomato. Some of the largest buttermilk biscuits in the city are baked fresh daily here. The menu of tried-and-true local essentials runs the gamut from gumbo and shrimp remoulade to po-boys and country-fried steak. Rotating daily

dinner specials feature jambalaya with andouille sausage, blackened catfish, and barbecue shrimp, among other dishes.

Red Fish Grill $$
115 Bourbon Street, New Orleans
(504) 598-1200
www.redfishgrill.com

Local artist Luis Colmenares's sculpted metal branches transform the wooden columns in the main dining room into encircling palms. All shapes and sizes of seafood are etched into the sea-colored concrete floor. Hanging on the exposed-brick back wall of the cocktail and oyster bar are half a dozen yard-high oyster half shells with mirrors inside; the backs of the artsy metal stools are adorned with alligators and crabs and fish, oh my. The tables are hand-painted in bright seafood designs. And the menu is divided into such categories as Bait (appetizers, soups, and salads), Fin Fish, Shell Fish, Go Fish (meat, pasta, vegetarian), and Overboard (dessert). Leave it to longtime restaurateur and proprietor Ralph Brennan of the Brennan restaurant family to create a comfortable bistro as whimsical to the eye as the remoulade-covered crabcakes and shiitake-and-grilled-shrimp quesadillas are pleasing to the palate. (See Mr. B's Bistro, Bacco, and Palace Cafe.) What Brennan and executive chef Robert Gregg Collier have concocted inside this renovated 1800s building, once home to D.H. Holmes department store, is a parade of heavenly delights using earthy crawfish, oysters, and pasta. Its Bourbon Street location draws a lot of walk-in tourists, but locals, too, have embraced this "casual New Orleans seafood" experiment. What is casual to Brennan, however, can seem downright otherworldly to out-of-towners unfamiliar with the creative heights so often reached by this former president of the National Restaurant Association. For proof pick from among these menu offerings: Creole-style sweet potato catfish; sesame-crusted salmon; gumbo with spicy alligator sausage; hickory-grilled redfish; and spring rolls filled with grilled chicken, shrimp, andouille sausage, and red beans in Chinese wrapper. The state-of-the-art kitchen's hickory wood-burning grill adds a smoky flavor to the grilled seafood and vegetable dishes. Lunch and dinner are served daily; brunch Sunday.

Remoulade $
309 Bourbon Street, New Orleans
(504) 523-0377
www.remoulade.com
Visitors strolling Bourbon Street who are looking for an affordable grazing menu of local flavors and a fun vibe, courtesy of Archie Casbarian (the restaurateur who put the famed Arnaud's next door back on the map), should look no farther. Casbarian's latest offering opened in 1994. New Orleans jazz is piped throughout the two-story century-old building and one-time jazz club venue, which features French doors, ceiling fans, wall sconces, and exposed brick walls and arches. Local staples include café au lait, beignets, red beans and rice, half-size po-boys dubbed "po-babies," boiled and fried seafood, and oysters on the half shell. Arnaud's famous remoulade sauce (the same kind found atop the celebrated restaurant's filet mignon Charlemond) tops the burgers and franks. Other offerings include smoked boudin, thin-crust 8-inch gourmet pizzas, Nachitoches (*NACK-ah-dish*) meat pies, and baskets of spare ribs. Mixed drinks, shooters, and a selection of "bayou potions guaranteed to ward off alligators" are served from behind the restored 1870s mahogany bar. Granite-topped tables and an open kitchen fit right in with the laid-back surroundings of Bourbon Street. Lunch and dinner are served daily until midnight.

The Rib Room $$$$
621 St. Louis Street, New Orleans
(504) 529-7045
Elegant 20-foot ceilings, exposed brick, gracious arches, and cypress barge-board walls from 19th-century keel boats set the stage for fine dining. The heady aromas wafting from the French rotisserie that dominates the back of the dining room

are proof you have arrived at a palais du boeuf non pareil. For generations the city's politicians, lawyers, and art dealers have made this French Quarter dining den on the ground floor of the Omni Royal Orleans Hotel a lunchtime favorite. And chef Anthony Spizale's prime rib and selection of rotisserie classics such as the chateaubriand, roti-assorti (English-cut prime rib, loin pork chop, and grilled lamb sausage), filet mignon, and lamb T-bone steaks seasoned with fresh herbs will tell you why. At night when the lights are turned down, the ambience changes from power-lunch buzz to pure hushed-tone romance. (For best seats—lunch or dinner—reserve a table overlooking Royal Street.) The menu stays the same with the addition of a few noteworthy seafood creations such as the roasted or grilled filet of salmon, crabcakes, and spit-roasted Gulf shrimp sautéed in a light butter with herbs and served with garlic sauce. Reservations are highly suggested for lunch and dinner, which are served daily.

Tujague's $$$
823 Decatur Street, New Orleans
(504) 525-8676
www.tujagues.com
In 1856 local butcher Guillaume Tujague, a native of Mazzeroles in southern France, opened this restaurant in the old Spanish armory on Decatur Street. He served hearty fare to dockworkers, butchers, and seamen who gave the French Market neighborhood its delightfully saucy character. Since that time U.S. presidents Roosevelt, Truman, and Eisenhower as well as France's Charles de Gaulle have dined at the city's second oldest restaurant. Politicians, artists, and travelers still rub elbows around the 1849 cypress bar—the oldest standing bar in the city and a classic in every sense of the word. The Latter family bought the restaurant in 1982 but the seven-course-only dinners for which the establishment is known are still built around such longtime staples as shrimp remoulade and beef brisket. While Tujague's can never be accused of impulsive innovation,

RESTAURANTS

Don't think that Creole and Cajun are the only two cuisines Big Easy restaurants have to offer. New Orleans is a multicultural melting pot, and its numerous ethnic restaurants offer foods of the world ranging from to Chinese and Cuban to Senegalese and Vietnamese. In fact, it's been said that the only type of food not available in New Orleans is Scandinavian.

patrons today have their choice of four traditional Creole entrees. Reservations are suggested, especially for weekend dining. Lunch at this more-than-200-year-old Street landmark is a far less fussy way to experience the ambience. Order the chicken and andouille pasta.

CBD/DOWNTOWN

Bon Ton Café   **$$$**
401 Magazine Street, New Orleans
(504) 524-3386
A brace of gaslights flank the canvas-canopied entrance to this popular establishment. Local dining connoisseurs first discovered this leisurely restaurant when it originally opened in the early 1900s. It closed for a spell only to be reopened in the 1950s by Al and Alzine Pierce when they arrived in New Orleans from their bayou home in south Louisiana's Lafourche and Terrebonne Parishes. Like many Acadian restaurateurs who have set up shop in the Big Easy over the decades, they brought their family recipes with them. Today the Pierces' nephew, Wayne, and his wife, Debbie, continue the family tradition of authentic Cajun cookery in the historic 1840s Natchez building. Amid a decor of red-and-white checkered tablecloths, wrought-iron chandeliers, shuttered window blinds, and exposed brick walls, guests will find many time-honed Bon Ton creations. Crawfish étouffée, crawfish bisque, shrimp and oyster jambalaya, and soft-shell crabs barely scratch

the surface. Other considerations are the filet mignon, shrimp Creole, and crawfish omelette. The Rum Ramsey cocktail, adapted from a recipe handed down from the early 1900s and known only to the owners, is famous. Lunch and dinner are served Monday through Friday, and reservations are "strongly urged."

Cobalt   **$$$**
333 St. Charles Avenue, New Orleans
(504) 565-5595
Bayona superstar chef Susan Spicer (see Bayona) has concocted what may well be one of the most eclectic, ingredient-savvy menus in town for this new restaurant located inside the midsize boutique Hotel Monaco. Where consulting chef Spicer and executive chef Brack May really shine is with their stone-ground cream-flavored grits (served with some dinner entrees as well as with breakfast), seared scallops with lentils in a citrus vinaigrette, and seasoned and grilled lamb or pork chops. More adventurous diners should check out the handmade goat cheese with white bean ravioli with butternut squash puree and sage–pumpkin seed pesto or the pan-roasted Maine salmon served in Spicer's martini sauce alongside roasted-garlic mashed potatoes. A Gehry-esque curvilinear aluminum fence separates the bar from the Art Deco dining room's barrel-vaulted ceiling and cobalt tile–accented walls, all of which gives this hot new venue a decidedly Big Apple cool. Breakfast, lunch, and dinner served daily.

Liborio Cuban Restaurant   **$$**
321 Magazine Street, New Orleans
(504) 581-9680
Simple and consistently prepared Cuban mainstays served in a Spartan dining room that often buzzes with Latin music and a lively crowd (especially during lunch) has helped this downtown spot earn its stripes. The restaurant moved to its current location from across the street, but hot meals still arrive in generous portions. The unique Spanish- and African-influenced cooking traditions of the Caribbean's largest island

have found a fitting home in a city that enjoys centuries-old ties to the region. Order a Honduran Port Royal beer served ice cold (or the nonalcoholic tamarind- and ginger–flavored Tamarindo) and dive into a traditional Cubano fried sandwich (pork, ham, and Swiss cheese on pressed grilled French bread) or the garlic roasted pork. The paella (with shrimp, lobster, crab, chicken, and fish) is mouthwatering and well worth the 45 minutes the kitchen cooks need to prepare this Andalusian-inspired version of New Orleans's jamba-laya. Or opt for the adventurous but satisfying pan-fried squid seasoned with onions, bell peppers, and red wine. Many dishes come with rice and peas (the Latin-Caribbean's answer to New Orleans's red beans and rice) and either sweet or green fried plantains, always tender to the fork. If your meal doesn't include the boiled yuca with garlic sauce, do yourself a favor and ask for it as a side order. Lunch is served Monday through Saturday; dinner Tuesday through Saturday.

Michaul's $$
840 St. Charles Avenue, New Orleans
(504) 522–5517, (800) 563–4055
www.michauls.com

"The most fun on two feet" is the motto. Every night there's a hot Cajun band jam-ming out born-on-the-bayou classics for diners looking to cut the rug. "Bring them dancin' shoes," says proprietor Al Babineaux, a native of Lafayette, the unof-ficial capital of Cajun Country. Popular bands such as Alan Fontenot and the Country Cajuns and Michaul's Mamou Brew provide the backbeat while Babineaux's wife, Michelle, and Barbara and Ron Borde-lon give free dance lessons to those of us born with two left feet. Before long you're dancing the two-step to "Joilen Blone" and "La Port a' Nadier" like a Cajun trapper after bagging the biggest gator in the swamp. Murals of bayou scenes add to the rustic decor of this popular restaurant, which opened in 1986. It's lively, boisterous, and a fun place to bring the family. Dance till midnight on Saturday, but first you'll

want to store up some energy from the large menu of mostly Cajun and New Orleans seafood appetizers and entrees. Topping the appetizers are fried alligator (served in a sauce piquante), artichoke Orleans (fried artichoke bottoms stuffed with shrimp and crabmeat dressing with a garlic-butter sauce), crawfish pies, and Cajun-style pork boudin sausage. House specials include spicy blackened shrimp and the herb-seasoned crabcakes in a creamy pepper sauce served over pecan rice. Traditional favorites like red beans and rice, roux-smothered crawfish étouffée, and deep-fried shrimp, oysters, catfish, and combo plates are served. Reservations are suggested for dinner Monday through Saturday.

The New Orleans Grill $$$$
300 Gravier Street, New Orleans
(504) 522–1992, (800) 262–2662
www.windsorcourthotel.com

One thing shared by the world's most impeccable dining legends is a liberation of geography. It is a restaurant's seamless savoir faire, say internationalists, that gives it a worldliness that would make it as at home in Istanbul and Paris as Vienna and Hong Kong—or New Orleans. Ranked as one of the finest restaurants in the United States and Europe, the New Orleans Grill is such a place. The Lalique table at the entrance greets guests to this famed culi-nary enclave on the second floor of the posh Windsor Court Hotel. But the focal point of this highly polished room is a marquetry screen of Windsor Castle com-missioned by Viscount Linley, son of the late Princess Margaret, for Windsor Castle. The elegant, softly lit, and unpretentious decor is accented by upholstered, dark-wood, straight-back chairs and light-colored linen tablecloths; an antique painting, *Girl on the Seashore,* dominates one wall. From people-watching during power lunches to romantic anniversaries celebrated in grand style, this continental oasis of refinement has been luring discriminating gourmets since it opened in 1984.

How to Crack a Crawfish

Some people call the little red crustaceans mudbugs, others crayfish, but by any name this Big Easy mainstay arrives at dining tables boiled, seasoned—and in the shell. Here's the skinny on how to avoid shell-shock: First, break off the head. This part of the crawfish is filled with marvelously seasoned fat juices from boiling, and most of us simply put the opening to our lips and suck. Next turn the tail on its back lengthwise between your thumbs and crack open the shell.

Gently squeeze the tip of the tail between your thumb and index finger and—bingo!—the crawfish meat should slide easily out of its shell. Mmmm. Traditionalists keep a cold Dixie longneck within arm's reach for celebratory swigs. By the way, it's correctly pronounced CRAW-fish, just like it's spelled.

Executive chef Jonathan Wright's menu includes an oxtail confit–tasso dumpling appetizer and such entrees as grilled Maine scallops in portobello mushroom reduction; pan-roasted grouper with artichoke-pancetta couscous; and Muscovy duck, crawfish, and orzo "jambalaya." Popular, too is Wright's chef's kitchen table, an intimate 10-course epicurean experience borrowed from European fine-dining tradition. Here guests can soak in the hustle and bustle of a working kitchen while enjoying an evening of food sampling, wine tasting, and culinary secrets. Breakfast and dinner are served daily; lunch is served Monday through Saturday. Arrive early to allow ample time for a martini at the Polo Lounge, the hotel's swank watering hole.

Le Salon in the hotel's lobby is nearly as famous for its traditional British tea as the New Orleans Grill is for its avant-garde repast. Taking tea in Le Salon includes a pot of classical tea and a three-course meal that begins with crustless tea sandwiches filled with smoked turkey, egg salad, cucumber, or salmon. Caviar and smoked canapés are served for a few extra dollars. Next comes the English currant and walnut scones and four spreads—sweet butter, lemon and curd, raspberry preserves, and clotted cream. Last, but not least, are the sweets—an array of chocolate-dipped strawberries, chocolate truffles, pecan tarts, cookies, and tea-cakes. Champagnes, aperitifs, and sherries are served by the glass. Sink into one of the overstuffed chairs and listen to the classical music, provided by a string trio or harpist, surrounded by some of the hotel's $8 million collection of 17th-through 20th-century art and antiques. Tea is served daily 2:00 to 4:30 P.M. (a tea and etiquette class is held Tuesday at 2:00 P.M.). Reservations are required for both the New Orleans Grill and Le Salon.

Palace Café $$$
605 Canal Street, New Orleans
(504) 523-1661
www.palacecafe.com
Located in the former Werlein's music store, Palace Cafe's building has been a local landmark since the turn of the 20th century. Nowadays it's classic and contemporary Creole and Cajun indulgences, not sheet music, that lure people to this lively, upbeat, grand Parisian-style brasserie owned and operated by Dickie Brennan Jr. of the famed New Orleans restaurant family. (This Brennan got his culinary start at Commander's Palace under the tutelage of Paul Prudhomme, now the proprietor-chef of K-Paul's.) Like

most of the family's new generation of eateries, which includes Mr. B's Bistro, Bacco, and Red Fish Grill, the accolades for this $2 million Palace coup haven't stopped since it opened its doors in 1991. The restaurant copped the prestigious Ivy award (the food industry's Oscar) from *Restaurants and Institutions* magazine, deeming the restaurant one of the top dining experiences in the United States. Brennan and the Palace Cafe have been on CNN's *On the Menu*, recognizing the restaurant for "being consistently voted some of the best food in the city and in the nation." Make reservations for one of the upstairs window-side tables during Mardi Gras, and enjoy a best-seat-in-the-house view of Canal Street below as a nighttime Carnival parade rolls by. The downstairs dining room offers a view of the open kitchen. Tasty favorites by executive chef Dourin Nesbit include molasses-glazed oven-roasted duck, crabmeat cheesecake, oyster pan roast, shrimp Tchefuncte, and, of course, the original white-chocolate bread pudding. Nesbit has also introduced an "on the lite side" menu popular among locals watching their girth. Reservations recommended. Lunch is served Monday through Friday; dinner is served nightly. Enjoy the live blues brunch Saturday and Sunday.

Restaurant August $$$$
301 Tchoupitoulas Street, New Orleans
(504) 299-9777
www.restaurantaugust.com

Among the city's consistently top-ranked newcomers is this gastronome's Vahalla and nationally praised retreat for the gourmand in us all. To set the right gustatory tempo, start off with award-winning executive chef John Besh's creative appetizers, particularly his three-way foie gras and terrine of artichokes, piquillo peppers, and sweet garlic with tomato confit. A changing menu of equally admirable entrees may be underscored by the Moroccan spiced duck with sweet corn polenta, duck foie gras and Folsom peaches, and the Parmesan-roasted

amberjack with crabmeat whipped potatoes and bouillabaisse. Personal favorites include the crispy veal sweetbreads with grilled lobster and French lentils, and porcini-crusted sea bass with orzo and Crowder pea risotto. Can't decide? Don't fret. Besh has whipped up a don't-miss tasting menu and tour de force of mouthwatering specialties fated to command the attention—and palate—of even hard-to-please culinary critics: chilled heirloom tomato consommé with lobster and caviar; grilled foie gras with piquillo peppers and nectarines; Chilean sea bass with veal sweetbreads; roasted saddle of Colorado lamb with panisse, artichokes, and ratatouille butter; and warm chocolate cake with spiced berries and golden beet ice cream. If this doesn't leave you breathless in New Orleans, nothing will. Lunch is served Monday through Friday and dinner Monday through Saturday.

Restaurant Cuvee $$$
322 Magazine Street, New Orleans
(504) 587-9001
www.restaurantcuvee.com

If in New Orleans "it seems every good adventure starts in a restaurant," perhaps it should come as no surprise that appetizers at this stylist bistro are found on the menu under "Preludes." And what preludes. If executive chef Bob Iacovone can be accused of anything, it is seducing epicures at this romantic, white-linen CBD venue with a sensual journey through gastronomies still to be explored. And little could better set the mood than his appetizer of rabbit confit crepe with butter-poached asparagus and lemon-thyme sabayon. Iacovone's Creole-continental menu of culinary spells whispers of the city's French and Spanish cooking influences. A solid example is the beef carpaccio with sweet corn-new potato salad, seared filet of beef with a garlic wild-mushroom andouille polenta cake. Other savvy gastronomes swear allegiance to Iacovone's butter-poached lobster and braised veal in a roasted garlic white-bean puree accompanied by steamed clams, dried chorizo, and rapini. But this humble diner found his Lyonnaise home away from home with each tender forkful of the chef's liver with caramelized onions, wild mushrooms, baby carrots, Brabant pota-toes, and a crispy parsnip thistle. Open for lunch Monday through Friday and dinner Monday through Saturday. Reservations recommended.

Travelers who visit the city during some of its peak tourism times—Mardi Gras, Jazzfest, the Sugar Bowl, and large conventions, for instance–will find securing reservations, especially at better restaurants, a challenge. One way around this is to make your reservations as soon as possible upon arriving—or even before, if possible.

Riverview   **$$$$**
555 Canal Street, New Orleans
(504) 581-1000
The highest possible altitude for local dining (unless you're circling the city in a Cessna while savoring crème brûlée) is the 41st-floor Riverview in the New Orleans Marriott. You may not be able to see as far away as Baton Rouge, but it's still a capital idea to soak up the bird's-eye view of the French Quarter and Mississippi River here over one of the house steaks, chops, or chicken specialties. Start off with the goat cheese–stuffed portobello mushrooms while perusing the entrees, many of which can be grilled or blackened to taste. A few shortcuts to smiles include the pan-seared salmon with fried oysters and citrus beurre blanc; the 14-ounce New York strip, served with Burgundy marrow sauce; and the veal chop stuffed with Fontina cheese, prosciutto, and sage cream sauce. The airy and casually well-dressed decor keeps the ambience light enough for a New Orleans–style dessert of crème brûlée, praline cheesecake, pecan tart, or banana walnut bread

pudding. Or drink in your after-dinner treat with a chocolate martini—shaken, not stirred—with Absolut, white crème de cacao, and Godiva chocolate liqueurs. A lounge with comfy chairs and sofas is an inviting place for before-dinner drinks while waiting for a table or just to enjoy the view. Dinner is served Tuesday through Saturday; brunch Sunday.

Top of the Dome Steakhouse   **$$$**
500 Poydras Plaza, New Orleans
(504) 561-1234
Even in a city known for its sinful culinary indulgences, this place takes the cake. Imagine sating your sweet tooth after dinner at an all-you-can-eat chocolate bar of lavish cakes, creamy truffles, and other sugary delights—all while enjoying the 32nd-floor view of the Big Easy from the city's only revolving rooftop restaurant. Now, that's decadence. But more than confections meet the palate at this popular chop house, squired away in the stratosphere of the sky-piercing Hyatt Regency, adjacent to the Superdome. A softly lit dining room at night serves up window-side romance as grilled and blackened beef creations make their way from kitchen to table. Sizzling examples of the kitchen's forte include the veal chop, filet mignon, New York strip, and prime rib. Swordfish steak, pecan-orange roasted chicken, and a catch of the day are served. Starters range from fresh oysters on the half shell and crawfish rémoulade to Louisiana lumpmeat crabcakes. For many locals this is the place to bring out-of-town visitors to show off the city from this culinary theater in the round. Dinner is served Tuesday through Saturday and reservations are suggested. The dessert hour stretches to midnight.

Veranda   **$$**
444 St. Charles Avenue, New Orleans
(504) 525-5566
Drop by for the popular Sunday champagne jazz brunch and ask for a table in the climate-controlled, French Quarter–style atrium enclosed by a massive glass

ceiling. Located on the lobby level of the Hotel Inter-Continental, the faux courtyard has brick floors, lush palms, gaslights, wrought-iron chairs, and white-linen table-cloths—just like the real thing in the French Quarter a few blocks away. But on weekends it boasts something rarely found at those traditional Creole establishments on the other side of Canal Street: a magician who goes table to table entertaining antsy youngsters with sleight-of-hand tricks. Grown-ups sans kiddies will find the atrium a quiet escape for dinner (unless the hotel is thronged with conventioneers). Executive chef Willy Cohn, who still rolls out the sauerbraten and other dishes from his native Germany during an annual Oktoberfest, prepares what many loyalists say are among the best Louisiana crabcakes in town. Others point to the Creole herb–crusted chicken breast with étouffée. Breakfast, lunch, and dinner are served daily; brunch Sunday. Reservations are recommended for brunch.

WAREHOUSE DISTRICT

Emeril's $$$$
800 Tchoupitoulas Street, New Orleans
(504) 528–9393
www.emerils.com
Proprietor-chef Emeril Lagasse's restaurant empire started inside this brick building and one-time factory in the heart of the Warehouse District. The menu developed by Lagasse, a former executive chef at Commander's Palace and one of the city's best-known culinary figures, is strong on inventive Creole dishes with plenty of contemporary flair. Comfy bent-wood chairs, polished hardwood floors, and abstract oil paintings are good signals that this is not your father's Creole restaurant. Many locals rely on the specials, but the standard menu deserves more than a quick look, especially if you like your red-fish pecan-crusted and served on grilled vegetables and shoestring potatoes with cane-syrup–glazed pecans and meuniére

butter sauce. Oyster lovers meantime can enjoy them paneed with sweetcorn maque choux, tomato jam, and bacon. Don't miss homemade andouille and Creole boudin sausages with beer-braised onions, mustard, and homemade Worcestershire sauce. Dinner is served daily, lunch Monday through Friday. Reservations are a must.

Mulate's $$
201 Julia Street, New Orleans
(504) 522–1492, (800) 854–9149
www.mulates.com
"Ask not what your culture can do for you, ask what you can do for your culture." Breaux Bridge native and proprietor Kerry Boutte is oft quoted as saying. For Boutte that means showing visitors as well as Cajun locals how to "pass a good time," as they say in Acadiana, when it comes to the traditional foodways of his people. Let's face it: Not everyone who visits the city has the time or budget to scamper off to Cajun country, one to three hours away (depending on which part you visit). The next best thing is to hunker down around one of the wooden tables at this lively, family-style restaurant opened in 1991 and decorated with bayou-themed paintings, murals, and bric-a-brac. Standbys range from fried seafood (shrimp, stuffed crabs, crawfish tails, and catfish) to boiled crawfish, gumbo, and blackened and grilled seafood entrees. Other feasts for hearty appetites include the cayenne-seasoned blackened rib-eye served with jambalaya. Bring your dancing shoes, as free, live Cajun music rules the roost nightly 7:00 to 10:30 P.M. Lunch and dinner are served daily.

Rio Mar $$
800 South Peters Street, New Orleans
(504) 525–3474
www.riomarseafood.com
In 2001 this hip Spanish entry snatched *Bon Appetit*'s award for best new casual restaurant in New Orleans. Native chef Adolfo Garcia's Iberian version of French bouillabaise, called zarzuela de Mariscos,

alone merits notable mention for its simmering saffron-spiced seafood broth topped by shrimp, clams, scallops, and fish. He offers four types of the classic Latin dish cerviche prepared in the style of Peru (with tomatoes and onions), Ecuador (shrimp and citrus juices), Panama (habañero peppers and lime), and Spain (octopus, olive oil, and paprika). For appetizers the open-shell, garlic-steamed mussels adorned with chorizo is a surefire winner. Top entrees include Serrano (ham)-wrapped yellowfin tuna in chickpea puree with Romesco sauce. Artful decor inside this "seafood destination" includes an open kitchen, Mediterranean-yellow and exposed-brick walls, terra-cotta floors, and original metalwork. Open for lunch Monday through Friday and dinner Monday through Saturday.

Taqueria Corona $
857 Fulton Street, New Orleans
(504) 524-9805

5932 Magazine Street (Uptown)
New Orleans
(504) 897-3974

3535 Severn Avenue, Metairie
(504) 885-5088

The Warehouse District location of this popular Mexican restaurant can be counted on for lively after-work and weekend-night crowds. In New Orleans the number of establishments serving consistently good traditional Mexican fare has never quite kept pace with the city's other ethnic restaurants. This place saves the day. The chips, for example, served with a choice of freshly made guacamole, pico de gallo, or cebollitas (charbroiled green onions), always arrive at the table crispy and fresh. The enchiladas and burritos (try the overstuffed California chicken burrito—lots of onions and cilantro) are flavorful. Patrons can wash down their combination plate or one of three kinds of pizza—beef taco, chicken taco, and Mexican (with ham, cheese, guacamole, and jalapeño sauce)—with tasty margaritas, sangria, or shots of that bad hombre, Jose

Cuervo. The strong suit of this relaxed establishment are the tacos, which are served in soft flour tortillas with freshly chopped cilantro and fresh pico de gallo on the side. They can be ordered with any number of tasty fillings: seasoned and fried fish filet bits with tartar sauce; chorizo; sautéed marinated Gulf shrimp; charbroiled lean pork; and spicy and tender beef tongue (highly recommended). The list of desserts is short and to the point: flan and arroz con leche (Mexican rice pudding). Lunch and dinner are served daily. Takeout is available.

FAUBOURG MARIGNY

Café Negril $$
606 Frenchmen Street, New Orleans
(504) 944-4744

De rigueur murals of reggae legend Bob Marley and faux Jamaican-style roadside bar motif set the stage for chef Cecil Palmer's (former owner of the now-closed Palmer's Jamaican Restaurant) distinctly Caribbean menu of meat, chicken, and fish dishes at the city's only Jamaican restaurant. Palmer, who hails from rural Manchester outside Jamaican capital Kingston, knows that the best way to serve jerk chicken is in a backcountry hot-pepper-and-onion sauce blended with demiglace. His jerk fish is marinated 24 hours with hot peppers, Jamaican pimento, and lime juice before it's sautéed and served in a hearty tomato-and-onion sauce. While the curried goat sometimes has a few too many bones, it's still a commanding version of this West Indian staple. On cold days the creamy Bahamian chowder and hearth-style pepperpot soup are perfect body warmers. The Red Stripe beer is served ice cold (tropical rum drinks are available, too). Open for lunch and dinner Wednesday through Sunday.

Feelings Café $$
2600 Chartres Street, New Orleans
(504) 945-2222
www.feelingscafe.com

The tropically lush, romantic courtyard crumbling with history has been a favorite among locals for years. For an untouristy spot in which to unwind with predinner cocktails, it has few equals. The courtyard surface features bricks recycled from the massive fireplace of the original D'Aunoy Plantation, built in 1795 and one of the first constructed in the historic Faubourg Marigny neighborhood. The main dining room is an 1860s Creole storehouse (a store below with the shopkeeper's residence directly above). Guests can dine in the courtyard (weeknights only), upstairs, or in the downstairs main dining room adjacent to the bar. For an extra touch of romance, when making reservations request one of the candlelit tables on the second-floor balcony that overlooks the courtyard. Romance isn't the only thing in the air though, as the aroma of house specials plus fried and grilled New Orleans seafood fills your senses. If you think you've tried the city's famed bivalve just about every way imaginable, think again: The oysters en brochette, available as appetizer or entree, is a tour de force of deep-fried, bacon-wrapped oysters served with sour cream and Creole mustard sauce. Open for dinner daily and lunch Friday and Sunday only.

Marisol $$$
437 Esplanade Avenue, New Orleans
(504) 943–1912
www.marisolrestaurant.com

The white-brick exterior and blue-and-white front-door awning make for a thankfully understated façade. After all, this is a favorite "secret" that at least one local keeps up his sports-coat sleeve for such times when he wants to impress globe-trotting pals and self-styled gourmands visiting from out of state. But not just because of the restaurant's intimate bistro decor of muted Provencal hues (and beautiful mural of sunflowers a la van Gogh) or the intimate fountain and gaslamp courtyard. Tucked on the edge of the French Quarter far from the madding crowd is owners Janis Vazquez and chef

Peter Vazquez's tour de force of "pure intense cooking" that is rooted in the terra firma of European cooking tradition. And this is precisely why Marisol is a wake-up call for savvy palates that have become weary from restaurants that translate European culinary craft into lackluster recipes. At Marisol an ever-changing menu means diners on one night will discover the Vazquez's foie gras dressed with sturgeon caviar, toasted brioche, and fig gelee; another night with fried potatoes and peach compote with jalapeños. Whether it's plantain-crusted salmon filet with black beans or slow-cooked lamb shank in a hot Indian vindaloo, Chef Peter nightly achieves his stated mission to "challenge the complacent palate." Consider yourself lucky if, on the night you visit, the Pacific sturgeon (wrapped in prosciutto with goat cheese gnocchi and tomato-saffron broth) is on the menu. Another European flourish of finesse the Vazquezes bring to the dessert side of the menu is the largest selection of international and domestic cheeses found in any New Orleans restaurant (and what Janis says is probably the second largest in the country). Whether your palate yearns for a French *chevre*, a Spanish *garrotxa*, an Italian *cimonino*, or Roaring Forties Blue from Australia's Tasmania island-state, a worldly mix of nearly 50 cheeses from 10 countries awaits the serious *amant de fromage*. This white-linen fine-dining venue also offers a tapas happy hour Wednesday through Friday. Up to 40 appetizer-size dishes range from tuna-and-escargot empanadas and mussels steamed with homemade chorizo to such traditional Spanish staples as *pescado en escabeche* (fish in a spicy vinegar-based sauce) and *patatas allioli* (cubed potatoes in garlic mayonnaise). Open for lunch Wednesday through Friday and dinner Wednesday through Sunday; jazz brunch Saturday and Sunday. Once a month, the restaurant hosts a yappy-hour dog party in the courtyard (only guests with pooches are allowed in the courtyard from 5:00 to 7:00 P.M.)

Praline Connection   **$**
542 Frenchmen Street, New Orleans
(504) 943–3934
www.pralineconnection.com
Walk into this intimate Faubourg Marigny restaurant with its stainless-stool ceiling fans, black-and-white tile floor, and a wait-staff adorned in flashy ties and fedoras, and one word comes to mind: slick. No doubt, this Creole soul food restaurant is one of the coolest places you'll ever eat in. And will you be glad you did. The fried chicken is crispy and delicious, and the meat loaf will make you think you're eating at your mama's house. Most meals include melt-in-your-mouth corn bread and a choice of beans or greens. Other best bets include barbecued ribs, hot chicken wings, and soft-shell crabs in this casual yet bustling setting populated with a mix of locals and tourists. No reservations are accepted, so to avoid the biggest crowds in this small dining room, take in a late lunch or early dinner. On your way out, stop into the adjacent candy shop to stock up on pralines and other goodies for the trip home. The Praline Connection Gospel and Blues Hall, at 907 South Peters Street (504–523–3973), is a 9,000-square-foot former engine factory where a raucous gospel brunch is served every Sunday. However, for lunch and dinner daily, the original location can't be beat.

Santa Fe   **$$**
801 Frenchmen Street, New Orleans
(504) 944–6854
This Latin restaurant was one of the first in the city to introduce a Creole flair to a largely Mexican menu. Purists will find a charity of traditional dishes such as carne asada, Spanish omelettes, pork-and-cheese quesadillas, and combo plates with enchiladas, chile rellenos, and tamales. The fried flour tortilla filled with chicken, sweet potatoes, and chili, covered with cheeses, and topped with a fried egg, is a surefire winner. The kitchen inside this two-story restaurant overlooking Washington Square turns up the creative heat on local flavors. For proof check out the flash-fried shrimp and crawfish fajitas and the crawfish (or spiced pork) tamales, which come topped with chili, Taos sauce, and cheeses. Another Mexican Creole creation is the Corquieta St. Jacques—scallops, shrimp, crabmeat, and mushrooms blended in a bed of duchess potatoes topped with a rich white wine sauce. If the spacious downstairs dining room is too noisy, opt for one of the cozy, organza-colored nooks up-stairs, with high ceilings, ceiling fans, Oriental rugs, and wicker and cane chairs. (Plus, the window views of Washington Square across the street are nice.) Dinner is served Wednesday through Saturday.

ESPLANADE

Cafe Degas   **$$**
3127 Esplanade Avenue, New Orleans
(504) 945–5635
www.cafedegas.com
Particularly in fall and spring, when the weather can be downright blissful, the covered deck of this fashionable bistro-style eatery in historic Esplanade Ridge is a pure delight. Named after the 19th-century French Impressionist Edgar Degas, who lived down the street for a brief time, this restaurant is ideal for lunch or dinner after visiting the nearby New Orleans Museum of Art. A large number of rotating daily specials augment the French-language menu (with English translations) of French specialties. The sometimes breezy venue is popular among hoi palloi and politicians who can be found dining on such creations as the roasted boneless duck breast with orange sauce, or the roasted Cornish hen served with pancetta, peppers, tomatoes, and rice pilaf. The crispy veal medallions and broiled escargot are popular. A selection of homemade desserts including Key lime pie is served. The restaurant is open for lunch Tuesday through Saturday and dinner daily; brunch Sunday.

Gabrielle $$$
3201 Esplanade Avenue, New Orleans
(504) 948–6233
www.gabriellerestaurant.com

The intriguing family tree that links many of the city's best-known chef-proprietors includes Greg and Mary Sonnier, who met while working under chef Paul Prud-homme at K-Paul's Louisiana Kitchen (see K-Paul's). Greg worked on the line; Mary was a sausage-maker. When Frank Brigt-sen left K-Paul's to open his own restau-rant (see Brigtsen's), he tapped Greg to be sous chef. In 1992 Greg set out on his own with Mary (now his wife) to open their own restaurant and named it after their daughter and Greg's grandmother. But that was only the beginning for the duo, who since have carved their own niche in the New Orleans dining scene and earned national kudos for their efforts. Mary's passion for gardening has resulted in the small garden outside the restaurant, which provides the herbs and flowers for many of Greg's creations. From the smoked chicken gumbo to the barbe-cue shrimp pie and Creole cream cheese–crusted lamb chops with Israeli couscous and black grape sauce, this culi-nary pair has earned a loyal following. (Mary handles the desserts.) The cracker-crusted rabbit wrapped in basil with shrimp, andouille, and tomato-basil pasta is among the best bets, as is the slow-roasted duck with exotic mushrooms in an orange-sherry sauce. The intimate dining room is brightened with mirrored panels and large windows. Menu changes daily. Dinner is served Tuesday through Satur-day; lunch Friday only. Reservations are recommended.

Liuzza's by the Track $
1518 North Lopez Street, New Orleans
(504) 943–8667

Ask any New Orleanian to rattle off the names of their favorite neighborhood joints, and this one invariably shows up in the top five, often winning by a nose against the Big Easy's most beloved and acclaimed down-home eateries (and that's

saying a mouthful). It's also among the spots New Orleanians who've moved out of state are eager to visit when they drop into town. And for good reason: Liuzza's menu hits the backstretch of cherished local dishes ranging from its acclaimed fried oyster salad and well-seasoned Cre-ole chicken and sausage gumbo to fresh sautéed shrimp and corn chowder with crawfish. Its moniker derived from the restaurant's proximity to New Orleans Fair Grounds Race Track, this homebred win-ner has proven itself a front-runner when it comes to its plethora of po-boys that include a don't-miss roast beef with "nos-tril-searing" horseradish so good *Gourmet* magazine in 2002 proclaimed it "the rea-son to come to New Orleans." Though the restaurant unfortunately flies below the radar of many unknowing tourists, Liuzza's is a true Insider's nook and a great place to rub elbows with locals. Don't bother jockeying for a table by the window as it's the energy of the lively din-ing room that helps make this neighbor-hood landmark simply unforgettable. Open for lunch Monday through Saturday and dinner Monday through Friday.

Restaurant Indigo $$$
2285 Bayou Road, New Orleans
(504) 947–0123
www.restaurantindigo.com

Some restaurateurs possess intuition when it comes to creating a romantic dining atmosphere that not only invites but also cultivates intimate conversation coupled with anticipation of sensual culinary delights to come. Owner Cynthia Reeves is such a restaurateur (in fact, she opened Restaurant Indigo on New Year's Eve 1999). Sculptured sconces, ceiling fans, high ceilings, and white linens, plus a pro-fessional yet unobtrusive waitstaff, trans-form the dining room into an elegantly understated retreat in which to savor executive chef Jared Katz's commanding (and always surprising) creations. For instance, Katz gives osso buco a memo-rable Euro-Creole makeover by serving the classic veal dish braised in grillades sauce over Gruyere grits. Ditto for the paneed rabbit tenderloin dressed to thrill with prosciutto, Fontina, and sage tossed with pappardelle (ribbon) pasta and baby vegetables. Katz the internationalist sends Britain's beef Wellington to France so it arrives at your table topped with *chevre duxelle* wrapped in a flaky pastry with foie gras demi. Other diners have raved about the poached Maine lobster with pickled watermelon rind and Katz's watermelon gazpacho. Favorite appetizers include poached mussels (in a spicy tomato and saffron white wine broth) and seared foie gras (served with caramelized shallots drizzled with Port reduction and Sauterne gastrique). Veranda dining is available. Open for dinner Tuesday through Sunday; brunch Sunday.

MID CITY

Christian's   **$$**
3835 Iberville Street, New Orleans
(504) 482-4924
www.christiansrestaurantneworleans.com
For more than two decades, the picturesque, flood-lit steeple of this former Lutheran church built in 1914 has served as a beacon for scores of hungry pilgrims. If you have to wait for a table, order a drink from the bar, where the crying room used to be, and relax on one of the two polished pews in the reception area. Today rows of truncated cone-shaped lamps hang from the original cathedral ceiling in the dining room, which is surrounded by Gothic stained-glass windows and hanging foliage. But the name of this award-winning restaurant has nothing to do with the fact that it's housed in a historic, renovated church. It is the name of cofounder Christian Ansel, who, along with Hank Bergeron, opened the original Christian's in Metairie in 1973 before moving four years later to this present Mid City landmark. Chefs Michael Foucqueteau and Roland Huet's largely Creole menu is a heavenly mix of New Orleans–style standbys and classic French cuisine. Sink

your fork into such Creole traditions as sautéed baby veal, bouillabaisse Marsellaise, and roasted loin chop. Slightly more adventurous diners may want to try the oyster-stuffed filet mignon or the shrimp Marigny (sautéed with pearl onions, mushrooms, sundried tomatoes, and garlic, then flamed in brandy and finished with a Dijon butter sauce). Homemade ice creams and fresh fruit ices are house specialties, but the homemade brownie served with vanilla ice cream, chocolate sauce, and roasted pecans is too sinful to pass up. The dress is casual, but jackets are preferred; jeans and shorts are not permitted after 5:00 P.M. Lunch is served Tuesday through Friday; dinner Tuesday through Saturday. Reservations are recommended.

Dooky Chase   **$$**
2301 Orleans Avenue, New Orleans
(504) 821-0600
New Orleans' premier Creole soul food restaurant, Dooky Chase is also the place where the movers and shakers of the city's African-American community meet. Edgar "Dooky" Chase and his wife, Emily, opened the restaurant in 1941. Over the years the eatery has grown from the best-kept secret of the black community to a restaurant of international renown, mostly because of chef Leah Chase's talent. Chase, the wife of Dooky Chase Jr., is a home-taught cook who creates such delicacies as breast of chicken a la Dooky, stuffed with oysters, baked in a marchand de vin sauce, and served with sweet potatoes. Locals and tourists alike can be found daily in the casually glamorous Dooky Chase dining room, which features a collection of African-themed art including stained-glass panels depicting life in black New Orleans. Other best bets at this restaurant, which features a full bar and short wine list, are fabulous fried chicken, red beans and rice, Creole gumbo, stuffed shrimp, and the fried seafood platter. Or, if you're really hungry, call ahead and order the Creole Feast. (*NOTE:* Tourists unfamiliar with the city are advised to take a cab

to this restaurant at night.) Lunch and dinner are served daily and reservations are recommended.

Five Happiness $
**3605 South Carrollton Avenue
New Orleans
(504) 482–3935**

When Five Happiness owner Peggy Lee first visited the Big Easy in the early 1980s, she found that local Chinese restaurants were serving rather bland fare. Knowing New Orleanians' love for spicy food, she decided to relocate to New Orleans her California-based restaurant, which specialized in Szechuan and Hunan fare. Since that time, this Mid City eatery has grown into one of the city's most popular Chinese restaurants, which on any given night can be found full of local families, couples, and students from nearby Loyola and Tulane Universities. The traditionally decorated dining rooms are comfortable and spacious at Five Happiness, which is one of the city's few Chinese restaurants featuring an extensive dim sum menu. Best bets include Szechuan shrimp, sizzling go bah, shredded pork in hot garlic sauce, pot stickers, hot and sour soup, and the Triple Delight—a combination of chicken, beef, and shrimp sautéed with vegetables in a brown sauce. The full bar features a short wine list and Chinese beer as well as specialty drinks such as the tiki bowl and mai tai. Combination lunch specials are available Monday through Saturday. Lunch and dinner are served daily. Reservations are accepted and recommended on weekend evenings.

Jacques-Imo's Café $$
**8324 Oak Street, New Orleans
(504) 861–0886**

This is the little soul-food den you've heard about where customers actually walk past the open kitchen to arrive at the covered-deck dining area out back. And, yes, that's owner-chef Jack Leonardi wearing a chef's jacket and Bermuda shorts. But peccadilloes such as those don't even scratch the surface of what

makes a meal at this popular Carrollton neighborhood spot so memorable. What does begin to tell the story of this always bustling den is fried chicken so outstanding devotees have described it as a near religious experience, and a national travel magazine dubbed it the best of its kind anywhere in the United States. But the lengthy regular and specials menu featuring old-school soul food and Creole standards (a must-have is the deep-fried roast beef po-boy) also shares the spotlight with an adventurous shrimp and alligator sausage cheesecake, paneed rabbit with oyster/tasso cream sauce, grilled duck, and pork chop stuffed with ground beef and shrimp. What this lively dining joint does, it does extremely well—consistently. And that's why visiting travel writers and food critics have joined locals in singing the praises of this humble establishment virtually from the moment it opened its doors. All together now: "Jock-a-mo fee-na-ne!" Open for dinner Monday through Saturday.

UPTOWN

Cafe Atchafalaya $$
**901 Louisiana Avenue, New Orleans
(504) 891–5271**

"Rather Southern specialties" are the bywords of this down-home neighborhood eatery tucked inside a yellow wooden building with multistriped awnings. And if anyone knows the ins and outs of Southern cookery (and hospitality), it's longtime restaurateur and kitchen veteran Iler Pope. When she was a fresh-scrubbed newlywed of 21, her mother paid a woman for a year to teach the recipe-challenged Pope to cook, she says. Pope caught on fast and has never stopped experimenting in the kitchen, all the while staying close to her Delta roots. Consider: A basket filled with a triple threat of just-baked French bread and Pope's famous jalapeño cheesebread and regular corn bread arrives at the Formica tables not long after guests do. Popular "sides" include black-eyed peas, turnip greens, and homemade Southern vegetables. The congenial and straightforward Mississippi native also knows a thing or two about chicken and dumplings, calves liver and onions, boiled brisket, barbecue shrimp, and country-fried steak. First-time visitors might also want to check out the hand-scrawled specials board for such dishes as the crabmeat-and-shrimp-stuffed soft-shell crab, which arrives swimming in a thick meunière sauce good enough for dipping the brabant potatoes. Not to be outdone is the pork chop stuffed with andouille cornbread dressing and served in a Jack Daniels–apricot glaze. The gumbo and its mercilessly hearty roux should be savored half a spoonful at a time. Lunch is served Tuesday through Sunday; dinner Tuesday through Saturday. Weekend brunch kicks off early Saturday and Sunday at 8:30 A.M., where the best-eats award goes to the eggs Atchafalaya—poached eggs with grilled andouille sausage served atop an English muffin smothered in hollandaise and Creole sauces.

Clancy's $$
6100 Annunciation Street, New Orleans
(504) 895-1111

This is the kind of tucked-back-in-a-neighborhood place that concierges recommend to savvy hotel guests when they ask for a locals' spot that oozes with character. The faded wooden CLANCY'S sign hanging outside dates to the days when this was a sandwich shop. Today this corner restaurant draws a stylish crowd; on the far wall of the main dining room, amid the ceiling fans, candles, white linens, and mirrors, are sketches of neighborhood regulars. Patrons looking for quiet seclusion can opt for one of the cozy "vintage" dining rooms upstairs, where the walls are lined with floor-to-ceiling wine racks. Elsewhere upstairs are framed Jazzfest posters and paintings by local artist Peter Bryant of the surrounding Uptown neighborhood. Oprah had the roasted garlic chicken when she dined here; Michael Jor-

dan, Larry Hagman, and Alec Baldwin have also dined on some of executive chef Brian Larson's creations. But you don't have to be famous to enjoy Chef Brian's veal liver Lyonnaise, smoked pork loin (with a Creole mustard and green peppercorn sauce), grilled baby drum with smoked salmon, or filet mignon (with Stilton and a red wine demiglace). Lunch is served Tuesday through Friday; dinner Monday through Saturday. Reservations are recommended.

Commander's Palace $$$$
1403 Washington Avenue, New Orleans
(504) 899-8221
www.commanderspalace.com

A local longtime food critic once wrote about the test he gives friends and restaurantgoers who say they've grown tired of this standard-bearer of Creole dining. He asks them simply whether they would prefer to dine at Commander's or (fill in the blank). Guess which one they pick 99 times out of 100? He explains that while some locals may grow tired of hearing about Commander's, no one ever tires of actually putting a napkin on his or her lap inside this legend. A generation of chefs who have gone on to make their own culinary marks in the city have worked the Commander's kitchen. Even the short list is impressive: Emeril Lagasse (see Emeril's and Nola), Paul Prudhomme (see K-Paul's), Frank Brigtsen (see Brigtsen's), Anne Kearney (see Peristyle), and Greg and Mary Sonnier (see Gabrielle). All have left their imprint—and vice versa. The menu still woos even the most hard-to-please palate with starters such as oysters simmered with apple-smoked bacon garnished with caviar and, of course, the restaurant's famous shrimp rémoulade. Likewise for entrees such as the rack of lamb, grilled veal chop, and pecan-crusted Gulf fish crowned with champagne-poached lump crabmeat with crushed corn sauce. This turquoise-and-white Victorian bastion of tradition is keeping up with the culinary times; good examples include the pan-seared foie gras and muscadine and chicory coffee-lacquered quail with blue crab stuffing, mixed potato hash, and baby mustard greens.

High society has called this Garden District landmark home ever since the Anglo-Saxons arrived in the 19th century to make their fortunes, put down roots Uptown, and stopped fighting the Creoles long enough to gain respectability. Founder Emile Commander was a practical man: He knew that all those new Americans would need a place to eat, preferably with an English-speaking staff. (The French-speaking Creoles across town in the French Quarter certainly weren't looking to cater to these brash upstarts.) By 1900 his restaurant, on the site of the former Livaudais Plantation, was already well known. It also attracted riverboat captains as well as "sporting gentlemen" who used the private upstairs dining room to rendezvous with beautiful women. The family dining room downstairs, however, maintained "impeccable respectability"—and a separate entrance. In 1974 four members of the Brennan family (Ella, Dottie, Dick, and John) bought the place, redecorated to brighten it up, and steered Commander's to its present-day glory. Chef Tory McPhail deserves credit for helping keep this establishment among the restaurants most often mentioned in the country and a shining pinnacle of a culinary city at its best. Lunch and dinner are served daily; a live jazz brunch is offered Saturday and Sunday. Reservations are required.

Copeland's $
4338 St. Charles Avenue, New Orleans
(504) 897–2325

1001 South Clearview Parkway, Metairie
(504) 733–7843
www.alcopeland.com
Families traveling on a budget (more than 30 entrees weigh in at under $12) as well as those with a yen for consistent Cajun fare with an occasional twist should check out this local chain restaurant. The lively vibe is casual. In 1983 this became Al

Copeland's first foray into the full-service restaurant business. Today the popular restaurant is usually packed, and you can count on at least a short wait on weekend nights. But it's worth it. The large menu offers burgers and sandwiches for the kids as well as sizzling steaks, chicken dishes, and a selection of Cajun and Creole seafood specialties including several blackened steak and seafood dishes. The spicy paneed veal Copeland with a creamy blend of pasta mixed with shrimp and Cajun-spiced tasso has always been a satisfying venture. The huge, hot buttermilk biscuits accompanying many of the dishes are homemade and flaky. The restaurant is open for lunch and dinner daily with a jazz brunch menu Sunday 11:00 A.M. to 3:00 P.M.

Delmonico's $$$$
1300 St. Charles Avenue, New Orleans
(504) 525–4937
www.emerils.com
Locals were happy indeed when this 104-year-old restaurant reopened its doors in June 1998 after a one-year hiatus. Current owner, superstar chef and Food Channel regular Emeril Lagasse, bought the restaurant from longtime owners Rose Dietrich and Angie Brown, and so far no one has been disappointed. The five dining rooms (one downstairs; four upstairs) have been completely redecorated in a contemporary style to give the place a casual elegance (jackets are recommended for gents). But pictures of the old restaurant hanging on the wall are reminders that the

Foodies and gourmands have several resources for keeping abreast of the local dining scene, thanks to weekly reviews by restaurant critic Brett Anderson in the Times-Picayune's "Friday Lagniappe" section and food critic Tom Fitzmorris' call-in radio program on WSMB 1350-AM Monday through Friday 4:00 to 7:00 P.M.

reborn Delmonico's isn't about to abandon its heritage anytime soon. Signature dishes include the oysters brochette with Brie-roasted mushrooms appetizer, soufflé spinach and Brie crepes, and Creole broiled prime filet mignon or dry aged prime rib-eye. Newcomers on the menu include banana leaf-steamed fish served with steamed rice, chile onion salsa, and sake soy glaze. Daily epicurean "tributes" range from stuffed quail with oyster dressing to pheasant under glass with truffle sauce. Many dishes are prepared tableside. Lunch is served Monday through Friday; dinner Monday through Saturday. The Sunday jazz brunch is popular. Reservations are highly suggested.

Jamila's Café $$
7808 Maple Street, New Orleans
(504) 866-4366

Just when you were beginning to wonder if all Mediterranean restaurants served more or less the same fare seemingly from cookie-cutter menus, along comes this cozy Maple Street retreat of mouthwatering Tunisian surprises. The appetizers alone will be enough to make even seasoned lovers of traditional Greek, Turkish, and Lebanese fare sit up and take note. Yet as satisfying as gourmands will find the *brik au thon* (filo dough stuffed with tuna, potatoes, parsley, and onions), it would be a pity not to explore the exotic swirl of flavors discovered in Jamila's *merguez,* the traditional Tunisian (and Algerian) lamb sausage. Best bets include the appetizers *ojja* merguez (sautéed homemade seasoned lamb sausage, caraway seeds, tomatoes, and bell peppers mixed with eggs) and grilled merguez (with lentils). As subtle yet recognizable as a North African wind is Jamila's fish chowder and signature *tajine* of lamb—boneless leg of lamb cooked in a traditional Tunisian terra-cotta dish and served with marinated garlic and saffron rice. The restaurant pays homage to Tunisia's cross-cultural ties with France courtesy of a grilled petite filet that arrives at the table alongside pommes

Lyonnaise. A succinct mix of traditional Mediterranean meat, fish, and vegetarian dishes served with couscous (steamed whole-wheat semolina) is available. Flamenco guitarists perform Friday nights; belly dancers on Saturday. Open for lunch Tuesday through Friday and dinner Tuesday through Sunday. Reservations recommended.

Kyoto $$
4920 Prytania Street, New Orleans
(504) 891-3644

Local sushi lovers debate their favorite restaurant ad nauseum, often using the salmon sashimi as a barometer for the overall freshness of fish served. This Japanese restaurant can live by that— everything from the salmon and yellowtail to the mackerel and eel consistently wins high praise from lunch and dinner patrons. Lovers of local seafood should try the soft-shell crab and crawfish rolls. Sit at the sushi bar or one of the tables in this uncluttered, well-lit dining establishment to order a la carte or off the full menu, which features a large appetizer section as well as numerous traditional Japanese noodle soups and grilled and fried dinners. People at your table not yet hooked on sushi can opt for such standbys as chicken, beef, or salmon teriyaki, sukiyaki, and tempura (including vegetarian) dinners. The ambience is usually subdued, even when the weekday lunch crowd piles in. The restaurant is open for lunch and dinner Monday through Saturday.

Lafitte's Restaurant $$
2031 St. Charles Avenue, New Orleans
(504) 524-0581
www.pontchartrainhotel.com

Many of the city's movers and shakers start their privileged days off right with a power breakfast here. This cozy "in" spot to the left of the lobby of The Pontchartrain Hotel is decorated in French country style with blue-tiled walls, white-shuttered windows, bent-back chairs, and white table linens. Photographs of loyal local guests decorate the walls of this trendy enclave, the setting for a portion of Anne Rice's *The Witching Hour*. Mornings the silverware clatters against china plates filled with roasted Granny Smith apples with maple-scented double cream, and banana and macadamia nut–stuffed French toast with raspberry sauce. Unfortunately, the cafe's legendary big brother across the lobby, The Caribbean Room, has closed except for banquets of 15 or more guests. But patrons can still taste several of that restaurant's famous dishes during lunch and dinner at the cafe. Best examples include Louisiana baby cakes made with crawfish, King rex filet crowned with crumbled bleu cheese and drizzled with a rich Creole buttersauce, and double-cut stuffed pork chop rubbed with fresh rosemary and stuffed with a creole corn bread dressing. The Caribbean Room's famous Mile High Pie ice cream blowout also makes an appearance on the cafe's menu—don't miss it. Breakfast, lunch, and dinner are served daily.

Nirvana $$
4308 Magazine Street, New Orleans
(504) 894–9797
One of the newest Indian restaurants on the New Orleans dining scene is putting smiles on the faces of fans of this flavorful cuisine. Large Hindu-themed paintings hang on blue walls above the blue and yellow chairs and white-linen tables. On nice days it's pleasant to sit at one of the sidewalk tables. In addition to a daily lunch buffet, the menu features customary Indian breads and rich soups, as well as curry and tandoori dishes, many available with lamb, chicken, fish, shrimp, or vegetarian. A large selection of traditional breads ranging from naan to roti and curries, including the sweet mango and notorious wildfire called vindaloo, are available on most dishes. Whether it's the coconut lamb curry or the spiced and roasted tandoori shrimp, it's hard to go wrong starting off with a hot bowl of thick mulligatawny (chicken and lentil) soup. Open Tuesday through Sunday for lunch and dinner.

Pascal's Manale $$
1838 Napoleon Avenue, New Orleans
(504) 895–4877
The photographs of well-known (and not-so-well-known) guests who have dined here that hang on the wall attest to the lure of this timeless restaurant owned and operated by the same family since 1913. The old-fashioned oyster and cocktail bar is lively and draws a spirited after-work crowd. But one look around the linen-covered tables reveals that this place is still the legendary home of one of the city's most delicious comfort foods—barbecue shrimp. Sixteen to 20 large fresh Gulf shrimp still in the shell (with heads on, too) are served in a peppery butter sauce. Be prepared to use your hands in the three-step eating process: Break off the head, pull the plump shrimp out of its shell, and dunk it into the spicy sauce. Savor. (A friendly waiter is always available to offer the novice instructions.) Freshly baked French bread is served on the side, and tradition calls for dunking doughy pieces of it into the warm, buttery nirvana that only seems to taste better the longer the meal lasts. Daily specials as well as traditional Italian, Creole, seafood, and steaks are served. Lunch is served Monday through Friday; dinner daily. (The restaurant is closed Sunday from Memorial Day through Labor Day.)

Semolina $
3226 Magazine Street, New Orleans
(504) 895–4260

5080 Pontchartrain Boulevard
New Orleans
(504) 486–5581
Pasta lovers may swoon when they see the menu—an eclectic mix of pasta dishes artfully blended with the flavors of the world. Such a global approach has earned this local chain restaurant a loyal following since the first location opened in 1991 in Covington on the north shore. The lengthy yet reader-friendly menu is thankfully divided into easy-to-digest categories: vegetables and cheese; shrimp

and seafood; chicken; meat; pan-seared entrees; and international favorites. (Breads, appetizers, and salads are served, too.) Even so, the choices are nearly overwhelming. Consider: In the chicken category alone are the cordon bleu (peppered and sautéed chicken, smoked ham, and garlic tossed with penne in a rich Dijon mustard cream sauce) and the Santa Fe (caramelized onion, bell peppers, black beans, hominy, green chiles, and cumin-seasoned chicken breast served over linguine with red-chili puree and masada lime cream, toasted tortilla chips, cilantro, and cheddar cheese). The large, attractively garnished plates nearly overflow with food. Venture to Greece if you'd like your rigatoni blanketed with roasted beef, lamb, and pork morsels sautéed in olive oil and topped with cool sour cream zitziki sauce, feta cheese, and Mediterranean olives. Lunch and dinner are served daily.

Tee-Eva's $
4430 Magazine Street, New Orleans
(504) 593-9955

This sidewalk take-out joint with the giant red and blue dots against a bright-yellow brick building almost screams when you pass in a car. Making things better is the fact that this funky little facade is tucked in the middle of a trendy section of Magazine Street elbow to elbow with chic boutiques and galleries. Tee-Eva's is best known for its homemade gumbo and jambalaya, to-die-for pecan pie, and more kinds of snowballs than you can shake a straw at. The red beans and rice are creamy and the stuffed bell peppers are filling. Don't miss the Creole cream cheese–flavored snowball. Opened in 1994, this Creole soul food landmark is open Tuesday through Sunday for lunch and dinner. No credit cards are accepted.

Vaqueros $$
4938 Prytania Street, New Orleans
(504) 891-6441

More than 20 top-shelf tequilas behind the bar earned this Uptown eatery a ranking as one of the top 20 tequila bars in the United States by Spirits & Cocktails magazine. The tequila offerings and the margaritas they help create at this establishment will never disappoint. Ditto for the well-seasoned (but not overly spicy) Southwestern menu offerings, which rely on more than two dozen kinds of blended chile peppers. In a city dominated by fried seafood and Creole delicacies, Vaqueros is a breath of fresh air. The corn and flour tortillas are made to order and come in plain, sage, and garlic. Strong suits include corn-fried oysters wrapped in a garlic-sage burrito; grilled Gulf fish with pineapple salsa; tequila-marinated lamb flank steak; fennel-crusted yellowfin tuna served with crabmeat quesadillas; a smoky rabbit étouffée with homemade chipotle tortillas; and ancho-glazed shrimp in a "tower" of black beans, goat cheese, and corn bread. Dinner is served Tuesday through Sunday; brunch Sunday. The covered patio is open for seating Thursday through Sunday nights and for Sunday brunch.

Winnie's Artsy Cafe $
3454 Magazine Street, New Orleans
(504) 899-3374

Even New York City's Tribeca-SoHo can't boast an art studio/cafe anywhere as much fun as what owner-chef-artist Michael Wingertner has fashioned at this new Uptown establishment. And, yes, everything inside and out of this retro eatery is for sale—right down to the colorfully hand-painted tables and chairs and playful tin-can columns. The festive Christmas tree lights are another matter. It wasn't long after Wingertner learned that his studio was zoned for restaurants that he set to work combining the best of both worlds for a clientele ranging from bohemians to the firefighters who pulled up in their laddered red truck on a recent Saturday and hopped off for lunch. "This is a five-year work in progress," Wingertner said.

Behind the deli-style counter is a kitchen that turns out some of the best breakfast quesadillas (Hummeggible: scrambled eggs, hummus, roasted red peppers, and cheddar) and burritos

(Winnie's Salmon Sunrise: scrambled eggs, smoked salmon, red onions, spinach, capers, and dill cream sauce) in recent memory. Diners can also custom make their breakfast from a roster of ingredients. Try the gourmet muffuletta lunch burrito made with ham, salami, provolone cheese, and olive salad. Grilled sandwiches and a nice selection of salads round out the imaginative menu. Lunch only is served Wednesday through Friday; brunch Saturday and Sunday.

CARROLLTON/RIVERBEND

Brigtsen's $$$$
723 Dante Street, New Orleans
(504) 861–7610
www.brigtsens.com
Frank Brigtsen, one of the city's heralded chefs, opened the doors to this converted shotgun cottage in a quiet Carrollton neighborhood in 1986 and has been swamped by loud applause ever since. Brigtsen, who still works five nights a week in the kitchen, where he personally prepares the lion's share of dinners, infuses Creole-Acadian cooking traditions with creative and seasoned twists. "Brilliantly creative" is a phrase often found simmering alongside descriptions of Brigtsen's culinary skills. It's hard to disagree after one taste of his rabbit tenderloin, served on an andouille Parmesan grits cake with Creole-mustard sauce or the blackened yellowfin tuna with smoked corn sauce and red bean salsa. The menu changes regularly, so be on the lookout for surprising kitchen experiments. Brigtsen says he learned many of his techniques during seven years under chef Paul Prudhomme at K-Paul's restaurant (see K-Paul's). "I was right next to the man watching every move he made, all the nuances, all the timing." Small, cozy rooms with whirring ceiling fans create an intimate yet informal dining experience. Dinner is served Tuesday through Saturday and reservations are suggested.

Cafe Volage $
720 Dublin Street, New Orleans
(504) 861–4227
Pistachio the Amazon parrot is often in his cage outside to greet visitors to this 1845 Creole cottage and today the home base of chef-proprietor Felix Gallerani. The Bologna native spent nearly two decades honing his culinary chops at some of the city's best-known hotel restaurants before opening this charming pocket of Continental and French cuisine. The cozy, six-table main dining room in front overlooks trendy Dublin Street; the spacious covered veranda out back features ceiling fans, hanging greenery, and a huge cypress gum tree growing out of the wood-slat deck. Celebs such as John Goodman and Sylvester Stallone have dined on Gallerani's short, simple, and traditional menu of pasta, chicken, fish, and veal dishes. Several house specials are served, including the Quasil a la Felix (roasted in a rosemary glaze), rib-eye strak (pan-sautéed with brandy, peppercorns, and cream), and pork filet Provençal (sautéed with garlic sauce). The cafe, listed on the National Register of Historic Places, is open for dinner daily and lunch Monday through Saturday. The price is right, and so is the ambience. Just ask Pistachio.

Camellia Grill $
626 South Carrollton Avenue
New Orleans
(504) 866–9573
It's easy to find the Camellia Grill. Go to the Riverbend, the area where St. Charles and Carrollton Avenues meets the Mississippi River, and look for the line. No doubt, there will be one protruding from the graceful white columns that front this traditional New Orleans favorite. Neighborhood families as well as college students from nearby Loyola and Tulane Universities can be found queuing up for the pleasure of snagging one of the tiny diner's 20 counter stools (the place's only seating). So why all the fuss? Because taking one of those seats is like sitting down to an old movie where waiters and cooks

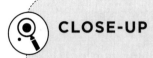

Po-Boys in Paradise

There's an old joke that goes: What's a New Orleanian's favorite seven-course meal? A po-boy and a six pack of Dixie beer.

While the highfalutin' may spend hours raving about the latest nouvelle cuisine, the average local knows that there's no dish more satisfying than the sloppy, overstuffed po-boy. In fact, satisfaction was the inspiration for this sandwich's invention. There are a couple versions of the origin of the po-boy sandwich, one of which is that during a streetcar strike financially strapped wives would make long sandwiches on enormous baguettes for their picketing husbands—the "po-boys." According to New Orleans historian Buddy Stall, during the Depression, when a large portion of the population fell on the worst of times, local merchants, brothers Clovis and Denny Martin, decided to concoct a sandwich that could fill an empty stomach for a nickel. They found that a sandwich made with French bread, lots of gravy, and scraps of meat did the trick. However, the pointy ends of the bread were wasted, so they called on baker John Gendusa to create a loaf that was longer and more slender. This came to be known as po-boy bread or New Orleans French bread. Within six months of its creation, the po-boy, or poor boy as outsiders call it, had become the most commonly eaten sandwich in the city.

Today, there are almost unlimited kinds of po-boys. For the novice, here are the basics: First, you have your fried seafood po-boys, the most common of which are shrimp, oyster, or soft-shell crab. For these the French bread is usually buttered and probably toasted. Appropriate condiments are ketchup and/or hot sauce. Next is the ham and cheese, usually with mynaz (that's local lingo for mayonnaise). Tell them you want it hot so that the cheese is melted and ask for a little Creole mustard, too. You'll be glad you did. Then there's the roast beef po-boy, best served hot with enough gravy and mynaz that both drip off the sandwich when you pick it up. And if you want lettuce, tomato, and pickle on your po-boy, ask for it "dressed." Got that, dawlin?

Following is a list of some of the places around town to find the best po-boys and other traditional New Orleans dishes. Bon appetit.

FRENCH QUARTER

Johnny's Po-Boys $
511 St. Louis Street, New Orleans
(504) 524–8129
A French Quarter institution since 1950, Johnny's is without a doubt the best place to get po-boys in the Vieux Carré. Rated by *Good Housekeeping* magazine as one of the "100 great values for your money" restaurants in the country (and that's really saying something in the French Quarter), "Mr. Johnny" DeGrusha serves 45 varieties of po-boys as well as breakfast (all day), home-style hot lunches, seafood, gumbo, and salads. The place is a favorite for take-out with French Quarter residents and also does a brisk tourist trade. DeGrusha, whose motto is "Even my failures are edible," is

always on hand asking visitors where they're from and how they like the food. (If they don't like it, he's been known to take it back and give them something else.) Try the hot roast beef po-boy, which is always delicious (and don't forget to ask for lots of gravy) or the seafood platter. One of the daily specials is a combination plate with red beans, jambalaya, and gumbo—a good introduction to local cuisine. Breakfast and lunch are served Monday through Friday till 4:30 P.M. and Saturday and Sunday till 4:00 P.M. No credit cards are accepted.

CENTRAL BUSINESS DISTRICT

Mother's $
401 Poydras Street, New Orleans
(504) 523-9656
A few blocks from the Convention Center, in the shadow of towering office buildings and hotels, sits an unobtrusive little brick structure with a small white sign reading, MOTHER'S WORLD'S BEST BAKED HAM RESTAURANT, EST. 1938. From the outside (and from the inside for that matter), it may not look like much, but generations of New Orleanians have been known to exhibit a Pavlovian-type mouth watering response to seeing that sign. A time-honored and secret family recipe produces a tender, sweet, crispy, caramelized ham that is the most popular item on the menu. The signature po-boy is the Ferdi Special—a combination of baked ham, roast beef "debris" (the part of the roast that falls into the gravy in the oven), shredded cabbage, and Creole mustard. Mother's makes more than 100 Ferdis every day. The dining room, with brick walls and concrete floors, is usually overflowing with diners as well as those standing in line, especially at lunchtime. A more pleasant alternative is to call ahead, place a take-out order, and eat the po-boy a few blocks away at the riverfront's Woldenberg Park. For breakfast, try Mae's omelette with the crusty ham, green onions, and mushrooms. Breakfast, lunch, and dinner are served daily. No credit cards are accepted.

MID CITY

Betsy's Pancake House $
2542 Canal Street, New Orleans
(504) 822-0213
Although terrific po-boys are available at lunchtime, breakfast at Betsy's is the real draw for an authentic "local" experience. This place is diametrically opposed to those $3.00-a-cup froufrou coffeehouses that seem to have popped up everywhere. The atmosphere can be downright raucous sometimes, with cell phones going off and regulars talking to one another across the room (or taunting waitresses just for the hell of it). It's sort of like Mel's Diner, except funny. There's nothing fancy here—just good down-home food freshly prepared, served by sassy waitresses, and enjoyed by everyone from cabbies to judges. The breakfast specials, served till 10:30 A.M. Monday through Friday, are only $3.00 and are sure to fill you up. The regular breakfast menu is available all day, and the daily lunch specials, ranging from $5.25 to $6.00, are really good. Best bets are the red beans and rice, beef tips, or the stuffed eggplant. Breakfast and lunch are served daily.

Liuzza's $
3636 Bienville Street, New Orleans
(504) 482-9120

Opened in 1947, Liuzza's is one of the city's best neighborhood restaurants. Visitors interested in mixing with real New Orleanians should definitely head to this Mid City favorite. A homey atmosphere created by owners who each worked in the place as young girls and eventually bought it is outshined only by the food. The Frenchuletta is Liuzza's answer to the muffuletta (a cheese, ham, salami, and olive salad sandwich served on a large round bun, which was originally the Central Grocery's answer to the po-boy). The Frenchuletta is basically the same thing, except that the meats are grilled and it's served on French bread. The closest thing to low-cal here is the spinach salad, which is topped with half a dozen fried oysters and artichoke hearts. Best bets also include the tenderloin of catfish in white wine and butter sauce served with a stuffed artichoke, the fried shrimp, and the soft-shell crabs. The full bar features a short wine list, but the preferred drink is beer served in a frosty 18-ounce glass goblet. Lunch and dinner are served Monday through Saturday. Credit cards are not accepted, but an ATM is located on premises.

Mandina's $
3800 Canal Street, New Orleans
(504) 482-9179
www.mandinas.citysearch.com

Down-home cooking is the name of the game at this locals' hangout, and you'd best leave your plastic at home. The sign outside says, NO CREDIT CARDS—ATM MACHINE INSIDE. This friendly neighborhood dining den has been serving up daily Creole, Italian, and Cajun specials plus burgers, deli and po-boy sandwiches, seafood, chicken, and steaks since its doors opened in 1932. The place bustles at lunch, and a lively crowd can always be found on weekend nights hunkered around the dinette tables under the whirring ceiling fans. Trout meunière and catfish amadine at half the price charged at upper-crust establishments can be found on the menu, as well as the locally famous "loaf"—a whole loaf of French bread gutted and filled with a choice of fried oysters, shrimp, catfish, or half-and-half (shrimp and oysters). Spaghetti and meatballs and homemade turtle soup share the menu alongside fried seafood platters, smothered chicken with mashed potatoes, and, on Tuesday, chicken breast stuffed with oyster dressing and served with candied yams. Thursday, it's delicious burccialone. Children's plates are on the menu. Come as you are. Lunch and dinner are served daily.

UPTOWN

Parasol's $
2533 Constance Street, New Orleans
(504) 899-2054
www.parasols.com

If ever a restaurant completely lacked pretension, it is this eatery that began as a bar next to the owner's home in the 1950s. Early on, patrons were handed their food through the house's kitchen window while they drank at the bar. Today the 50-seat restaurant has rightfully earned a stellar reputation for serving sumptuous New Orleans po-boys. The walls are green, as are the vinyl tablecloths, commemorating the special place Parasol holds in the city's mammoth St. Patrick's Day festivities, when the line of people runs long and the beer runs green. The crowd of mostly locals and some tourists most often chooses the hot roast beef po-boy with lots of seasoned gravy. Other best bets include the shrimp po-boy, oyster po-boy, hot sausage po-boy, and the seafood platter. Parasol's is open for lunch and dinner Monday through Saturday; Sunday evening during football season. Reservations are accepted but generally not necessary.

Uglesich's $
1238 Baronne Street, New Orleans
(504) 523-8571
Expect a long wait for a table in this hole in the wall, but once you taste the barbecue oysters and fried green tomatoes, you'll know why. Besides, the wait gives you time to down a dozen oysters on the half shell, shucked right before your eyes, at the bar. Food preparation time is also slow, as everything is made fresh to order. Best bets include the grilled fish plate and the crawfish étouffée. Check the blackboard for daily specials. As could be expected, dress is casual. But more important, when deciding what to wear, bear in mind that when you leave Uglesich's your clothes will smell like you've been deep-frying seafood all day. *NOTE:* This restaurant is not in a good neighborhood. For safety's sake, park in the secured, adjacent parking lot. Despite all the negatives, Uglesich's is a very popular spot and extremely crowded at noon. As service continues weekdays only till 4:00 P.M., a late lunch is recommended. Credit cards are not accepted.

CARROLLTON/RIVERBEND

Ye Olde College Inn $$
3016 South Carrollton Avenue
New Orleans
(504) 866-3683
This Carrollton restaurant has been a popular dining spot since it opened 68 years ago. It's the kind of place New Orleanians who have moved away go to when they're home visiting. Despite its name, you won't find many students hanging out here. In fact, on any given night an overwhelming percentage of patrons are members of the Social Security set. Nothing fancy, the brightly lit restaurant is a simple place with simple food—and a lot of it. The menu, full of good, old-fashioned New Orleans dishes made fresh daily on the premises, seems to go on forever in this "home of the oyster loaf" (which novices should not even attempt without some help). Best bets include the shrimp remoulade, fried seafood platter, oysters, charbroiled chicken salad, chicken-fried steak sandwich, and fried chicken made to order. The red beans and rice are pretty good, too. (They must be—the restaurant sells 60 pounds of them every Monday.) If you're still having trouble making a choice, ask somebody at the next table for advice. Chances are they've been eating here their whole lives. Lunch and dinner are served daily.

OLD METAIRIE

The Galley $$
2535 Metairie Road, New Orleans
(504) 832-0955
Homemade corn and crabmeat soup, hot boiled shrimp and crawfish, and a lengthy

specials board of home-style Italian and Creole dishes are found at Vicki and Dennis Patania's patio restaurant in the heart of Old Metairie. What really put this casual family eatery on the map, though, are the same plump, soft-shell crab and catfish filet po-boys the husband and wife team have served since 1977 at the New Orleans Jazz and Heritage Festival. The overstuffed po-boys served in freshly baked French bread are among the best in town. The recipe for the fry batter is a closely guarded family secret. Seafood baskets and platters filled with soft-shell crab, stuffed crab, catfish, shrimp, or oysters are popular standbys as well as the roast beef and seafood po-boys. Vicki's soups are famous among regulars, who keep the lively main dining room and patio crowded most nights. Her corn-and-crabmeat, oyster-artichoke, corn-and-crawfish, eggplant-and-shrimp, and three-cheese soups rule the roost. Vicki is always trying something new in the kitchen to come up with new dishes for the specials board, which offers 8 to 15 items nightly. Fettuccine, crabmeat au gratin, white beans and catfish, and pecan-fried catfish with sweet potato fries show up on a regular basis. The establishment does a booming to-go business. Opened in 1990, The Galley serves lunch and dinner Tuesday through Saturday.

LAKEFRONT

The Po-Boy Bakery $
5321 Franklin Avenue, New Orleans
(504) 282-9203

For those finding themselves at the University of New Orleans or the Lakefront Airport, this Gentilly establishment is a good place to stop for a real New Orleans lunch—not to mention a bit of history. It is located across the street from the Milne Boys' Home, where a young man named Louis Armstrong learned to play the cornet after being sent there for shooting a gun. The walls of this friendly neighborhood po-boy joint are covered with UNO sports memorabilia, a poster from the 1984 World's Fair, a photograph of the Jesuit High School class of '38, and a picture of the Pope. Before ordering a sandwich, though, ask to see the size of the bread on which it will be made. A medium could easily feed two people. Here the sandwich to end all sandwiches is Will's Chamber of Horrors, made with roast beef, ham, turkey, American cheese, Swiss cheese, onions, lettuce, tomatoes, and Italian dressing. If you're looking for a hot home-style dinner, daily specials include lasagna, shrimp Creole, and beef stew.

Lunch and dinner are served daily till 8:00 P.M. and Sunday till 5:00 P.M. No credit cards are accepted.

in crisp uniforms dispatch orders and service with the kind of aplomb that's so rare these days it could almost be considered an art form. All food is made to order on grills in plain view, which is also part of the fun. Best bets include the hamburgers and omelettes (served anytime) stuffed with ham and oozing with cheese. And don't forget the fresh pies baked daily. Open daily for breakfast, lunch, and dinner and open till 2:00 A.M. on weekends, the Camellia Grill is also popular for late-night eating. No alcohol is served, and no credit cards are accepted.

La Madeleine $

601 South Carrollton Avenue
New Orleans
(504) 861–8662

1327 St. Charles Avenue, New Orleans
(504) 410–8500

Jackson Square, New Orleans
(504) 568–0073
www.lamadeleine.com

Take an early morning streetcar ride down St. Charles Avenue and jump off here for breakfast. This corner cafe, located on the streetcar line at the Riverbend where St. Charles and Carrollton Avenues meet, opens at 7:00 A.M. when the freshly baked French and sourdough breads and baguettes are coming out of the oven. Dine alfresco at one of the outside tables for a view of the passing streetcar while opening your eyes with a cup of French-roast coffee, latte, espresso, or cappuccino. The breakfast menu features omelettes, French toast, and eggs cooked to order, as well as numerous homemade pastries, Danish, scones, and flaky croissants. Late-risers can beat the heat at a window table inside this cozy eatery of exposed beams and brick columns. A French-flavored selection of satisfying and inexpensive lunch and dinner items includes the tomato basil soup and the chicken friand (with mushrooms, grated Swiss, and béchamel sauce sandwiched between layers of pastry crust topped with creamy mushroom sauce). Follow in the footsteps of Europeans and grab a late-night dinner—the place stays open till 10:00 P.M. weekdays, 11:00 P.M. weekends. You won't have to dig deep into your pockets for the portobello poulet crepe (rosemary rotisserie chicken with porto-bello mushrooms and broccoli, wrapped in a crepe) or the shrimp and spinach crepe with pesto cream sauce. The popularity of this modest-size establishment has seen it branch into the suburbs in recent years, but it still remains hands-down one of the best values in town.

Mat & Naddie's Café $$

937 Leonidas Street, New Orleans
(504) 861–9600

"Where Freret (Street) meets the river," might mean something to locals, but out-of-town visitors might have a hard time finding this place. Instead, head down St. Charles Avenue (away from the French Quarter and Downtown) to River Road, turn right, and head 4 blocks to Leonidas Street. It's on the corner to your right. Look for the pistachio-green wooden building with a short white picket fence and the blue neon restaurant name above the door. Inside, polished hardwood floors, ceiling fans, and a brick fireplace in the middle of the main room add to the casual, stylish charm of dining in this ren-ovated 1852 cottage. (The picture on the foyer wall of the building's exterior 10 years ago shows how much it's changed for the better.) The tidy menu created by proprietor-chef Michael Schramel offers dishes influenced by local, Continental, and ethnic cookery. The saffron and sage–marinated pork chop arrives stuffed with telegio and proscuitto; the Indone-sian tiger prawns are flavored with garlic, chili, ginger, and Chef Mike's secret spice blend. Fun starters include the Viet-namese spring rolls and the Louisiana shrimp and crawfish cake. Lunch is served Tuesday through Friday; dinner Tuesday through Saturday.

Upperline $$$

1413 Upperline Street, New Orleans
(504) 891–9822
www.upperline.com

Proprietor and longtime restaurateur JoAnn Clevenger is one of the indefatiga-bly charming figures on the local fine-dining scene. She encourages patrons to ask questions and explore her 40-year rotating collection of artwork, which includes paintings, sculpture, and pottery. Some regulars have referred to the estab-lishment as a fun after-hours museum. Clevenger often hands out a list of her

RESTAURANTS

New Orleans is home to some of the most affable and gracious restaurateurs found anywhere in the country. Just ask any local who has enjoyed the good fortune of meeting Iler Pope of Café Atchafalaya or JoAnn Clevenger of Upperline. Especially at smaller venues patrons will discover that the chance to chat with the proprietor makes the dining experience all the more memorable. Don't be bashful.

---

favorite things to see and do in New Orleans to guests as they depart. A mostly local clientele is found inside this 1877 town house, which offers a classy, warm mood framed by fresh-cut flowers, an Art Deco bar, high ceilings, and lace curtains—all Clevenger-inspired artistic touches. The sophisticated, award-winning menu is exciting but never stuffy thanks to executive chef Ken Smith. Winners abound: fried green tomatoes in a zesty shrimp remoulade; spicy shrimp with jalapeño corn bread; duck gumbo; seared salmon with crawfish bouillabaisse and aioli; and braised lamb shank in Burgundy with saffron risotto. Clevenger hosts theme and historical wine dinners throughout the year as well as her famous garlic "festival" in June and July. Located at the corner of Upperline and Prytania Streets, the restaurant opened in 1983, and dinner is served Wednesday through Sunday. Reservations are highly recommended. Upperline is usually closed during the first two weeks of August.

LAKEFRONT/ BUCKTOWN/LAKEVIEW

Deanie's Seafood   **$$**
1713 Lake Avenue, New Orleans
(504) 831-4141
www.deanies.com
For generations Bucktown Harbor at the 17th Street Canal has been the docking point for fishers bringing in the catch of the day. Not surprisingly, several fine seafood restaurants have grown up around the place. This right-off-the-lakefront Bucktown spot doesn't boast a river view, but once you start eating, you won't care. The meal starts off on the right track with hot, steamy new potatoes, which are served instead of bread in this casual, bright, and airy eatery. If there's any room left after devouring the tasty spuds, try the barbecue shrimp, and you won't even have to ask for lots of French bread to dip in the buttery sauce. As at many other Lakefront restaurants, the portions are generous and delicious. Some other best bets are the crawfish étouffée, crabmeat au gratin, stuffed flounder, and the broiled stuffed shrimp dinner. Expect to wait in line for dinner, especially on weekends. Lunch is the least crowded time to go. Plus, you'll be sure to have time to visit the adjoining Deanie's Seafood Market, an excellent place to get some of that spicy seafood to take back home. Shipping is also available. There is now a second location at 841 Iberville Street in the French Quarter.

R&O's Pizza Place   **$**
216 Old Hammond Highway, New Orleans
(504) 831-1248
People always look as though they're having a good time in this crowded, noisy Bucktown restaurant, and no wonder. The mostly local, family crowd knows that they can expect some of the best po-boys and simple specialty dishes in town. The large, airy restaurant has been expanded several times, and each time the customer base has expanded with it. This is not a place for intimate conversation, but if your family wants to go out with a baby who sometimes cries and a brother who talks too loud, no one will even notice. Although it's called a pizza place, the sandwiches are the real star. Try the roast beef po-boy dripping with gravy and mynaz (y'at-speak for mayonnaise); the stuffed crab Parmesan po-boy with lots of red gravy and mozzarella; or the soft-shell crab po-boy that almost melts in your

mouth. Other good bets are the R&O Special po-boy with ham, roast beef, and Swiss cheese or the Italian combo po-boy with Italian sausage, meatballs, red gravy, and mozzarella cheese. Some of the sandwiches may seem a bit pricy, but keep in mind that a "whole" could easily feed two people. If you're a novice, stick to the "half." Lunch specials such as eggplant Parmesan, Roland Jr.'s seafood stew, and veal Parmesan are served Monday through Friday. Lunch and dinner are served Wednesday through Monday.

Sid-Mar's $$
1824 Orpheum Street, New Orleans
(504) 831–9541
www.sidmarsofbucktown.com
A thin stretch of land runs along the 17th Street Canal, which separates New Orleans from Metairie at Lake Pontchartrain. On one side is the Bucktown Harbor, where seafood fishers still set out every morning to bring in the catch that Lakefront restaurants serve. At one time, this entire area on the Metairie side of the canal, known as Bucktown, was a small fishing village. Today, most of it is a suburban bedroom community, except for those little boats docked at Bucktown Harbor. Overlooking the harbor is Sid-Mar's, an unpretentious seafood restaurant that has changed little since its heyday in the 1960s. Here guests can sit on the screened porch for a view of the harbor. The airy dining room, filled with mostly local families, is almost completely devoid of decor. Of course, the owners probably figured that no one would notice, as just about everybody in the place always seems right in the middle of devouring a mound of boiled seafood piled on the table in front of them. The grilled fish, fried shrimp, or oyster po-boys; seafood gumbo; and oyster soup are also good choices, as are the changing daily specials. The full bar features a short wine list, but pitchers of beer are generally the drink of choice here. Friday and Saturday evenings are the restaurant's busiest time. For evening meals, weekdays are best.

Lunch and dinner are served Tuesday through Sunday.

Steak Knife $$$
888 Harrison Avenue, New Orleans
(504) 488–8981
www.thesteakknife.com
Between Downtown and Lake Pontchartrain lies the small upper-middle-class bedroom community of Lakeview, which boasts a couple of restaurants worth exploring. The Steak Knife is Lakeview's upscale restaurant; it's where mom and dad go when they get dressed up and hire a sitter. The fact that the new digs the restaurant moved into a few years ago used to be a bank actually works in its favor. The financiers left behind fine wood paneling and lots of marble. These, combined with subdued lighting, make for a romantic setting. As the name implies, the Steak Knife once specialized in beef only, but a few years ago the menu was expanded. All the steak dishes are still good, and other best bets include the jumbo shrimp Bordelaise sautéed with mushrooms, garlic butter, white wine, and brandy; grilled lamb chops with minted demiglace, served with celery garlic mashed potatoes; and the extraordinarily tender osso buco, served in a red wine reduction sauce with fettucine Alfredo. Also try the coconut shrimp and the lump crabmeat fritters. The Steak Knife is also the only place in Lakeview to hear live jazz music, which is played Friday and Saturday nights starting at 8:00 P.M. There is no cover charge. Weeknights are the least crowded. Expect heavy traffic early Friday and Saturday. (If you go during this time, give your car to the valet or you could drive around awhile looking for a space.) Dinner is served daily, and reservations are recommended.

Tony Angello's Ristorante $$
6262 Fleur de Lis Drive, New Orleans
(504) 488–0888
Tony Angello's serves Creole Italian cuisine, a tiny bit of heaven created by the marriage of two great cooking styles and

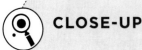

Olé! The Nuevo Wave of New Orleans Cuisine

The globe-trotter was midway into his first-ever dinner at Laurentino's, savoring forkfuls of simmering seafood *fideua* and *patatas allioli,* when he remarked to his companion: "Unbelievable—this is just like dining in Barcelona." Not the Barcelona of the pricy nouvelle cafes found amid the Catalonia capital's chichi dining scene, mind you. But rather the Barcelona of Catalan soul food savvy travelers seek out on the *carrer* less traveled in the ancient Mediterranean seaport's storied Barrio Gothic. Unbelievable, too, was Laurentino's location: the far corner of a stubby strip mall tucked on the fringe of suburban Metairie. Blink and you'll miss it.

What is impossible to miss, however, is the culinary mouth-quake Iberian gastronomy has unleashed in recent years on the East and West Coasts. And this white-hot megatrend is gaining ground in New Orleans, challenging the dining status quo while offering an armada of bona fide, full-bodied tastes of Espana. Though it's been more than 200 years since Spain ruled Louisiana, several restaurants have stepped smartly into the bullring with a full-blown tapas dinner menu (Vega Tapas Café, 2051 Metairie Road, Metairie; 504-836-2007), a tapas happy hour (Marisol, 437 Esplanade Avenue, New Orleans; 504-943-1912; see Restaurants chapter), and a mixed menu of Spanish and Latin American specialties (Rio-Mar, 800 South Peters Street, New Orleans;

504-525-3474; see write ups in this chapter).

But it's Barcelona native Xavier Laurentino who oversees the only restaurant in the metropolitan area—and perhaps the entire Third Coast—specializing in the authentic foods of Catalonia, Spain's northeasternmost province. A quintessentially Mediterranean cuisine, Catalan recipes reflect a legacy of cross-cultural contact with Greeks, Romans, Arabs, and Sicilians, not to mention plenty of influences from southern France. Laurentino comes by it naturally. The longtime New Orleans resident and seasoned restaurateur opened his establishment (4410 Transcontinental Drive, Metairie; 504-779-9393) armed with family recipes handed down for generations. "My father," he says, "was an honest and humble man who taught me how to cook and instilled in me the love for honest and simple food."

Catalan food may indeed be historically peasant-simple, but under Laurentino's stewardship it becomes a cuisine rich in nuance and subtext. Take, for instance, paella Valenciana, "the flagship of Spain's gastronomy that originated centuries ago on the delta of the Ebro River," he explains. Iberia's best example of one-pan cooking and a sophisticated, Old World predecessor to jambalaya, paella is a deftly seasoned rice dish blended with seafood, chicken, meat, or a combination. But the Catalan version of paella is a country cousin called fideua (feh-du-AH) that replaces rice with angel hair pasta for a lighter and subtle alternative that better absorbs the flavors and creates a heavenly twist on Spain's national dish. Swirl in a dollop of allioli (the Spanish word for the French aioli, or garlic mayonnaise) for your first bite of fideua, which arrives at your table in an individual *paellera,* or paella pan, and your palate will dance a Sardana.

To be sure, Catalan cuisine is as old—if not older—than many of its European counterparts. Some of the region's cooking traditions can be traced to the 14th century, when Barcelona ruled a mini-empire that stretched from Sicily and Malta to the French regions of Rousillon and Cerdagne and parts of Greece. Hundreds of years ago, tapas were free tidbits on a slice of bread large enough to cover the top of a wine glass as a sort of lid, ostensibly to keep flies out of the wine. (*Tapa* is Spanish for lid or cover.) Some historians say tapas were born when Spanish King Alfonso X was so ill he could only eat small bites of food with wine between meals. Others claim the humble food was the mother of invention that gave sustenance to farmers and laborers so they could work until the job was done and it was time to eat the main meal of the day.

Either way, Laurentino's tapas bear the Catalan stamp of authenticity. The patatas allioli (cubed potatoes slowly fried to a golden brown and drizzled with home-made allioli), as well as the Mediterranean olives and thin slices of robust Manchego cheese, served on Catalan garlic-tomato bread, for instance, are as good as (if not better than) what a traveler might find at a beachside joint in Calella de Palafrugell or a hip tapas bar in Tarragona. Ditto for the savory slices of Serrano (Spain's proscuitto) and pan-seared marinated pork loin medallions. "This is one of the most famous tapas in Spain," says Laurentino. Indeed, if the proprietor were any more true to his school, the restaurant would have to stay open past midnight as is the custom in Barcelona and larger cities throughout Catalonia.

The globe-trotter was by no means the only one singing the praises of Catalan cuisine. In 2003 a Sunday *New York Times Magazine* cover story titled "The Nueva Nouvelle Cuisine: How Spain Became the New France" proclaimed Catalonia the epicenter of nouvelle cuisine. Meantime, *Los Angeles Times* restaurant critic and *Saveur* magazine editor Coleman Andrews's 1999 book, *Catalan Cuisine: Europe's Last Great Culinary Secret,* is a 352-page love-fest celebrating the food traditions of a province settled by ancient Greeks in sixth century BCE and by the Romans 300 years later.

Accolades notwithstanding, most nights the affable Laurentino oversees his two-person kitchen staff while making the rounds with customers. The globe-trotter warmed a glass of Spanish Grand Duque de Alba brandy in his hands and smiled at the proprietor. "Your food . . . transports me," he said.

Laurentino beamed. "That makes me happy," he said, standing beside a pair of colorful murals depicting the photogenic Costa Brava coastline of his native homeland. "So very happy."

RESTAURANTS

If you visit this predominantly Catholic city during Lent, be prepared for longer-than-usual waits at seafood restaurants on Friday. During Lent, the 40 day period of fasting and penitence from Ash Wednesday to Easter, the faithful abstain from eating meat on Friday. Locals of all persuasions recognize the day by dining out en masse.

found only in New Orleans. At first glance, this signless restaurant could be mistaken for a large house on a corner lot in west Lakeview. But the crowds headed for the door with smiles on their faces give the place away. Inside, a welcoming attitude, subdued lighting, and attentive service make this a popular date spot and always a good experience even before you take the first bite. Sit back and relax with one of the fine Italian wines the restaurant offers by the glass or bottle, and then say the magic words: "Feed me, Mr. Tony." This will be followed by a series of small courses, such as stuffed shells, lobster cup, soft-shell crab, spinach salad, soup, cannelloni, veal with peppers and mushrooms, and eggplant Tina—each more delicious than the last. There are several versions of "feed me" from which to choose, as well as a full a la carte menu. Dinner is served Tuesday through Saturday, and reservations are recommended to avoid a long wait. Jackets are not required, but "dressy casual" attire is suggested.

West End Café $-$$
8536 Pontchartrain Boulevard,
New Orleans
(504) 288-0711

West End Café is a newcomer by New Orleans standards. This Lakefront restaurant opened 12 years ago. There's no lake view here, but the staff makes up for that by creating a casual and fun environment. The place combines the feel of a neighborhood family restaurant with the menu of a seafood house. The staff is attentive, and the menu offers a variety of traditional New Orleans dishes, po-boys, and daily specials. Best bets include fried catfish, oysters, and shrimp as well as the crawfish pie, crabmeat au gratin, the tenderloin of trout, and seafood fettuccine. For the hearty eater, sandwiches are another good alternative, including smoked pork loin on wheat toast, soft-shell crab, or seafood platter po-boys, and the traditional, roast beef, ham, oyster, or shrimp po-boys. The full bar includes a short wine list. There's also a kids menu for children under 12. Start the weekend right with such breakfast indulgences as the kitchen-sink omelette with shrimp, crawfish, onions, peppers, mushrooms, ham, and cheese or pain perdu (the original French toast). And, this being New Orleans, breakfast can be accompanied by your choice of a Bloody Mary, screwdriver, or mimosa. Lunch and dinner are served daily. Breakfast is served Saturday and Sunday.

NIGHTLIFE ⊗

New Orleans nightlife is world renowned—so much so that it would be hard to believe that the city could live up to its reputation. However, one thing New Orleans has always been good at is throwing a party. And not just at Mardi Gras time. Locals are always up for a good time. In fact, they make it a priority. Therefore, just as it is hard to find a bad meal in the Big Easy, it is equally difficult to find an entertainment venue where people aren't having fun.

Though some are better than others, the following listings should provide a pretty good time. They were chosen for uniqueness or simply being the best at what they do. There's every type of after-dark diversion, from the gentility of sipping martinis on a Victorian porch to the recitations of beat poets and folk singers who seem to have just stepped out of a time machine; the smooth sounds of traditional jazz to the raucous fun of a Cajun fais do do; the flamboyance of a "best butt" contest at a gay dance club to the charm of a Celtic Christmas show. One thing's for sure: If you can't have fun in New Orleans, you can't have fun anywhere.

Now get out there—and make sure you're back by dawn.

FRENCH QUARTER

Bombay Club
830 Conti Street, New Orleans
(504) 586-0972
www.thebombayclub.com
People don't meet in this stylish club; they rendezvous. Subdued lighting, intimate booths, and live piano music make this one of the most elegant bars in town. There's a full selection of domestic and French wines as well as 85 different signature martinis including the Breathless, made with Skyy vodka and white crème de cocoa along with a splash of Godiva liqueur and served in a chocolate-rimmed glass; the James Bond 007 features Absolut vodka, Boodles gin with a splash of Dubonnet—shaken, not stirred—and served with a lemon twist; the Cajun King martini has Absolut pepper and citron with dry vermouth and spiced Tabasco olives. And don't miss out on the more than 30 premium cigars in stock. The Thursday night happy hour offers two-for-one drinks and domestic beer as well as a free buffet. Jackets are required in the evenings.

Cats Meow
701 Bourbon Street, New Orleans
(504) 523-1157
www.catsmeow-neworleans.com
When the Cats Meow opened its doors in 1989, karaoke was somewhat of a novelty. And believe it or not, 15 years later this place is still packed pretty much every night with guests singing their hearts out. The music is a mix of hits from the '50s to today, including rock, disco, dance, and hip-hop. Happy hour runs 4:00 to 8:00 P.M. weekdays and 2:00 to 8:00 P.M. on weekends and features three-for-one drinks. Housed in a structure dating to the 1820s, the bar also features two balconies overlooking Bourbon Street as well as an intimate courtyard.

Chris Owens 500 Club
500 Bourbon Street, New Orleans
(504) 523-6400
The show opens at 8:30 P.M. Monday through Saturday when the house band Latin Rhythms takes the stage. At 10:00 P.M. the undisputed Queen of Bourbon Street makes her appearance. What ensues is an energetic and entertaining floor show performed to the hilt by Ms. Owens much as she has for as long as most people can remember. In fact, a

much-loved (if admittedly rude) pastime in New Orleans is trying to guess this beloved star's age. One thing's for sure, whatever that age is, she defies it in spades. She could be Dick Clark's sister. Not to be missed by those who enjoy dancing and a good nightclub act "like in the old days."

The drinking age in New Orleans is 21, but you can get into the clubs legally at 18. Many places charge a cover for 18 to 21 year olds to make up for the lost drink revenue.

Fritzel's European Jazz Pub
733 Bourbon Street, New Orleans
(504) 561-0432
www.geocities.com/fritzelsjazz
An unobtrusive yet historic building constructed in 1831 provides an intimate setting for talented local musicians as well as touring international jazz groups. House bands are led by clarinet and soprano saxophone maestro Jacques Gauthe on Friday and Saturday and by cornet and piano virtuoso Jamie Wight on Sunday. The eclectic crowd of tourists and locals combined with German beers and well-chilled Schnapps make for a lively European pub atmosphere. No wonder this is an after-hours hang out for "off duty" musicians looking for a late-night jam. There's a one-drink minimum at this club, where the music starts around 10:00 P.M.

The Funky Butt
714 North Rampart Street, New Orleans
(504) 558-0872
www.funkybutt.com
On the outskirts of the French Quarter this swanky jazz and blues club is named for the turn-of-the-20th-century hall where Buddy "King" Bolden led the band and helped usher in the jazz age. The hip Art Deco club offers some of the city's hottest live music and Creole food nightly. The club faces Congo Square in Armstrong Park, which was once a meeting place for the city's slaves where they would perform for themselves the music of Africa. A must for New Orleans music aficionados, this club is off the beaten path. Take a cab.

House of Blues
225 Decatur Street, New Orleans
(504) 529–BLUE
www.hob.com
This national chain, inspired by the original Dan Aykroyd/John Belushi Blues Brothers movie, hit a high note when it opened in the French Quarter—in part because blues music, the club's original focus, has always found a spiritual home here. However, most of the credit for the club's popularity would have to be given to the big-name acts—Bob Dylan, Eric Clapton, Wynton Marsalis—it has brought into the city. Nightly concerts also feature well-known local groups as well as promising unknowns. A word of warning for those who have been walking around the French Quarter all day and who actually want to sit down to listen to music: Get here when the club's doors open at 8:00 P.M. to snag one of the few church pew seats on the music hall's balcony. Preshow dinner is also available in the club's restaurant, which is decorated with primitive art as well as the faces of great contemporary musicians in plaster relief. Burgers, pizzas, salads, and specialty sandwiches dominate the menu. The restaurant also offers daily lunch; a Sunday gospel brunch takes place in the hall.

Lafitte's Blacksmith Shop
941 Bourbon Street, New Orleans
(504) 523-0066
Dating to the 1770s, this dank and dusky bar is housed in one of the city's oldest buildings that lore tells us once belonged to pirate Jean Lafitte and his band of frisky privateers, who supposedly stored their ill-gotten booty there. It's the kind of place that still feels like a pirate could walk in the door any minute and where people can find privacy in the quiet, darkened corners created by the crumbling

walls and exposed beams. In a world that seems increasingly phony, this place is still the real thing.

Margaritaville Cafe/Storyville Tavern
1104 Decatur Street, New Orleans
(504) 592-2565
www.margaritaville.com
Singer Jimmy Buffett developed a love for New Orleans through stories he heard from his grandfather, a steamship captain who frequented the city's port, and later when Buffett started his musical career here. His laid-back Margaritaville Cafe/Storyville Tavern in the French Quarter is the place to find performances by such local talent as swamp blues singer Coco Robicheaux and R&B guitarist Irvin Bannister. Live music is offered daily from 3:00 P.M. to midnight with no cover charge. The cafe features a varied menu with local delicacies as well as themed specialties such as the "Brown Eyed Girl" Triple Chocolate Pie.

The Napoleon House
500 Chartres Street, New Orleans
(504) 522-4152
www.napoleanhouse.com
By 1821 Napoleon Bonaparte had seen his empire reduced to the tiny island of St. Helena, where he found himself in exile. His reign over the hearts of French expatriates, however, had remained undiminished. In New Orleans, no less than Mayor Nicholas Girod and pirate Jean Lafitte sipped absinthe and hatched plots to rescue their hero. Ships were readied, the mayor had his home enlarged to properly accommodate an emperor, and who knows what would have happened if Napoleon hadn't had the bad taste to die before the mission could be completed. Today, the mayor's 1797 home, at the corner of St. Louis and Chartres in the French Quarter, is a National Historic Landmark where generations have gathered to practice the art of civilized drinking. Walls covered with peeling paint and yellowed oil portraits might lead one to believe that the place hasn't been spruced up since

Want to check out the latest on the local music scene? Visit www.offbeat.com, Web site of Offbeat Magazine—*the authority on local music, with club listings, reviews, and a public message board.*

the 19th century, but this timeworn look, along with the piped-in classical music and subdued lighting, are part of the pub's shadowy charm. Be sure to order a Pimm's Cup, the house specialty. This tangy gin concoction is equally good when sipped sitting next to the open French doors on a rainy afternoon or over a cozy, candlelit table on a hot summer night. For the hungry, there's a reasonably priced menu of salads and sandwiches.

O'Flaherty's Irish Channel Pub
514 Toulouse Street, New Orleans
(504) 529-1317
www.celticnationsworld.com/oflahertys.htm
This Celtic gem in the heart of the French Quarter opened in 1989, when musician Daniel O'Flaherty made his way to the Crescent City from Ireland. The proprietor's easy manner and Celtic charm have carried over into the atmosphere of his intimate pub that serves Guinness on tap and authentic Irish coffee. Also enjoy home-style Irish stew and shepherd's pie during the nightly serenade of traditional Irish folk music performed by O'Flaherty and a talented group of regulars. As part of the pub's annual Christmas show (presented nightly during the holiday season), the musicians sing and tell stories of their Hibernian childhoods. Traditional Irish dancing takes place in the pub on Saturday nights.

Oz
800 Bourbon Street, New Orleans
(504) 593-9491
www.ozneworleans.com
A gay dance club, Oz often sports a mixed crowd who dance the night away

to club music from the '70s to the '90s spun by popular DJs such as Tim Pflueger. There are manager's drink specials all night, and at 11:30 P.M. the games begin. On Tuesday join host Bianca DelRio's for her Dooty Duffel in which the room's best butt wins three days and two nights at the Grand Casino on the Mississippi Gulf Coast. Wednesday is drag show night, when the Ladies of Oz take the stage. Monday night presents the Gay Gong/Game Show with your host Barry Bareass. Audience members show off their talent and/or name that tune to win the top prize of $100.69.

The Palm Court Jazz Cafe
1204 Decatur Street, New Orleans
(504) 525-0200
www.palmcourtcafe.com
Jazz for grown-ups is an appropriate description of this elegant setting featuring exposed brick walls covered with a collection of music-themed photographs, linen tablecloths, a classic mahogany bar, and mosaic tile floors. The club, located in an old French Market warehouse, offers a variety of Creole dishes as well as live traditional jazz music five nights a week at 8:00 P.M. And don't miss the records and CDs from the GHB family of labels for sale in back. The cover charge is $4.00, and reservations are highly recommended.

Pat O'Brien's
718 St. Peter Street, New Orleans
(504) 525-4823, (800) 597-4823
www.patobriens.com
Pat O's, as locals call it, is the home of the original Hurricane—first served more than half a century ago. And visitors can begin sipping this taste of New Orleans (a fruit punch and rum powerhouse guaranteed to knock even the most seasoned drinker off his game) when the bar opens at 10:00 A.M. daily. B. H. Pat O'Brien opened his first drinking establishment a block from the saloon's current location in the early part of the 20th century. Unfortunately, there was a little Constitutional amendment in place at the time called Prohibition. Mr.

O'Brien's Club Tipperary was one of New Orleans's many speakeasies that were open only to those who knew the secret password "Storm's Brewin'." With the 1933 repeal of Prohibition, the business turned legit and took on the moniker it would retain, Pat O'Brien's—a name that has been synonymous with fun for generations. Whether you want to sit at the piano bar or outside around the courtyard fountain, getting here early is a good idea to avoid waiting in line. Open till the wee hours, Pat O's is also a great last stop of a night on the town.

Preservation Hall
726 St. Peter Street, New Orleans
(504) 522-2841, (504) 523-8939
www.preservationhall.com
There are two universal truths associated with this traditional jazz hall: (1) You will wait in line to get in, and (2) you will be glad that you did. This dilapidated French Quarter landmark is the closest thing you will find to a living museum. Inside the small, dimly lit club, jazz lovers stand or sit on the floor to experience America's only original art form in its purest rendition. A number of the regular musicians are in their 70s or 80s and helped develop jazz during the early part of the last century. Shows are nightly 8:00 P.M. to midnight and admission is $5.00. Be forewarned, this is simply a performance hall. No alcohol is served, but guests are welcome to bring their own and Pat O'Brien's is conveniently located right next door. (See the Close-up in this chapter for more information.)

Storyville District
125 Bourbon Street, New Orleans
(504) 410-1000
This new club was the brainchild of the folks who bring us the annual New Orleans Jazz & Heritage Festival and the famous Brennan restaurant family. The idea was to return a little class, in the form of traditional jazz (with such talent as The Dirty Dozen Brass Band) and Creole food, to bawdy Bourbon Street. The place is a winner, offering nightly live music begin-

ning at 11:30 A.M. and playing 'til whenever, with no cover. Happy hour, weekdays from 3:30 to 6:30 P.M., offers two-for-one drinks and 25-cent oysters on the half shell.

CBD/WAREHOUSE DISTRICT

Club 360
World Trade Center
2 Canal Street, 33rd floor
(504) 595-8900

This revolving lounge at the top of the World Trade Center has had a number of incarnations. The latest is comfortable and contemporary with an upscale flare. The best feature of this club is the panoramic view of the city and Mississippi River seen through the floor-to-ceiling windows, and the room almost imperceptibly revolves. This is also a fun place to dance or just relax in a cushy club chair and watch the world go by.

For more intimate affairs, the center stationary portion of the room offers curtained private booths for four to six people. A control panel allows guests to adjust lighting and music levels, and there's a closed-circuit video screen that broadcasts a view of the dance floor.

Club 360 is located in the World Trade Center at the foot of Canal Street. Hours are weekdays 11:00 A.M. to midnight and weekends 1:00 P.M. 'til whenever.

Howlin' Wolf
828 South Peters Street, New Orleans
(504) 529-5844
www.howlin-wolf.com

The Howlin' Wolf is the rock club in New Orleans, booking the top touring groups and lots of underground must-see shows. It's where serious musicians go to hear music. The spacious house, which has no seats (thanks to a recent renovation that vastly increased its size), is decorated with old movie posters and also hosts alternative groups, country bands, and even the likes of the Mexican Elvis, El Vez.

Hyttops Sports Bar & Grill
Hyatt Regency
500 Poydras Street, New Orleans
(504) 299-1169
neworleans.hyatt.com

Looking for a place to have a beer and catch a game? It just makes sense that there'd be a sports bar in the hotel next to the Superdome. There's no mistaking what this place is with team uniforms, sports equipment and life-size posters of athletes adorning the walls. And if that weren't enough, the bar features 16 (count 'em, 16!) wide-screen satellite televisions, video games, foosball, shoot-the-hoop, and backgammon. (Not really sure how backgammon wormed its way in there, but whatever.) All NFL, NBA, NHL, Major League Baseball, and college games are shown via Direct TV. The hearty menu includes burgers, shrimp po-boys, Cajun chicken fingers, Ultimate nachos, and buffalo wings.

Hyttops is located on the third floor of the Hyatt, next to the Mint Julep Lounge. Hours are Monday through Thursday and Sunday 11:00 A.M. to 1:00 A.M., Friday and Saturday 11:00 A.M. to 2:00 A.M.

Le Chat Noir
715 St. Charles Avenue, New Orleans
(504) 581-5812
www.cabaretlechatnoir.com

Vintage street lamps on the 700 block of St. Charles Avenue light the way to Le Chat Noir, New Orleans's only European-style cabaret. When guests enter this restored turn-of-the-20th-century, building they first find Bar Noir, which fronts the Cabaret Room. With its top-drawer

In the mood for a torch song? Le Chat Noir in the Central Business District is the city's only European-style cabaret, featuring a variety of entertainment including theater, cabaret acts, and music. Performance schedules change weekly. Call (504) 581-5812.

CLOSE-UP

Preservation Hall

"If there's only one place I go," the American expat visiting from Berlin said wagging his finger, "it's Preservation Hall to hear some authentic New Orleans jazz." Timing is everything. Had the friend blown into town 40 years ago, he would have found that the local traditional jazz scene had nearly played its own funeral. At the time few venues existed for the aging musicians who played the joyous improvisational music born in the wee hours of the 20th century inside the bars and bordellos of the Big Easy's legendary Storyville red-light district.

Fortunately, the late Allen Jaffe, a dyed-in-the-clef jazz lover from Pennsylvania, moved to New Orleans and opened the dilapidated landmark on St. Peter Street known as Preservation Hall in 1961. Traditional New Orleans jazz was given a rebirth. "Those who predicted an end to local jazz at phases from the 1920s, through the 1940s revival, and by the end of the 1960s were simply wrong," writes local musician and jazz historian Dr. Michael White in the Louisiana Endowment for the Arts' *Cultural Vistas* magazine in 1991. "It seems that New Orleans jazz as a living tradition will have a future."

Today that future meets the past inside Preservation Hall, a dusky, dimly lighted enclave crowded nightly with jazz lovers happy to sit on a hard wooden bench or the floor for a chance to experience what is perhaps the Crescent City's most enduring legacy. And we're not talking only about music. Many of the regular musicians are in their 70s and 80s. As performers they stand—and sit—as living proof that the city's venerated cool cats of improvisation, playing elbow to elbow with jazz heirs half their age on the cramped stage, still make the "roof shake and the walls come a-crumblin' down." The intergenerational ensemble that is the Preservation Hall Jazz Band carries the torch of this century-old legacy nightly from 8:00 P.M. until midnight. Sets last about 35 minutes with a brief intermission. Admission is $5.00.

Traditional New Orleans music was handcrafted by the city's African-American jazz pioneers, such as Buddy Bolden, Jelly Roll Morton, Kid Ory, Joe "King" Oliver, and Louis Armstrong, to name only a few. Today the city's jazz bands—the outgrowth of New Orleans's post-Civil War brass bands—still feature a

liquor menu, striking black-and-white mosaic tile floor, and expansive windows that offer a view of the St. Charles Streetcar, the Bar Noir is a sophisticated place to enjoy a drink, listen to live piano music, or peruse the pictures of past performers on the Wall of Fame. House specialty drinks include Cosmopolitans and the Black Cat. The bar generally opens Tuesday through Saturday at 7:00 P.M. or one hour before showtime.

front line of trumpet, clarinet, and trombone backed by a drums-bass-banjo rhythm section. For visitors who have never heard songs like "St. Louis Blues," "Closer Walk with Thee," "St. James Infirmary," or "Mood Indigo" performed live, it can be a near-transcendental experience.

Be forewarned: Preservation Hall is not a nightclub or bar. Few, though, are likely to lament the absence of booze and food. The real attraction is center stage when this no-frills, near-mythical landmark's changing roster of leading local jazz musicians honors the roots of what historians have called America's only truly original art form.

Don't let long lines stretching down the block hit a sour note. Jazz has been around 100 years—it's not going anywhere. And neither should you. Grab a rum-and-punch Hurricane at Pat O'Brien's next door and strike up a conversation with other like-minded music fans in the queue. Before long the friend visiting from Berlin was exchanging addresses with the backpacking college kids from France and the white-haired retired couple from Ohio. Once inside, visitors are invited to listen to as many sets as they wish. And it's worth the wait.

After all, the city's sultans of swing— then and now—remind the listener what it means to hear New Orleans.

Preservation Hall is home to the city's legacy of jazz as well as nightly performances by local groups such as the Preservation Hall Jazz Band. COURTESY OF NEW ORLEANS METROPOLITAN CONVENTION AND VISITORS BUREAU, INC./ MICHAEL TERRANOVA

The Cabaret Room is reminiscent of elegant 1940s nightclubs with candles flickering atop linen-draped tables. The room is venue for a wide variety of interesting theater, cabaret acts, and music with the performance schedule changing weekly. Table reservations are suggested for all shows with doors opening half an hour before showtime. Dress code is casual dressy. Jeans and shorts are not permitted.

NIGHTLIFE

At some point in the night you are bound to come across a kid in the French Quarter who wants to bet you that he knows where you got your shoes. Don't be a sucker. Instead of taking the bet, just tell him the proper answer, which is: "I got 'em on my feet."

A $6.00 service charge is added to all tickets, but guests receive a $5.00 drink credit with it. Festive nonalcoholic drinks are also available. Park in the adjoining lot.

Loa
International Hotel
221 Camp Street, New Orleans
(504) 553-9550
www.ihhotel.com
Located in the International House boutique hotel, Loa is just a couple of blocks from the French Quarter but light-years away from Bourbon Street. Lit only by candles set on old plaster shelves and furnished with sumptuously upholstered sofas, Loa exudes the glamour of an upscale martini bar slightly softened by New Orleans's signature laissez-faire.

Dress is always stylish. Loa is open daily 5:00 P.M. until whenever.

Loft 523
523 Gravier Street, New Orleans
(504) 200-6523
www.loft523.com
Loft 523 is the name of both this 18-room boutique hotel and the bar within it. The building is a converted dry goods warehouse, and designers went to much trouble to make it visually interesting. In the bar that look is achieved with an eclectic mix of old exposed brick walls, slightly crooked raw wood columns, and cushiony contemporary furniture. Enjoy cocktail hour perched by the large windows facing the street—perfect for watching the local and visiting glitteratti pass by.

Open Tuesday through Saturday 5:00 P.M. until whenever.

Mulate's
201 Julia Street, New Orleans
(504) 522-1492
www.mulates.com
If you don't have time to make your way out to Acadiana, Mulate's is the closest thing in town to an authentic Cajun dance hall. That's probably because the original Mulate's in Breaux Bridge, Louisiana, is one. This spacious club offers lots of dancing room and tons of friendly people to make sure you get that two-step right. This place can be a whole lot of fun; the spicy Cajun food is pretty good, too.

Whiskey Blue
W Hotel
333 Poydras Street, New Orleans
(504) 525-9444
www.whotels.com
Dim lights, black-and-white photos of old jazz greats, and low-slung leather stools—all the stylish brainchild of upscale bar designer Rande Gerber. And all set the cool mood of this upscale nightspot in the oh-so-hip W Hotel. The drinks are a bit pricey, but the company is worth it if sophistication does it for you. Sit at a short table or try out the queen-size bed that sits in the center of the room.

Dress is casual to dressy but always chic. Hours are Monday through Saturday 4:00 P.M. to 4:00 A.M., Sunday 4:00 P.M. to 2:00 A.M. Valet parking available.

The Wine Loft
752 Tchoupitoulas Street, New Orleans
(504) 561-0116
www.thewineloft.net
This Warehouse District hotspot is a quiet, sophisticated place to relax and enjoy good conversation over your choice of an impressive wine selection and gourmet cuisine. Offerings include more than 200 wines by the bottle and 70 by the glass. The delightful menu features upscale versions of local favorites such as a soup of Louisiana blue crab and creamy brie; New Orleans–style barbecue shrimp in a puff pastry dome; and succulent oysters pre-

pared three ways: feta baked, classique gratinee, or casino-style. Yum!

With exposed brick walls and soft suede-covered furniture, the atmosphere is casually elegant and sure to impress anyone you bring there.

The Wine Loft opens daily at 5:00 P.M. The kitchen stays open late. It's about 3 blocks upriver from Poydras Street in the Warehouse District. Valet parking is available.

FAUBOURG MARIGNY

Café Brasil
2100 Chartres Street, New Orleans
(504) 949–0851

Café Brasil was one of the first trendy and casual music clubs in the Faubourg Marigny, the neighborhood adjacent to the French Quarter. A mostly young and diverse clientele can be found here dancing to mostly jazz, R&B, Latin, and Caribbean beats with crowds always spilling out into the street.

Snug Harbor
626 Frenchmen Street, New Orleans
(504) 949–0696
www.snugjazz.com

With performers such as jazz pianist (and father of Wynton) Ellis Marsalis and singer Charmaine Neville, as well as talented, lesser known musicians, Snug Harbor is one of the city's premier jazz clubs. Arrive early to snag a good view in the rustic, two-tiered seating area. Hungry or just want to avoid the cover charge? Then sit in the dining room that serves juicy burgers and fried seafood, or hoist a few at the bar. The show is piped into both. This is also a favorite after-hours place for musicians. Shows begin nightly at 9:00 and 11:00 P.M. Cover charge varies.

MID CITY

Mid City Lanes Rock 'N Bowl
4133 South Carrollton Avenue
New Orleans
(504) 482–3133

Caution: This is not your father's bowling alley. Mick Jagger, Nicole Kidman, Tom Cruise, Brad Pitt, and Susan Sarandon have partied here. And why not? How many places on earth can you listen to down-and-dirty blues, finger-snapping zydeco, or alternative grunge while sipping brewskies, tripping the light fantastic, and trying to keep the bowling ball out of the gutters for a change?

The dance floor and bowling lanes are filled with a typical New Orleans mix of nightcrawlers ranging from middle-aged professionals to college students with just enough pocket change for a few bottles of beer.

The building, located in a strip mall at the intersection of Carrollton and Tulane Avenues, may not be much to look at from the outside, but inside is a different story. Weekends, live music on two stages—one upstairs where the bowling lanes are, the other downstairs—keeps the place jumping and the eardrums ringing till the wee hours. Artist Tony Green's mural artistry surrounds a cozy cluster of tables adjacent to the dance floor, ideal for people watching.

Mid City Lanes Rock 'N Bowl opens at noon and closes at 12:30 A.M. Tuesday, 1:00 A.M. Wednesday, 1:30 A.M. Thursday, and

Looking for a rockin' and bowlin' good time? Mid City Lanes Rock 'N Bowl mixes hot licks and lane tricks, and the best time to arrive is 11:00 P.M. or later on Friday and Saturday, when the place is buzzing with fun and wall-to-wall nightcrawlers.

Coffee Klatch

New Orleanians consider good coffee pretty much a birthright, so no self-respecting native will recommend any of those caffeine-come-lately froufrou coffeehouses whose only focal point is an overpriced cup o' joe. There has to be more than that in the offing, or locals will just stay home and drink the really good coffee they all know how to make. Following are a few coffeehouses worthy of your time.

The Neutral Ground
5100 Daneel Street, New Orleans
(504) 891-3381
www.neutralground.org
Claiming the title of New Orleans' oldest coffeehouse, this time warp and cleverly named spot definitely marches to the beat of its own drummer—who can some nights be found at the microphone spouting original poetry about a romance gone wrong while accompanying himself on

the bongos. Serving good strong coffee, teas, and pastries, the Neutral Ground also features nightly entertainment, whether poetry or a variety of music. There are tarot card readings on Saturday, open mike on Sunday, and free massages Friday and Sunday. Take time to check out the paintings and sculpture that abound. Play a game of chess or just relax on one of the lumpy old couches and enjoy the retro feel of this fun, offbeat place. Open nightly.

True Brew
200 Julia Street, New Orleans
(504) 524-8441
The fun of True Brew comes from the fact that it is a coffeehouse with a theater in back. So there's always lots going on. Up front, you'll find a comfortable atmosphere, and a good variety of coffees, salads, sandwiches, pastries, and cocktails! There's also entertainment almost every

2:30 A.M. Friday and Saturday. The weekend cover charge depends on which band is performing. Bowling is extra.

UPTOWN

The Columns
3811 St. Charles Avenue, New Orleans
(504) 899-9308
www.thecolumns.com
There is no more civilized activity than sipping a martini or other cocktail of choice while sitting on the Victorian porch of the elegant Columns Hotel, feeling the gentle night breeze on your face, and watching the streetcars clank down oak-

lined St. Charles Avenue. As many locals (if not more) as hotel guests can be found any given night passing a trés genteel time on the porch or in the ornate Victorian lounge of this charming 20-room hotel, housed in one of the last remaining examples of turn-of-the-20th-century Louisiana plantation architecture.

Dos Jefes Uptown Cigar Bar
5535 Tchoupitoulas Street, New Orleans
(504) 891-8500
As may be expected, the crowd here is mostly young and male. They come to enjoy the 50 brands of stogies on hand, the rustle of the banana trees on the patio, and the live music nightly.

night, including live music and stand-up comedy.

The intimate theater produces a lot of New Orleans–themed shows, especially those that lightheartedly poke fun at local traditions and customs. These shows are a good place to get a little insight into the Big Easy mind-set. The occasional drama also makes its way to the boards here; and if Roberts Batson's long-running one-man show *Amazing Place, This New Orleans* is still up when you visit, see it. It runs Saturday at 4:30 P.M. Tickets are $20.

This Central Business District coffee-house is open weekdays 6:30 A.M. to 9:00 P.M., weekends 8:00 A.M. to around 2:00 or 3:00 A.M.

Z'otz
2003 Royal Street, New Orleans
(504) 943-9689
This quirky little shop takes its name from the Mayan glyph that looks like a bat. Bats fly at dusk and dawn between their cave underworld and the heavens. Thus the Z'otz represents those in-between or crossover moments in life. (This is already so much better than places where they think saying "grande" instead of "large" passes for interesting.) And this 24-hour Bohemian retreat is as interesting as its name. Housed in an early 19th-century Creole cottage with faded paint, exposed beams, and secondhand furniture, Z'otz offers an intriguing selection of beverages including bubble tea and yerba mate. The crowd is mixed, from lots of artist-type regulars to lucky straights who happen to wander by.

Along with quenching your thirst, Z'otz also features a lending library and, for insomniacs, late-night movies every night around 1:00 A.M. The shop is conveniently located in the same building as the Royal Launderette, which is also open 24 hours, at the weird little intersection of Royal, Touro, and Kerlerec Streets in the Marigny.

F&M Patio Bar
4841 Tchoupitoulas Street, New Orleans
(504) 895-6784
It may not look like much from the outside, but this Uptown bar is a popular place for locals who are staying up late. It's got the perfect combination of ingredients for a middle-of-the-night outing: a terrific jukebox, cheese fries, and an open attitude toward tabletop dancing. The main portion of the bar is living-room comfortable, and the tropical patio fluctuates between tranquil and bustling, depending on the time of night and the crowd. There's also a photo booth to record your New Orleans all-nighter for posterity.

Tchoupitoulas Street, which runs along the river, is not the best place to be late at night. Park close to the bar or, better yet, cab it. You'll be in no condition to drive when you leave there anyway. Open pretty much all night, every night.

Maple Leaf
8316 Oak Street, New Orleans
(504) 866-9359
This music scene staple features top talent and a narrow dance floor that tends to become even more so as the night progresses—generally until the crowd spills out into the street or onto the patio. A broad range of bands can be heard here, including those that play Cajun, zydeco,

R&B, and Latin. This a popular spot for the drinking and dancing Uptown college crowd who don't seem to mind the lack of personal space and who apparently don't have to get up in the morning.

A few years ago Tip's opened a French Quarter location at 233 North Peters Street (504-895-8477), which concentrates on traditional New Orleans music with popular local acts nightly.

Tipitina's
501 Napoleon Avenue, New Orleans
(504) 897-3943
www.tipitinas.com
One of New Orleans's oldest music clubs, Tipitina's was formed as a home stage for Professor Longhair near the end of his career. From there it had grown to be one of the city's premier musical venues until the House of Blues began providing competition. Still, it's the place to hear good local and occasionally touring rock and R&B bands. And don't miss the sweaty good time of the Sunday fais do do (traditional Cajun dancing) with Bruce Daigrepont and his band from 5:00 to 9:00 P.M.

METAIRIE

CopaCabana
4609 Airline Drive, Metairie
(504) 780-0212
Basically the only reason to go out to the suburb of Metairie at night is this authentic Latin nightclub. The music is loud, and the crowd is friendly. Unescorted women never have to worry about not being asked to dance in this fun club, where every guy seems to move like a professional. Free dance lessons are periodically given in the early evenings. Call for schedule.

SHOPPING ✦

In the Big Easy the next closest rival for your money after dining is likely the city's A to Z of eclectic retail shops. Collectors of fine antiques, vintage and upscale clothing buffs, nostalgia fiends, dyed-in-the-wool craft nuts, and single-minded hobbyists alike could not ask for better hunting grounds. From custom-made perfumes and hand-stitched European-style finery to rare 18th-century books and imported Balinese bamboo furnishings, New Orleans seems to offer a little bit of everything under the subtropical sun.

Anyone who has traveled abroad knows of shopkeepers in some cities, which shall remain nameless, who have elevated to high art the ill treatment of customers—even those who speak fluent French. Fortunately, the prevailing warm winds of bona fide Creole hospitality that sweep through New Orleans have a way of making the easily intimidated out-of-town shopper feel right at home, even in the city's haute retail enclaves like Sak's Fifth Avenue, Gucci, Macy's, and Lord and Taylor, to name but a few. Visitors likewise can duck into a third-generation antiques shop just to admire a Tiffany tea service and expect to be accorded the same treatment as a major collector. Or step into one of this waterfront's funky bric-a-brac shops; if you're lucky you might meet one of the colorful characters—and there are plenty—for which the city is known.

And fun? Just as the Crescent City's hot dining spots and even hotter nightclubs are the stuff of legend, so too are the myriad shops every bit as diverse and unique as the people who own them. Shop owners in this heavily touristed town are accustomed to the ways of travelers from all over the world. And they enjoy breaking the ice with newcomers and putting them at ease, usually with a polite "Where y'all from?" It's all part of this port city's more than 300-year-old tradition of commerce and trade.

Unlike most other sections in this book, this chapter is organized by three main shopping districts—the French Quarter, Warehouse District, and Uptown—followed by some of the city's better known shopping complexes located in the French Quarter and riverfront. While additional retail clusters exist throughout the metropolitan area, those selected for this chapter were chosen, among other reasons, for their ease of accessibility and diversity. We'll start in the Faubourg Marigny (a neighborhood adjacent to but technically outside the French Quarter). Next we'll wind our way leisurely down the Quarter's main shopping streets (Royal, Decatur, and St. Peter, to name a few). You're going to meet some interesting locals along the way, people who help make a New Orleans shopping spree unlike anything you've experienced. Let's burn some plastic.

FRENCH QUARTER

Arcadian Books and Prints
714 Orleans Street, New Orleans
(504) 523–4138

Desmond Russell opened this funky trove of Francophile tomes half a block off Royal Street in 1981 and today carries thousands of rare and secondhand French-language volumes in philosophy, science, religion, drama, and history. In the fine tradition of secondhand bookstores, a couch near the stacks has seen better days and invites an angle of repose for anyone eager to peruse Balzac, *The Confessions of Jean Jacques Rousseau,* and other rediscovered literary gems. Floor-to-ceiling shelves stock a wide array of books in English on local subjects, including Louisiana, the South, horticulture, art, and regional cooking.

Arius Art Tiles
504 St. Peter Street, New Orleans
(504) 529-1665
www.ariustile.com
Lovely ceramic tiles handcrafted by artists
in Santa Fe, New Mexico, are the specialty
of this tidy Jackson Square shop. Collectors and browsers alike should check out
the hand-painted artworks incorporating
Latin, Hebrew, Southwestern, Mayan, mystical, jazz, and Native American themes. A
line of New Orleans–themed tiles includes
fun scenes of the French Quarter and
Bourbon Street, Cafe du Monde, crawfish
boils, and Mardi Gras. One wall features
several multitile murals, including a brilliantly colored Amazon rain forest teeming
with red and gold macaws in flight.

California Drawstrings
812 Royal Street, New Orleans
(504) 523-1371
Owner Linda Keenan must have reasoned
that visitors to humid New Orleans would
need a place to buy lightweight, "climate-
appropriate" cotton and linen threads.
Immediately. Some call it resortwear, others cruisewear, but the selection of California Drawstring and Blue Fish label
breezy dresses, shorts, tops, and separates in this season's vibrant tropical colors seem tailor-made for Big Easy
heatwaves. Batiks and Moroccan dresses
should add a splash of adventure to any
event. The Southern Comfort Cotton side
of the business offers a large selection of
men's linen and cotton casual shirts and
shorts as well as even more casual tropical
and Hawaiian shirts.

Central Grocery Co.
923 Decatur Street, New Orleans
(504) 523-1620
Sitting elbow to elbow with locals and
tourists alike at one of the two narrow
counters in the back of this Tusa family–
owned Italian market while munching on a
muffuletta sandwich has been a tradition
almost from the day this place opened in
1906. Several establishments (including
this one) lay claim to being the originator

of the popular Italian-bread feast overstuffed with provolone cheese and deli
meats and topped with tangy olive salad.
Sidestepping the controversy, it's safe to
say the mighty muffuletta certainly helped
put this enterprise on the map as well as
in the hearts of New Orleanians.

Don't stop at the sandwiches though.
Floor-to-ceiling shelves are stocked with
gallon-size containers of imported extra-
virgin olive oil, balsamic vinegars,
Agostino Recca anchovy fillets, tins of
mackerel and codfish, grape leaves, and
other cooking essentials from the Mediterranean. Hanging from a small wooden
beam above the deli counter near the
front door are Sicilian Filzette- and
Citterio-brand salami, prosciutto, mor-
tadella, panchetta, hot or sweet coppa-
cola, and boneless baccala. Cajun-style
andouille and boudin sausage and tasso
ham abound.

Civil War Store
212 Chartres Street, New Orleans
(504) 522-3328
Pop quiz: Who, besides the Confederacy,
printed currency during the Civil War to
distinguish itself from the North? If you
correctly answer, "Loyal Southern states
such as Texas, Louisiana, Mississippi, and
Alabama, and even many cities," step up
to the glass counter display of 1860s
moolah. Talk about inflation, though: A
$5.00 bill printed by the Confederacy or a
Southern state during the Civil War today
can fetch up to $2,000 (though most of
what's for sale is quite affordable). Other
history can be learned—and purchased—
at this one-room shop specializing in rare
Civil War–era collectibles.

Gleaming sharpshooter pistols (they
still work) compete for attention with
Confederate-era bonds and stamps, diaries,
and scribbled autographs, as well as a
wall of gallant swords. Owner Hardie
Maloney also sells ancient Roman coins
dating to the reign of Gordian III in A.D.
238, U.S.-minted coins from the 1880s to
the present, and silver dollar–size Spanish
pieces of eight (worth less than a buck

back then and $50 today). You don't have to be a die-hard Civil War buff to appreciate the irony of a box full of battlefield shrapnel found at a place called Bloody Angle.

Crescent City Books Inc.
204 Chartres Street, New Orleans
(504) 524-4997
A roaming Siamese cat named Ali Baba keeps tabs on the first-floor volumes, while upstairs, not one but six ghosts reportedly haunt the fiction racks. Now that's teamwork. But don't count on the specter of trashy beach novels anytime soon at this bastion of scholarly used and antiquarian books. Unless, of course, your idea of skimpy summer reading is *William Harborne and the Trade with Turkey: 1578-1582.*

Since 1992 art and history lovers, gallery owners, and academicians alike have found a friend at this pleasantly crowded two-story bookseller. Joe Jackson stopped in once and within seconds had scooped up an entire collection of Robertson Davie's works. Ceiling fans whir over shelves stocked with an A to Z of world history (organized by era as well as by country), the body politic of Latin America and Caribbean cultures, ancient and modern architecture, contemporary and 19th-century criticism, and many other topics. The War Room is dedicated to books on all the major 20th-century conflicts fought by the United States.

Museum curators and scholars routinely shop here for classical and academic monographs as well as the kind of rare, backbreaking tomes that cost a bit more than last year's best-selling hardback. But that, too, is available in the fiction section on the second floor. Just watch out for things that go bump in the night.

Dashka Roth
332 Chartres Street, New Orleans
(504) 523-0805
www.dashkaroth.com
This two-story shop specializes in an exclusive line of originally designed, hand-

Looking for a unique shopping experience? Perhaps it's time to pick up a paddle. Neal Auction Co. (4038 Magazine Street, New Orleans; 504-899-5329) and New Orleans Auction Galleries (519 Julia Street, New Orleans; 504-566-1849) host auctions throughout the year as well as previews—a great place to mingle while checking out that collection of rare stereoscopic viewing cards. Both auction houses offer catalogs upon request.

crafted Judaica in eye-catching mixed metals and thousand-year-old fused glass from Israel. Jewelry and objets d'art crafted by two dozen local and national Judaica artists include menorahs, chais, wedding dreidels, Shabbat candle holders, mezuzah pendants, tzedakah (charitable donation) boxes, Stars of David, and Seder cups hand-painted with the ancient ketubah, or marriage contract. One of the menorahs is a replica of the one presented to Bill Clinton for Hanukkah in 1993 at a White House ceremony by the children of Washington, D.C.'s Jewish Community Center. The shop opened at its current location in 1994 and features a fine selection of non-Judaica, mixed-metal jewelry and earrings by more than 50 artists, plus owner Dashka Roth's own creations.

Dixon & Dixon of Royal
237 Royal Street, New Orleans
(504) 524-0282, (800) 848-5148
www.dixon-antiques.com
Time may wait for no one, but the largest selection of tall-case clocks in the United States will certainly chime your pants off. A 19th-century, 8-foot mahogany clock designed by Pennington of Liverpool welcomes guests entering the shop. Walk on by, though, or else the idea of dropping $18,500 for this British masterpiece will start to make bloody good sense. Edward Hall, who owns the portion of the shop devoted to clocks, specializes in fully restored 18th- and 19th-century English, Scottish, and Dutch tall-case clocks and

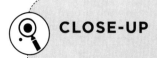

French Market

It had been raining and it seemed doubtful the sparse Saturday afternoon crowd at the French Market would hit typically elbow-to-elbow density any time soon. At least that's what we thought until we tried to sweep into Loretta's, a praline confectioner tucked near the Ursuline Street entrance of the 5-block-long historic covered market. Instead we found ourselves pulling up the rear of a line that stretched from the glass counter all the way to the front door. But French Market connoisseurs know even long waits are aptly rewarded when they leave with a little white paper bag filled with New Orleans's ubiquitous solution for a sweet tooth in need of sustenance: pralines.

But these weren't just any pralines, mind you. The traditional Southern candy likely made fresh that morning beckoned from tidy trays behind the counter in a quintet of flavors—coconut, rum, chocolate, peanut butter, and regular. We opted for the peanut butter and rum versions before setting off to explore this beloved landmark and venue for conducting commerce since 1791.

News welcomed by all in March 2004 was the city's announcement of a three-phase revitalization plan for the country's oldest open-air marketplace. The plan calls for upgrading the buildings and public facilities, constructed in the 1930s during the Works Progress Administration. Despite its lengthy past, none of the original French Market structures built during 18th-century Spanish Colonial rule exist due to centuries of conflagrations, hurricanes, and floods. Another goal is to open the market to the riverfront streetcars that operate just on the other side of a nearby dividing concrete wall. Perhaps the most laudable objective will see the city trying to lure farmers back to a market that in recent years has seemed to have a little bit of everything—except a lot of produce. "A gaggle of T-shirts, tchotskes, and hot sauce," a friend and recent visitor observed, "but not much in the way of fruits and vegetables."

Even so, the French Market (1100 North Peters Street, New Orleans; 504–522–2621) is still among top spots locals playing tour guide love to bring out-of-town guests. This simple act of hospitality hasn't hurt the reputation of this sprawling smorgasbord anchored by a community flea market and farmer's market, plus dozens of specialty retail shops, restaurants, and cafes. Consider: Tourism-related Web sites are rife with "expert reviews" and visitor testimonials giving above-average to high marks for the popular attraction's local color ("Does the chayote vendor singing opera take requests?" the friend asked) and bargains, notably on jewelry, leather, sunglasses, folk art, and Carnival and jazz-themed souvenirs. Others applaud the bounty of andouille sausage and pre-packaged

Louisiana foodstuffs that help more than a few out-of-state tourists whip up jambalaya and gumbo back home for their Mardi Gras parties.

Also in abundance are shelves of Cajun and Creole cookbooks and numerous kiosks hawking more different brands and varieties of hot sauce than one might imagine possible in a free market governed by supply and demand. Many bottles bear names sufficiently off-color that you'd be hard-pressed to find a polite New Orleanian who would subject dinner guests to indelicate sobriquets such as Red Ass and Butt Blaster. But at these same kiosks is where eagle-eye shoppers can snare Louisiana's Tabasco and Melinda line of peppery condiments, jars of Arnaud's Original Remoulade Sauce (from the legendary French Quarter restaurant of the same name), and noteworthy imports such as Jamaica's Busha Brown line of jerk seasoning. Shrimp, crawfish, and crab boil seasonings are in abundance. Elsewhere, martini lovers will find the perfect accoutrements for the classic cocktail thanks to the local Boscoli family's Creole marinated cocktail onions and jalapeno-stuffed jumbo olives. The Louisiana Creole Tomato Festival is held at the market each June to pay homage to the tart and juicy tomato grown chiefly in the parishes surrounding New Orleans.

Hands down, the cultural crowning glory of this outdoor commercial strip in the lower French Quarter is Café du Monde (1039 Decatur Street, New Orleans; 800–772–2927; www.cafedu monde.com). The city's oldest coffee shop, established 1862, is open 24/7 and serves two New Orleans mainstays: café au lait, a rich brew made with chicory-laced dark-roasted coffee; and the square, French-style donut known as beignet, best enjoyed heavily dusted with powered sugar (for this reason it's best to leave your black threads at home). The menu's only concession to modernity seems to be the introduction of iced coffee in 1988. Pray you get a table near the sidewalk. For here is among locals' (and certainly tourists') favorite places to watch the whirl go by. Just beyond is the French Quarter "theater" of horse-drawn carriages, street performers, sidewalk musicians, and artists, not to mention views of Jackson Square and St. Louis Cathedral, all punctuated by the occasional sound of a paddle wheeler horn blowing off steam. Nearby is Latrobe Park, a people-watching greenspace accented by sunken seating, a fountain, and a statue honoring the man who designed the city's first waterworks.

Whether your explorations find you standing in line for a rum-flavored praline or hunkered with friends around a table at Café du Monde, the French Market is a generous serving of New Orleans. And indisputable proof why America's most European city has long been a place best savored by the senses.

setting them up anywhere in the mainland United States. Oil paintings by American and European masters flirt with English and French armoires and other fine furnishings from the past 200 years. An eclectic trove of late-Edwardian, Art Deco, and 18th-century objets d'art is found alongside somewhat more tactile treasures like Napoleonic, Victorian, and estate jewelry. Fine Oriental rugs are displayed, not rolled up, rather as they might be found in someone's home.

The Entertainment Gallery
537 Royal Street, New Orleans
(504) 588-1777
www.s2art.com
For anyone who has ever lamented that they just don't make 'em like they used to, the Entertainment Gallery has an answer: "We do." Recreations, not "compromised reproductions and tattered antiques," of hundred-year-old Parisian street advertisement posters in exquisitely vibrant colors on crisp, fresh paper is the specialty of this well-lighted shop. Here the Golden Age of Posters (1865–1939) lives again in hand-drawn, limited edition lithographs produced by expert chromists. So, too, do the original artists' beguiling Art Nouveau beauties and stunning Art Deco vamps, stylized avatars of the Belle Epoque and the emerging Industrial Age.

In the final production stages, a team of artisans slowly "pulls" each lithograph, one color at a time, in perfect registration,

on rare 19th-century French-made Marinoni Voirin lithography presses at New York's prestigious S2 Atelier. These are the same presses used to produce the subtly blended and richly textured original Golden Age posters. Each lithograph contains the date and signature in the place of the contemporary artist and bears the S2 Atelier and Entertainment Gallery symbols. As director Katrina M. Schmidt points out, these re-creations are priced to preserve the original spirit of poster collecting.

Esoterica
541 Dumaine Street, New Orleans
(504) 581-7711, (800) 353-7001
www.onewitch.com
Some occultists appreciate household gadgets that are both handy and macabre. This probably explains the skeleton beer bottle openers stashed behind the counter, just looking to pop the top on a cold bottle of Voodoo beer. Handy and macabre also describes the bookrack. Browsers will find a large selection of tomes for the Wiccan on their gift list, such as *The Complete Book of Witchcraft, The Pagan Book of Days, Aleister Crowley's Magick,* and Tarot dictionaries. Brass chalice sets and earthy handmade brooms with cypress handles are found alongside chicken-foot necklaces, herbs, camphor candles, incense, and a selection of pentagram-shaped jewelry and earrings.

Faulkner House Books
624 Pirate's Alley, New Orleans
(504) 524-2940
William Faulkner lived in this 1840 four-story Creole house while writing his first novel, *Soldiers' Pay.* The main room features original brick walls, 16-foot ceilings, and double French doors with fanlight. Upstairs is the private residence of owners Joe DeSalvo and Rosemary James, who opened their business in 1990 on Faulkner's birthday, September 25. Rosemary, a poet, hosts "Words of Music," an international writers confer-

ence that attracts some of the world's greatest authors.

Specialties include used and rare books, with a focus on local authors, poetry, first editions, and, of course, the entire collection of Faulkner's works. This bookseller's homage to the man DeSalvo calls "the dean" of Southern literature shares shelf space with Tennessee Williams, Ernest Hemingway, George Bernard Shaw, Oscar Wilde, and many others. The few, the proud, the waggish might want to consider a copy of the *Algonquin Literary Quiz Book* as a cocktail party icebreaker.

Fleur de Paris
712 Royal Street, New Orleans
(504) 525-1899, (800) 229-1899

From silk and linen to cotton and lace, elegant finery fit for the Southern belle in any woman are specialties of this corner shop known for its chic, eye-catching window displays. Beaded evening gowns and bridalwear fashioned by in-house designers overlook cocktail dresses, separates, and antique-style lingerie. Check out the unique custom-made hats with European-style ribbons, flowers from Paris, and South American feathers and other stylish accessories for the modern woman who thinks locally and dresses globally.

The Frame Shop and Gallery
1041 Bourbon Street, New Orleans
(504) 581-1229

3030 Severn Avenue, Metairie
(504) 454-8256

This funky street-corner shop keeps alive the fading art of museum-quality custom framing. The same staff that has worked here since the establishment first opened its doors in 1970 is well known for meticulous craftsmanship when putting the finishing touches on an original painting or sketch, photograph, poster, or print. Imaginative framing concepts are a specialty. Not long ago a woman's Flamenco fan (a treasured family relic salvaged from the attic during spring cleaning) was given

new life with an eye-catching shadow-box display. Another artful solution for a small Turkish tribal rug from Istanbul: Hold the textile between two panes of glass (trimmed with a faux-gilt wood frame) to create the effect of the hand-woven kilim "floating" in mid-frame. Inventory includes black-and-white art photography, Jazzfest and Mardi Gras posters, original works by notable local artists, and one of the French Quarter's largest selections of quality antique European prints from the 1500s through the Art Deco 1920s. Compared to the suburban sheen of the shop's Metairie strip-mall location, the no-frills ambience of the French Quarter venue is pure Bohemian rhapsody—right down to the back-shop buzz of a rotary saw creating new frames and the earthy scent of freshly cut wood mingling in the air.

French Antique Shop Inc.
225 Royal Street, New Orleans
(504) 524-9861
www.gofrenchantiques.com

As the name implies, this shop specializes primarily in 19th-century and later treasures from France. And, as discriminating antique collectors will attest, the timelessness of handcrafted works of art from this era has rarely been matched. Start with the stately collection of Baccarat crystal and French bronze chandeliers for some irrefutable elegance. Then work your eyes down to the gorgeous hand-carved cherry-wood and mahogany armoires, marble mantels, and provincial gold-leaf mirrors, fine porcelains, and marble statuary.

Hové Parfumeur Ltd.
824 Royal Street, New Orleans
(504) 525-7827
www.hoveparfumeur.com

Mrs. Alvin Hovey-King, who turned a lifetime of perfume and ingredient collecting into an exclusive enterprise, founded the oldest perfume manufacturer in the city in 1931. Today third-generation owner William van Calsem oversees what may well be the best smelling place in the

French Quarter, offering 52 proprietary fragrances and scented oils for men and women, all under a 150-year-old bronze hanging light fixture from the Quadroon Ballroom of the Bourbon Orleans Hotel. Fragrances sold inside this historic Creole house, built in 1813, are available in both perfume and cologne, and each comes in a lovely Williamsburg pink box. Popular scents have been formulated into creamy solid perfumes, rich bath and body oils, soaps, and body powders. Hové-made soaps come in magnolia, vetivert, and tea-olive aromas. Sachets, gift baskets, pot-pourris, and a fine selection of antique straight razors are available.

The Kite Shop
542 St. Peter Street, New Orleans
(504) 524-0028
From beautifully hand-painted Balinese silk creations to those emblazoned with Charlie Brown's face, the second oldest shop of its kind in the United States features perhaps the most intriguing selection of kites anywhere in the city. Duffers accustomed to tree magnets will want to check out the line of windless kites (it's about time), 6-foot graphite Prism Ions, box-shaped numbers called The Cube (designed to dart and tumble in the wind), and the Delta wing–shaped squadron ready for stealth action. The shop, on the Canal Street side of Jackson Square, offers decorated minikites as well as New Orleans–themed fly-by-days with Mardi Gras masks and crawfish.

Louisiana Loom Works
616 Chartres Street, New Orleans
(504) 566-7788, (800) 889-8281
It's hard to find another shop in the French Quarter where passersby are treated to the sight of an 1893 Amish jack loom in warp drive. The easygoing husband-and-wife team of Walt and Rhonda Rose say it takes about four hours to set up the loom. Walt handles the thread patterns while Rhonda shreds the half-size bolts of fabric for making the hand-loomed rag rugs that decorate the shop's walls and hardwood

floors. The tradition has its roots in Scandinavia, say the owners, but it's the shop's second loom that keeps modern-day custom orders flying out the front door. Custom-made rugs take two weeks from ordering to delivery and cost about 5 cents per square inch. Feel free to ask questions—the Roses never blush when it comes to sharing their passion for their time-honored craft.

Lucullus
610 Chartres Street, New Orleans
(504) 528-9620

3932 Magazine Street, New Orleans
(504) 894-0500
Lucullus was the Roman general who returned from battle in order to take up feasting (a man after every New Orleanian's own heart, if one ever existed). He became famous as much for the style with which he celebrated his banquets as for the food. Today, Lucullus has been reborn in his spiritual home, New Orleans, in this shop carrying culinary antiques, artworks, and objets d'art. English and other Continental antiques from the 17th, 18th, and 19th centuries depict or complement the grand pursuit of gastronomy. One room centers on an open-hearth kitchen that displays cooking equipment and utensils from the last 200 years. An interesting display of glassware, silver, and porcelain can be found arranged on antique tables and sideboards. Even the paintings on the walls carry out the food motif. The Chartres Street location occupies a charming 19th-century French Quarter building, which retains much of its original architectural detail.

Moss Antiques
411 Royal Street, New Orleans
(504) 522-3981
This quiet and understated antiques shop offers truly elegant visions in the form of Napoleonic-style mahogany armoires and 19th-century drop-front secretaries. Other items include burled-walnut and crystal inkwells, stately Provençal oak desks and

cabinets, and oil paintings and decorative artworks. Imagine a spirited game played on an oak-and-brass Victorian cribbage board while sipping tea served in a five-piece Sheffield silver service. Perhaps a French-walnut grandfather clock hand-crafted in Europe at the turn of last century would keep players from tarrying while one of the shop's century-old crystal chandeliers helped shed some light on the game.

M. S. Rau Antiques
630 Royal Street, New Orleans
(504) 523–5660, (800) 544–9440

To step into this institution, opened in 1912, is to understand the art of how best to present one of the finest collections of antique European and American treasures in the city. Third-generation proprietor Bill Rau's grandparents started the business, and today serious art buyers and collectors from around the world patronize this establishment. Wedgwood, rare pink diamonds and other highly select jewelry, English and French furnishings, porcelains, whiskey flasks, and objets d'art like Fabergé enamel bell pushers are specialties. Renowned craftsman Paul DeLamerie produced the silver candlestick holders in the locked glass case in 1713.

A collection of rare antique canes includes one French number used to hold a camera high above crowds. The photographer meantime looked into a tiny mirror in the staff, which reflected what the camera saw overhead. In one room are exquisitely handcrafted German, Swiss, and American music boxes. Another room features some top contenders from Europe's golden age of furniture; another, Russian and British sterling tea sets and 19th-century macro-mosaic table plaques.

New Orleans Famous Praline Co.
300 Royal Street, New Orleans
(504) 525–3370
www.neworleanspralines.com

Hope springs eternal for nonchefs when food essentials like boxed mixes for jambalaya, étouffée, and gumbo are near at hand. This brightly lit and well-organized outlet for Creole and Cajun cooking lore features recipe books, hot sauces (and gator-emblazoned oven mitts ideal for wrestling even hotter dishes), a wide selection of utensils, assorted local condiments, and Louisiana coffee.

The Quarter Stitch Needlepoint
630 Chartres Street, New Orleans
(504) 522–4451

Whether it's Christmas stockings, pillows, throw rugs, Beatrix Potter animals, or something in between, this shop carries entire kits needed to save—and make—a stitch in time. Needlepoint fans can select from designs crafted by local artists such as Clementine Hunter, featuring New Orleans and Mardi Gras scenes, plantation homes, Creole cottages, magnolias, even festive crawfish boils. Then choose from a selection of custom-dyed yarns in cotton, wool, rayon, and acrylic. It couldn't be easier. Starter kits for youngsters are available as well as gift sets, complete sweater and angel kits, and six-strand embroidery floss.

Rendezvous Inc.
522 St. Peter Street, New Orleans
(504) 522–0225

Unless you're a Munchkin, you'll have to stoop over to open the double French doors of this chandelier-lit shop: The doorknob is 15 inches from the ground. Don't ask. Once inside this agreeable shop, visitors quickly learn that elegant linens and lace—not stature—are the name of the game. Specialties include lace window suncatchers with artful designs ranging from hearts and wedding chapels to tulips and butterflies. Fans of finery will also discover an A to Z of Battenburg and cotton goods: tablecloths, runners, doilies, aprons, placemats and napkins, pillow covers, christening dresses, vests, and women's collars and shawls. Pragmatists shopping on a sweltering day might do well to beat a path to the shop's parasols or men's linen handkerchiefs. Shirts for boys and sundresses for girls are alongside baby booties, ruffle bonnets, lace-and-glass picture frames, and wedding

Malls

Whether you love 'em or hate 'em, the American mall has endured over the decades to become one of the most convenient ways to shop since the invention of the catalog—and it's certainly faster. In New Orleans two venues of distinction are a far cry from the sprawling complexes typically found in the suburbs: Jackson Brewery and the Riverwalk Marketplace. These are designed with imagination and offer a level of fun—and location right on the Mississippi River—worthy of praise from even the most discriminating international visitor with plastic to burn.

Jackson Brewery
620–624 Decatur Street, New Orleans
(504) 566-7245
www.jacksonbrewery.com

Not many malls can boast of a strolling jazz band that serenades shoppers as they sample a mall version of Louisiana culture, from Creole cooking and zydeco CDs to Mardi Gras memorabilia and locally handcrafted art and jewelry. This former brewery and proud home to Jax Beer from 1891 to 1974 stands tall on the Mississippi River, reborn in 1984 as a French Quarter shopping complex across from Jackson Square and between Toulouse and St. Peter Streets.

Affectionately known as Jax Brewery, this four-story complex today is home to more than 50 specialty shops, restaurants, and cafes. Attractions include the New Orleans School of Cooking (a three-hour Cajun cooking class with recipes and a full meal), Gumbo Kids (custompainted T-shirts and accessories for the

accessories such as ring bearer pillows and garters.

Rothschild's Antiques
241 Royal Street, New Orleans
(504) 523-5816

321 Royal Street, New Orleans
(504) 523-2281
www.rothschildsantiques.com
This fourth-generation family-owned business, presided over by Michael D. Greenblatt, prides itself on representing, with integrity, elegant chandeliers made from 1880 to 1920. Greenblatt even sheds some light on the subject: Any chandelier with down-turned lighting fixtures was made in the 1880s or later, after the invention of electricity. Why? Anyone who unknow-

ingly suggests that people in their otherwise right mind would burn candles upside down, he says, has more than a few wires crossed. Greenblatt also oversees a handsome selection of 18th- and 19th-century French and English handcrafted furnishings as well as on-site custom work.

Royal Antiques Ltd.
309 Royal Street, New Orleans
(504) 524-7033
www.royalantiques.com
Walk through the stately rooms of 18th-and 19th-century antique masterworks and notice the contrast of a 250-year-old, ceiling-topping Louis XV armoire next to a French country farm table. Other worldly footnotes of handcrafted grace inside this

little ones), Victoria's Creations (vintage-style clothing, jewelry, hats, and accessories), Bayou Country General Store (plenty of hot sauces and Cajun-themed cooking accessories), Virgin Megastore, and Mostly Mardi Gras (a good selection of New Orleans and Mardi Gras memorabilia, ranging from ceramic and feather masks to party favors and second-line umbrellas).

And what New Orleans shopping experience is complete without—you guessed it—food? Peckish shoppers should head to the food court for French Market Candy Creations (good pralines), Hotsey's Grill for burgers and hot dogs, and New Orleans Fried Chicken (both the Southern-fried and rotisserie-style chicken is worthy of any lunch). Call ahead to get a Jax discount card for discounts, exclusive offers, gifts, and other benefits offered by participating stores and restaurants.

Riverwalk Marketplace
Poydras Street at the Mississippi River, New Orleans
(504) 522-1555
www.riverwalkmarketplace.com
Here's a good example of the inherent wisdom of converting a former riverfront land-sore into a breezy enterprise where the Mississippi River and the nearby docks, when lined with cruise ships, seem like the best view in town. In fact, the nearly half-mile-long wall of floor-to-ceiling windows offers one of the best panoramas of the Mississippi in town. Three levels and more than 140 shops and one-of-a-kind pushcart vendors later, you can catch yourself coming and going at the food court on Level C. Buy a daiquiri to go and step outside onto the promenade to recharge your battery. Popular shops include The Disney Store, Banana Republic, Structure, Tabasco Country Store, Masks and Make Believe, Victoria's Secret, and Evan's Creole Candy.

nearly century-old institution include English riding crops, French brass-bound cider jugs, Rococo gold-leaf mirrors with distressed glass, and early-19th-century Chinese red-lacquer cabinets with secret drawers. An 1896 Russian samovar is limited these days to serving illumination in its new assignment as an elegant lamp, perfect for shining light on a reading of *Anna Karenina*.

Royal Cameo Glass
322 Royal Street, New Orleans
(504) 522-7840
www.royalcameo.com
Owner Paula Schaffer offers marvelously detailed examples of the lost art of cameo glassmaking, with works by noted national artists Kelsey Murphy, Ulla Darni, Paul

Cunningham, and Greg Dietrich. All artwork in this family-owned studio is hand-blown by the artists. Some of the best in the bunch are Murphy's hand-carved layered colored glass pieces and Darni's reversed floral paintings and sconces.

Southern Candymakers
334 Decatur Street, New Orleans
(504) 523-5544, (800) 344-9773
www.southerncandymakers.com
The heavenly aroma of warm, mouthwatering pralines will tempt even the most strident Sugar Busters® devotee to break with the pack and run with the diet devil. This candymaker understands that variety is the spice of life when it comes to satisfying a sweet tooth. Five kinds of yummy pralines (original creamy, chocolate,

peanut butter, cinnamon, and rum and coconut) are fresh-made daily, along with 18 varieties of chocolate-covered clusters and a dozen kinds of fudge and heavenly hash—all cooked from scratch.

Up the sin ante with white-chocolate peanut butter cups so good that *Bon Appetit* magazine requested the recipe. Or try the Mississippi Mud (dark and milk chocolates swirled with fresh caramel) and dark chocolate–covered almond toffee. Not to be outdone are the white chocolate–dipped dried apricots and triple-dipped Oreos (in white and dark chocolates and caramel). A selection of traditionally prepared saltwater taffy includes a most nontraditional flavor and hands-down favorite: Jamaican rum.

Three Dog Bakery
827 Royal Street, New Orleans
(504) 525-2253
A bakery for dogs that sells Ciao Wow Cheese Pizzas, Scotti Biscotti, and Whole Kitten Caboodle? For owner Jane Rogers, the paw-sibilities are endless when it comes to creating these and other tail-wagging treats for the four-legged best friend in our lives. Also popular is her Bark 'N Fetch line of all-natural, fresh-baked cookies in peanut butter, vegetable-beef, carob chip, cheese-and-herb, apple-cinnamon, and "slow-basted BBQ" flavors. Rogers has even compiled her recipes in a cookbook titled *Short Tails & Treats from Three Dog Bakery.* Decorative gift baskets, ceramic and metal feeding dishes, aprons, and greeting cards about—and, yes, even for—dogs are available as well as celebration cakes inscribed with "Welcome Home from the Kennel" and "Good Boy (name)!"

Virgin Megastore
620 Decatur Street, New Orleans
(504) 671-8100
www.virginmega.com
At first blush this supersize music outlet looks so much like, well, the future. Clusters of wall-mounted TVs broadcast the

message of the medium while people hunker around the CD listening stations lining every wall on each of the three levels. High ceilings, brick walls, and indirect lighting provide urban flourishes while the espresso at the second-floor coffee shop adds a jolt of caffeine. Be prepared to spend time here.

This massive emporium carries virtually everything under the sun from the world of contemporary music, from jazz and blues to alternative and hip-hop. Besides CDs, music lovers will find laser discs, new releases, and even used LPs for under $20 a pop. Noteworthy, too, is the huge selection of music from around the planet, organized by country, and as nearby as the second floor. It won't take a passport to track down that hard-to-find CD of Iranian singer *Googoosh or Music of the Whirling Dervishes,* performed by Turkey's sultans of swing. Ditto for obscure Senegalese singer-songwriters as well as rare recordings of Antonio Carlos Jobim, Gilberto Gil, and other bossa nova pioneers. The third floor is a bookstore devoted to slick zines and new and classic volumes covering pop culture, jazz, erotica, spirituality, the occult, photography, art, travel, humor, and local interests. Magazines run the gamut from Gothic lifestyle, film, and fashion to music of every kind.

FAUBOURG MARIGNY

American Aquatic Gardens
621 Elysian Fields Avenue, New Orleans
(504) 944-0410
www.americanaquaticgardens.com
Stressed-out police officers and firefighters occasionally visit to spend a few minutes strolling the peaceful horticultural vignettes created by owners Rich Sacher and Bill Dailey. "It's a quiet place," Sacher says of his magnificent water gardening complex. Even those with boring jobs and brown thumbs will dig this upscale "gardener's garden," a city block–size outdoor Eden of exquisite display ponds (with full

kits available), limited-edition sculpture fountains and statuary, Oriental statues and pagodas, and classic English arbors, archways, and trellises. No pink flamingos need apply.

Sacher and Dailey opened their business in 1991 with no idea it would turn into such a success. It was "a hobby that ran amok," says Sacher, who has spent more than 40 years growing water lilies. He used to sell them out of his home until too many customers started banging on his front door. Today he grows and sells his exotic water lilies in a dozen aboveground ponds in the greenhouse out back, along with enchanting ponytail palms and rare Louisiana irises and potato vines.

Elsewhere are elegant handmade teak benches and spirit houses from Thailand and pottery from Vietnam and Italy.

A red, cathedral-shaped corrugated tin building designed by Tulane University architecture professor Gene Sisek houses accessories such as wrestling cherubs (though they look like they're kissing), books on gardening and horticulture, Buddha busts, hand-painted ceramic light fixtures for wall mounting, crystal, dinnerware, and even oil paintings. Ample on-site parking is available, as is shipping of most items anywhere in the United States.

UPTOWN

Aesthetics & Antiques
3122 Magazine Street, New Orleans
(504) 895–7011
Ever wonder where some of those "I Like Ike" campaign flyers and "I've Contributed to Goldwater" bumper stickers went to die? Look no further. This offbeat repository of bric-a-brac from the early to mid-20th century also pays homage to more than just the politics of the day. Just in time for that 19th-hole cocktail is a golf ball the diameter of an LP, which opens on hinges to reveal a decanter and six shot glasses just waiting for a bartender. Make it a double. The shop's wicker picnic baskets

are tailor made for splendor in the grass. Just add a petite pair of glass salt-and-pepper shakers from the 1940s and rose-tinted Depression glasses for the wine. Better get some film for the Brownie.

Aidan Gill for Men
2026 Magazine Street, New Orleans
(504) 587–9090
www.aidangillformen.com
At Aidan Gill for Men, discerning gentlemen will discover stylish shaving and toiletry accessories and for-the-modern-man items ranging from passport covers and silver cufflinks to decorative champagne bottle stoppers. A selection of old-fashioned shaving implements include silver-handled whisks and razors, mildly scented shaving creams, skin care lotions, and other men's personal care and bath products. In the back, customers can enjoy a haircut and hot-towel shave while sipping complimentary single-malt scotch and reading the latest issue of *Maxim*. Here Gill displays his obelisk *Monument to the Unknown Barber,* which bears the inscription AL BARBERO DESCONOCIDO.

Behind the glass counters is where the Dublin native keeps the large collection of old electric shavers, metal hair dryers, and straight razors he began amassing long before his move from Ireland to the Big Easy in the 1990s. On the wall is a framed print of Irish writers, turn-of-the-20th-century newspaper articles about shaving, and sketches of hairstyles that haven't seen the light of day since the 1950s. The outdoor sitting area is where Gill and his clientele "hatch our revolutions" while smoking cigars and admiring the towering St. Alphonsus Church next door. "There are two 'dead' words in here—unisex and PC," Gill says only half-jokingly. Make no mistake—men behaving gladly (like men) will find this venue a guilty pleasure.

Anne Pratt
3937 Magazine Street, New Orleans
(504) 891–6532
Since 1995 this artist's eclectic gallery of

ethnic art has featured hand-beaded Haitian banners in exquisitely rich colors and funky little painted chairs full of balanced whimsy. The award-winning Pratt has spent mucho time in Mexico and was so enchanted by the beauty of its artists' crucifixes that she had to bring some home. Other Spanish colonial artistic expressions imported from Mexico include a headboard made from a wrought-iron balcony. Custom-designed and hand-crafted silver and gold jewelry as well as Old World–style iron-and-wood decorations for the home, loft, or office round out Pratt's devotion to the art of following one's personal compass.

As You Like It Silver Shop
3033 Magazine Street, New Orleans
(504) 897–6915, (800) 828–2311
www.asyoulikeitsilvershop.com

Hundreds of active and inactive silver patterns fill elegant dark-wood cabinets and gleaming shelves, such as ornate 1854 Imperial Chrysanthemum by Gorham Co. and 18th-century Francis I by Reed & Barton. This 34-year-old business features a fine selection of tea sets, champagne goblets, salt and pepper shakers, candelabra, and trays.

Aux Belles Choses
3912 Magazine Street, New Orleans
(504) 891–1009
www.abcneworleans.com

Owners Bettye Barrios's and Anne Gauthier's love of European flourish and elegant pragmatism has given this shop all the warmth of a French country kitchen in springtime. And just in case you're having one of those wish-I-were-in-the-south-of-France kind of days, the blue-and-white Provençal-print kitchen napkins are stored in the drawers of the antique French cabinet near the front of the store. Other homey touches include old-fashioned scales, notepaper, linens, pottery, tin watering pitchers for the garden, European soaps, and biscuit cutters. Dried-flower arrangements are offered in the back.

The Bead Shop
4612 Magazine Street, New Orleans
(504) 895–6161

Glass beads and bead jewelry of all types from around the world are tucked inside this attractive green cottage. A feast of color in the round is found in Venetian glass and crystal from Austria and the Bohemian region of the Czech Republic. In addition to a selection of loose beads are "Tin Cup" necklaces (popularized by the movie of the same name), Russian and Baltic amber jewelry (look in the glass-top wooden box), sequin-and-bead art from Haiti, craft books, and handwoven baskets, rugs, and throw pillows. Customers are encouraged to custom design and make their own bead jewelry on the spot. Those with more time on their hands might want to enroll in one of the design classes offered by owner Nancy Campbell.

Beaucoup Books
5414 Magazine Street, New Orleans
(504) 895–2663

If the book *La Reina de los Cordenados* doesn't ring a bell, it's probably because the Anne Rice novel is better known by its English title, *The Queen of the Damned.* (The title *Cocina Dieticica del Dr. Atkins,* however, should be a snap.) Owner Mary Price has assembled a large selection of American best-sellers in Spanish, as well as books by Latin authors, including Isabel Allende, Julia Alvarez, Manuel Scorza, and Gabriel Garcia Marquez. Spanish-language children's short stories and coloring books are on hand as well as English-language selections on parenting, self-help, photography, poetry, cooking, health, travel, architecture, and history. In the back is a separate room for children's books plus—just for kiddies—a sleeping mattress with a few stuffed animals strewn about.

Belladonna
2900 Magazine Street, New Orleans
(504) 891–4393
www.belladonnadayspa.com

Walk into this unisex day spa and head

upstairs to check out the quiet hallway of opaque Japanese *shoji* doors that open to softly lighted tiled rooms used for facials, massages, aromatherapy, and other pamperings. The late New Orleans designer Roy Fairman created the second-floor respite from the workaday world for owner Kim Dudek, who opened the full-service facility in 1995. Jacuzzis, Vichy showers, and 120-jet hydrotubs augment salt rubs, seaweed wraps, and aromatherapy. The first floor is where personal, bath, and beauty products are found alongside stylish sleepwear and booths for pedicures and manicures. An outdoor Zen tea garden features a gurgling fountain, low-slung table, and floor cushions tailor made for the urban escapist. Sexually segregated lockers, saunas, and steam showers are available, as are complimentary kimono, flip-flops, towel, and shampoo.

Bon Montage
3719 Magazine Street, New Orleans
(504) 897–6295

Owners Muzzy Labouisse and Anne Vickery have fashioned an upscale mix of sophisticated interiors, gifts, and children's wear. Stylish clothing in sizes infant to 4 includes jumpers, sailor suits, separates, dresses, and baby cloths. Birch chests hand-painted with French Quarter balcony scenes and marble-patterned interiors seem tailor made for storing toys; ceramic cookware with shrimp and crawfish designs look ready to help any chef whip up a culinary storm. Check out the line of My Pool Pal bathsuits for infants and toddlers, with built-in floaties, and hand-knit baby blankets (the infant's name can be hand-stitched on the front). Once a year, usually just before Christmas, the owners offer a special: two-for-one silhouettes of your child in less than five minutes. Decoupage plates, wedding invitations and birth announcements, stuffed animals, and Beanie Babies round out the inventory.

Cameron Jones
2127 Magazine Street, New Orleans
(504) 524–3119

The Manhattan vibe of the avant-garde, forward-looking, and simply cool furnishings and accessories today's design—not designer—conscious urban dweller will make anyone wish they owned an Upper East Side loft to decorate from the ground up. This longtime Magazine Street fixture is among the best places in town to check out all those sleek and drool-worthy *articles essentials* found between the pages of hip shelter zines such as *Architectural Digest* and *Dwell*. From specialty room dividers, hip lighting, trendy mirrors, and retro occasional chairs and end tables to a polished metal entertainment bar from which to prepare the hottest cocktails raising expectations at Big Apple nightclubs, this establishment is a sure-fire cure for the aesthetic blues.

The least crowded time to cruise the shopping corridors of Uptown's Magazine Street and Royal Street in the French Quarter is weekdays before noon. This is a time when tourists are sleeping off the previous night's excesses and the city is yawning awake over its second cup of coffee. The mercury is at its lowest point of the day.

Cool Stuff
2855 Magazine Street, New Orleans
(504) 897–9466

Does your pulse quicken at the thought of an Eisenhower-era Hawaiian shirt so loud it would deafen Don Ho at 20 paces? Or perhaps a pair of capri pants straight out of Laura Petrie's closet and a mirrored disco ball to boot? At this vintage clothing and accessories store, which covers the 1940s to the 1970s, the past isn't so long ago after all. And it's certainly one of the most devil-may-care places on the street for grown-ups looking to play dress-up. Don't forget to try on one of the fully lined World War II–era bomber jackets. If anything can conjure the roar of B-52s taking off from an airfield at dawn, it's one of these well-worn babies.

Home Hook and Ladder
4100 Magazine Street, New Orleans
(504) 895–4480
www.homehookladder.com

It stands to reason that when two of the city's longtime antiques dealers team up for a new enterprise, it's likely to generate excitement. And that's exactly what has happened since owner Sandra D. Freeman and manager Michael D. Stoehr opened this establishment in 1998. The building, a virtual jinx for a succession of ill-fated restaurants over the years, was originally a firehouse called Home Hook and Ladder No. 1 (hence the new company's name), which was designed in 1884 by noted New Orleans architect James Freret. Today the brick structure's original archways and high ceilings are well lighted thanks to walls of windows facing Magazine and Marengo Streets.

More important, the 3,500-square-foot showroom of 18th- and 19th-century French and English dining tables, armoires, mirrors, dressers, sideboards, and accessories reflects the years Free-man and Stoehr each spent cultivating contacts throughout Europe. Many of the pieces are one of a kind. A case in point is the 9-foot-high French "cat and mouse" mirror, circa early 1800s, with hand-carved bas-relief of instrument-playing mice trying to awaken a sleeping cat—all in walnut.

Importicos
5523 Magazine Street, New Orleans
(504) 891–6141

Look no further if you ever wondered how a modern-day Balinese chieftain might decorate his jungle abode before *Architectural Digest* arrives for a cover shoot. Indonesian chic at this Uptown gallery is defined by stately and sturdy bamboo furnishings for adults (even kiddy furniture is available), bronze art and candle holders, statuary, silver jewelry, batik clothing, vases, and framed indigenous paintings and pictures. Music lovers can listen before they buy from a selection of world beat, Latin, and Caribbean music CDs.

Jon Antiques
4605 Magazine Street, New Orleans
(504) 899–4482
www.jonantiques.com

Enter on the Cadiz Street side of the building and take your time browsing the directly imported Georgian and French furnishings, ironstone porcelains, partner desks, settees, step bookcases, and satin-wood tea caddies with original locks. A 1759 six-volume Bible set and 18th-century wooden linen press are two examples of the one-of-a-kind items carried by owner Jon Strauss. Yew-wood glove boxes sit alongside other antique boxes in mahogany and cherry wood, many of which have been transformed into handsome humidors with cedar linings. Check out the 18th-century cutlery box featuring the Prince of Wales's crest of feathers and coronet.

Maple Street Book Shop
7523 Maple Street, New Orleans
(504) 866–4916

Discerning local and national authors as well as dyed-in-the-wool bookhounds say this privately owned pocket of literary paradise is one major reason New Orleans is "a great bookstore city." Walk past the azalea-twined wrought-iron fence and up the front steps, and notice the photographs of Martin Luther King Jr., Paul Prudhomme, and Walker Percy on the exterior wall. Open the cabinlike screen door and be greeted again—this time by the entire collection of Louisiana literary legend Walker Percy, who gave posthumous life to the New Orleans–set classic, *A Confederacy of Dunces,* following the death of author John Kennedy Toole. A photograph of a smiling Percy holding a bulging Maple Leaf–logo paper bag is testament to the close relationship this popular establishment enjoyed with the late author.

Cozy, well-lit rooms with floor-to-ceiling shelves offer everything from Eudora Welty and Alice Walker to photography, spirituality, music, limited-edition volumes, and self-help (BEFORE IT'S TOO LATE, the sign reads). Visitors will know they are in the travel section when they see the Russian-language map of the Moscow subway system. Ancient and Renaissance classics are well represented, as are local cookbooks, fiction and nonfiction, mysteries, criticism, women's issues, and essays.

Maple Street Children's Book Shop
7529 Maple Street, New Orleans
(504) 861-2105
www.maplestreetbookshop.com
Next door to the Maple Street Book Shop is this counterpart for youthful readers of all ages. Be sure to check out the section of imaginative New Orleans–themed books such as *Haunted Louisiana* by Christy L. Vivano, *The Cajun Night Before Christmas* talking book (with Gaston the green-nosed alligator), and *The Jazz of Our Streets* by Fatima Shaik and E. B. Lewis, which tells the story of the birth-place of jazz with watercolors and poems. *If Only I Had a Horn,* by Roxane Orgill teaches youngsters about jazz pioneer Louis Armstrong; Angela Shelf Medearis's *Rum-A-Tum-Tum* tells of the excitement of a second-line parade through the eyes of a child. The up-and-coming musician in the family will find inspiring high notes in the book *Wynton Marsalis: Gifted Trumpet Player,* the only artist to ever win Grammys for best classical and jazz recordings in the same year. If all else fails, there's always Dakota Lane's *Johnny Voodoo.* According to the back cover: "Johnny is so mysterious, and so beautiful. People say all sorts of things about him. Which things are true and which are lies?" Best let a pint-size reader be the judge.

Martin Wine Cellar
3827 Baronne Street, New Orleans
(504) 899-7411

714 Elmeer Street, Metairie
(504) 896-7300
www.martinwine.com
If your favorite martini leaves you shaken *and* stirred, you must have discovered the jalapeño-stuffed jumbo Spanish olives and Creole marinated onions sold at this pop-

ular store. Join the crowd. There is always a buzz inside this mustard-colored Uptown shop on Saturday afternoon, when loyal locals browse aisles full of domestic and international wines and liquors, gourmet food items and hot sauces, Jamaican jerk seasoning, Brazilian mustard glazes, Creole coffees, and local seasonings and dressings (try the mango or passion fruit vinaigrettes by Consorzio).

Weekend cooking demonstrations, informal wine tastings, and microbrewed beer samplings create an upscale atmosphere accented by a pleasant selection of cheeses ranging from double-cream havarti to crumbly Spanish cabrale. Gourmet cookies, biscotti, and shortbreads target the sweet tooth, while a crowded deli section offers to-go or dine-in specialty pastas, salads, and sandwiches. The Nova Delight—Norwegian smoked salmon and cream cheese with onion and capers on pumpernickel or a bagel—is particularly good.

Mayan Import Co.
3000 Magazine Street, New Orleans
(504) 269-9000, (888) 372-2100
www.mayanimport.com
Honduras takes a bow at this emporium specializing in cigars and handcrafts from the Central American country that gave the world the great Mayan city of Copan. This in no small way is due to co-owner David McCammon's love affair with Honduras, says business partner Graymond Martin. Sixty percent of the shop's cigars are imported from Honduras and include such well-known labels as Santa Rosa, Don Fortunato, Valle de Maya, Punch, and Indios. Also from Honduras are mahogany room dividers and decorative boxes, leather handbags, and colorful baskets and tortilla warmers woven from shredded palm leaves called junca. Looking to customize your favorite smokes? The shop uses state of the art computer software to convert business logos, photographic images, and/or monograms into custom cigar labels for advertising and personal use (minimum 10 labels per order).

Mignon Faget Ltd.
3801 Magazine Street, New Orleans
(504) 891-2005
www.mignonfaget.com
Native artisan Mignon Faget's brilliantly crafted jewelry, which includes those designs on architecture and nature (such as marine life and horticulture), has won her nationwide critical acclaim and megasales in boutiques from coast to coast. Her upstairs studio and workshop produce the downstairs creations, which include the Louisiana Collection of locally familiar icons ranging from Creole cottages to streetcars.

Musica Latina
4714 Magazine Street, New Orleans
(504) 895-4227
Don't expect to find cushy high-tech listening booths or a froufrou coffee bar at this tiny (and blessedly unfettered) music shop. It opened in 1969 and is located on an oft-overlooked-by-tourists downscale stretch of this Uptown street. What you *will* find, pure and simple, is one of the largest selections of Latin music cassettes and CDs as well as hard-to-find LPs anywhere in the city. The Honduran-born husband-and-wife team of Juan Suarez and Yolanda Estrada Suarez carry virtually every Latin music style under the tropical sun: salsa from Puerto Rico; merengue from the Dominican Republic; bossa nova from Brazil; Garifuna dancehall punta from Honduras; tango from Argentina; folk music from the Peruvian Andes; sardana and flamenco from Spain; and much more. Spanish-language newspapers and periodicals are available.

New Orleans Cypress Works
3110 Magazine Street, New Orleans
(504) 891-0001
This new kid on the block has already cultivated a loyal following, due to the skilled artisans who can take a 150-year-old cypress barge plank and transform it into a dining table with stories waiting to be told. It's hard to resist running a caressing hand slowly over one of the rustic tables, armoires, headboards, and other furniture—all custom-crafted from cypress and pine architectural pieces found at demolished old New Orleans homes. Shoppers will find that everything from hutches and game tables to 10-foot mirrors suitable for a swank foyer feature old-time nail-less jointery. Many pieces are available in one of the three levels of wood "stress."

On the Other Hand
8204 Oak Street, New Orleans
(504) 861-0159
It's worth a stop at this haute couture consignment boutique just for the chance to meet owner Kay Danné, whose unflinching Southern grace and hospitality have been charming shoppers since 1987. Looking for a stylish number by Chanel, Donna Karan, or Yves St. Laurent (to name but a few of the designer brands) but at a to-die-for price? Chances are you'll find it here among the more than 3,500 dresses, Mardi Gras ball gowns, prom and evening dresses, fur coats, hats, scarves, and shoes that overfill six rooms in Danné's Victorian shotgun house, located in Riverbend. Wedding gowns and vintage clothing complete the mix. "There's a story behind every dress," Danné says of her inventory. For an elegant shopping treat, stop by on Saturday afternoon when the owner hosts one of her patio wine-and-cheese soirees, with a guest pianist.

Parcels and Post
5721 Magazine Street, New Orleans
(504) 891-8402
Wondering how you're ever going to take home that swelling car trunk full of souvenirs and gifts? Give yourself a break from feeling like a beast of burden by stopping off at this full-service packaging and shipping enterprise. If you've got it, they can ship it—anywhere—via U.S. Post, Federal Express, and Airborne Express. Services include packaging, crating, gift-wrapping, faxing, copying, custom boxing, motor- and

air-freight, and pickup and delivery. They've even got a selection of greeting cards in case you just remembered Aunt Jeanne's birthday was last month.

The Private Connection/Pieces
3927 Magazine Street, New Orleans
(504) 899–4944

If the *New York Times* calls it "the most cheerful shop on the street," it's almost worth dropping by just to see if the newspaper is wrong. But we'll save you some time—go. This is the kind of place where art feels good—and there's a reason why. In 1988 owner Clifford Henrotin opened this import shop to combine his passion for adventure travel to Indonesia with the region's fine and folk arts. (If Santa's listening, one of the 6-foot plastic banana trees posing as a cartoon jungle dream would look smashing in the studio of one writer who has been very good this year.) Hand-crafted Balinese teakwood and Burmese rosewood furniture and architectural pieces include century-old regal beds; animal-shaped tables; and intricate, brightly colored old wooden panel doors. Batiks, copper stamps, and hand-painted mobiles also are sold.

Ruby Ann Tobar-Blanco
3005 Magazine Street, New Orleans
(504) 897–0811, (800) 826–7282

This New Orleans native creates reasonably priced jewelry, accessories, and objets d'art from rare and unusual materials that speak to the artist in "the language of color and texture." The colors of gemstones, pearls, sterling, hand-blown glass, and other fine materials are combined to create simplicity, luxury, and a sense of timelessness. Especially striking are the bracelets and earrings crafted from a mix of freshwater pearls, American glass, and sterling silver and necklaces incorporating handblown glass and bronze. At other times the artist uses hand-painted glass and silver to create one-of-a-kind earrings; garnet beads and

carved bone become unique necklaces of pure imagination. Tobar-Blanco's other creations include coral and silver Nepalese prayer-box pendants, Ethiopian crosses made from Mediterranean deepwater coral, and faux antique pueblo pottery.

Scriptura
5423 Magazine Street, New Orleans
(504) 897–1555

What globe-trotter wouldn't appreciate an elegant leather-bound journal in which to jot down the vagaries of travel? Or perhaps a specialty book for scribbling impressions of memorable (and not-so-memorable) wines, restaurants, and cigars enjoyed along the way? (A limited-edition copy of *The Hand Made Cigars Collector's Guide and Journal* might help the novice get the lingo down.) This well-lit shop also specializes in custom monogrammed stationery seals and sealing wax. "Essential papers" run the gamut from beautifully boxed stationery from France, Italy, and Japan to lovely cards for "notes and queries." Other treasures include fountain pens in Venetian glass and carved wood, hand-bound scrapbooks in rich textured fabrics, and archival quality photo albums with recycled acid-free paper.

Thomas Mann Gallery
1804 Magazine Street, New Orleans
(504) 581–2113
www.thomasmann.com

Thomas Mann's "techno-romantic" jewelry has earned him coast-to-coast kudos from fans that include Robert DeNiro. Sterling, nickel, copper, and brass are transformed into striking Mann-made museum-quality sculpture, amulets, tabletop art, earrings and pendants, teapots d'art, and eye-shaped mirrors, as well as art based on nature. Works by other artists include a selection of handcrafted Studio Inferno martini glasses with blue Greek torsos, which are really something to shake a swizzle stick at.

Utopia
5408 Magazine Street, New Orleans
(504) 899-8488
www.utopianola.com
Unique (yet comfortable) women's clothing, home accessories, and exclusive hand-
crafted pine furnishings—all with an artful
spin—are just some of the specialties
found inside this Greek Revival cottage,
tucked behind a wrought-iron fence in the
heart of Magazine Street's shopping district. Narrow vertical "chimney" cabinets
are colorfully hand-painted and can be
found alongside artsy-chic linen dresses in
pastel shades and recycled metalwork.
Bookshelves are lined with local cookbooks and a selection of upscale bath
products.

Villa Vici
2930 Magazine Street, New Orleans
(504) 899-2931
Anyone eager to add the contemporary
lines of cotton and linen slipcover furnishings to their bedroom and home will want
to run their hands over the stylish (and
washable) couches and chairs of this
upscale "two-of-a-kind" shop. Breezy
canopy beds and living space ensembles
from North Carolina and California share
floor space with locally crafted art lamps
and imported Italian and French reproductions of Mediterranean urns and vases.
If you see something you like, buy it—this
window-front shop's inventory changes
regularly.

Westgate
5219 Magazine Street, New Orleans
(504) 899-3077
www.westgatenecromantic.com
Death has its moments—typically the final
ones—but some people may find this
enterprise a tad beyond their pale. First,
this mid-19th-century, two-story Greek
Revival house, tucked amid a nondescript
tree-shaded block of low-slung homes, is
downright impossible to miss: It's painted
black and purple. Signs on the front
door—GREETINGS FROM THE HOUSE OF DEATH

and DEATH IS SWEET—may give some people
pause. Fear not. Ever since it opened in
1990, everyone who has entered this
macabre gallery-museum devoted to
necromantic art and literature has exited
very much alive.

Be prepared for a truly otherworldly
experience, though, thanks to the owners-
curators, who say the name Westgate was
chosen because it symbolizes the journey
"home." And what a home it is. Interior
walls are painted black and accented with
painted lightning bolts, while tangles of
fake cobwebs hang from the ceiling. On
one wall is a sculpture with a dozen or so
clustered skull faces, whose empty eye
sockets seem to follow visitors around the
room. The black cat that roams the place
is named Damien and, yes, that's a real
coffin—complete with a skeleton inside—
against the parlor wall. A cache of goodies for sale includes paintings depicting
intimate encounters with angels of death,
copies of *Bloodsong* magazine, how-to
books on necromantic rituals, and objets
de la morte, such as a skeleton couple in
bed titled *The Last Date*.

Whole Foods Market
5600 Magazine Street, New Orleans
(504) 899-9119

3135 Esplanade Avenue, New Orleans
(504) 943-1626
www.wholefoods.com
Despite this mega-grocer's motto of
"Whole foods, whole people, whole
planet," it's the eye-popping selection of
international cheese that drew raves from
one recent first-time shopper. With an
estimated 225 varieties of domestic and
international cheese that run the gamut
from Swiss Emmenthaler and Spanish
Manchego and Zamorano to hard-to-find
Basque Idiazabal and more than two
dozen French varieties of the fermented
curd, it's like stumbling upon a European
cheese monger's shop in the middle of a
modern supermarket. Plus, the white-
jacketed staff not only knows their fromage
but also offers a free bite to those curious

about the flavor of an unfamiliar cheese. But cheese is by no means the only staple shoppers will find at this 40,000-square-foot emporium, which opened in 2003 at the site of the completely restored old bus barn on Magazine Street.

Meticulously arranged displays of gorgeous fresh seafood and meat are reminiscent of the Rialto Bridge outdoor market in Venice. Elsewhere a cornucopia of natural food includes a nice selection of organic juices and the city's hands-down largest selection of whole grains, ranging from bulgur wheat, pearled barley, and millet to nearly 50 kinds of bulk granola (the pumpkin seed version might make for a good Halloween breakfast). A coffee bar and gourmet food-to-go section give this Austin, Texas-based international company's Uptown location a trendy vibe, along with a licensed message therapist offering 10- to 30-minute neck and shoulder massages—no appointment necessary—for about $1.00 per minute. Especially on Saturday the tables and chairs out front offer a pleasant venue for enjoying coffee or a meal while soaking in the buzz of Magazine Street. When the firm bought Whole Food Co. on Esplanade Avenue, the name changed to Whole Foods Market, but the parent company kept open the doors of the far smaller but perennially popular spot tucked in Bayou St. John neighborhood.

Winky's/UPstairs
2038 Magazine Street, New Orleans
(504) 568-1020

This is two shops in one. Downstairs is Winky's, a swing kid's paradise featuring spats, porkpie hats, '40s-style retro dresses, and other clothing and accessories for those who like to kick dance the Charleston to "Take the A-train." Upstairs is UPstairs, a decidedly funky and quirky mélange of retro bric-a-brac cleverly converted into wall clocks. Name the item and chances are it's been pressed into service as an electrical timekeeper—old bingo cards, green olive cans, ham tins, Chinese Checker boards, old purses, and more.

Wirthmore Antiques
3727 Magazine Street, New Orleans
(504) 269-0660
3900 Magazine Street, New Orleans
(504) 899-3811
www.wirthmoreantiques.com

A 19th-century hand-painted Swedish tall-case clock near the front door greets visitors to this "accidental" store. As owner Gay Wirth explains it, curious shoppers kept sticking their noses into this former warehouse, where she used to store furniture for her other shop on Magazine Street. Before long she converted the warehouse into the second Wirthmore retail outlet. French Provincial furnishings from the 18th and 19th centuries include armoires with double-sculpted moldings, beautiful walnut panetieres (awaiting fresh loaves of French bread), and grille doors with *chapeau gendarme* bonnets. Wirth scours the highways and byways of France's Normandy and Burgundy regions for treasures that range from a Louis XV–style bibliotheque with coquillage feet to blue-and-white dinner plates circa 1920 from a Provence restaurant.

Yvonne La Fleur
8131 Hampson Street, New Orleans
(504) 866-9666
www.yvonnelafleur.com

The black stretch limousine parked at the curb and the uniformed chauffeur standing at the front door spoke volumes about the kind of clientele seduced by this chandelier-lit dreamscape of femininity. A cozy interior of Victorian-style salons, each decorated according to the creative whim of owner Yvonne La Fleur, would make even the snobbiest European on a shopping spree feel right at home. Chandeliers, antique baby carriages, an Art Deco settee, and a mirrored wet bar serve as the backdrop for La Fleur's custom millinery. Most of it is fashioned from her collection of veilings and turn-of-the-20th-century flowers from France, silk ribbons from Switzerland, antique feathers from Germany, "and other elegant touches

from around the world." The Yvonne La Fleur Private Collection features silk dresses, sportswear, suede, one-of-a-kind evening gowns, and exclusive wedding dresses and bridesmaid's gowns. Other specialties are hand-tailored hats, lingerie, fragrances, bath products, jewelry, and linen apparel.

ATTRACTIONS AND ACTIVITIES

Pull up a comfy chair. The year was 1930 and the city's first German consul, an erudite statesman named Rolf L. Jaeger, who possessed both a polished pedigree and protocol skills, had just settled into his swank Italianate digs on St. Charles Avenue. It was only fitting that Gov. Huey P. Long wished to properly receive the city's esteemed new diplomat. The meeting was to take place in the governor's suite at the downtown Roosevelt (now Fairmont) Hotel.

When Jaeger was ushered into the governor's suite, he was shocked to discover his host, Louisiana's highest-ranking elected official, attired only in a pair of green silk pajamas. Long's dress code might have passed muster with some of his backwoods cronies, but Jaeger the nobleman would have none of it. This flagrant slap in the face of international diplomacy caused the German consul to pop his cork.

Long tried to recover from his faux pas with profuse apologies. However, Louisiana's most colorful politician—and one of the country's most stalwart populists—had a knack for putting things in perspective. When asked a few weeks later if the incident amounted to political suicide, he reportedly answered, "Yeah. When they find out I sleep in silk pajamas and not cotton, I'll be ruined in Winn Parish."

Seven years later, when the dashing Baron Edgar von Spielgel arrived in New Orleans as the newly appointed German consul for the South, he set up shop in the same St. Charles Avenue mansion that Jaeger had called home. The baron, a highly prestigious addition to the Garden District social scene, was feted at afternoon teas and black-tie soirees almost from the time he set foot in the city. By the time World War II was over and von Spielgel had long since pulled up stakes and returned to Europe, though, an interesting discovery had been unearthed: The good baron had been Hitler's second-highest ranking spy in the United States. Today the elegant home in which the German consuls Jaeger and von Spielgel resided, the stately Van Benthuysen–Elms Mansion, is open for tours and underscores the always intriguing, sometimes quirky history lurking behind so many New Orleans "attractions."

For a city its size, New Orleans nearly breaks the mold when it comes to ways to have a good time that don't require Bill Gates's bank account or spending two hours in gridlock. Museums and historic homes? We got 'em coming out of our crawfish tails. Riverboat cruises and a world-class zoo and aquarium? Ditto. Plantation mansions? Fiddle-dee-dee. Historic cemeteries? Pshaw. Moreover, the opening of Harrah's casino, Six Flags New Orleans amusement park, and the nationally heralded D-Day Museum has added diversity to the city's enviable roster of noteworthy attractions.

If New Orleans doesn't have it all, it certainly has most of it. And so far nobody has complained, as evidenced by the fact that the city can barely keep pace with the demand for new hotels and convention center space. Visitors who arrive by plane are often stunned by the number of airport bars passed en route to baggage, but that's just the city's friendly way of saying, "Pssst, c'mere."

While the following list of activities is by no means complete, it is nevertheless comprehensive and reflects the scope of attractions that has made and kept New

ATTRACTIONS AND ACTIVITIES

Orleans one of the nation's premier and laudable tourism cities. Always call ahead to verify times and admission costs, but be patient as many New Orleanians are unaccustomed to the harried tempo of out-of-towners, even those on vacation.

PRICE CODE

Our price is based on admission for one adult.

$	$0 to $10
$$	$11 to $20
$$$	$21 to $50
$$$$	More than $50

Audubon Aquarium of the Americas $$
1 Canal Street, New Orleans
(504) 581-4629, (800) 774-7394
www.auduboninstitute.org
Enter the Audubon Aquarium of the Americas' underwater world and explore more than one million gallons of fresh- and saltwater exhibits representing the Caribbean Sea, the Amazon rain forest, and the Gulf of Mexico. Stroll through a sunlit tunnel surrounded on three sides by a Caribbean reef, where the colors of the coral are reflected in a dazzling collection of tropical fish. In the Amazon rain forest, soothing waterfalls and tropical birds lull you. But watch out: Piranhas, anacondas, and stingrays also populate the region.

Don't forget to catch a glimpse of the sharks as they glide through the shadows of pylons of a Gulf of Mexico oil rig replica. The aquarium houses one of the world's most diverse shark collections, from Australia's odd-looking wobbegongs

Spring and fall months are the best time to enjoy the city's multitude of outdoor attractions and activities. So don't let summer sneak up on you—start planning now by making a list of things you want to do when New Orleans's weather is at its year-round best.

of the Coral Sea to sleek blacktip reef sharks that prowl the Pacific Ocean. You can even pet a baby nurse shark. Don't miss the freak show that is the Living in Water gallery of flashlight fish that glow in the dark and four-eyed anableps. The aquarium opens daily at 9:30 A.M. Closing hours vary.

Audubon Louisiana Nature Center $
Joe Brown Park
5601 Read Boulevard, New Orleans
(504) 246-5672, (800) 774-7394
www.auduboninstitute.org
If overindulgence is starting to take its toll on your liver and cholesterol level, it may be time to head back to nature. And the nearest nature call in New Orleans is 15 minutes from downtown off I-10, where visitors can work off their Hurricane drinks and deep-fried oyster po-boys with a hike on one of the center's three walking trails. The .3-mile Discovery Trail (approximate walking time: 30 minutes) and 1.4-mile Adventure Trail (one hour) are both ground-level trails. The 0.8-mile Wisner Loop Trail (45 minutes) is a handicapped-accessible elevated boardwalk. Self-guided trail manuals are available for each of the trails at the information desk and are helpful for those eager to learn about the flora and fauna.

Visitors can check out from the information desk at no charge a Discovery Kit, a canvas shoulder bag that includes binoculars, field guides, a bird call, a dip net, magnifying lens, and an activity guide. Or take a guided trail walk on Sunday at 3:00 P.M.

At the Interpretive Center visitors can learn more about reptiles and amphibians at the Snakes 'N' Stuff exhibit, visit the Discovery Loft for a "touching" experience, hear more about the animals at the 11:45 A.M. Birds of Prey program, 1:15 P.M. Reptile program, and 4:00 P.M. Mammal program. Guided bird walks are held Saturday 10:30 A.M. Don't forget to stop by the greenhouse and butterfly garden, as well as the Interpretive Garden to spy on the squirrels, rabbits, birds, butterflies, and the occasional "surprise" visitor (no, not Anne Rice) who drops by to feed in the Urbina Wildlife Garden.

Adventurers can voyage to other planets or watch laser light dance to the rhythms of popular music at the center's planetarium at 11:00 A.M. and 12:30, 2:00, 3:30, and 4:30 P.M. Shows are included in the price of admission. Laser rock concerts are held Friday and Saturday at 9:00 and 10:30 P.M. and midnight (additional admission).

The Entergy/LP&L Science Resource Center offers teachers and students a variety of natural history and science research material, including books, periodicals, and brochures. The nature center also hosts numerous children's and family programs, activities, clubs, camps, and festivals throughout the year, which are well worth exploring.

To get to the Louisiana Nature Center take I-10 east to exit 244 at Read Boulevard. Go south (right) on Read, turn left into Joe Brown Park at Nature Center Drive, and follow the signs to the nature center entrance. Restrooms, a gift shop, and snack vending machines are available.

Audubon Zoo $–$$
6500 Magazine Street, New Orleans
(504) 581–4629, (800) 774–7394
www.auduboninstitute.org
The 58-acre Audubon Zoo, consistently rated among the nation's best, features 1,500 animals representing 360 species—many of which are rare or endangered—in natural habitat exhibits. At the new, $2.2-million Jaguar Jungle, visitors walk past an ancient Meso-American bas-relief glyph of a jaguar while spider monkeys swing on vines and a jabiru stork clicks its beak looking for a mate—all in the shadows of a Mayan temple. The 1.5-acre exhibit uses a mix of zoology and history to tell the story of Central America's exotic animals and that region's 4,000-year-old Mayan civilization. The extravagant Jaguar Jungle was fashioned after the zoo's popular Louisiana Swamp Exhibit, which showcases the state's indigenous wildlife,

including a rare white alligator, as well as human life on the bayou. Both exhibits underscore a trend among the nation's progressive zoos to focus on education in addition to entertainment.

Other exhibits include the Komodo Dragon, Reptile Encounter, the Tropical Bird House, World of Primates, and Butterflies in Flight, as well as those devoted to the animals of North and South America, Africa, and Asia. New attractions include the Pacific Coast Adventures exhibit and a seahorse "gallery."

The zoo opens daily at 9:30 A.M. and closes at 5:00 P.M. (6:00 P.M. weekends in summer). The Audubon Institute offers discounts to individuals who wish to visit more than one of its four attractions—Audubon Zoo, Audubon Aquarium of the Americas, IMAX Theater, and Audubon Louisiana Nature Center.

Bayou Barn $–$$
7145 Barataria Boulevard,
Crown Point, New Orleans
(504) 689–2663, (800) 862–2968
www.bayoubarn.com
Looking to "dance your gumbo off"? A zydeco music–fueled dance and food party, called "fais do do" by Cajuns, blows the roof off the Bayou Barn pavilion on Bayou Des Familiies February through December on Sunday noon to 6:00 P.M. (live music starts at 2:00 P.M.). Cost is $10 (children under 12 free) and includes free Cajun two-step dance lessons and a dinner of alligator jambalaya, gumbo, rice, bread, and soft drink.

Located at the junction of Louisiana Highways 45 and 3134 in the heart of Barataria, once home to that Jean Lafitte and his swamp-based profiteers, Bayou Barn also offers daily guided swamp tours and rental canoes to see the alligators, snakes, and other wildlife in the Jean Lafitte National Historic Park and Preserve—all less than 30 minutes from downtown New Orleans. Guided swamp tours, minimum two persons, include lunch.

To get here take the Crescent City Connection over the Mississippi River to

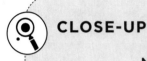
National D-Day Museum

This long overdue museum opened its doors in June 2000 to national fanfare worthy of the heroes who fought what many historians believe to be the one of the most important battles in history. Operation Neptune sent the largest armada in history—5,333 ships and landing craft carrying 175,000 troops—across 100 miles of the churning English Channel to assault Hitler's Atlantic Wall at Normandy. The National D-Day Museum (www.ddaymuseum.org), located in a renovated four-story 19th-century warehouse at 934 Magazine Street in the Warehouse Arts District, is one of the most acclaimed museums of its kind to open in the United States in the past decade. The 70,000-square-foot exhibit space, housed in the former Louisiana Brewery, constructed in 1856, takes visitors through state-of-the-art interactive exhibits intermixed with oral histories from veterans worldwide, photographs, hands-on activities, and film footage never seen before.

Most important, the museum shines a light on the events leading up to and including the fog-shrouded morning of June 6, 1944, the D-day of World War II, when the Allies landed on the beaches of Normandy, which eventually led to victory in Europe. Designed to inspire "future generations to learn life lessons—teamwork, the value of democracy, unsung bravery—from the most complex military operations ever staged," the museum also presents such sensitive issues as the African-American experience at home and abroad in a straightforward manner.

A room-size diorama of the air and sea armada conveys the size and complexity of the invasion force. This exhibit-rich repository of the most historic day of World War II will leave visitors with a better idea of what it was like to ride aboard a Higgins Boat, storm the beaches of Normandy, fly an Allied glider into France, and fight your way through hedgerow country. The museum also presents a collection of personal stories through recorded oral histories of war workers, air raid wardens, and other ordinary Americans who contributed to the war effort at home.

Other exhibit highlights include:

- A reproduction Higgins landing craft built by volunteers, many of whom worked on these boats during the war.
- A 110-seat theater where the Academy Award–nominated documentary film *D-Day Remembered,* produced by the museum, is shown seven times daily.
- Aircraft, vehicles, weapons, uniforms, home-front materials, and other significant artifacts.
- Interactive galleries featuring electronic maps, minitheaters, photomurals, text panels, and original artifacts that allow visitors to see a piece of D-day firsthand.

A new 5,000-square-foot exhibit, "The D-day Invasions in the Pacific," describes the amphibious invasions as they were

A reproduction LCVP (Landing Craft Vehicle Personnel), or Higgins boat, built from original World War II plans by former Higgins employees, is displayed in the Louisiana Memorial Pavilion of the National D-Day Museum. NATIONAL D-DAY MUSEUM

fought across the vast expanse of the Pacific Ocean. The exhibit combines photos, videos, artifacts, animated maps, newspaper headlines, and interactive touch screens and oral histories to tell the story of the sacrifice and courage of the men and women who fought in the Pacific Theater. Visitors will be able to see "the details of how Americans fought the Japanese in leading our troops to victory," said Dr. Gordon H. "Nick" Mueller, president of the museum.

From amphibious landings, hand-to-hand jungle combat, and naval battles to fighter and bomber strikes and submarine warfare, this latest edition to the National D-Day Museum embodies the American spirit and the country's fight for freedom and democracy at a crossroads of world history. In the documentary *Price for Peace,* the voices of the American and Japanese veterans who spent time in the Pacific Theater discuss their emotions and perceptions of their respective enemy. *Price for Peace* was coproduced by Steven Spielberg and museum founder, historian, and late author Stephen E. Ambrose.

the Westbank Expressway; turn left at Barataria Boulevard and follow the four-lane divided road out of the city and into the country until you reach Bayou Barn—it's on the left and well marked.

Blaine Kern's Mardi Gras World $-$$
233 Newton Street, Algiers Point
(504) 361-7821, (800) 362-8213
www.mardigrasworld.com
Go behind the scenes of Mardi Gras to see the world's largest fleet of Carnival floats and the artists who create them. Nearly 500,000 square feet of Carnival "dens" are the working studios of international artists and sculptors who form the largest float-building company in the world. Tours allow guests to try on authentic Mardi Gras costumes, visit the prop shop where artists create the giant papier-mâché sculptures that adorn floats, watch floats being constructed, and get a glance at Captain Eddie's S. S. Endymion, the world's biggest float, which measures 240 feet long and is adorned with tens of thousands of fiber-optic lights.

Mardi Gras World is open daily 9:30 A.M. to 5:00 P.M. The 45-minute tours begin every hour. Last tour starts at 4:30 P.M. To get here take the Canal Street Ferry to Algiers Point. A free shuttle bus meets every ferry.

Canal Street Ferry $
Canal Street at the Mississippi
New Orleans
One of the most romantic views of the city is the one from the Canal Street ferry at night. During the day it's the simplest way to experience the Mighty Mississippi, especially if you don't have 1.5 hours for a steamboat ride. Drive or walk aboard and get a panoramic view of the city during the short ride to Algiers Point. Once there check out Blaine Kern's Mardi Gras World, where Carnival floats are built and stored. The Canal Street Ferry leaves the dock on the hour and half hour. Cost is $1.00 per car round-trip and is free for pedestrians.

Cookin' Cajun Cooking School $$
1 Poydras Street, Riverwalk
New Orleans
(504) 586-8832, (800) 786-0941
www.cookincajun.com
Looking to get your hands literally into some of those heavenly local dishes you'll be writing about in postcards to your co-workers back in Muncie? Grab an apron and let chef Susan Murphy of the Creole Cajun New Orleans Cooking School demonstrate a thing or two about local staples like shrimp remoulade, oysters Rockefeller, Creole bread pudding with Amaretto sauce, fried eggplant fingers, chicken andouille gumbo, and Grandpere's praline parfait. With the Mississippi River serving as the backdrop for this Riverwalk market store, visitors pay $20 for a two-hour class in which they eat what the chef prepares after watching step-by-step preparations of a classic Creole-Cajun menu that blends the best of the city's Spanish, French, and Caribbean heritage. Breakfast, lunch, cocktail hour, and dinner classes are available and accommodate up to 75 persons. Cooking school students get 10 percent discount off the Louisiana cookbooks, spices, and hot sauces, as well as pralines made fresh daily and gourmet gift baskets, sold at the adjoining Creole Delicacies Gourmet shop.

Global Wildlife Center $
26389 Louisiana Highway 40, Folsom
(985) 624-9453
www.globalwildlife.com
The Global Wildlife Center is a 900-acre nonprofit home to more than 2,000 free-roaming animals from all over the world—that's more hoofed stock than in all Louisiana zoos combined and the largest free-range facility in the country. Zebras, antelope, camels, bison, and other animals enjoy dominion over the land, while visitors are "contained" in covered wagons pulled by tractors. During the 90-minute tour a guide entertains and educates participants about the center's species and wildlife preservation. Along the way, the

wagon stops and the animals approach. Where else can you hand-feed a giraffe?

The preserve, originally a private collection of exotic animals, opened to the public nearly 12 years ago. Global Wildlife Center is open year-round. Call for hours, tour times, and availability. To get here take I-10 west to the Causeway exit. Take Causeway north and proceed over the 26-mile Causeway over Lake Pontchartrain to St. Tammany Parish and I-12. Head west on I-12 to exit 47 (Robert exit). Turn right on Highway 445 (north) and proceed for approximately 11 miles to Highway 40 East. Turn right; the stone entrance to the park is 1.5 miles on the left.

Harrah's Casino
**512 South Peters Street, New Orleans
(504) 533-6000
www.harrahs.com**
Lady Luck smiled on New Orleans in October 1999 with the opening of Harrah's Casino. But visitors will find more than row upon row of slot machines and gaming tables for blackjack, craps, roulette, and other popular pastimes for people hoping to hit it big in the City that Care Forgot. From the towering artificial oak tree and statue of a jazz trumpeter in the Jazz Court reminiscent of a French Quarter courtyard, to the three Mardi Gras floats and thrice-nightly Carnival parades, to four performance stages with live entertainment nightly, including vintage jazz and Dixieland, there is no question that this new casino is set right in the heart of the Big Easy. The New Orleans–themed and decorated gaming den is located on the edge of the French Quarter, near the foot of Canal Street and bordered by Convention Center Boulevard and Poydras and South Peters Streets.

If you're looking for the notorious rum-smuggling pirate Jean Lafitte, matey, head to Smuggler's Court. The Barataria Cove section of the food court features a replica of a beach-wrecked 18th-century pirate's ship with Lafitte at the helm and the sound effects of exotic birds, ghostly skeletons, and waves gently lapping a

rocky beach. A special effects storm cycles every 20 minutes, enhanced by real wave action (don't worry, patrons stay dry), fog, wind, and moving clouds. Open 24/7, Harrah's has a 1,550-space parking garage across from the casino at Convention Center Boulevard and Poydras Street.

House of Broel Victorian
Mansion and Dollhouse Museum $
**2220 St. Charles Avenue, New Orleans
(504) 522-2220
www.houseofbroel.com**
To step inside this three-story Victorian mansion and museum-home built in the 1850s is to sample the kind of gracious Southern hospitality envisioned by Bonnie Broel, a Polish countess and fashion designer who bought the home in 1970. The oak-shaded St. Charles Avenue landmark at Jackson Avenue, located just minutes from downtown New Orleans and the French Quarter, is a special occasion and bridal salon known also for Broel's collection of exquisite gowns, lavish Mardi Gras queens' gowns, and seven restored, elaborately detailed dollhouses, many with antique pieces.

The original two-story antebellum home, an example of high Victorian architecture and woodwork, was the city home of wealthy plantation owners. Tobacco millionaire Simon Hernsheim added the stately first floor 40 years later. The center hall showcases an original mirror embellished with an intricate border of tobacco leaves fashioned in gold. The ballroom features ornate chandeliers and original black-marble fireplaces and is the site of many private weddings and parties. The mansion and museum are open for tours Monday through Saturday 10:00 A.M. to 5:00 P.M.

IMAX Theater $
**1 Canal Street, New Orleans
(504) 581-4629; (800) 774-7394
www.auduboninstitute.org**
Put yourself in the driver's seat, going more than 200 miles per hour with NASCAR 3D while watching one of IMAX

Theater's swear-you-were-there movies. The French Quarter theater, adjacent to the Audubon Aquarium of the Americas, opened in 1995 and features 354 "front row" seats for viewing its 5.5-story screen—three times the size of a regular movie screen. Several seats provide a rear-view, closed-captioned system for the hearing impaired. Current larger-than-life flicks include *Dolphins, The Mysteries of Egypt,* and *Everest.* IMAX shows begin daily at 10:00 A.M. Call ahead, though, because they are subject to change without notice. Advance purchase is recommended but not required. The Audubon Institute offers discounts to individuals who wish to visit more than one of its four attractions—Audubon Zoo, Aquarium of the Americas, IMAX Theater, and Louisiana Nature Center.

Kliebert's Alligator and Turtle Farm $
41083 West Yellow Water Road
Hammond
(985) 345–3617, (800) 854–9164

This working farm, dotted with duckweed and clove-covered ponds, was opened to the public in 1984. The Klieberts have been raising turtles for nearly 40 years and alligators for more than two decades. The most popular attraction of the guided tour is the alligator-breeding pond, where visitors can gawk at 250 gators lounging at the water's edge. The largest of the gators, is 16 feet and weighs 1,200 pounds. Around June 1 every year the females begin building nests by piling dirt and grass in mounds 2 feet high. They lay eggs only once between June 15 and July 1. After hatching, the gators are sold for their meat and hides or to breeders in Florida. "By raising them and finding ways to market them," say the Klieberts, "we contribute to their ultimate survival."

More than 17,000 of the farm's turtles produce more than one million eggs each year. Hatchlings are exported and sold for aquariums, children's pets, and food. Special times to visit are April to July during turtle egg-laying season and June 15 to July 1 during alligator egg-laying time. Alli-

gator Day at the farm is held every fall and features free food and entertainment. The gift shop sells gator heads, teeth, feet, jewelry, back scratchers, and just about any gift you can imagine made out of alligator or turtle parts. The farm is open daily noon till dark, March 1 through October 31. To get to Kliebert's, take I–55 north to the Springfield exit. Cross over Louisiana Highway 22 west, turn right onto the Interstate Service Road north, and follow the signs.

New Orleans Multicultural
Tourism Network
2020 St. Charles Avenue, New Orleans
(504) 523–5652
www.soulofneworleans.com

Looking for New Orleans soul in all the right places? A call to the New Orleans Multicultural Tourism Network (NOMTM) can help. The mission of the NOMTM is to promote the diversity of the city and region through its ethnic cultures, heritage, products, and services within the hospitality, travel, and tourism industries. Another goal is to encourage leadership, career, and business opportunities at all levels of the hospitality and tourism industries. Whether your interest lies in exploring the historic Faubourg Treme (America's oldest black neighborhood), the city's best soul food spots, jazz, the heritage of Mardi Gras Indians, or the tradition of second lines, the tourism network can help steer you in the right direction. Call to request a free copy of the 128-page, full-color booklet *The Soul of New Orleans Visitors Guide.*

New Orleans School of Cooking $$$
524 St. Louis Street, New Orleans
(504) 525–2665, (800) 237–4841
www.neworleansschoolofcooking.com

"Our chef is completely bonkers!" While we rarely recommend exploiting anyone's compromised state of mental health for the sake of a good time, visitors are encouraged by the owners to enjoy the Southern humor at one of its three-hour cooking demonstrations. Creole cooking is everyday family fun and no more so than in a melting pot city like New Orleans. Learn the ins and outs of cooking gumbo or bananas Foster in the time-honored Creole tradition that mixes French, Spanish, African, and Indian food cultures. Everyone leaves the class with a full belly and a recipe. Classes are held daily 10:00 A.M. to 1:00 P.M. A two-hour class is offered Monday though Saturday 2:00 to 4:00 P.M. Classes are limited so it's best to make a reservation.

New Orleans School of Glass Works & Printmaking Studio $–$$$$
727 Magazine Street, New Orleans
(504) 529–7277
www.neworleansglassworks.com

Housed in a restored 19th-century storefront, GlassWorks is the South's largest contemporary facility featuring glass sculpture, glass casting, lampworking, stained glass, printmaking, and bookbinding. The school offers free daily demonstrations of Venetian-style glassblowing. Since its opening in 1990, GlassWorks has been the site of exhibitions highlighting the works of emerging as well as prominent artists including the luminous vitrography of Dale Chihuly, the delicate botanical works of Paul Stankard, and the sensual designs of Richard Royal. Have your hand cast in glass, pick out a piece of colorful glass artwork to take home, and chat with an artist. Then get in on the act by signing up for one of the weekend beginner classes. GlassWorks is open Monday through Saturday 11:00 A.M. to 5:00 P.M. (closed Saturday during summer). Admission is free but donations are welcome. No reservations are necessary to see the free demonstrations. Classes are scheduled throughout the year, require reservations, and cost approximately $100 to $198 for two-day sessions.

Old Ursuline Convent $
1100 Chartres Street, New Orleans
(504) 529–3040
www.accesscom.net/ursuline

Constructed in 1745, the Old Ursuline Convent, the oldest building in the Mississippi Valley and the only one to survive French colonial times, is 25 years younger than New Orleans but 25 years older than the United States. Its history is a microcosm of early life here. The Ursuline nuns were both saints and pioneers when they opened the doors of their convent to the orphaned children of the French colonists slaughtered at Fort Rosalie, a pitifully long list of names still visible in the convent's yellowing archives: Louise Chalante, Francoise Caillon, Marie Le Pris, and so on. Here the nuns conducted an academy for the daughters of wealthy plantation owners and the city's Creole aristocracy. It was within these walls that the beautiful Baroness Micaela Almonaster de Pontalba (see the 1850 House) received her schooling. But the sisters also extended their generosity to the less fortunate as well by teaching young black and Indian girls how to make silk fabrics.

The great fire of 1788, which swept away the St. Louis Cathedral and 856 homes in the French Quarter, also threatened the convent, but Pere Antoine with the aid of a "bucket brigade" saved not only this building but also the adjoining Royal Hospital and barracks. It was inside the chapel in 1815 that the nuns and relatives of the men fighting with Andrew Jackson's forces at the Battle of New Orleans spent the night in prayer before the statue of Our Lady of Prompt Succor. New Orleans is a city that never forgets, and each year a solemn mass is offered in thanksgiving for the astounding American victory despite unbelievable odds.

The adjacent St. Mary's Church, the restored old Chapel of the Archbishops, was erected in 1845 and is still used as a house of worship. Especially noteworthy is how it has served successively as a church for French, Spanish, Creole, Irish, German, Slavic, and Italian congregations as well as for Native Americans and the black Sisters of the Holy Family. The old organ pipes in the choir loft serve merely as decorations, as there is no console. Guided tours are offered Tuesday through Friday 10:00 and 11:00 A.M. and 1:00, 2:00, and 3:00 P.M. Saturday; and 11:15 A.M. and 1:00 and 2:00 P.M. Sunday.

St. Charles Avenue Streetcar   **$**
2817 Canal Street, New Orleans
(504) 242-2000
www.regionaltransit.org
If you've never ridden a streetcar, New Orleans is a good place to start. You haven't lived till you've sat on wood-slat seats, feeling the breeze blow on your face through the huge open windows while this electric-powered green giant shakes and rattles as it rolls down St. Charles Avenue. Just think, you're travel-ing around the city the same way New Orleanians have done since before the Civil War. Riding the streetcar is one of the best ways to leisurely soak up the oozing charm of St. Charles Avenue, not the least of which are the famous thor-oughfare's canopies of moss-draped oak trees, Garden District mansions, Audubon Park, and Tulane and Loyola Universities. If you ride the streetcar all the way to the end and back, the whole trip will take about 90 minutes. Best times to ride are late morning and early afternoon when it's least crowded. Catch the streetcar at Canal and Carondelet Streets. It costs $1.25 per person each way, and exact change is required.

Six Flags New Orleans   **$$$**
12301 Lake Forest Boulevard
New Orleans
(504) 253-8000
www.sixflags.com
Whether you prefer to rock, roll, rotate, twist, tilt, or free-fall (or all of the above), chances are there is a ride with your name on it at Six Flags New Orleans. Six Flags's purchase of Jazzland in 2002 not only rescued the city's only amusement park but also pumped new adrenaline into what is fast becoming a favorite attraction among locals and visitors. 2003 saw the debut of two new state-of-the-art roller coasters: Batman: The Ride, with its ski-lift–style chairs that soar 105 feet into the air through corkscrews and hairpin turns

at speeds of 50 mph; and The Jester, with its 1,936-foot steel track that sends riders on a 79-foot drop and five 360-degree vertical loops—backward! Batman and Jester share the Six Flags New Orleans sky with other high speed thrill rides such as the 65-mph wooden-track Mega Zeph and the Zydeco Scream's boomeranging inverted loops. Others who prefer the spine-tingling chills of sheer vertical drops strap into the Sonic Slam or free-fall (not all the way down, of course) 180 feet from the top of the Skycoaster over (but not into) the water basin. Tamer spirits mean-time can enjoy a heron's-eye view of the city from the top of the 90-foot-tall Big Easy Ferris Wheel or swing back and forth—higher and higher—on the high seas aboard Lafitte's Pirate Ship. Family fun has never seemed quite so, well, fun. Suffice to say, Six Flags New Orleans also is proba-bly the best place in town to overcome acrophobia.

Even classic amusement park fun gets its due thanks to bumper cars (Beach Bang Up) and a carousel (Mardi Gras Menagerie), as well as water-splash and twister rides (Spillway Splashout and Muskrat Scrambler, respectively). Visitors can also experience a virtual pirate encounter as well as the sensation of ris-ing through a swamp (this one features a colorful alligator character). A children's section is chockablock with pint-size rides. Youngsters can also root for Batman while he tracks down Gotham City's biggest vil-lains. Plenty of shows and events through-out the park include the "American Rock" revue at the Orpheum Theatre on Main Street, performances by Rockin' Country at Gator's LaCroix's Dockside Café, and a chance to sing along with Bugs Bunny, Daffy Duck, Sylvester, Tweety, Foghorn Leghorn, and the rest of the gang at the new Looney Tunes Theater. (If you've got tykes in tow, they'll want to get to the park early when the Looney Tunes gang is on hand to sign autographs.) The park also offers rentals for lockers, strollers and wheelchairs, plus numerous shopping and souvenir venues and food outlets virtually everywhere you turn. Six Flags New Orleans, located 12 miles from downtown New Orleans, operates seasonally. Call for days, times, and admission. To get here take I-10 east to the Lake Forest Boulevard offramp. Follow the sign.

HOME SWEET HOMES

New Orleans's elegant old homes are time-honored barometers of architecture, culture, and taste, each of which contributes a chapter to the 300-year-old story of the city's mostly well-heeled Creole and American families, as well as the laudable ethic of savvy preservation efforts among those who knew good real estate when they saw it. How any of these relics survived the seemingly nonstop calamity of fires, hurricanes, war, and economic downturns is almost anyone's guess.

But survive they did. Historic preservation in New Orleans is an ongoing, time-consuming, dollar-sapping endeavor that brings together concerned citizens for a common cause. In the past, the city often has been accused of laziness in regards to these and other such efforts—and it shows. Some historic homes worthy of restoration in historic districts look as though they are ripe for joining the crackhouse roster. Some have been bulldozed for new construction. Fortunately, nonprofit groups such as the Preservation Resource Center have stepped in to offer potential homeowners the chance to buy and restore century-old Victorian camelback homes in blighted neighborhoods on the verge (hopefully) of a renaissance.

Following are some of the most painstakingly restored, preserved, and attended-to homes in the city. Don't miss them.

Beauregard-Keyes House $
1113 Chartres Street, New Orleans
(504) 523-7257
The kind of compact architectural scale historic New Orleans homes are known for is admirably exemplified by this house, occasionally referred to by those who know about such things as "a fascinating old raised cottage." Though not a cottage by common standards, this house stands as a stunning example of the raised Creole cottage.

Located opposite the Old Ursuline Convent, this yellow-with-white-trim house built in 1826 by well-heeled auctioneer Joseph Le Carpentier and designed by architect Francois Correjolles, like so many others of its ilk, has a checkered history of passing through numerous owners' hands, falling into disrepair, and eventually being restored to its former glory. The fate of this house, however, was almost worse: In 1926 the owner announced plans to demolish it and erect a macaroni factory.

Pasta's loss was New Orleans's gain. The fact that noted Confederate General P. G. T. Beauregard had once lived here for 18 months following his return to New Orleans after the Civil War aroused the interest of a group of patriotic women, who begged and borrowed funds to save the house. In 1944 well-known novelist Frances Parkinson Keyes rented the house and eventually took it over from the preservation group and started work on its badly needed restoration until it was once again a stately edifice. Four years later the Keyes Foundation was set up and the house entrusted to its care. Keyes made the "cottage" her winter residence for a quarter of a century and wrote several of her 51 books here, including *Dinner at Antoine's, The Chess Players, Madame Castel's Lodger,* which was about General Beauregard, and *Blue Camellia.*

The ballroom, parlor, library, halls, bedrooms, and rear gallery were completely restored by New Orleans architect Richard Koch, director of the Historic American Buildings Survey in Louisiana. But perhaps the most interesting artifacts in the house built by a Spanish architect for a French auctioneer are the heirloom pieces in the Beauregard Chamber, which belonged to the general and his family. Docents in period costumes lead guided tours Monday through Saturday 10:00 A.M. to 3:00

P.M. A gift shop carries a selection of Frances Parkinson Keyes's books.

Gallier House Museum $
1118-1132 Royal Street, New Orleans
(504) 525-5661
www.gnofn.org/~hggh

Noted New Orleans architect James Gallier Jr. wasted no time in fashioning this elegant French Quarter town house for his Creole wife, Aglae, and their four small daughters back in 1857, a time when the young designer was eager to execute his innovative ideas about residential comfort and convenience. For example, because ventilation was important for comfort during New Orleans's long hot summers, Gallier incorporated a skylight and ceiling vents into his 19th-century design, which can still be seen in this completely restored house-museum.

The exterior has typical Creole cast-iron work, while the interior blends a traditional town house floor plan with Gallier's own ingenuity, such as the composite columns and the unusual plaster cornice work of the double parlor. The collection includes a complete bedroom suite by master cabinetmaker Prudent Mallard and parlor chairs by John Henry Belter.

Gallier's eclectic and stylish design reflects the latest of Victorian taste, with fine New Orleans–made mahogany and rosewood furniture, colorful wool carpets woven on antique looms in England, period French wallpaper, and hand-painted window shades. Utilitarian items such as a cypress icebox, ironing equipment, and a fly-catch appear in their proper places.

A National Historic Landmark and the third museum in Louisiana to be accredited by the American Association of Museums, Gallier House opened to the public in 1971 after extensive archaeological and documentary research. Recently hailed by the *New York Times* as "one of the best small museums in the country," Gallier House offers unique insights into the lifestyle of a bygone era. The museum complex includes two adjacent 1830s commercial buildings converted into exhibit space for Victorian art and a museum shop.

Gallier was born in England in 1827, the son of an Irish architect-builder who brought his family to America in 1832. The father, James Gallier Sr., became a successful architect with the building of Municipality Hall, built in 1845 and now known as Gallier Hall in his honor. In 1849 the senior Gallier turned his practice over to his son, who is best remembered as the designer of one of the city's most elaborate facilities, the famous French Opera House, which was destroyed by fire in 1919. Other examples of James Gallier Jr.'s architectural skill include his Bank of America building, built in 1866 on Exchange Place and probably the first in New Orleans to have a structural cast-iron front, and the Florence A. Luling House, built in 1865 and later used as the Jockey Club. Docents lead guided tours Monday through Saturday 10:00 A.M. to 4:00 P.M. and present an accurate and engaging interpretation of life in the prosperous and cosmopolitan New Orleans of the 1850s.

Hermann-Grima House $
820 St. Louis Street, New Orleans
(504) 525-5661
www.gnofn.org/~hggh

This handsome two-story brick mansion, designed by Virginia architect William Brand for Samuel Hermann in 1831, is generally considered to be the best example in the Vieux Carré of American influence on New Orleans architecture—and one of the most elegant residences in the Crescent City. The complex includes a working 1831 French kitchen complete with oven, potagers, and open hearth, an unusual cast-iron cistern, the last private stable in the French Quarter, and original parterre beds filled with fragrant flowering plants. Some of the amenities include marble mantels, faux bois doors, and hand-carved wooden friezes in the parlor and dining room.

Samuel Hermann came to Louisiana from Germany the year after the Louisiana

Purchase and settled in New Orleans in 1815. Fifteen years later he had amassed a substantial fortune as an entrepreneur, banker, and broker, and his newfound wealth was amply expressed in the splendid mansion on St. Louis Street. Hermann's successes were not immune to the Panic of 1837, and he was forced to sell his home in 1844 to prominent New Orleans judge Felix Grima. The house remained in the Grima family until 1921. After restoration, the house opened to the public in 1971 and today depicts the lifestyle of a prosperous Creole family in the years from 1830 to 1860. Elegant furnishings include family portraits, fine American and Rococo Revival pieces, English loom–woven wool carpets, and silk damask draperies reproduced by Scalamandre from an 1830s pattern.

On Thursday from October to May, volunteer cooks prepare meals in the restored kitchen following period recipes. History becomes palpable as visitors see egg whites whipped with birch whisks, smell gumbo simmering on the potager, and feel the intense heat and bustle of an urban 19th-century kitchen. Each December the house is authentically decorated with fresh boxwood garlands, apple topiaries, festive table settings, and a tree with handmade ornaments for Christmas and New Year's celebrations. This National Historic Landmark is open for tours Monday through Friday 10:00 A.M. to 4:00 P.M.

Pitot House Museum $
1440 Moss Street, New Orleans
(504) 581–3824, (504) 915–0815
www.pitothouse.org
It's easy to miss this plantation house, the only one in New Orleans open to the public on a regular basis, because of the distractingly pretty scenery of nearby Bayou St. John. So double back and take a peek inside one of the few West Indies–style houses that lined the bayou in the 1700s—you won't be disappointed. With its stucco-covered, brick-between-post construction and double-pitched hipped roof, the Pitot House was restored to its original

18th-century condition by the Louisiana Landmarks Society in the 1960s and is furnished with Louisiana and American antiques from the period. The Louisiana Landmarks Society was founded in 1950 to promote the preservation of Louisiana's historical and architectural heritage.

James Pitot bought the typical colonial Louisiana house in 1810 as a country home for his family. He was the first mayor of the incorporated City of New Orleans in 1804–05, and later appointed a parish court judge by Louisiana's governor. Within easy walking distance from the New Orleans Museum of Art in City Park, the house is open for tours Wednesday through Saturday 10:00 A.M. to 3:00 P.M.

The Van Benthuysen-Elms Mansion $
3029 St. Charles Avenue, New Orleans
(504) 895–5493
www.elmsmansion.com
If the Italianate walls of this antebellum mansion could talk, they might have a few asides to offer about Oprah Winfrey, Liberace, Xavier Cougat, and other luminaries who have celebrated special events over the decades in this historic landmark in the heart of the Garden District. The three-story house was built on St. Charles Avenue in 1869 for Watson van Benthuysen Jr., who just so happened to be president of the company that operated the St. Charles Avenue streetcar line. Flourishes illuminating the grand foyer include hand-carved woodwork and inlaid floors of Flemish oak, a freestanding staircase with an unusual newel post, gold-plate sconces, and an authentic copper wind chime that once hung from the ceiling of a Chinese temple.

And yes, the Empire Room does feature 24-karat gold Doré sconces and hand-stenciled, hand-painted canvas wall coverings and furnishings. The Louis XVI Room houses an imported hand-carved mantel of Carrara marble, imported French mirrors and consoles, 48-foot grand ballroom lead-glass windows, and a ceiling fashioned after that of Brussels's town hall.

ATTRACTIONS AND ACTIVITIES

*From jazz and food to religion and soci-
ety, and so much in between, the contributions of African Americans past and
present have given New Orleans a heart
and soul all its own. And one of the best
ways to explore and experience what
makes the Big Easy unlike any other
place in the world is by taking one of
the city's black heritage tours.*

But for us the most interesting nugget
of nuance by far is that the house was
used as the German consulate between
World Wars I and II. Imagine in 1930 the
look on the face of the first consul, Rolf L.
Jaeger, when he was received by then-
Gov. Huey P. Long in his Roosevelt Hotel
suite wearing only green silk pajamas.
Jaeger was furious.

It gets stranger. In 1937 the dashing
and oh-so-aristocratic Baron Edgar von
Spielgel, a submarine commander in
World War I, arrived in New Orleans as the
newly appointed German consul general
for the Southern states. By 1946 von
Spielgel, who was back in Europe, was
identified by *Times-Picayune* reporter
Meigs O. Frost as "Hitler's No. 2 spy and
sabotage commander in the United
States," whose aim had been to wreck the
port of New Orleans, vital to the war
effort. Luckily for us, von Spielgel was
apparently no better a saboteur than
Long was a diplomat. The house is open
for tours Monday through Friday 10:00
A.M. to 2:00 P.M. Tours last approximately
20 to 30 minutes.

MUSEUMS: THE "OTHER" HOUSES OF WORSHIP

The Arsenal $
600 St. Peter Street, New Orleans
(504) 568-6968
lsm.crt.state.la.us
Looking to earn extra points toward your
New Orleans coffee merit badge? The
best place for field research (after Cafe du

Monde, of course) may be the Arsenal,
home to the exhibit "Freshly Brewed:
The Coffee Trade and the Port of New
Orleans." Entry to the museum, built in
1839, is through the Cabildo. The Arsenal,
which occupies the original 1769 site of
the Spanish arsenal, also presents special
and short-term exhibitions, lectures, seminars, and interactive programs for both
adults and children.

The Louisiana State Museum is one of
the region's best values. In New Orleans
visitors may purchase single building tickets or purchase tickets to two or more
properties and receive a 20 percent discount. Visitor guides are available to each
of the buildings. Plan on at least 45 minutes
per building. Optional guided tours, at no
extra cost, take about the same time and
require at least 24 hours' advance notice.

All buildings are open Tuesday
through Sunday 9:00 A.M. to 5:00 P.M. All
state museums are wheelchair accessible
except for the 1850 House. Special accommodations for viewing the house are
offered to individuals who request them.
All visitors who have other special needs
are asked to call in advance to allow
museum staff to make arrangements.

The Cabildo
701 Chartres Street, Jackson Square
New Orleans
(504) 568-6968
lsm.crt.state.la.us
The Cabildo, built from 1795 to 1799 as the
seat of Spanish colonial government in
New Orleans, was the site of the Louisiana
Purchase Transfer, which brought the territory into America's fold and opened up a
vast new frontier for a young country's
explorers, such as Meriwether Lewis and
William Clark. Besides doubling its land
mass, America also got a cosmopolitan
city in the deal, thank you very much, on
December 20, 1803, when the transfer was
officially signed in the Cabildo's Sala
Capitular, or counsel chamber. Because no
artifacts of the event exist, the museum
has re-created what the chamber might
have looked liked, reproducing furnishings

based on a brief surviving inventory and other research. The chamber was also home to the State Supreme Court from 1868 to 1910 and the site of several nationally important rulings, such as those in the cases of *Plessy vs. Ferguson* and the Slaughterhouse Cases, post–Civil War decisions with far-reaching civil rights implications.

Beginning with European settlers' encounters with Native Americans and progressing through the Civil War and Reconstruction, exhibits ranging from Napoleon's death mask, one of only four in existence, to Colonial era domestic items incorporate a charismatic "people" perspective. For example, the "Iberville Stone," located on the first floor, was recovered from Ft. Maurepas, the first permanent French site in Louisiana, settled by Pierre LeMoyne Sieur d'Iberville not long after he reached the mouth of the Mississippi River on Shrove Tuesday (Louisiana's first Mardi Gras) in 1699.

Battle of New Orleans buffs will want to check out the second-floor exhibit of battle relics, weapons, authentic uniforms, a lock of Andrew Jackson's hair, and even the drum of Jordan Noble, a free black man who helped lead Jackson's ragtag army into battle. (Historical note: Free people of color composed about 40 percent of New Orleans's pre–Civil War population, contributing significantly to the city's skilled labor force. Many owned businesses, engaged in professions, and amassed estates.) Adding historical dimension are objects recalling an infamous facet of this era: the proliferation of piracy and smuggling spearheaded by Jean Lafitte and his Baratarian profiteers. A video and fiber-optic map help visitors navigate the complex history.

A French Opera House bell, a bamboula, such as those used at African-American celebrations, and an unusual chordophone, a prototype of the banjo, represents origins of the state's musical traditions. Elsewhere, a leech jar and other medical and scientific equipment, as well as a child's casket, attest to the omnipresent specter of disease and death in the mid-19th century when Louisiana had the highest death rate among states and New Orleans's mortality led other American cities. Plantation life and all its gentility and horror is presented on the third floor in an exhibit that juxtaposes fine china and silver with a slave auction block and iron collar used to restrain slaves.

Confederate Museum $
929 Camp Street, New Orleans
(504) 523–4522
www.confederatemuseum.com
This one-room cypress-walled memorial to Confederate veterans opened its doors on Jan. 8, 1891, and is the oldest museum in the state. Louisiana philanthropist Frank T. Howard constructed the hall as a meeting place for Confederate veterans to reflect on their Civil War stories and to house and protect their relics. He wished that the building and its collection might forever proclaim "how a brave people and their descendants hold the name and the fame of their heroes and martyrs with the admiration undiminished by disaster or defeat and with love unquenched by time."

The Memorial Hall Foundation—Confederate Civil War Museum, located at Lee Circle near Howard Avenue not far from the French Quarter, houses the largest collections of Civil War artifacts in the nation with more than 100 Confederate battle flags, a large array of uniforms, and numerous rare Louisiana-made swords. On display are personal items of such famous figures as Jefferson Davis, Robert E. Lee, P. G. T. Beauregard, Brazton Bragg, and Frank Gardener. Hours are Monday through Saturday 10:00 A.M. to 4:00 P.M.

The 1850 House $
523 St. Ann Street, New Orleans
(504) 568–6968
lsm.crt.state.la.us
It was in 1850 that the Baroness Micaela Almonaster de Pontalba first opened the doors of the two magnificent row houses, patterned after stately French architecture of the period, she had designed and built.

Among the most beautiful—and free—attractions/activities in a city surrounded by water is watching a sunset. Whether it's from the steps of the French Quarter's Moonwalk or along The Point at West End, you'll have the best seat in the house for enjoying nature's daily taps.

They flank Jackson Square on St. Ann and St. Peters Streets. She inherited the land from her father, Don Andres Almonaster y Roxas, a wealthy Spaniard who rebuilt the Cabildo, Presbytere, and St. Louis Cathedral after the fire of 1788 destroyed those buildings along with most of the old city.

The baroness hired noted local architect James Gallier Sr. to design the row houses (though she dismissed him shortly before construction was begun and finished it herself), Henry Howard to work on the architectural drawings, and Samuel Stewart as the builder. When the Pontalba buildings, constructed to stop the increasing deterioration of the old part of the city that had begun in the 1840s, were completed, each contained 16 separate houses on the upper floors and self-contained shops on the ground floors. The cartouches that decorate the cast-iron railings were designed by her and signify the Almonaster and Pontalba families.

The matching block-long structures added style and dimension to the Place d'Armes (later renamed Jackson Square at the urging of the baroness to commemorate General Andrew Jackson, hero of the Battle of New Orleans). After the Civil War the Pontalba buildings fell into disrepair and, by the turn of the century, had become tenements. New Orleans philanthropist William Ratcliffe Irby bought the Lower Pontalba building from the Pontalba heirs in 1921 for $68,000 and willed it to the Louisiana State Museum in 1927. The City of New Orleans ultimately acquired the Upper Pontalba building on the opposite side of Jackson Square. Extensive restoration of the buildings took place under the Works Progress Adminis-

tration in the 1930s while renovation of the interiors occurred in 1955. The museum has re-created what one of these residences might have looked like during the antebellum era and depicts family life—minus the family—during the most prosperous period in the city's history. The original tenants of the 1850 House were A. A. and Isaac Sovia.

The Historic New Orleans Collection $
533 Royal Street, New Orleans
(504) 523-4662
www.hnoc.org
Visitors step through the patio of this French Quarter town house from the late 1800s and into the house-museum of the collection's founders, General and Mrs. L. Kemper Williams. Remodeled for 20th-century living, the house is filled with antique furniture and Chinese porcelains arranged in harmony with contemporary pieces, all of which reflect the gracious 1940s lifestyle of its owners.

This museum and research-exhibit complex includes the Merieult House, built in 1792—one of the few in the French Quarter to have escaped the conflagration of 1794. Beautiful high-ceilinged rooms showcase rare archival photographs, books, and documents from the Williams's collection; other exhibits include documents from the Louisiana Transfer of 1803, maps that show the growth of the city from the original "old square," and an 18th-century self-portrait of Bienville, cofounder of the city of New Orleans. Rooms are organized to provide a chronological history of the city.

Not to be missed is the nearby Williams Research Center at 410 Chartres Street, owned and managed by the same private nonprofit foundation that oversees the Historic New Orleans Collection. The reading room offers access to the bulk of the Williams's collection of books, maps, manuscripts, paintings, prints, drawings, photographs, and artifacts on the history of New Orleans and Louisiana.

The Historic New Orleans Collection and the Williams Research Center are open, free of charge, Tuesday through Saturday 10:00 A.M. to 4:30 P.M. Guided tours are given during the same days at 10:00 and 11:00 A.M. and 2:00 and 3:00 P.M. Children under 12 are not admitted.

Longue Vue House and Gardens $
7 Bamboo Road, New Orleans
(504) 488-5488
www.longuevue.com

Locals are immensely proud of this historic Greek Revival city-estate, former home of the late cotton broker, businessman, and philanthropist Edgar Bloom Stern and his wife, Edith, daughter of Julius Rosenwald, the Sears magnate. Designed by architects William and Geoffrey Platt, the house is surrounded by eight acres of simply superb gardens created by Ellen Biddle Shipman, referred to in her green-thumb circle as the dean of American women landscape architects.

The magnificent twin hearts of Longue Vue gardens are the Spanish Court and its Moorish flourish inspired by the 14th-century Generalife Gardens of the Alhambra in Spain, and somewhat less formal Wild Garden with its "forest walk," both of which are framed by horticultural displays and lyrical fountains. A Discovery Garden for children opened four years ago. Beautiful manicured lawns feature a who's who of New Orleans horticulture: live oaks, magnolias, camellias, azaleas, roses, sweet olives, crape myrtles, and oleanders.

The house itself is an elegant nod to Shipman, who had more than a hand in the interior design, which relies heavily on American and English antiques, needlework, French and Oriental carpets, and a notable British and Continental cream ware pottery collection. Longue Vue's Tuscan columns, circular spaces, and classical molding and friezes are a strong reminder of late-18th-century country houses—the kind really rich people could afford. Visitors are welcomed by a circular vestibule with turn-of-the-19th century Chinese bamboo and cane chairs, the same kind seen at the Brighton Pavilion in England, bottom-lit niches (a mid-20th-century

architectural conceit), and classically inspired circular spaces.

Many of the architectural elements that characterize the exterior of the house are displayed in the center hall, including Doric columns flanking the steps leading down from the circular vestibule into the hall, which serve as introductions to the major rooms. The oak and elm sideboard circa 1750 belonged to Mrs. Stern's mother and came from England.

Some of the more notable rooms also reflect the owners' tastes and include Mrs. Stern's flower arranging room, a library of Norwegian spruce paneling from an 18th-century house in Surrey, England, and a dining room with 19th-century Chinese rice paper, Georgian millwork, Turkish Oushak rugs, and a color scheme of aquamarine, rose, and ecru that reflects the fashionable colors of the late 1930s. Setting the table are examples of the Sterns' Wedgwood "Queen's Ware" collection, one of the largest in the United States.

Not to be outdone is the second-floor drawing room overlooking the gardens, where the Sterns entertained distinguished visitors that included Eleanor Roosevelt, John and Bobby Kennedy, and Pablo Casals. The mantelpiece was carved circa 1800 as a memorial to George Washington. The carpet, Aubusson; the draperies, chinoiserie-patterned chintz. A pair of matched antique Anglo-Irish chandeliers hang from the 14.5-foot ceiling; the walls are covered with an arabesque-patterned damask from Scalamandre in New York. Even the oak chest of drawers, edged with ebony moldings and brass-bail handles, has a pedigree: It was created in 1770 by John Linnell, a fashionable London cabinetmaker who had supplied furniture for Castle Howard in Yorkshire, as well as Osterly Park in Middlesex. The lovely walnut music box created by A. Penelet & Co. of Geneva, Switzerland, in the 1860s, is equipped with six interchangeable cylinders, each having eight songs.

A personal favorite among the rooms is the gift-wrapping room, designed as a place to receive mail and to wrap holiday and birthday gift packages. The cabinets were custom made to hold wrapping paper and other needed items. Visiting hours are Monday through Saturday 10:00 A.M. to 4:30 P.M. (last tour 4:00 P.M.), and Sunday 1:00 to 5:00 P.M. (last tour 4:15 P.M.). Building on the tradition of community service established by the family, Longue Vue has programs for school children and older and disabled adults. Ongoing educational programs for both adults and children include those on the decorative arts and horticulture, summer gardening classes, workshops, seminars, and lectures.

This is exactly how the lady of the house wanted it. One of Mrs. Stern's final philanthropic gestures was the creation of a nonprofit foundation to maintain her house and gardens for the public to enjoy. When she died at age 85 in 1980, 21 years after her husband's death and less than 10 months after the house was opened, she expressed the wish "that my house and garden will serve some public use." Here's to you, Mrs. Stern.

Louisiana State Museum $
751 Chartres Street, New Orleans
(504) 568-6968, (800) 568-6968
lsm.crt.state.la.us
To enter into the Louisiana State Museum and its historic structures is to venture through a gateway to Louisiana's past. One of New Orleans's top attractions, the state museum is actually a collection of nine structures throughout Louisiana, five of which are located near Jackson Square in the heart of the French Quarter: the Cabildo, the Presbytere, the Old U.S. Mint, the 1850 House, and the Arsenal. We will focus on these.

Flanking the St. Louis Cathedral are the twin Cabildo and Presbytere buildings, both national historic landmarks whose collections and exhibits showcase turning points in Louisiana history, as well as the ongoing evolution characterized by dramatic social change and cultural diversity. Standing at the statue of Andrew Jackson in Jackson Square facing St. Louis Cathe-

dral, the Cabildo is on your left and the Presbytere is on your right.

Musée Conti $
(The Wax Museum)
917 Conti Street, New Orleans
(504) 525-2605, (800) 233-5405
www.get-waxed.com
The tradition of wax figures dates back to ancient Babylon and has continued throughout the ages. Alexander the Great commissioned a personal wax sculptor a century before the birth of Christ, and the art was common in ancient Rome. European medieval fairs always featured a collection of wax figures. And New Orleans has the Musée Conti, proof that this is indeed the most European city in America, not because of its name, but rather its contents. Other cities tout wax museums whose biggest draw is a figure of George Burns. The Musée Conti, on the other hand, tells the tale of New Orleans and depicts everything from the city's founding to the legendary Battle of New Orleans, to the mysterious world of voodoo. Just for fun there's also the Haunted Dungeon with more than 20 monsters.

The painstaking, European-style craftsmanship that went into creating this French Quarter facility is unparalleled in the United States. Ordinary beeswax was combined with a secret chemical compound and infused coloring to create the remarkably lifelike figures; each strand of human hair, imported from Italy, was attached with a special needle. All male figures were given full beards. Look closely and notice that even the clean-shaven ones have a faint stubble. Only the most natural-looking, medical glass eyes were used. They were imported from Germany, a country long famous for supremacy in creating optical glass.

Note also the size of the figures. They may appear smaller than life-size but they are accurately portrayed. The human race has steadily gained in average height with the biggest jumps recorded in the last 100 years. The museum is open Monday through Saturday 10:00 A.M. to 5:00 P.M.,

Sunday noon to 5:00 P.M., and for private appointments. The museum is located on Conti Street between Burgundy and Dauphine Streets in the French Quarter.

**New Orleans Fire Department
Museum and Educational Center $
1135 Washington Avenue, New Orleans
(504) 896–4756
www.tmc.tulane.edu/oehs/firemus.htm**
Built in the 1850s, the Washington Avenue Firehouse was home to the City of Lafayette firefighters and their valiant fire horses that often could be heard galloping through the streets of what was to become Uptown New Orleans. The mighty steeds pulled a steam-driven pump made of gleaming brass seated atop a wooden chassis painted shiny red. Later known as Chalmette No. 23, the station was the city's last to trade in its horses for motorized transport in the Roaring '20s and remained a viable firehouse for another half century. In 1995 the building underwent extensive restoration and opened as a museum full of historic memorabilia. See a real hand-drawn ladder truck and a fire-alarm telegraph, both of which predate the Civil War, as well as the collection of authentic firefighting equipment used over the last 150 years. The museum is open Monday through Friday 9:00 A.M. to 2:00 P.M. Groups of six or more should call ahead to check on guide availability. Admission is free but donations are welcome. To get to the museum, take the St. Charles Avenue streetcar to Washington Avenue. Walk up Washington past Commanders Place, toward the Mississippi River about 5 blocks.

**New Orleans Historic
Voodoo Museum $
724 Dumaine Street, New Orleans
(504) 523–7685
www.voodoomuseum.com**
Cynics may take one look around inside the dusky foyer, where voodoo dolls in little cardboard coffins are sold alongside good-luck herbs, wealth candles, and love potions, and wonder when the zombies

are going to show up moaning for blood. But anyone who has read John Tallant's book *Voodoo in New Orleans* or Harvard ethnobotanist Wade Davis's accounts of his scientific exploration of voodoo in Haiti, *The Serpent and the Rainbow,* simply knows better.

Voodoo is a bona fide religion practiced seriously in New Orleans even to this day. And owner-curator Charles Gandolfo's museum offers the curious and skeptic alike one of the best places to discover the history and modern-day practices of this ancient and deeply spiritual African belief system. Memorial prayer altars, displays of occult objects including African and Caribbean masks as well as gris-gris and ju-ju from around the world, "spirit boxes," a live python, and, of course, a portrait of voodoo queen Marie Laveau tell the story of voodoo in New Orleans. Guided tours of the museum are conducted daily 10:00 A.M. to dusk.

**New Orleans Museum of Art $
P.O. Box 19123, City Park, New Orleans
70124-4603
(504) 488–2631**
Maybe size really doesn't matter. But a recently completed $23.5 million expansion project, which added 55,000 square feet to City Park's largest structure, sure has given locals something to crow about—and more room to roam. Founded in 1910 with a gift to the city from philanthropist Isaac Delgado, NOMA, the city's oldest fine art organization, has a permanent world-class collection of more than 35,000 objects valued in excess of $200 million. And with its recent expansion, the museum's strong suits—French and American art, photography, glass, African works, and Japanese paintings from the 17th- to 18th-century Edo period—only continue to grow.

The facility's comprehensive study of French art includes such treasures as groups of work by French Impressionist Edgar Degas, who visited maternal relatives in New Orleans in 1871 and painted in a house on Esplanade Avenue just 12

New Orleans Historic Voodoo Museum

Some years back a close friend living in Florida was gripped by a downturn in economic circumstances. After deliberating the dilemma a few days, the guiding light of reason revealed a uniquely Big Easy solution: gris-gris. Traditionally, gris-gris (pronounced GREE-GREE) is a red felt bag filled with secret scented herbs, briefly flamed, blessed by a priestess, then tied with a black ribbon. The individual needing help in matters of love, health, court cases, or, in this instance, finances, carries it. But how does even the most sympathetic of friends come by one of these time-honored, "protective" voodoo charms?

In this city that place is the New Orleans Historic Voodoo Museum at 724 Dumaine Street. This dusky French Quarter museum celebrating nearly 30 years keeps alive the flickering flame of ancient voodoo traditions while promoting the understanding and modern teachings of this oft-maligned mystical religion. Newcomers take note: Don't refer to it as "spooky."

Voodoo—or, voudou, as the Lousiana-French spell it—was brought to New Orleans in the 1700s by shackled slaves from West Africa, Haiti, and Santo Domingo stripped of virtually everything save for their deeply rooted spiritual beliefs. The religion has been practiced in New Orleans for nearly 300 years but reached its zenith in the late 19th century when Creole hairdresser Marie Laveau's secret nighttime rituals on the banks of Bayou St. John earned her the reputation as the city's voodoo queen—and someone not to be trifled with.

"Voodoo is such an important part of New Orleans history," John T. Martin, who is in charge of the museum's special rituals, said, adding, "We aren't here to recruit, we're here to enlighten."

Far from the laughable and even racist stereotypes presented in Hollywood B-movies, voodoo, at its heart, is a deeply spiritual and rich belief system that for centuries was passed down by African elders to youth in the oral tradition. When voodoo-practicing slaves in the New World were forced to convert to Christianity, they incorporated some Catholic traditions, initially for the sake of appearances lest they be punished or even put to death. One tradition that took hold, though, was the use of altars to pray to saints to intercede to God for favors. This practice closely paralleled the ancient voodoo custom of praying to the spirits of nature—wind and rain, lightning and thunder, rivers and oceans, animals and trees—for the same reason. It was a match made in heaven.

Consider: Laveau, a devout Roman Catholic who died in 1881, often would conduct her rituals after Mass in the gardens behind St. Louis Cathedral, said Martin. Controversy has always surrounded her exact place of burial. But it is widely believed that St. Louis Cemetery No. 1 is the final resting place of one of New Orleans's most intriguing and, according to accounts of the day, bewitchingly beautiful historical characters.

New Orleans Historic Voodoo Museum is where visitors can learn more about this religion as well as buy gris-gris bags. JAMES GAFFNEY

Today people from all over the world seek out the museum and its owner-curator Charles M. Gandolfo, an artist and historian, to learn about the religion's animism-meets-Catholicism roots in New Orleans. In one room of the museum is the "wishing stump," a carved totem reportedly used by Laveau for her rituals at Bayou St. John to attract ancestors and repel evil spirits. Visitors bring offerings as well as pictures of friends and family who have petitioned the spirits, or loas, for health, wealth, love, and reconciliation. Nearby is the 100-pound Burmese python, Zombie, named after Laveau's snake, and the same kind of altar used by practitioners of the Spanish-Caribbean version of voodoo, called santeria.

Other rooms feature an 1850s-style parlor where gris-gris bags are meticulously prepared and Haitian paintings, Gandolfo's original artworks, occult masks, and a "witchstand" incense burner dating to the 1600s are displayed among other artifacts. Visitors who pay $15 can observe and participate in one of the two-hour public rituals occasionally hosted by Martin in his third-floor home above the museum. During the hypnotic, drum-fueled damballah dance, a live python is passed among willing participants.

"It's a full-blown ritual for healing or for reconciliation," says Martin. "The drumming becomes very sensuous and driving, and it's amazing what it does to people—it's mesmerizing." On the night of June 23, St. John's Eve, visitors meet at the museum and are escorted to a secret courtyard destination for an ancient ritual commemorating the growing season of the planting cycle.

"I don't think there is anything wrong about being skeptical," Martin said when asked what he tells voodoo cynics, "but I think people need to make themselves aware of other religions and practices and views."

As for the fate of the Florida friend who received the gris-gris? Life couldn't be better. Call it a coincidence.

blocks from the museum. Works by the masters of the School of Paris include paintings and sculptures by Picasso, Braque, Dufy, and Miró.

A unique Arts of the Americas collection surveys the cultural heritage of North, Central, and South America from the pre-Columbian through the Spanish colonial periods, with special emphasis on objects from the Mayan civilization of Mexico and Central America, and paintings and sculpture from Cuzco, the Spanish Viceregal capital of Peru. A display of American art is found in a suite of period rooms featuring 18th- and 19th-century furniture and decorative arts.

One of the more popular collections in this 130,000-square-foot gem is the work of Peter Carl Fabergé (1846–1920), master jeweler to the last czars of Russia, on loan from the Matilda Geddings Gray Foundation. Three Imperial easter eggs, as well as the famous jeweled Imperial lilies-of-the-valley basket, crafted in 1896 for the Empress Alexandra Feodorovna, highlight this exhibit.

Besides enhancing New Orleans's reputation as a major tourist and convention center, NOMA also plays an important role as an educational resource. Each year the museum opens its doors to more than 25,000 schoolchildren for free guided tours, and on Thursday 10:00 A.M. to noon

any Louisiana resident with valid identification gets in at no charge. NOMA's museum-on-wheels, "Van Go," serves as an educational liaison between the museum and the New Orleans area.

A good place to rest tired feet is at the Courtyard Cafe, which offers a light menu of salads and sandwiches, and, more important, a view overlooking City Park's scenic lagoons and giant live oaks. Hours are Tuesday through Sunday 10:00 A.M. to 5:00 P.M. except Thursday when the hours are 12:30 to 8:30 P.M. Louisiana residents enter for free from 5:00 to 8:00 P.M. on Thursday only. On occasion there may be an additional charge for major international exhibits. NOMA is located in City Park, convenient to the City Park/Metairie Road exit of I-10. The museum may be reached by public bus via the Carrollton Avenue or Esplanade bus lines of the RTA. Ample free parking is available, and the museum is fully accessible to the handicapped.

New Orleans Pharmacy Museum $
514 Chartres Street, New Orleans
(504) 565-8027
www.pharmacymuseum.org
In 1823 Louis J. Dufilho Jr., America's first licensed pharmacist, built his apothecary on Chartres Street in the French Quarter. The walled courtyard contained a botanical garden, which supplied medicinal

herbs for the pharmacy. As was common, Dufilho worked as both a pharmacist and a doctor. In fact, in those days the pharmacist was sort of a chemist-of-all-trades who also blended perfumes, cosmetics, and housepaint available only at the apothecary. The museum still has Dufilho's curved glass cosmetics case filled with century-old face paint and perfume bottles. The museum also contains hand-blown antique glass jars containing crude drugs and herbs as well as voodoo powders and gris-gris potions.

Mayor Robert Maestri bought the building in 1937 and donated it to the city to be converted into a Napoleonic museum honoring Napoleon. Why? Maestri had heard the legend that the structure had been built by pirate Jean Lafitte and his brother, Alexandre, as the future home for the French emperor after they rescued him from a prison on St. Helena. But the legend was false. Once city officials discovered the truth, the place was instead turned into a pharmacy museum. The building, located on Chartres Street between St. Louis and Toulouse Streets, is open Tuesday through Sunday 10:00 A.M. to 5:00 P.M.

The Old U.S. Mint $
400 Esplanade Avenue, New Orleans
(504) 568–6968
lsm.crt.state.la.us
What earns this national historic landmark, constructed in 1835 during the presidency of Andrew Jackson, its stripes is the fact that it is the only building in the United States to have served both as a U.S. and a Confederate Mint. President Jackson, hero of the Battle of New Orleans, advocated the establishment of a mint in New Orleans to provide much-needed hard currency for Western expansion, as well as to wrest power from Eastern bankers who wanted to consolidate their resources in that part of the country.

New Orleans was a good choice for a mint. In the 1830s it was the fifth-largest city in the nation and the largest in the South and West. The city was also home to one of the United States' most active ports, attracting goods and people from all over the world; more foreign trade was transacted in New Orleans at this time than in any other part of the country. It didn't hurt either that New Orleans was situated near recently discovered gold deposits in Alabama. The Greek Revival–style Mint and its Ionic porticos and simple classic lines were designed by renowned architect William Strickland and its construction supervised by two New Orleanians— Benjamin F. Cox, a master carpenter, and John Mitchell, a master mason and builder.

The Mint's originally hand-powered coining machinery was replaced in 1845 with steam power, a sign of the ever-widening influence of the Industrial Revolution. Interestingly, when structural flaws began to show in the mid-1850s, officials hired P.G.T. Beauregard, a recent West Point engineering graduate, to fireproof the building and add masonry flooring and iron beams to the edifice. Beauregard is best known as the commander of the Confederate forces that fired upon Fort Sumter on April 12, 1861, igniting the Civil War.

Louisiana had already seceded from the Union, and the Mint was transferred to the Confederate States Army for its own coinage operations. Later it was used to house Confederate troops. In 1879, following Reconstruction, the Mint reopened and its labor force of coiners, melters, pressers, cutters, and rollers set to work. Conditions were harsh, as windows were kept shut to prevent even the slightest draft from disturbing the delicate balances that weighed money. According to a May 31, 1891, report in the *New Orleans Daily Tribune*, ". . . the only air in the room (enters) through ventilators and gauze wire doors opening on the gallery; but even these must be closed if the breeze blows too strongly, and one may imagine what is in that room—thirty-nine people breathing the same impure air and (inhaling) the poisonous silver dust into their lungs." Not fun.

The Mint ceased operations in 1909 and its machinery moved to Philadelphia after the federal government decided that facilities in San Francisco and Denver were more than adequate to meet demands. In 1966 Uncle Sam transferred the property to the State of Louisiana, and between 1974 and 1981 the Mint was transformed into a museum and research center devoted to Louisiana history.

Today the Mint is home to a notable exhibit: the "New Orleans Jazz" exhibit, which tells the story of this Big Easy–born art form from its humble street origins to current world renown through vintage photographs, authentic recordings, and the lovingly worn instruments of such musical legends as Louis Armstrong and Sidney Bechet. The Old U.S. Mint is within easy walking distance of Jackson Square and is located across the street from the French Market at the Mississippi River. Open Thursday through Sunday 9:00 A.M. to 5:00 P.M.

The Presbytere $
751 Chartres Street (Jackson Square)
New Orleans
(504) 568-6968
http://lsm.crt.state.la.us
Capuchin monks of St. Louis Cathedral were supposed to be (but never were) the first residents of the Presbytere, built in 1791 to match the Cabildo (Town Hall). The lower floor, completed in 1797 by philanthropist Don Andres Almonester y Roxas, was rented for shops. Under the administration of Baron de Carondelet, it was used for governmental purposes.

It wasn't until 1813 that the second floor was added by the wardens of St. Louis Cathedral and the Presbytere was completed, the result of a lawsuit between the church and Almonester's widow. The matter was settled in 1801 when King Charles of Spain relieved the Almonester family from any obligation to complete the Presbytere. Rear wings were added in 1840, and seven years later the mansard roof and cupola were added to complement the scale of the newly rebuilt cathedral and the proposed new Pontalba buildings. The City of New Orleans pur-

chased the building in 1853 and used it as a courthouse until 1911. The cupola was destroyed in a hurricane four years later and was not rebuilt.

The Presbytere today is home to eclectic exhibits of Louisiana's quixotic heritage past and present. If men's and women's evening wear from the turn of the last century to the present doesn't grab your attention, you will certainly be interested in the collection of rare and historic maps, colonial era paintings, and an exhibit called "In the Eye of the Beholder," which features medical instruments, folk art, mourning jewelry, and World War I weapons. They also have an exhibit called "Carnival Time: Mardi Gras in Louisiana."

RIVERTOWN MUSEUMS

Cannes Brulee Native
American Center $
303 Williams Boulevard, Kenner
(504) 468-7231, (800) 473-6789
Rivertown's most distinctive museum, the outdoor Cannes Brulee, is located behind the Wildlife Museum and showcases the traditions of the area's first inhabitants. Native Americans who wear traditional dress and demonstrate their cultural heritage through the presentation of rituals, domestic and occupational crafts, and native foods run this history exhibition (Saturday 9:00 A.M. to 4:00 P.M.). The site features a palmetto hut, a chickee (pole house with raised platform floor and palmetto roof), a mud and moss house, and a variety of pirogues. The look of the place is continuously changing as crops grow, bear fruit, and wither among the resident population of turkeys, ducks, rabbits, and chickens.

Visitors are invited to join in such activities as mud-oven construction, singing, dancing, beading, and cooking. There are also seasonal ceremonial events throughout the year. Cannes Brulee is the name given to the area by early European explorers. Meaning "burnt cane," the Europeans so dubbed the area after coming across Native Americans who would cut and burn river cane to help drive out small game.

Louisiana Wildlife Museum and Aquarium $
303 Williams Boulevard, Kenner
(504) 468-7231, (800) 473-6789
Alligators, turtles, egrets, and eels are just a part of this museum's extensive collection of more than 700 preserved (stuffed) animal specimens including birds, reptiles, and mammals presented in natural habitat exhibits. A 15,000-gallon freshwater aquarium gives visitors the opportunity to get an up-close view of the state's marine life from perch to turtles. A scale model oil rig and a full-size escape capsule are popular features of the Gulf of Mexico exhibit.

The Mardi Gras Museum $
415 Williams Boulevard, Kenner
(504) 468-7231, (800) 473-6789
The Mardi Gras Museum brings Carnival to life year-round with the most extensive array of memorabilia, photographs, videos, and costumes ever assembled on the subject. Miniature float replicas, elaborate costumes, giant walking figures, and a huge papier-mâché king cake make a great introduction to the so-called greatest free show on earth. Visitors step into Mardi Gras in a street-scene reproduction complete with all the sights and sounds of New Orleans's most popular party. Self-guided tours include the 20-minute Richard Dreyfus–narrated video *Farewell to the Flesh,* as well as 13 other videos shown throughout the museum, which highlight the traditions of Mardi Gras. Live costume-making and float-building demonstrations are scheduled periodically.

Rivertown
415 Williams Boulevard, Kenner
(504) 468-7231
www.rivertownkenner.com
A 4-block riverside stretch of Williams Boulevard in Kenner, 25 minutes from downtown New Orleans (if you're traffic lucky), is home to an impressive cluster of six modest-size, family-friendly museums: the Toy Train Museum; the Mardi Gras Museum; the Saints Hall of Fame; the Science Center, Planetarium, Observatory, and Space Station; the Wildlife and Fisheries Museum and Aquarium; and the Cannes Brulee Native American Center. The Children's Castle and the Rivertown Repertory Theatre are also located here.

Spend a half to full day exploring some or all of Rivertown's museums, all of which are open Tuesday through Saturday 9:00 A.M. to 5:00 P.M. If you plan to visit all the Rivertown museums, purchase a budget-stretching, pay-one-price pass, available at the Rivertown Welcome Center (415 Williams Boulevard). The passes are good for one day. To get here take I-10 west to the Williams Boulevard exit. Turn left (south) on Williams Boulevard and follow the street all the way down until you cross the railroad tracks. Free parking is available.

Saints Hall of Fame $
415 Williams Boulevard, Kenner
(504) 468-7231, (800) 473-6789
Even if you're not a Saints fan, you can enjoy a variety of hands-on (or "feet-on" in the case of the field goal–kicking station) exhibits while testing your knowledge of sports trivia. The museum is unique in NFL cities as a museum by and for fans. Exhibits include tributes to John Gillam's kickoff return touchdown on the opening play of the team's first game and Tom Dempsey's 65-yard record-setting field goal. NFL film highlights can be viewed in the Saints Theater, which features wooden bleachers from old Tulane Stadium, the team's home in days before the Superdome.

Science Center Observatory, Planetarium, and Space Station $
409 Williams Boulevard, Kenner
(504) 468-7231, (800) 473-6789
Tour a life-size NASA space station prototype, the only one of its kind, at this Rivertown museum. The museum's newest exhibit includes live demonstrations, a flight

simulator, and astronaut-training gyroscope; a time line of everyday products originally invented for the space program; Internet links to other space centers around the country; and, believe it or not, live video transmissions from NASA astronauts.

The center offers hands-on exhibits centered on science as it is used in daily living, such as hurricane tracking (which qualifies as a daily living situation in New Orleans), human physiology, and the "secret science" found inside walls. The center is also home to a state-of-the-art planetarium and observatory featuring 30-minute narrated sky shows. Open Friday and Saturday evenings (weather permitting), the observatory offers a view of the stars and constellations through the largest public telescope in Louisiana. Call (504) 468-7229 for current schedules and conditions.

Toy Train Museum $
519 Williams Boulevard, Kenner
(504) 468-7231, (800) 473-6789
Adjacent to the Illinois Central Gulf railroad tracks is this turn-of-the-20th-century building chock-full of hundreds of model trains, with some dating to the 1800s. There's even a train playscape for the little ones, featuring a half-scale caboose playhouse, a make-believe circus, a train engine, and the Dixie Diner, where youngsters can enjoy a play meal.

TOURS: IF IT'S TUESDAY, THIS MUST BE BARATARIA

Most people who think of themselves as savvy travelers would likely blanch at the idea of crowding into an air-conditioned tour bus for three hours to watch the city they came to explore pass before their eyes through polarized window glass. But as both frequent travelers and local yokels, we've found two universal truths regarding tours:

First, whether staying in a new city for a long weekend or two weeks, a general

tour provides a much-needed lay of the land, and that is certainly true in crescent-shaped New Orleans, where geography can often seem baffling. Sometimes even a half-day city tour with a halfway decent guide can provide a good base in history on which to build (though the ones we recommend are among the city's best, naturally) while helping the newcomer nail down points of interest worth exploring again later and at a leisurely pace either by car or on foot. Second, a focused tour of, say, the city's cemeteries will flesh out more of the details and nuances of one aspect of the city than will a more general excursion.

Not surprisingly, in a tourism-based city like New Orleans, the variety of tours is nearly endless. Stroll the French Quarter at sunset and admire its shadowy architecture. Head up River Road into Plantation Country for a glimpse back at antebellum life. Explore the vast contributions of African Americans to the city's diverse social and cultural fabric. Take a paddle wheel cruise from the French Quarter upriver to the zoo. Or paddle a canoe through a Barataria bayou, scanning the cypress-covered banks for graceful, long-legged egrets and sunbathing box turtles, as well as hungry gators patrolling for both, as you go.

Whether it's on foot, in a bus coach or old-fashioned carriage, or aboard an authentic paddle wheeler or Cajun trapper's swamp boat, there are almost as many ways to tour New Orleans as there are things to see. And, please, don't worry—not all of your tour companions will be attired in Mardi Gras–colored purple, green, and gold soccer shirts and alligator-head hats bought on Bourbon Street. And you ...? Here are but a few suggestions—a complete list would be exhaustive and redundant. Many more can be found at your hotel's lobby brochure rack or by asking at the front desk or by contacting the Metropolitan Convention and Visitors Bureau at (504) 566-5011.

French Quarter Walking Tours $
701 Chartres Street, New Orleans
(504) 523-3939
www.frenchquartertour.com
As far as walking tours go, this one provides an excellent overview of French Quarter history and architecture while enabling visitors to help support the Louisiana State Museum. This memorable two-hour walk with a city-licensed Friends of the Cabildo guide starts at the 1850 House Museum Store at 523 St. Ann Street in the French Quarter's Jackson Square and includes admission to two of the Louisiana State Museums: the Cabildo and the 1850 House. Proceeds from tour fees benefit the Friends of the Cabildo, a nonprofit volunteer group organized in 1956 to support the state museum. Customized tours of private homes, the Garden District, and plantations can be arranged on a group basis 30 days in advance.

Gay 90s Carriages Inc./
Royal Carriages $
1824 North Rampart Street, New Orleans
(504) 943-8820
Established in 1941, this is probably the oldest carriage tour operator in the city and definitely one of the most romantic ways to take in the French Quarter. All those honeymooners can't be wrong. The half-hour open-air ride in an authentic carriage starts at the riverside entrance to Jackson Square, across the street from Cafe du Monde, and winds through the French Quarter at a leisurely pace that exasperates most local motorists unlucky enough to get stuck behind the clip-clopping mules. Or simply flag a passenger-free carriage driver anywhere on the street. Some carriages hold up to six passengers.

Le Monde Creole $$
624 Royal Street, New Orleans
(504) 568-1801
www.lemondecreole.com
The 200-year history of five generations of one of New Orleans's oldest Creole families

is recounted during this unique guided storytelling, which offers an intimate glimpse behind the closed doors of secluded and mysterious courtyards. Tickets for tours departing Monday through Saturday at 10:30 A.M. and 1:30 P.M., and Sunday 10:00 A.M. and 1:30 P.M. can be purchased in the shop of Le Monde Creole at 624 Royal Street at the rear of the courtyard.

Le'Ob's Tours
4635 Touro Street, New Orleans
(504) 288-3478
www.leobstours.com
What sets this company apart from the pack is that its tours relate the stories of contributions of French, Irish, Spanish, Greek, Italian, German, African, and Native American settlers from the 1700s to the present. Driving tours vary in length and cost.

Magic Walking Tours
Vampire and Ghost Hunt $$
714 North Rampart Street, New Orleans
(504) 588-9693
www.neworleansmagicwalkingtours.com
It would be hard to disagree that a legacy of death, suffering, decadence, mysticism, voodoo, and vampirism makes New Orleans perhaps the most haunted city in the United States. And this perhaps is best underscored in St. Louis Cemetery No. 1. First-time travelers here who have been subjected to ghost and cemetery tours in other cities may understandably arch a suspicious brow. But people interested in exploring the final resting place of Homer Plessey and voodoo queen Marie Laveau can rest assured. This tour operator promises "no phony vampires, no rubber snakes, no drunken 'guides' in shabby costumes, no quack ghostologists, or vampirologists with phony degrees." Seems ironic that in New Orleans's most historic "city of the dead," this company lives up to its word. This two-hour walking tour leaves Pirate's Alley Cafe at 622 Pirate's Alley (on the side of St. Louis Cathedral in the French Quarter) at 10:30

Treat your taste buds to a Creole-Cajun cooking class and learn firsthand some time-honored New Orleans recipes. Add hot sauce. Then plunge your fork into a plate of spicy chicken-and-sausage jambalaya or dip your spoon into a zesty bowl of fresh okra gumbo. Add more hot sauce. Afterward, write a postcard home saying, "Can't talk—mouth exploded."

A.M. and 1:15 P.M. Nightly vampire and ghost hunt tours start at 8:00 P.M. from Lafitte's Blacksmith Shop at 941 Bourbon Street at St. Phillip Street. No reservations are needed. Just show up and have fun.

New Orleans Tours $$$
4220 Howard Avenue, New Orleans
(504) 592-0560
One of the largest motorcoach tour operators in the city, this company offers several comprehensive daily tours to suit nearly any taste, budget, and schedule. Motorcoach tour packages include a city and riverboat combo; half- and full-day Plantation Country; New Orleans and French Quarter; and swamp. Walking tours include the Garden District or French Quarter. Check with your hotel for exact pickup times.

Southern Seaplane Inc. $$$$
1 Coquille Drive, Belle Chasse
(504) 394-5633
www.bayou-airtours.com
For a real Louisiana high, try a flightseeing trip aboard a seaplane that takes passengers on a fly-by over the city's French Quarter and Superdome before heading south to the bayous and marshes of pirate Jean Lafitte's Barataria. If the 35-minute flight seems too brief, a two-hour trip flies to Kraemer for a 60-minute ground tour of this Cajun town and surrounding wildlife. A five-hour tour is available. All flights are subject to cancellation in the event of bad weather—thank goodness. This Belle Chasse air-charter tourist

company on the West Bank of Jefferson Parish, one of the largest in the Gulf South, has been in business since 1954.

Tours by Isabelle $$$-$$$$
P.O. Box 740972, New Orleans 70174
(504) 391-3544, (877) 665-8687
www.toursbyisabelle.com
This company prides itself on small but highly personalized half- to full-day explorations of the city, plantations, and bayous aboard a passenger van staffed by knowledgeable and licensed guides who speak English, French, Spanish, German, or Italian, depending on the group. The company promises to "make you fall in love with Louisiana," but even if you don't, the tour still provides an intimate alternative to large bus tours. Tour options include a half-day city tour; a combo city tour plus Longue Vue House and Gardens; the plantation tour, which includes Oak Alley, Madewood, and Nottoway; the 90-minute bayou tour with a Cajun guide-trapper; and the "grand tour," which takes in Oak Alley and Destrehan plantations plus a trapper's boat excursion along Bayou Chevreuil in Kramer. Individuals are encouraged to call between 8:00 and 10:30 A.M. to reserve space for any of the tours.

OL' MAN RIVER

New Orleans
Steamboat Company $$-$$$
2 Canal Street, New Orleans
(504) 586-8777, (800) 233-2628
www.neworleanssteamboat.com
Sure, it's a Twain thing, but it would be more than a small shame not to get swept away at least once by the mighty Mississippi during a visit to the Big Easy. And one of the safest and most comfortable ways to do this, while savoring some of the beauty and romance of New Orleans, is by taking a short trip aboard either the steamboat *Natchez* or the riverboat *John James Audubon.*

The 265-foot, three-deck steam sternwheeler *Natchez* holds 1,600 passengers and takes visitors on two-hour cruises twice daily, departing from the Toulouse Street Wharf across from Jackson Square. The harbor/jazz cruise departs 11:30 A.M. (returning 1:30 P.M.) and 2:30 P.M. (returning 4:30 P.M.) and includes a narration of the highlights, live jazz by the Steamboat Stompers, and optional lunch.

A dinner/jazz cruise boards passengers at 6:00 P.M., leaves at 7:00 P.M., and returns at 9:00 P.M., and features music by the Dukes of Dixieland and casual buffet-style dining.

One of the best ways to take in two of the city's world-class attractions is aboard the *John James Audubon,* which has four round-trip cruises daily departing the Audubon Aquarium of the Americas for a 7-mile upriver excursion to the urban Eden of Audubon Zoo. Passengers have four options: cruise-only; cruise and aquarium; cruise and zoo; and cruise, aquarium, and zoo. Cruises depart from the aquarium at 10:00 A.M., noon, 2:00, and 4:00 P.M.; return departures from the zoo are at 11:00 A.M., 1:00, 3:00, and 5:00 P.M. Snacks and beverages are sold on all cruises, and an onboard gift shop sells the usual souvenirs.

A cruise aboard either the *Natchez* or the *John James Audubon* is a fun and leisurely way to soak up, figuratively speaking, a different view of the French Quarter and the bustling Port of New Orleans while passing amid the towboats, ferries, domestic and international freighters and frigates, and other watercraft that make the Mississippi one of the most trafficked rivers in the world. Guide narrations are provided at no additional charge. Both boats have air-conditioning and heating and offer inside and outside seating. To play it safe it's a good idea to call ahead to verify departures and to make reservations.

SWAMP THINGS

Airboat Tours by Arthur $$–$$$
4262 Highway 90 East, Des Allemands
(800) 975-9345
www.airboattours.com

Just 45 minutes (if you're boogying—coming out of Downtown can be slow) west of New Orleans in St. Charles Parish, Capt. Arthur Matherne waits to take you on a thrilling airboat ride through the swamps from a small fishing village that will make you feel like you've gone back in time. Matherne guides passengers deep into the marsh while sharing tales of his lifelong experiences of fishing for alligators, crab, shrimp, and frogs in Bayou Gauche.

This leisurely and educational experience can turn into a ride on the wild side when Matherne revs up his 400-horse-power engine and turns the bayou into a raceway. Matherne, a U.S. Coast Guard–approved captain, will also customize tours for hunting, fishing, or just to enjoy the sunset. Tours are by appointment only with a maximum of 32 passengers. Half-hour, one-hour, and 90-minute tours are available.

Honey Island Swamp Tour $$–$$$
106 Holly Ridge Drive, Slidell
(985) 641-1769
www.honeyislandswamp.com
Located on the Pearl River boundary between Louisiana and Mississippi, the Honey Island Swamp is one of the wildest and most pristine river swamps in the United States; nearly 70,000 acres are designated as a permanently protected wildlife area. See alligators, bald eagles, waterfowl, herons, egrets, raccoons, nutria, mink, otters, and a host of other marsh wildlife on the area's most popular swamp tour. Explore the deeper, harder-to-reach bayous and sloughs of the swamp interior known so well by primary guide Dr. Paul Wagner, a wetlands ecologist and environmental consultant. Wagner has fished, hunted, and studied the Honey Island area (named for a small island within the swamp known for its swarming bees), bordered by tupelo gum and bald cypress trees, for nearly three decades.

Don't forget to take your camera on this two-hour narrated adventure offered year-round every morning and afternoon. Customized tours for birding, duck hunting, nighttime, or special occasions are available. Call for departure times and to make required reservations. If you'd rather let them do the driving, tours with New Orleans hotel pickup are available for an extra charge. A gift shop, Cajun food, and restrooms are available at the dock. To get to the swamp take I-10 east across Lake Pontchartrain to Gause Boulevard at exit 266. Head east for 2 miles to the traffic light at the intersection of Louisiana Highways 190 and 1090 (Military Road). Turn left and drive 1 mile north on Louisiana Highway 1090 to the I-10 Service Road. Turn right and follow the service road 1.5 miles to where it ends at Pearl River. Parking is on the left.

Jean Lafitte Swamp Tour $$-$$$
Route 1, Box 3131, Marrero
(504) 689-4186, (800) 445-4109
www.jeanlafitteswamptour.com
A native tour guide spins tales of the legends and lore of Louisiana's still untamed wilderness while a covered 60-passenger flatboat glides beneath a canopy of moss-draped cypress trees. Named for the famous buccaneer who helped the Americans beat the British at the Battle of New Orleans, this ecotour takes visitors into the heart of southeast Louisiana's swamplands, billed as the "home of the white nutria." Swamp boats depart daily at 10:00 A.M. and 2:00 P.M. Hotel pickups (for an extra fee) begin at 8:30 A.M. Call (504) 587-1719 for reservations. To get here cross the Crescent City Connection (Mississippi River Bridge) and continue on the Westbank Expressway 7.5 miles to the

Barataria Boulevard exit. Turn left and continue down Barataria 3.5 miles to Louisiana Highway 3134 (the Lafitte-Larose Highway), turn left and drive 5 miles. The swamp tour site is on the left.

Lil' Cajun Swamp Tour $$-$$$
Louisiana Highway 301, Crown Point
(504) 689-3213, (800) 725-3213
www.lilcajunswamptours.com
The biggest draw of this swamp tour is to "see, hold, and have your picture taken with Julie the alligator." Of course there's also the beauty of the swamps, bayous, and marshes of Cajun country aboard the *Lil' Cajun*. At the helm narrating is Capt. Cyrus Blanchard, a French- and English-speaking Cajun who shares his experiences of life on the bayou. Refreshments are served and restroom facilities are available onboard—a consideration when traveling with children. Two-hour tours depart daily, rain or shine, at 10:00 A.M., noon, and 2:00 P.M. March through November; noon only November through March. Call to make reservations. Transportation is available from your hotel for an additional fee. Discount coupons can be printed out from the Web site. To get to the *Lil' Cajun* take the Crescent City Connection (Mississippi River Bridge) to the Westbank Expressway and exit at Barataria Boulevard. Turn left at Barataria Boulevard; go to the Lafitte/Larose Highway (McDonald's is on the corner) and take a left; proceed for about 4.5 miles, then turn right on Louisiana Highway 301. The *Lil' Cajun* is right next to Frank's Boat Launch.

KIDSTUFF 👥

Riddle: What do you call a place where you can have your picture taken with an alligator, tour a life-size NASA space station model, and have exotic animals literally eating out of your hand?

Answer: New Orleans.

The Big Easy truly has earned the reputation of "sin city." (Yes, they even sell beer at kids' baseball games here, but *only* to adults.) For the most part, though, this is a town of close-knit families. And when we're not at one another's backyard crawfish boils and barbecues, we like to go out and have fun. Luckily, the city boasts an almost endless supply of natural wonders and creative artists to capture any young person's—and parent's—imagination. The following is a list of interesting ways for kids to spend time in the Big Easy. But remember, in New Orleans, fun is like chocolate—even a little is still pretty delicious.

And away we go . . .

PRICE CODE

Our price is based on admission for one adult.

$ $0 to $10
$$ $11 to $20
$$$ $21 to $50
$$$$ more than $50

Blaine Kern's Mardi Gras World $–$$
233 Newton Street, Algiers Point
(504) 361–7821, (800) 362–8213
www.mardigrasworld.com
Go behind the scenes of Mardi Gras to see the world's largest fleet of Carnival floats and the artists who create them. More than 500,000 square feet of Carnival "dens" are the working studios of international artists and sculptors who form the largest float-building company in the world.

Tours include trying on authentic Mardi Gras costumes, visiting the prop shop where artists create the giant papier mâché sculptures that adorn floats, watching floats being constructed, and getting a glance at Captain Eddie's S. S. Endymion, the world's biggest float, which measures 240-feet long and is adorned with tens of thousands of fiber-optic lights.

Mardi Gras World is open daily 9:30 A.M. to 5:00 P.M. The 45-minute tours begin every hour. The last tour starts at 4:30 P.M. To get there take the Canal Street Ferry to Algiers Point. A free shuttle bus meets every ferry.

Canal Street Ferry $
Canal Street at the Mississippi River
New Orleans
There is a ferry landing where Canal Street meets the Mississippi River. If you don't have 90 minutes or money for a steamboat ride, this is the simplest way to experience the Mighty Mississippi. Climb aboard and take in the panoramic view of the French Quarter during the short ride across to Algiers Point. While there, check out Blaine Kern's Mardi Gras World, where Carnival floats are built and stored. The Canal Street Ferry leaves the dock on the hour and half hour. The first ferry of the day begins its 15-minute trip from Algiers at 5:45 A.M. and the last ferry leaves Canal Street at midnight. It costs $1.00 per car round-trip and is free for pedestrians.

St. Charles Avenue Streetcar $
2817 Canal Street, New Orleans
(504) 242–2600
www.regionaltransit.org
If you've never ridden a streetcar, New Orleans is a great place to start. You haven't lived till you've sat on wood-slat seats with reversible backs (so that you can face either direction), feeling the breeze blow through the large windows on your face while this electric-powered green streetcar shakes and rattles as it

i *Looking for a kid-friendly place to eat authentic New Orleans seafood? Try Anthony's Seafood and Lobster House in the Riverwalk, touted as having more high chairs than any other restaurant in town.*

rolls down St. Charles Avenue. Just think, you're traveling around the city the same way New Orleanians have for more than 100 years.

And there's a lot to see along the way, including beautiful mansions, some of which look like giant gingerbread houses.

Around the 6500 block of St. Charles Avenue, get off and have a look around Audubon Park, named after naturalist John James Audubon who was famous for his detailed drawings of birds. (Be on the lookout for his artwork when visiting some of the city's museums.) It's a great spot for a picnic lunch or a leisurely stroll. If you walk all the way through the park to Magazine Street, you'll reach Audubon Zoo, which is guaranteed to be one of the best you've ever seen. Don't miss it. (See the listing later in this chapter.)

If you decide to stay on the streetcar, ride down to the Riverbend where St. Charles Avenue intersects with Carrollton Avenue. Get off here, then walk across the street and up onto the levee for a view of the Mississippi River. There are also several places to eat at the Riverbend, but the coolest is the Camellia Grill, an old-fashioned diner where everybody sits at the counter. They serve terrific burgers and omelettes that you get to watch the cooks prepare on the grill right in front of you. When you come out of the diner, notice the big white building across Carrollton Avenue. This is the Lusher Extension School (sixth through eighth grade). It is the oldest building in America being used as a school. Originally it was the courthouse when this area was the town of Carrollton.

If you ride the streetcar all the way to the end and back, the entire trip will take

about 90 minutes. The best times to ride are late morning and early afternoon when it's least crowded. You can catch the streetcar at Canal and Carondelet Streets. Each time you get on, you pay $1.25 per person each way, and exact change is required.

YOU ART TO SEE THIS

Louisiana Philharmonic Orchestra $
Orpheum Theater
225 Baronne Street, New Orleans
(504) 523-6530
www.lpomusic.com
Take part in the musical adventures of *Jack and the Beanstalk, Hansel and Gretel,* and, of course, *Peter and the Wolf.* In fact, come early to experience the musical instruments "petting zoo." It's all part of the LPO's Saturday morning Family Discovery concert series. Each season, the orchestra presents a trio of performances for young children, often featuring the Delta Festival Ballet as well as young musicians. An hour before the show, orchestra members introduce children to a variety of instruments and the sounds they make. This hands-on approach to music appreciation is called the Petting Zoo. The Family Discovery series is one of the fun ways that the only full-time professional orchestra in the Gulf South works to develop its audience. Call for program and performance dates.

New Orleans School of GlassWorks
& Printmaking Studio $-$$$$
727 Magazine Street, New Orleans
(504) 529-7277
www.neworleansglassworks.com
Don't pass up this Warehouse District gem just because it sounds too highfalutin' to be fun for children. Anyplace that combines creativity and blow torches was made for kids. Have your hand cast in glass, admire colorful glass artwork that will make you think of what Dr. Seuss would have created had he been a sculptor, or watch a glassblowing demonstration (it's sort of like blowing a giant

bubblegum bubble). Then get in on the act by signing up for one of the weekend beginner classes.

The school is very kid-friendly. During the summer it conducts workshops in kiln-fired glass, printmaking, beadmaking, metal sculpture, and stained glass for children ages 9 to 16. Classes are offered weekly and designed for traveling families. Glassblowing is available for the same age group during spring break and winter holidays.

Housed in a restored 19th-century storefront, GlassWorks is the South's largest contemporary facility featuring glass sculpture, glass casting, lampworking, stained glass, printmaking, and bookbinding. The school offers free daily demonstrations of Venetian-style glassblowing. Since its opening in 1990, GlassWorks has been the site of exhibitions highlighting the works of prominent as well as emerging artists, including the luminous vitrography of Dale Chihuly, the delicate botanical works of Paul Stankard, and the sensual designs of Richard Royal.

GlassWorks hours are Monday through Saturday 11:00 A.M. to 5:00 P.M. (closed Saturday during the summer). There is no admission charge but donations are welcome. No reservations are necessary to see free demonstrations. Classes, scheduled year-round, require reservations and cost approximately $100 to $198.

MUSEUMS THAT AREN'T A DRAG

Louisiana Children's Museum $
420 Julia Street, New Orleans
(504) 523–1357
www.lcm.org
Strike a pose, then walk away and watch your shadow remain on the wall. "Make groceries" (local jargon for grocery shopping) in a pint-size supermarket with carts, produce, and a cash register. Anchor a newscast in a real KidWatch television studio. It's all everyday fare at this "please touch" imagination station in the Warehouse District, rated among the

nation's top 10 children's museums by both *Parenting* and *Your Family* magazines. Discover more than 100 hands-on exhibits, daily art activities, and educational as well as entertainment programs for all ages.

In the Lab, kids learn about the physics of simple machines by lifting their own weight with the help of a pulley, or discover the importance of fitness by climbing the Rock Wall or riding a bike with Mr. Bones in Body Works. Youngsters can experience firsthand the challenges faced by the physically handicapped by shooting hoops from a wheelchair or identifying textured surfaces while blindfolded. Even toddlers get to climb, crawl, and explore in a playscape expressly for 1- to 3-year-olds.

This place is so much fun, they rent it out for grown-up parties at night. Really. Museum hours are Tuesday through Saturday 9:30 A.M. to 4:30 P.M., Sunday noon to 4:30 P.M., and Monday (summer only) 9:30 A.M. to 4:30 P.M. All kids under 16 must be accompanied by an adult. To get to the museum from Canal Street, take Magazine Street toward Uptown to Julia Street (about 9 blocks). Take a left on Julia Street, and the museum is just ahead on the right.

Musée Conti (The Wax Museum) $
917 Conti Street, New Orleans
(504) 525–2605, (800) 233–5405
www.get-waxed.com
New Orleans has been called the most European city in America, and the Musée Conti is proof. Not because of its name but its contents. Other cities tout wax museums whose biggest draw is a figure of George Burns. The Musée Conti, on the other hand, tells the tale of New Orleans and depicts everything from the city's founding to the legendary Battle of New Orleans, to the mysterious world of voodoo. Just for fun there's also the Haunted Dungeon, with more than 20 monsters.

The painstaking, European-style craftsmanship that went into creating this

French Quarter facility is unparalleled in the United States. Ordinary beeswax was combined with a secret chemical compound and infused coloring to create the remarkably lifelike figures; each strand of human hair, imported from Italy, was individually attached with a special needle. All male figures were given full beards. Look closely and notice that even the clean-shaven ones have a faint stubble. Only the most natural-looking, medical glass eyes were used. They were imported from Germany, a country long famous for supremacy in creating optical glass.

Note also the size of the figures. They may appear smaller than life-size, but they are accurately portrayed. The human race has steadily gained in average height, with the biggest jumps recorded in the last 100 years.

The tradition of wax figures dates back to ancient Babylon and has continued throughout the ages. Alexander the Great commissioned a personal wax sculptor a century before the birth of Christ, and the art was common in ancient Rome. European medieval fairs always featured a collection of wax figures. And in New Orleans we have the Musée Conti located on Conti Street in the French Quarter between Burgundy and Dauphine Streets. Don't miss it. The museum is open Monday through Saturday 10:00 A.M. to 5:00 P.M., Sunday noon to 5:00 P.M., and for private appointments.

New Orleans Fire Department Museum and Educational Center $ 1135 Washington Avenue, New Orleans (504) 896-4756 www.tmc.tulane.edu/oehs/firemus.html
Fighting fires was quite a challenge before the invention of the automobile and the telephone. Learn how they did it at the Fire Department Museum, housed in an authentic firehouse built in the 1850s. See a pre–Civil War hand-drawn ladder truck and fire-alarm telegraph, as well as an authentic collection of firefighting equipment used over the last 150 years, all

while picking up important pointers on fire safety.

The firefighters' valiant steeds once galloped through Uptown streets (then called the City of Lafayette) pulling a steam-driven pump made of gleaming brass atop a shiny red wooden chassis. Later known as Chalmette #23, the station in the Roaring '20s was the city's last to trade in its horses for motorized transport and remained a viable firehouse for another 50 years.

In 1995 the building underwent extensive restoration and was opened as a museum full of historic memorabilia. Admission is free (donations are accepted) and museum hours are Monday through Friday 9:00 A.M. to 2:00 P.M. Groups of six or more should call ahead to check on guide availability. To get to the museum take the St. Charles Avenue streetcar to Washington Avenue and walk up Washington toward the Mississippi River past Commander's Palace Restaurant, about 5 blocks.

RIVERTOWN MUSEUMS

A 4-block riverside stretch of Williams Boulevard in Kenner, 25 minutes from downtown New Orleans, is home to an impressive cluster of six modest-size family-friendly museums: the Toy Train Museum; the Mardi Gras Museum; the Saints Hall of Fame; the Science Center, Planetarium, Observatory, and Space Station; the Wildlife and Fisheries Museum and Aquarium; and the Cannes Brulee Native American Center. The Children's Castle and the Rivertown Repertory Theatre are also located here.

Spend a half to full day exploring some or all of Rivertown's museums and Children's Castle (www.rivertownkenner.com). All the museums are open Tuesday through Saturday 9:00 A.M. to 5:00 P.M. If you plan to visit all the Rivertown museums, purchase a budget-stretching pay-one-price pass, available at the Rivertown Welcome

Center (415 Williams Boulevard). To get here take I-10 west to the Williams Boulevard exit. Turn left (south) on Williams Boulevard and follow the street all the way down until you cross the railroad tracks. Free parking is available.

Cannes Brulee Native American Center $
303 Williams Boulevard, Kenner
(504) 468-7231

Rivertown's most distinctive museum, the outdoor Cannes Brulee is located behind the wildlife museum and showcases the traditions of the area's first inhabitants. This history exhibition is run by Native Americans who wear traditional dress and demonstrate their cultural heritage through the presentation of rituals, domestic and occupational crafts, and native foods (Saturday 9:00 A.M. to 4:00 P.M.). The site features a palmetto hut, a chickee (pole house with raised platform floor and palmetto roof), a mud and moss house, and a variety of pirogues. The look of the place is continuously changing as crops grow, bear fruit, and wither among the resident population of turkeys, ducks, rabbits, and chickens.

Visitors are invited to join in such activities as mud-oven construction, singing, dancing, beading, and cooking. There are also seasonal ceremonial events throughout the year. Cannes Brulee was the name given to the area by early European explorers. Meaning "burnt cane," the Europeans so dubbed the area after coming across Native Americans who would cut and burn river cane to help drive out small game.

Children's Castle $
503 Williams Boulevard, Kenner
(504) 468-7231

Opened in 1995, the Children's Castle is one of several attractions in Kenner's historic Rivertown district. The 16-block area is mostly made up of museums (all of which are worth visiting), but the Children's Castle is where the art of live performance reigns supreme. Shows

Don't miss the Wax Museum (officially Musée Conti; see write-up in this chapter). It's a great way to get a quick lesson in the city's history, and the realistic wax figures are mesmerizing. The kids will love the monsters in the Haunted Dungeon.

featuring musicians, magicians, puppets, and storytelling are presented every Saturday. The castle also offers performance workshops and myriad other activities focused on stimulating young imaginations and providing family entertainment. The castle's second floor houses a state-of-the-art broadcast facility that sends castle shows out over Cox Cable Channel 10. Shows are every Saturday at 11:30 A.M. and 1:00 P.M. Call for reservations.

Louisiana Wildlife and Fisheries Museum and Aquarium $
303 Williams Boulevard, Kenner
(504) 468-7231

Climb up a papier mâché tree house and observe Louisiana wildlife through binoculars. Alligators, turtles, egrets, and eels are just a part of this museum's extensive collection of more than 700 preserved (stuffed) animal specimens including birds, reptiles, and mammals presented in natural habitat exhibits. A 15,000-gallon freshwater aquarium gives visitors the opportunity to get an up-close view of the state's marine life, from perch to turtles. A scale model oil rig and a full-size escape capsule are popular features of the Gulf of Mexico exhibit.

The Mardi Gras Museum $
415 Williams Boulevard, Kenner
(504) 468-7231

Miniature float replicas, elaborate costumes, giant walking figures, and a huge papier mâché king cake make a great introduction to Mardi Gras, dubbed the biggest free show on earth. The Mardi Gras Museum brings Carnival to life year-round with an extensive array of memorabilia, photographs, videos, and costumes. Visitors step into Mardi Gras in a street-scene reproduction complete with all the sights and sounds of New Orleans's most popular party. Self-guided tours include the 20-minute Richard Dreyfus-narrated video *Farewell to the Flesh,* as well as 13 other videos shown throughout the museum that highlight the traditions of Mardi Gras. Live costume-making and float-building demonstrations are scheduled periodically.

ℹ️ *If you're planning to take the kids to the Rivertown museums listed in this chapter (and you should), visit their Web site, www.rivertownkenner.com, to find out about special events taking place while you're here. The site also offers games for the kids!*

Saints Hall of Fame $
415 Williams Boulevard, Kenner
(504) 468-7231
Even if you're not a Saints fan, you can enjoy a variety of hands-on (or "feet-on" in the case of the field goal–kicking station) exhibits, while testing your knowledge of sports trivia. The museum is unique in NFL cities as a museum by and for fans. Exhibits include tributes to John Gillam's kickoff return touchdown on the opening play of the team's first game and Tom Dempsey's 65-yard, record-setting field goal. NFL film highlights can be viewed in the Saints Theater, which features wooden bleachers from old Tulane Stadium, the team's home in pre-Superdome days.

Science Center Observatory, Planetarium, and Space Station $
409 Williams Boulevard, Kenner
(504) 468-7231
Tour a life-size NASA space station prototype, the only one of its kind, at this Rivertown museum. The exhibit includes live

demonstrations, a flight simulator, and astronaut-training gyroscope; a time line of everyday products originally invented for the space program; Internet links to other space centers around the country; and, believe it or not, live video transmissions from NASA astronauts.

The center is geared to kids age 6 and older and offers hands-on exhibits centered on science as it is used in daily living, such as hurricane tracking (which qualifies as a daily living situation in New Orleans), human physiology, and the "secret science" found inside walls. The center is also home to a state-of-the-art planetarium and observatory featuring 30-minute narrated sky shows. Open Friday and Saturday evenings (weather permitting), the observatory offers a view of the stars and constellations through the largest public telescope in Louisiana.

Toy Train Museum $
519 Williams Boulevard, Kenner
(504) 468-7231
Adjacent to the Illinois Central Gulf railroad tracks is this turn-of-the-20th-century building chock-full of hundreds of model trains, some dating to the 1800s. There's even a train playscape for the little ones, featuring a half-scale caboose playhouse, a make-believe circus, a train engine, and the Dixie Diner, where youngsters can enjoy a pretend meal.

THE GREAT OUTDOORS

Audubon Aquarium of the Americas $$
1 Canal Street, New Orleans
(504) 581-4629, (800) 774-7394
www.auduboninstitute.org
They're huge and tiny, they glow in the dark, and they're deadly. See the country's largest collection of jellyfish when you enter the riverfront aquarium's underwater world that includes more than one million gallons of fresh- and saltwater exhibits representing the Caribbean Sea, the Amazon rain forest, and the Gulf of Mexico.

Stroll through a sunlit tunnel surrounded on three sides by a Caribbean reef (sort of like snorkeling without getting wet), where the colors of the coral are reflected in a dazzling collection of tropical fish. Soothing waterfalls and tropical birds lull you in the Amazon rain forest. But watch out, the region is also populated by piranhas, anacondas, and stingrays. Then get a much different perspective watching sharks glide through the shadow of a replica of an offshore oil rig in the Gulf of Mexico.

The French Quarter aquarium houses one of the world's most diverse shark collections, from Australia's odd-looking wobbegongs from the Coral Sea to sleek blacktip reef sharks that prowl the Pacific Ocean. You can even pet a baby nurse shark, if you dare. Don't miss the freak show that is the Living in Water gallery, which includes flashlight fish that glow in the dark, four-eyed anableps, and penguins, which are, well, just plain funny.

The aquarium is open Sunday through Thursday 9:30 A.M. to 6:00 P.M., Friday and Saturday 9:30 A.M. to 7:00 P.M. The Audubon Institute offers discounts to individuals who wish to visit more than one of its four attractions—Audubon Zoo, Aquarium of the Americas, IMAX Theater, and Louisiana Nature Center.

Audubon Louisiana Nature Center $
Joe Brown Park
5601 Read Boulevard, New Orleans
(504) 246–5672, (800) 774–7394
www.auduboninstitute.org
The name really says it all at this little urban oasis, just 15 minutes from downtown in eastern New Orleans. Check out free of charge from the information desk a Discovery Kit, a canvas shoulder bag that includes binoculars, field guides, a bird call, a dip net, magnifying lens, and activity guide. Then take a hike on one of the center's three walking trails. The 1.25-mile Adventure Trail and 1.4-mile Discovery Trail are both ground-level trails; the 0.8-mile Wisner Loop Trail is a handicapped-accessible elevated boardwalk. Self-guided trail manuals are available for each of the trails at the information desk and are helpful for those eager to learn about the flora and fauna. Take a guided bird walk on Saturday at 10:30 A.M. or a guided trail walk on Saturday and Sunday at 3:00 P.M.

In the Interpretive Center kids can learn more about reptiles and amphibians at the Snakes 'N' Stuff exhibit; visit the Discovery Loft for a "touching" experience; and hear more about the animals at the 11:45 A.M. Birds of Prey program, 1:15 P.M. Reptile program, and 4:00 P.M. Mammal program. Don't forget to stop by the greenhouse and butterfly garden, as well as the Interpretive Garden to spy on the squirrels, rabbits, birds, butterflies, and occasional "surprise" visitors who drop by to feed in the Urbina Wildlife Garden.

Adventurers can voyage to other planets or watch laser light dance to the rhythms of popular music at the center's planetarium at 11:00 A.M. (Saturday only) as well as 12:30, 2:00, 3:30, and 4:30 P.M. Saturday and Sunday. Shows are included in the price of admission.

The nature center also hosts numerous children's and family programs, activities, clubs, camps, and festivals throughout the year, which are well worth exploring.

The nature center is open Tuesday through Friday 9:00 A.M. to 5:00 P.M., Saturday 10:00 A.M. to 5:00 P.M., and Sunday noon to 5:00 P.M. Restrooms, a gift shop, and snack vending machines are available. To get to the Louisiana Nature Center take I-10 east to exit 244 at Read Boulevard. Go south (right) on Read, turn left into Joe Brown Park at Nature Center Drive, and follow the signs to the nature center entrance.

Audubon Park $
6500 St. Charles Avenue, New Orleans
(504) 861–2537, (800) 774–7394
www.auduboninstitute.org
Originally part of a plantation, this 400-acre park has been a part of New Orleanians' lives since it was the site of the 1884 World's Fair. It features shimmering lagoons, fragrant gardens, recreation areas,

KIDSTUFF

> ℹ️ *For those traveling with the newly potty trained, who sometimes can't wait: The only public restrooms in the French Quarter (not inside a "customers only" business) are conveniently found at the back of the building that houses the Café du Monde on Decatur Street and on the second floor of Jax Brewery.*

an array of local wildlife, and 4,000 live oaks and other majestic trees. Cross Magazine Street and discover the Audubon Zoo.

Audubon Zoo $-$$
6500 Magazine Street, New Orleans
(504) 581-4629, (800) 774-7394
www.auduboninstitute.org
Check out the new tree house and rope bridge on Monkey Hill, the city's highest point, built by WPA workers to show local kids what a hill looks like. Or walk past an ancient Meso-American bas-relief glyph of a jaguar while spider monkeys swing on vines overhead and a jabiru stork clicks its beak looking for a mate—all in the shadow of a Mayan temple pyramid. No, you're not in an Indiana Jones movie, but rather Audubon Zoo's Jaguar Jungle. The 1.5-acre exhibit uses a mix of zoology and history to tell the story of Central America's exotic animals and that region's 4,000-year-old Mayan civilization.

The extravagant Jaguar Jungle was fashioned after the 58-acre zoo's popular Louisiana Swamp Exhibit, which showcases the state's indigenous wildlife, including a rare white alligator, as well as human life on the bayou. Both exhibits underscore a trend among the nation's progressive zoos to focus on education in addition to entertainment.

Audubon is consistently rated among the nation's best zoos and features 1,500 animals representing 360 species—many of them rare or endangered—in natural habitat exhibits. Exhibits include the Komodo Dragon, Reptile Encounter, Tropical Bird House, World of Primates, and

Butterflies in Flight, as well as those devoted to animals of North and South America, Africa, and Asia.

The zoo opens daily at 9:30 A.M. and closes at 5:00 P.M. (6:00 P.M. weekends in summer). The Audubon Institute offers discounts to individuals who wish to visit more than one of its four attractions—Audubon Zoo, Aquarium of the Americas, IMAX Theater, and Louisiana Nature Center.

City Park $
1 Palm Drive, New Orleans
(504) 482-4888
www.neworleanscitypark.com
More than a century ago, philanthropist John McDonogh bestowed to the City of New Orleans a 100-acre tract of land in Mid City, which has evolved into the fifth-largest municipal park in the country. Today the park encompasses 1,500 acres and accommodates 10 million annual visitors. The Carousel Gardens amusement area and Storyland are two of the best reasons for visiting City Park with children.

Since the turn of the last century, children have enjoyed the "flying horses" of the amusement area's antique carousel. One of only 100 wooden merry-go-rounds left in the United States and the last in Louisiana, the carousel is listed on the National Register of Historic Places. Other rides include two miniature antique trains, a Ferris wheel, bumper cars, a 40-foot fun slide, the Lady Bug roller coaster, tilt-a-whirl, the toy helicopter ride, and antique cars. Hours vary. Ride tickets are purchased separately in addition to admission, or visitors can purchase a wristband good for unlimited rides all day.

Storyland, a fairy tale theme park rated one of the top 10 playgrounds in the country by *Child* magazine, gives kids the chance to climb into the mouth of Pinocchio's whale, have a pretend sword fight aboard Captain Hook's ship, or fish in the Little Mermaid's Pond, all beneath the approving gaze of Mother Goose as she flies amid the limbs of ancient oaks.

Stick around for one of the daily puppet shows at Rapunzel's castle. Storyland is open Wednesday through Sunday. Call or check the Web site for varying seasonal hours.

City Park also offers recreational activities such as canoeing, fishing, tennis, and horseback riding. (See the Parks and Recreation chapter for details.) Or visit City Park just to sit under beautiful moss-draped live oak trees, eat an ice cream cone, and feed the ducks.

Global Wildlife Center $
26389 Louisiana Highway 40, Folsom
(985) 624-9453
www.globalwildlife.com
Where else can you feed a giraffe? The Global Wildlife Center is a 900-acre non-profit home to more than 3,000 free-roaming animals from all over the world—that's more hoofed stock than in all Louisiana zoos combined and the largest free-range facility in the country.

Zebras, antelope, camels, bison, and other animals have the lay of the land while visitors are "contained" in covered wagons pulled by tractors. During the 90-minute tour, a guide entertains and educates visitors about the different species as well as wildlife preservation. The really fun part, though, comes when the wagon stops and you get to feed the animals.

The preserve, originally a private collection of exotic animals, opened to the public 12 years ago. Global Wildlife Center is open daily year-round; call for wagon tour times and availability.

The center is located about one hour north of New Orleans. To get here take I-10 west to the Causeway exit. Take Causeway north and proceed over the Causeway toll bridge to St. Tammany Parish and I-12. Go West on I-12 to exit 47 (Robert exit). Turn right on Highway 445 (north) and proceed for approximately 11 miles to Highway 40 east. Turn right, and the stone entrance to the park is 1.5 miles down on the left.

IMAX Theater $
1 Canal Street, New Orleans
(504) 581-4629, (800) 774-7394
www.auduboninstitute.org
Put yourself in the driver's seat, going more than 200 miles per hour with NASCAR 3D, or just feel like you're on another planet when *Journey into Amazing Caves* explores the rugged caverns of the Grand Canyon and more. These are two of IMAX Theater's swear-you-were-there movies. The French Quarter theater, adjacent to the Aquarium of the Americas, opened in 1995 and features 354 "front row" seats for viewing its 5.5-story screen—three times the size of a regular movie screen. Several seats provide a rearview, closed-captioned system for the hearing impaired.

IMAX shows are hourly beginning 10:00 A.M. daily. Call ahead, though, because they are subject to change without notice. Advance purchase is recommended but not required. The Audubon Institute offers discounts to individuals who wish to visit more than one of its four attractions—Audubon Zoo, Aquarium of the Americas, IMAX Theater, and Louisiana Nature Center.

Kliebert's Alligator and Turtle Farm $
41083 West Yellow Water Road
Hammond
(985) 345-3617, (800) 854-9164
The Klieberts have been raising turtles for 35 years and alligators for more than a quarter century. This working farm, dotted with duckweed and clove-covered ponds, opened to the public in 1984. The most popular attraction of the guided tour is the alligator breeding pond, where visitors can gawk at 250 gators lounging near water's edge. The largest of the gators is 16 feet and weighs 1,200 pounds. Around June 1 every year the females begin building nests by piling dirt and grass in mounds 2 feet high. They lay eggs only once between June 15 and July 1. After hatching, the gators are sold for their meat and hides or to breeders in Florida.

More than 17,000 of the farm's turtles produce more than one million eggs each year. Hatchlings are exported and sold for aquariums, children's pets, and food.

Special times to visit are April to July during turtle egg-laying season, and June 15 to July 1 during alligator laying time. Alligator Day at the farm is held every fall and features free food and entertainment. The gift shop sells gator heads, teeth, feet, jewelry, back scratchers, and just about any gift you can imagine made out of alligator or turtle parts.

The farm is open daily noon till dark March 1 through October 31. To get to Kliebert's take I-55 north to the Springfield exit. Cross over Louisiana Highway 22 west and turn right onto the interstate service road north and follow the signs.

Woldenberg Riverfront Park $
Riverfront, New Orleans
It's always good to know where the wide-open spaces are when traveling with kids. Adjacent to the aquarium and IMAX Theater, these 17 acres of urban green space, public artwork, and brick pathways offer an up-close view of the Mississippi River and, perhaps more importantly, a place to relax while the kids run around when visiting the French Quarter. Festivals and open-air concerts are held here throughout the year.

ON THE WATERFRONT

Airboat Tours by Arthur $-$$$$
4352 Louisiana Highway 306
Des Allemands
(800) 975-9345
www.airboattours.com
Just 45 minutes west of New Orleans in St. Charles Parish, Capt. Arthur Matherne waits to take you on a wondrous airboat ride through the swamps from a small fishing village that will make you feel as if you've gone back in time. Matherne guides you deep into the marsh while sharing tales of his lifelong experiences of fishing for alligators, crab, shrimp, and frogs in Bayou Gauche.

This leisurely and educational experience can turn into a ride on the wild side when Matherne revs up his 400-horsepower engine and turns the bayou into a raceway. Matherne, a U.S. Coast Guard–approved captain, will also customize tours for hunting, fishing, or just to enjoy the sunset. Tours are by appointment only with a maximum of 32 passengers.

Honey Island Swamp Tour $$-$$$
Crawford Landing at the
West Pearl River, Slidell
(985) 242-5877, (985) 641-1769
www.honeyislandswamp.com
See alligators, bald eagles, waterfowl, herons, egrets, raccoons, nutria, mink, otters, and a host of other marsh wildlife on the area's most popular swamp tour. Located on the Pearl River, which forms the boundary between Louisiana and Mississippi, the Honey Island Swamp is one of the wildest and most pristine river swamps in the United States; 70,000 acres of it is a permanently protected wildlife area.

Explore the deeper, harder-to-reach bayous and sloughs of the swamp interior known so well by primary guide Dr. Paul Wagner, a wetlands ecologist and environmental consultant. Wagner has fished, hunted, and studied the Honey Island area (named for a small island within the swamp known for its swarming bees), bordered by tupelo gum and bald cypress trees, for nearly three decades.

Don't forget to take your camera on this two-hour narrated adventure offered year-round every morning and afternoon. Customized tours for birding, duck hunting, nighttime, or special occasions are available. Call for departure times and to make required reservations. If you'd rather let them do the driving, tours with New Orleans hotel are available at an additional charge.

A gift shop, Cajun food, and restrooms are available at the dock. To get to the swamp take I–10 east across Lake Pontchartrain to Gause Boulevard at exit 266. Head east for 2 miles to the traffic light at the intersection of Louisiana Highways 190 and 1090 (Military Road). Turn left and drive 1 mile north on Highway 1090, cross over the interstate and immediately turn right onto Crawford Landing Road. Drive 1.5 miles to where it ends at Pearl River. Parking is on the left.

Jean Lafitte Swamp Tour
Lafitte-Larose Highway, Marrero
(504) 689–4186, (800) 445–4109
www.jeanlafitteswamptour.com
Named for the famous buccaneer who helped the Americans beat the British at the Battle of New Orleans, this ecotour guides visitors through the heart of southeast Louisiana's swamplands, known as the home of the white nutria. A native guide spins tales of the legends and lore of Louisiana's still untamed wilderness while a covered 60-passenger flatboat glides beneath a canopy of moss-draped cypress trees.

Swamp boats depart daily at 10:00 A.M. and 2:00 P.M. Hotel pickups begin around 8:30 A.M. Call (985) 592–0560 for reservations. Transportation from downtown hotels is available at an additional charge. To get here cross the Crescent City Connection (Mississippi River Bridge) and continue on the Westbank Expressway 7.5 miles to the Barataria Boulevard exit. Turn left and continue down Barataria 3.5 miles to Louisana Highway 3134 (the Lafitte-Larose Highway); turn left and drive 5 miles. The swamp tour site is on the left.

Lil' Cajun Swamp Tour $$
Louisiana Highway 301, Crown Point
(504) 689–3213, (800) 725–3213
www.lilcajunswamptours.com
The biggest draw of this swamp tour is to "see, hold, and have your picture taken" with "Julie" the alligator. Of course there's also the beauty of the swamps, bayous, and marshes of Cajun country aboard the *Lil' Cajun.* At the helm narrating is Capt.

Rated one of the country's top 10 play-grounds by **Child** *magazine, City Park's Storyland is where kids can climb inside the mouth of Pinocchio's whale or fish in the Little Mermaid's pond. And don't miss the adjacent Carousel Gardens where visitors can ride 100-year-old "flying horses" or take a miniature train ride through the park.*

Cyrus Blanchard, a French- and English-speaking Cajun who shares his experiences of life on the bayou.

Refreshments are served and restroom facilities are available onboard—a consideration when traveling with children. Two-hour tours depart daily, rain or shine, at 10:00 A.M. and 2:00 P.M. Call to make reservations. Discount coupons can be printed out from the Web site.

To get to the *Lil' Cajun* take the Crescent City Connection (Mississippi River Bridge) to the Westbank Expressway and exit at Barataria Boulevard. Turn left at Barataria Boulevard to the Lafitta-Larose Highway (McDonald's is on the corner); take a left, proceed for about 4.5 miles, and turn right on Louisiana Highway 301. The *Lil' Cajun* is right next to Frank's Boat Launch.

New Orleans
Steamboat Company $–$$$
2 Canal Street, New Orleans
(504) 586–8777, (800) 233–2628
www.neworleanssteamboat.com
One of the best ways to take in two of the city's world-class attractions is aboard the riverboat *John James Audubon,* which offers four round-trip cruises daily departing the Aquarium of the Americas and traveling 7 miles upriver to the urban Eden of the Audubon Zoo. A cruise aboard the *John James Audubon* is a fun and leisurely way to soak up a different view of the French Quarter and the bustling Port of New Orleans, while passing amid the towboats, ferries, domestic and international freighters and frigates, and other water-

> **i** *Definitely take the kids out for beignets and cafe au lait (or chocolate milk) at Café du Monde on Decatur Street in the French Quarter. Then duck around back to watch those deep-fried taste treats being made through the cafe's display window.*

craft that make the Mississippi one of the most trafficked rivers in the world. Guide narrations are provided at no additional charge. The boat has air-conditioning and heating and offers inside and outside seating. Snacks and beverages are sold on all cruises, and an onboard gift shop sells the usual souvenirs.

Passengers have four options for the cruise only. You can also choose value packs that include cruise and aquarium; cruise and zoo; and cruise, aquarium, and zoo. Cruises depart from the aquarium at 10:00 A.M., noon, 2:00 and 4:00 P.M.; return departures from the zoo are at 11:00 A.M. and 1:00, 3:00, and 5:00 P.M. To play it safe it's a good idea to call ahead to verify departures and to make reservations.

THE ARTS

New Orleans abounds with great artists surrounded by a population that truly understands and appreciates their work. However, unlike other communities of artists, these probably never come in contact with a bow, a leotard, or a period costume. Instead they take food and with inspired levels of cunning and craft create the magic of barbecue shrimp, bread pudding, or a hot roast beef po-boy.

And that's just the folk art.

Among the most accomplished of these truly brilliant artists whose work touches millions of waistlines each year would be such luminaries as Paul Prudhomme, Susan Spicer, and just about everybody's mama. As a result, the Big Greasy may not have quite as developed a fine arts scene as, say, cities where people think that eating is something you do just to survive.

If you are looking for the New Orleans arts scene, you will find that it is small. However, it is full of artists who have been forced to find ways to reach and cultivate an audience of people who would just as soon go out to dinner. Often performances are accompanied by open discussions between musicians or dancers and audience members about the opera or ballet that they've both just experienced.

Professional artists regularly bring their work to schools, facing, perhaps for the first time, the challenge of figuring out how to move a child. The city's orchestra, which is owned and operated by its musicians, regularly performs under less than ideal circumstances when it could just as easily never leave the comfort of the Orpheum Theater. But then it would never reach that audience who will only hear music played out in the suburbs, at a country plantation home, or in a park. Yes, the New Orleans art scene is small—but it's full of inspiration.

DANCE

Delta Festival Ballet
3850 North Causeway Boulevard
Metairie
(504) 836–7166
Delta Festival Ballet is Louisiana's only resident professional dance company, with a school and a junior company. The company performs at various venues from its New Orleans home to Reserve, Louisiana, and Biloxi, Mississippi. With more than 50 ballets and divertissements in its repertoire, ranging from 19th-century classics to rock ballets, Delta Festival is also the official dance company of the New Orleans Opera Association. The company's annual Christmas presentation of *The Nutcracker* in conjunction with the Louisiana Philharmonic Orchestra is a local favorite. Ticket prices are approximately $10 to $40, depending on performance. The box office is open Monday through Friday 9:30 A.M. to 4:30 P.M. Call for the performance schedule.

New Orleans Ballet Association
305 Baronne Street, New Orleans
(504) 522–0996
www.nobadance.com
The core of the ballet association's programs at the Mahalia Jackson Theatre of the Performing Arts in Armstrong Park is the performance series—the presentation of professional guest companies showcasing a diverse range of dance from classical to modern. Past performers include the Jose Limon Dance Company, the Pittsburgh Ballet Theatre, Maria Benitez Teatro Flamenco, the Twyla Tharp Dance Company, and the Urban Bush Women. The association offers a full season of performances and a series of one-hour lecture/demonstrations for students. Each performance is followed by the popular INFORMance, a free dialogue with artistic directors or company members, open to

If you're into long-term planning, check out the three-month arts calendar in the Times-Picayune's "Bon Vivant" section.

all ticket holders. Tickets start around $26.00. Students and seniors get a $7.00 discount. The box office is open Monday through Friday 9:00 A.M. to 5:00 P.M.

FILM

The New Orleans Film Festival
843 Carondelet Street, New Orleans
(504) 523-3818
www.neworleansfilmfest.com
The NOFF is best known for its annual film festival (see Annual Events and Festivals), which exhibits more than 130 movies and videos, many of which are produced by regional artists. Throughout the year the society also presents multi-cultural film and video screenings, industry workshops, and lectures by guest speakers. Screenings, held at various venues around town, include a French Film festival each spring. Call for dates and times.

The Prytania Theatre
5339 Prytania Street, New Orleans
(504) 891-2787
www.theprytania.com
The Prytania is the only single-screen neighborhood movie theater left in the state; it's the kind of place where a person (not a machine) often answers the phone and movie times out front are written with a marker on posterboard. The original Prytania Theatre was built on this Uptown corner in 1915, and before that movies were shown here under a tent. Reel old-timers remember the early days of talkies, when the streetcar would pass in front and make the sound record skip. The movie house went through various incarnations until a new local owner saved it from the wrecking ball in 1997. Today, the theater shows "Hollywood movies with an art flair," which generally means those predicted to be big at the box office. Saturday-morning kiddie

matinees and periodic screenings of classic films are also offered. This landmark also cohosts the New Orleans Film Festival, the French Film Festival, and the Jewish Film Festival.

Zeitgeist Theatre Experiments
1724 Oretha Castle Haley Boulevard
New Orleans
(504) 525-2767
www.zietgeistinc.org
Zeitgeist Theatre Experiments is a volunteer, nonprofit, cultural arts organization offering alternative art exhibits in a variety of disciplines as well as an odd assortment of independent films in an intimate 90-seat theater that shares space with Barrister's Gallery. From *The Girl Next Door,* about the trials and tribulations of a rising porn star, to a documentary on a jazz great, *Louis Prima: The Wildest!,* this is the place to find offbeat cinema.

GALLERIES

French Quarter

Bee Galleries featuring Martin LaBorde
509 Royal Street, New Orleans
(504) 587-7111
www.beegalleries.com
Twenty-seven years ago, artist Martin Laborde stood at the top of an ancient Mayan pyramid in Mexico and had what he describes as a "mystical experience." The result was Bodo, a cartoonish, pointy-hatted character in wizard's robes who flies, floats, and glides across midnight canvases, like a child on a dream journey. Sometimes he takes along a dog. "Bodo is what I want to be," says this longtime favorite New Orleans artist who enjoys a deeply loyal following (his murals adorn the exterior wall of the Upperline restaurant Uptown). LaBorde's international following is matched only by the many awards he has garnered, including the prestigious Pushkin Medal of Honor from the Hermitage Museum in Leningrad.

Bryant Galleries
316 Royal Street, New Orleans
(504) 525–5584, (800) 844–1994
www.bryantgalleries.com

"Art is the pouring of all your knowledge, your culture, your religion, and your moral philosophy into building aesthetic pleasure," says renowned artist Juan Medina. "The more universal your culture, so it will be with your art."

For years collectors throughout the United States and Europe have been mesmerized by the complexity of Medina's graphics, based on his interests in philosophy, science, and religion. And a visit to this gallery is good chance to view the artist's work.

Upstairs, the animated cartoon and comic strip devotee will find Valhalla: Original production sketches and cels as well as hand-painted limited edition prints of Bugs and Daffy, Fred and Barney, Pinocchio and Jimminy Cricket, Mickey Mouse, Winnie the Pooh, and many other favorites born in the art studios of Disney, Warner Brothers, and Hanna-Barbera. No one will need a magic bag of tricks to figure out the appeal of the Friz Freleng–autographed cels of the "wonderful, wonderful" Felix the Cat. Skating on thin ice are Charlie Brown and the whole Peanuts gang in original sketches from *A Charlie Brown Christmas*. Astro takes Elroy out for a "walk." Rut-roh.

Ed Dwight's negative-space sculpture of jazz legends makes it look as though seemingly disconnected parts of Satchmo's hand, trumpet, and face are floating in air. Glass artist Martha Wolf meantime offers a menagerie of fanciful animals—mostly lions and gators and elks, oh my!—she created by using heat (and a bit of imagination) to melt pieces of colored glass.

Carriageway Gallery
536 Royal Street, New Orleans
(504) 581–4180

A native New Orleanian of Creole and Cajun heritage, artist Myrl D'Arcy found her artistic inspiration during a childhood alternately spent playing on the flagstone streets of the French Quarter and in the shade of Louisiana's cypress bayous. A self-taught painter in the Impressionist tradition, D'Arcy employs several media; however, her preference is oils. Though she has spent four decades traveling and painting around the world, her true passion is found in her French Quarter street scenes, courtyards, and lace balconies as well as her moonlit swamps. The gallery deals exclusively in D'Arcy's work, which includes limited-edition, hand-tiled lithographs, each signed by the artist.

Galerie Louisiane
910 Royal Street, New Orleans
(504) 581–4596
www.fredrickguessstudio.com

What a nice flip of the coin it is to walk past a Royal Street gallery and see an artist through a pair of open French doors, sitting at his easel, brushes in hand, working on his newest creation. Artist/owner Fredrick Guess doesn't mind the ebb and flow of people while he works in his sunny gallery of brilliantly colorful New Orleans mindscapes—his favorite subject. In fact, the inquisitive interruptions help bring the New Orleans newcomer back down to earth and helps him see new possibilities in whichever canvas happens to be propped on the wooden easel. Ask him about how he chooses his expressive colors. Guess is likely to answer by mixing a few acrylics on his palette with a fingertip, then smudging it on a piece of paper to show off the results. Concentration indeed seems the least of this artist's concerns as you marvel at the contemporary impressionism Guess lends his Creole cottages, Carnival balls, Mardi Gras Indians, voodoo altars, and French Quarter moments.

A Gallery for Fine Photography
241 Chartres Street, New Orleans
(504) 563–1313
www.agallery.com

Joshua Mann Pailet's paradise for photography lovers moved in 2003 to this new, softly lighted location, but the venue

Want to know what's going on this week? Check the critics' picks and pans, not to mention the weekly arts and entertainment calendar, in the "Lagniappe" section of Friday's Times-Picayune and the "Gambit" on Monday.

remains a favorite haunt for collectors searching for a rare print by lens pioneers such as Henri Cartier-Bresson, Robert Doisneau, and Eduard Steichen. (In case you were wondering, Cartier-Bresson's classic 1932 photograph titled "Behind the Gare, St.-Lazare, Paris" today fetches a cool $175,000. By comparison, Steichen's 1906 "The Flatiron" seems almost a steal at $12,500.) Here Herman Leonard's timeless takes on jazz legends like Louis Armstrong, Billie Holiday, Duke Ellington, and Dexter Gordon can be found alongside Yousuf Karsh's 1958 photograph of Robert Frost.

More than 5,000 photographs including museum-quality salt prints, daguerreotypes, and panoramas join rotating exhibits, such as E.J. Bellocq's "Storyville Portraits: 1911–1913" and Sandra Russell Clark's tour de force of old New Orleans cemeteries. Vintage photogravures include those from the legendary Harriman Alaska Expedition of 1899, as well as 19th-century North American Indians. The first floor also features a selection of art photography books covering the American and French styles, jazz, the South, even truck stops found on the hard road of life.

Upstairs is a second-floor gallery of exhibits of contemporary photographers including signed-and-numbered prints by Annie Leibowitz and the late Helmut Newton. Josephine Sacabo's "Ophelia's Garden" offers an ethereal collection of dreamscapes writer Stephanie Mallarme has described as "an inner mural to protect herself from the brilliant indiscretions of the afternoon." The works of other photography legends found throughout the 4,000-square-foot establishment include Gordon Parks, Scavullo, and Eisenstaedt.

The gallery also has a user-friendly Web site that enables visitors to check its complete inventory by artist, medium, subject, and price (after registering with your e-mail address and a password).

Hanson Gallery
229 Royal Street, New Orleans
(504) 524-8211
www.hansongallery-nola.com
It's not only *Yellow Submarine* artist Peter Max's annual exhibits of dozens of acrylic pop-culture observations that make artist/owner Scott Hanson's track-lit hardwood-floor gallery stand out from the pack. Hanson's own sculpture has given the establishment a heart-shaped globe and bronze leather jacket to be reckoned with. Painter LeRoy Neiman's sports impressions hang nicely not far from beautiful human-form Lucite and acrylic sculptures by Fredrick Hart. The remarkable range of original artwork by living artists (with the exception of the occasional Pisarro, etc.) includes Caribbean-motif and French-scape serigraphs. Upstairs the huge second-floor windows in this 205-year-old building overlook Royal Street's Saturday afternoon mix of antiques hunters and browsing tourists.

Kurt E. Schon, Ltd.
523 Royal Street and 510 St. Louis Street
New Orleans
(504) 524-5462
There isn't a blue dog or red cat to be found in this showcase of 17th, 18th, and 19th-century artwork. For four decades the Schon gallery has specialized in Victorian art—paintings that reflect the high standards of quality, strength, and professionalism upheld by the influential Royal Academy, which flourished during the reign of Queen Victoria from 1837 to 1901. In 1966 the gallery began collecting Barbizon paintings, which originated in a small village in the Fountainbleau forest. There, in 1825, a small group of artists broke with 300 years of tradition and began painting landscapes in a new way. Examples of

Schon's original collection can now be found in museums around the world. In case you hadn't guessed, this gallery is no place for dilettantes.

La Belle Galerie &
The Black Art Collection
309 Chartres Street, New Orleans
(504) 529–3080

This 9,000-square-foot building is purportedly the largest gallery in the United States featuring African-American art. Permanent displays include paintings and limited-edition prints by local and national artists, antique African artifacts, music-related photographs, and official Mardi Gras posters and Jazz Festival prints. The gallery also offers custom framing and shipping worldwide. A 3,000-square-foot exhibition space upstairs is available for social or business gatherings.

Michalopoulos
617 Bienville Street, New Orleans
(504) 558–0505
www.michalopoulos.com

The almost psychedelically distorted depictions of French Quarter and Uptown architecture seen in James Michalopoulos' acrylics, oils, and serigraphs in bright primary colors can put a discerning smile on the face of even the most jaded been-there-seen-that collector of unique contemporary art. His expressionistic and "gestural" style seem to make his houses breathe and move like the people who inhabit them. Over the years many have tried to emulate his style, but none have succeeded in nailing the essence of New Orleans as captured by Michalopoulos's linear-defying brush. In addition to architectural renderings, his subjects include landscapes, automobiles, and figures. Michalopoulos, thrice commissioned to create the official poster for the New Orleans Jazz and Heritage Festival, also has prints and posters available of his works.

Rodrigue Studio
721 Royal Street, New Orleans
(504) 581–4244, (800) 899–4244
www.georgerodrigue.com

The Blue Dog is everywhere at this gallery, the New Orleans home of artist George Rodrigue's yellow-eyed, cobalt-blue-with-white-snout canine. She appears in all of his paintings, sitting in the same position and with the same expression. *People* magazine described it as "the stunned look of Wile E. Coyote." The been-there-done-that Blue Dog is the Cajun artist's humorous canvas mascot and appears in the foreground of Acadian shacks (*Tee George's Cabin*), draped in an American flag cape (*My Security Blanket*), and decked out in a tuxedo and shoulder-to-shoulder with a woman with long flowing hair (*Wendy and Me*). The 54-year-old New Iberia native also folds New Orleans into his paintings. Sometimes the pooch du jour fronts a trio of felines in Carnival purple, green, and gold (*Mardi Gras Cats*) or is adorned in Rex-like regal red velvet (*Mardi Gras '96*).

The short-haired phenomenon seen in Munich, Tokyo, and Carmel galleries is Rodrigue's late dog Tiffany. The black-and-white spaniel-terrier's likeness was first transformed to blue in 1984 when the painter was illustrating a werewolf for a collection of Louisiana swamp ghost stories titled *Bayou*. The story goes he sold his first blue-dog painting for $2,500 at a Beverly Hills gallery, which gave him the impetus he needed to open his own gallery in New Orleans. If the immense commercial appeal of Rodrigue's blue-dog

Can't figure out what that artist is trying to say? Free (with admission) tours of the New Orleans Museum of Art's permanent collection and special exhibitions are conducted by knowledgeable docents at 11:00 A.M. and 2:00 P.M. daily except on Thursday.

paintings, lithographs, and prints is any indication (collectors include Whoopi Goldberg, Tom Brokaw, Delta Burke, and former Louisiana Gov. Edwin Edwards), Tiffany is not likely to be found barking up the wrong tree anytime soon.

Sutton Galleries
519 Royal Street, New Orleans
(504) 581-1914
The insightful bronze sculptures of African-American jazz and blues musicians by artist Paul Wegner dovetail nicely with this brightly lit shop's collection of fine French oil paintings of turn-of-the-last-century cityscapes and the Riviera.

In addition to fine jewelry and objets d'art is a selection of Poupeé Millet's captivating human figures, each handcrafted with intricate ceramic faces and adorned in myriad exotic fabrics; some have fanciful headdresses.

Warehouse District

Arthur Roger Gallery
432 Julia Street, New Orleans
(504) 522-1999
www.arthurrogergallery.com
Combining the works of established local artists such as Elemore Morgan, George Dureau, and Francis Pavy with a show by New York artist Peter Halley was original enough to make this one of the Warehouse District's most prominent galleries. It also earned Arthur Roger a place among the nation's best in *The 1998 Art Market Guide*. It is, according to the guide, "a relatively new hybrid: a gallery that retains its regional flavor while showing enough established artists to have a national identity."

Contemporary Arts Center
900 Camp Street, New Orleans
(504) 523-1216
www.cacno.org
Anchoring the Warehouse Arts District is the CAC, established in 1976 by a group of artists who recognized the city's desperate need for space in which to showcase alternative and experimental works. The center has no permanent collection; five rotating exhibits each year by local and international artists present a wide range of genres. Past exhibits have included contemporary Japanese sculpture, a mausoleum installation by local glass artist Mitchell Gaudet, and color photographs by national icon William Eggleston and local emerging talent William Greiner. Other well-received showings have included paintings by artists of the Visionary Imagist school, conceptual works by Robert Tannen, a voodoo hut by African-American artists Betye and Allison Saar, and a sod house by sculptor Herb Parker. The center also sponsors "open" exhibitions by local artists who have submitted works related to a particular theme. The main Lupin Foundation Gallery on the second floor and three smaller first-floor galleries provide the 10,000-square-foot center with ample show space, especially for its multiple exhibits.

LeMieux Galleries
332 Julia Street, New Orleans
(504) 522-5988
www.lemieuxgalleries.com
Honduran artist Luz Maria Lopez's bold, colorful canvases bursting with ancient Mayan symbolism beckon visitors to this intimate gallery specializing in contemporary Louisiana and Third Coast artists. Self-taught painter Leslie Staub's whimsical, plaster-icon framed drawings from her children's book, *Whoever You Are*, adorn a back wall, and Shirley Rabe Masinter's realistic urban landscapes in watercolors and oils add sobriety to the mix. LeMieux also represents sculptors Kim Bernadas, Kinzey Branham, Mark Derby, Sara Moczygemba, and Sybille Reretti.

Marguerite Oestreicher Fine Arts
726 Julia Street, New Orleans
(504) 581-9253
Look for an eclectic mix in this gallery specializing in historical and contemporary artworks—from 50 works on paper created

in the 1920s and 1930s by Edward Hage-
dorn (a recluse who died in 1982 and never
showed his work except for the few pieces
that hang in museums) to life-size alligators made from tires found along the highway. International, national, regional, and
emerging artists are represented including
Milton Avery, Sally Avery, and daughter
March Avery. Don't miss the courtyard
sculptures and extra exhibition space in
the former slave quarters out back.

YA/YA Inc.
601 Baronne Street, New Orleans
(504) 529–3306
www.yayainc.com
The colorful building reflects the childlike
exuberance of Young Aspirations/Young
Artists. This collective of youthful artists
began in 1988 as a group of inner-city
high school students who recycled furniture with their own original artwork. Today
the group is renowned from Tokyo to
Amsterdam for its funky furniture work,
original fabric prints, and sculpture. A core
group of 30 high school and college students produce the vivid and energetic
works found in this intimate space. (See
Close-up in this chapter.)

Uptown

Anton Haardt Gallery
2858 Magazine Street, New Orleans
(504) 891–9080
www.antonart.com
This funky new addition to Magazine
Street's outsider-art scene has a few surprises up its sleeve. And the high-grade
retro kitsch, folk-art dolls, and metal Hui-
choi Indian masks are only the beginning.
Other high notes include the whimsically
hand-painted (though non-playable)
acoustic guitars by Alabama artist Mose
Tolliver (whose works are exhibited at the
Corcoran Gallery of Art) and a selection of
Sybil Gibson's hand-painted grocery bags
that were rediscovered shortly after the
artist's death. The works of nearly two
dozen largely Southern artists found

*Most Warehouse District galleries take
part in coordinated openings the first
Saturday of each month from 6:00 to
9:00 P.M.*

throughout the cozy venue include owner
Anton Haardt's own symbolic and highly
evocative acrylics, mixed media, and
assemblages, a self-described "visual
scrutiny of existence through the dissection
of detail." As Birmingham, Alabama, art
critic James Nelson noted of Haardt's work,
"(Her) images suggest figures ripped from
multiple layers of wallpaper in a Victorian
boarding house." No matter your aesthetic
leanings, contemporary Deep South artwork couldn't ask for a better home.

Carol Robinson Gallery
840 Napoleon Avenue, New Orleans
(504) 895–6130
www.carolrobinsongallery.com
Take a streetcar ride down St. Charles
Avenue to Napoleon Avenue. Then walk
past Anne Rice's St. Elizabeth's Home to
this restored turn-of-the-20th-century,
two-story house on the corner of
Napoleon and Magazine Streets. Established in 1980, this gallery represents the
works of regional, national, and international artists with ties to New Orleans in
oil and watercolor paintings, ceramics,
sculpture, photography, and glass. The
gallery's goal is to showcase diversity in
art in a relaxed and friendly atmosphere.
Visitors are encouraged to take their time
viewing the sizable collection.

Shadyside Pottery of New Orleans
3823 Magazine Street, New Orleans
(504) 897–1710
A native New Orleanian, Charles Bohn
has traveled extensively throughout the
United States, Europe, and Asia. He began
working in pottery in 1972 and studied
with Shoji Takahara in Japan. Back home,
he updated the art of raku, an ancient
Japanese firing technique that produces
beautifully unique pieces. Each piece is

YA/YA

Framed by a towering row of gray-cast office buildings in the oh-so-serious Central Business District, this art gallery's brightly painted door shutters seem to burst with color and proclaim to passersby that this place is *all* that. Inside the main studio are everyday household items such as chairs and tables ablaze with paintings of a school yard, bright skies, or an alligator—all the result of unleashed youthful imaginations.

Quite simply, this place is where you come to get your YA/YAs out.

The studio at 628 Baronne Street is the home of Young Aspirations/Young Artists, better known as YA/YA. The group began 14 years ago when artist Jana Napoli joined forces with commercial art teacher Madeleine Neske to develop a project for students at L. E. Rabouin Career Magnet, a Central Business District high school where 75 percent of the mostly African-American student population are classified as academically or economically disadvantaged. Students were asked to draw pictures of downtown buildings, which Napoli then showed at her gallery, inviting area businesspeople to the show. To almost everyone's surprise, some of the pictures sold and YA/YA was born.

Since then the young artists' group has expanded its repertoire beyond its signature funky furniture to include murals as well as the designing and printing of fabric sold and licensed to manufacturers. In 1995 the group was commissioned by Swatch to design a watch commemorating the 50th anniversary of the United Nations. Consequently the group was hired to design and manufacture 582 slipcovers for the U.N. General Assembly room. Two years later, YA/YA artists created the stage set for the New Orleans Opera Association's touring production of *Porgy and Bess*. The group's work has received coverage in more than 80 publications, including the *New York Times, New York Magazine, Vogue, Life,* and *Fortune*. They've appeared on *Sesame Street* and MTV's *House of Style*.

But the program is about a lot more than picking up a brush and counting the bucks. More than 30 Rabouin students and recent graduates attend daily art training sessions after their regular classes and on weekends. Students must maintain a C average to join and earn Bs to be a part of the group's traveling shows. All artists take part in the entire process from creating the art and entering shows to writing up sales, doing

quickly fired to about 2,000 degrees, then plunged into a smoke chamber where flames and smoke change the colors and design. The unpredictability of the finished pieces is part of the appeal. Each work is signed by the artist. Some historians attribute raku's roots to the 15th-century Japanese tea ceremony, while others claim Korean roof tile makers created the unique handling efforts.

inventory, and even cleaning up the studio. It's all part of the master plan to develop entrepreneurs with marketable skills as well as artists.

Students must earn their way into varying levels of mastery. At the entry level, students work on chairs and small wood sculptures. As apprentices they work on commissioned projects like the Swatch job. Some are hired as paid administrative interns, and those who attain the highest level of skills are granted membership in the YA/YA Professional Guild. The eldest of this group form the core of mentors for younger students.

"The only roadway out of being trapped in your environment is to build access to the world," says Napoli.

Napoli oversees the distribution of this nonprofit organization's earnings. Fifty percent of proceeds earned from artwork goes to the student, 20 percent is put back into the program to purchase supplies and materials, and 30 percent is placed in trust for students' college education.

Many of the program's artists have landed careers in the real world. Mural painter Lionel Milton, for example, has worked for film director Spike Lee as well as for TV sitcoms *Living Single* and *The Jamie Foxx Show*. He has since opened his own design studio.

Future plans include opening the YA/YA program to other high school stu-

Young artists create vivid work at the popular YA/YA Gallery. JAMES GAFFNEY

dents citywide while continuing to expand the artist group's product line. An Italian company recently purchased the rights to a YA/YA motif for a line of porcelain ware. For many of these young artists, who 16 years ago might not have even known what porcelain ware was, YA/YA is more than just a dream. It really is all that.

Thomas Mann Gallery I/O
1812 Magazine Street, New Orleans
(504) 581–2113
www.thomasmann.com
Contemporary American craft leader

Thomas Mann's "techno-romantic" jewelry and eclectic furnishings have been igniting the imagination of serious collectors and lovers of forward design for 30 years. And the largest selection of the internationally acclaimed artist's award-winning works is found at his Magazine Street gallery in Uptown's Lower Garden District. Brilliant examples of Mann's sculptural—and highly wearable—objets d'art include his "space frame" brooches and one-of-a-kind "caged necklaces" combining "technical ephemera" such as quartz and non-precious metals like nickel, brass, and copper. Mann has also designed what may be among the most unique collections of mirrors and one-of-a-kind men's cufflinks and tuxedo studs seen anywhere. The gallery also showcases the works of more than 40 U.S. and international artists including Boris Balley's chairs and bowls made from recycled highway signage, and contemporary tribal lamps incorporating metal, mahogany, and paper shades.

MUSEUMS

New Orleans Museum of Art
City Park, 1 Collins Diboil, New Orleans
(504) 488-2631
www.noma.org
Maybe size really doesn't matter. But a $23.5-million expansion project that added 55,000 square feet to City Park's largest structure sure has given locals something to crow about—and more room to roam. Founded in 1910 with a gift to the city from philanthropist Isaac Delgado, NOMA, the city's oldest fine art organization, has a permanent world-class collection of more than 35,000 objects valued in excess of $200 million. And with its expansion, the museum's strong suits—French and American art, photography, glass, African works, and Japanese paintings from the 17th- to 18th-century Edo period—only continue to grow.

The facility's comprehensive study of French art includes such treasures as groups of work by French Impressionist Edgar Degas, who visited maternal relatives in New Orleans in 1871 and painted in a house on Esplanade Avenue just 12 blocks from the museum. Works by the masters of the School of Paris include

paintings and sculptures by Picasso, Braque, Dufy, and Miró.

A unique Arts of the Americas collection surveys the cultural heritage of North, Central, and South America from the pre-Columbian through the Spanish colonial periods, with special emphasis on objects from the Mayan civilization of Mexico and Central America and paintings and sculpture from Cuzco, the Spanish Viceregal capital of Peru. A display of American art is found in a suite of period rooms featuring 18th- and 19th-century furniture and decorative arts.

One of the more popular collections in this 130,000-square-foot gem is the work of Peter Carl Fabergé (1846–1920), master jeweler to the last czars of Russia, on loan from the Matilda Geddings Gray Foundation. Three Imperial Easter eggs, as well as the famous jeweled Imperial lilies-of-the-valley basket, crafted in 1896 for the Empress Alexandra Feodorovna, highlight this exhibit.

Besides enhancing New Orleans's reputation as a major tourist and convention center, NOMA also plays an important role as an educational resource. Each year the museum opens its doors to more than 25,000 schoolchildren for free guided tours. NOMA's museum-on-wheels, "Van Go," serves as an educational liaison between the museum and the New Orleans area.

A good place to rest tired feet is at the Courtyard Cafe, which offers a light menu of salads and sandwiches and, more importantly, a view overlooking City Park's scenic lagoons and giant live oaks.

Hours are Tuesday through Sunday 10:00 A.M. to 5:00 P.M. except Thursday, when the hours are 12:30 to 8:30 P.M. Admission is $6.00 adults; $5.00 seniors; $3.00 children. Louisiana residents enter for free from 5:00 to 8:30 P.M. on Thursday only. On occasion there may be an additional charge for major international exhibits. NOMA is located in City Park, convenient to the City Park/Metairie Road exit of I-10. The museum may be reached by public bus via the Carrollton Avenue or

Esplanade bus lines of the RTA. Ample free parking is available, and the museum is fully accessible to the handicapped.

Ogden Museum of Southern Art
925 Camp Street, New Orleans
(504) 539–9600
www.ogdenmuseum.org
The arts district's newest museum offers rotating exhibits of Southern-themed art from the 18th through 20th centuries. The museum is set in a renovated 1888 building designed by renowned local architect Henry Hobson Richardson and a newly constructed connecting five-story gallery. The Warehouse District museum is open Tuesday through Sunday 9:30 A.M. to 5:30 P.M., Thursday until 8:30 P.M.

MUSIC

Cathedral Concerts
Christ Church Cathedral
2919 St. Charles Avenue, New Orleans
(504) 895–6602
Begun in 1974 as part of this Episcopal church's outreach effort, the Cathedral Concerts encompass a wide variety of musical offerings performed by talented local musicians, including baroque, classical, jazz, and contemporary. An interesting aspect of the series is the post-concert reception during which audience members have the opportunity to talk with performers. The hourlong concerts are generally held on Sunday at 4:00 P.M. There is a church nursery provided for younger children. Cathedral Concerts are free, although donations are appreciated. For more information, call the church office Monday through Friday 9:00 A.M. to 5:00 P.M.

Louisiana Philharmonic Orchestra
Orpheum Theater
129 University Place, New Orleans
(504) 523–6530
www.lpomusic.com
As the only full-time professional orchestra in the Gulf South, the LPO goes out of

The city's orchestra, ballet association, and other groups of performers often sponsor talks between the audience and artists either before or after a show. They are educational and fun. Ask if one is scheduled for the show you're attending.

its way to serve and develop its audience. A 16-concert classical series and the relaxed-fit "Beethoven and Blue Jeans" are performed in the historic and beautifully restored Orpheum Theater. The "Casual Classics" programs are held at the Pontchartrain Center, a stone's throw from Lake Pontchartrain in the suburb of Kenner. The cabaret-style table seating (in addition to bleachers) and bring-a-picnic casualness have helped earn the series a loyal following. The "Southern Serenades" concerts take place on the elegant grounds of stately River Road plantation homes. Many performances include a pre-curtain "Words on Music" session in which orchestra members discuss the evening's selections. The Saturday morning Family Discovery series includes a trio of performances for young children that typically feature the Delta Festival Ballet as well as young musicians. An hour before the show, orchestra members introduce children to a variety of classical instruments and the sounds they make. This hands-on approach to music appreciation is called the Petting Zoo. Ticket prices are approximately $7.00 to $62.00, depending on the series. The box office is open Monday through Friday 9:00 A.M. to 5:00 P.M. Call for program and performance dates.

The New Orleans Opera Association
Mahalia Jackson Theatre of the
Performing Arts
801 North Rampart Street, New Orleans
(504) 529–2278
www.neworleansopera.org
North America's first grand opera was staged in the Big Easy, and New Orleanians

enjoyed the highest quality performances until the old French Opera House burned down in 1919. In 1943 a group of local music lovers, bent on reestablishing opera in the city, created the New Orleans Opera Association. Today the association presents three or four professional offerings each season. Operas not in English are accompanied by projected supertitles. Ticket prices are $30 to $100, with a $10 discount for students. The box office at 305 Baronne Street is open Monday through Friday 9:00 A.M. to 5:00 P.M.

The Trinity Artist Series
Trinity Episcopal Church
1329 Jackson Avenue, New Orleans
(504) 522-0276
www.trinityc.net
The Trinity concerts are performed by local as well as touring musicians. Programs have included performances by such notables as jazz artists Ellis Marsalis and the Moses Hogan Chorale; blues musicians Earl King and Marva Wright; and touring shows by the Paris Opera Boys Choir and the Tibetan Monks. A season highlight is always the Bach-a-Thon, a 24-hour concert celebrating the music of J. S. Bach, performed from midnight to midnight on or around his birthday, March 21. The church's classic pipe organ is also a mainstay of the series. Trinity performances take place every Sunday at 5:00 P.M. and last about an hour. The programs are free; however, donations are gladly accepted. For more information, call the church office during regular business hours.

In New Orleans, it's hard to find a bad meal and easy to find a good show for free. The Cathedral Concerts and the Trinity Artists Series often showcase topflight talent; the Louisiana Philharmonic Orchestraa periodically performs in City Park and at Zephyr Field.

THEATER

The Contemporary Arts Center
900 Camp Street, New Orleans
(504) 523-1216
www.cacno.org
In the heart of the Warehouse Arts District, the CAC produces plays by emerging and established contemporary playwrights. This one-time ice-cream factory is also a venue for local theater groups—for instance, the Alliance for Community Theater's Black Theater Festival, the Dog and Pony Theater Company, and Theatre Louisiane. Performances are held in two theaters: the main Freeport-McMoRan Theater, a technically well-equipped space with seating for 165; and the 100-seat experimental-type BankOne Theater. The center also hosts a monthly Playwrights' Unit's Staged Reading Series, where works-in-progress by local artists receive staged readings and peer critique. Ticket prices vary. Box office hours are Monday through Saturday 10:00 A.M. to 5:00 P.M.; Sunday 11:00 A.M. to 5:00 P.M.

Le Petit Theatre
616 St. Peter Street, New Orleans
(504) 522-2081
www.lepetittheatre.com
Founded in 1916 when a group of amateur theater-lovers began putting on plays in one of the group's drawing rooms, Le Petit is the oldest continuously operating community theater in the United States. Housed in an 1822 Spanish Colonial–style building, just down the street from St. Louis Cathedral, the little theater offers a full season of plays and musicals performed by an all-volunteer cast as well as productions associated with the Tennessee Williams Festival in March. There are also children's shows in the adjoining theatre—Teddy's Corner. Acting legend Helen Hayes said, "Le Petit Theatre is not just good community theater—it is magnificent community theater." (Coincidentally, the theater's 460-seat auditorium is

named for the celebrated actress.) Tickets tend to range from around $10 to $21, depending on the show. Box office hours are Monday through Friday 10:30 A.M. to 5:30 P.M.

Rivertown Repertory Theatre
325 Minor Street, Kenner
(504) 468-7221
www.rivertownkenner.com/theatre.html
Located in the historical Rivertown museum district, this 300-seat theater presents mostly traditional favorites such as Cole Porter's *Anything Goes, Born Yesterday,* and *Guys and Dolls,* September through May. The playhouse was built in 1994 and features a dining area with an optional precurtain buffet catered by Messina's, a popular local restaurant. Ticket prices are $20.00 for adults; $18.00 for seniors and students age 13 to 21; $10.00 for children age 6 to 12. (Tickets cost $2.00 more for musicals.) The optional buffet is $16. Group rates are available. Box office hours are Tuesday through Friday 10:00 A.M. to 4:00 P.M.

The Saenger Theatre
143 North Rampart Street, New Orleans
(504) 525-1052
www.saengertheatre.com
Constructed in 1927 for a whopping $2.5 million, the Saenger Theatre became one of the grand movie palaces of Hollywood's Golden Age. Today it is the New Orleans home for touring Broadway shows, concerts, and other special productions. But during any event the Saenger itself is an exquisite part of the show. The 4,000-seat landmark designed by Emile Weil is considered his greatest achievement in "atmospheric"-style theaters (which give the illusion of being outdoors). "Clouds" and more than 150 tiny ceiling lights in constellation patterns make audiences feel as though they're sitting under a beautiful night sky surrounded by Italian baroque architecture. The lobby's crystal chandelier once hung in the Palace of Versailles'

famed Hall of Mirrors. The theater originally owned a dozen of the chandeliers but sold off 11 to finance renovations. Another unique feature is the theater's 778-pipe Wonder Organ custom-designed for the Saenger's acoustics and the largest such instrument ever built by the Robert Morton Co. The Saenger is designated a New Orleans historic landmark and is found on the National Register of Historic Places. Ticket prices vary and can be purchased at the Saenger box office Monday through Friday 10:00 A.M. to 5:30 P.M., or through TicketMaster at (504) 522-5555.

Southern Repertory Theatre
333 Canal Street, New Orleans
(504) 522-6545
www.southernrep.com
"Dedicated to the Southern mystique," Southern Rep seeks to "capture the legend of Southern life and display it on stage." This Actors' Equity house founded in 1986 by Loyola University professor Rosary O'Neill produces regional as well as classic works in an intimate setting. Performances take place Thursday, Friday, and Saturday at 8:00 P.M. with Sunday matinees at 4:00 P.M. Ticket prices are $19 to $30 for adults; $15 for students and seniors. Box office hours are Tuesday through Saturday 10:00 A.M. to 6:00 P.M.

ARTS SUPPORT AND CLASSES

The Arts Council of New Orleans
225 Baronne Street, New Orleans
(504) 523-1465
www.artscouncilofneworleans.com
The Arts Council is a private, nonprofit organization providing programs and services to artists, arts organizations, the business community, and city government. Established in 1975, it is the official arts agency of the City of New Orleans. Programs and services include an arts business center designed to enhance the

marketing and entrepreneurial abilities of arts organizations; grants provided to 200 organizations annually; the Urban Arts Training Program, a job-training program for disadvantaged teenagers; and Percent for Art, the city's public art program. Office hours are Monday through Friday 9:00 A.M. to 5:00 P.M.

**New Orleans School of Glass
Works and Printmaking Studio
727 Magazine Street, New Orleans
(504) 529-7277
www.neworleansglassworks.com**
Since its opening in 1990, GlassWorks has been the site of exhibitions highlighting the works of prominent as well as emerg-

ing artists. Past exhibits include the luminous vitrography of Dale Chihuly, the delicate botanical works of Paul Stankard, and the sensual designs of Richard Royal. Free daily demonstrations of Venetian-style glassblowing in the South's largest contemporary facility feature glass sculpture, glass casting, lampworking, stained glass, printmaking, and bookbinding—all housed in a restored 19th-century storefront. Have your hand cast in glass; pick out a piece of colorful glass artwork to take home; chat with an artist. Then get in on the act by signing up for one of the weekend beginner classes. Donations to this nonprofit organization are welcome.

ANNUAL EVENTS AND FESTIVALS

Is it any wonder that a sassy, freewheeling city forever checking its pulse against the meter of some eternally offbeat, funky tempo would have found so many jubilant ways to ritualize its heartfelt love of life, music, and food? New Orleans has festivals and events to celebrate everything under the sun and stars. In fact, the city denies itself nothing for the sake of a good time, and the Big Easy will even offer a warm smile and breezy nod of understanding for those who might arch their brow in judgment of our characteristically carefree ways.

Ironically, we can chalk up at least part of our Big Easy heritage to religion. As a city settled by predominantly French and Spanish Catholics, New Orleans never quite grasped the Protestant work ethic like the rest of the country did. This, no doubt, explains why this unabashedly flamboyant and European-like enclave possesses such a seductive and masterful flair when it comes to letting the good times roll at the drop of a crab. This ethos was ingrained in the city's psyche early on, and by the time those somewhat stuffy, style-starved Americans from the Colonies began arriving here in the early 1800s following the Louisiana Purchase, New Orleans simply twirled its parasol over its shoulder and continued along its merry Creole way.

Many outsiders think of the Big Easy as an oversize frat party that uses the Superdome as a beer keg. Without a doubt the city can parade, dance, and eat up a storm like nobody's business. In fact, it takes a full calendar year for the City that Care Forgot to pack in with near-spiritual devotion all the best life has to offer, set against a backdrop of trombone-sliding brass band funk, spicy sausage jambalaya, and sunny days. But New Orleans more than anything else is a city of celebrations. If it offers hot eats, cool tunes, and just the right spin of light-hearted fun, chances are someone has built a festival around it. Outsiders wonder how we manage to get any work done. We wonder why we bother.

Not one but two parades, spaced a weekend apart and held in the Irish Channel and Old Metairie, respectively, celebrate the patron saint of Ireland with kisses and cabbages. In the French Quarter, dog lovers and their costumed canines in the Krewe of Barkus as well as the Bourbon Street Awards' drag-and-leather contest keep the campish possibilities of Mardi Gras on a long leash indeed. Enjoy sweet Creole tomatoes? The Great French Market Tomato Festival offers a weekend-long tribute to the region's heralded accept-no-substitutes cooking mainstay. Or join locals at the Greek Festival to pay tribute to the culture that gave the world philosophy—and the ouzo needed to understand it—all while munching on stuffed grape leaves and dancing to bouzouki music. The Essence Music Festival, which draws some of the nation's top entertainers from the worlds of rhythm and blues, soul, and hip-hop, has already earned its stripes as a major attraction and tourist draw.

You can't miss locals at the New Orleans Jazz and Heritage Festival. We're the ones dressed more casually than Californians at a surf wedding, dancing our heinies off or striking up friendly conversations with out-of-towners while waiting in line at a food booth for some shrimp remoulade or alligator-on-a-stick. When Carnival season officially kicks off on January 6, it doesn't stop until midnight on

Mardi Gras after more than 70 parades, thousands of king cakes, high-society balls, and downscale street parties later. During this time the Big Easy turns fantasy into reality and reveals to the world the true colors of its beautifully adulterated, quixotic soul: purple, green, and gold.

New Orleanians also make room on the social calendar for special occasions a little more serious but truly just as fun. A shining example is the Tennessee Williams Literary Festival, a tour de plume of the life and times of the author who gave the world *Night of the Iguana* and *A Streetcar Named Desire,* the famous play set in New Orleans about that always-shouting-about-something couple next door, Stanley and Stella Kowalski. The annual 10K Crescent City Classic helps locals burn off calories, while Art for Arts' Sake opens the art season with a nighttime "Artwalk" of more than 60 Uptown, French Quarter, and Warehouse District galleries hosting open houses. Celebration in the Oaks trumpets the arrival of the holiday season with a dazzling display of one million lights decorating City Park's centuries-old live oaks. And on December 31 the city kisses another year good-bye with its New Year's Eve countdown in the French Quarter outside Jackson Brewery on the Mississippi River. And then we start all over again. Got aspirin?

JANUARY

Nokia Sugar Bowl
Sugar Bowl Drive, New Orleans
(504) 525-8573
www.nokiasugarbowl.org
New Orleans Item newspaper publisher Colonel James M. Thomson and sports editor Fred Digby hatched the idea for a New Year's Day college football game in New Orleans in 1927. It took eight years to develop public and financial support for the project. On January 1, 1935, in the depths of the Depression, the first Sugar Bowl Football Classic was held at Tulane Stadium. Tulane's Green Wave, which were

undefeated in the South, were pitted against the only undefeated Northern team, Pop Warner's Temple University Owls. Tulane prevailed, 20–14, before a crowd of 22,026 who had paid $1.50 to $3.50 per person admission. A tradition was born. The Sugar Bowl was the subject of the first live TV program in New Orleans, in 1953, which was broadcast coast to coast. Seven years later it was the first game televised in color across the United States.

Over the years the Sugar Bowl has hosted several national champions and a virtual who's who of legendary football coaches including Frank Broyles, "Bear" Bryant, Bobby Bowden, Bob Devaney, Vince Dooley, Woody Hayes, "Shug" Jordan, Johnny Majors, Joe Paterno, and Bud Wilkinson.

In 1995 Nokia became the game's title sponsor and, subsequently, the Nokia Sugar Bowl signed a deal with the Orange, Fiesta, and Rose Bowls, stating that beginning in January 1999 each bowl would host a national championship once in the following four years. This agreement was designed to allow for the best possible bowl games while maintaining conference contractual obligations, plus increase the likelihood of an actual college championship game between the two highest-ranking teams. The Dome, home of the Sugar Bowl, seats around 77,000 in its expanded football configuration. Tickets for the Sugar Bowl usually go on sale in August and are sold through Ticketmaster at (504) 522-5555 or (800) 488-5252.

FEBRUARY

Lundi Gras
Woldenberg Park/Spanish Plaza
New Orleans
(504) 565-3033
www.auduboninstitute.org
As a city famous for cherishing tradition, and no more so than during Carnival season, it seemed only a matter of time before the celebration of Lundi Gras, which

lasted from 1872 until the beginning of World War I in 1917, was reborn in high style. Today Lundi Gras, or Fat Monday, the day always preceding Mardi Gras, is sort of a minifestival within a festival. Revitalized in 1986, it features the city's two premier Carnival organizations—Rex and Zulu.

Thousands of locals and tourists alike are lured to the daylong outdoor festivities starting at 10:00 A.M. at Woldenberg Park on the banks of the Mississippi River and including music, food, and, of course, some Carnival ceremony. Traditional New Orleans brass bands, Mardi Gras Indians, and local rhythm and blues singers lay down the soundtrack for dancing Lundi-goers, while boiled crawfish, po-boys, filé gumbo, alligator-sausage-on-a-stick, and other local foodstuffs provide another taste of what Carnival is all about. Characters such as the Witch Doctor and Mr. Big Stuff from the Zulu Aid and Pleasure Club, the city's oldest African-American Carnival krewe, second-line through the festival every hour. At 5:00 P.M., make way for the ceremonial arrival of King and Queen Zulu by way of the Mississippi River.

After the arrival of Zulu, the second phase of Lundi Gras moves upriver to Spanish Plaza for the 6:00 P.M. arrival of Rex, or King of Carnival, by Coast Guard cutter and a flotilla of riverboats to an official welcome from the Mayor of New Orleans, the consular corps, and other officials and dignitaries. Hizzoner reads a proclamation that officially turns the City that Care Forgot over to Carnival's Main Man, Rex, for 24 hours until the equally official end of Mardi Gras, which occurs at midnight on Fat Tuesday.

MARCH

New Orleans Spring Fiesta Association
826 St. Ann Street, New Orleans
(504) 581–1367, (800) 550–8450

To glimpse the procession of horse-drawn carriages with the Spring Fiesta Queen and her court as it makes its way through the French Quarter under an azalea-filled afternoon is to experience the genteel, small-town side of New Orleans pageantry. For more than six decades this March event has welcomed the graciousness of spring with four days of guided tours of select, highly historic, and architecturally significant homes in the French Quarter, Garden District, and Plantation Country. Mind your manners.

The centuries have seen passions kindled and passing fancies dwindle inside the city's mercilessly romantic Victorian-style Creole homes, Garden District mansions of Italianate grandeur, and former slave quarters renovated with tasteful Greek Revival flourishes. And this festival is a unique way to explore the history and romance always in fashion behind the curtains of New Orleans' architectural legacy. Tickets for the various tours as well as the gala that follows Saturday's presentation of the queen's court in Jackson Square and "Night in Old New Orleans" parade of carriages through the French Quarter are available through the New Orleans Spring Fiesta Association.

St. Patrick's Day
Irish Channel and Old Metairie

Nobody begs, steals, or borrows any excuse to have a parade like the Irish, and where else but in New Orleans would they have mustered the blarney to hold two processions a week apart for the same occasion? Equally important, how many places can paradegoers count on catching cabbages, carrots, and potatoes for an Irish stew from float-riding Hibernians as part of an annual bash held in the name of Celtic pride?

Everyone is a leprechaun for the day as a convoy of floats and trucks festively decorated with all manner of lucky charms and four-leaf clovers rumble down city streets. Walking club members twirl white and emerald-green umbrellas and hand out paper roses in exchange for a peck on the cheek and an "Erin Go Braugh!" Wear a "Kiss me, I'm Irish" button and try to catch the eye of a green-vested float rider scanning the crowd and maybe you'll catch enough plastic cups, doubloons, and beads to make even your non-Irish friends green with envy.

The first shamrock-festooned event is probably the larger of the city's Irish parades and falls on the Saturday before St. Patrick's Day. It rolls aptly enough through the Irish Channel, where many of the city's Irish immigrants settled in the 1800s, looking like one of those old-fashioned, waving-from-atop-the-back-of-the-convertible kind of neighborhood parades from a bygone era. The Irish Channel is bordered by Jackson and Louisiana Avenues, Magazine Street, and the Mississippi River. The parade usually starts at 2:00 P.M. Saturday at the corner of Race and Annunciation Streets, rolls up Magazine Street to Louisiana Avenue, heads down Louisiana to Prytania Street, where it makes a U-turn back to Annunciation, down Annunciation to Washington Avenue, and ending at the corner of Washington and Tchoupitoulas Street.

Anyone who hasn't had their fill of green beer can catch the smaller parade at 6:00 P.M. that evening, which rolls from Molly's At The Market, 1107 Decatur Street in the French Quarter, and runs along Decatur, Royal, and Bourbon Streets. Molly's, a venerated watering hole, long popular with local media types, keeps the drinks and good cheer flowing.

Old Metairie weighs in with its own high-stepping, beer-sippin'-guys-handing-out-flowers-for-kisses parade the following Sunday at noon. The route of this popular 30-year-old Jefferson Parish parade is crowded but no more so than on Metairie Road. Green spaces and parking places are jammed with RVs and pick-ups parked door handle to door handle overnight as well as families out for a day of fun with their charcoal grills, coolers, lawn chairs, and sun umbrellas.

Arrive early and count on spending three hours to see the entire parade, which includes nearly two dozen floats, more than 30 trucks, seven minifloats, and a dozen marching bands. This spectacle enjoys a reputation for thumbing its collective nose at the silly notion of sobriety. In the past it wasn't uncommon for some paraders to duck into each bar on the route for a not-so-quick glass of kelly-green cheer. By the time they had reached Metairie Road, the procession had turned into a highly unsteady state of affairs. Some members of the Jefferson Parish City Council have even proposed a ban on alcohol consumption by parade participants as a result of reports of excessive drinking. One council member said the message of the parade should not be "getting dead drunk."

Old Metairie's parade begins near Archbishop Rummel High School on Severn Avenue and 41st Street in Metairie, rolls south on Severn, and turns east when it gets to Metairie Road. It continues down Metairie Road, turns left onto Focis Street, and proceeds up Focis to the intersection of Focis and Canal Streets, where it disbands.

Many clubs and bars offer St. Patrick's Day fun, but for a week's worth of sing-alongs, storytellers, dart games, Irish folk music, jigs, and reels, plus a few pints of stout to top things off, head to O'Flaherty's Irish Channel Pub at 514 Toulouse Street in the French Quarter. Call ahead for a schedule of St. Patrick's Day–related events.

Tennessee Williams/New Orleans Literary Festival
938 Lafayette Street, New Orleans
(504) 581-1144
www.tennesseewilliams.net
The name sounds highbrow, but by the time you've finished screaming your brains out in the Stella and Stanley Shouting Contest, you're far wiser to the ways of our little corner of the world. And that world likes to honor its own—in this case America's legendary playwright and the literary heritage of the city he called his "spiritual home." This weeklong March festival is a lightning rod for high-typing literary figures as well as those of us whose favorite Tennessee moment is the Natalie Wood skinny-dipping scene in the screen adaptation of *This Property Is Condemned*.

Highlights include nearly three dozen literary panels, theatrical productions, poetry readings, musical events, and an expansive book fair, as well as literary walking tours of the French Quarter, jazz and New Orleans movie sites, St. Louis Cemetery No. 1, and Anne Rice's haunts. Nearly a dozen master classes have been combined into the three-day French Quarter Literary Conference, where aspiring writers and avid readers alike can glean writing tips firsthand from some of their favorite authors.

Most events take place at Le Petit Theatre du Vieux Carré, 616 St. Peter Street, which serves as festival headquarters. Neighboring French Quarter venues—the Cabildo, the Historic New Orleans Collection, 21 Supper Club, O'Flaherty's Irish Pub, the Monteleone Hotel, and the Palm Court Jazz Cafe—also host various events. A Literary Panel Pass for admission to all weekend discussions as well as one-day passes are available. Individuals can register for one or more 90-minute master classes or for the entire French Quarter Literary Conference, which includes all master classes, a Festival Panel Pass, and two evening receptions. Tickets to other theater events are available.

The festival ends on a thunderous note during the popular Stella and Stanley Shouting Contest, better known as the "Stell-Off," with prizes awarded to the best interpretation of the warring mates in *Streetcar*. A bevy of wannabe Stanleys bellow to the lovelorn Stella and Stanley who stand on a balcony at the historic Pontalba Apartments in Jackson Square.

APRIL

Crescent City Classic
8200 Hampson Street, New Orleans
(504) 861–8686
www.ccc10K.com
Even a city renowned for its unbridled indulgence of sensual and gastronomic pleasures can muster the discipline to host what has become a major spectacle of endurance drawing top runners from all over the world. As one might expect in New Orleans, this 10K road race, which begins on Decatur Street at Jackson Square and ends at the entrance to City Park, also draws its share of walkers and others in costume who prefer to take their time and get nowhere fast. An estimated 20,000 persons participate in this mid-April race. Live music, food booths, and sporting gear tents await contestants at the end of the race. Come out and watch someone set a world record— either for best time or for the amount of jambalaya and beer consumed at the finish line.

French Quarter Festival
400 North Peter Street, New Orleans
(504) 522–5730, (800) 673–5725
www.frenchquarterfestivals.org
Didn't the city just celebrate Mardi Gras less than two months ago? Yes, Virginia, but by April we're in major party withdrawal. And for many New Orleanians the annual French Quarter Festival is the perfect sort of post-Lenten fete between Carnival's end and when Jazzfest pumps up the jam in late April. Far from being merely some warmed-over affair, though, this highly popular festival's breezy blend of outdoor springtime fun in the city's most historic district lasts only a weekend, but it serves up what we cherish most about our Big Easy good times—food, music, and still more food.

Since 1983 this festival, named the best in Louisiana by *Offbeat* magazine readers in 1995 and 1996, has earned its gold-cluster crawfish tails as a major event offering more than 100 hours of free musical entertainment, "the world's largest jazz brunch" (with more than 60 booths serving up specialties from the city's best restaurants), tours of private French Quarter courtyards, and fireworks over the Mississippi River. Concerts, a battle of the jazz bands, a bartender's competition, the Pirate's Alley Art Show, and second-line parading take place throughout the Vieux Carré and Woldenberg Riverfront Park.

Kick back on the grass in Jackson Square with some crawfish-stuffed bread, red beans and rice, or grilled chicken livers with hot-pepper jelly—or all three, no one's watching—while listening to live jazz, gospel, zydeco, and classical music on one of several music stages. Amble over to the International Stage on Bourbon Street and catch a German oompah band or Irish folk group, then head to the Royal Street Stage, where the Louisiana Philharmonic Orchestra trumpets the classics. Grab some café au lait and mosey over to the French Market along Decatur Street to hear some live Cajun and zydeco groups.

Whatever you do, though, you'll be doing it in good company: More than a quarter-million people attend the three-day Friday-to-Sunday event each year. And for those who track such things, a University of New Orleans survey found that 40 percent of festivalgoers gave the festival a 10 rating; 47 percent rated it 8 or 9. To festival hounds like us, that's the equivalent of a cheery thumbs up from *Consumer Reports.*

New Orleans Jazz and Heritage Festival
Fair Grounds Race Course, New Orleans
(504) 522-4786
www.nojazzfest.com
A friend takes no small amount of pride in the fact that he has yet to miss a single day, much less a nanosecond, of this two-weekend food- and music-drenched blowout since it started in 1970. Come rain or career, the poster child for New Orleans's mother of all festivals each year

The internationally renowned Jazzfest held the last weekend in April and first weekend in May is one of the hottest tickets in town—and not just because of the music. The weather this time of year can include rain and/or scorching heat. So come prepared—bring an umbrella (a disposable plastic raincoat isn't a bad idea either) as well as sunblock, sunglasses, and bottled water.

dons his straw hat, sunglasses, T-shirt, and suspendered jeans and heads out to the Fair Grounds armed with his meticulously color-coded performance schedule of what acts he's going to see and when.

Devotees of this festival, which draws jazz lovers and die-hard foodies alike from all over the world, understand completely. Munching on spicy crawfish bisque, catfish amandine, stuffed artichokes, Creole-stuffed crabs, sweet potato pie, boudin sausage, blackened redfish, or a barbe-cued alligator po-boy while shaking your booty to an A-list of music powerhouses is enough to knock the flip-flops off just about anybody.

Dress in your favorite boppin' attire. In recent years Jazzfest's heavyweight muscle has been buffed by an ever-widening roster of both cutting-edge and venerated local and international performers from the worlds of gospel, jazz, Latin, blues, reggae, Afro-Caribbean, ragtime, salsa, bluegrass, zydeco, rock, hip-hop, and alternative music. Nonstop performances presented simultaneously on 12 stages throughout the Fair Grounds Race Track keep the joint jumping from 11:00 A.M. to 7:00 P.M. Whether it's the likes of B.B. King and the Neville Brothers or community gospel choirs and African-inspired dance collectives, the event was recently named the country's best music festival by *Poll-star* and is all but guaranteed to crease the face of even the most hard-to-please fest snob.

A new multitiered, air-conditioned grandstand features the Music Heritage Stage as well as the folk and African heritage stages, spotlighting the diversity of Louisiana's culture with contemporary arts-and-crafts exhibits, video presentations, cooking demonstrations, a variety of music performances, and "intimate interviews." Brass bands and marching clubs begin and end their parades in this area.

Souvenir hounds should head to the Louisiana Heritage Fair on the racecourse infield for one-of-a-kind hand-painted silk clothing, fanciful leather masks, jewelry, photographs, and sculptures. The Congo

Square African Marketplace highlights the vibrancy of indigenous African culture through original artwork, crafts, and music performances.

Jazzfest is held Friday through Sunday in the last week in April and Thursday through Sunday in the first week in May. But if you can't always get what you want at the Fair Grounds, an evening concert series of top-name acts is also held at venues throughout the city, including the Kiefer UNO Lakefront Arena, the Morris F.X. Jeff Municipal Auditorium at Armstrong Park, and the Praline Connection Gospel & Blues Hall at 907 South Peters Street.

Jazzfest producer/director Quint Davis gives the event an added educational spin with a series of free music and cultural workshops open to the public and held at local schools and colleges as well as the Mahalia Jackson Theatre for the Performing Arts.

Jazzfest began in 1970 when 300 musicians entertained a crowd half that number at New Orleans's historic Congo Square. Music legends Mahalia Jackson, Duke Ellington, Pete Fountain, and Al Hirt performed—all brought together by producer George Wein, founder of the Newport Jazz Festival. Today nearly 10,000 musicians, cooks, and craftspeople entertain more than 400,000 persons each year during the rollicking, fun-filled 10-day event.

Parking is available. New Orleans Tours Inc. operates a continuous round-trip Jazzfest Express bus service from the downtown Sheraton New Orleans, Superdome, French Quarter, and City Park to the Fair Grounds Race Course during festival days 10:45 A.M. to 7:30 P.M. Call (800) 380–3378 for cost. The Regional Transit authority operates public bus routes to the Fair Grounds. For information call (504) 248–3900. Taxis also offer convenient transportation at a special-events rate, which varies year to year, or the meter reading, whichever is higher. Festival tickets are available through Ticketmaster or by mail. Browse the Web site for up-to-the-minute information, photographs, online chats,

and much more. Better yet, meet you at the Gospel Tent.

MAY

Greek Festival
1200 Robert E. Lee Boulevard
New Orleans
(504) 282–0259
www.greekfestnola.com
If Greek folk dancing mixed with shouts of "opa!" and seasoned with tasty dishes of spring lamb, souvlaki, and Athenian salad sound like fun, this fund-raising festival may be your cup of ouzo. Just phyllo the crowds. Each year since 1973 more than 15,000 festivalgoers have sampled the alpha-to-omega roster of fun, which includes gourmet foodstuffs like pastitsio (pasta and ground meat), spanakopita (spinach pie), tiropita (cheese pie), dolmades (rice-stuffed grape leaves), gyro and baklava sundaes, as well as all manner of Hellenic imports, from clothing and Greek vases to gold and silver jewelry.

This community festival is held during Memorial Day weekend at the Hellenic Cultural Center at Holy Trinity Cathedral. Built in 1864 and reconstructed in 1985 after a fire, Holy Trinity Cathedral is the oldest Greek Orthodox Church in the United States and is located on Robert E. Lee Boulevard at St. Bernard Avenue. The festival also offers tours of the Holy Trinity Cathedral and features both a 1 mile and 5K Olympic Run to benefit the cathedral. (For registration information call 504–282–0259.) Admission is $5.00 at the gate, $3.00 in advance; children under 10 free. Hours are Friday 5:00 to 11:00 P.M., Saturday 11:00 A.M. to 11:00 P.M., and Sunday 11:00 A.M. to 9:00 P.M.

New Orleans Wine and Food Experience
P.O. Box 70514, New Orleans 70112-1909
(504) 529–9463
www.nowfe.com
Since 1991 gourmands and gourmets alike have united for four days under the banner

of nonprofit culinary good deeds called the New Orleans Wine and Food Experience. Full registration is nearly $435, but what participants get in return is well worth the hassle of digging up a pair of elastic-waist pants: two grand tastings with more than 800 vintages and specialties of more than 100 of the city's best-known restaurants Saturday and Sunday at the Ernest N. Morial Convention Center; four food and wine seminars; and the "Royal Street Experience," during which French Quarter antiques shops and art galleries hold open house with yet more wine tastings and food.

Local palates got a first taste of this event in 1991 when a group of food and wine enthusiasts (of which the city has plenty) got together with some of the great chefs of New Orleans as well as some of the top vintners and wineries in the country. The "experience" begins with grand multicourse vintner dinners at more than 30 restaurants, which include multiple wines from a particular vineyard with a principal, often the winemaker, on hand to explain the wine before each course. Vintner dinners are $85, and reservations and payment are made directly to the restaurant. Typically, more than 5,000 people from almost every state and several foreign countries are in attendance. Proceeds benefit the Louisiana Restaurant Association's School-to-Career program.

JUNE

The Great French Market
Creole Tomato Festival
1008 North Peters Street, New Orleans
(504) 522-2621
www.frenchmarket.org
It may sound small-town to say, but Louisiana's luscious, sweet, and unbelievably tasty homegrown Creole tomatoes are worth biting home about. If this festival holds high its namesake, it's only because the state's tomatoes form the backbone of so much local cooking. Like its luminary counterparts, the Florida orange and California avocado, the Mississippi Delta soil-grown Creole tomato is heralded by virtually everyone who has ever enjoyed the good fortune of its company. And the idea of throwing a free outdoor party at the French Market in June to celebrate the sacred vegetable-fruit with live music, cooking demonstrations, crafts, and face painting, with a few clowns tossed in to boot, seems as good a reason as any to duck chores for the day.

The International Arts Festival
City Park, New Orleans
(504) 367-1313
www.internationalartsfestival.com
Perhaps it's all those balmy days, overgrown banana trees, and easygoing rhythms that earned New Orleans its moniker as the Northernmost Island in the Caribbean. Or maybe it's the fact that both cultures—New Orleans and the Caribbean—share a similar disdain for life not lived to the fullest. In some parts of the Caribbean it's called "limin," patois for taking it easy. In our neck of the Caribbean it's called "laissez les bon temps rouler"—let the good times roll. Either way, this festival dips its straw hat to the Big Easy–West Indies link with renowned reggae artists, authentic island foods, and traditional Caribbean crafts, all at Marconi Meadows in City Park each year during the second weekend in June.

Whether you stir it up or legalize it, this 18-year-old Jazzfest-meets-Reggae Sunsplash house party can set even us off-island types to swaying like banyan trees in the tradewinds. And it's not just because of the good spirits. The nirvana-like mix of cool reggae and pulsing calypso, soca, and World Beat rhythms, when added to spicy Jamaican jerk chicken, curried goat, and steamy coconut-and-crab callaloo soup, could make anyone feel as though he or she has gone to Blue Mountain heaven. And heaven knows you might as well browse the craft booths for a new silk-screen T-shirt of Bob Marley to wear to the office next Casual Friday. Tickets are available at

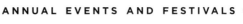

Ticketmaster, and admission is free for children under 12.

JULY

Essence Music Festival
Sugar Bowl Drive, New Orleans
(504) 522-5555
www.essence.com

This three-day celebration and tour de force of African-American culture and music has become a powerhouse draw for locals and travelers alike during one of the city's traditionally slow tourism months. Consider: An estimated 175,000 attendees pump a reported over $80 million into the local economy during this major early-July event, which started in 1993. Holding this event in the home of the African-American jazz legacy made a lot of sense to festival organizers, the New York–based Essence Communications Inc., publisher of *Essence* magazine. But they went a step farther: In addition to standing-room-only performances by leading blues, jazz, soul, and hip-hop artists at the Louisiana Superdome, the festival also offers a roster of empowerment seminars at the Ernest N. Morial Convention Center. Tickets are available at Ticketmaster at the number listed above.

AUGUST

Satchmo SummerFest
400 North Peters Street, New Orleans
(504) 522-5730, (800) 673-5725
www.satchmosummerfest.com

The most famous trumpet player in the history of modern music is feted as only he could be celebrated in the city of his birth. This five-day August event offers music lovers and jazz fans the chance to experience and explore the life and times of Louis "Satchmo" Armstrong, who helped put jazz on the map nearly a century ago. Most of the events take place in and around the Louisiana State Museum's Old U.S. Mint at 400 Esplanade Avenue in

The newest reason to brave the August heat is the Satchmo SummerFest, a weekend-long celebration of New Orleans native and jazz pioneer Louis "Satchmo" Armstrong through food, free music, and special events. The event is held early in the month in the French Quarter in and around the Old U.S. Mint. See ya there!

the French Quarter. This food and free-music festival also features seminars on Armstrong's music and legacy, a club crawl, art and photo exhibits, a jazz Mass, and second-line parades. From brass bands to big bands, continuous live music on three stages will keep the joint jumpin' when the city's newest festival, launched in 2001, reminds us what a wonderful world it is.

SEPTEMBER

Southern Decadence
French Quarter, New Orleans
(504) 522-8047
www.southerndecadence.com

For some cities family barbecues and last-minute trips to the beach mark the end of summer. In New Orleans, however, it's the time when hundreds of castanet-playing, whistle-blowing drag queens parade through the French Quarter serving up a silver platter full of attitude, all in the name of fun. This always colorful and highly anticipated parade kicks up its heels—literally—at 2:00 P.M. the Sunday before Labor Day when the grand marshal arrives with his entourage and begins leading the rowdy boys and girls of summer on a secret route through the French Quarter. One year this outrageous group's walk on the wild side took them through St. Louis Cathedral—during Mass. Another year they teased tourists in the lobby of the Fairmont Hotel.

What began as an informal march back in 1973 from Matassa's Bar to 2110

Barracks Street has become one of the city's favorite expressions of lifestyle freedom, one which draws an estimated 125,000 revelers and contributes a reported $96 million to the local economy. People looking for more information are encouraged to contact *AmBush Magazine* at the number listed above or visit the Southern Decadence Web site.

New Orleans festivals are renowned for good times, great food, and, as one might expect in the Big Easy, lots of booze. If you enjoy alcohol, do so responsibly. And if you've had too much to drink, do yourself and everyone else a favor: Don't drive; call a cab. This may be a freewheeling city, but that doesn't mean the police won't bust drunken drivers.

OCTOBER

Art for Arts' Sake
900 Camp Street, New Orleans
(504) 523-1216

Time to dry-clean the spaghetti-strap black Halston or give that special Armani suit a once-over with the lint brush. The art season is officially opening, and we don't want to be seen looking, um, unstylish while browsing the wine-and-cheese open house hosted by local art galleries, do we? No matter how you dress to paint the town, though, this annual citywide extravaganza, started in 1980 to benefit the Contemporary Arts Center, has become one of the year's best excuses to explore what New Orleans's visual artists are creating for, well, arts' sake. Participating in the "Artwalk," held on the first Saturday in October, are more than 50 commercial galleries on Magazine Street in Uptown, Julia Street in the Warehouse District, and Royal Street in the French Quarter, open from 6:00 to 9:00 P.M. Side-

walks are pleasantly crowded with everyone from window-shoppers to serious patrons. A free bus shuttle provided by the Magazine Street Merchant Association runs a continuous loop from Race Street in the Lower Garden District to Joseph Street Uptown and is designed to alleviate some of the gridlock of drivers cruising Magazine Street for a parking space. Riders can disembark at any corner.

Gumbo Festival
1701 Bridge City Avenue, Bridge City
(504) 436-4712
www.hgaparish.org/gumbofestivities.htm

For every food there is a season, and the murky, densely flavored valedictorian of Louisiana's down-home school of cooking is no exception to the roux. The annual Gumbo Festival, held the second weekend in October in Bridge City, proclaimed in 1973 by then-Gov. Edwin Edwards as the Gumbo Capital of the World, offers the chance to pay homage to 2,000 gallons of this stewy, roux-based heaven out of Africa cooked fresh daily. Gumbo, or "gombo," is a native name for okra, a popular ingredient in the dish, among the Bantu tribes of Africa.

The festival, started in 1972 by the Rev. Monsignor J. Anthony Luminais and parishioners of Holy Guardian Angels Church, is a small-town tour de force of gumbo served a variety of ways, including with okra, seafood/sausage, chicken/sausage, duck, poule d'eau, and z'herbs. New Orleans–style red beans and rice with sausage, jambalaya, and hamburgers, hot dogs, and homemade cakes and candy round off the food booth menus. Live entertainment includes the usual complement of Cajun/zydeco, country, jazz, blues, and rock music, a midway, craft booths, souvenirs, carnival rides, and a 5K Bridge Run held Saturday morning over the Huey P. Long Bridge, which spans the Mississippi River. Don't be bashful, the Beautiful Child Contest is now open to all age groups.

The Gumbo Festival is held in Bridge City on the west bank of Jefferson Parish across the Huey P. Long Bridge. To reach the bridge take I-10 west from downtown New Orleans 15 to 20 minutes to the Clearview Parkway exit. Follow the clearview parkway south sign at the off-ramp, which will loop around onto Clearview Parkway heading toward the Mississippi River. Take Clearview Parkway all the way to the end and enter the bridge when you see the well-marked sign. The narrow-enough-to-be-one-lane two-lane divided bridge was built in 1935 and shakes a little, especially when tractor-trailer rigs whiz past at perilous speeds. But it's a short drive over the Mississippi River and into Bridge City and well worth the effort for this festival. Admission is $2.00 per person, per day; children under 5 free. Parking and onstage entertainment are free.

Mensaje Spanish Festival
Zephyrs Stadium, 6000 Airline Drive Metairie
(504) 734-5155
www.mensajefestival.com
The city's Latin-American and Latino communities step into the spotlight during the second and third weekend in October with the Mensaje Festival, a celebration of the culture, folkways, food, music, and dance of 14 Hispanic countries in the Western Hemisphere. Since 1979, this annual fund-raiser for the Archdiocese of New Orleans' Hispanic Mensaje ministry has offered a lively and colorful multicultural experience. Sample a freshly baked pupusa from El Salvador or rice and peas from the Dominican Republic while watching Garifuna dancers from Belize perform in folkloric costumes — you'll get the idea. Live entertainment typically features more than three dozen performers such as international Latin headliners Jon Secada and Caroline Lao, as well as the city's hottest Latin bands, including Los Babies del Merengue and Ritmo Caribeno. More than two dozen rides help keep the youngsters entertained at this increasingly popular event held at Zephyrs Stadium that drew more

than 30,000 visitors in 2003. Hands down this is the best event year-round in New Orleans in which to immerse yourself in local and international Latin culture, a feast for the senses that will leave you saying, "Ole!" Admission is $5.00; children under 12 free.

New Orleans Film Festival
843 Carondelet Street, New Orleans
(504) 523-3818
www.neworleansfilmfest.com
As a film festival city, it may not be that long before New Orleans starts nudging its way into the spotlight dominated by Cannes, Sundance, Toronto, and Telluride. Until then, the 16-year-old New Orleans Film Festival quietly dims the lights in mid-October, flips on the projector, and rolls the global gamut of celluloid culture, from high-flung, full-length independent features to fast, cheap, out-of-control art-house flicks. But no matter how you like your popcorn buttered, this volunteer-driven labor of love sponsored by the nonprofit New Orleans Film Society, founded in 1989, is a cinematic feast for the devotee of experimental film as well as the merely curious moviegoer who couldn't care less that Igmar and Ingrid Bergman weren't related.

More than 30 major feature-length regional premiers are held at the Canal Street Landmark Cinema (dubbed the "Big House" during the festival) at 333 Canal Place at the edge of the French Quarter. Screenings of nearly 90 independent and low-budget movies from around the region and the world that people are not likely to see anywhere else are held at the Contemporary Arts Center at 900 Camp Street, the Entergy IMAX Theatre at the Aquarium of the Americas at 1 Canal Street, and Prytania Theater at 5339 Prytania Street in the Garden District. Cinema 16's Independent Filmmakers' Showcase is the competitive part of the festival and presents features, shorts, documentaries, animation, music videos, and experimental films of all lengths in 16mm, Super-8, and video formats.

Special events include galas, cocktail parties, and gatherings for local and visiting filmmakers and industry guests as well as late-night events with live music from local bands. Directors and other industry pros hold panel discussions on everything from funding and producing to distributing the independent film, documentary filmmaking, and how to obtain an agent. The closing-night party is a chichi celebration typically held at a Warehouse District nightclub. Tickets for movies are available at Canal Place Cinema and the Prytania Theater box office, and a cover charge is required for the Saturday and Thursday closing-night parties held at locations announced at least a week before the festival begins. The cost for weekend workshops varies, so call ahead.

NOVEMBER/DECEMBER

Celebration in the Oaks
1 Palm Drive, New Orleans
(504) 482-4888

If any part of New Orleans looks like a fairy-tale wonderland during the holidays, it's City Park when the greenspace's centuries-old live oaks are bedecked, adorned, and otherwise strung branch to trunk with more than one million twinkling Christmas lights, fanciful ornaments, and mirrored objets d'art. Each year an estimated 500,000 people visit Celebration in the Oaks, and the line of cars waiting to enter the 2-mile driving tour often extends

---

The city looks magical during the holidays. Special holiday events beloved by locals include candlelight caroling in Jackson Square, driving or walking through "Celebration in the Oaks," where City Park's centuries-old oaks are decorated with thousands of lights and ornaments, and strolling the Fairmont Hotel's marvelously decorated block-long lobby. Bring the kids!

---

out onto Wisner Avenue. But it's worth the wait, especially if traveling with children. Visitors can also park their cars and take a walking tour, which should include a stop at the Christmas tree-lined and festively decorated Botanical Gardens and Storyland. Here kids and grown-ups alike can enjoy a cup of hot chocolate and other refreshments in between rides on the park's historic carousel of antique wooden horses, tilt-a-whirl, giant slide, and roller coaster. Santa, of course, visits nightly to hear youngsters' holiday wish lists. Caroling, a live Nativity, real snow, and fireworks on various nights (always call for dates) round off the events, which run from the day after Thanksgiving. The park is open for nighttime driving and walking tours from 5:30 to 10:30 P.M. Driving tours cost $12.00 per car; walking tours, $5.00 per person; children under 3 free.

Christmas New Orleans Style
400 North Peters Street, New Orleans
(504) 522-5730, (800) 673-5725
www.christmasneworleans.com

During the holidays the city rolls out the red holly berries with a Santa sack full of fun under the banner "Christmas, New Orleans Style," from decorated hotel lobbies and old New Orleans homes and traditional Creole reveillon dinners to a night of candlelight caroling in romantic Jackson Square. Festivities kick off in early December with tree-lighting ceremonies held at the French Market at the corner of St. Philip and Decatur Streets and at Lee Circle and continue throughout the month with holiday tours of old New Orleans homes Uptown and in the French Quarter, hosted by the Preservation Resource Center at (504) 636-3040 and French Quarter Festivals at (504) 522-5730, respectively. For other holiday walking tours call Friends of the Cabildo at (504) 523-3939, St. Louis Cathedral at (504) 525-9585, and St. Catherine of Siena in Old Metairie at (504) 831-1166. Or see how the Creoles decorated their Victorian homes during Christmas in the 19th century with tours of the Gallier House Museum, 1118 Royal Street, and Hermann-Grima, 820 St. Louis Street. Call (504) 525–5661.

Peckish? Try one of the four- or five-course, fixed-price reveillon lunches or dinners offered by a growing number of restaurants citywide through Christmas Eve. This French tradition, revitalized locally in 1987, lasts three weeks and hearkens back to the mid-1800s when Creole families would follow Christmas Eve Midnight Mass at St. Louis Cathedral with a simple, breakfast-till-dawn feast of eggs, sweetbreads, daube glacé, and filled cakes. Today, in theory, the reveillon menu should feature once-a-year or otherwise unique dishes not normally available at the restaurant. Unfortunately, in reality some but certainly not all participating restaurants simply choose to repackage their regular menus.

Duck into the Fairmont and stroll this venerated hotel's block-long lobby of manger scenes, flocked Christmas trees, and an angel hair "snow tunnel" decorated with more than 30,000 lights. Then duck into the Fairmont's famed Sazarac Bar for a little holiday cheer. Elsewhere the city's churches, universities, and performing arts organizations host productions of *The Nutcracker, Messiah,* and holiday music programs.

Christmas Eve Bonfires
River Parishes
(800) 367–7852
www.festivalofthebonfires.org
Legend has it that the early Cajuns who settled upriver from New Orleans in a region called the River Parishes burned huge Christmas Eve bonfires along the riverbanks to light the way for Papa Noël and his sled team of alligators. Another version says the bonfires were lit for people returning from Mass on the opposite side of the Mississippi River. Either way, the tradition continues today each Christmas Eve night as an estimated 100 towering infernos burn for hours on the west side of the levee along the Mississippi

Among the most unique holiday celebrations anywhere in the country is the Festival of the Bonfires held in the River Parishes 34 minutes from New Orleans. During Christmastime up to 100 towering tepee-shaped bonfires constructed along the Mississippi River levee are lighted to help guide the way for Papa Noel following a centuries-old tradition.

River in Vacherie, Lutcher, and Gramercy at Louisiana Highway 44, a one-hour drive west of New Orleans on I-10. Residents of St. John the Baptist and St. James parishes spend weeks building the huge wooden structures, which can be counted on for warmth on a cold Christmas Eve night. Ample street parking is available, and there is no charge to walk along the levee and enjoy mingling with the locals and tourists who turn out for this special event. A Festival of the Bonfires is usually held the second weekend in December at the Lutcher/Gramercy Knights of Columbus Home on Louisiana Highway 51 in Lutcher.

New Year's Eve
Jackson Brewery
620–624 Decatur Street, New Orleans
(504) 566–7245
www.jacksonbrewery.com
Seriously, could a street-party city like New Orleans end the year on anything but a bang? (And, no, we're not referring to those shameful few who choose to discharge firearms into the sky at midnight.) The countdown action takes place in the French Quarter, where a lighted ball drops from the top of Jackson Brewery to the whoops and hollers of cheering midnight revelers. This Third Coast celebration may not be as well known as its Time Square counterpart, but at least in New Orleans partygoers can count on being surrounded by tons of places in which to grab—what else?—the first meal of the New Year. Pop the bubbly and pass the crawfish.

MARDI GRAS

A couple of years ago, following a traditional breakfast of eggs Sardou and Bloody Marys in the palm-flanged courtyard of the French Quarter's Louis XVI Restaurant, we ambled outside to greet the beckoning cloudless day and outrageous revelry. Our tight-knit, costumed coterie featured a Sultan of Schwing, a French maid, a tigress, and a pair of regally attired faux royalty—Hapsburgs, no doubt. We mamboed toward Bourbon Street as The Meters' impossibly funky version of "New Suit" blared from a stereo perched on a fern-framed, bead-bedecked balcony overhead. *"Every year at Carnival time we make a new suit . . . "* Then we turned the corner and came face to face with ground zero of the greatest free show on Earth: Mardi Gras.

Comically ribald, kaleidoscopic extravagances were everywhere: gorillas in surgical greens; bikini-clad women (and men); wizards and princesses; more-than-a-bit-suggestive Monica Lewinsky and Bill Clinton duos; multicolored Styrofoam dinosaurs; drag queens in stunningly beautiful costumes; and leather-and-bondage entourages. A group in white butcher aprons pushed their Jeffrey Dahmer Deli Cart past a Bible-thumping evangelist who was trying to prop up an 8-foot neon-lit crucifix while shouting into his Mr. Microphone. OK, so maybe your mama never told you there'd be days like these, but any celebration that results in the official day-long closing of local city, state, and—gasp!—federal offices is bound to be, well, different.

In Carnival tradition, hooch-addled, hormone-crazed college guys shouted "Show your t*ts!" to women on balconies, who were all too happy to oblige before tossing plastic beads to the depths of frat-like depravity. Such are the microeconomics of Carnival. And it wasn't even noon

yet. We swam the sea of elbow-to-elbow humanity—claustrophobics should stay at home—to the Bourbon Street Awards, a fancifully staged theatrical presentation of elaborate, elegant, and erstwhile campy drag costumes. On Judy, on Liza, on Joan, on Bette! *"Every year at Carnival time we make a new suit . . . "*

But the out-of-town sibling visiting from Southern California had seen it all before. During Carnivals past she has been lured into an impromptu dance with a New Orleans police officer, greeted by whoops and hollers inside Pat O'Brien's courtyard bar while removing her sweater (only) to beat the heat, and playfully strewn with Silly String on Canal Street while trying to catch a prized gilded coconut from a Zulu float rider. She has joined in spontaneous second-line dancing and once snuck in behind a marching band during a parade, accompanied by a local who knew better than to engage in this highly illegal activity. She has gorged on time-honored Carnival mainstays like Popeye's fried chicken and beignets and has quaffed a cistern's worth of rum-and-fruit-juice Hurricanes. Along the way she learned the finer points of scooping up the choice beads a Bacchus parade float tossed out on to the sidewalk, but not before nearly being rushed to the hospital with a badly sprained finger. And she's a soccer mom.

For one day each year New Orleans is the hot dog the rest of the country wants to run wild with through the streets. During Carnival the Big Easy takes no prisoners—except, of course, those who flagrantly break the law. Unless someone urinates on public streets or gets into a fight, two of the most common violations, the city lets its hair down and encourages revelers to do likewise. For example, drinking alcohol is allowed on the streets of the

French Quarter (year-round, not just during Mardi Gras), so long as partygoers have a plastic "go cup." Bars provide these free of charge. Boozing it up while behind the wheel of a car, though, is a Carnival no-no.

Truth is, Carnival's orderly chaos is a virtually seamless event for the vast majority of millions of visitors, thanks largely to the heightened presence of local police working round the clock. For more information, consult your common sense or watch the episode of *Cops* filmed in New Orleans during Mardi Gras.

Note that if your travel plans include coming to New Orleans for Carnival, you'd best plan on booking a hotel reservation no later than six months before Mardi Gras. Many hotels, especially in the French Quarter, require a minimum four- to five-night stay—usually the Friday or Saturday night before Fat Tuesday through Mardi Gras night. Less-restrictive reservation policies can usually be found in smaller hotels and motels located in surrounding suburbs.

HISTORY

It was New Orleans's founders—the Lemoyne brothers, Iberville and Bienville—who brought Mardi Gras from France to the New World in 1699. Historians tell us that Mardi Gras was a raucous affair even during the early 1700s. In fact, the celebration had become so mired in danger by 1817 that city officials were forced to ban masking altogether. No one is entirely sure as to the year of the first formal parade, but most people put it around 1835 or 1838. The most widely cited of the earliest reports of the time, which appeared in the *Daily Picayune* in 1838, refers to "a procession of masked figures through the public streets with every variety of costumes from Harlequin to the somber Turk and wild Indian. Yesterday was a jolly day in our city."

The Song of Mardi Gras

In 1872 His Imperial Highness, Grand Duke Alexis Romanoff Alexandrovitch, was touring the United States on a buffalo hunt when he spied a young musical-comedy actress named Lydia Thompson in a New York performance, according to Robert Tallant in his book *Mardi Gras.* The elegant Grand Duke, as renowned a lover as he was a sportsman, was smitten. Thompson was headed to New Orleans for a performance days before Mardi Gras, and Alexis was hot on her heels. Buffalo? Pshaw!

In New Orleans, meantime, a group of prominent citizens quickly formed a Carnival organization called the School of Design and chose a King of Carnival to welcome the Duke. Little did Alexis and Thompson know that the local grapevine had been burning with word of their reported romance and that plans had been hatched to celebrate their love during the parade.

During the first Rex parade, an estimated 10,000 maskers lined a route that stretched more than a mile, according to Tallant. Each marching band that passed the City Hall reviewing stand, where the Duke sat with city officials, performed the song "If Ever I Cease to Love." It was the same song Thompson had sung during her New York stage performance seen by the Duke—and, also, later privately during her rendezvous with him. While the romance between the pair faded, "If Ever I

Despite what you think you know about Carnival in the French Quarter, stronger enforcement of laws prohibiting public sex (and even total public nudity), especially on Bourbon Street, has made such Fat Tuesday indulgences a far riskier venture for hookup-seeking revelers. A word to the wise: Get a room—if you can find one!

Cease to Love" did not; today it remains the song of Mardi Gras.

The Krewe

By midcentury the frivolity became somewhat more organized with the formation of the first formal Carnival organization, the Mistick Krewe of Comus. For the record, the word "krewe," the name for Carnival organizations that stage the parades, now appears in *Webster's Dictionary* and is defined as "a fanciful spelling of crew, generalized from the Mistick Krewe of Comus . . ." Surely no more fitting tribute to Carnival's enduring contribution to the international language of fun can be found anywhere.

Krewes are private social organizations. Membership in krewes is by invitation only, and membership criteria depends on those established by each krewe. The number of members in each krewe varies widely, ranging from fewer than 300 for smaller new krewes such as Vesta to longtime Carnival groups like Endymion that boasts more than 5,000 members.

Many krewes do not exist simply to put on a parade one evening during Carnival season—they're year-round social clubs. Krewes hold dances, crawfish boils, and other social gatherings through the summer and fall. These events usually bring in a little extra profit, which helps fill the krewe's coffers while giving members and their

families an opportunity to socialize. Many krewes hold a coronation dance in the fall, where the Queen and Maids for the coming year are presented and the King is chosen. Krewes that hold such a dance often choose their king by lot from the members of a more exclusive "King's Club."

Several krewes have also gone into the "ball business" in the off-season. New Orleans attracts many large conventions. These folks want to get a taste of what Mardi Gras is all about, so the organization holding the convention will contract with a krewe to present their ball one evening at a hotel. This is great fun for the krewe, since the King, Queen, and Court get a chance to wear their costumes once again. It's also a good fund-raising opportunity for the krewe, since they can charge the organization holding the convention a good bit of money for staging the ball.

The early 20th century saw the creation of the premiere African-American Carnival krewe—the Zulu Social Aid and Pleasure Club. In 1910 Zulu presented its first parade, and its king, William Story, spoofed the traditional all-white Uptown Carnival organizations by carrying a banana stalk scepter and wearing a lardcan crown. The organization began the tradition of celebrity krewe kings in 1949 when Louis Armstrong rode as King Zulu. Zulu's tongue-in-cheek take on Mardi Gras has made it one of the most popular and enduring of all Mardi Gras parades. In fact, the most highly prized throw is still—and will likely always be—one of the Zulu's gilded coconuts. Ironically, the Zulu Social Aid and Pleasure Club, once forbidden to parade down Canal Street in segregated New Orleans, is now the first krewe to hit the streets Mardi Gras morning, preceding Rex, the very kind of old guard Carnival organization Zulu set out to mock.

By the 1980s the roster of krewes had exploded following the addition of suburban, women's, and neighborhood Carnival organizations, plus the appearance of the first "superparades"—Endymion and Bacchus. New Orleans's contribution to revelry rolls very tall indeed, especially when

Carnival season commences January 6, the 12th night after Christmas, also known as the Feast of the Epiphany, when the three Wise Men are said to have visited the Christ Child. Festivities end at midnight on Fat Tuesday. The fluctuating dates of Easter and, as a result, the preceding Lent season mean that Mardi Gras can take place anytime between February 3 and March 9.

the streets are filled with triple-decker and superfloats, such as the 120-foot-long and 18-foot-high "Leviathan" of the Krewe of Orpheus, founded by entertainer and New Orleans native Harry Connick Jr. in 1993.

Today more than five dozen krewes parade in the New Orleans metropolitan area during the Carnival season, with as many as 13 rolling on a single night. For the most up-to-date schedule of parade dates and times, check out the *Times-Picayune*'s annual Mardi Gras supplement, published typically two weeks prior to Fat Tuesday.

Krewes are not the only organized tribute to the season, as half a dozen walking clubs hit the streets on Mardi Gras. The most well-known group is Pete Fountain's Half Fast Walking Club, a tradition since 1961. Dubbed "the Prince of Mardi Gras," the clarinet-wielding jazz musician and his rollicking entourage start off at Commander's Palace at 7:45 A.M.—or thereabouts, depending on how long breakfast lasts—and wind their way through the French Quarter. The Krewe of Barkus, a French Quarter extravaganza of costumed canines, has become one of the season's paw-ticularly popular parades. Junior and senior high school marching bands are also a parade mainstay of this $800 million annual party known as Mardi Gras. The perennially popular and national award-winning St. Augustine High School band is among the best and certainly the most popular.

Likewise, the Mardi Gras Indians contribute their own special flair to the season, one every bit as rich in Carnival tradition as krewes. For more than a century many in the city's African-American community have dressed like Native Americans, singing and dancing down neighborhood streets while playing tambourines and bells. Members of various "tribes," including the well-known Wild Magnolias and Creole Wild Wests, work throughout the year creating their gorgeous ostrich- and peacock-plumed headdresses and costumes of sequins, beads, satins, velvet, and metallic cloth. These

For the most up-to-date schedule of parade dates and times, check out the Times-Picayune annual Mardi Gras section, typically published two weeks prior to Fat Tuesday.

painstakingly handcrafted costumes are startlingly beautiful and exquisitely elaborate in detail. These neighborhood marching organizations commemorate that time when local African slaves seeking freedom found refuge and safety with neighboring Native American tribes such as the Choctaws.

Today during their parades, youths known as spy boys run ahead of the group, on the lookout for an "enemy" tribe, which dates to a time when competing tribes literally warred in the streets. Next in rank are the "flag boys" who carry the tribe's banner. Remember the song "Iko Iko," popularized by New Orleans's Dixie Cups? "My flag boy and your flag boy are sitting by the fire/my flag boy told your flag boy, 'I'm gonna set your flag on fire.'" The head of the tribe, naturally, is the "Big Chief."

Segregation

Like many other old-line Southern institutions, segregation was an accepted way of life when it came to membership in Carnival organizations. But in 1988 segregation of Carnival krewes officially came to a screeching halt when the New Orleans City Council issued its historic and then highly controversial antidiscrimination ordinance. The ordinance forbade any parading organization from restricting its membership on the basis of race. (It was—and still is—permissible to exclude individuals on the basis of gender.) The ordinance was based on a ruling by the U.S. Supreme Court, which upheld the rights of cities to ban racial discrimination in clubs where business contacts are made. As a result, three of the city's oldest krewes—135-year-old Comus, 120-year-old Momus, and 111-year-old Proteus—opted out of the city's annual parade lineup. Many locals decried the loss of these cherished old-line krewes as the end of Mardi Gras as the city knew it. Fortunately, the Carnival gestalt turned out to be bigger than the sum of its krewes. Rex, at the time the only remaining member of the Big Four krewes, pledged to adhere to the new law and open its membership. And 1999 saw the return of Proteus, pledging to do likewise. Life goes on.

CARNIVAL BASICS

When to Find Mardi Gras

During Mardi Gras, historians and morning-after revelers alike may look around and ask the same question: How did we get here? The roots of pre-Lent feasting and frolicking that grew up to become Mardi Gras can be found in ancient Christendom's attempts to fold the ceremonies of Europe's pagans into a new religion observing the passion and crucifixion of Christ. Mardi Gras, or Fat Tuesday, is the last big party of the Carnival season and takes places the day before Lent begins on Ash Wednesday.

Throws

Masked float riders dress in themed costumes and toss what are known as "throws" to the eagerly outstretched hands of revelers who fill the parade route. The most traditional—and, by far, the most numerous—throws are plastic bead necklaces and colored aluminum coins called doubloons. Over the decades more throws were added to the roster that now boasts plastic krewe-themed cups, MoonPies, panties, giant cigars—you name it.

If a throw has fallen to the ground, the safest way to pick it up while avoiding having your fingers stomped—we're not kidding—is to first step on it to stake your claim. When the crowd clears and the dust settles, bend down and pick it up. Remember, everything is fair game at a parade, and the most prudent way to catch a throw is to get the attention of a float rider, preferably with the traditional Carnival cry, "Throw me something, Mister!" It also doesn't hurt if you can jump like Michael Jordan. And just in case you want to show off your doubloon smarts, New Orleans artist H. Alvin Sharpe and Rex member Ford Thomas Hardy invented the wildly popular aluminum doubloon back in 1960.

Die-hard legends of St. Charles Avenue paradegoers often stake out a spot on the neutral ground (median to the rest of the country) with chairs and coolers the night before Fat Tuesday, all but guaranteeing a secured prime location for catching beads. Be forewarned: Police in recent years have taken a dim view of the ubiquitous wooden ladder, retrofitted with safety seats for youngsters, hogging public space hours before the parade even rolls.

Mardi Gras is not just about the ribald and not-so-subtle innuendo found on the flagstones of the French Quarter. Family-oriented fun is best found along the parade routes of St. Charles Avenue in Uptown, Canal Street in Mid City, Veterans Boulevard in Metairie, and elsewhere in

the suburbs of the west bank of Jefferson and Orleans Parishes and the north shore of St. Tammany Parish. Here, lawn chairs, homemade ladder-seats for tykes, and coolers full of fried chicken and soda pop are the norm. Rarely does anything rise above a PG rating. What does rise to excruciating levels is the noise from the rolling, music-blaring vans fronting local dance school groups who march in between the floats.

The King Cake

The king cake is Carnival's food du jour—a round Danish or coffee-cake pastry traditionally covered in icing in the Mardi Gras colors of purple (for justice), green (faith), and gold (power). Nowadays the once-simple pastry can be found filled with everything from pralines to cream cheese to raspberry jam—sometimes all three. A king cake can also be found in virtually every office during Carnival season. And the co-worker who winds up with the little plastic baby (another bastion of this baked goodie) inside his or her slice is obliged to bring the next cake to work. By the end of Mardi Gras, many locals would rather not have to even look at another king cake until the following year.

Many believe that the first king cakes were served on the Feast of the Epiphany, January 6, as part of a religious celebration, and the trinkets inside represented the gifts of the Magi. In Louisiana the first king cakes were baked by early French settlers as part of private family customs.

On the Epiphany in 1870, a king cake was served to eligible single girls at the first Ball of the Twelfth Night Carnival Club. Presumably, the young lady who found the golden bean inside her slice of cake was crowned the Queen of the Carnival.

Bakeries in the 1930s began making the cakes at the request of some krewes, yet king cakes weren't made for general consumption. Mass production of king

Among the smartest ideas for Bourbon Street–bound tipplers Fat Tuesday is taking a cab between your hotel (or house) and the French Quarter. This way you know that you and your entourage will have a safe ride home. You'll save a little on the cost of parking and a lot on the time and headache spent finding a parking space.

cakes began after World War II, and the cake has retained a venerable position in Carnival tradition ever since.

Today king cake sales gross millions of dollars annually, and visitors can send them as gifts.

Queen of the Carnival

For New Orleanians, January 6 is typically when a former debutante finds a small gold bean—in lieu of a small plastic baby—in her slice of king cake at the Twelfth Night Revelers Ball, held at the Municipal Auditorium, and ends the mystery as to who will be Queen of Carnival that year.

While the men of the Twelfth Night Revelers Ball are still getting dressed for their ball, which begins promptly at 9:00 P.M., The Phunny Phorty Phellows, a group of primarily 30- and 40-something folks, are already rolling on their streetcar ride announcing that the carnival season has begun.

The Twelfth Night Revelers Ball is a private invitation-only affair; The Phunny Phorty Phellows ride the streetcar hollering at those they meet along the way. Of course, there's no rule that says one cannot imbibe a bit of the grape while riding along the streetcar route, from the Car Barn on Willow Street down Carrollton and St. Charles Avenues to Canal Street, then back to the Barn (there's a designated driver, after all), so the Phellows do indeed have a merry time.

In contrast to New Orleans, Carnival events on the north shore of Lake Pontchartrain offer a downsized change of pace thanks to a roster of family-oriented rural parades and even a couple of boat parades featuring theme-decorated vessels with costumed riders (yes, they still toss beads and doubloons!) that ply the local rivers and bayous.

By the time the streetcar is parked back in the Barn, the Phellows (there's lots of women Phellows by the way—no sexist organization, this one) have disembarked, and the Twelfth Night Revelers have chosen their Queen, the rest of us are counting the days to our krewe's functions, the first king cake someone brings to the office, or the first parade in our neighborhood. By day, New Orleans is more or less a normal place to live, but by night the city won't be calm and quiet until Ash Wednesday.

Each year most Carnival organizations, or krewes, select a queen. And the Twelfth Night Revelers, the second-oldest Carnival organization in New Orleans, is no exception. Where the Twelfth Night Revelers differ from the vast majority of their Carnival counterparts is the fact that each year's maids of honor are all college juniors and, equally important, former debutantes with pedigree. No one in the Carnival social club known as the Twelfth Night Revelers knows ahead of time which maid of honor from the elite ranks of New Orleans high society will be the lucky woman who finds the gold bean and thus be crowned queen. Of this everyone is certain, though: Regardless of who gets the bean, the woman who is hailed as queen at the Twelfth Night Revelers Ball is not likely to soon forget the spectacular, once-in-a-lifetime evening of royal pomp and pageantry dedicated in her honor.

ALL GOOD THINGS MUST COME TO AN END

And the end of Mardi Gras tolls at midnight on Fat Tuesday, when a patrol of the city's finest, linked arm to arm, front a Patton-like division of slow-moving street sweepers, rumbling down Bourbon Street and sucking up tons of garbage, while admonishing good-till-the-last-drop revelers to call it a night. By the next morning, Ash Wednesday, the city is nearly perfectly still (and unbelievably pretty clean). Bleary-eyed tourists, many with beads still around their necks, crawl into hotel cabs to be whisked to the airport to catch planes back home. The city's faithful Catholics meantime head off to church before work for their traditional ashes, which marks the solemn beginning of the 40-day season of Lent. For many New Orleanians this time of religious sacrifice is celebrated each Friday with a traditional feast of succulent seafood at local restaurants.

But that's getting ahead of the story. As the tigress-attired sibling from Southern California emerged from Lafitte's Landing bar on Bourbon Street, she surveyed the crazy kebab of pierced drag queens and the trio of men dressed like cherubs-gone-S&M who were clinging to a corner lamppost, posing for pictures with their cute little bows and arrows. "Oh, we're definitely not in Kansas anymore," the soccer mom said as a grin creased the black whiskers painted on her cheeks.

And it wasn't even noon yet. *"Every year at Carnival time we make a new suit . . ."*

PARKS AND RECREATION

Whether you find yourself sitting in front of the fireplace of a waterfront cabin, paddling a canoe down a moonlit swamp, or lounging in the limbs of an ancient oak tree, New Orleans area parks will make you feel like you've discovered where the South's natural charm originated.

There are three major greenspaces around the city, so visitors never find themselves too far from the opportunity to run barefoot in the park. They are favorite places among locals for picnicking, relaxing, and even the occasional frolic. City Park, the granddaddy of municipal parks, is in Mid City, Audubon Park is Uptown, and Woldenberg Riverfront Park is on the edge of the French Quarter.

PARK IT— MUNICIPAL PARKS

Audubon Park
6500 St. Charles Avenue, New Orleans
(504) 861-2537
www.auduboninstitute.org
Originally a plantation, this 400-acre park has been a part of New Orleanians' lives since it was the site of the 1884 World's Fair. It features shimmering lagoons, fragrant gardens, recreation areas, an array of local wildlife, and 4,000 live oaks and other majestic trees. A new golf course opened here in 2003. Cross Magazine Street and discover the adjacent Audubon Zoo.

City Park
1 Palm Drive, New Orleans
(504) 482-4888
www.neworleanscitypark.com
More than a hundred years ago, philanthropist John McDonogh bestowed on the City of New Orleans a 100-acre tract of land in Mid City, which has evolved into the fifth-largest municipal park in the country. Today the park encompasses 1,500 acres and accommodates 10 million annual visitors. The Carousel Gardens amusement area and Storyland are two of the best reasons for visiting City Park with children.

Since the turn of the last century, children have enjoyed the "flying horses" of the amusement area's antique carousel. One of only 100 wooden merry-go-rounds left in the United States and the last in Louisiana, the carousel is listed on the National Register of Historic Places. Other rides include two miniature antique trains, a Ferris wheel, bumper cars, a 40-foot fun slide, the Lady Bug roller coaster, tilt-a-whirl, the toy helicopter ride, and antique cars. Hours vary and admission is $1.00. Ride tickets are purchased separately, or visitors can pay $8.00 for a wristband good for unlimited rides all day.

Beneath the approving gaze of Mother Goose as she flies amid the limbs of ancient oaks, young visitors can climb into the mouth of Pinocchio's whale, have a pretend sword fight aboard Captain Hook's ship, or fish in the Little Mermaid's Pond in Storyland, a fairy-tale theme park rated one of the top 10 playgrounds in the country by *Child* magazine.

Then stick around for one of the daily puppet shows at Rapunzel's castle. Storyland is open various days depending on the season. Admission is $2.00 per person. Children under age 2 are admitted free.

Adults won't want to miss City Park's Botanical Garden. Art Deco–inspired fountains, ponds, and sculptures with both mythological and natural themes punctuate the seasonal splashes of color pro-

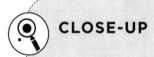

CLOSE-UP

City Park

Mention City Park to locals and watch their eyes light up as they recall childhood thrills atop the flying horses, teenage revelry in Tad Gormley Stadium, or, perhaps, a lover's first kiss beneath a thousand-year-old oak tree. The French Quarter may be this town's center, but City Park is its heart.

New Orleanians have gathered beneath its canopy of live oaks—so named because the species stays green year-round—since the area was part of the Allard Sugar Plantation in the 1700s. Actually it was even before that, when the Accolapissa and Biloxi Indians, who traded along the banks of adjacent Bayou St. John, made their homes in the then-swampy oak-filled forest.

The park served as the focal point of Creole passions in the 18th and 19th centuries and was the site of many gentlemen's affairs d'honneur, or duels. The practice of defending one's (or a loved one's) honor with swords was so common among Creoles that duel listings appeared in local newspapers, much like today's sports matchups. Though the practice may seem barbaric, it was considered quite civilized. The pair fenced, and when blood was drawn the matter was settled. The most popular dueling spot was beneath what was appropriately dubbed the Dueling Oaks.

Americans began arriving in droves in the early 1800s following the Louisiana Purchase. Like the ostentatious designs of their Garden District homes, the Americans' contribution to dueling—the use of

pistols—seemed simply over the top to Creole sensibilities. By 1890 dueling in the park was outlawed.

Women today might be hard-pressed to find a man willing, much less able, to draw a sword for their honor, but they can still find the Dueling Oaks. They're located northeast of the park's New Orleans Museum of Art on Dueling Oak Drive, among one of the largest collections of mature live oaks in the world, 250 of which are registered with the Live Oak Society. The eldest of these ancient trees is the McDonogh Oak, named for the philanthropist who bequeathed the park's original 100-acre tract to the city in 1850. The tree is approximately 1,000 years old.

Over the last 150 years, this tract of land has evolved into the fifth-largest urban park in the United States, encompassing 1,500 acres and boasting magnificent architecture and gardens, delightful play areas for the city's children, and topflight recreation facilities, including impressive golf, tennis, and track centers, plus two football stadiums, softball diamonds, soccer fields, and riding stables. All the while, this almost magical place has never ceased to spark people's imaginations.

In 1907 the Peristyle, an elegant open-air dance floor, was built. This Greek-style colonnade was designed to frame the view of the moonlit lagoon while graceful Creole couples waltzed the night away.

If botanical gardens are to plants what museums are to art, then City Park's version of horticulture is a masterpiece.

City Park's stone bridges are surrounded by one of the nation's largest collection of live oak trees. COURTESY OF NEW ORLEANS METROPOLITAN CONVENTION & VISITORS BUREAU, INC./ ANN PURCELL

When it opened in 1936 during the Depression, the botanical gardens became the city's first public garden featuring a classical combination of art and nature. Art Deco–inspired fountains, ponds, and sculpture with both mythological and natural themes punctuate the seasonal splashes of color produced by native botanical favorites. Exotic imports in this lush 10-acre site were set aside for "the indulgence of man and nature." Much of the garden was created by Works Progress Administration workers following the artistic vision of architect Richard Koch, landscape architect William Wiedorn, and sculptor Enrique Alferez.

One of the park's most popular draws is the Carousel Gardens amusement area, home to one of the few remaining wooden carousels in the country. The masterwork of famed carousel carvers Looff and Carmel, this turn-of-the-20th-century wonder is listed on the National Register of Historic Places, and its extensive 1988 restoration garnered nationwide attention and praise from the National Trust for Historic Preservation. But to locals it's simply the flying horses, a part of childhood for so many. When the carousel is not being rented out for kids' birthday parties, it's often the site of grown-ups-only cocktail socials.

But why in a city that has so many places to party would adults choose a child's merry-go-round? Perhaps it has to do with the memory of a time when they were so little they had to be lifted into the saddle. Then the music would play and they'd feel the breeze on their faces while flying high through the air on their beautiful wooden steeds as City Park taught yet another generation what it feels like to be alive.

duced by native botanical favorites and exotic imports in this lush 10-acre site set aside for "the indulgence of man and nature." Mostly built by Works Progress Administration workers under the creative direction of architect Richard Koch, landscape architect William Wiedorn, and sculptor Enrique Alferez, the botanical garden opened in 1936 as the city's first public garden featuring the classical combination of nature and art. A popular venue for weddings, the Botanical Garden is also the center of the city's horticultural education, with regular seminars and workshops for both adults and children presented in its garden study center. The elegant Pavilion of the Two Sisters houses a horticultural library and a unique gardener's gift shop. Admission is $5.00 for adults and $2.00 for children ages 5 to 12. Hours vary.

City Park also offers such recreational activities as canoeing, fishing, tennis, and horseback riding. See individual listings for details. Or visit City Park just to climb the branches of a beautiful moss-draped live oak tree, eat an ice-cream cone, swing, and feed the ducks. The park is open at night and is the site of one of the city's most popular haunted houses at Halloween. At other times, though, it doesn't seem too smart to hang out in any park after dark.

For more information on City Park, check out the Close-up in this chapter.

Woldenberg Riverfront Park
French Quarter Riverfront
Adjacent to the Aquarium of the Americas and IMAX Theater, these 17 acres of urban greenspace, public artwork, and brick pathways offer a terrific view of the Mississippi River. Festivals and open-air concerts, including the Zulu Lundi Gras celebration during Carnival and the springtime French Quarter festival, are held here.

For a romantic rendezvous, why not make a date to meet under the thousand-year-old McDonogh Oak at City Park? It's easy to find. Just park at the Timken Center concessions building, cross the arcing stone bridge over the lagoon, take a left, and follow the path a short ways. The McDonogh Oak is on the right side of the path and identified by a small plaque.

A STATE OF BLISS— STATE PARKS

Louisiana State Parks
Office of State Parks, P.O. Box 44426, Baton Rouge, LA 70804
(888) 677-1400
(877) 226-7652, reservations
www.lastateparks.com
Louisiana State Parks offer travelers the opportunity for overnight camping, hiking, and swimming. Five such sites—St. Bernard State Park in Violet, Bayou Seg-

nette State Park in Westwego, Fairview-Riverside State Park in Madisonville, Fort Pike State Commemorative Area in the Rigolets, and Fontainebleau State Park in Mandeville—are located within an hour's drive of New Orleans.

All parks are open daily, year-round with staff members on call 24 hours. Improved campsites feature electricity and water; unimproved sites do not. Certain on-site facilities are closed seasonally, so call ahead. The number for the central system for making reservations for any state park facility is listed above.

Bayou Segnette State Park
7777 Westbank Expressway, Westwego
(504) 736–7140, (888) 677–2296
Thirty minutes across the Mississippi River from New Orleans is an unusual blend of natural recreation and urban comfort. Swampland meets marsh, and nature enthusiasts can observe wildlife while children play in the wave pool. Facilities include 98 improved campsites, 20 waterfront cabins (with air-conditioning, screened porches, and fishing piers), a massive group camp, playgrounds, picnic tables, pavilions, and a wave pool. A conference room rounds out the facility. Boat launches provide access to both fresh- and saltwater fishing with catches of bass, catfish, bream, redfish, and speckled trout.

Admission to the park is $2.00 per car with up to four people, plus 50 cents for each additional person. Camping is $12 per night. To get here, cross the Mississippi River Bridge to the Westbank Expressway, and continue west on U.S. 90 to Westwego.

Fairview-Riverside State Park
Off Louisiana Highway 22, Madisonville
(985) 845–3318, (888) 677–3247
North of New Orleans on the other side of Lake Pontchartrain, this park is a tranquil setting on the banks of the Tchefuncte River. The waterfront park is surrounded by mossy live oaks, piney woods, a cypress swamp, and the historic Otis House. Catches of bass, bluegill, bream,

and white perch can be landed by boat or along the banks of the Tchefuncte. However, channel catfish, speckled trout, and crabs are more abundantly found where the river meets Lake Pontchartrain. Upstream the river is wide and free of obstacles for water-skiing. Accommodations include 81 improved campsites as well as 20 tent sites. For boaters, there is a public launch in Madisonville, less than 2 miles away and only a few minutes from the park by boat. For landlubbers there are picnic tables, grills, pavilions, and a playground. Admission to the park is $2.00 per car with up to four people, plus 50 cents for each additional person. Camping is $12 per night for improved sites and $10 for tent sites.

Fontainebleau State Park
Louisiana Highway 190, Mandeville
(985) 624–4443, (888) 677–3668
Just across Lake Pontchartrain from New Orleans is this 2,809-acre park, which has provided a much-needed urban escape for 50 years. The entry drive, with its stately live oaks, leads visitors past ruins of an old sugar mill, historic plantation, and brickyard. This lovely park is bordered on three sides by Lake Pontchartrain as well as the wetlands and woods of bayous Cane and Castine.

Located near the tail-end of the famed Mississippi Flyway, part of the North American continent's immense migratory corridor, the park's trails offer outstanding bird-watching. Facilities include 126 improved campsites, 200 unimproved sites, a primitive group camping area, three group camps, lodge, swimming pool, beach, picnic tables, grills, pavilions, sailboat ramp, playground, and restrooms. Cycle, hike, or horseback ride down 9 miles of the 31-mile Tammany Trace—an old railroad track converted into a paved trail which passes through the park. Fontainebleau also features a 1.25 mile nature trail for hiking.

Admission to the park is $2.00 per car with up to four people, plus 50 cents for each additional person. Camping is $10 per night for unimproved sites, $12 per night for improved sites.

Don't miss City Park's new five acre sculpture garden featuring 60 works by major 20th-century European, American, Israeli, and Japanese artists, gifts from the Besthoff Foundation, combined with works from the New Orleans Museum of Arts permanent collection. The sculptures are among meandering footpaths, pedestrian bridges, lagoons, and Spanish moss–laden 200-year-old trees. Open Tuesday through Sunday for free.

Fort Pike State Commemorative Area
Louisiana Highway 90, Lake Catherine
(985) 662-5703, (888) 662-5703

Fort Pike, named for explorer and soldier General Zebulon Montgomery Pike, who discovered Pike's Peak, is a historic site strategic for U.S. defense in the country's early years.

Constructed between 1819 and 1826, this was one of six masonry forts built on coastal Louisiana to protect New Orleans from seaborne invasion. The remains feature enclosed casemates (brick vaults within the walls) with long exit tunnels. A curved structure overlooks the rigolets (pronounced *rig-o-LEES*), a narrow passage of wetlands east of New Orleans between Lake Pontchartrain and the Gulf of Mexico.

The original citadel, a two-story soldiers' barracks, still stands with the outer walls of the fort. Enter the facility by crossing a dry moat and passing through the sally port and stroll through arched casemates, climb to the top of the perimeter wall overlooking the Rigolets, or visit the museum and exhibits housed in the citadel. The site also offers a picnic area with tables, pavilion, boat launch, and restrooms. Guided tours are available, as are periodic special events. Fort Pike is located on old Louisiana Highway 90, formerly the Old Spanish Trail, approximately 23 miles east of downtown. Take Louisiana Highway 90 east from downtown New Orleans.

St. Bernard State Park
501 St. Bernard Highway, Braithwaite
(504) 682-2101, (888) 677-7823

Just 19 miles south the French Quarter in St. Bernard Parish, this is the only state park located next to the Mississippi River. The woods, surrounding wetlands, and man-made lagoon system give visitors the chance to get back to nature without venturing too far from the city. The park offers 51 improved campsites, a pool, a covered pavilion, a large grill, picnic tables, and restrooms. A clearly marked (but rather short) nature trail takes the hiker across rustic bridges and throughout the park.

There is no charge for admission to the park. Swimming is available May through August and costs $2.00. Campsites are $12 per night. To get here: Take I-10 east to LA 47 south, turn left on LA 46 through Violet and Poydras, then right on LA 39 South. Or, from the French Quarter, take North Rampart Street (LA 46) south through Violet and Poydras and then right on LA 39 south.

LOOK OUT, IT'S THE FEDS—NATIONAL PARKS

Jean Lafitte National Historical Park and Preserve
419 Decatur Street, New Orleans
(504) 589-2133
www.nps.gov/jela

There's only one national park in the New Orleans area, but it's everywhere. Jean Lafitte National Historical Park and Preserve, named after that rascally pirate-turned-patriot-turned-pirate, is composed of three parts: the Barataria Preserve on the West Bank near Crown Point, dedicated to the natural and cultural history of the region's uplands, swamps, and marshlands; the Chalmette Battlefield, 6 miles southeast of New Orleans and the site of the 1815 Battle of New Orleans; and the New Orleans Visitor Center in the French Quarter's French Market, which interprets the history of New Orleans and Louisiana's Mississippi Delta region. Sit back, relax, and enjoy your federal tax dollars at work.

Barataria Preserve
Louisiana Highway 45, Crown Point
(504) 589-2330

The Barataria Preserve is dedicated to the culture of the people, past and present, who have made the delta their home, as well as the unique ecosystem that sustained them. It preserves a portion of that environment containing natural levee forests, bayous, swamps, and marshes. Though wild and teeming with wildlife, this wilderness is not pristine. Evidence of prehistoric human settlement, colonial farming, plantation agriculture, logging, commercial trapping, fishing, hunting, and oil and gas exploration overlay much of this former wilderness.

The preserve encompasses 20,000 acres of hardwood forest, cypress swamp, and freshwater marsh. Eight miles of hard-surface trails include a 2.5-mile boardwalk that winds through three distinct ecosystems—a cypress swamp, palmetto forest, and marsh. Natural history walks are conducted Sunday through Friday at 1:30 P.M.; group tours of the park are available.

Nine miles of canoe trails, closed to motorized boats and accessible only by three canoe launch docks, will give you an up close and personal view of the swamps and marshes. Guided canoe treks take place Sunday at 8:30 A.M., and moonlight canoeing is offered monthly on the night before and the night of the full moon, both by reservation only. Another 20 miles of waterways are open to all boats. Canoe rentals are available just outside the park, and a number of public and private boat launches provide access for motorboats.

The visitor center is open daily 9:00 A.M. to 5:00 P.M., with extended hours during daylight saving time. Trails are open

daily 7:00 A.M. to 7:00 P.M. To get to the park: Cross the Mississippi River Bridge to the Westbank Expressway and exit at Barataria Boulevard (Louisiana Highway 45). Turn left and drive approximately 8 miles to reach the park.

Chalmette Battlefield
8606 St. Bernard Highway, Chalmette
(504) 281-0510

The Chalmette unit preserves one of the country's most significant battle sites, which saw a decisive American victory over the British at the end of the War of 1812. Adjacent to the battlefield is the Chalmette National Cemetery. Take a self-guided tour, which begins at the visitor center, where exhibits and an audiovisual program explains the importance of the battle. Next, follow the 1.5-mile tour road that features six stops incorporating various features of the battlefield. A free brochure tells about the significance of each stop.

Two additional structures in the park worth noting are the Chalmette Monument and Beauregard House. The cornerstone of the monument, dedicated to the American victory, was laid in January 1840 shortly after Andrew Jackson visited here to commemorate the 25th anniversary of the battle. Construction did not begin until 1855 and was completed in 1908. The Beauregard House, built 18 years after the battle, is a beautiful example of French-Louisiana architecture and is named for its last private owner, Judge René Beauregard.

Battle of New Orleans talks take place daily at 11:15 A.M. and 2:45 P.M. Living-history demonstrations are presented Saturday mornings. Call for times. Although there is a small family picnic area in the southwest corner of the park, any kind of organized games or recreational activities are considered inconsistent with the site's historical character and are not permitted. To get to the park: Take I-10 east to the Chalmette exit (LA 47). Head south to St. Bernard Highway and turn right.

RECREATION

Sure, we like to drink and party here, but the truth is New Orleans embraces outdoor recreation as much as the next city, and its roster of activities—from biking and diving to golfing and tennis—is enough to cure even the worst case of cabin fever. The following list should be enough to get you started and keep you going for as long as you like.

PRICE CODE

Our price is based on admission for one adult.

$	$0 to $10
$$	$11 to $20
$$$	$21 to $50
$$$$	More than $50

Bike Rentals

Bicycle Michael's $
622 Frenchmen Street, New Orleans
(504) 945-9505
www.bicyclemichaels.com
This neighborhood bike shop in the Faubourg Marigny, across Esplanade Avenue from the French Quarter, has been renting 21-speed GT and Fuji mountain and hybrid bikes, as well as Tandem-brand professional cycles for athletes, since it opened 19 years ago.

Rates start at $7.50 per hour. The owners suggest BYOH—bring your own helmet—to guarantee a comfortable fit, although helmets can be rented for $5.00 a day. Hours are Monday through Saturday 10:00 A.M. to 7:00 P.M. and Sunday 10:00 A.M. to 5:00 P.M. Rentals include locks. A major credit card is a must.

French Quarter Bicycles $
522 Dumaine, New Orleans
(504) 529-3136
www.fqbikes.com
If pedaling around the French Quarter and then down Esplanade Avenue to City Park

to feed the ducks is what a beautiful Saturday afternoon calls for, call on this mountain bike rental outlet. With an inventory of 18 to 20 cycles, there's always something on hand. Hours are Monday through Friday 11:00 A.M. to 7:00 P.M. and Saturday and Sunday 10:00 A.M. to 6:00 P.M. (closed Sunday in summer). A major credit card and $200 deposit is required. Call first to check availability, as reservations are not accepted.

Boating/Instruction

Bayou Sauvage National
Wildlife Refuge $
17158 Chef Menteur Highway, New Orleans
(985) 882-3881
southeastlouisiana.fws.gov/bayou
sauvage.html
This 22,000-acre U.S. Fish and Wildlife Service preserve is located just 15 minutes from downtown in the area called eastern New Orleans. Visitors are welcome to bring their own canoes and enjoy the preserve's waterways Monday through Friday 7:30 A.M. to 4:00 P.M. Guided adventures, including canoe trips, are available at no charge. Call for times.

City Park Boating $
City Park, 1 Palm Drive, New Orleans
(504) 483-9371
www.neworleanscitypark.com
Pedal boats can be rented from the dock on the lagoon behind the museum for excursions on the park's 11 miles of scenic lagoons. Identify, or simply enjoy, several species of ducks, geese, swans, and native Louisiana egrets while gliding along the banks of Old Bayou Metairie. Boat rentals are $5.00 per person per hour.

Jean Lafitte National Historical
Park and Preserve $
Barataria Unit, Louisiana Highway 45
Crown Point
(504) 589-2133
www.nps.gov/jela
Nine miles of canoe trails, closed to

motorized boats and accessible by three canoe launch docks, allow up close and personal exploration of the swamps and marshes. Guided canoe treks take place some Saturday mornings, and moonlight canoeing is offered monthly on the night before and the night of the full moon, both by reservation only. Another 20 miles of waterways are open to all boats. Canoe rentals are available just outside the park, and a number of public and private boat launches provide access for motor boats.

Murray Yacht Sales $$$$
7356 West Roadway Drive, New Orleans
(504) 283–2507
www.murrayyachtsales.com
Twelve hours of entry-level instructions—8 hours of it on a boat—over a weekend (Saturday and Sunday 9:00 A.M. to 3:00 P.M.) will put the budding seafarer on course for American Sailing Association–certified basic keelboat sailing. Tuition of $225 includes instruction, boat rental, textbook, study guide, and certification. Reservations are secured with a $100 deposit accompanying the registration form. The balance is due one week before class begins.

Diving

Chag's Scuba Center $$$$
4740 Veterans Boulevard, New Orleans
(504) 455–8636
www.chags.com
For 15 years this scuba center has been helping both local and out-of-town novices get their fins wet. The $99 tuition includes lectures and pool instructions necessary for the certification dive in Destin, Florida. There are additional costs: $150 to $175 to purchase basic equipment such as custom-fitted mask, snorkel, and fins; $75 to rent dive buoyancy compensator, regulator, cylinder, and neoprene wet suit for classes and dive certification; $80 to $100 for dive certification boat

fees; and $60 for motel and food during certification. All of which brings the total fee to anywhere from $564 to $609.

Harry's Dive Shop $$$$
4709 Airline Highway, Metairie
(504) 888–4882
www.harrysdiveshop.com
Entry-level open-water scuba diver classes are held in the heated indoor Olympic-size pool at this Metairie combination diving school/dive shop. Classes are held weekdays and weekends. Cost is $299 and includes qualification for YMCA, NAUI, and SSI certification; textbook; and use of tank and regulator during the course.

Students must provide mask, snorkel, fins, boots, and weight belt, as well as all equipment for required open-water dives, which must be completed within six months of completing the course.

Fishing

Watching the sun rise above the coastal marshlands of southeast Louisiana on a cloudless morning while heading out on a flat-bottom boat to some of the world's best fishing waters is a surefire way to heal an achy-breaky hook. The good news is this Sportsman's Paradise earned its state moniker, as well as a secure place in hearts of novice and experienced fishers alike, in part because of the region's plentiful lakes, bays, bayous, and marshes, not to mention the nearby Gulf of Mexico, all blessed with an abundance of finfish. The bad news is that anglers may catch their limit before the beer runs out.

Year-round warm temperatures keep local inland-water and deep-sea fishing charters, many located within a 35-mile radius of New Orleans, operating during all four seasons. There are many within 35 miles of Downtown. Inland-water fishing in particular offers a unique glimpse of marsh coastal wildlife—alligators, otters, nutrias, minks, egrets, blue herons, ospreys, pelicans, and raccoons.

Native captains know the region's fishing spots like the back of their hands. Experience the windswept barrier islands and cypress swamps to Lake Borgne, Black Bay and, farther south, the Gulf of Mexico. (Ever fish from a boat anchored near a towering offshore oil-rig platform? The pylons covered in barnacles are like an all-you-can-eat buffet attracting some of Neptune's tastiest pals. Just drop them a line.) Here the rod-and-reel fan can spin-, fly-, and bow-fish a who's who of Louisiana's catch du jour: redfish, bass, speckled trout, flounder, king mackerel, red snapper, amberjack, white trout, pompano, and cobia, to name just a few.

The cost for many but not all charters includes rod and reel, fishing license, soft drinks, bait, ice and gas, fileting and bagging, and instruction. Some charters provide transportation to and from hotels. Either way it's always a good idea to check in advance—and to get directions—when making a reservation. A nonresident special-guide fishing license costs $5.50 (good for unlimited trips taken on consecutive days) and can often be purchased from the charter captain or at the marina. A three-day fishing license purchased independently costs $26.50. Advance notice may be necessary to arrange for fishing licenses for out-of-town anglers.

Check to see if the captain is certified and his boat approved by the United States Coast Guard. In many instances custom charters can be arranged. The following are but a sample of the available charters. For more information visit the Web site www.sportmans-paradise.com. Happy fishing.

Bourgeois Charters $$$$
2724 Sievers Drive, Marrero
(504) 341-5614
www.neworleansfishing.com
This fishing charter 30 minutes from New Orleans on the west bank of Jefferson Parish offers the chance to fish the same wildlife-filled bayous that pirate Jean Lafitte roamed more than 175 years ago. Groups of 2 to 60 persons depart the

Sea-Way Marina in Lafitte aboard Capt. Theophile Bourgeois's 22-foot boats, specially designed for shallow-water draft, and head deep into the bayou for fly- and spin-fishing for speckled trout, drum, and flounder. Charters depart at 5:00 A.M. (returning 11:30 A.M.) and 1:00 P.M. (returning at dark).

Overnight accommodations in a two-bedroom bed-and-breakfast Cajun cabin complete with optional personal chef and fishing trips are available.

Capt. Nick's Wildlife Safari $$$$
102 Arlington Drive, Luling
(504) 361-3004, (800) 375-3474
www.captnicks.com
Looking for a private swamp safari or "fishing adventure"? A five-boat fleet of flat-bottom and bay boats, which can accommodate 2 to 30 passengers, takes fishers from Joe's Landing in Lafitte into the inland saltwater marshes, where redfish, flounder, and drum come out to play. Getting here is a snap: This charter has shuttle vans that stop at all the major hotels in New Orleans, as well as residences upon request.

Everything, even round-trip transportation, is included in the $175 per person cost (minimum 2 persons; maximum 30). Guides have thermal insulated jumpsuits to loan passengers should the weather turn cold. Charters run from 6:00 A.M. to 1:00 P.M. and from 12:30 to 6:30 P.M. Reservations are recommended but not mandatory.

Capt. Phil Robichaux's Saltwater Guide Service $$$$
4775 Jean Lafitte Boulevard, Lafitte
(504) 689-2006
www.rodnreel.com/captphil
Not far from the town of Lafitte, 30 minutes south of New Orleans, is the Barataria-Terrebonne Estuarine Complex, which contains 34 percent of the state's marshlands and is one of the largest, most dynamic estuary systems in the United States. Robichaux's signature-edition 25-foot Bay Quest boat is equipped with a

TV fishing guide and a Great White trolling motor. Five additional charter boats are available.

Year-round, eight-hour daily charters depart from the Lafitte Harbor Marina at a cost of $400 for the first two people and $50 for each additional person. There is a $150 deposit per group. Customers must furnish their own food, beverages, and license, all of which are available at the marina. Everything else is included.

Charter Boat Teaser $$$$
2625 Fawnwood Drive, Marrero
(504) 341–4245
www.rodnreel.com/teaser

Don't let the name fool you—this charter can be counted on to deliver the goods. Capt. Mike Frenette, a 27-year fishing veteran, steers his new 36-foot Contender from Venice on the west bank of Jefferson Parish to the mouthwaters of the Mississippi River for blue marlin, blackfin, and big eye tuna, grouper, barracuda, trigger fish, and jack crevalle. Anglers with more domestic tastes can fish the inland marshes and passes for largemouth and striped bass, flounder, and speckled trout.

Daylong charters cost $200 to $300 per person and can accommodate up to six passengers. A six-person group costs $1,200. Overnight accommodations at the Teaser Clubhouse cost $60 per person and include snacks, nonalcoholic beverages, dinner buffet, breakfast, and in-house chef. Three-, five-, and seven-day packages are available.

Frenette is a fishing guide who knows how to hook audiences: Besides his own local cable program, he hosts a weekly fishing segment on WVUE-TV channel 8 and has appeared on ESPN's *Salt Water Journel* and TNN's *Great American Outdoors*.

City Park Fishing $
City Park, 1 Palm Drive, New Orleans
(504) 482–4888
www.neworleanscitypark.com

Bass, catfish, and perch make their homes in the lagoons of City Park. Fishing per-
mits are required and are easily obtained at the park's boating and fishing office on a lagoon dock behind the museum. City Park's Big Bass Fishing Rodeo, the oldest freshwater fishing contest in the country, is held each spring. This popular event features Cajun music, barbecue, and trophies for the catch of the day. Daily fishing permits cost $2.00 for adults, $1.00 for kids under 16. Yearly permits are $50 and $25, respectively.

Escape Fishing Charters $$$$
210 Blackfin Cover, Slidell
(504) 643–5905
capthook@bellsouth.net.

Capt. Tim Urson Sr. heads out from the venerated Isleño Blackie Campo's marina in Shell Beach, located at the tail end of lower St. Bernard Parish, aboard his 25-foot Privateer to some of the most hallowed fishing grounds in all of southeast Louisiana: Black Tank, Snake and Lonesome Islands, Batteldore Reef in Lake Borgne, and Black Bay. Ursin, a member of the Louisiana Charter Boat Association, charges full-day, year-round rates of $100 per person, plus $75 for expenses for up to five persons May 1 to October 1; $50 November 1 to April 1.

Fishing Guide Services $$$$
7301 Downman Road, New Orleans
(504) 243–2100
www.fishing-boating.com/fishingguide services

Anyone who promises a 10-fish minimum catch must be on to something good. Capt. A. D. "Dee" Geoghegan has more than 35 years' experience fishing the waters of southeast Louisiana and specializes in light-tackle saltwater fishing in Breton Sound, Chandelur Isle, and the Louisiana marsh aboard his 26-foot Privateer open-hull *Fish Stalker*. Cost is $350 for up to three persons, plus $40 each for gas, live bait, fish cleaning, and rental rods. Overnight accommodations with private baths and central heat/AC for up to eight are available at Capt. Dee's waterfront fishing camp in Shell Beach.

Fishunter Guide Service Inc.   **$$$$**
1905 Edenborn Avenue, Metairie
(504) 837-0703
www.fishunterguideservice.com
The father-son team of Capt. Nash
Roberts III and Capt. Nash Roberts IV,
both college-educated biologists, take
anglers year-round for light-tackle fishing
in the shallow (1 to 1.5 feet depth) interior
marshes and bays that border New
Orleans. The 21-foot Neumann Custom
Marsh Max boat departs at safe light from
either Delacroix Island (on the east bank
in lower St. Bernard Parish) or Port Sul-
phur (on the west bank of Jefferson
Parish), returning at 2:30 P.M. Cost is $350
for two people, $400 for three, and $450
for four. Call at least two weeks ahead of
time to make a reservation.

Fitness Centers

Cureton's Sports Club
524 Metairie Road, Metairie
(504) 835-7121
www.curetons.com
Pumping iron in this longtime Old Metairie
establishment is a breath of fresh air and a
return to the days when people came to
gyms to actually work out, not strut around
in fancy gear or fuss over their Greek salad
at the heart-healthy rooftop restaurant. The
only real compromise this no-frills facility
makes to modern convenience are the six
TV sets in the first-floor cardiovascular
room, which members can tune to through
their hands-free radio headsets.

Another plus is that this multistory
facility has more than a dozen rooms,
each with a specific exercise focus or type
of equipment. Classes are offered in aerobics (step and low-impact), stretching and
toning, and martial arts/self-defense, to
name just a few. Other amenities include
an indoor track, racquetball drives, indoor
heated swimming pool, a women-only
workout room, personal trainers,
whirlpools, saunas, and steam rooms.

Compared with some other health
clubs in the area, this one is a bargain.
Annual memberships start around $250.

The club is open Monday through Friday 6:00 A.M. to 10:00 P.M., Saturday 8:00
A.M. to 6:00 P.M., and Sunday 10:00 A.M. to
6:00 P.M. A second location at 1712 Vegas
Drive in Metairie is open Monday through
Friday 6:00 A.M. to 11:00 P.M., Saturday
7:00 A.M. to 9:00 P.M., and Sunday 9:00
A.M. to 9:00 P.M. Members are allowed full
use of both facilities.

Elmwood Fitness Center
701 Poydras, New Orleans
(504) 588-1600

1200 South Clearview Parkway, Harahan
(504) 733-1600

111 Veterans Boulevard, Metairie
(504) 832-1600
www.elmwoodfitness.com
If space ships had fitness centers, they
would probably resemble these spanking
clean, energetic, state-of-the-art facilities.
The New Orleans location on the 13th
floor of One Shell Square in the Central
Business District offers a nice view of
downtown while hitting the treadmills and
other cardiovascular equipment. This location is open Monday through Friday 5:30
A.M. to 9:00 P.M. and Saturday 8:00 A.M. to
4:00 P.M.

The Harahan location on Clearview
Parkway at Elmwood is affiliated with
Ochsner Hospital and has more than 100
pieces of cardiovascular machinery,
indoor/outdoor food service, sand-
volleyball drives, a pro shop, kidsport and
seniors activities, gymnastics, and health
fairs. Hours are Monday through Friday
5:30 A.M. to 10:00 P.M., Saturday 8:00 A.M.
to 8:00 P.M., and Sunday 8:00 A.M. to 7:00
P.M. The Metairie location on Veterans
Boulevard is open Monday through Friday
5:30 A.M. to 10:00 P.M., Saturday 8:00 A.M.
to 4:00 P.M.

All three locations offer classes in aerobics, spinning, aqua, self-defense, and

boxing as well as personal trainers, massage therapy, sauna, Jacuzzi, locker rooms, and child care. Month-to-month memberships and a 30-day money-back guarantee are available.

New Orleans Athletic Club
222 North Rampart, New Orleans
(504) 525-2375
neworleansathleticclub.com

Long before the advent of fitness centers, there were athletic clubs. And this one, established in 1872 and located on Rampart Street on the edge of the French Quarter, is the oldest in New Orleans and the second-oldest in the United States. Originally a white men's–only facility called the Young Men's Gymnastic Club, this is where some of the city's most prominent citizens come to tone up their flabby abs.

Aerobics, spinning, yoga, Pilates, fencing, and boxercise classes augment the club's Nautilus equipment, cardiovascular area, three free-weight rooms (including an "antique" weight room), and four racquetball/handball drives. Other amenities include a basketball gym, sundeck with roof track, indoor climate-controlled pool, personal trainers, and a full-service salon offering everything from pedicures to massage and aromatherapy. Rates are $50 to $60 per month for singles (plus $500 initiation fee) and $85 for couples ($500 initiation fee). The first additional family member costs $22; $10 for each member thereafter.

Golf

Even in New Orleans a reference to "clubs" doesn't always mean late-night forays into smoke-choked dens of bluesy ennui. Whether a weekly fanatic or a twice-a-year duffer, golf for many people is a powerful lure that often defies explanation. The temptation among nongolfers to paint this game as an escape from weekend chores, as well as foreplay for

19th-hole martinis and calamari, is par for the course.

But anyone willing to sidestep the plaid pants and Polo shirt–stuffing love handles would have to acknowledge that in New Orleans golf is truly something to write home about. The following sampling of available courses should drive home the point. See you at the clubhouse.

Audubon Park Golf Course
Audubon Park
6500 Magazine Street, New Orleans
(504) 212-5290

The city's newest golf course combines more than a century of history with the latest in golf course design. The Denis Griffiths design features contoured fairways, manicured Tif Eagle greens, four lagoons, and exquisite landscaping on a par 62, 4,198-yard layout set among 100-year-old oak trees.

The Audubon Park Golf Course is located just minutes from downtown New Orleans. Audubon Park is on the St. Charles Avenue streetcar line, across from Tulane University, and among some of the most beautiful homes in uptown New Orleans. The park was the site of the 1884 World's Fair, and world-famous Audubon Zoo is located across Magazine Street from the golf course. Hours of operation are Wednesday through Monday 7:00 A.M. until dusk, Tuesday 10:00 A.M. until dusk. Greens fees, which include tax, are $22 for Louisiana residents on weekdays, $27 for nonresidents. On weekends, it's $29 for residents, $35 for nonresidents. Cart rental is $22.

Bayou Oaks Driving Range
City Park, 1 Palm Drive, New Orleans
(504) 483-9394
www.neworleanscitypark.com

This 100-tee double-decker driving range has night lighting and is open Monday through Friday 9:00 A.M. to 10:00 P.M., Saturday and Sunday 8:00 A.M. to 10:00 P.M. PGA pro instruction and club rentals are available. A small bucket of balls costs

$5.00, a large bucket is $7.00, and a jumbo bucket is $9.00.

Bayou Oaks Golf Courses
City Park, 1 Palm Drive, New Orleans
(504) 483-9396
www.neworleanscitypark.com
City Park boasts the largest municipal golf facility in the South. More than 200,000 rounds are played annually on its four 18-hole courses. Named "the place to play in the city" by *Golf Digest*, Bayou Oaks offers electric carts, individual and group lessons by PGA pros, club rentals, a fully stocked pro shop, and the Clubhouse restaurant. Bayou Oaks is open daily sunup to sundown, except Christmas Day. Daily rates are $8.00 to $22.00.

Eastover Country Club
5690 Eastover Drive, New Orleans
(504) 245-7347
www.eastovercc.com
Joe Lee, whose credits include three of the five courses at Walt Disney World Resort, designed the 6,800-yard Eastover around a tricky network of lakes and lagoons, which probably have more balls lying at the bottom than crawfish. The hole that has caused the greatest resettlement of crustaceans is the 16th—a 545-yard par-5 crisscrossed by water and rated by *Golf & Travel* as among the best in the city. The tee box is perched on an island, which requires a long and daring drive to cut off the lake and as much of the dogleg right as possible. An accurate iron is needed to lay up into a narrow throat about 175 yards from the green.

Rated by *Golf Digest* as among the best courses in town, the links-type Eastover is 12 miles east of downtown New Orleans between Bayou Sauvage Wildlife Refuge and Lake Pontchartrain off the I-10 Bullard Avenue exit. The course is open Tuesday through Friday 7:30 A.M. (first tee time 8:00 A.M.) to 6:00 P.M., and Saturday and Sunday 6:30 A.M. (first tee time 7:00 A.M.) to 6:00 P.M. Fees are $88 per player plus tax and include cart.

Lakewood Country Club
4801 General DeGaulle Drive
New Orleans
(504) 393-2610
www.lakewoodgolf.com
"Lakewood is a great driving golf course—very tight [and] demands accuracy off the tee," Tom Watson is quoted as saying. Anyone eager to play in the footsteps of the legends—Watson, Jack Nicklaus, Seve Ballesteros, and Lee Trevino, among others—will want to check out this 7,100-yard Robert Bruce Harris–designed course, which has hosted 26 PGA tour events. The championship 18-hole par-72 golf course, nestled between century-old oak and cypress trees, offers tight fairways and smooth, quick greens. Course is open Monday 9:00 A.M. to 5:00 P.M. and Tuesday through Sunday 7:00 A.M. to 5:00 P.M. Rates are $62.13 Monday through Thursday and $78.48 Friday through Sunday. Fees include cart and tax.

Oak Harbor Golf Club
201 Oak Harbor Boulevard, Slidell
(985) 646-0110
oakharborgolf.com
The 6,885-yard layout of this "beauty and the beast," situated 2 miles from scenic Lake Pontchartrain and built in the tradition of PGA West, Oak Tree, and Kiawah Island courses, earned *Golf Digest*'s nomination for best new course when it opened in 1992. The Pete Dye–inspired Lee Schmitt design makes use of railroad ties and bulkheads around the many bayou waterways that intersect the layout, a worthy adversary to even scratch golfers, but plays a manageable 6,261 yards from the regular men's tees. Sound strategy is always a premium on this championship course 20 minutes east of downtown New Orleans off I-10, as danger lurks in the form of water that comes into play on 12 of the holes. The course is open daily 7:30 A.M. to 6:00 P.M., and fees are $59 weekdays and $69 weekends, including cart. Club rentals cost $25.

Horseback Riding

Equest Farm
City Park, 1001 Filmore Avenue
New Orleans
(504) 483-9398
www.equestfarm.com
Hop into the saddle amid the oak trees of New Orleans's favorite park and learn the ropes of handling a horse. One-hour guided trail rides through the park cost $30. Horseback riding lessons are available as well at the stable on Filmore Street near the golf course. Classes are held year-round. Fees are $30 per hour for group lessons and $40 per half hour for private lessons. Riding camps for children during holidays and evening lessons are available.

Softball

City Park Softball Center
City Park, 1 Palm Drive, New Orleans
(504) 483-1720
www.neworleanscitypark.com
Batter up! The City Park Softball Center features four regulation softball fields and a concessions building complete with satellite television and four state-of-the-art softball/baseball batting cages. Ball diamonds and soccer fields available for league or tournament rental are also located in the park. The batting cage rate is $1.00 for 16 balls. Leagues play here almost every night. Hang out with your glove and a team may take you on as a ringer.

Team Sports for Kids

Interested in getting your kids involved in team sports? Here are a couple of options.

The Jefferson Parish
Recreation Department
East Jefferson: (504) 736-6999
West Jefferson: (504) 349-5000
www.jeffparish.net

Along with playground sports activities, the recreation department offers more classes—from dancercize to tennis lessons—than some small colleges. Call for schedules.

The New Orleans
Recreation Department
1340 Poydras Street, New Orleans
(504) 299-4170
www.new-orleans.la.us/home/nord
NORD offers football, basketball, soccer, and baseball/softball league play as well as a variety of other sports and exercise classes. Call for schedules.

Tennis

City Park Tennis Center
City Park, 1 Palm Drive, New Orleans
(504) 483-9383
www.neworleanscitypark.com
The largest public tennis facility in the South, the City Park Tennis Center has been named one of the top 25 municipal tennis facilities in the nation by *Tennis* magazine. As many as 70,000 people play tennis yearly on the center's 36 lighted hard and clay courts. The facility offers individual as well as group lessons by U.S. Professional Tennis Association pros, a full-service pro shop, and racquet rentals. Court rentals range from $6.50 to $7.50 per hour.

Track

City Park Track
City Park, 1 Palm Drive, New Orleans
(504) 482-4888
www.neworleanscitypark.com
This 400-meter international track was designed as a practice surface for the 1992 U.S. Olympic Track & Field Trials held in adjacent Tad Gormley Stadium. The eight-lane polyurethane track is open daily to the public, except during special events.

SPECTATOR SPORTS

Spectator sports are a big draw in the Big Easy. In fact, local sports fans are so enamored of their favorite pastime that their devotion is extended even to local sportscasters.

Hap Glaudi was one of those old-time newspaper sportswriters who made the switch to broadcasting in the early days of local television. In his later years, he hosted the Saints post-game radio show called *The Point After,* during which fans would call in and talk about, mostly, what they thought the problem was with the team. Glaudi, who started covering sports in this town when he was still a student at Jesuit High School, arguably knew more about local athletics than anybody else. But he never took issue with the fans on his show. He would just "um-hum" his way through even the most lunatic of callers.

When Glaudi died, the show's name was changed to *Hap's Point After*—which makes it, perhaps, the only memorial radio talk show in the world. In fact, so beloved was Glaudi that callers still sometimes begin their conversations with current host Buddy Diliberto: "Yeah, Hap, I was thinking . . ."

And Diliberto never corrects them.

Get the major league stars of tomorrow to sign your glove today at the Zephyrs' autograph booth, which opens 30 minutes before game time.

BASEBALL

New Orleans Zephyrs
6000 Airline Drive, Metairie
(504) 734-5155
www.zephyrsbaseball.com

The New Orleans Zephyrs baseball team played its inaugural season at Zephyr Field in 1997, which then-team president Rob Couhig called "the crown jewel of minor league baseball."

Fans of this Houston Astros AAA affiliate watch minor league ball in style April through September. The new $20 million, 10,000-seat (with chairbacks) ballpark features the largest scoreboard in all of minor league baseball, 16 VIP suites, a covered party area adjacent to seating, and a fan swimming pool with two hot tubs.

Spectators are also treated to a variety of theme nights that include fireworks shows, dollar beer, and hat and T-shirt giveaways. And the team's a contender, winning the AAA World Series in 1998. This combination of merriment and mastery has proven unbeatable, attracting more than half a million fans during the regular season. This breaks the city's last baseball attendance record, set in 1947 when the now-defunct New Orleans Pelicans (named after the state bird) drew 400,036 fans at Pelican Stadium.

Gates open 90 minutes before game time.

Most Zephyrs games are broadcast on WTIX–FM 94.3.

Tickets range from $5.00 to $9.50 with $1.00 off for seniors and kids under 12. To buy tickets to any of the Zephyrs 71 home games, call Monday through Friday 9:00 A.M. to 6:00 P.M., Saturday 10:00 A.M. to 4:00 P.M., or visit the box office at the ballpark.

To get to Zephyr Field from New Orleans: Take I-10 west toward Baton Rouge. Exit at Clearview Parkway and head south. Turn right on Airline Drive and after two stoplights you will see the stadium's two big signs on the left. Turn at the first one.

FOOTBALL

New Orleans Saints
Louisiana Superdome
Sugar Bowl Drive, New Orleans
(504) 731-1700
www.neworleanssaints.com

The National Football League awarded its 16th franchise to New Orleans on All Saints Day, November 1, 1966. And the team's been in need of a prayer practically ever since. The squad has seen its highs (Tom Dempsey's 1970 league record–setting 63-yard field goal on the last play of the game to defeat Detroit 19-17) and lows (their dismal 1980 1-15 season).

But the real story of the Saints has always been the fans who have stuck by the team through the worst of times and, well, the worst of times. Although pulling for perennial losers certainly has developed the fans' sense of humor. In the early '80s, when it seemed that things couldn't get any worse, fans still showed up but wore paper bags over their heads and nicknamed the team "The Aints."

The January 1997 announcement of Mike Ditka as the Saints' 12th head coach brought a new sense of optimism to die-hard fans. But by early November, there appeared on the front page of the Monday *Times-Picayune* a picture of Ditka with his hand over his face, following his 4-8 team's loss to the Falcons. The legendary coach was quoted as saying, "I don't have it anymore."

By January 2000, Saints owner Tom Benson apparently decided that he agreed with Ditka, who had produced a three-year record of 15-33 (including his final 3-13 season), and fired the Hall of Famer along with the rest of the coaching staff and general manager Bill Kuharich. In early February, new G M Randy Mueller hired Pittsburgh Steelers defensive coordinator Jim Haslett for the head coaching spot. And with Haslett, who was the Saints' linebacker coach and defensive coordinator in '95 and '96, the team began to rebuild. By the end of the 2000 season the Saints were NFC West

The Zephyrs boast different promotions every night of the week. On "$1,000 Tuesday," they give away—guess what?—$1,000. "Thirsty Thursday" offers live music and $1.00 beers. Friday features a post-game fireworks show; for some reason they don't call it "Fireworks Friday."

champs, garnering well-deserved praise for Mueller, whom owner Tom Benson fired for no apparent reason two years later. So the team begins to rebuild—again. They ended the 2003 season a dismal 8-8 with no playoff spot.

All together now: "Our Father, who art in heaven . . ."

The Dome seats about 69,000 for Saints games, and with the organization not fielding a winning team since 1992, tickets are becoming easier and easier to get. They are available at the team's training and administrative facility at 5800 Airline Drive in Metairie, but the easiest place to get them is the Superdome box office, Gate A, ground level. (As you drive past the Dome on Poydras Street, you will see a long ramp at the front of the building. Drive under the ramp to find the box office.) The Superdome box office is open Monday through Friday 8:30 A.M. to 5:30 P.M. and two hours before kickoff. Single game tickets cost $65 to $150. Call the Saints ticket office at (504) 731-1700 or Ticketmaster at (800) 488-5252.

If you don't have tickets, you can hear sportscaster Jim Henderson give play-by-play and former Saints quarterback Archie Manning provide color commentary on WWL-AM 870. Away games are telecast on WVUE-TV Fox 8.

If you're going to a Saints game and want to park in the Dome garage, arrive two hours before kickoff when the doors open. Or check out the New Orleans Centre next door, which offers a food court and shopping.

Most of the Dome's 5,000 parking spaces are reserved for season ticket holders; however, two garages are open for individual parking during Saints games. The cost is $12.

The Superdome is located on Poydras Street at the foot of the Central Business District. It's 27 stories high with a dome-shaped roof measuring more than nine acres. It's pretty hard to miss.

New Orleans VooDoo
New Orleans Arena, New Orleans
(behind the Superdome)
(504) 731-1700
www.govoodoo.com

In May 2003, Saints owner Tom Benson announced that he would bring an Arena Football League expansion team to the city. The New Orleans VooDoo kicked off its inaugural season the following February.

Fans responded enthusiastically to this fast, high-scoring sport, played on a walled 50-yard field with eight players on each side. With tickets as low as $6.00 and players who will stay after the game to talk or sign autographs, games have become a family affair with a fun atmosphere. And we haven't even mentioned the organization's lively dance team, the VooDoo Dolls, of course.

At this writing, the VooDoo had just played their last regular season game to a standing-room-only crowd of 17,030. Better yet, they beat the Austin Wranglers, 38–21, clinching the Southern Division title and the fourth seed in the playoffs.

And we have a winner!

Games are broadcast in English on WSMB 1350-AM and in Spanish on WFNO

If you're in town February through May, don't miss a chance to see the New Orleans VooDoo play. This Arena Football League team puts on a great show, and the fans have a really good time. And, hey, with tickets as low as $6.00, a game can fit into anybody's travel budget!

830-AM. The VooDoo play at the New Orleans Arena, located directly behind the Superdome. Tickets, which range from $6.00 to $42.00, are sold at the club's training facility, 5800 Airline Drive in Metairie, and at the Superdome ticket office, Gate A Ground Level. Season tickets go on sale each year in early fall, with individual game tickets available in late January.

Sugar Bowl
Louisiana Superdome
1500 Sugar Bowl Drive, New Orleans
(504) 525-8573
www.nokiasugarbowl.com

The idea of a New Year's Day college football game in New Orleans was hatched by New Orleans Item newspaper publisher Colonel James M. Thomson and sports editor Fred Digby in 1927. It took eight years to develop public and financial support for the project.

Then on January 1, 1935, in the depths of the Depression, the first Sugar Bowl Football Classic was held in Tulane Stadium. Tulane's Green Wave, which were undefeated in the South, were pitted against the only undefeated Northern team, Pop Warner's Temple University Owls. Tulane prevailed, 20–14, before a crowd of 22,026 fans who had paid $1.50 to $3.50 each to get in. A tradition was born.

The Sugar Bowl was the subject of the first live television program in New Orleans, in 1953, which was broadcast coast to coast. Seven years later it was the first game televised in color across the United States.

Over the years, the Sugar Bowl has hosted several national champions and a virtual who's who of legendary football coaches, including Frank Broyles, "Bear" Bryant, Bobby Bowden, Bob Devaney, Vince Dooley, Woody Hayes, "Shug" Jordan, Johnny Majors, Joe Paterno, and Bud Wilkinson.

In 1995 Nokia became the game's title sponsor and, subsequently, the Nokia Sugar Bowl signed a deal with the Orange, Fiesta, and Rose Bowls, stating that beginning in January 1999 each bowl would host a national championship once in the following four years. The title game took place at the Sugar Bowl when LSU beat Oklahoma, 21–14, making the championship extra sweet for all the local Tiger fans. This agreement was designed to allow for the best possible bowl games while maintaining conference contractual obligations, plus increase the likelihood of an actual college championship game between the two highest ranking teams.

The Dome, home of the Sugar Bowl, seats around 77,000 in its expanded football configuration. Tickets for the Sugar Bowl usually go on sale in August and are sold through Ticketmaster. Tickets generally cost around $150. Call Ticketmaster at (504) 522–5555 and (800) 488–5252.

BASKETBALL

New Orleans Hornets
New Orleans Arena, New Orleans
(504) 525–Hoop, (800) HORNETS
www.nba.com/hornets
Offering virtually everything except someone's firstborn, the City of New Orleans finally snagged a new National Basketball Association team in 2002 (to replace the one Utah snagged from us a couple of decades ago).

October 30, 2002, marked the inaugural tip-off of the New Orleans (formerly Charlotte) Hornets in their new home, the New Orleans Arena. Ironically, they hosted the Utah Jazz.

"We're bringing New Orleans a winner," said Hornets co-owner George Shinn when the agreement was announced. "Our team has had a winning record for the past nine years. . . . We are totally committed to bringing a championship caliber team to New Orleans."

On May 4, 2004, the Hornets lost to the Miami Heat in the first round of the playoffs, ending a 41–41 regular season, as well as the employment of coach Tim Floyd.

Oh well, maybe next year.

Want to get out to Zephyr Park but I–10 is backed up? Just take Airline Drive. Go down Tulane Avenue (which runs parallel to Canal Street, a few blocks upriver). Tulane Avenue turns into Airline Drive immediately after crossing Carrollton Avenue. Keep going. The field is right past Clearview Parkway, on the left.

Hornets games can be seen on Cox Sports Television (cable channel 37) and heard on WRNO 99.5 FM.

The arena is the green stadium at the rear of the Superdome on Poydras Street. Monday through Saturday home games will begin at 7:30 P.M., with Sunday night games at 6:00 P.M. Tickets cost $18.50 to $200.00.

EQUESTRIAN

Fair Grounds Race Course
1751 Gentilly Boulevard, New Orleans
(504) 944–5515, (800) 262–7983
www.fgno.com
The Fair Grounds, America's third-oldest Thoroughbred race course, offers 88 days of racing from Thanksgiving through March. The Racetrack, as locals call it, celebrated its 126th year of racing in 1997 with the grand opening of a new six-story, 217,000-square-foot facility featuring a 4,000-seat grandstand, box seats, and a clubhouse where spectators can enjoy gourmet dining while watching a photo finish through floor-to-ceiling windows (reservations and jackets required). There's also an oyster bar and a cocktail lounge offering a view of the paddock and the New Orleans skyline.

Grandstand admission is $1.00; clubhouse admission is $4.00. Gates open at 11:30 A.M. First post is Thursday through Monday at 12:30 P.M. Last race is approximately 5:30 P.M.

The Fair Grounds Race Course is located near City Park at 1751 Gentilly

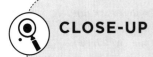

Louisiana Superdome

It was November 1965 and New Orleans Mayor Vic Schiro, a one-time Hollywood bit player known for telling his staff, "Just give me my lines and I'll go out there and ham it up," was behind in his race for reelection. He was running against former police chief and popular city councilman Jimmy Fitzmorris. Public sentiment held that Schiro had botched citywide emergency preparations during Hurricane Betsy less than four weeks before Election Day, a major political misstep that also proved devastating to the city. To make matters worse, Schiro had to stop campaigning to have his appendix removed.

Something had to be done.

Political consultant David Kleck stepped in with a campaign promise to beat all others: If there's anything New Orleanians love as much as food, it's sports. So why not promise to build a domed stadium? Businessman and civic promoter Dave Dixon had been talking about it for years, but he'd never received any backing.

Thus was hatched "A Fireside Chat with Sunny [Schiro's wife] and Vic," a live half-hour broadcast from the mayor's Lakefront home, featuring hizzoner clad in his sick-bed pajamas and robe. Schiro went before the cameras and made his grand declaration to build a domed stadium. He was followed by Dave Dixon showing drawings of the proposed structure and, finally, eastern New Orleans real estate developer Marvin Kratter, who agreed to give the city a tract of suburban land on which to erect this monument to the mayor's imagination. (The Schiro campaign had convinced Kratter to donate the land in order to increase the value of his adjoining property.)

The program aired two days before the election. Next-morning headlines blazed the announcement and, according to former *Times-Picayune* political columnist Iris Kelso, one broadcaster even went so far as to state, "New Orleans will have the greatest stadium in the world, thanks to Mayor Vic Schiro." In a case of Louisiana politics-as-usual, Schiro's big promise got him reelected, but he never made any attempts to push forward the Superdome project. Gov. John McKeithen picked up the ball, and with his backing the Superdome was finally built in downtown New Orleans in the early '70s.

Completed in 1975 at a cost of $163 million, the Louisiana Superdome is the world's largest indoor arena. The stadium sits on 13 acres with the entire facility encompassing 52 acres. It stands 27 stories high, and the roof (the largest of its kind) covers 9.7 acres. The stadium is the home of the New Orleans Saints, the Nokia Sugar Bowl, and Tulane University football. It's where the pope addressed 80,000 schoolchildren, a president (George H. Bush) was nominated, and the largest indoor concert audience in history (87,500) saw the Rolling Stones perform in 1981.

The Dome has played host to more Super Bowls (six) than any other stadium, three NCAA Final Four tournaments (two of which set attendance records), and was the site of Walt Disney Studios' world

The Louisiana Superdome has hosted world-class sporting events, a Republican National Convention, and the largest indoor concert in history. COURTESY OF NEW ORLEANS METROPOLITAN CONVENTION & VISITORS BUREAU, INC./RICHARD NOWITZ

premiere of *The Hunchback of Notre Dame.*

The structure is so big that seats were designed to be different colors so that to a television camera the stadium would look full, even if some of the stands were empty. The stadium is also credited with spurring the development of the lower Poydras Street corridor and, consequently, the expansion of the city's Central Business District.

In his book *Superdome: Thirteen Acres that Changed New Orleans,* author Marty Mule points out: "Until the Louisiana Superdome was built, urban renewal was rarely associated with the construction of sports arenas. Now Balti-more, Cleveland, and others have made new stadiums the centerpiece of a refurbished downtown, the magnet for attracting visitors and suburbanites into the city center."

Though the $163 million expenditure to build the Dome was widely criticized at the time, a study of the facility's 20-year economic impact concluded that nearly $4.6 billion has found its way into state coffers via the stadium. "It is hard to imagine a better return on an investment," said University of New Orleans economist Dr. Timothy Ryan, the study's author.

If only Vic Schiro could see it now.

Boulevard, New Orleans. To get there from downtown, take Esplanade Avenue (which runs along the northwest border of the French Quarter) away from the Mississippi River to Broad Street, turn right, then left at Gentilly Avenue. The racetrack is on the left.

VENUES

The Louisiana Superdome
1500 Sugar Bowl Drive, New Orleans
www.superdome.com
The Louisiana Superdome is located on Poydras Street at the foot of the Central Business District. For more information on the Dome, see the Close-up in this chapter.

New Orleans Arena
1501 Girod Street, New Orleans
www.neworleansarena.com
Adjacent to its towering big brother the Louisiana Superdome, the New Orleans Arena (affectionately dubbed the Dome's Mini Me) opened with much fanfare in October 1999. The state-of-the-art 19,000-seat arena is home to Tulane University basketball and the New Orleans Hornets. (The venue is also designed for concerts.)

DAY TRIPS 🚗

QUE PASA, ISLEÑOS? THE SPANISH DESCENDANTS OF LOWER ST. BERNARD PARISH

St. Bernard Parish, named for Gov. Bernardo de Galvez, has been dubbed "Louisiana's Spanish Treasure" due to the legacy of its earliest colonial settlers from the Canary Islands—the Isleños. While French settlers inhabited the upper regions of the parish in the early 1700s, it was these Spanish immigrants from the Canary Islands who arrived nearly 80 years later to help stave off British invasion, carving a community out of a swamp wilderness in the lower part of the parish along Bayou Terre-aux-Boeuf. The land was harsh and inhospitable. Still, these poor yet resourceful settlers soon earned reputations as expert trappers, fishers, farmers, ranchers, and boat builders, according to parish historian William Hyland. Lower St. Bernard, flanked by deltas and bayous, Lake Borgne, the Mississippi River, and Breton Sound, provided the Isleños with a cash crop of oyster, shrimp, crab, and other seafood. Many modern-day Isleños living in fishing communities such as Delacroix, Reggio, Shell Beach, and Yscloskey can point with pride to the local multimillion-dollar commercial fishing industry, no less a tribute to the legacy of their 18th-century ancestors.

By the 1830s local Isleño farmers were supplying the new colony of New Orleans upriver with sweet potatoes, onions, pumpkins, and other food staples. During the 19th century many Isleños, such as the Nunez, Estopinal, and Marrero families, became prosperous large-scale sugar planters and built beautiful homes in the area, some of which can still be seen today. Only about 300 Isleños, mostly elders, still speak Spanish, and many fear that the heritage and folkways of their close-knit communities are being lost to the passage of time. Efforts to preserve Isleño culture for generations to come is underscored by the lively annual Isleño Festival (see below), held on the grounds of the modest museum of the same name and coordinated by the Los Isleños Heritage and Cultural Society. Besides Isleño culture and untouristed fishing villages, visitors to lower St. Bernard Parish will also discover scenic oak alleys and picturesque plantation homes (though all are private and not open for public tours), as well as the Chalmette National Historical Park—site of the Battle of New Orleans. Because most of the historic homes do not have identifying plaques or visible addresses, it's highly advisable to get a free copy of the *Discover St. Bernard* tourism brochure, which includes full-color pictures of the homes and other historic points of interest as well as a map of where to find them. For a copy of the map call the St. Bernard Tourism Commission at (504) 278-4242.

Getting There

The best way to explore the Isleños community of lower St. Bernard Parish, 20 miles from downtown New Orleans, is on a driving tour. The best days to explore the area are Wednesday through Sunday, when the Isleños Museum is open. The museum takes only a half hour to browse but provides a valuable glimpse into the history and culture of the community. Getting to lower St. Bernard Parish is a snap. Take I–10 east toward Slidell to the I–510 on-ramp. Take I–510 to Chalmette (the only direction you can go). The interstate turns into Paris Road; follow Paris Road all the way to where it ends in Chalmette at the intersection of St. Bernard Highway, also known as Louisiana Highway 46.

(You'll see the signs for the Chalmette Ferry Terminal and the St. Bernard Parish Prison.) Turn left and head east.

Attractions

One of the most striking aspects of the redbrick ruins of the **De La Ronde Plantation** house may be its location—on the neutral ground of St. Bernard Highway just west of Paris Road, near the entrance to Chalmette National Historical Park. (In New Orleans we refer to medians as neutral grounds, after those on Canal Street that once served as a "neutral" space between the French Quarter and the new American section of the city.) Col. Pierre Denis de la Ronde, a leader of the Louisiana militia, built the plantation in 1805 and 16 years later planted the alley of oaks that stretches from the house to the Mississippi River. The plantation home was used by the British as a temporary hospital and headquarters during the Battle of New Orleans; the remains of British General Pakenham were carried here after the battle.

The **Chalmette National Historical Park and Chalmette National Cemetery** (8606 West St. Bernard Highway; 504–589–4428; www.nps.gov/jela) is the site of the 1815 Battle of New Orleans—the final battle of the War of 1812. (See Parks and Recreation.) The park was established in 1939 after a 45-year effort waged by the Chalmette chapter of the United States Daughters of 1812. They were also responsible for construction of the Chalmette Monument in 1909. (The obelisk had been designed 55 years earlier by Newton Richards, but construction was interrupted by the Civil War.) Museum exhibits

and audiovisual programs at the visitor center tell the story of the battle. Park rangers present talks on the area's history while an annual reenactment illustrates American soldier life during the War of 1812. On the grounds is the antebellum Beauregard House, built in 1812 and once owned by René Beauregard, son of General P.G.T. Beauregard.

Continue down St. Bernard Highway, past the Kaiser smokestack to the right, and soon you'll be in Meraux and driving under a picturesque alley of live oaks (on the south side) and pecan trees (on the north side) known as Docville Oaks. Photo hounds with a yen for sun-dappled country roads will most likely want to stop for pictures. Just be careful—rumbling tanker trucks travel the highway between the area's oil refineries. The trees were planted in the 1930s by Dr. Louis A. Meraux, for whom the town and oaks are named. He had them transported via Model A wreckers from nearby Olivier Plantation. Meraux, who was also parish sheriff from 1924 until his death in 1938, is regarded as the father of modern-day St. Bernard for the many new schools and roads built under his guidance.

If you packed a picnic, you'll want to take Louisiana Highway 39 off St. Bernard Highway in Violet and head to **St. Bernard State Park** (www.crt.state.la.us/crt/parks/stbernard/stbernard.htm). On your immediate right after crossing the railroad tracks is the Mississippi River Crevasse, a small but deep, tree-lined body of water formed in 1922 when the river broke through the levee. The crevasse is on the site of the former Poydras Plantation, once owned by 19th-century philanthropist Julian Poydras. Continue down Louisiana Highway 49 till you see the sign on your left for the entrance to the state park (see Parks and Recreation).

As you continue your journey down St. Bernard Highway, you'll come to a fork in the road. Keep to your left, as this is where St. Bernard Highway turns into Old Bayou Road. The first historic home, **Sebastopol,** will be on your right. This plantation home was built in 1830 by Pierre Marin, a native of Spain, and Evariste Wagan. While the single-story frame house is not overwhelming as far as plantation homes go, it was used as the St. Bernard branch of the Citizen's Bank of Louisiana in 1836. Two decades later Ignatius Szymanski, a Polish refugee and Confederate Army colonel, named it Sebastopol in honor of the stunning Russian defeat in a battle of the Crimean War. Today it is a private home and not open for tours.

Large tracts of land on which thriving sugarcane plantation homes like Sebastopol were built were sold by Isleño families, who later retreated to the lower reaches of the parish to Shell Beach and other fishing communities.

Beauregard Middle School will always have jurisprudence on its side—namely because the school is housed in the **Old Courthouse,** a stately three-story Federal-style building designed by the Freret brothers and constructed in 1915 for the sum of $64,893. The structure served as the parish courthouse until 1938. Vicente Nunez, the son of Canary Island native Esteban Nunez de Villavicencio, originally donated the property to the parish in 1848. Esteban Nunez was the progenitor of the politically influential Nunez family of St. Bernard Parish.

Farther down Old Bayou Road to the left is the modest **Ducros Historical Museum and Library** (504–682–2713) and its next door neighbor, the Museo de Los Isleños—better known as the **Los Isleños Heritage and Multicultural Park** (504–682–0862; www.losislenos.org). Both museums, 1345–57 Bayou Road, are free and open Wednesday through Sunday 11:00 A.M. to 4:00 P.M.

Ducros, built by the Gutierrez family in 1800 using traditional brick-between-post construction, houses a modest but locally important historic collection of 18th-century artifacts from nearby St. Bernard Village, as well as 2,000-year-old pottery shards. A piece of iron track laid in the 1840s for the Mexican Gulf Railroad (one

of the earliest in the South), which ran from Poydras to Shell Beach, is also on display. The library, named for Dr. Louis Alfred Ducros, who lived in the house from 1905 to his death in 1948, also has a collection of books on local history.

The tidy, four-room Los Isleños Heritage and Multicultural Park was established in 1980 by Marie Louise Molero O'Toole and Mael Molero Quatroy. The museum pays tribute to the Spanish immigrants from the Canary Islands who settled the lower St. Bernard coast between 1778 and 1785. Life among the swamps and marshes was harsh, but the Canary Islanders, or Isleños, soon established a reputation as consummate muskrat and nutria trappers, oyster and shrimp fishers, and boat builders. Exhibits include rare Works Progress Administration photographs of Isleño life in the marshes and replicas of hand-carved boats.

Other reflections of Isleño heritage are found among the wall maps showing the yearlong transatlantic route from the Canary Islands to Louisiana as well as authentic folk costumes. A sign in front of the museum displays the names of the eight ships—including the *Sacramento,* the *Sagrado Corazon de Jesus,* the *Santa Faz,* and the *Trinidad*—that transported an estimated 2,000 Canary Islanders to Spanish Louisiana. The immigration was part of a grand colonization scheme by King Charles II of Spain and headed by Pierre Phillippe de Marigny. He donated to Spain a huge parcel of land bisected by Bayou Terre-aux-Boeuf ("land of oxen") from Poydras to Lake Borgne and the Mississippi Sound. By 1780, when the region was renamed San Bernardo in honor of Gov. Bernardo de Galvez, more than 700 Isleños were living here. By the 1840s, Italian immigrants began arriving, followed by Germans and Filipinos.

A 20-year, $5.4 million master plan will create a 26-acre Isleño village. A 200-seat multipurpose center opened in 2000. Walk behind the museum and visit the board-and-batten structure the Coconut Island Store, the first of several old structures from the area relocated onto the grounds as part of the re-created village. A bar and grocery built in the 1920s (and vacant since the '50s), the Coconut Island was dubbed the "Bucket of Blood" for the weekend-night fistfights that broke out inside. The Isleños were nothing if not passionate.

Other historic local structures relocated to the museum grounds include the Estopinal House (and separate kitchen building), constructed of hand-hewn cypress posts and bousillage, a mud-and-moss mixture originally used by Native Americans. The bousillage was placed between posts and used as insulation. The Estopinal House, circa 1800, is identical in floor plan to the original homes built by the Spanish government for Isleño colonists in St. Bernard in the 1780s. The structure will be restored as a house museum, depicting life in the earliest days of Isleño colonization in Louisiana. Future plans call for additional historic structures as they become available.

For a real treat visit the grounds of the museums during the annual **Isleño Festival** held during the third weekend in March. Modern-day descendants of Canary Islanders roll out the welcome mat with traditional taste treats like *caldo* (Spanish soup), oyster fritters, and potatoes en salsa verde. Folk musicians from the Canary Islands are usually on hand to perform while volunteers in period costumes hold living-history demonstrations on palmetto-thatch hut building and hand-carved model boat construction. Also on display are traditional home remedies. Don't miss it.

It wasn't until 1842 that sugarcane plantation owner Laurent Millaudon built **Creedmore,** a Greek Revival plantation home on Old Bayou Road and today a well-shaded private residence. The structure, including several outbuildings such as the overseer's house, stables, and privy, is visible from the road. The private residence of **Magnolia Plantation** (reportedly the oldest home in the parish) is easy to miss because in some ways it barely

resembles a plantation. Today the original French windows and gallery are hidden behind a spacious redbrick- and window-enclosed front porch. Towering magnolias flank this private home, built in 1794 by Antonio Mendez not long after he and Manuel Solis developed new sugarcane cultivation techniques.

Not too far down Old Bayou Road on the right side is the **St. Bernard Cemetery** and its cluster of bleach-white above-ground tombs dating to 1787. To read the family names chiseled into the smooth granite tombs is to learn the roll call of the proud Isleños immigrants from the Canary Islands who settled lower St. Bernard Parish south of New Orleans in the 18th century—names like Melerine, Alfonso, Molero, Nunez, Estopinal, and others. In fact, Gran Canaria native Joseph Messa, a farmer, was the first to be interred at the St. Bernard Cemetery, one of the oldest in Louisiana. St. Bernard's first sheriff, Francois Garic, a veteran of the Battle of New Orleans and a sugar planter, is buried here, as well as the family of General P.G.T. Beauregard and a Revolutionary War soldier who died in 1815. Across the highway from the cemetery, which is still in use today, is the **St. Bernard Church,** originally built in 1785 as the first ecclesiastical parish church south of New Orleans. The modern-day Greek Revival structure was built in 1857 and its facade remodeled in 1915.

The privately owned **Kenilworth Plantation,** with its six truncated square columns (a design originating in colonial French Haiti), double-hip pitched roof, and brick-between-post construction, stands as one of the area's most enduring examples of antebellum architecture. Set at the back of a grassy oak-dotted lot, the French- and Spanish-colonial mansion was built between 1816 and 1819, fastened together by mortising and wooden pegs—and without a single nail.

When Old Bayou Road dead-ends at the Louisiana Highway 624 intersection, take a right. Follow the lazy turns of the two-lane road, which runs alongside Bayou Terre-aux-Boeuf to the right. Keep your eye on the left because the lone brick sugarmill chimney—all that remains of the Ruiz plantation—is nearly hidden behind the magnolia trees. Renamed **Hopedale Sugar Mill** after its namesake village community, this former glint in the eye of the Industrial Revolution was powered by a steam engine in the 1870s. Antebellum forts and prehistoric Indian mounds are nearby but accessible only by boat.

Yet another fork in the road leads travelers either to the fishing community of **Delacroix Island** or those of **Shell Beach, Yscloskey,** and **Hopedale.** Explore both byways (Delacroix and Shell Beach are only 10 minutes away in either direction) as they each run alongside scenic Bayou Terre-aux-Boeuf and fleets of skiffs and private shrimp and oyster boats. Arrive in the afternoon and watch deckhands off-load the day's catch. On a sunny day you're likely to pass a family or two, perched atop ice coolers on the grassy road shoulder with fishing poles in hands. The aptly named **End of the World Marina** (you can't miss the large sign) also serves as the end of the road in Delacroix Island, named for one-time "island" owner Francois Dusuau Delacroix. Take time to enjoy the bayou view before turning around and heading to Shell Beach and Yscloskey. Usually by late afternoon the green trawling nets of tall-rigged shrimp boats there are "wings up" at the eleven and one o'clock positions.

Across the vast expanse of Bayou Yscloskey from Shell Beach are the ruins of **Fort Proctor** on a spit of shell-strewn marsh. Construction of the fort's three-tiered tower (originally reached by a drawbridge over an inner moat) began in 1856 at the direction of Captain P.G.T. Beauregard. The outpost, designed to safeguard New Orleans against invasion from the bayous of Lake Borgne, is a vivid reminder of the area's strategic military importance. Outbreak of the Civil War prevented the roof and second-story floor from being built. Ironically, a garrison of black Union soldiers occupied the fort in 1865. Plans

over the years to turn the fort into a recreational facility never materialized, and today the only way to visit the abandoned structure is to charter a private boat. In recent years the quiet, countrified charm of Shell Beach has caught the eye of the well-to-do. **Proctor's Landing,** for example, is a small but growing development of new, modern-style homes built on pylons with massive decks overlooking the bayou. Property values are rising throughout the community, and some have suggested that it won't be long before Waverunners outnumber fishing boats.

Fortunately for landlubbers a local landmark and culinary tribute to home-cooked gluttony called *Rocky and Carlo's* can be found on dry land at 613 West St. Bernard Highway in Chalmette (504–279–8323). Check your heart-healthy diet at the door and prepare to binge—you won't be alone. Take a seat, dawlin'. Families pack the joint especially on Sunday afternoon for Sicilian and New Orleans house specialties like the Wop Salad, fried chicken, roast beef po-boys, and the eatery's famous fresh-baked macaroni and cheese. Just as famous are the king-size portions prepared by kitchen cooks behind the order counter, which are guaranteed to satisfy the heartiest of appetites. Order a Barq's root beer—another tradition—with your smothered pork chops, and enjoy the down-home ambience of this local landmark, which opened in 1965.

ST. TAMMANY: OVER THE BRIDGE AND THROUGH THE WOODS

Thirty miles north of New Orleans across Lake Pontchartrain sits St. Tammany Parish, where visitors can find the natural delights of a weekend in the country. The original inhabitants of these piney woods, which locals call the north shore, were the Choctaw Indians. The area was part of the vast Louisiana Territory that Napoleon sold to the United States in the early 19th century. At that time it was named for

For more information on attractions and special events in the great outdoors north of the lake, call the St. Tammany Parish Tourist and Convention Commission at (800) 634-9443.

Delaware Indian Chief Tamanend, who was renowned for his virtue.

Even before that time, though, settlers—mostly via New Orleans—were drawn to the area by its abundant sources of water. The earliest industries were boat building, farming, brick molding, and timber. In antebellum times, St. Tammany boomed as a resort community with hotels, inns, and restaurants frequented by wealthy New Orleans Creoles who came to partake of the "healing" artesian waters in the town of Abita Springs or simply to holiday in the fresh outdoors on l'autre cote du lac—the other side of the lake. Daily boat excursions from the city were popular, and by 1880 people were able to travel here by rail.

The 1956 completion of the 24-mile Lake Pontchartrain Causeway Bridge, the world's longest bridge completely over water, made the drive only a 60-minute commute to New Orleans. In recent years, thousands of New Orleanians have relocated to the north shore, making St. Tammany the state's fastest growing parish.

There are two ways to get to the north shore from New Orleans. I-10 east takes drivers to Slidell on the east side of the parish, and the Causeway (which is off I-10 west at the Causeway Boulevard exit) takes visitors to west St. Tammany and the towns of Mandeville, Madisonville, and Covington. The following are suggestions of at least twice as many activities as can be done in a day, so take your pick and enjoy your day in the country.

Slidell, Louisiana

Settled in 1850, Slidell offers natural attractions and scenery. First, there's

Fort Pike in the Rigolets. Named for the explorer who discovered Pike's Peak, this fort was built in the early 19th century to protect New Orleans from seaborne invasion. (See Fort Pike State Commemorative Area in the Parks and Recreation chapter for details). While in Slidell, don't miss the Honey Island Swamp Tour (see Attractions). Considered one of America's most pristine river swamps, the area is teeming with wildlife, including alligators, waterfowl, and mink.

Mandeville, Louisiana

From Slidell, take I-12 west to the town of Mandeville (or go straight to Mandeville from New Orleans via the Causeway). Founded as a summer retreat by Bernard de Marigny, one of New Orleans's most prominent Creoles, Mandeville offers Fontainebleau State Park (see Parks and Recreation) for hiking, bird-watching, and picnicking. Excellent for cycling or horseback riding, 9 of the 31 miles of the Tammany Trace, a 200-foot wide wooded trail that follows the old Illinois Central railroad bed, passes through the park. For more information call (800) 43-TRACE.

Mandeville is also a good place to enjoy a lunch of fresh local seafood while overlooking the lake at Alex Patout's Restaurant (2025 Lakeshore Drive; 985-626-8500).

Madisonville, Louisiana

A few minutes west of Mandeville (take scenic byway Louisiana Highway 22) is Madisonville. This quaint waterfront town, situated at the mouth of the Tchefuncte River, was established in 1810 and named for President James Madison. It is home to the annual Wooden Boat Festival that attracts the largest gathering of antique, classic, and contemporary boats in the South. The Fairview-Riverside State Park (see Parks and Recreation) is also here,

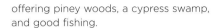

offering piney woods, a cypress swamp, and good fishing.

Covington, Louisiana

About 10 minutes up Louisiana Highway 21 is the town of Covington. Established in 1813, Covington scenically sits where the Bogue Falaya and Tchefuncte Rivers meet. Stroll through the shops and galleries of Covington's quaint historic district, and don't miss **H. J. Smith's Son's General Store** at 308 North Columbia Street. Family owned and operated since 1876, this shop is more museum than store. It has everything from ox yokes and cast-iron stoves to plantation bells and cypress swings. Then tour the region's only winery, **Pontchartrain Vineyards** (985–892–9742), just outside town on Highway 1082, where fine table wines are produced. The tour includes tasting in an Old World, French Provençal tasting room.

At the end of the day, before heading back to New Orleans, stop back in Madisonville and enjoy dinner at **Friends on the Tchefuncte** (407 St. Tammany Street, 985–845–7303), in a beautiful riverdock setting. From there, cruise on back across the Causeway to the city.

PLANTATIONS: THE WAY WE WERE

Call it political correctness. Call it long overdue. Either way, a growing number of River Road plantation homes between New Orleans and Baton Rouge are beginning to acknowledge stories of the African slaves who almost single-handedly—and, it should be remembered, without any say in the matter—constructed the antebellum's so-called grandeur of the Old South.

Any story of the African experience in southeast Louisiana can only make a visit to Plantation Country richer, not to mention more accurate. Some tours include visits to historic on-site slave quarters. Consider: It was in one of Laura Planta-

tion's 150-year-old slave cabins that the West African folktales of "Compair Lapin," better known in English as the legendary "Br'er Rabbit," were first told on the American continent.

Plantation Country still offers an unparalleled glimpse of what unlimited time, wealth, ego, free labor, and architectural largesse could create in this one-time backwater territory. Ironically, the smoke-belching refineries that today dot the petrochemical corridor along River Road also remind us that time waits for no one.

Many antebellum homes throughout southeast Louisiana's Plantation Country offer overnight accommodations, a romantic way to savor the historic opulence, architecture, and elegance of a time when self-pampering was the order of the day—and night.

**Destrehan Plantation
13034 River Road, Destrehan
(985) 764–9315
www.destrehanplantation.org**
What makes this home noteworthy, at least in the historic scheme of things, is that Destrehan is the oldest documented plantation left intact in the lower Mississippi Valley. And that's saying a mouthful. This multicolumned tribute to Louisiana's antebellum glory was built in 1787 and acquired five years later by Jean Noel Destrehan, the son of a French aristocrat statesman, from his father-in-law, Robin de Logny. These names mean something down here, trust us.

Destrehan had his own statesman stash, and in 1810 he didn't bat an eye at the cost of embellishing this stately mansion with two additional wings. After all, he had the bucks. During his off time he had perfected the process for granulating sugar and, thus, helped launch the most profitable industry in the history of the Louisiana plantation economy. No layabout, he.

From 1830 to 1840 the facade and interior were changed during a major renovation, and today the Greek Revival–style house showcases Destrehan's hand-hewn cypress timbers, *bousillage-entre-poteau* construction, and West Indies–style roof. Destrehan Plantation, listed in the National Register of Historic Places, is also a popular site for dinner parties and special evening occasions, when only costumed guides who intrigue visitors with the history of the house and its ghosts will do.

Located 8 miles from New Orleans International Airport, Destrehan is best reached by taking I-310 to the River Road exit. Head east on River Road and you can't miss it or the house's twin redbrick chimneys. Tours are daily 9:00 A.M. to 4:00 P.M. Tickets cost $10.00 for adults, $5.00 for teens, and $3.00 for kids 6 to 12. A gift shop sells books by Louisiana authors, locally made handcrafts, and specialty products. A fall festival is held the second weekend of November.

Houmas House
40136 Louisiana Highway 942, Darrow
(225) 473-7841
www.houmashouse.com
In its heyday more than 20,000 acres of surrounding sugarcane fields made fortunes for men like Ireland native John Burnside, who bought Houmas and 12,000 acres for $1 million in 1858. The British subject saved his home from the ravages of the Civil War by declaring immunity, thus avoiding occupation by Union forces. The move helped Houmas flourish as the greatest sugar producer in Louisiana in the late 1800s under Col. William Porcher Miles.

The house was built in 1840 by John Smith Preston, and movie buffs will recognize the blinding-white three-story, 14-columned home as the setting for the classic film *Hush, Hush, Sweet Charlotte,* starring Bette Davis and Olivia de Havilland. The Greek Revival masterpiece has also been featured in national magazines including *Life, House Beautiful,* and *National Geographic.* Preston purchased the house from his wife's father, Revolu-

tionary War hero General Wade Hampton of South Carolina, who had acquired the property in 1812.

The original four-room dwelling at the rear of the house, characteristic of both Spanish and rural French architecture, was built in the late 1700s by Alexander Latil after he purchased this tract of land along the Mississippi River from the Houmas Indians. The structure was later attached to the great house by a porte cochere, or arched carriageway.

The grand old home fell into disrepair after the Depression and was purchased and restored in 1940 by Dr. George Crozat of New Orleans for his country estate. Today the home, listed on the National Register of Historic Places, is furnished with the late Crozat's collection of 1840s-era museum pieces of early Louisiana craftsmanship. The formal gardens have been returned to their former beauty beneath magnolias and 200-year-old moss-draped oak trees.

Daily guided tours are conducted 9:00 A.M. to 5:00 P.M. Admission is $20 adults and $10 children. To reach Houmas House, 60 miles from New Orleans, take I-10 west and exit at Louisiana Highway 44 to Burnside, turn right on Louisiana Highway 942 and drive 4 miles.

Laura Plantation
2247 Louisiana Highway 18 River Road
Vacherie
(225) 265-7690, (888) 799-7690
www.lauraplantation.com
Perhaps the most important legacy of this Creole plantation is not its opulence but rather the fact that inside its six historic 150-year-old slave cabins were first told the West African folktales of "Compair Lapin," better known in English as the legendary "Br'er Rabbit," by Senegalese slaves. This two-story restoration-in-process, built in 1805, is surrounded by sugarcane fields and is home to the largest collection of artifacts—more than 5,000 pieces—belonging to a single Louisiana plantation family. Objects include clothing, toiletries, business and

slave records, Carnival and mourning heir-looms, and the retold stories of Laura Locoul, the 1805 owner-manager. All of which enables visitors to glimpse the daily workings of 18th- and 19th-century planta-tion life, as well as a detailed look at one extended Creole family. Unlike most of its River Road cousins, Laura has been only partially renovated, but its weathered walls add an authentic air of untouched history to the 45-minute guided tours conducted daily 9:00 A.M. to 5:00 P.M. in English or French. Admission is $10.00 adults; $5.00 children age 6 to 17.

Madewood
4250 Louisiana Highway 308
Napoleonville
(504) 369-9848, (800) 375-7151
www.madewood.com

The origin of this wonderfully restored, two-story Greek Revival mansion con-structed in 1818 on Bayou Lafourche is rooted in sibling rivalry. Madewood was built over a period of eight years by the youngest of three sons of a wealthy North Carolina planter to outdo the architectural splendor of his older brother's Woodlawn home. But, as luck would have it, the youngest brother died of yellow fever before Madewood, designed by noted architect Henry Howard, was completed.

Be that as it may, what really sets this 21-room Plantation Country charmer apart from its competitors is the reputation of current owners Keith and Millie Marshall for treating overnight visitors staying in one of the greathouse guest rooms to a unique experience: a library wine-and-cheese reception followed by a sumptu-ous multicourse candlelit dinner in the large dining room and, later, brandy in the parlor. Some guests opt for a more secluded stay in one of three informal suites in Charlet House, a restored raised cottage built in the 1820s on the planta-tion grounds, which features a family cemetery and carriage house.

Not to be outshined by nearby Houmas House, site of the movie *Hush, Hush, Sweet Charlotte*, Madewood lured

Hollywood to its breezy gallery and mas-sive white columns for the filming of *A Woman Called Moses*, starring Cicely Tyson. Tours are available daily 10:00 A.M. to 4:00 P.M. at a cost of $6.00 for adults and $4.00 for children. Madewood is located 2 miles south of Napoleonville on Louisiana Highway 308, 74 miles from New Orleans and 20 minutes from Houmas House.

Nottoway Plantation
30970 Highway 405, White Castle
(225) 545-2730, (866) 527-6884
www.nottoway.com

If Southern grandeur has a name, it's Not-toway. That in no small part was due to the great wealth of prosperous sugar planter John Hampden Randolph, who in 1849 commissioned what today is the largest and certainly one of the finest homes in the entire South. Nottoway, sim-ply put, is an American castle whose Ital-ianate and Greek Revival architecture and 22 enormous columns epitomize antebel-lum luxury and magnificence. Randolph also saw to it that his splendid 53,000-square-foot home with 64 rooms brought innovative and unique features to the South, including indoor plumbing, gas lighting, and coal fireplaces.

Ten years after construction began, Nottoway was completed to accommo-date Randolph's 11 children. Situated on a 7,000-acre sugar plantation, this aristo-cratic house, with its intricate lacy plaster friezework, hand-painted Dresden porce-lain doorknobs, hand-carved marble man-tels, Corinthian columns of cypress wood, crystal chandeliers, and 65-foot Grand White Ballroom, was saved from total destruction during the Civil War by a kindly Northern gunboat officer who had once been a guest of the Randolphs. The current owner, Paul Ramsey of Sydney, Australia, continues an authentic restora-tion begun in 1980.

Guided tours are daily 9:00 A.M. to 5:00 P.M. Admission is $10.00 for adults and $4.00 for children 6 to 12; children under 5 free. A restaurant and overnight accommodations in one of 13 guest rooms, each with private bath and entrance, are available. Room rate includes bottle of sherry; morning wake-up call with sweet potato muffins, orange juice, and coffee; plantation breakfast; and guided tour of the mansion. To reach Nottoway take I-10 west and exit at Louisiana Highway 22. Turn left on Louisiana Highway 70 and follow the signs across the Sunshine Bridge, 14 miles north through Donaldsonville on Louisiana Highway 1.

Oak Alley Plantation
3645 Louisiana Highway 18, Vacherie
(225) 265-2151, (800) 442-5539
www.oakalleyplantation.com
To stand at the wrought-iron gates to the entrance of this River Road plantation near the levee and gaze down its quarter-mile alley of 28 evenly spaced, 300-year-old live oak trees, believed to be at least 100 years older than the great house, is to experience firsthand perhaps the most spectacular antebellum setting in the entire Mississippi Valley. If nothing else, it's probably the most photographed plantation house in Louisiana.

Fluted Doric columns surround the two-story Greek Revival house originally named Bon Sejour and built in 1837 by Jacques T. Roman III, reportedly because he was so enamored of the oaks. The traditional interior floor plan leads visitors to a second-floor gallery overlooking the alley of oaks. Jefferson Hardin bought the deteriorating house in 1914 and sold it in 1925 to Andrew Stewart, whose restoration gained for Oak Alley its designation as a National Historic Landmark. The house is furnished as it was during Stewart's ownership.

Oak Alley is open for tours daily March through October 9:00 A.M. to 5:30 P.M.; November through February 9:00 A.M. to 5:00 P.M. Tickets are $10.00 for adults, $5.00 for ages 13 to 18, and $3.00 for ages 6 to 12. Take I-10 west to the Gramercy exit 194 and take Louisiana Highway 18 (River Road) to Vacherie. Oak Alley is located

between St. James and Vacherie, 60 miles from downtown New Orleans.

Ormond Plantation Manor Home
13786 River Road, Destrehan
(504) 764-8544
www.plantation.com
In the 1800s travelers visiting Louisiana's sugarcane plantation had three basic ways of getting around: They could buy passage aboard a steamboat plying the Mississippi River, hire a horse-drawn coach and take their chances on the primitive River Road, or ride the railroad through the swamp. Overnight accommodations along the way for most were dependent upon the hospitality of plantation owners, who often smiled kindly at their visiting guests whether they be peddlers or friends and family. The oldest West Indies–style Creole plantation on the Mississippi River sits on 16 acres in the heart of Louisiana's German Coast and was once such a place of respite for weary travelers, as well as soldiers headed to the Battle of New Orleans.

The house was constructed using bricks between cypress studs (*briquettes entre poteaux*—brick between posts) on the front and rear walls, cemented brick columns to support the front porch, or gallery, with wood columns on the second floor supporting the roof. Two wings, or garconnieres, were built around 1811 by Col. Richard Butler, who had bought the plantation home a few years earlier from the original owner, Pierre d'Trepagnier, and renamed it after his ancestral home, Castle Ormonde in Ireland.

Ghost stories and mysteries abound at Ormond. For example, in 1798 d'Trepagnier was reportedly summoned from a family meal by a servant to meet a gentleman, supposedly attired in the uniform of a Spanish official, and never returned. No trace of d'Trepagnier was ever found. Must have been some poker game.

Ormond has three rooms used for bed-and-breakfast, all furnished with period antiques. Accommodations include chilled wine with fruit and cheese tray, wake-up call, breakfast, and guided plantation tour. An on-site restaurant offers an a la carte menu. Ormond is open for public viewing with guided tours daily 10:00 A.M. to 3:00 P.M. Admission is $5.00 for adults, $4.00 seniors, $3.00 children 6 to 12. Take I–10 east to I–310 and get off at the St. Rose/Destrehan exit; turn right at River Road.

San Francisco Plantation House
Drawer AX, Reserve
(985) 535–2341, (888) 322–1756
www.sanfranciscoplantation.org
Back in the 1820s, Elisee Rillieux had the idea to put together a large plantation out of smaller properties. Edmond Bozonier Marmillion, whose family owned some estates in the neighborhood, liked what he saw so much that he snatched it off the market in 1830 and commenced construction two decades later. Today this galleried house, originally called St. Frusquin, a name derived from the French slang *sans fruscins*—"without a penny in my pocket"—has only a dining room and various service rooms on the ground floor. The main living room is on the second floor as was often the Creole custom. Marmillion's son Valsin and his wife, the former Louise von Seybold, whom he met during a trip to Bavaria, decorated the home in 1860.

In 1879 Achiulle D. Bougere bought the plantation, renamed it San Francisco, and in 1905 sold it to the Ory family. For a while this plantation seemed gone with the wind, but a $2-million complete restoration in the 1970s returned this belle of the ball to its rightful place on the River Road plantation corridor. Ceiling murals, faux marbling, and graining reflect the interior splendor that once was, while Gothic windows, ornate grillwork, and gingerbread trim characterize the facade. Those tracking the Battle of the Plantations take note: Flanking the exterior of the house are onion-domed blue-and-white water cisterns that look like miniature Russian Orthodox churches. Daily 30- to 40-minute tours are conducted every 15

minutes from 9:40 A.M. to 4:40 P.M. at San Francisco Plantation, located on River Road about 1 mile past the Marathon Oil Refinery. Admission is $10.00 for adults; $5.00 for children 13 to 18; $3.00 for children 6 to 12; kids under 6 are admitted free.

CAJUN COUNTRY: HOUMA GOOD TIMES

In the 18th century the British swept into Nova Scotia and shoved the French settlers out. This homeless band left Acadia and moved southward to set up an outpost along the coast of the colonial French territory of Louisiana. These Acadians kept their language and their culture and made new lives for themselves as the Cajuns of South Louisiana. Many of them ended up an hour southwest of New Orleans in the modern-day city of Houma, named for the Houmas Indians who originally settled the area. Houma is the seat of Terrebonne Parish, the second largest in Louisiana. More than half of Terrebonne's 2,000 square miles is made up of bayous, lakes, and salt marshes. The area offers the closest taste of Cajun Country to New Orleans as well as ample evidence of why Louisiana is called a Sportsman's Paradise. In fact, the bounty and beauty of this rich subtropical delta so enchanted the Acadians that they named it "Terrebonne," French for "good earth."

Terrebonne Parish is located on the last great delta created by the Mississippi River more than 2,500 years ago and is home to the largest, most productive estuary system in the world. People here have long been connected to the local bayous. Pirate Jean Lafitte and adventurer Jim Bowie were known to retreat to the mystery of the region's moss-draped waterways. Civil War soldiers adapted to the land using a local plantation home as a hospital and converted Spanish moss into sutures. The Acadians chose the area because it was so secluded.

To reach Houma from New Orleans, cross the Crescent City Connection (the

Mississippi River Bridge) and continue down U.S. Highway 90. It's a straight shot that takes about an hour. For a good area overview, stop at **Southdown Plantation,** which houses the **Terrebonne Parish Museum** and its oral history room. Exhibits chronicle the contributions made by various cultures in the area and showcase the unique Cajun lifestyle. The house itself, built in 1858, is beautifully decorated and displays a collection of 135 Boehm and Doughty porcelain birds as well as a re-creation of local U.S. Sen. Allen J. Ellender's private Washington office. (Ellender served in Congress from 1937 to 1972.)

No one should miss **the swamp** on their visit to Terrebonne Parish. The variety of tours include those on foot, by boat, and by air—and now even by train. The two most popular tours are those offered by "Alligator" Annie Miller's Sons and Ron "Cajun Man" Guidry. Miller's sons still steer a boat full of visitors into the moss-draped cypress swamp, cut the engine and, then, as if calling a dog sing out, "Come on, Baby!" as a 7-foot alligator swims up to get its reward—a piece of raw chicken they place on a stick they hold just above the water. "When Annie's sons call," say locals, "the gators come like children to an ice cream truck." **Alligator Annie's Sons' Swamp and Marsh Tours** is at 3718 Southdown Mandalay Road, Houma; (985) 868-4758 or (800) 341-5441.

Ron "Black" Guidry, on the other hand, is known as the Cajun crooner. While swamp-cruising visitors gaze at alligators, possums, and cranes, Guidry, a former Green Beret and Louisiana State Trooper, plays guitar and sings Cajun songs. If you're feeling lonely, it won't be for long because Guidry's dog, Gator Bait, a Louisiana catahoula who rides along, is

sure to give warm welcome. **A Cajun Man's Swamp Cruise** is at 3109 Southdown Mandalay Road, Houma; (985) 868-4625.

In Gibson, 15 miles west of Houma, there is another fun option for exploring the swamp and learning about Cajun life on the bayou: the **Wildlife Gardens** at 5306 North Bayou Black Drive (985-575-3676). The Wildlife Gardens is a swamp zoo featuring native plants and animals including rare duck species. The walking tour features an authentic trapper's cabin and B&B cabins for overnight accommodations.

Take U.S. Highway 90 back to Houma and head south on Louisiana Highway 56 to begin a picturesque 80-mile driving tour of **Bayou Country.** Travel down Louisiana Highway 56 until you reach Louisiana Highway 315 for the return trip. Along the way are sugarcane fields, moss-draped cypress trees, the swamp maple, redbud, and various fruit trees. See eagles, egrets, herons, owls, and seabirds—all of which flock to this fertile delta located within the Mississippi Flyway, the migratory path of waterfowl and geese from 32 states and 3 Canadian provinces.

At the Bayou **Dularge Marina,** visitors will find a small fishing village where many locals make their living repairing boats and making nets. See miles of campboats, oyster lugger boats, shrimp boats, and various pleasure boats. The marina offers a rest stop, refreshments, fuel, visitor information, and the opportunity to experience the charm of local Cajun conversation. Five miles from the junction of Louisiana Highways 56 and 57 is **LUMCON,** a marine biology research facility. Visitors are welcome to stop and view the marsh from the facility's observation tower, free of charge.

Back in Houma, the kids may be ready for a splash at **Waterland USA** before heading home. The seven-acre water park on Louisiana Highway 311 (985-872-6143) features a 52-foot tower and 32-foot slide, wave pool, miniature golf, and batting cages. Hungry? The food is hearty and fresh from the water pretty much anywhere along the way in these parts. In particular, check out **A-Bear's Cafe,** which also features live Cajun music on Friday nights; 809 Bayou Black Drive in Houma. Call (985) 872–6306.

SLIP-SLIDING AWAY ON THE MISSISSIPPI GULF COAST

Where do many Big Easy residents head off to when the walls start closing in? For more than 150 years the Mississippi Gulf Coast has been a home away from home for locals seeking an escape from the rattle and hum of big-city life. First-timers are easily smitten by the area's breeze-swept sandy beaches of rickety, private wooden piers and the raucous gulls that scout overhead for fish in the calm, warm seas. Travelers along the coastal scenic drive lined with oak-framed antebellum mansions and stately summer homes with screened verandas can look out to the horizon and see shrimpers and sailboats silhouetted in the late afternoon sun. Shopping and historic districts compete for attention with lively beach bars, brash souvenir shops, and a dozen neon-lit floating casinos (with more on the way) in the third-largest gambling mecca in the country.

Affectionately dubbed the Redneck Riviera, the Gulf Coast stretches from Waveland eastward through Bay St. Louis, Pass Christian, Long Beach, Gulfport, Biloxi, and Ocean Springs on U.S. Highway 90 along a 26-mile curve of man-made white-sand beach. Variety is the spice of life on this sun-drenched Mississippi coastline where the Deep South meets the Gulf of Mexico. **The Mississippi Gulf Coast Coliseum & Convention Center,** for example, is big enough to lure heavy metal troubadours like Van Halen and just small-town enough to host local craft shows and the annual Crawfish Festival. The region has offered shelter from the storm for such eccentric and nationally acclaimed artists as the late painter Walter Anderson and potter George Ohr, who

ran a Cadillac dealership in his later years. One watering hole celebrates Christmas in July (and the owner gets riled if anyone cuts in on his one-man jukebox sing-alongs). And sometimes it seems as though the casual seafood restaurants overlooking the area's picturesque harbors are as plentiful as the beach kiosks that rent waverunners and umbrellas.

Anglers anxious to get their hooks into the Gulf's legendary bounty of succulent redfish, flounder, king mackerel, red snapper, grouper, and cobia will find more than 70 fishing charter boats at the Gulfport Small Craft Harbor, Biloxi Small Craft Harbor, Broadwater Marina, and Point Cadet in east Biloxi. Capt. Mike McRaney, who owns and operates the 42-foot *Outrageous* at Point Cadet Marina (228–875–9462), is part of the growing breed of charters using sonar to pinpoint the Mississippi's catches du jour.

The umbilical cord linking the Crescent City and the Mississippi Gulf Coast reaches back to 1699 when French explorer and New Orleans founder Pierre LeMoyne d'Iberville landed in Biloxi and established the first permanent European settlement in the Louisiana Territory for King Louis XIV. Iberville established Biloxi (*buh-LUX-see*) as the third capital of the colonial French megacolony, which stretched north to Canada, east to the Alleghenies, and west to the Rockies. Prior to the Civil War, wealthy 19th-century New Orleanians rode the Louisiana-Nashville Railroad to their gracious Greek Revival and West Indies–style planter's homes located on the Gulf Coast. Confederate President Jefferson Davis spent the last 12 years of his life at Beauvoir, a national historic landmark in Biloxi, which is open for tours.

Waveland

This "Hospitality City," population, 5,600, is a popular weekend getaway for New Orleanians and year-round home for Big Easy retirees who bought smaller vacation homes here when property values were affordable. For travelers packing a carload of restless kids, however, the main lure is **Buccaneer State Park,** 2 miles south of U.S. 90 at 1150 South Beach Boulevard, (228) 467-3822. A shaded picnic area lush with moss-draped oaks offers plenty of picnic tables, barbecue grills, a covered shelter, and a children's playground with slides and teeter-totters. Admission is $2.00 per vehicle with up to four persons (25 cents for each additional person). At 0.5 mile farther down Beach Boulevard, youngsters can beat the heat at the **Buccaneer Bay Waterpark,** (228) 467-3822. The five-acre park includes a dual-flume, 300-foot twisting water slide, wave pool, kiddie pool for nonswimmers, a large sundeck, locker rental, and rental tubes. The park is open daily 11:00 A.M. to 6:45 P.M. between March 1 and Labor Day, and admission is $9.00 for adults and $7.50 for children ages 3 to 12. The pine-tree–shaded campground features a supervised, foot-deep wading pool for youngsters, a snack pavilion offering burgers and pizzas, two lighted tennis courts, 50 picnic sites, and the Pirate's Alley 0.5-mile circular nature trail. The campground has 149 pads for RV camping with picnic tables, grills, and water/electrical hookups (rate is $12.00, add $1.00 for sewage), bathhouses, and laundry facilities.

To get here, take I-10 east from downtown New Orleans approximately one hour, over Lake Pontchartrain, and past the city of Slidell. At the juncture of I-10 and I-59/I-12, stay on I-10 heading east to the town of Bay St. Louis in Mississippi. Exit at Highway 607 south, turn right, and continue for approximately 3 miles to the town of Waveland, Mississippi (waveland .ms.us).

Bay St. Louis

This thriving community (bay-st-louis .ms.us) of more than 400 local and transplanted New Orleans artists was recently rated as among the best art towns in America. But Bay St. Louis, population 9,000, also offers a slow-paced way of life and homespun seafood eateries. To sample it all, and then some, make a beeline for **Old Town Bay St. Louis,** the 3-square-block waterfront district on Main Street off Highway 90 near Beach Boulevard. Park your car and browse—this quaint arts, antiques, and dining enclave is well worth the time to experience on foot. (Don't miss Old Town Bay St. Louis's art walks held the second Saturday of each month from 6:00 to 8:00 P.M. with featured artists, refreshments, and live music.)

Local antiques hounds found a new friend when **Charbonnet & Charbonnet Antiques Unlimited** opened at 216 Main Street (228-466-9931). Among the newest kids on the block in Old Town Bay St. Louis, the 2,000-square-foot antiques emporium specializes in custom-ordered, custom-made reproduction furnishings hand-crafted from centuries-old cypress and long-leaf Southern pine barge board salvaged from dilapidated New Orleans homes. Stumped? Customers can peruse the store's photo albums of reproductions to find just the right piece to accent a home with Southern charm. Other eye-catchers include authentic late-1800s Romanian hutches hand-painted the color of Gypsy wagons, as well as antique armoires, headboards and sideboards, and bookshelves. Don't miss the collection of whimsical face masks ideal for guests at your next dinner party who want to disguise themselves as flappers and dandies, fez-wearing Turks, and Golden Age vamps. Open Monday through Saturday.

The Purple Snapper (111-A Main Street; 228-467-7703; www.purplesnapper.com) is one of the newest additions to the local gallery scene, offering a colorful palate of works by Gulf Coast artists. The diminutive shop features a mix of acrylics, watercolors, black-and-white art photography, and other one-of-a-kind and mixed-media artworks.

Ellis Anderson's **Quarter Moon Gallery,** at 146 Main Street (228-467-7279), offers an eye-pleasing mix of locally designed reticulated sterling-silver and gold jewelry by McLees Baldwin and Carol Maschler. Anderson's own unique selection includes one-of-a-kind cufflinks and tuxedo studs. One room features original-dyed and handwoven millinery by Tracy Thompson and Barbara Lundy Stone. A second gallery with a side-street entrance offers black-and-white photography by James W. deBuys as well as paintings by local artists. Hours are Friday and Saturday 11:00 A.M. to 5:00 P.M. and the rest of the week by appointment.

Giving a literary spin to Old Town is the eclectic **Old Books & Curiosities,** 126 Main Street, (228) 467–9791. Owners Nancy Marie and Zoe Bowers stock more than 7,000 rare and out-of-print hardback books on history, philosophy, religion, poetry, and other subjects. Visitors browsing the floor-to-ceiling shelves of dusty tomes may stumble upon a copy of *Liturgy for Episcopal Sunday Schools,* printed in 1846, or an 1845 volume of Eugene Sue's *The Wandering Jew.* Old sheet music, postcards, and magazines round out a pleasant selection of ephemera.

Foxy the Finnish Spitz is always on hand to greet visitors to owner Pye Parson's aptly named **Sol Garden** (111 Main Street; 228–463–1200), a "Zensational" New Age-flavored garden and sanctuary accessories shop and spirited new arrival on the Old Town scene. Here serenity takes the form of yoga mats and scented candles, bamboo and foliage, wind chimes, and unusually shaped ceramic pots and art vases from Vietnam, Indonesia, and Malaysia, all designed to turn any garden or sanctuary space into a meditative retreat. Best bets include the Chinese "rain chains," a 6-foot vertical "fountain" consisting of 20 copper "cups" that overflow with rain water when hung outdoors. Open daily.

Not to be missed across the street is the ground zero of the Bay St. Louis art gallery scene—**Serenity.** Owner Jerry Dixon opened his fine arts gallery, 126 Main Street, (228) 467–3061, in 1986 to

give local artists a place to show their work. Today, the 3,000-square-foot establishment is one of the oldest and best known in the area. It showcases the work of 150 local and Southern artists in 12 large rooms linked by narrow hallways. Artwork includes Jeanne Warner's and Dot Copeland's rural scene watercolors and Joseph Anthony Pearson's nude sketches and portraits. Also on hand are Alexander Brown's handcarved cypress alligators (that is, when they're not on loan to the George Ohr Museum & Cultural Center), mosaic tables by Elizabeth Vaglia, and Connie Boussom's oil paintings and one-of-a-kind ceramics and metal sculpture.

Also not to be missed is the '30s-era stucco **train depot,** where part of Tennessee Williams's *This Property is Condemned,* starring Robert Redford and Natalie Wood, was filmed. To reach the depot take Main Street to Toulme Street, turn left, and follow Toulme Street until it turns into Blaize Street at the bend in the road. Drive over the railroad tracks and you'll see the green building on your right. Across the street at 136 Blaize Avenue is the newest entry to the dining scene, **Bay City Grille** (228–466–0590). Many locals have put this casual dining spot, which offers a selection of po-boy and chicken sandwiches, burgers, deep-fried seafood (including shrimp, oyster, and catfish platters), and pastas, at the top of their list. House specialties not to be missed include the snapper Margarita (broiled and seasoned with rosemary, cilantro, cracked black pepper, and fresh lime and served with homemade papaya salsa) and the sour mash barbecued chicken (two chicken breasts smothered in homemade whiskey sauce).

Popular Beach Boulevard waterfront restaurants include the local legend **Trapani's Eatery,** 116 North Beach Boulevard, (228) 467–8570. An energetic crowd of Big Easy day-trippers and locals fill this brightly lit dining landmark known for its New Orleans–style po-boys, steaks, and seafood platters. The Crescent City leaves its mark on the menu with other dishes such as soft shell crab, crawfish étouffée (fresh crawfish tails and Creole veggies blended in a light roux), blackened shrimp (served with a pasta Bordelaise), and eggplant Delacroix (medallions of eggplant lightly fried with bread crumbs and topped with sautéed shrimp and veggies with hollandaise and Parmesan cheese). Traditional Italian pasta dishes and sides, including squash casserole and twice-baked potatoes, round out the menu. The restaurant is housed in a building constructed in 1906, which survived both the Hurricane of '47 and Camille in 1969.

Regulars may miss the weekend-night performances by **Dock of the Bay** (www .dock-of-the-bay.com) co-owner Jerry Fisher, former singer with Blood, Sweat and Tears (his last gig was New Year's Eve 1998), but the menu he created with wife Melva still packs a punch. This casual waterfront-deck dining establishment, 119 North Beach Boulevard (228-467-9940), opened in 1967 and offers one of the best views of the bay, day or night, as well as the whistling trains crossing the bay bridge to Pass Christian and beyond. A creamy homemade okra and shrimp gumbo (from Melva's recipe) and hearty oyster-artichoke soup are good segues into a selection of steaks, seafood platters, pastas, catches of the day (grilled, broiled, sautéed, fried, or blackened), and house specialties like Gumbo-laya (jambalaya surrounded with a moat of Melva's gumbo). Cassette tapes and CDs of Jerry Fisher & the Music Co., Fisher's now-defunct house band, are available.

One of the most photogenic accommodations on the Mississippi Gulf Coast, the distinctive **Bay Town Inn** (www.bay towninn.com), is a two-story West Indies–style planter's house built in 1899 that offers an unobstructed waterfront view framed by a massive oak tree, garden trellis, and white picket fence. Seven individually decorated guest rooms (two downstairs, $105 each; six upstairs, $90 each) feature antiques, 12-foot ceilings, ceiling fans, private baths, and such ameni-

ties as hand-ironed pillowcases and full-course breakfasts. Nos. 1 and 2 face the bay and are decorated in deep greens and burgundy. Some rooms have four-poster beds and all have queen beds (except No. 2, which has a king). This historic home at 208 North Beach Boulevard (800–533–0407) also has two front-porch swings ideal for catching up on reading or for enjoying a commanding view of the bay.

Another bed-and-breakfast, **The Heritage House** (116 Ulman Street, 228–467–1649), is within easy walking distance to Beach Boulevard and Main Street. Guests at this century-old house, known by locals as the Drake Home for its builder E. F. Drake, a prominent civil engineer and Bay St. Louis resident, stay in one of the three spacious second-floor bedrooms decorated with antique furnishings. Rates are $95, $110, and $125 and include offstreet parking, complimentary Southern breakfast, soft drinks and bottled water, and cable TV and telephones in each room. Present-day owners Winston and Alma Levy invite guests to stroll their relaxing gardens, which include 100-year-old live oaks, camellias, magnolias, and azaleas.

Pass Christian

Besides its pretty harbor, mercifully uncrowded beaches, and laid-back ambience, one of the best things about this small residential community, known affectionately as "The Pass" (pronounced *Pass Kris-tee-ANN*), is its 3-mile Scenic Drive, which runs alongside coastal Highway 90. The drive offers visitors a close-up view of waterfront antebellum mansions and Creole cottages. Many of these gracious homes, which survived the wrath of Hurricane Camille, were built by well-heeled New Orleans merchants in the 19th century and today rise from manicured lush front lawns shaded by towering oak, pine, and magnolia trees. Some of the homes are on the National Register of Historic Places, such as 1835 **Grass Lawn** (702 East Beach Boulevard, 228–868–5907), which offers tours Monday, Wednesday, and Friday 10:00 A.M. to 4:00 P.M. The massive two-story Greek Revival mansion, with an eight-column facade, first-floor veranda, and second-floor gallery, is hard to miss.

The Pass (pass-christian.ms.us/) was once an internationally known resort area. Six U.S. presidents have vacationed at The Pass, including Woodrow Wilson, who resided in the "Summer White House" on Scenic Drive, and Theodore Roosevelt, who came often to sail, write, and visit friends. If you want to be in that number, stay overnight at proprietors Tony and Diane Brugger's charming and unpretentious **Harbour Oaks Inn,** 126 West Scenic Drive, (228) 452-9399. The three-story Greek Revival house has covered first- and second-floor porches and a deep backyard with gigantic live oaks draped with Spanish moss. Guests staying in one of the five individually furnished rooms, decorated with antiques and period furnishings, can enjoy views of the Pass Christian Yacht Harbor, beaches, and the Mississippi Sound across the street. Amenities include private baths and full breakfast as well as the chance to make friends with the Bruggers' gentle horse, Bucky. The equine is so popular that Tony once quipped: "If anything ever happens to [Bucky], I might as well close the place down." Other amenities include complimentary wine and beverages made available to guests from the first-floor kitchen adjacent to the antique-filled billiards room. Rates are $83 to $128, and children ages 12 and older are welcome.

The best place to browse among the works of 175 Gulf Coast, regional, and national artists is **Hillyer House,** 207 East Scenic Drive, (228) 452-4810. The gallery specializes in artisan collections of hand-crafted jewelry, pottery, and blown glass. Earrings, necklaces, bracelets, and more in gold, silver, and porcelain have been hand-made by more than four dozen jewelers such as Courtney Miller and Jan Palombo. (Don't forget to check out Gulf Coast artist M. Milleur's pewter "gumbo necklaces" with dark-gray hematite beads and seed

pearls.) Among the hand-sculpted ceramics are sealife-themed pitchers, vases, platters, and wine coolers by Matt Brabham and Connie Mickle. Handblown glass includes pastel-colored oil lamps and sailboat-etched wine glasses in radiant colors. By the way, the 15-inch high polished brass cargo lanterns really work. Hours are Monday through Saturday 10:00 A.M. to 5:00 P.M. and Sunday noon to 5:00 P.M.

Long Beach

Pick up Highway 90 at the end of Scenic Drive and the next town you'll come to is Long Beach (long-beach.ms.us), the self-proclaimed Radish Capital of the World in the early 1900s. Two of the most popular attractions include the 500-year-old, 50-foot **Friendship Oak** (www.gp.usm.edu/oak.htm) at the University of Southern Mississippi Gulf Coast campus (730 East Beach Boulevard; 228–865–4500) and **Wolf River Canoes** (www.wolfrivercanoes.com), 21652 Tucker Road (228–452–7666), for leisurely guided tours of the local swamps and waterways. Cost is $36 per canoe (two-person minimum); children under 12 can sit in the center for free. Call for departure times.

Hungry? A second-level dining room view of the Mississippi Sound, Long Beach Harbor, and the nesting tern beach sanctuary have helped make **Steve's Marina Restaurant,** 213 East Beach Boulevard (228–864–8988), a new favorite among locals and visitors who used to dine here when it was The Chimney's. Hit this establishment at sunset and enjoy a predinner drink on the deck. The mostly seafood menu features shrimp dishes as well as trout, yellowfin tuna, flounder, and soft-shell crab. House specialties include blackened red snapper Cat Island, stuffed with seafood and topped with shrimp, crabmeat, artichoke hearts, and mushrooms in a lemon-butter sauce and served over pasta. Other surefire winners include deep-fried veal cutlets and seafood au gratin featuring jumbo lump crabmeat and shrimp baked in a rich cheese sauce. Open Sunday through Thursday 11:00 A.M. to 9:00 P.M. and Friday and Saturday 11:00 A.M. to 10:00 P.M.

Gulfport

Two points of pride among the 64,000 residents of Mississippi's second-largest city are (1) the town celebrated its centennial anniversary in 1988; and (2) the State Port at Gulfport is the largest banana importer in the country. That said, Gulfport (www.gulfcoast.org) is also a fun place for kids, and the best place to start is the **Marine Life Oceanarium** (www.dolphins rus.com); you can't miss the sign on the right-hand side of Highway 90 at the end of Highway 49. Families have been coming to Marine Life (228–864–2511), since 1956 to watch the high-jumping bottlenose dolphin shows, California sea lion skits, and colorful South American rain forest macaws. Divers in the Gulf of Mexico reef tank exhibit swim among sharks and stingrays while feeding the loggerhead sea turtles. Youngsters meantime can reach for the stars—starfish, that is—along with horseshoe crabs, sand dollars, and other sea life at the touch pool. Marine Life is open year-round daily 9:00 A.M. to 6:00 P.M. during the summer (9:00 A.M. to 4:00 P.M.), and admission is $13.75 for adults, $10.75 for seniors, and $8.50 for children ages 3 to 11. Children under 3 are admitted free. Shows run continuously all day, and a snack bar is available.

If all that marine action makes your brood eager to jump into the thick of things, head to **Wet Willy's,** 1200 Beach Boulevard, (228) 896–6592. This waterpark offers three 400-foot water slides, which empty into a 30,000-gallon wave pool as well as a kiddie pool. The park is open daily from Memorial Day to Labor Day 9:30 A.M. to 9:00 P.M. and costs $6.50 per hour for adults and children age 5 and older; youngsters aged 2 to 5 free. The $12 all-day pass is a bargain. Directly across the street is **Fun Time USA** (228–896–7315), an

amusement park with rides, miniature golf, bumper boats, go-karts, and an arcade. The park is open March 1 through Labor Day Sunday through Thursday 9:00 A.M. to 1:00 P.M. and Friday and Saturday 9:00 A.M. to midnight, with some winter hours. There is no charge for admission, and guests pay as they go. Miniature golf costs $4.00 per person (regardless of age); all rides cost $1.00 except the tilt-a-whirl and go-karts, which cost $2.00 per ride.

The state's first hands-on children's museum is found at the **Lynn Meadows Discovery Center,** 246 Dolan Avenue; (228) 897–6039. Turn left off Highway 90 onto Dolan Avenue and it's 1/2 block on the right-hand side. Simulation is the name of the game here. Youngsters can meet the R.U. Healthy fitness robot, become a news reporter and make a video, shop for seafood and garden veggies at a grocery store, operate a crane, trawl the Gulf for shrimp, and even load a bunch of bananas into an 18-wheeler tractor-trailer rig. The History Attic lets kids learn what it was like to live in the 1890s, while youngsters with a yen for science can deflect a tornado, make a square wheel roll, and defy gravity. Not to be left out, toddlers can join a group of teddy bears on a bayou camp "picnic." The center is open Tuesday through Saturday 10:00 A.M. to 5:00 P.M. Admission is $6.00 for all ages.

Ship Island is the most historically significant and visited of the four major barrier islands (the others are Cat, Horn, and Petit Bois) rimming Mississippi Sound about 10 miles offshore. Visitors can tour the remains of historic **Fort Massachusetts,** built in 1858. Travelers can surf-fish, swim, and sunbathe at the **Gulf Islands National Seashore,** known for its warm tidal pools and wind-shaped sand dunes crowned with sea oats. Visitors will find a beach snack bar, picnic pavilions, shower and restrooms, and rental beach chairs and umbrellas. During the War of 1812, 60 British ships with nearly 10,000 troops rendezvoused at Ship Island prior to an unsuccessful attack on New Orleans.

The island was a POW camp for Confederate soldiers and a base for the U.S. Second Regiment—one of the first African-American combat units to fight in the Civil War.

Ship Island is best reached by taking the Ship Island Excursions (www.msship island.com) passenger ferry (228–864–1014 or 866–466–7386), which departs the Gulfport Harbor daily during summer months at 9:00 A.M. and noon, returning at 3:40 and 6:15 P.M. Fall and spring departures are Monday through Friday at 9:00 A.M., returning at 3:40 P.M.; Saturday and Sunday at 9:00 A.M. and noon, returning at 3:40 and 6:15 P.M. Call ahead—departure and return times may vary depending on season. Round-trip fees are $18.00 for adults; $9.00 children aged 3 to 10; and $16.00 seniors aged 62 and older. It's a good idea to buy tickets for the popular Skrmetta family-owned and -operated ferry excursion at least one hour prior to departure. Onboard snack bars and restrooms are available.

As snowbird golfers from the Midwest and Canada attest, some of the Gulf Coast's 21 public golf courses are among the best in the country. And one of the least expensive is **Pine Bayou Golf Course** at the Naval Construction Battalion Center, 5200 CBC Second Street, (288) 871-2494. The greens fee (including cart) is $18 to $24. While there, visit the **Seabee Museum;** (228) 871-3164. The 1,000-acre Naval Construction Batallion Center was established in 1942 and is home to the Atlantic Fleet Seabees, which includes 90 Marines of the Fourth Platoon Reinforcement, the Fourth Amphibious Assault Battalion, and Fourth Marine Regiment.

Biloxi

The French explorer Iberville landed in what is now modern-day Biloxi (www .biloxi.ms.us) on February 13, 1699. Since that time eight flags—namely, those of France, Britain, Spain, the Republic of Florida, Mississippi Territory, State of Mis-

sissippi, Confederate States of America, and United States of America—have flown over the area. By the mid-1850s Biloxi was arguably the Deep South's most popular coastal resort. New Orleans newspapers of the period were filled with advertisements proclaiming the amenities of the area's fine hotels: fresh seafood daily, live bands, banquets, and balls. As the most widely recognized Gulf Coast town, this city of 54,000 residents plays host to the lion's share of the region's casinos (see Close-up in this chapter), the last home of Jefferson Davis, the historic Biloxi Lighthouse, and a museum of artworks by the late George Ohr, "the Mad Potter of Biloxi" (the late artist delighted in the moniker).

The **Ohr-O'Keefe Museum of Art** (www.georgeohr.org), 136 G. E. Ohr Street, Biloxi (228–374–5547), pays homage to the Dali-like eccentric artist who used to wrap his 2-foot-long moustache around his ears while toiling at his potter's wheel. A permanent display of 175 fanciful pots, many shaped like hula girls and whirling dervishes, joins exhibits by local and national artists. The artist who went virtually unrecognized until his death and who owned a local Cadillac dealership was anything but modest. Ohr billed himself the "unequaled, unrivaled, undisputed greatest art potter on earth." Today a George Ohr pot can fetch up to $35,000—more than he earned as an artist his entire life. Orh's work, warehoused in boxes at his dealership, wasn't discovered until 1972, after his death, when visiting New Jersey resident James Carpenter bought 5,000 pots for $350,000. Today Ohr's pots are displayed in the Smithsonian, the Metropolitan Museum of Art, the Los Angeles County Museum, and the Victoria and Albert Museum in London.

It's impossible to miss the historic **Biloxi Lighthouse** (228–435–6308), one of the most famous icons on the coast—and perhaps the only lighthouse in the world situated in the middle of a four-lane highway. Located on Highway 90 (Beach Boulevard) at the foot of Porter Avenue, the towering white structure is topped by

Luck of the Draw

The Gulf Coast's floundering tourism industry got a well-needed shot in the arm when the region's first casino—Isle of Capri—opened in Biloxi in August 1992. Today nearly a dozen casinos on barges moored to docks (many with adjacent high-rise hotels) have created an economic boom that has seen average annual incomes jump $3,000 and the average sale price of homes skyrocket from $70,000 to more than $100,000. Call it the luck of the draw. Southern daytrippers, including shuttle vans full of New Orleanians, flock to the casinos in droves to see the national headliners and high-kicking showgirls. B.B. King, Ray Charles, and The Four Tops have performed here as well as Engelbert Humperdinck, Johnny Mathis, Joan Rivers, Wayne Newton, and Don Rickles. Many casinos have added brewpubs (featuring casino-brewed beer), shopping complexes, cabarets, kid-oriented arcade and game rooms, and restaurants ranging from all-you-can-eat buffets to fine dining. All casinos are open 24 hours and require no admission. The legal gambling age is 21. Many casinos offer free shuttle service to nearby hotels and motels. The following casinos are grouped alphabetically by cities reached driving west to east on Highway 90 (Beach Boulevard).

BAY ST. LOUIS, MISSISSIPPI

Casino Magic Bay St. Louis
711 Casino Magic Drive, Bay St. Louis
(800) 562-4425
www.casinomagic-baystlouis.com
National headliners from Milton Berle to Hootie and the Blowfish have revved up visitors to this casino's entertainment complex, which, oddly enough, doesn't

have a name. Pool tournaments and boxing also pack them in. A new 14-story, 201-room Bay Tower opened in 2002. Camp Magic keeps restless youngsters occupied while parents cruise the establishment's 1,100 slots and 40 game tables as well as an Arnold Palmer–designed 18-hole golf course. The casino also features five restaurants, an RV park, and 50-slip marina.

GULFPORT, MISSISSIPPI

Copa Casino
777 Copa Boulevard
(off Beach Boulevard), Gulfport
(228) 863-3330
www.thecopacasino.com
If any of the area's gambling establishments are ever forced to bail due to a hurricane, this one may stand the best chance of surviving. After all, it's the coast's only permanently docked cruise ship casino. Walk the gangway and cruise this brightly lit ship's 700 slots and 26 game tables, which include a number of (almost unheard of) 10-cent slots. The Copa Showroom plays host to live Top 40 and pop music, while the 24-hour Cabana Cafe and Coffee Shop offers a menu of po-boys and seafood platters. For barbecue dinners and home-style lunches check out Uncle Floyd's Barbecue & Buffet.

Grand Casino Gulfport
3215 Beach Boulevard, Gulfport
(800) 946-7777
www.grandgulfport.com
Three gambling floors, five restaurants, an America Live! entertainment complex, and outdoor Grand Pavillion Theatre featuring live music and comedy with national acts, plus a Kids Quest and Grand Arcade add

up to fun for the whole family. Overnight accommodations are available in the 400-room, 17-floor hotel, which features a full-service spa and indoor pool. The 600-room Oasis Hotel offers a three-acre pool and water area.

BILOXI, MISSISSIPPI

Beau Rivage
875 Beach Boulevard, Biloxi
(228) 386-7111, (888) 567-6667
www.beaurivage.com

The newest resort casino on the Gulf Coast has raised the bar for luxury accommodations and resort amenities. From the massive lobby arboretum of blooming azaleas, evergreens, and other foliage, all sunbathed by the sun streaming through the glass ceiling, to the five fine-dining restaurants with inspired decor ranging from walls of Thai bamboo to walls lined by huge aquariums of tropical fish, this 1,780-guest room resort has made a splash ever since it opened in 2000. Gamblers will find every possible game of chance under the sun—and lots of them. But those who prefer to keep their hands off Lady Luck will have no problem finding fun, whether it's sunning around the Romanesque outdoor pool, relaxing at the Mediterranean-style, sexually segregated spa and sauna, or simply enjoying the Gulf of Mexico view from their guest room, with oversize bathrooms accented by Spanish and Grecian marble, hand-finished wood, luxurious bath towels, and a step-in shower for two.

Boomtown
676 Bay View Avenue, Biloxi
(228) 435-7000
www.boomtownbiloxi.com

This country-western themed facility has 1,000 slots, 25 tables, and a 24-hour all-you-can-eat buffet. Freshly baked breads and pies are found at the coffee shop. The Boots Cabaret offers national acts, including live comedy and music.

Casino Magic Biloxi
195 Beach Boulevard, Biloxi
(228) 387-4600, (866) 867-7711
www.casinomagic.com

A 378-room hotel (with fitness center, indoor pool, outdoor spa, sundeck, gift shop, and jewelry store) is the latest addition to this casino, which features 1,100 slots and 40 game tables. The Eclipse Showroom offers the headliners, while two restaurants tempt gamblers with a variety of seafood and steaks.

Grand Casino Biloxi
265 Beach Boulevard, Biloxi
(228) 436-2946, (800) 946-2946
www.grandbiloxi.com

Parents can drop the kids at the arcade or the indoor jungle gym in Kids Quest before trying their luck at the casino's 2,000 slots and 90 game tables. Brulo's New Orleans Seafood Co. and L.B.'s Grill (plus six other restaurants) will help keep the batteries charged before heading to the Biloxi Grand Theatre for stage shows that include singers, musicians, comedians, and even boxing matches. Two hotels include the adjacent 12-story, 500-room Islandview (345 Beach Boulevard) and the new 500-room Bayview (280 Beach Boulevard) directly across the street.

Imperial Palace
850 Bayview Avenue, Biloxi
(228) 436-3000, (800) 436-3000
www.ipbiloxi.com

Imperial features headline acts as well as six-screen cinema, 10 restaurants, 100 restored classic cars on display, and a shopping "esplanade." The 1,200-room, 32-story casino hotel offers 1,600 slots and 64 gaming tables.

Isle of Capri
151 Beach Boulevard, Biloxi
(228) 435-5400, (800) 843-4753
www.isleofcapricasino.com
This casino rolls out the tropical motif with live Caribbean music in the atrium of its 370-room resort as well as fun dining at the Calypso Buffet and Tradewinds Grill. Put on a straw hat and try your hand at one of the 1,200 slots and 42 game tables.

Palace Casino Resort
158 Howard Avenue, Biloxi
(228) 432-8888, (800) 725-2239
www.palacecasinoresort.com
This 236-guest room luxury resort hotel that opened May 2000 features a 500-seat theater with fast-paced production shows and headliner entertainment. Local casinogoers say the hardest choice at this establishment is not which of the 1,000 slots or more than 30 game tables to play in the three-story gambling area, but rather where to eat. A quartet of restaurants includes Point Grille, Palace Café & Bakery, Palace Buffet, and, for fine dining, Jazzmin's.

The President Casino Broadwater Resort
2110 Beach Boulevard, Biloxi
(228) 388-2211, (800) 843-7737
www.presidentbroadwater.com
Even ardent gamblers may want to edge past the 950 slots and 38 game tables to check out the free entertainment (which occasionally includes national acts) presented in the Vegas Showbar Lounge. Three restaurants (including Audree's, the President's Buffet, and the Oyster House) offer ample dining opportunities. The 800-room President Broadwater Resort features eight tennis courts, an 18-hole golf course, and charter fishing boats.

Treasure Bay
1980 Beach Boulevard, Biloxi
(228) 385-6283, (800) 747-2839
www.treasurebay.com
This replica of an 18th-century pirate ship will bring out the buccaneer in any gambler eager to beat Lady Luck at one of the casino's 1,130 slots and 40 game tables. Coast magazine rates Scalawag's Showbar, which features national and regional acts, as the area's "best live music venue." If that doesn't float your boat, there's a four-star poker room, five restaurants ranging from fine dining to buffets, virtual reality games at Captain Kidd's Video Arcade, and a 268-room hotel with sports and hockey bars, Jacuzzi, and tropical swimming pool with water slides.

a weathervane and has been a symbol of the city's maritime industry since it was erected in 1848.

History buffs will want to set aside time to visit **Beauvoir-Jefferson Davis House and Presidential Library,** 2244 Beach Boulevard (800-570-3818), the final home of Confederate President Jefferson Davis. In 1877 the aging Davis accepted an invitation by then-owner Sarah Dorsey to write his memoirs at the 52-acre seaside estate. Two years later Davis and his wife, Varina, bought Beauvoir from Dorsey for $5,500, and in 1881 he published his memoirs as *The Rise and Fall of the Confederate Government*, followed by *A Short History of the Confederate States of America*.

Beauvoir (www.beauvoir.org), a national historic landmark overlooking Mississippi Sound, includes the 1851 Greek Revival residence and outbuildings, nature trails, a Victorian antique rose garden, a Confederate cemetery, a 10,000-volume library, and a museum exhibiting Civil War and Jefferson Davis memorabilia. The museum chronicles Davis's life beginning with his boyhood and West Point education and ending with his retirement at Beauvoir. On display is the catafalque used to support and carry the copper-lined wooden casket with the body of Jefferson Davis during his funeral procession in New Orleans. Visitors can also read original letters penned by Davis during his stints as both a U.S. congressman and senator in the 1840s. Other artifacts include the Davis family prayer book, the young Davis's Latin grammar book, and the shawl worn by the defrocked Confederate president at the time of his dawn capture by Union soldiers. Beauvoir is open daily 9:00 A.M. to 5:00 P.M. and admission is $7.50 adults; $4.50 children age 6 to 16; seniors $6.75. The self-guided tour includes a 29-minute videotape, which provides a historical overview.

If the Gulf waters prove too tame for your liking, jump on the huge triple-flume water slides at **Slippery Sam's,** 1782 Beach Boulevard, (228) 435-3140. Grown-ups and kids alike can also take a ride on the wild side on one of the water park's new double-speed slides. Bumper boats and a kiddie pool are on hand for the little ones. The park is open May through September daily 10:00 A.M. to 9:00 P.M. Admission is $7.00 per person per hour; $8.00 for two hours; $14.00 all day. Kids under age 4 pay half price.

For a hands-on seafood experience, hop aboard the Biloxi **Shrimping Trip's Sailfish** (www.gcww.com/sailfish) at the Biloxi Small Craft Harbor on Highway 90

at Main Street, (800) 289-7908. The 70-minute tour in the calm protected waters between Deer Island and the Biloxi shoreline lets passengers participate in a real shrimping "expedition" that includes casting a net to catch blue crabs, flounder, stringrays, squid, and other sea life. Cost is $12.00 for adults and $8.00 for children age 4 to 12. Children age 3 and under are admitted free. Call for departure times.

One of the best dining experiences on the entire Mississippi Gulf Coast is to be found at **Mary Mahony's Old French House** (228-374-0163) across the street from Beau Rivage casino and resort. John Grisham mentions this venerable landmark and one-time headquarters of the Louisiana Territory in his books *The Runaway Jury* and *The Partner*. French colonist Louis Fraiser constructed the building in 1737, and its original high ceilings, wooden-pegged cypress columns, heart-pine floors, and exposed walls of handmade brick are characteristic of Creole homes in the French Quarter. Diners who know what's good for them will want to try the shrimp remoulade, seafood gumbo, stuffed catfish, and bread pudding with rum sauce. Other signature dishes at this fine-dining establishment include Sisters of the Sea au gratin (fresh lump crabmeat and shrimp in a creamy cheese sauce); half-lobster Georgo (blended with shrimp in a cream sauce, teased with a hint of brandy and served en coquille); and red snapper stuffed with shrimp and crabmeat au gratin. Hours are Monday through Saturday 11:00 A.M. to 10:00 P.M.

Even if you don't dine at Mary Mahoney's, it's worth a visit just to see the spectacular 2,000-year-old oak tree "Patriarch" towering above the French Quarter–style courtyard. Nearby is the historic **Old Magnolia Hotel,** 119 Magnolia Street, the coast's oldest extant antebellum hotel and today home to the **Biloxi Mardi Gras Museum;** (228) 435-6245. The museum tells the story of Gulf Coast Carnival celebrations and traditions with a

Day-trippers looking to escape New Orleans's urban sprawl for the lazy beaches and warm coastal waters of Louisiana's neighbor to the east can call the Mississippi Gulf Coast Convention & Visitors Bureau. The bureau, at 135 Courthouse Road in Gulfport, Mississippi, can be reached by calling (888) 467–4853.

display of festive costumes and old photographs. Hours are Monday through Saturday 11:00 A.M. to 4:00 P.M. and admission is $2.00 for adults; $1.00 for seniors, students, and children; kids age 6 and under are admitted free.

Biloxi's **Green Oaks** (www.gcww.com/greenoaks), built in 1826 and the area's oldest beachfront residence, is a bed-and-breakfast listed on the National Register of Historic Places. More important, perhaps, is that guests who stay in one of the two historic homes' eight guest rooms will find 14-foot ceilings, fine antiques, and family heirlooms as well as all the modern conveniences—private bath, cable TV, and dataport telephones. Some rooms feature antique or wrought-iron four-poster queen or double beds, hand-stenciled walls, fireplaces, and screen doors, which open to the front porch. Other amenities include nightly turndown, complimentary afternoon tea, and gourmet breakfast served with antique linens, china, and crystal. Rates at Green Oaks, 580 Beach Boulevard (888–436–6257), are $140 to $150 per night.

Another waterfront bed-and-breakfast of distinction is the **Father Ryan House** (www.frryan.com), 1196 Beach Boulevard, (800–295–1189), built in 1841 and best spotted by the towering palm tree (planted in 1906) growing literally from a hole cut into the front-porch steps. This two-story columned manor is named for Father Abram Ryan, a Confederate army chaplain and poet who lived here for several years after the Civil War. Eight guest rooms (four downstairs, four upstairs) are individually decorated in early-19th-century

antique and hand-carved period furnishings and feature four-poster beds, private baths, color TV, and down comforters. Rooms Nos. 5 and 6 upstairs have spa baths, mosquito netting over beds, and dormers that open onto private balconies overlooking the landscaped front gardens and Mississippi Sound. The second-floor public area features cool Mexican floor tile, a cozy library with sofa and chairs, and a full kitchen (with breakfast nook) for guests. Double French doors open onto a balcony. Special touches include homemade lemonade and pastries. Room rates are $100 to $175 per night.

The **Santini-Stewart House Bed & Breakfast Inn** (www.santinibnb.com), 964 Beach Boulevard (800–686–1146), was built in 1828 by wealthy New Orleans merchant John Blight Byrne. Joseph Santini purchased this early example of the "American cottage" in 1867, and it remained in the family until 1972. Present-day owners James and Patricia Dunay have decorated each of the four first-floor guest rooms with warm, distinctive contemporary flourishes that reflect their desire to make visitors feel at home. Rooms feature polished pine-wood floors, 12-foot ceilings, color cable TVs, and private baths with pedestal sinks. Guests must use the telephone in the first-floor lobby, which is decorated with Louis XVI–style reproduction furnishings, brass chandeliers, and a fireplace. The two-room honeymoon cottage out back features a king-size bed, spa tub, wet bar, and private porch. Amenities include afternoon tea or wine and cheese served on the porch as well as deluxe complimentary breakfast presented in an elegant dining room with sterling silver and china. Unfortunately, the highway off-ramp directly across Beach Boulevard from this lovely Caribbean-yellow painted home, listed on the National Register of Historic Places, obscures views of the beach and water. Rates are $90 Sunday through Thursday (Honeymoon Cottage $125) and $125 Friday and Saturday (Honeymoon Cottage $155).

Ocean Springs

If you do only one thing in Ocean Springs (www.oceansprings-ms.com), it should be to visit the **Walter Anderson Museum** (www.walterandersonmuseum.org), 510 Washington Avenue, (228) 872-3164. Anderson, regarded as the region's premier artist, was a fierce Gauguin-like recluse whose inspired paintings and drawings of Gulf Coast animals, plants, and people put him on the map of 20th-century American artists. Anderson used to row his 12-foot skiff filled with paints and brushes 10 miles out to Horn and Chandeleur Islands to work. Andy Warhol collected Anderson's artworks, and today more than 150 examples of his carvings, ceramics, sketches, and paintings—including numerous vibrant watercolors of seashells, herons and gulls, swallow hawks and myrtle warblers, crabs and pumas—are on display. A wonderful "day in the life" mural discovered after the artist's death depicts Anderson's Gulf Coast world and is regarded as his most important work. The mural, originally painted on the walls and ceilings of a small room in Anderson's cottage, was painstakingly reconstructed and attached to the museum. The museum, located in the historic downtown district and next door to the Ocean Springs Community Center, is open Monday through Saturday 9:30 A.M. to 4:30 P.M. and Sunday 12:30 to 4:30 P.M. from October to April, and Monday through Saturday 9:30 A.M. to 5:00 P.M. and Sunday 12:30 to 5:00 P.M. from May to September. Admission is $5.00 adults; $3.00 seniors; and $2.00 children under 18. Admission is free on the first Monday of each month.

LIFE'S A BEACH AND THEN YOU FRY

When it comes to bagging rays close to home, New Orleanians are never bashful about piling the car with sun block, straw hats, and trashy novels for a quick fix on the Mississippi Gulf Coast. Surfers and boogie-board enthusiasts may be surprised to discover that the Gulf, rimmed by barrier islands, is flat-calm, shallow (walk out a quarter mile and you're still only knee-deep), and usually bathtub warm. Leave the wet suits at home. A lack of waves and dangerous undertows makes Mississippi's beaches, in theory at least, among the safest and most swimmer-friendly anywhere. Watersports including aquacycles, sunfish sailboats, waverunners, parasailing, paddleboats, and kayaks (plus umbrellas and beach chairs) can be rented on the beach usually in front of the larger hotels.

Free public beach parking is available from Bay St. Louis to Biloxi (although parking is prohibited from midnight to 6:00 A.M. in the parking bay in front of the Coliseum Holiday Inn in Biloxi). Permits for bonfires, a popular nighttime activity, are available from the city fire departments in Ocean Springs (288-875-4063), Bay St. Louis (288-467-4736), and Waveland (288-467-9353). In Bay St. Louis bonfires are permitted between Bay Oaks and Washington Street only. A $25 deposit is required and refunded if the site is cleaned before noon the following day. Permits cost $30 ($25 is refunded following cleanup within 24 hours) in Pass Christian, Long Beach, Gulfport, and Biloxi. Caution: The fine for not having a permit is $25 to $500.

RELOCATION

The relocation information in this book starts in this chapter with information on neighborhoods and real estate. Also see the Retirement, Health Care and Wellness, Education, Mediua, and Worship chapters for information important to relocators.

New Orleans is a mosaic of neighborhoods. One of the cornerstones of development here was the growth in the 19th and 20th centuries of working- and middle-class ethnic neighborhoods of immigrant populations—Irish, Italian, German, French, Spanish (including Canary Islanders, known locally as Isleños), descendents of the city's earliest Creole and African-American inhabitants, and, most recently, Vietnamese. During the past 55 years, a confluence of population growth, demographic shifts, economic upswings and downturns, and social change has transformed some neighborhoods dramatically, while others have barely been touched by the passage of time. Meantime, the development and growth of suburbs, some of which were wooded wetlands only three decades ago, has been nearly mind-boggling.

REAL ESTATE

Compared with other cities of similar size and infrastructure, New Orleans offers a sizeable and affordable middle- and upper-middle-class housing market, especially for people relocating from the Northeast, Pacific Northwest, and West Coast accustomed to inflated housing prices.

Newcomers to the area will find the state's homestead exemption a tax-friendly and money-saving aspect of home ownership. Homeowners are exempt from paying state property taxes on the first $75,000 of the value of their home. For example, an individual who lives in a $100,000 home

pays taxes on $25,000 of the value; $125,000 for a $200,000 home, and so on. This can add up to a significant savings for the young family shopping for that first three-bedroom home, as well as the retiree on fixed income eager to downsize his postwork years by moving into a condo or town house.

In Orleans Parish, where property taxes are paid forward, the homestead exemption offers another excellent way to stretch the home-buying dollar. Since mortgage companies escrow a year of property taxes when a home is purchased, a reduced property tax bill enables buyers to spend less up front for their home.

The homestead exemption has long been one of the live wires of Louisiana politics—touch it and you're dead. Opponents say the exemption robs state coffers of tax revenues urgently needed for Louisiana's cash-strapped public school system, highways, and other infrastructure. Supporters say the exemption helps build strong communities by removing an onerous tax burden of home ownership for working- and middle-class families struggling to get—and keep—a leg up on the American dream.

In the 1980s the United States enjoyed, at least on paper, its biggest economic boon since World War II. During that same period the booming Louisiana oil patch went bust and turned more than a few rural millionaires with oil wells in their backyards into paupers, while offshore rig workers who once earned lawyer-level incomes took a number at one of the state's increasingly crowded unemployment offices. The so-called trickle-down theory of Reaganomics, in reverse, was not a pretty sight. Thousands of hardworking people in other sectors of the labor market lost their jobs and, in some instances, their homes, as the local economy's downward spiral only seemed to pick up steam. Housing markets took a nosedive.

While no one can pinpoint exactly when the turnaround happened, it was sometime in the 1990s. Optimism in the housing market increased. Today sellers have a slight edge in the market, say real estate experts, and there simply isn't enough property to keep up with demand. First-time homebuyers taking advantage of low-interest loans have helped fuel this trend. "In 1990 our real estate books were two volumes, now it's half that," said a local real estate expert. "It's a seller's market—in a heartbeat."

Newcomers from large cities who are accustomed to long commutes will also discover it's fairly easy and economical to find suitable housing only 10 to 25 minutes from work. For north shore residents who commute to work in New Orleans and drive the Causeway over Lake Pontchartrain or Interstate 10 from Slidell, the commute is about 45 minutes.

Like the rest of the nation, New Orleans is also seeing a diversification of the "typical" homebuyer. Today it's rare to find a neighborhood that has only large families, with kids all about the same age attending the same schools. Here, as elsewhere, a typical homebuyer in both suburban and urban areas is just as likely to be a single woman or man, a single parent, or an unmarried straight or gay couple. People are also buying their first homes at a younger age, recognizing the importance of developing a secure financial future beginning as soon as possible. Here comes the new neighborhood.

Not surprisingly, architecture varies greatly in this 300-year-old city, and a 1,000- to 1,500-square-foot house that people would still regard as "nice" can be had for $100,000-plus. Newcomers from Southern California or New York City who arrive here with heavy-duty home equity under their belts often discover they can live like virtual land barons—with more than enough left over for his and her tan-

Among the most vexing pests is the notorious Formosan termite, which can inflict substantial and costly damage. Solution? Many wise homeowners contract with a reputable termite pest control company for regularly scheduled inspections, preventive care, and (if necessary) treatments.

ning beds or holiday shopping trips to the Big Apple's F.A.O. Schwartz.

But what of the neighborhoods?

NEIGHBORHOODS

French Quarter

The French Quarter is certainly New Orleans at its most colorful. But unlike Uptown, the French Quarter prefers to keep some of its most charming attributes tucked away like a secret. Magnolia-shaded courtyards accented with lovely fountains hide behind a high brick fence or wrought-iron gate.

Architecture dates to the 1700s, and some homes feature century-old, hand-carved cypress-beam ceilings and brick or slate floors, double parlors, paneled bookcases, floor-to-ceiling guillotine windows, and wrought-iron balconies. Another feature not uncommon to residents is the scent of a Lucky Dog, that widely-scoffed-at-but-secretly-indulged French Quarter vendor frank, being devoured by a tourist ambling by on the sidewalk, his camera about the size of a button against his unregulated midriff. Renovation is a popular pastime for homeowners with the time and money—and many of the French Quarter's well-heeled residents have plenty of both.

Even with a lack of off-street parking (though the creation of special parking permits for residents has helped), real estate in New Orleans's second most picture-postcard section goes for a ransom worthy of King Louis XIV. A joke overheard in the company of Realtors chatting about the price of French Quarter housing: I've got a no-bedroom for $90,000. Now, double that amount and the reality of starting prices will start to sink in.

Uptown

The Uptown area includes the Garden District (Upper and Lower), Bouligny, and University area. Each has a distinct personality, but what pulls them all together is the unparalleled charm that pervades Uptown's sleepy oak-lined streets and architecture—from Victorian, Greek-, and Spanish-Revival mansions to far more modest camelbacks and Victorian shotgun doubles. A camelback features a second floor but only at the back of the house (thus the "camelback" hump), a design feature that at one time helped residents finagle out of a tax levied on homes with complete second floors. A shotgun house refers to how someone could stand at the door, shoot a gun and the bullet would go through every room and exit the back door. Simply put, every room in the house, from the living room and kitchen to the bedroom, is situated in a linear fashion.

With few exceptions real estate here fetches a pretty penny. The same three-bedroom home costing $175,000 in Lakeview could easily snare twice that amount Uptown. Far more opulent homes long ago topped the million-dollar mark. And why not? This is unquestionably one of New Orleans's most postcard-perfect surroundings, epitomized perhaps by the sight of one of the city's leaf-green streetcars click-clacking down St. Charles Avenue under moss-draped oaks past Audubon Park on one of those mercilessly idyllic spring days.

Nowhere else does the city's characterization as an architectural "checkerboard" fit so snugly as it does Uptown amid the area's lush kaleidoscope of myrtles, azaleas, camellias, and bougainvillea. One street is filled with stately French Gothic and antebellum-style plantation homes, any of which would be right at home on the cover of *Architectural Digest*. Two blocks away and you swear you've stumbled upon a Caribbean island neighborhood, where West Indies–style wooden cottages in pastel turquoise, yellows, and greens are framed by overgrown front-yard banana trees that shade jalousied windows and a lazy pooch too busy slumbering to bark.

Residents with an Uptown address are allowed to be a little smug. After all, they live nearby some of New Orleans's best-known restaurants, from elegant old-line French Creole establishments to greasy-spoon after-hours hangouts. And if anyone ever publishes a map of the city's legendary mix of bars, Uptown watering holes will be showcased every bit as prominently as some of the area's monied denizens are at a Rex Carnival ball. A seemingly nonstop calendar of cultural and social events, as well as private social fetes, doesn't hurt Uptown's quietly sophisticated allure either. Whether it's black-tie galas like the popular Zoo to Do fund-raiser or the annual Art for Art's Sake nighttime walkabout, where Magazine Street's antiques shop and gallery owners serve wine and cheese and keep their doors open till—gasp!—9:00 P.M., this part of town is arguably New Orleans at its best.

Old Metairie

Many experts believe that the latest local tear-down-and-rebuild craze got its start not in New Orleans but rather in Old Metairie, one of the oldest sections of east bank Jefferson Parish. With the notable exception of that part of Old Metairie nearest Metairie Country Club, the lion's share of this neighborhood was composed mostly of wooden 1940s and 1950s cottages, some three- and four-bedroom homes, and a sprinkle of Federal-style Georgian brick houses.

Some of the oldest residents here are also some of the very first. They moved in during the post–World War II building boom, a time when the G.I. Bill and economic optimism was motivating New Orleanians to take that tentative first step into the strange new world just over the Orleans Parish Canal: the 'burbs.

Today, the "new" Old Metairie is defined in part by the demolition of charming and old (or puny and obsolete, depending on perspective) homes and their replacement by two- and three-story property-line-to-property-line houses costing $350,000 to $1 million or more. Cloned driveways are filled with SUVs, BMWs, and Volvo station wagons. Old Metairie has been embraced by many— but certainly not all—New Orleanians looking for a post-urban slice of nouveau oak-draped grace. Whether the area is destined to become the Uptown of the 21st century is anyone's guess. Nevertheless, Old Metairie is certainly trying its darndest considering the appearance in recent years of a slew of coffeehouses, upscale boutiques, interior decorating shops, and chichi spas. Resales are up, and the market looks the strongest it's been in years. "To think that people are buying a $250,000 house (in Old Metairie), and scraping it off to build another, more expensive house is startling," said a local Realtor. Stay tuned.

Elsewhere on the east bank of Jefferson Parish is a mix of homogeneous, mostly middle-class, cookie-cutter subdivisions of single-story three- and four-bedroom brick homes. Corridors of apartments and town houses are often conveniently located near I-10 or Veterans Boulevard's grotesquerie of strip- and anchor-store malls, fast-food drive-thrus, franchise restaurants, car dealerships, health clubs, pawn shops, and bank branch offices. Neighborhoods on the lakeside of West Esplanade Avenue,

meantime, feature four-bedroom family and executive-style houses within easy reach of the Lake Pontchartrain levee trail popular among joggers, cyclists, and those out for a sunset walk.

Kenner

The popularity of Kenner, one of the fastest-growing cities in Louisiana, has grown in recent years with the addition of The Esplanade mall, the Pontchartrain Center entertainment and convention complex, and the Treasure Chest casino. Ongoing public works projects to ease traffic congestion has resulted in the widening of Kenner's main arteries, Williams and Loyola Boulevards, a new I-10 off-ramp at Power Boulevard, and a new Williams Boulevard and I-10 interchange.

Lakeview

Bordered by Bayou St. John, Robert E. Lee, and Canal Boulevards, the Lakeview area is consistently and highly regarded for the affordability and mix of housing in quiet, tree-lined, middle-class neighborhoods, as well as the diversity of its residents. Lakeview is close to many good public schools, the University of New Orleans, Lake Pontchartrain, and the West End restaurant and nightlife corridor, yet less than 15 minutes from the French

Many young families buying their first home find they get more bang for the buck in one of New Orleans's numerous suburbs, where the cost of a three-bedroom house can be considerably less than the price of a comparable residence in town. These include Metairie, Kenner, the West Bank of Jefferson Parish, parts of St. Tammany Parish, and St. Bernard Parish.

RELOCATION

> *Upscale urbanites might want to check out the hot apartments and condominiums available in the Warehouse Arts District, which during the past 15 years has seen numerous old brick warehouses and factories converted into oh-SoHo-hip residences.*

Quarter's riverfront Woldenburg Park—all for about one-half the price, or less, of its breeze-swept Lakefront neighbors only blocks away.

Another of Lakeview's selling points is its healthy inventory of single-story, two- to three-bedroom family homes. Most of them come with living rooms big enough for that entertainment unit from Kirschman's, as well as junior's piano, and ample backyards for that Labor Day luau but not so large the gardener has to show up Saturday morning with a six-person crew.

Expect to pay between $175,000 and $200,000 for a 2,000-square-foot ranch-style home to more than $325,000 for one of those two-story, Georgian-style architectural gems tucked away on one of Lakeview's sleepy streets, where the oak trees are a little older and a little bigger.

Gentilly

Gentilly's golden age was probably from the 1940s to the mid-1970s, and many of the mostly slab-foundation stucco houses typically built on 50-by-120-foot lots are one by one being renovated and updated with new roofs and modern kitchens and expanded to add on that extra bedroom or bathroom. Streets are wider and have fewer potholes than many sections of town.

A necklace of upscale neighborhoods—Lake Vista, Lake Shore (East and West), Lake Oaks, Lake Terrace, and so on—rim Lake Pontchartrain to Robert E. Lee Boulevard and characterize the dynamic Lakefront housing market. Some people are buying and tearing down some

of the area's original columned and executive-style homes costing $200,000 and up and replacing them with magnificent single- and two-story mansions costing $500,000 to $1 million or more. These new homes come with more bathrooms, more bedrooms, and most likely more tranquilizers to ward off mortgage anxiety. It's a safe bet, though, that many owners will keep the area's existing low-slung, postmodern Frank Lloyd Wright–era homes just as they are, along with the terrazzo floors and oh-so-lavish pool and patio ensembles.

West Bank

The opening of the twin span of the Mississippi River bridge, officially named but rarely called the Crescent City Connection, has significantly opened up the West Bank of Jefferson Parish as a desirable and affordable location. Commute times to New Orleans from major West Bank cities such as Algiers (which is part of Orleans Parish), Marrero, Gretna, and Westwego have been cut in half. Once viewed as suburban sprawl, the West Bank's attractiveness has soared among homeowners looking to get the most bang for their home-buying buck and a stable resale value. A 2,200-square-foot, four-bedroom, two-and-a-half-bath home with two-car garage, for example, costs about $125,000. Many homes can be found in the $100,000 range. Those looking for the country club life will find it at English Turn. As one Realtor pointed out, the West Bank offers "all the conveniences of Metairie without the crowds and hassle." For some people this is a good thing.

North Shore

Whether the result of a conspiratorial mass exodus from New Orleans or simply normal demographic shifts, development on the north shore region of the metropolitan area has exploded over the past 15 years and shows few signs of slowing. The once rural but still pine tree–dotted communities of Mandeville, Covington, Madisonville, Abita Springs, and Folsom have become bedroom communities du jour. Convenience is a factor: These towns are linked to New Orleans by the 26-mile twin-span Causeway (the nation's longest, for those keeping track) over Lake Pontchartrain. Popularity has fueled construction of new homes and subdivisions, such as the exclusive gated community of Beau Chene on the Tchefuncte River, and growth of new local business.

Lured by the promise of relaxed, country-style living near the lake and solitude far from the big city, new residents are plunking down $100,000 and more for large lots on which to build custom homes, while others are buying older homes. Adding to the area's popularity are modest- to fine-dining establishments (including several notable ones right on the lake and the Tchefuncte River), boating and recreation opportunities, and a manicured lakefront of sleepy oaks, quiet gazebos, greenspaces, and bicycle paths.

The north shore community of Slidell, 20 minutes south of Covington-Mandeville, has seen the development of Oak Harbor and other new fresh-scrubbed subdivisions, some with homes right on a lake canal highly coveted by weekend boaters and other water enthusiasts. Slidell is linked to New Orleans via I–10, and inbound traffic both frustrates and confounds commuters almost daily when they hit that inexplicable slowdown at the top of the interstate's humped "high-rise" over the Industrial Canal.

REAL ESTATE FIRMS

New Orleans is home to hundreds of real estate offices and thousands of agents, but finding the best broker or Realtor for your particular needs can be tricky business. Does he or she possess an understanding of the particular kind of house

you're interested in—a lakefront condominium, an antebellum home, or a three-bedroom family house in the 'burbs, for example? Is he or she versed in the history and nuance of the neighborhoods you prospect, with a sensitive finger on the market's sometimes-elusive pulse?

These professionals take pride in leading locals and newcomers alike gently by the hand through the often-complicated maze of buying a home. If in doubt, call the New Orleans Metropolitan Association of Realtors (504–885–3200), the Better Business Bureau of Greater New Orleans Area Inc. (504–581–2842), and the Chamber of Commerce/New Orleans and the River Region (504–527–6900).

The following real estate companies were selected for several reasons. First, they are among the best in the region. Second, they are representative of similarly reputable firms offering similar services in the metropolitan area. Third, space limitations preclude a complete listing of all real estate agencies and their offices.

Century 21 Patio Realty
534 Oaklawn Street, Metairie
(504) 837–8180
www.century21.com
Specializing in residential and investment properties, leasing, and management, this agency was formed in 1974 and is one of nine independently owned and operated Century 21 offices throughout the metropolitan area. Twenty-five agents and a full range of relocation services are available to help individuals moving into Orleans and Jefferson Parishes, including those needing help with short-term residential leasing while shopping for or building their dream home.

French Quarter Realty
1041 Esplanade Avenue, New Orleans
(504) 949–5400
www.fqr.com
Anyone searching for that historical or otherwise special property in the French Quarter, the adjacent Faubourg Marigny district, and Uptown's Lower Garden

District should consider a firm whose agents are well versed in those neighborhoods. The company's dozen or more agents have in-depth knowledge about the individual property histories and architecture in three of New Orleans's most significant neighborhoods. Agents also keep their ears close to the ground for current news on neighborhood associations, zoning law changes, and anything else that can impact the housing market. To get a better picture of what this real estate agency has to offer, check out the property listings with photographs at its Web site.

Grady Harper Inc. Realtor
726 Fern Street, New Orleans
(504) 861-4551
From young entry-level homebuyers to middle-aged third-home shoppers, from new construction to century-old homes, this family-owned New Orleans establishment has been keeping its finger on the housing market's pulse for nearly half a century. Relocation kits include information from the Chamber of Commerce, the latest news on neighborhood schools and churches, and listings on a range of available housing, from midpriced family dwellings in Metairie in Jefferson Parish to stylist show-homes in upscale Uptown and Lakeview.

Latter & Blum
840 Elysian Fields, New Orleans
(504) 948-3011
www.latter-blum.com
Whether it's an antebellum mansion in the Lower Garden District, a University-area bungalow, or a home in a spanking new subdivision, this local company with 23 offices helps take the hassle out of home buying with its high-tech computer network, Virtual Mortgage. The agent takes clients online to a real-time video conference with a lender, anywhere in the country, which in minutes locks buyers in to the best interest rates and tells them how much they qualify for. Paperwork, including amortization schedules, is faxed. Other

services include relocation packages with city maps, information on schools as well as local history, utilities companies, public services, and transportation.

Liberty One Realty
10001 Lake Forest Boulevard
New Orleans
(504) 246-7926
www.libertyonerealty.com
Whether it's the riverboat casinos, a nature center and wildlife refuge, the Six Flags New Orleans theme park, or the serenity of nearby Lake Pontchartrain, eastern New Orleans and its modern subdivisions are experiencing resurgence in popularity among homebuyers. And the professionals at this real estate firm, located on one of eastern New Orleans's main thoroughfares, know the local market inside and out. Orientation tours and briefings on local churches and schools will help bring prospective homebuyers up to speed on the area's varied $50,000 to $300,000 housing inventory.

Parkway Realty
2140 St. Bernard Avenue, New Orleans
(504) 944-7755
www.parkwayrealty.com
Whether it's downtown housing from the low 30s to the high 90s, affordable new construction in eastern New Orleans, or rental property virtually anywhere, this real estate firm's four agents can put newcomers who are on a budget into a centrally located home of their choice. Listings are varied, and agents are equipped to handle questions about local schools and churches.

Prudential Gardner Realtors
7934 Maple Street, New Orleans
(504) 861-7575
www.prudentialgardner.com
This New Orleans–based, privately owned company founded in 1958 is expanding its roster of 13 offices and 760 agents with the recent acquisition of another local Realtor. Whether it's a condominium, a family home, or new construction, home-

buyers count on this full-service Realtor to lead them through the residential ropes. The Realtor is part of a 1,000-member relocation network that includes major oil companies. Other services include information packets, relocation guides, computerized market analysis, and a Web site of homes in the market.

RE/MAX N.O. Properties
8001 Maple Street, New Orleans
(504) 866-7733
www.remax-neworleansproperties-la.com
RE/MAX may not be a New Orleans homegrown company, but this privately owned international firm specializing in residential, commercial, and industrial real estate can certainly crow about its size— 75,000 agents nationwide and new offices recently opened in Singapore and Ireland. With more than 300 agents in eight offices throughout the metropolitan area, RE/MAX celebrates its success with a commitment to "highly personalized service," including customized relocation.

TLC Realty Inc.
2119 Elysian Fields, New Orleans
(504) 944-2100, (800) 860-2345
www.tlcrealty.com
Name the homeowner who doesn't need a little tender loving care. This full-service residential and commercial real estate and property management company is well versed in handling the complex needs of homebuyers moving into the area. Whether looking for home sweet home in the city or the suburbs, finding the right house at the right price and close to public schools is the key to success for this eight-agent firm, in business since 1984. Free customized relocation kits are available by writing to the company's Elysian Fields address.

Tommy Crane Inc.
3702 Bienvielle Street, New Orleans
(504) 899-8666, (877) 899-8666
www.tommycrane.com
While this company is not the first to offer a real estate Web site, Tommy Crane's is

certainly one of the most consumer-friendly of its kind in the area. Anyone with a computer and Internet access can go to the Web site for a detailed account of the metropolitan-wide housing market, which includes not only the history of various areas but also a complete listing of homes. Specialty areas include Uptown, the City Park/Bayou St. John area, and Old Metairie. The five-agent firm does not cover the West Bank but will make referrals. Relocation kits for prospective clients looking for anything from an entry-level home to short-term rental leases include a copy of the *Home Buyers Guide*, published by the *Times-Picayune*, city maps, and overviews of local attractions. Clients can also count on familiarization tours of city neighborhoods.

APARTMENTS AND RENTAL HOUSING

New Orleans has an abundant and diverse mix of furnished and unfurnished apartment and rental housing with an equally satisfying range of amenities. Some rental units in megacomplexes come with ceiling fans, balconies, carpet, washer and dryer facilities, a clubhouse, and pool. A few offer off-street parking with card-coded gate entry and video camera surveillance. Monthly rents range from $300 to more than $1,000, depending on location and amenities, and most require security deposits (extra for a pet) and a lease.

Whether renting a swank lakeshore condo, a quaint Uptown shotgun double, a close-to-the-busline Metairie efficiency apartment, or something in between, the area has several apartment and rental-home finder agencies. All of them are full-service companies offering newcomers help in finding any apartment or rental home to suit their needs while providing information on everything from local schools and restaurants to historic points of interest. Below is a sample listing.

ADA Rental Guide of New Orleans
2121 North Causeway Boulevard, Metairie
(504) 831-8680

Since 1984 this widely distributed quarterly guide—published January 1, April 1, June 1, and October 1—has been helping singles, couples, and families moving into the area find the right apartment. People living anywhere in the United States can call toll-free (800) 277-7800 to receive a free issue of the publication, which includes 68 pages of apartment listings, photographs, and Web site addresses of available units.

Apartment Finders
3101 North Causeway Boulevard, Metairie
(504) 834-1200

This free finder service specializes in locating for newcomers and residents everything from unfurnished efficiencies to unfurnished four-bedroom apartments in New Orleans and in Metairie and Kenner in Jefferson Parish. The agency does not provide finder services for the West Bank of Jefferson Parish.

Apartment and Home Hunters Inc.
2901 Ridgelake Drive, Metairie
(504) 835-7368

Employees at this firm will pick up prospective renters at the airport and provide personalized tours of both utility- and non-utility-paid apartment complexes as well as rental homes, furnished and unfurnished, primarily on the East Bank of Jefferson Parish, New Orleans, and in outlying LaPlace, at no charge. Many clients are able to find what they are looking for in one day. The company prides itself on helping renters with special requirements—from an apartment with private washer-dryer that allows pets to a house with a two-car garage—find the place that best suits their needs.

The Times-Picayune
3800 Howard Avenue, New Orleans
(504) 826-3279
www.nola.com

The daily newspaper uses a three-pronged approach to its coverage of the dynamic local real estate market. A Saturday real estate tabloid covers the nuts and bolts of the local market, from who's doing what and where to renovation trends to tips on inexpensive remodeling projects. The Sunday real estate broadsheet keeps readers abreast of the ebb and flow of the market, with practical how-to advice for buying and selling a home, as well as features on what makes the city's neighborhoods tick. Both the tabloid and broadsheet sections include residential home and rental apartment listings. *The Home Buyer's Guide,* published every two weeks, offers a comprehensive and detailed 140-plus page digest of listings, each with pictures, of housing throughout the metropolitan area.

RETIREMENT 🌴

Lazy hours spent in a veranda rocking chair basking in a gloriously breezy afternoon or stoop-sitting to soak up the easygoing neighborhood rhythm is a favorite pastime for locals of all ages. But don't think for one moment that residents here turn their backs on the active life once they bounce that first grandchild on their knee or qualify for AARP membership and senior discounts at local restaurants. Today in New Orleans, retirement is a time for life-enhancing opportunities—personal growth, a second career, taking classes at local colleges and through special programs, volunteerism, starting a business, community activism and advocacy, or taking home a gold medal at the Louisiana Senior Olympics.

For many people the Crescent City is an ideal backdrop for retirement. Key reasons include relatively affordable housing and inexpensive cost of living; enviable range of dining and cultural opportunities (for example, admission to the New Orleans Museum of Art is free on Thursday evenings to anyone with a valid Louisiana identification); warm climate and compact geography; state-of-the-art hospitals and ancillary health care services; and a small but growing number of retirement communities. In fact, the booming, pine tree–dotted north shore bedroom community 30 minutes across Lake Pontchartrain from New Orleans has repeatedly been ranked as one of the 10 best places to retire in the United States.

Numerous community agencies meantime provide older adults with a critical safety net of social services, ranging from free and/or home-delivered meals and transportation to job training. Metropolitan-wide senior centers offer a daily roster chock-full of fun activities and social opportunities designed to help people enjoy the best years of their lives.

The Silver-Haired Legislature, local chapters of the American Association of Retired Persons, the Older Women's League, and other seniors-only advocacy groups help make the voice of older New Orleanians heard by policymakers at the local, state, and national levels. New Orleans is a sound place to retire.

EDUCATION

Some area universities offer discounts to seniors. See "Colleges and Universities" in the Education chapter.

ELDERHOSTEL

Elderhostel is a nonprofit organization dedicated to serving the educational needs of adults age 55 and older. It's also a great way to get to see and learn about a city at minimal cost. Two Elderhostel programs in New Orleans are sponsored by the Jewish Community Center and the Center for New Orleans Studies/People Program (*NOTE:* this is not the same as the People Program listed below).

Center for New Orleans Studies
People Program Elderhostel
832 South Clearview Parkway, Jefferson
(504) 733–3550
www.elderhostel.org
One of the largest Elderhostel programs in the country, the Center for New Orleans Studies offers 5- and 10-day tutorials on the city. Part I consists of the historical trends and accidents culminating in present-day New Orleans. Explore the city with instructors who are experts in local literary figures and architecture as well as the Big Easy's festivals and food. Part II builds on the first experience, further exploring history, culture, and litera-

ture with the addition of voodoo practice and Cajun history as well as a glimpse of New Orleans music through discussions with and performances by homegrown musicians.

Jewish Community Center Elderhostel
5342 St. Charles Avenue, New Orleans
(504) 897-0143
www.elderhostel.org
This five-day program of lectures and field trips explores New Orleans's rich history, from art and architecture to food, frivolity, and music, all the while learning about the impact of the Jewish community on the city. People learn how Jews, who began arriving after the Louisiana Purchase in 1803, became successful business owners and professionals whose accomplishments and philanthropic activities are still evident by the museums, schools, and hospitals that bear their names.

The People Program
1200 Mirabeau Avenue, New Orleans
(504) 288-3171
www.peopleprogram.org
Established in 1974 by the Sisters of St. Joseph, the People Program is a nonprofit, nonsectarian organization that offers adults age 50 and older more than 140 classes, five days a week for 15 weeks in the fall and spring. With classes held on the oak-shaded grounds of the St. Joseph Provincial House near Lake Pontchartrain, the program's goal is to provide opportunities for individuals to share knowledge and experiences, express creativity, and develop new interests. Members pay a nominal fee each semester, which entitles them to attend as many classes as they can schedule. Study subjects include yoga, chess, bridge, Spanish, French, German, Italian, ballet, tap dancing, belly dancing, creative writing, braille, bowling, perspective drawing, oil painting, water color, Brazilian embroidery, keyboard, physical fitness, clogging, computers, cooking, estate planning, tai chi, quilting, line dancing, guitar, scripture study, and wood carving.

EMPLOYMENT

The Senior Community Service Employment Program (SCSEP)
936 Front Street, Cottonport
(888) 926-1739
www.experienceworks.org/scsep.html
This program provides temporary work experience for people age 55 and older who have limited financial resources. Sponsored by the American Association of Retired Persons, the program gives clients the opportunity to develop and sharpen skills while searching for permanent employment. Participants receive on-the-job training for 20 hours each week at nonprofit or public service host agencies while working with SCSEP staff to find a job. Training positions include activities coordinator, bookkeeper, cashier, clerk/typist, custodian, data entry clerk, day care worker, driver, food service worker, groundskeeper, mechanic, receptionist, salesperson, security guard, and teacher's aide. Participants receive temporary work experience to improve marketable skills and develop new ones, the opportunity to establish a current work history, help in developing job search skills and locating a permanent job, paid sick leave and holidays, worker's compensation insurance, a yearly physical exam, and a year's free AARP membership.

RECREATION

For other recreational activities including golf and fishing, see the Parks and Recreation chapter.

The Greater New Orleans Regional Senior Olympics
University of New Orleans, Lakefront
(504) 280-3159
www.gnoso.com
Each fall, the regional Senior Olympics take place in New Orleans in preparation for the state Olympics held in October in Baton Rouge. Anyone age 50 and older is eligible to compete in such events as badminton, bowling, cycling, horseshoes,

shuffleboard, table tennis, track and field, volleyball, basketball, crafts, golf, recreational walking, swimming, and tennis.

SERVICES

Several area hospitals offer programs specifically geared toward seniors. For more information see the Health Care chapter.

American Association of Retired Persons
301 Main Street, Suite 1012, Baton Rouge
(866) 448-3620
www.aarp.org

Although AARP offers a number of chapters throughout the New Orleans area, the closest information office is in Baton Rouge, the state capital. For information on the chapter closest to you, call the above toll-free number. With 30 million members, AARP is the largest advocacy group for older adults in the United States. Membership in local chapters provides opportunities to socialize and volunteer as well as subscriptions to the monthly *AARP Bulletin* and the bimonthly magazine; access to the organization's home-delivery prescription drug service; free membership for a spouse; travel discounts on lodging and car rentals; free information-packed guide books; auto, home, life, and health insurance; AARP Visa and MasterCard; and investment and annuity programs.

AARP's 55 Alive/Mature Driving Program
301 Main Street, Suite 1012, Baton Rouge
(866) 448-3620
www.aarp.org

This comprehensive eight-hour course teaches about the normal age-related changes that affect vision, hearing, and physical strength and, as a result, driving ability. Teachers provide tips on how to compensate for some of these changes. Drivers age 50 and older are welcome to join the course, which is taught in two

The AARP-sponsored Senior Community Service Employment Program helps people age 55 and older with limited financial resources to gain temporary work experience while sharpening skills needed to search for permanent employment. For more information call (225) 924-4091.

half-day sessions. Curriculum reminds drivers of skills and techniques they once learned but perhaps fail to use regularly and updates them on the rules of the road. Some insurance agencies give discounts for older drivers who have completed the course.

AARP Tax Aide
301 Main Street, Suite 1012, Baton Rouge
(866) 448-3620
www.aarp.org

Through AARP's Tax Aide program, volunteers trained to understand how the tax code impacts mature adults, provide free personal income tax assistance to older people. The service helps middle- and low-income taxpayers complete basic federal and state tax forms February 1 through April 15. The program is conducted at community sites or at home for housebound participants.

The New Orleans Council on Aging
2475 Canal Street, New Orleans
(504) 821-4121

The Council on Aging is a private non-profit corporation that serves as the Area Agency on Aging for Orleans Parish, providing a comprehensive array of social, recreational, and nutritional services for the city's estimated 85,000 residents age 60 and older. Many of the council's services are provided through neighborhood senior centers. These facilities are focal points for a broad spectrum of outreach educational and social programs. Most centers are open a minimum of six hours a day Monday through Friday and offer a grocery shopping service; health education seminars,

The Louisiana Silver-Haired Legislature is always looking for new ideas from people interested in championing the cause of older adults at the state level. Each year representatives in the Silver-Haired Legislature develop an agenda of senior-related issues with which to lobby state lawmakers. For more information contact the Governor's Office of Elderly Affairs in Baton Rouge at (800) 259-4990 or the New Orleans Council on Aging at (504) 821-4121.

screenings, and dental services; regularly scheduled in-house recreational activities such as arts and crafts, bridge, exercise, and dances; off-site museum visits; and picnics. Free hot meals served midday are offered at all centers as well as a number of other meal sites. Donations are accepted. Call the council office to find the most convenient senior center.

An estimated 900 homebound older adults receive delivered hot meals. However, this popular program has a need-based waiting list of up to a year. The council also helps individuals needing assistance with housekeeping, home health care, home repair, legal aid, housing placement, companion services, and emergency payment of utility bills.

VOLUNTEERING

The Green Project
2831 Marais Street, New Orleans
(504) 945-0259
This nonprofit organization's mission is to develop and sustain community-based solutions to urban environmental problems. Currently the group offers recycled paint and building materials at low cost. The building materials and paint exchange is the place to drop off extra lumber, bricks, doors, sinks, and paint. These are cleaned and/or repaired (or, in the case of paint, remixed) and sold to renovators for a small fee. This helps keep recyclable

items out of landfills and helps play a positive role in rebuilding the city.

Volunteers are needed in all areas of the organization. On site, they sort paint and building materials and assist customers. Off-site jobs include manning booths at festivals, researching grant opportunities, writing newsletters, calling other volunteers, and assisting with office tasks such as maintaining the database. Store hours are Monday through Saturday 9:00 A.M. to 5:00 P.M.

The Lake Pontchartrain Basin Foundation
3838 North Causeway Boulevard
Metairie
(504) 836-2215
www.saveourlake.org
The 630-square-mile Lake Pontchartrain is part of a vast ecosystem called the Lake Pontchartrain Basin. Spanning 4,700 square miles, the basin also encompasses Lakes Maurepas and Borgne as well as a number of freshwater rivers and bayous and part of the Gulf of Mexico, forming the largest contiguous estuary in the Gulf Coast region. The foundation is a membership-based citizens organization representing the public's independent voice in restoring and preserving the basin. Highlights of the group's successes include coordinating an extensive monitoring program to track pollutants in lakes and canals, helping reduce agricultural runoff in north shore rivers by constructing dairy waste retention lagoons, and planting sea grass beds to replace those destroyed by hurricanes and shoreline development. Volunteers are needed throughout the year for restoration as well as educational projects.

The Louisiana Eldercare Volunteer Network
P.O. Box 80374, Baton Rouge 70898-0374
(800) 259-4990
Interested in helping other older citizens in need? The Louisiana Eldercare Volunteer Network, sponsored by the Governor's Office of Elderly Affairs, provides services to help older adults age in place

while maintaining their freedom and dignity. Projects can include organizing a church group to paint an older person's house or helping a senior fill out a Medicare form. Volunteers work in nursing homes, legal services, health care instruction, education, cooking and gardening, foster grandparenting, senior companion programs, and churches. Volunteers of all ages are welcome.

The Retired and Senior Volunteer Program
2475 Canal Street, New Orleans
(504) 821-4121
www.seniorcorps.org

Each year nearly 500,000 older-adult volunteers in 800 cities nationwide provide more than 80 million hours of free service valued at more than $1 billion through the Retired Senior Volunteer Program. Far more important is the fact that those hours were spent mentoring at-risk youth, making hospital visits, teaching English to immigrants, organizing neighborhood watch groups, and helping people recover from natural disasters. Want to be in that number? A program of the New Orleans Council on Aging, RSVP helps people 55 and older put their skills and experience to work for their community through a network of more than 60 government offices, social service agencies, health care institutions, cultural attractions, and schools. Volunteers serve from a few hours up to 20 hours per week. Benefits include free insurance coverage for personal liability, accident, and auto during volunteer hours; a yearly recognition party; and a quarterly newsletter that includes volunteer opportunity notices.

The Service Corps of Retired Executives
365 Canal Street, New Orleans
(504) 589-2356
www.score.org

Miss the office? The Service Corps of Retired Executives gives you the chance to get back into the game by pairing retired executives with small-business owners in need of advice. This Small Business Administration-sponsored program needs experts in virtually every area of free enterprise. SCORE volunteers lead in-depth counseling and training to help small-business owners identify problems, determine the causes, and find solutions. Low-cost workshops on such topics as starting a home-based business, purchasing a franchise, or defining a marketing and advertising strategy are led by these expert volunteers. Others offer free, confidential one-on-one counseling sessions with owners either in person or through e-mail. The program has more than 12,400 retired volunteers nationwide.

i

If you discount it, will they come? You bet. Many of the city's restaurants, hotels, movie theaters, car rental outlets, and even colleges take a little off the top if you're over a certain age (usually 55, 60, or 65) or a member of the American Association of Retired Persons. If in doubt about whether a discount is offered, just ask.

RETIREMENT COMMUNITIES

The Atrium at Lafreniere
6555 Park Manor Drive, Metairie
(504) 454-6636

Located on the edge of Lafreniere Park in the suburb of Metairie, the Atrium offers 80 efficiency, one-, and two-bedroom apartments with full kitchens and plush carpeting. The focal point of this restricted-access community is the lushly landscaped, temperature-controlled two-story atrium, adorned with soothing fountains and aviary, goldfish pond, and artwork. The dining room serves continental breakfast as well as a midday meal. All apartments feature free basic cable television, light housekeeping, beauty/barber shop, free laundry facilities,

Big Easy history and aging dovetail during the tutorials sponsored by the People Program/New Orleans Study Center Elderhostel, the largest Elderhostel program in the country. Class topics range from local literary figures, voodoo, and architecture to New Orleans' festivals and food. For more information call (504) 887-7333.

emergency call system, transportation, camera-monitored entrances, personal health consultation, and weekly social activities. Fees are charged monthly.

Christwood
100 Christwood Boulevard, Covington
(985) 898-0515
www.christwoodrc.com
Located on 58 landscaped acres in piney St. Tammany Parish north of Lake Pontchartrain, Christwood is a nonsectarian continuing-care retirement community. The facility features 118 apartments as well as more than 20,000 square feet of common living, dining, and recreational space. The Arbor health center has separate living and dining areas in both the assisted living and nursing wings. At Christwood, the emphasis is on civility. A pillared *porte cochere* makes for an elegant entryway into an inviting atrium, while arches and weather-vaned cupolas add points of interest.

Residents are invited to entertain their guests in the library and a private dining room. The main dining room features chandeliers, crystal, and crisp linen. Apartments provide a view of the landscape through large bay windows or from private balconies. One-, two-, and three-bedroom apartments are available. Features include 9-foot ceilings, emergency call system, modern kitchen, basic cable television, 20 meals per person per month, laundering service, light housekeeping, and guest accommodations. Pets allowed in first-floor apartments. Christwood requires an up-front buy-in as well as monthly fees

that include unlimited lifetime nursing care.

Lambeth House
150 Broadway Street, New Orleans
(504) 865-1960
www.lambethhouse.com
Lambeth House is a continuing care retirement community located in Uptown New Orleans, offering one-, two-, and three-bedroom apartments as well as a dining room, activity room, auditorium, fitness center, gallery, business center, and a private walled courtyard. Apartment amenities include fully equipped electric kitchens with microwaves, washer and dryer, mini-blinds, and balconies (select apartments). Fees include flexible meal plans, security, utilities, activities, maintenance, housekeeping, a 24-hour call system, and unlimited lifetime nursing care. Lambeth requires a buy-in plus monthly fees.

The Landing at Behrman Place
3601 Behrman Place, Algiers
(504) 361-1088
Located across the Mississippi River in Algiers, the Landing offers studio, one-, and two-bedroom apartments with carpet, drapes, kitchenette, full bath, and an emergency call system. Rates include three meals a day, weekly housekeeping, scheduled transportation, cable TV, security, recreational activities, and outings. Other amenities include private dining area for special occasions, bed linens, bath towels, free laundry facilities, beauty/barber shop, library, chapel, activity and craft rooms, exercise room, and large-screen TV room. Monthly fees are required.

Nouveau Marc
1101 Joe Yenni Boulevard, Kenner
(504) 469-7988
Located near Lake Pontchartrain in the East Jefferson surburb of Kenner, Nouveau Marc features studio, one-, and two-bedroom apartments with kitchenette, large private bath (two-bedroom apartments

have two baths), spacious bedroom closet, and emergency pull cords. Rates include three meals a day, paid utilities, satellite TV, free laundry facilities, trans-portation to shopping centers and doctor's appointments, weekly housekeeping, linen service, and planned activities. Fees paid monthly.

HEALTH CARE AND WELLNESS

In a TV commercial for a local hospital, groups of New Orleanians are shown doing what many New Orleanians do best: eating, drinking, and (yes) smoking. The narrator says, "If ever a city needed a great hospital . . ." No kidding. After all, one day the backlash from all of those artery-clogging oysters Bienville and roux-thickened étouffées—not to mention the cigarettes and booze—is bound to come banging at the front door. Perhaps it's only fitting that the city that forgot to close its bars can trace the roots of two longtime hospitals to an early 19th-century Irish nun and a World War I-era Baptist missionary. What does catch one off guard is the story of the late philanthropist Elizabeth Miller Robin. She was stricken by polio as a toddler and grew up to build in New Orleans the state's only children's hospital, designed originally to provide care to children hit by a poliomyelitis epidemic. When it comes to hospitals in the Big Easy, necessity is the mother of invention.

Today more than two dozen acute-care facilities of various sizes throughout the New Orleans five-parish metropolitan area provide state-of-the-art health care to more than 1.5 million area residents. Hospital growth tempered by managed care virtually guarantees a topflight facility or satellite clinic is always nearby ready to provide treatment in a cost-conscious environment. Whether it's organ transplantation, limb reattachment, treatment for reproduction disorders, or physical therapy, local hospitals, doctors, and other health care professionals offer a broad spectrum of services, procedures, and treatments.

Health care cost cutting is the name of the game nationwide, and local hospitals have responded with aggressive community outreach efforts to promote prevention and wellness through seminars, workshops, health fairs, and screenings. Many hospitals offer special membership programs for senior adults, while the influx of aging baby boomers has seen the development of hospital-based fitness centers and wellness programs. Other hospitals have opened new specialized treatment centers and rehabilitation units to improve patient care. Several progressive hospitals are incorporating elements of holistic health and alternative medicine formerly relegated to the sidelines of modern Western science.

Exciting scholarly research is conducted by local and international scientists at the city's medical centers and teaching hospitals. A good example is the discovery by Tulane researchers in 1989 of a vaccine against simian immunodeficiency virus. The vaccine has been hailed as a breakthrough in the fight against AIDS. A Louisiana State University Medical Center ophthalmologist meantime became the first person in the world to perform laser surgery to correct poor vision. New Orleans has a lot to be proud of in the physicians and other health care practitioners who heal the sick, as well as the researchers who are finding better ways of doing so in the future.

In this chapter we will focus on many of the hospitals within the New Orleans area and outline the uniqueness of each facility set against the local health care landscape. Remember, this is meant to serve only as an overview of New Orleans

Numbers for Health-related Questions or Emergencies

Look to these phone numbers for help. Crisis lines are answered 24 hours a day.

Life-threatening, police, and fire emergencies:	911
AIDS Counseling:	(800) 590-2437
AIDS Testing:	(800) 584-8183
AIDS Statewide Hotline:	(504) 821-6050,
	(800) 992-4379
Al-Anon:	(504) 888-1356
Alcoholics Anonymous:	(504) 779-1178
Alcohol Abuse Helpline:	(800) 278-8962
American Cancer Society:	(504) 465-8405
American Diabetes Association:	(504) 899-0278
American Lung Association:	(504) 828-5864
American Red Cross:	(504) 620-3105
Arthritis Foundation:	(800) 283-7800
Gamblers Anonymous:	(504) 431-7867
Narcotics Anonymous:	(504) 899-8840
New Orleans Health Department:	(504) 565-6900
Overeaters Anonymous:	(504) 366-3230
Poison Control Center:	(800) 256-9822

acute-care hospitals. Check the Yellow Pages for freestanding specialized treatment centers, such as physical therapy and outpatient clinics, home health agencies, alternative medicine practitioners, substance abuse treatment facilities, mental health professionals, and other health care providers.

ALTERNATIVE CLINICS

American Back Institute
734 Veterans Boulevard, Metairie
(504) 833-2225
www.backpaininstitute.com
This institute specializes in treatment of the spine using state-of-the-art technol-

ogy including the VAX-D, which has been demonstrated to be effective in 71 to 74 percent of 778 patients who participated in a recent study. Other disciplines include prolotherapy and chiropractic. The clinic also offers a large and varied referral base including conventional and alternative medicine specialists.

Metairie Pain and Acupuncture Clinic
3216 North Turnbull Drive, Metairie
(504) 888-5449
For nearly a quarter century, this clinic has been providing patients with nonsurgical alternatives to pain management, specializing in nerve blocks and acupuncture. Dr. Jerry S.Y. Yong is one of only a few

acupuncturists licensed in Louisiana to practice the ancient Chinese healing art.

CHIROPRACTIC

Achievement Therapeutic Services
3320 Hessmer Avenue, Metairie
(504) 366-7246
www.drpace.com
Dr. Kenneth S. Pace, DC, treats a wide variety of patients with joint pain, whiplash, sports injuries, and neck pain using the most modern techniques available to chiropractic medicine. Pace combines his extensive knowledge of biomechanics and state-of-the-art equipment and diagnostic techniques.

Chiropractic Health Center
101 Clearview Parkway, Metairie
(504) 454-2000
www.chirohealthcare.com
Since 1986 this clinic has been treating patients requiring short- or long-term corrective chiropractic treatment. From junior high school students with sports-related injuries to oil rig workers with back and neck pain, the Chiropractic Health Center team provides state-of-the-art treatment. Other ailments treated include headache and shoulder pain, pinched nerves, and sciatica.

Discover Chiropractic
4600 South Claiborne Avenue
New Orleans
(504) 525-6659

2629 North Causeway Boulevard
Metairie
(504) 834-2926

Many local hospitals offer a broad range of on-site community health- and wellness-related seminars, lectures, and workshops, often free to the public. To get the pulse of the latest trends in diagnosis, treatment, and prevention, call the hospital nearest you for a list of upcoming topics.

The team of Drs. Patrick McNeil, Paul Gordon, Jeff Miller, and Ben McNeil offer spinal corrections and other chiropractic treatments for a variety of disorders including disc injuries, headaches, dizziness, and migraines. The clinic, which also has a staff physician, offers emergency appointments and X-ray facilities.

HOSPITALS

Children's Hospital
200 Henry Clay Avenue, New Orleans
(504) 899-9511
www.chnola.org
Pint-size patients can count on big help at Louisiana's only full-service pediatric hospital, which opened its doors in 1955. Originally called Crippled Children's Hospital, the facility cared for the thousands of children left disabled as a result of the polio epidemics that followed World War II. The epidemics hit hard in Louisiana, which lagged behind in providing care to children. Thousands contracted polio—including the woman who would become the hospital's founder, the late Elizabeth Miller Robin. After a bout with polio at age 2, she spent many of her childhood months in the hospital and for the rest of her life was dependent on crutches. Years later, motivated by the challenges she encountered as a child, Robin set out to establish a hospital exclusively for handicapped children. The daughter of a prominent New Orleans physician, she used her powers of persuasion to fulfill her dream. "Liza was as strong-willed as anyone I've ever known—and she was great at convincing others," recalled Harry Kelleher Jr., a local attorney who later became chairperson of the hospital's founding board. "She would walk into a room with her crutches and fiery red hair and begin to talk about helping children. And it was virtually impossible to say no."

Nearly half a century after it opened, this well-respected health care provider further expanded its impressive range of services with the opening of the Research

Institute for Children, a joint project of Children's Hospital and Louisiana State University Medical Center in New Orleans. The institute has been awarded more than $3 million in research grants, primarily from the National Institutes of Health, to be a national testing laboratory and center for the study and prevention of type-I (insulin-dependent) diabetes. Over 350 medical centers nationwide are participating in the study. Other innovations include the establishment of the Children's Health Care Network, a physician-hospital organization consisting of a partnership between community-based pediatricians, Children's Hospital, and the LSU Healthcare Network.

"No child's case is too big or too serious," states the nonprofit hospital's brochure. Critical-care youngsters with broken bones and cancer to those born prematurely are but a few examples of the more than 7,800 inpatient and 170,000 outpatient visits in 2002. Patients, referred to this facility from more than 1,600 doctors each year, come from 40 states and 5 foreign countries. Developments at this 201-bed hospital in recent years include a new youth sports medicine program as well as clinics for genetic and metabolic disorders and general pediatrics. Critical care services include a 25-bed pediatric intensive care unit, an 8-bed spinal unit, and a 21-bed neonatal intensive care unit. The hospital's emergency care center is staffed around the clock by board-certified pediatricians, with the availability of a full range of pediatric subspecialists. The hospital has opened a satellite location, The Metairie Center, in the New Orleans suburb of Metairie in Jefferson Parish. Construction under way will double the size of the emergency room.

Nowadays the pediatric transport team uses a helicopter in addition to ground ambulances for emergency dispatchments day and night. The hospital was among the first in the state to provide a new epilepsy treatment for patients 12 years and older. A 380-physician staff includes 250 pediatric subspecialists. The

hospital is also the home of The Parenting Center, a program providing resources, education, and counseling to parents, and an emergency care center staffed 24-7 by fully trained pediatricians.

Why not donate the priceless gift of time to a local hospital in need of volunteers? Many health care organizations have volunteer and auxiliary groups that are always looking for individuals who have a couple of hours a week to help out.

Doctors Hospital of Jefferson
4320 Houma Boulevard, Metairie
(504) 849–4000
www.doctors-jefferson.com
This Jefferson Parish East Bank hospital located in Metairie was founded by a partnership of doctors in 1984 to meet the health care needs and expectations of this growing suburban community. Today more than 500 doctors representing every major medical and surgical specialty spearhead this 138-bed acute-care facility, a member of the Tenet Louisiana Health System. The hospital was one of the first in the area to use lasers in vascular, gynecological, and general surgical procedures, and the first to use lasers to break up kidney stones. Outpatient services include electrocardiograms, lab tests, physical and occupational therapy, ultrasound technology, nutrition counseling, cardiopulmonary stress testing, pulmonary rehabilitation programs, nuclear medicine, X-ray, magnetic resonance imaging, and CAT scans.

Specialty areas include orthopedics and sports medicine, from total joint replacement to arthroscopic surgery. The hospital is home to the Gulf South Knee Center, a program that provides education, treatment, and rehabilitation of knee pain. The Cardiac Cath Lab specializes in the detection of circulatory blockages that could lead to stroke, loss of function or strength in the legs, and impairment of other body functions. Well-known for its

Physician Referral

The following are at-a-glance physician referral telephone numbers for hospitals listed in this chapter.

Children's Hospital:	(504) 896-9460
Doctors Hospital of Jefferson:	(800) 522-6363
East Jefferson General Hospital:	(504) 456-5000
Lakeland Medical Center:	(504) 243-4373
Lakeside Hospital:	(504) 885-5433
Meadowcrest Hospital:	(800) 836-3848
Memorial Medical Center:	(800) 968-3638
Ochsner Medical Institutions:	(504) 842-3155
St. Charles General Hospital:	(888) 836-3848
Touro Infirmary:	(504) 897-7777
Tulane University Medical Center:	(504) 988-5800

experience in laser and balloon angioplasty, the institute continues to develop new treatments and diagnostic methods. The hospital offers a series of educational lectures focusing on important health and wellness topics. The popular (and free) Inside Medical Series, which features lectures by members of the hospital's medical staff, is held on the first floor in the staff development auditorium. Call for dates and times. A variety of self-help groups, ranging from Alcoholics Anonymous to cancer, lupus, and epilepsy support groups, meet at the hospital on a regular basis. Doctors Urgent Care, located next door to the hospital, handles

Today hospital-based membership programs targeted to older adults offer such perks as newsletters, access to medical information and hospital fitness centers, and various discounts. To get the most out of life in the mature lane, call local hospitals for the lowdown on their senior membership programs.

both medical emergencies and minor injuries. Call (504) 849-8780.

On a regional level, Doctors Hospital, along with other Tenet HealthSystem facilities, have introduced two wellness and membership programs for older adults and women.

East Jefferson General Hospital
4200 Houma Street, Metairie
(504) 454-4000
www.eastjeffhospital.org
Since 1971 this nonprofit, 525-bed community hospital has provided tertiary care to residents of the East Bank of Jefferson Parish and surrounding communities. More than 800 primary care and specialist physicians spearhead the broad-based medical staff at this facility, which was awarded accreditation with commendation by the Joint Commission on Accreditation of Health Care Organizations, the body's highest recognition. The facility also receives vital support from more than 1,000 volunteers, some of whom have been with the hospital since its inception. Centers of excellence include Cardiovascular

Services, Diabetes Management Center, The Wound Center, Regional Cancer Center, Rehabilitative Services, and Woman & Child Services.

A modern outpatient facility, the 228,000-square-foot Joseph C. Domino Health Care Pavilion opened in 1997 to accommodate the large number of patients needing same-day surgeries and laboratory procedures such as gastrointestinal endoscopy. Departments occupying the pavilion's four floors include laboratory and diagnostic radiology, same-day surgery, gastrointestinal endoscopy. Other hospital services offered include an emergency department, ambulance transportation, and intensive care unit. A 38,000-square-foot wellness center for older adults offers a variety of fitness and health education programs such as cardiovascular exercises and aquatic therapy. Mature adults will find innovative programs tailored to meet their special wellness and health education needs at the hospital's Elder Advantage program.

The Yenni Pavilion houses radiation therapy, outpatient chemotherapy, and MRI.

During the past three decades, the hospital has devoted millions of dollars in community benefits such as indigent care and support for the prison medical units. The hospital also provides the Jefferson Parish Public School System with registered nurses and substance abuse and intervention facilitators, and helped fund the Jefferson Community School's science lab.

The hospital's participation in the evolving Integrated Physician Network of primary care doctors and specialty physicians, as well as partial ownership of the Southeast Medical Alliance and its insurance products, puts the facility in a good position to seek managed care contracts.

This publicly owned service district hospital is governed by a 10-member volunteer board of directors appointed by the Jefferson Parish Council and Parish President. More important, with more than two decades of service and the steadfast

loyalty of the community, East Jefferson General has earned a reputation as a health care "jewel" of the East Bank.

Lakeland Medical Center
6000 Bullard Avenue, New Orleans
(504) 241-6335
www.lakelandmedcenter.com
This 180-bed acute-care facility offers a full range of services including inpatient and outpatient treatment and care, rehabilitation, skilled nursing, and home health services. The campus has three medical office buildings and houses the Fertility Institute of New Orleans, Center for Orthopedic and Sports Medicine, Lakeland Center for Fitness and Rehabilitation, and Crescent City MRI Center. Specialized cardiology services include cardiac catheterization lab, cardiac rehabilitation, electrocardiograph, and open-heart and minimally invasive heart surgery. Women's services include obstetrics and gynecology, infertility services, breast diagnosis center, labor and delivery suites, and the WomanCare Midwife Center. The hospital's sleep disorders clinic is staffed by a board-certified physician. New services include a transitional care center featuring a skilled nursing facility and rehabilitation unit.

Lakeside Hospital
4700 I-10 Service Road, Metairie
(504) 780-8282
www.lakesidehospital.com
In the 1960s and 1970s this hospital earned its stripes as a 14-bed specialty center for maternity and newborn care. More than 86,000 deliveries later, Lakeside is a 122-bed, state-of-the-art health care provider located in Metairie on the East Bank of Jefferson Parish. More than 250 full-time employees and 400 staff physicians work at the campus's three medical office buildings. The Women's Network, a comprehensive care system, offers a centralized system for coordinating patient education, screening, diagnosis, and treatment services related to women's health needs. Lakeside was the first hospital in the area with the new

Advanced Breast Biopsy Instrumentation and is a regional ABBI training site. The hospital was also the first in the market to have fully digitized radiography and fluoroscopy capabilities. Pioneering procedures have included the transvaginal sling procedure used to treat incontinence as well as the direct-oocyte sperm transfer for the treatment of infertility. The hospital has ICU and telemetry units, a state-of-the-art urgent care center with five exam rooms, remodeled medical and surgical wings, and a new sports medicine center.

Meadowcrest Hospital
2500 Belle Chasse Highway, Gretna
(504) 392-3131
www.meadowcresthosp.com
Located on the West Bank of Jefferson Parish, 5 miles from New Orleans across the Mississippi River, this 203-bed hospital, which opened in 1984, provides general medical and specialized surgical treatment. Tertiary medical care includes an emergency department, intensive and coronary care units, maternity services, and the West Bank's only level-III neonatal intensive care unit. Other specialty centers and services include heart surgery, SinuClear laser surgery, outpatient surgery, obstetrics, occupational health programs. Meadowcrest is part of the Tenet Louisiana Health System, a provider of health care services in the New Orleans area.

Memorial Medical Center
Baptist campus:
2700 Napoleon Avenue, New Orleans
(504) 899-9311
www.memmedctr.com

Mercy campus:
301 North Jefferson Davis Parkway
New Orleans
(504) 483-5000
This medical center is the blending of two historic health care institutions and their integration into the Tenet Louisiana HealthSystem, a provider of health care in the New Orleans area. The two facilities include campuses Uptown (formerly

Southern Baptist Hospital) and Mid City (formerly Mercy Hospital), plus satellite medical offices in Algiers, Metairie, and New Orleans's Lakeview neighborhood. The foundation of Mercy Hospital can be traced to 1030s Ireland where Catherine McAuley, an orphan and founder of the Sisters of Mercy, inherited a fortune from her guardian. Her organization spread to the United States and New Orleans in 1869 with the opening of a school for children and a local clinic. In 1924, Mrs. Leon Soniat donated to the Sisters of Mercy her estate on Annunciation Street, site of the original hospital. Mercy Hospital moved to its current location at the corner of Jefferson Davis Parkway and Bienville Street in 1953.

The roots of Southern Baptist Hospital reach back to the turn of the century. In 1917 a young Baptist missionary raised an important question at the Southern Baptist Convention: "What about a Baptist hospital in New Orleans?" The question was answered with a commitment by the convention to build a hospital with a fund established with the help of the Archbishop of New Orleans and individuals of all denominations. In 1926 a 248-bed hospital was opened, with numerous wings added during the century that doubled the facility's inpatient capacity. The merger of Mercy and Southern Baptist Hospitals in 1994 created the largest private hospital in the New Orleans area, with 726 beds and a dual-campus advantage. Management of the facilities also merged to become Christian Health Ministries, and two medical staffs became one.

Today a staff skilled in all specialties, including neurosurgery, neonatal intensive care, heart surgery, and home health care, provides an extensive range of state-of-the-art inpatient and outpatient services, including an innovative Women's Pavilion and bone marrow transplantation unit. In 1997 the medical center, in conjunction with the LSU Medical Center's Stanley S. Scott Cancer Center, became one of the few sites in the United States to offer computer-enhanced radiation therapy to treat prostate cancer. In other developments, hospital neurosurgeons implanted a vagus nerve stimulation device to treat epilepsy—the first procedure of its kind in Louisiana since the Food and Drug Administration approved the device. The hospital, the tertiary flagship of the Tenet Louisiana HealthSystem and one of the premier facilities of the national Tenet HealthSystem, has acquired the acute-care and outpatient surgical facility known as Eye, Ear, Nose & Throat Hospital.

Ochsner Medical Institutions
1516 Jefferson Highway, Jefferson
(504) 842–3000
www.ochsner.org

Twins born in separate years? The birth of twins Timothy and Celeste Keys of New Orleans set a world record by being delivered 95 days apart. Timothy was delivered at Ochsner on October 15, 1994, followed by his sister, Celeste, on January 18, 1995. David Watkins, a 19-year-old Louisiana State University football player, made national headlines as well when he received a heart transplant at Ochsner, not only giving him the chance to survive but also enabling him to continue his education and the hope of one day returning to athletics. The odds were against 4-month-old Guillermo Rodriguez of Honduras living to see his first birthday. The infant was born with life-threatening congenital heart disease and time was running out. But the odds took a 180-degree turn when Rodriguez arrived at Ochsner for life-saving surgery in 1996, which was performed by pediatric cardiologist Dr. Albert Gutierrez.

These and other success stories underscore the national and international reputation earned by this premiere health care facility, which opened its doors in early 1942 in a wooden complex known as "Splinter Village," a former military hospital at the foot of the Huey P. Long Bridge. The five physicians and surgeons who founded Ochsner Clinic—Alton Ochsner, Guy Caldwell, Edgar Burns, Francis Le-Jeune, and Curtis Tyrone—were all eminent specialists and professors at Tulane University School of Medicine. By 1946 the hospital had become a thriving multispecialty clinic and a nonprofit foundation responsible for running the hospital and directing the institution's research and medical education programs. Thirty-five years ago the hospital undertook a $60-million expansion to meet increases in patient volume. In 2000 Ochsner opened a $47-million critical care tower designed to provide patients with state-of-the-art critical care.

Numbers tell part of the story: For more than half a century Ochsner Foundation Hospital and Clinic have been widely recognized as centers of excellence in research, patient care, and education. *U.S. News & World Report* has continuously named Ochsner one of America's Best Hospitals (1990, 1996, 1997, 1998, and 1999). The hospital received the NRC Consumer's Choice Award for the New Orleans region and the Consumer's Choice Award for heart care services. As the fifth largest heart transplantation program in the country, Ochsner reached a milestone in 2000 by completing its 500th transplant, joining the ranks of only five other transplant programs nationwide.

The 443-bed teaching hospital is one of the largest non-university-based physician training centers in the country, serving not only the New Orleans community but also a large international patient base from South and Central America. Ochsner Clinic is one of the nation's largest multispecialty health care groups with 32 locations throughout southeast Louisiana. More than 450 staff physicians treat an estimated one million patients each year and train another 250 doctors as part of the facility's graduate medical education program, one of the largest in the United States. The hospital opened the first of its six north shore clinics in Mandeville in St. Tammany Parish.

Of the Ochsner clinics throughout southeast Louisiana, seven are located in the New Orleans area and handle minor emergencies and illnesses. Clinic hours are Monday through Friday 8:00 A.M. to 5:00

or 5:30 P.M. (depending on location), and many have Saturday hours 8:00 A.M. to noon. To make an appointment call Ochsner Clinic Algiers, 3401 Behrman Place, Algiers (504-371-9323); Ochsner Clinic Kenner, 2120 Driftwood Boulevard, Kenner (504-443-9500); Ochsner Clinic Lapalco, 4225 Lapalco Boulevard, Marrero (504-371-9355); Ochsner Clinic Metairie, 2005 Veterans Boulevard, Metairie (504–836-9820); Ochsner Clinic New Orleans East, 5701 Deer Park Boulevard (504–243-6022); Ochsner Pediatric Center/New Orleans East, 6030 Bullard Avenue (504–246-5700). After-hours clinic appointments can be made 24/7 by calling one of the registered nurses who staff the Ochsner On Call physician referral service at (504) 842-3155 or (800) 231-5257.

i

Some New Orleans hospitals specialize in the treatment of children and women; others offer general medical and specialized surgical treatment. To find out which facility best suits your and your family's health care and medical needs, always ask the hospital before making an appointment to see a doctor.

St. Charles General Hospital
3700 St. Charles Avenue, New Orleans
(504) 899-7441
www.stcharleshospital.com
This Uptown hospital opened its doors in 1972 as a 163-bed general acute-care facility and today employs more than 277 people plus a 285-doctor medical staff. The hospital, a member of the Tenet Louisiana HealthSystem, offers a full range of specialized services and treatments in every major medical specialty from allergy to vascular surgery. Specialized programs include a weight management center, an adult day care center, a two-chamber hyperbarics unit, SinuClear laser surgery, a 16-bed skilled nursing facility and 10-bed long-term acute unit, 24-hour emergency services, community education lectures, and Foot Conservation Center.

Touro Infirmary
1401 Foucher Street, New Orleans
(504) 897-7011
www.touro.org
The oldest private nonprofit hospital in the city, Touro Infirmary was founded in 1852 by Judah Touro, who envisioned a multispecialty facility offering a complete range of general medical and surgical services. The hospital made medical history in 1888 when Dr. Rudolph Matas, the father of modern vascular surgery, performed the first successful surgical repair of an aortic aneurysm. Today this 350-bed Uptown medical complex and teaching hospital has 500 physicians who staff state-of-the-art centers of excellence including cardiopulmonary and mental health services, obstetrics and gynecology, physical medicine and rehabilitation, and cancer treatment. The hospital's chest-pain emergency room, which opened in 1993, was the first of its kind in the New Orleans area and is designed to quickly diagnose and treat symptoms related to heart attacks. A family birthing center features beautifully designed and appointed labor, delivery, and recovery rooms as well as a level-III neonatal intensive care unit, a breast pump station, and perinatology services. Fast one-stop outpatient surgery in a private atmosphere is provided at the hospital's freestanding Prytania Surgery center at the corner of Prytania and Delachaise Streets. The satellite Touro Lakefront Medical Center is located in the Hibernia Bank building at Elysian Fields Avenue and Robert E. Lee Boulevard. The center is staffed by board-certified physicians specializing in internal medicine, nephrology, pulmonary medicine, ophthalmology, and chest and vascular surgery. For appointments call (504) 282-3434.

Tulane University Hospital & Clinic
1415 Tulane Avenue, New Orleans
(504) 588–5800
www.tuhc.com

Several of the world's top physicians were educated here. A 1977 winner of the Nobel Prize in Medicine works and teaches here. Important medical breakthroughs were discovered here, not the least of which was Dr. Rudolph Matas's development of a lifesaving surgical procedure for aneurysms—back in 1888. More than 170 years of health care delivery and medical research tradition is nothing to sneeze at.

In 1834 William Harrison was president and the first Mardi Gras parade was still three years down the road. Seven ambitious New Orleans doctors banded together to form the Medical College of Louisiana, the first of its kind west of the Allegheny Mountains and the forerunner of Tulane University Medical Center. Today the medical center is regarded as one of the finest teaching, research, and patient care centers in the country.

Several divisions make up the medical center located in the heart of the Central Business District nearby the French Quarter: the School of Medicine (with 1,700 faculty and 1,500 students), the School of Public Health and Tropical Medicine (established in 1910), the Tulane Regional Primate Research Center, the U.S.-Japan Cooperative Biomedical Research Laboratories, University Health Services, and the 300-bed Tulane University Hospital and Clinic. More than 250 hospital and clinic physicians see nearly 200,000 patients annually. Specialties include cancer and oncology, cardiology, neonatology, pediatrics, surgery, OB/GYN, international health, and infectious diseases. Seven centers of excellence include DePaul/Tulane Behavioral Health Center, Tulane Cancer

In the coming years a historic consortium forged by LSU and Tulane medical centers will create a comprehensive cancer treatment facility in New Orleans, offering patients access to a greater number of clinical research trials and promising treatments that observers say may one day rival such regional powerhouses as Houston's M.D. Anderson and Birmingham's University of Alabama medical centers.

Center, Tulane Hospital for Children, Tulane Institute of Sports Medicine, and Tulane-Xavier National Women's Center, Tulane Inpatient Rehabilitation center, and Tulane Center for Abdominal Transplant. The outpatient surgery facility is one of the newest and largest in the South.

With its proximity to downtown and the French Quarter, Tulane's emergency department sees many out-of-town visitors who need medical assistance. Services are available around the clock.

Tulane has been on the forefront of numerous important breakthroughs, such as in 1917 when the medical school awarded degrees to its first women graduates, and in 1969 when it was the first institution in Louisiana to transplant organs, beginning with the state's first kidney transplant. In 1989 Tulane researchers developed a vaccine against simian immunodeficiency virus, hailed as a breakthrough in the fight against AIDS. Another innovation is the hospital's community outreach: The Professionals At Tulane program allows anyone to call a central number—(504) 988–5800—and receive quick, accurate, and dependable health information, physician referrals, and registration for free classes and seminars.

EDUCATION 🎓

NEW ORLEANS PUBLIC SCHOOLS

The story of public schools in New Orleans is about as happy as a Tennessee Williams play. Orleans Parish (wholly composed of the City of New Orleans) and neighboring suburb Jefferson Parish educate approximately 66,000 and 53,000 students in public schools, respectively. Students in both systems routinely score below the national average on standardized tests and, periodically, newspaper articles appear telling of new businesses' reluctance to relocate to the area because of the lack of skilled and educated workers.

In Orleans Parish, with a majority of students eligible for free or reduced lunch (read: poor), the system has fought an uphill battle for quite some time. However, during the tenure of Superintendent of Schools Morris Holmes (1993–1998), things went from bad to worse. His promise of higher standardized test scores when he first took office turned to scandal four years later. At first school board members cheered advances made in this area—until a panel of local and national experts found the rise in test scores to be "statistically impossible." (Second graders at one school scored in the 95th percentile for reading on the California Achievement Test, when the same group scored in the 29th percentile the previous year.) The pressure on principals to achieve was reportedly so intense that "questionable testing practices" were found to be widespread.

Holmes received a $25,000 raise that year, bringing his salary to run a financially strapped school system up to a whopping $147,500 and making him one of the highest paid superintendents in similarly sized markets in the nation. Later the same year, the school board decided to buy out Holmes's contract with a package that couldn't be considered anything but generous in light of the fact that critics had called for his dismissal.

The summer of 1999 saw the beginning of a new era when retired Marine Colonel Al Davis took over the beleaguered school system as its CEO. In his first year, Davis, or "The Colonel" as he was known throughout the system, created small task forces to assess the needs of individual schools, shortened the time line for removing poorly performing employees, and devised a strategic plan to drive budget and policy decisions for the next five years.

Although The Colonel earned the respect of many veteran educators, defying the odds turned out to be an insurmountable obstacle—even for a former Marine. He resigned in 2002.

In the spring of 2003 new superintendent Tony Amato took the helm, diving headfirst into the system's academic problems by introducing a dizzying number of initiatives. He supplied new reading and math curricula to lower schools and demanded that an hour and a half each day be devoted to these subjects. He also established themed specialty programs to boost student achievement as well as enrollment.

Near the end of his first year, Amato announced plans to abolish a number of

---

There are a handful of excellent public magnet schools in New Orleans, the brightest star of which is Benjamin Franklin High School. The school, which regularly places students in the country's best colleges, is the kind of place private school kids transfer to when they hit ninth grade. For more information call the Orleans Parish School Board at (504) 304–5680.

---

middle schools and add those sixth-, seventh-, and eighth-grade classes to nearby elementary schools. And Amato has plowed ahead with his initiatives.

At the beginning of his second year in office, Amato declared his intention to begin concentrating on the financial mess the school system has been in for as long as anybody can remember. And in May 2004, it appeared he might get a little help when the state legislature introduced a bill that would transfer much of the system's financial decision-making power from the school board to the superintendent. As of this writing, the legislation, which is backed by the governor, has made it through committee and is expected to be passed. It just may be that the schoolchildren and parents of Orleans Parish finally have found the right man for the job.

Keep your fingers crossed.

Jefferson Parish, though not experiencing as chaotic a season as Orleans, has similar problems with low scores and high drop-out rates. (The latest statistics show Orleans Parish with a 14 percent high school dropout rate and Jefferson with 16.7 percent.) Problems that people moved out of the city to escape 30 years ago have made their way to the suburbs, resulting in little difference between the two systems.

Of course it is possible to get a decent education in either parish. Both have a handful of schools where students do quite well even by national standards. These successful schools generally have no more money than those schools that fail. What they do have, practically without exception, is a large percentage of students from middle-class families, a dedicated and talented faculty and staff, and a high level of parental involvement. Anybody out there listening?

PRIVATE SCHOOLS

The following is an overview of area private schools which, in the form of Catholic schools, have been educating New Orleans children since long before the public school system was established and, for that matter, decades before the United States was established. Not surprisingly, Catholic schools make up the majority of today's private institutions. An elementary school education tends to run approximately $2,000 to $3,000 per year with high school in the $4,000 to $6,000 range. Almost all non-Catholic private schools in New Orleans cost more.

Elementary

St. Anthony of Padua
4601 Cleveland Avenue, New Orleans
(504) 488-4426
www.stanthonyofpadua.net
Established by a Spanish Dominican priest in 1915, *St. Ant-nee* has been educating New Orleans's elementary students for more than 80 years. Everybody in the city knows someone who either went to school there or whose brother got married at the church. Over the years, the school has received numerous honors, including the Exemplary School Award from the U.S. Dept. of Education, the National Distinguished Principal Award, and the Walt Disney Co. American Teacher Award. But what really makes St. Anthony stand out (besides its excellent technology program) is the school's multi-ethnic faculty and student body. New Orleans is still a segregated town in some respects, and St. Anthony, whose student population is approximately 50 percent Caucasian, 30 percent African American, and 20 percent Hispanic or Asian, is one of the few private elementary schools that gives children the opportunity to learn in a diverse and culturally enhanced environment. The school is located in Mid City near the end of Canal Street in a neighborhood reflective of the school's ethnicity. However, the school's approximately 359 students in preschool through eighth grade come from four civil parishes and

Moving to town and suburbs bound? Contact the Jefferson Parish School Board at (504) 349-7600 to find out your district school.

60 church parishes, some of which have schools of their own.

In lower elementary classes, the approach is Montessori, center-based, small-group learning. Upper elementary grades concentrate on the development of a solid foundation in core academic subjects as well as sharpening analytical and problem-solving skills. Middle school emphasis is placed on preparing for high school through advanced study including eighth-grade Latin and algebra classes for high school credit. Curriculum includes reading, English, math, computer, science, social studies, spelling, handwriting, and religion. Cultural enrichment programs and extracurricular activities feature band, choir, ballet, sports, fine arts, keyboard, foreign language, altar service, choir, student council, cheerleading, quiz bowl, and drama club.

Technology is the biggest feather in the school's thinking cap. With national averages of student/computer ratios at 13:1 (25:1 at the state level), St. Anthony's boasts an overall 4:1 student/computer ratio in the form of two state-of-the-art computer labs as well as computer learning centers in each classroom. Every student from preschool through eighth grade participates in an age-appropriate computer curriculum during a minimum of four class periods each week in third through eighth grade.

Average class size is 20 students, with the preschool through kindergarten programs supported by additional paraprofessional aids. The 38-member faculty includes Dominican nuns as well as lay teachers, several of whom hold master's degrees. The staff also includes a social worker and a speech therapist.

Trinity Episcopal School
1315 Jackson Avenue, New Orleans
(504) 525-8661
www.trinityno.com

For students at Trinity Episcopal School, the educational journey begins in "the big pink house," a colonnaded two-story Garden District mansion. It's easy to find—right through the gate, past the tree house and tire swing in the towering oak tree out front. In current youth vernacular, going to school at Trinity is pretty sweet. Approximately 400 children, in preschool through eighth grade, are taught by 70 impressively educated teachers, two-thirds of whom have master's or higher degrees and who have graduated from such schools as Dartmouth, Tufts, Radcliffe, NYU, and Tulane. (Even the security guard and receptionist have degrees.) To say the least, this level of faculty is rare in local elementary education.

A low student-teacher ratio is complemented by an advanced curriculum geared to above-average students.

Preschool and kindergarten classes, with 18 to 22 students, each have two full-time teachers and a third who rotates among four classes. Preschool meets for half days. Kindergarten dismisses at noon Monday, Wednesday, and Friday and 3:00 P.M. Tuesday and Thursday. Optional afternoon enrichment programs on short days cover music, art, and creative play.

With 20 to 23 students, first- through eighth-grade classes focus on language arts, math, social studies, science, and foreign language, balanced with the study of fine arts, computer, physical education, and religion. Students attend chapel daily. Whole language and phonics are used to teach reading in groups of five to seven students. Employing the highly acclaimed University of Chicago Everyday Mathematics curriculum, lower grade teachers devote an hour each day to math. The use of computers is incorporated into core curriculum rather than taught as a separate subject. Students use computers to learn reading, word processing, and desktop publishing programs in lower grades and multimedia and Internet authoring programs in upper grades. Those students in fifth through eighth grades study French or Spanish, plus a semester of Latin in both seventh and eighth grades. The school's outdoor education program culminates in the students' final year with an eight-day wilderness trip.

Trinity students typically score five percentage points higher on standardized tests than similar independent schools, and more than half of its seventh graders consistently qualify for the highly selective Duke Talent Search. The school's students routinely go on to the best local high schools and have even been accepted at such prestigious institutions as Exeter and the Anglo-American School in Moscow.

One doesn't have to have gone to Trinity to be smart enough to know there's no free lunch. In fact, Trinity is closer to the filet mignon end of the menu. With an annual price tag of more than $8,000 (higher than most other private high schools cost), Trinity is one of the most expensive schools in the city. Financial aid is available; however, no full-tuition grants are given. It's not easy to get in, either. The intensive admissions procedure includes testing, recommendations from previous teachers, and observation of prospective students either in their current classrooms or during a day trip to Trinity (this goes even for preschoolers). Trinity is a member of the Independent Schools Association of the Southwest.

Middle

Christian Brothers School
8 Friedichs Avenue, City Park
(504) 486-6770
cbs-no.org
Christian Brothers is unique in two ways: It is New Orleans's only private school for boys exclusively serving the middle grades (fifth through seventh), and it's the only school located in City Park, tucked amid the park's centuries-old oaks. The faculty consists of Catholic Christian Brothers as well as lay teachers whose approach is modeled after St. de La Salle, who conceived of education as "a fraternal relationship between the teacher and the student." The low student-teacher ratio allows educators to take a personal interest in each student, sharing "his interests, his worries, his hopes," according to a school brochure. "They are not so much schoolmasters instilling a set of teachings as older brothers who help him to become aware of what the Spirit is seeking within himself, what his own abilities are, and, little by little, how he may discover his true place in the world." And all in a school full of adolescent boys. God love 'em. Daily curriculum includes religion, English, math, reading and literature, spelling, social studies, science, Spanish, and physical education. Computer science is offered. All applicants must take an entrance exam.

Elementary through Secondary

Academy of the Sacred Heart
4521 St. Charles Avenue, New Orleans
(504) 891-1943
www.ashrosary.org
Sacred Heart is a Catholic college prep school for girls in preschool through 12th grade. Founded in 1887 by the Religious of the Sacred Heart, the school educates 820 students with a faculty of 125. The preschool program emphasizes development of a positive attitude toward learning as well as fundamental readiness skills. Preschoolers attend half days, kindergartners full days. Ballet, gymnastics, and piano are offered after school. In the lower school (grades one through four), a whole language approach is taken to reading. Students also study math, science, social studies, religion, music, art, foreign language, physical education, and computer

science. In the middle grades students continue with their core curriculum, adding a peer support program as well as such electives as publications, hand bells, quiz bowl, drama, film, furniture refinishing, clown ministry, community service, and stock market. High school students can enroll in honors classes as well as advanced placement biology. All Sacred Heart graduates generally attend college. In recent years they have been accepted at Baylor, Bryn Mawr, Cornell, Columbia, Johns Hopkins, and Stanford.

Parents who want their children to attend private school in New Orleans must plan ahead. Most private schools hold "Open House" for prospective students and parents between September and November (for the following year), with the application process following in January and February.

Ecole Classique
5236 Glendale Street, Metairie
(504) 887-3507
www.ecoleclassique.com
Founded in 1956, Ecole Classique is a private, coeducational elementary and secondary school with the purpose of preparing students to enter college. All the school's educational aims are directed toward that goal from the moment a child enters kindergarten. Ecole's Children's Center oversees preschoolers through kindergartners and is staffed by a director and 26 support personnel. Student teacher ratios range from 8:1 for 2-year-olds to 13:1 for kindergartners. Children are grouped together according to age or development level in interactive center-based classrooms.

In kindergarten through third grade, students are in self-contained programs with a single educator teaching all subjects. Grades four through six are com-

pletely departmentalized (students change classes) and staffed by degreed and certified teachers. Some students attend classes in the resource center, based on teacher recommendation, where the student-teacher ratio is 1.1 to 5.1. Seventh through 12th grades are also departmentalized, with courses offered on three levels: honors, middle, and academic. Students are required to take both the SAT and ACT prior to graduation.

Extracurricular activities include key club, national honor society, yearbook staff, and academic games. Athletic teams include football, volleyball, track, golf, basketball, cross-country, soccer, baseball, tennis, and swimming.

Isidore Newman School
1903 Jefferson Avenue, New Orleans
(504) 899-5641
www.newman.k12.la.us
When financier and philanthropist Isidore Newman founded the Isidore Newman Manual Training School in 1903, he envisioned a superior education for the children of New Orleanians as well as those of the Jewish Children's Home. He hoped to provide skilled, competent, and well-trained labor for the local workforce. In the next 100 years, this Uptown institution developed into one of the city's finest college prep schools. The population has grown almost tenfold from 125 to 1,140 students in prekindergarten through 12th grade. The original Jefferson building, where early grade levels meet, now opens onto an 11-acre campus of 14 buildings set against a backdrop of playgrounds, patios, greenspaces, and an athletic playing field. Curriculum is infused with technology in every classroon, part of a network of 450 computers schoolwide administered by six full-time computer teachers.

The school offers a challenging academic curriculum that emphasizes sequential development of courses in basic disciplines—English, math, science, foreign language, history, the arts, computer science, and physical education.

Advanced placement classes and electives include film history, architecture, and photo journalism. Foreign languages offered include French, Spanish, Latin, and Chinese. A hands-on approach means that a first grader may learn such principles as weight, length, and volume by making a "rice baby." By middle school, he masters budgets, proportions, and scale by designing a playground for classroom presentation. By the time the student reaches upper school, he is comfortable using a calculator to graph interest on his investment account.

More than 60 team sports are offered to 7th through 12th graders, and the school's debate team has won three national titles. The school's library boasts 47,000 volumes, and the media center offers additional technological resources such as tapes, slides, albums, cassettes, and CDs.

Most of Newman's graduates attend college, with 60 percent earning advanced degrees. Recent college choices of Newman graduates include Amherst, Boston University, Columbia, Cornell, Dartmouth, Georgetown, Harvard, Princeton, and Yale. The educational background of the school's faculty, who have an average 15.2 years of teaching experience, is equally impressive. They are graduates of Princeton, Art Institute of Chicago, William and Mary, Columbia, and Oxford.

The school's admissions process is tough and similar to that of Trinity (see above), with a price tag of more than $10,000 a year at the high school level. Financial aid is available.

Metairie Park Country Day School
300 Park Road, Metairie
(504) 837-5204
www.mpcds.com
Everyone knows that the most successful schools are generally the ones with the most parent involvement. At Country Day, folks took it a step further. This kindergarten-through-12th grade school, situated on 14 acres in a quiet, residential

Most Catholic schools offer tuition discounts for parents who regularly contribute a certain amount to the parish church. It generally costs the same, except that church contributions are tax deductible and tuition generally is not.

neighborhood of the Metairie suburb, was founded by a group of parents in 1929. Country Day is a nonsectarian, college prep day school with an enrollment of 725 boys and girls. One hundred percent of Country Day graduates pursue a college degree and are accepted by some of the nation's best colleges and universities each year. The average class size at Country Day is 12 to 15 students. Honors and advanced placement classes are offered in all disciplines. An emphasis is placed on fine arts at every grade level. The school is the New Orleans leader in Orff music education, and its jazz band has performed on tour in London and Paris. The technology program includes a campus-wide network that rivals any other school in the Southeast.

Country Day athletic teams and individual students have achieved a great deal of success, including three National Merit Finalists in one recent year as well as state track and javelin champions. With nearly 90 percent of middle school students and 75 percent of upper school kids playing, the school's teams have won several state championships and dozens of district titles.

Ursuline Academy
2635 State Street, New Orleans
(504) 861-9150
www.ursulineneworleans.org
Ursuline Academy was established in 1727 by the Ursuline nuns as the first school for girls in the United States. Holistic education is designed to educate the whole person—spiritually, intellectually, socially, and physically. Ursuline is a private, independent Catholic school with an 11.5-acre campus

EDUCATION

If you're moving to town with an eighth grader who will attend private school, you'll want to check out both elementary and high schools. While most private lower schools go through eighth grade, most high schools now begin there as well.

in Uptown New Orleans. The school museum displays documents from Presidents Jefferson and Madison as well as religious artifacts dating from the Spanish colonial period to the present day. The campus also includes the National Shrine of Our Lady of Prompt Succor, whose statue has been venerated by New Orleanians for more than 150 years. Many locals believe it was Our Lady of Prompt Succor who protected the city during the great fire of 1812 and the Battle of New Orleans in 1815.

Currently, the school educates 720 girls, toddlers through 12th grade, with an average class size of 20 students. Ninety-nine percent of graduates go on to college. The school has been recognized by the U.S. Dept. of Education as a National School of Excellence and is a member of the National Honor Society of Secondary Schools and the National Catholic Education Association. It has been recognized locally as a model school for technology.

Eligible high school students can enroll in honors, accelerated, or advanced-placement courses. An active fine arts program offers students diverse opportunities in visual arts, speech, and drama as well as both vocal and orchestral music programs. In 1993 and 1995, the high school choir traveled to Rome to share mass with and perform for Pope John Paul II.

Extracurricular activities and sports teams include French club, science club, newspaper, orchestra volleyball, basketball, softball, soccer, tennis, and track.

High Schools

Archbishop Blenk High School
17 Gretna Boulevard, Gretna
(504) 367-2626
www.blenkhs.org
Archbishop Blenk High School, located across the Mississippi River from New Orleans on the West Bank of Jefferson Parish, was founded in 1962 by the Marianite Sisters of Holy Cross. Today, this U.S. Dept. of Education National Blue Ribbon School of Excellence educates approximately 600 girls in 8th through 12th grade. The school offers general, college prep, honors, and advanced-placement courses as well as championship athletic programs and extracurricular activities. The student-teacher ratio is 17:1. The average ACT composite score for seniors is 21. Approximately 96 percent of them go on to college, with 30 to 45 percent receiving scholarships. Recent graduates were accepted at such schools as William Carey, Baylor, Boston University, George Washington, University of Texas, and Florida State and earned more than $2 million in scholarships.

A unique aspect of Blenk is the schoolday. Ahead of its time, the school more than 20 years ago began following a "flexible block" schedule. Much like a college schedule, this approach allows students to fit both classes and independent study into day schedules. The system is designed to teach students to manage their time wisely and to better prepare them for university life.

Brother Martin High School
4401 Elysian Fields Avenue, New Orleans
(504) 283-1561
www.brothermartin.com
Brother Martin is a private Catholic school for boys in 8th through 12th grade. The school has a lay and religious faculty and is under the direction of the Brothers of the Sacred Heart, who have educated children in New Orleans since 1869. The

school philosophy states: "The most important aspect of any Catholic education is the development of Christian values and the transmission of the Catholic heritage. We accept this task as the call of the Church and as the primary goal of our school apostolate." Students study basic subjects in either an honors or academic curriculum. Recent graduates have been accepted at Rice, USC, University of Virginia, and Yale. The school library has more than 23,000 books, 100 periodicals, and online access to public and university library collections and the Internet. Admission is based on "desire to attend," overall elementary school record, recommendations of elementary principal and teachers, and an interview with the applicant and his parents.

De La Salle High School
5300 St. Charles Avenue, New Orleans
(504) 895–5717
www.delasallenola.com
Founded in 1949, De La Salle is named for St. John Baptist De La Salle, who founded the Christian Brothers, the order that runs the school. The school is the only coeducational Catholic high school in New Orleans, serving 750 students in grades 8 through 12. De La Salle, a U.S. Dept. of Education National School of Excellence, offers a curriculum anchored by four-subject, 90-minute schedules each semester, incorporating math/science and language/social studies. Study levels include honors, college prep, basic, and a program for students with learning disabilities. All faculty members have degrees, and 60 percent hold advanced degrees. Student-teacher ratio is 18:1. The last five graduating classes earned a total $15 million in scholarships and grants and were accepted at Yale, USC, the Citadel, Baylor, Harvard, and Penn State, among other schools.

The school's symphonic band earned 63 Superior medals in solo and ensemble festival competition, and 26 band members received the All-American Scholar Award. *The Maroon Legend,* the school's

yearbook, was one of only four books to receive an All Louisiana rating. Extracurricular activities include academic games, art club, bowling, campus ministry, dance team, key club, drama club, and National Honor Society. The school offers 12 interscholastic athletic programs. A student must have a cumulative 2.0 average and no discipline or attendance problems to be considered for admission. The process also includes a personal interview and transcript review.

Holy Cross School
4950 Dauphine Street, New Orleans
(504) 942–3100
www.holycrosstigers.com
Established in 1879 as St. Isidore's College, Holy Cross (as it was later called) is the second oldest Holy Cross institution in America—beat out only by a place in South Bend, Indiana, called Notre Dame University. As has been the trend among Catholic high schools in recent years, Holy Cross has expanded to include a middle school. Sixty-four faculty members with degrees from Notre Dame, St. Edward's, Tulane, and Loyola Universities educate 850 students in 5th through 12th grades. Average middle school class size is 22; high school is 29. The school offers a broad curriculum that includes an honors program and comprehensive college prep courses. Recent graduates have attended such universities as Auburn, Emory, George Washington, and Vanderbilt.

In the fifth grade students begin learning computer skills such as programming and word processing in a technology lab equipped with 35 PCs. The library/media center houses 30,000 volumes and a computerized access system for magazine reference as well as computers reserved for student use. High school electives include accounting, anatomy, journalism, law studies, marketing, psychology, and instrumental music. The Holy Cross's band program has been part of the school since 1894. The band includes several performing groups and has helped a high percentage of students earn music scholarships to college since 1989. Admission to Holy Cross is based on transcripts, standardized test scores, conduct, and interview.

St. Augustine High School
2600 A.P. Tureaud Avenue, New Orleans
(504) 944-2424
www.purpleknights.com
St. Augustine, the only historically black, all-male Catholic high school in Louisiana, was founded in 1951 by the Society of St. Joseph, also known as the Josephites—a religious order dedicated to the service of African Americans. "St. Aug" has graduated more than 6,000 men who have gone on to hold both community and national leadership positions, such as Peace Corps deputy director, U.S. Navy commander, U.S. Attorney, Court of Appeals judge, news director, Orleans Parish Civil Sheriff, and Mayor of New Orleans. The school offers young men in 8th through 12th grade a mix of academics, athletics, and extracurricular activities to produce a well-rounded individual.

All students are required to take four years of math, English, religion, science, history, economics, computer science, foreign language, and business law. More than 95 percent of graduates go on to college, with 26 percent receiving scholarships. The school has educated six Presidential Scholars and nine National Merit Scholars. Students have studied at such schools as Rice, Tulane, Howard, Michigan State, and Xavier. St. Aug's band, the Marching 100, is nationally known for being "the best band in the land" and is the most-requested high school band in the city. They have performed in numerous Mardi Gras parades and at the Theatre for the Performing Arts—always to enthusiastic audiences. They also appeared in the movie *The Big Easy. Many* band members receive college scholarships.

St. Mary's Dominican High School
7701 Walmsley Avenue, New Orleans
(504) 865-9401
www.stmarysdominican.org

The tradition of Dominican education was born in New Orleans in 1860 when seven young Dominican sisters arrived from Dublin to educate daughters of Irish immigrants. Despite the Civil War the nuns within five months had established St. Mary's Dominican Academy, a "select school" for girls, founded for literary, scientific, religious, and charitable purposes. Today the Carrollton school continues its pursuit of academic excellence through a traditional yet innovative college prep curriculum. The U.S. Dept. of Education recognized Dominican as an Exemplary School in 1989 and as a National Blue Ribbon School in 1996. Curriculum includes a variety of electives as well as advanced placement classes in a number of subjects. The student-teacher ratio is 11:1. Nearly half the faculty hold a master's or doctorate degree.

An estimated 99 percent of students go on to four-year colleges including Carnegie-Mellon, Clemson, Columbia, Oxford, Georgetown, Harvard, and Yale. Admission is based on cumulative school records with special attention given to math, English, and reading grades as well as attendance, conduct, and standardized test scores.

Special Schools

St. Michael's Special School
1522 Chippewa Street, New Orleans
(504) 524-7285
The Archdiocesan Department of Special Education was founded in 1964 with St. Michael's Special School for Exceptional Children as its focal point. The school is designed to help students with significant difficulties in learning. The program employs a low student-teacher ratio, specialized techniques in ungraded levels, and an atmosphere of love, order, and relaxation. The elementary program serves children age 5 to 16 in an academic climate. The secondary, vocationally oriented level works with students age 16 to 21. Academics are balanced with job-

training skills to prepare young adults for the world of work. After age 21, students attend the Joy Center, a sheltered activity facility at which they follow the school schedule but also take part in work-related activities. They deliver balloon bouquets to hospitals, decorate for lunch-eons, recycle Carnival beads, create sea-sonal jewelry and T-shirts, and do limited contract work.

CHILD CARE

New Orleans is a very family-oriented town. Consequently, there are a number of family child care homes. These home-based caretakers are often women who after having a baby decide to care for children in their home rather than return to the office. Whether looking for a family child care home or a traditional day care center, experts suggest visiting prospective facilities during the day, unannounced, to get a feel for the atmosphere and care level. Ask yourself: Do the children seem happy? Are they clean? Is the staff-child ratio acceptable? What kind of food are they being fed? Is the facility bright and cheerful? Are there appropriate toys? Have safety concerns been dealt with? And, most important, would I feel comfortable leaving my child here?

Child Care Resources
1720 St. Charles Avenue, New Orleans
(504) 586-8509
www.agendaforchildren.org/pages/
resources.shtml
This resource and referral service is a pro-gram of Agenda for Children, a statewide nonprofit child advocacy agency. The service provides parents with information about child care options, including cen-ters, family child care homes, summer camps, nursery schools, and before/after-school programs. The service also coun-sels parents on how to evaluate and locate quality child care. The counselor discusses the kind of care the parent

wants, where and when it is needed, and any other requirements. The parent is then referred to at least three child care pro-grams from a computerized database along with a checklist of what to look for. Referrals are free of charge.

COLLEGES AND UNIVERSITIES

Ironically, for a town whose public school system is envied by no one save for resi-dents of Mississippi, the City that Educa-tion Forgot has a lot of colleges. Following is an overview of what degree-seekers will find in post-secondary New Orleans.

Delgado Community College
501 City Park Avenue, New Orleans
(504) 483-4400
www.dcc.edu
With its main campus located across the street from City Park, this community col-lege is named for Issac Delgado, a busi-nessman who left most of his estate to found a trade school for boys in 1909. Old Issac wouldn't recognize the place today. Delgado currently is a state-supported, comprehensive community college edu-cating more than 16,000 men and women at multiple locations throughout the New Orleans area. Delgado is the largest and oldest two-year college in the state and is widely recognized for its constantly expanding curriculum and involvement in community programs.

Increasingly, students planning to seek four-year degrees find themselves spend-ing their first two years at Delgado, where transferable credits cost just a little more than half of those at state universities. Along with core curriculum courses, Del-gado offers 50 associate degrees and 22 certificate programs in allied health and nursing, early childhood education, busi-ness, technology, and skilled labor. The school also offers a wide variety of non-credit classes, from auto mechanics to genealogy.

CLOSE-UP

New Orleans Center for Creative Arts

With the possible exceptions of Louis Armstrong and Mozart, great musicians are not born, they are made. And in this cradle of jazz, that creation takes place at the New Orleans Center for Creative Arts. Since 1974 high school students with talent in music, dance, theater, creative writing, or visual arts have learned the meaning of discipline and rigor in this artistic haven that has produced the likes of singer Harry Connick Jr. and Wynton Marsalis, the first jazz musician to win a Pulitzer Prize. A media arts program incorporating film, video, and audio curricula was added in 2001.

In a city whose public education system could politely be described as wanting, NOCCA is a real star. And so are its students. After making it through a tough audition process, students sign a contract acknowledging the academic and artistic requirements they will be expected to meet. Each year, more than 800 teenagers from 100 public and private schools around the New Orleans area take half a day of classes at their "regular" schools, then spend the other half of the day at NOCCA for practice, practice, practice. Ninety-eight percent of them go on to college, with more than 70 percent earning scholarships.

"NOCCA had a profound influence on me," Connick said. "The teachers put the tool belt on me, gave me a hammer and nails. They gave me everything I needed to build what I had to do." Of course, students haven't always crooned about every aspect of the place. Until recently, NOCCA was housed in an old elementary school where the music practice room was a piano in a closet. Drama students had no theater, and dancers were forced to "explore space" in a classroom built for third graders. In a financially strapped school system, a nonprofit advocacy group called Friends of NOCCA (now the NOCCA Institute) sponsored fund-raisers to pay for toe shoes, band equipment, and a visiting artist program. Each year more than 70 professional artists from

Loyola University New Orleans
6363 St. Charles Avenue, New Orleans
(504) 865-3240, (800) 4-LOYOLA
www.loyno.edu
Loyola University New Orleans, founded in 1912, is one of 28 Jesuit colleges in the United States and one of the largest Catholic universities in the South. Its rich history and Jesuit influence date back to the early 18th century, when the members of this religious order were among the city's first settlers. The school's 20-acre campus offers a mix of Tudor-Gothic and contemporary architecture, set off by broad expanses of greenspace and walkways, located on prestigious St. Charles Avenue in the university section of Uptown. The university's 5,500 students include 3,500 undergraduates from all 50 states, the District of Columbia, Puerto Rico, and 59 foreign countries. Approximately 1,000 students live on campus.

With a typical class size of 22 students, the university stresses the Jesuit around the country conducted master classes and extended residencies. But after 26 years of "making do," it was decided that enough was enough.

"When you're dealing with the arts, especially now with the proliferation of computers and all the other technology, it's important that you have a space that's designed for what you are trying to do," said Marsalis. He should know, being the only musician to win Grammys for both jazz and classical recordings in the same year.

Thanks to the State Legislature and the NOCCA Institute, in 2000 students left their dilapidated Uptown location to move a few miles downriver of the French Quarter. On the border of two old neighborhoods—Faubourg Marigny and Bywater—sits their new school, a $23 million, 125,000-square-foot facility featuring not one, but three theaters (a 300-seat proscenium theater, a fully equipped "black box" experimental theater, and a jazz performance hall). Two of the riverfront campus's five buildings are new; the other three are renovated and revitalized

warehouses, part of the old New Orleans Cotton Press, where Louisiana's favorite cash crop was baled and shipped in the 1830s. The facility features a state-of-the-art writing lab, set and prop building areas, three kilns for pottery classes, TV and recording studios, three major dance studios, and a movement studio.

To many involved with the school, there was no better way to start the new millennium. "In the new century, if we hope to be competitive in the best sense of the word, we have to spur the imagination of American youngsters," said former NOCCA instructor and jazz legend Ellis Marsalis, "and there's no better way to do that than through the arts."

And if NOCCA was able to produce Wynton Marsalis and Harry Connick Jr. with pianos in closets, what will it do with state-of-the-art technology? "I'll tell you what we'll do," said then-Friends of NOCCA executive director Kenneth Ferdinand. "We'll produce more Wynton Marsalises and more Branfords (Marsalis) and more Harry Connicks and . . ."

tradition of liberal arts education in all majors. The Loyola College of Music is nationally acclaimed for the quality of its outstanding performance and music education curricula.

The university is one of three in the country that pioneered programs incorporating environmental considerations into business education. The department of mathematics and computer science is technologically strong with a student-

computer ratio of 15:1. (The average for private universities is 45:1.)

Eighty-nine percent of full-time faculty hold a doctoral degree or a terminal degree in their field.

In recent years Loyola has consistently ranked among the top regional colleges and universities in the South and one of the top 60 in the country, according to *U.S. News & World Report*'s special issue "America's Best Colleges." The school was also named one of "America's 300 Best Buys" in Barron's "Best Buys in College Education." Barron's also ranked it in the top 7 percent of 1,500 colleges and universities.

Distinguished alumni include Col. John Bourgeois, former director of "The President's Own" Marine Band; Louisiana Supreme Court Judge Pascal Calogero; jazz pianist Ellis Marsalis; former mayor of New Orleans and former secretary of the U.S Dept. of Housing and Urban Development, Moon Landreiu; and Prime Minister of Belize, Manuel A. Esquivel.

Our Lady of Holy Cross College
4123 Woodland Drive, New Orleans
(504) 394-7744, (800) 259-7744
www.olhcc.edu

A small band of nuns, the Marianites of Holy Cross, arrived in New Orleans from LeMans, France, in 1853. An ambitious bunch of educators, they began establishing schools throughout the state. In order to supply teachers to the schools, the Holy Cross Normal College was established in 1916. Today, nestled on 15 tree-shaded acres, Our Lady of Holy Cross College is located in Algiers (a tiny portion of New Orleans on the West Bank of the Mississippi River). The coed liberal arts college educates 1,450 full- and part-time students. Along with education (still the school's strong suit), the school offers master's and bachelor's degree programs in business, humanities, and natural and social sciences. Nearly 74 percent of the 39 full-time and 84 part-time faculty hold terminal degrees. The student-faculty ratio is 22:1.

Tulane University
6823 St. Charles Avenue, New Orleans
(504) 865-5000
www2.tulane.edu

Right next door (and basically dwarfing) Loyola is Tulane University's 110-acre campus, marked by traditional Romanesque and Georgian academic halls dating from the turn of the last century and accented by grassy quadrangles and oak-lined walks. Tulane was established in 1884, when the public University of Louisiana was reorganized as a private school, and named in honor of benefactor Paul Tulane, a wealthy merchant who bequeathed $1 million to endow a university for the city where he had earned his fortune. Two years later, Josephine Louise Newcomb founded Newcomb College at Tulane as a memorial to her daughter, Harriet Sophie. As the first degree-granting women's college in the nation to be established as a coordinate division of a men's university, Newcomb became the model for other women's colleges, including Barnard and Radcliffe.

Tulane began with schools of liberal arts and sciences, law, medicine, and graduate studies. Over the years it added schools of architecture, business, social work, public health, and tropical medicine. The school recently earned the prestigious Carnegie Research I University designation, based on number of Ph.D.s and total dollar value of research grants. With a student-teacher ratio of 11:1, 98 percent of faculty hold the highest degrees in their fields.

With 7,862 undergraduate and 5,114 graduate students, Tulane is consistently ranked in the top quarter of major universities and among the top 25 for value by *U.S. News & World Report*. For freshmen the average SAT and ACT scores are 1250 to 1390 and 28 to 31, respectively.

Distinguished alumni include U.S. Rep. Robert L. Livingston Jr., chair of the House Appropriations Committee; former U.S. Ambassador to the Vatican and Congresswoman Lindy Claiborne Boggs; Philip L. Carroll, president of Shell Oil Co.; U.S. Rep. Newt Gingrich; Michael DeBakey, renowned cardiac surgeon who performed the first American heart transplant; Harold Rosen, inventor of the first synchronous satellite; and the late Howard K. Smith, a Rhodes Scholar and ABC News anchor.

The University of New Orleans
2000 Lakefront, New Orleans
(504) 280–6595, (800) 256–5–UNO
www.uno.edu
Established in 1958 as part of the Louisiana State University system to bring public-supported higher education to the state's largest urban community, the University of New Orleans sits on a 195-acre parklike campus along the shores of Lake Pontchartrain, as well as the 200-acre east campus, which houses the UNO Arena. UNO has fully accredited programs in business studies and nationally recognized programs in hotel, restaurant, and tourism administration as well as jazz studies under the leadership of jazz great Ellis Marsalis. The College of Engineering boasts one of only five naval architecture and marine engineering programs in the nation and the only one in the South; the college of education is the state's largest and one of Louisiana's top producers of certified teachers. Eighty percent of the school's 750 faculty members hold doctorates.

Nearly 70 percent of UNO's 17,000 students (including 13,000 undergraduates) from 48 states and 80 countries, receive some form of financial aid. Half the student body is over age 25. Minority students make up 30 percent of the student body. Most students live off campus, although the school does offer both coed dorms and married student housing. The UNO Children's Center is an early childhood education program for children ages 12 months to 5 years. Special student rates are available.

Xavier University
1 Drexel Drive, New Orleans
(504) 486–7411
www.xula.edu
Founded in 1915 by Katherine Drexel of the Sisters of the Blessed Sacrament (nuns dedicated to serving the educational needs of Native and African Americans), Xavier is the only historically black Catholic university in the United States. And that's the least of its distinctions. Under the direction of Dr. Norman Francis, who became the school's first African-American lay president in 1968, Xavier has grown into a science powerhouse. For example, 25 percent of the nation's estimated 6,500 African-American pharmacists were trained at Xavier. The school's pre-med graduates have an 80 percent acceptance rate at medical and dental schools, more than twice the national average. For the past decade, Xavier has sent more African Americans to medical school than any other college in the country (twice the number of students sent by second-place Howard University). Xavier's Campus Partners program, through which college students are matched with kids in sixth through eighth grade for the purposes of academic assistance, cultural awareness, and help with education and career planning, was adopted by President Clinton as a model for a national program.

The campus, with a mix of contemporary architecture and Gothic design, is located in the residential neighborhood of Mid City. Current enrollment is near 4,000 students, of whom about 3,143 are enrolled in the College of Arts and Sciences. Approximately 84.9 percent are African American. Xavier has 226 full-time faculty members and a student-teacher ratio of 14:1. More than a third of the faculty are African American, and 90 percent hold the highest degrees in their fields.

MEDIA 📺

A slow news day in New Orleans can seem as rare as a Moon Walk saxophonist without enough tips for a root beer and a dozen oysters on the half shell at the Acme Oyster House. In a city where political skirmishes are as predictably biting as the mosquitoes, the Big Easy always makes much ado about something. Our indefatigably quirky culture, a journalist's Valhalla if one ever existed, is more than enough to keep the local media—20 print publications, 10 TV stations, and nearly three dozen radio stations—hopping in double-four time. After all, it's not every day that a 90-year-old Ninth Ward barber mourns the closing of his childhood snowball stand.

Local publications reflect the diversity of its multiethnic readership, whether it's *La Prensa and Aqui!* for the Hispanic population or *Louisiana Weekly* and the *New Orleans Tribune,* which covers news of interest to the city's—and the nation's— 12th largest African-American community. Over the past quarter century, the city has watched the growth of weekly, biweekly, and monthly publications and the merger of its two daily newspapers into the *Times-Picayune,* one of the country's oldest.

The weekly *Gambit* can be counted on for pointed political commentary and essays, while the weekly *CityBusiness* covers local commerce. The Catholic *Clarion Herald* provides local and national news of interest to the city's Catholic-majority population, while the slick *New Orleans Magazine* weighs in each month with its urbane and humorous take on the local scene. *Prime* gives the city's older readers a monthly glimpse of life on the other side of 50.

NEWSPAPERS

Daily

The Times-Picayune
3800 Howard Avenue, New Orleans
(504) 826-3279
www.timespicayune.com
Like a growing number of other big cities, New Orleans is a single daily newspaper town. The *Times-Picayune,* since its merger with the *States-Item,* has stepped up to the plate with its editorials and investigative, political, environmental, and community news reporting. Delivered each morning by 6:00 A.M., the newspaper has a daily circulation of 254,000 and a Sunday circulation of 281,760. More important, the newspaper has begun to really walk the walk: Voted by *Time* magazine as among the most improved daily newspapers in the country, the *Times-Picayune* won its first two Pulitzer Prizes in 1997— one for Walt Handelsman's editorial cartoons, the other for a major environmental series on the world's oceans. Part of the Newhouse family's media empire of daily newspapers, magazines, and book publishing houses, the *Times-Picayune* has other numerous strong suits, including its entertainment tabloid "Lagniappe" (Friday), Food (Thursday), and Sports, as well as Travel, Book, and "TV Focus" sections (all Sunday). Community-specific *Picayune*

ℹ️ *Newcomers often fret when they hear about this region's hurricane season, which officially runs from June 1 to November 30. But don't worry—be happy. Local media are diligent to a fault when it comes to covering weather disturbances in the Gulf of Mexico that have the potential to develop into hurricanes. In fact, many radio and TV stations and the local newspaper typically make available free hurricane tracking maps.*

---

sections on Thursday and Sunday zero in on local neighborhood and school news. Monthly home-delivered subscriptions cost $11.00; annual subscriptions cost $132. Newsstand cost is 50 cents.

Weekly

Clarion Herald
1000 Howard Avenue, New Orleans
(504) 596-3035
www.clarionherald.org
Archbishop Cody founded this 75,000-circulation tabloid, published every other Wednesday and one of the first in the country to use offset printing for photography. The official newspaper of the eight parishes of the Archdiocese of New Orleans reaches an estimated 210,000 Catholics. The *Clarion Herald,* which takes strong editorial stands on a range of local and national social and political issues, has been selected by the Catholic Press Association as one of the top 10 Catholic newspapers in the country. Columns include editorials by New Orleans Archbishop Alfred C. Hughes, movie reviews, national and international news by the Catholic News Service, sports by Buddy Diliberto, history by Buddy Stall, as well as local youth, school, and church news. Subscriptions cost $15 a year for 26 issues.

Data News Weekly
3501 Napoleon Avenue, New Orleans
(504) 822-4433
This African American–owned and -operated free Saturday newspaper itself on being "a pipeline to the people," with its man-on-the-street interviews, and a "Spiritually Speaking" column, as well as national and local news coverage with a focus on entertainment, food, music, and sports. Established in 1966, this newsweekly has received awards for its monthly magazine–style, single-theme "Impact" edition, which focuses on topics ranging from health care and politics to college campuses and local business.

Looking for love or companionship in all the Big Easy places? Check out the weekly personals tucked in the back of Gambit Weekly *and the* Times-Picayune's *Friday "Lagniappe" section.*

Circulation is 20,000 three weeks of the month; 30,000 for the fourth-week "Impact" edition.

Gambit Weekly
3923 Bienville, New Orleans
(504) 486-5900
www.bestofneworleans.com
This free weekly with a 50,000 circulation is as much a part of the urban landscape as the coffeehouses, record stores, and bistros through which it's distributed each Monday. The city's most widely recognized alternative tabloid keeps readers tuned in to the local art, film, and food scenes, while its often insightful investigative political reporting can be counted on to point out the good, the bad, and the ugly of local politics.

Louisiana Weekly
2215 Pelopidas Street, New Orleans
(504) 282-3705
www.louisianaweekly.com
Coverage of business, health, lifestyle, religion, and entertainment is the hallmark of this broadsheet founded in 1925 by local African-American businesspersons. Distributed on Saturday by subscription and at newsstands, news racks, and many convenience and retail drug stores, the 66,000 paid-circulation weekly is the oldest African American–owned newspaper in southern Louisiana. Cost: 50 cents.

New Orleans CityBusiness
111 Veterans Boulevard, Metairie
(504) 834-9292
www.neworleanscitybusiness.com
Since 1980 this weekly local business-to-business publication has covered the bottom line, from minority-owned start-up

companies and emerging women entrepreneurs to the region's huge oil and gas
and tourism industries and the movers
and shakers who make it all happen. The
paper won awards for its breaking story
on the sales tax scandal that rocked City
Hall. The popular annual supplemental
"Book of Lists" features the top companies in a multitude of industries. This
12,000- to 13,000-circulation tabloid is
published on Monday and available
through newsstands and an estimated
300 vending machines throughout the
Central Business District, Uptown, and
Metairie. Cost is $1.50 per issue and
$69.00 a year for subscription.

Monthly, Bimonthly, and Quarterly

Arts Quarterly
Collins Diboll Circle #1, New Orleans
(504) 488-2631
Members of the New Orleans Museum of
Art receive this 15,000-circulation quarterly arts journal free of charge. Others
can pick up copies at the museum's front
desk or pay $10 a year to have four annual
issues—published January 1, April 1, July 1,
and October 1—delivered at home. Highlights in each issue of this award-winning
oversize tabloid, founded in 1978 and published by NOMA, include the museum's
programs and exhibits, upcoming lectures
and education films, music news, and a
calendar of events.

OffBeat
421 Frenchmen Street, New Orleans
(504) 944-4300
www.offbeat.com
Locals have been keeping plugged into
the city's blues, jazz, traditional, folk, alternative, and rock music scenes ever since
this monthly music newspaper opened its
doors in 1988. *OffBeat* rarely hits a sour
note with readers with its monthly nightclub and entertainment listings, as well as
its unique spin on local culture, food, art,

and film. An estimated 51,000 copies
(71,000 during the annual New Orleans
Jazz and Heritage Festival) are distributed
free of charge at newsstands and about
500 hotels, restaurants, music venues,
coffee shops, and other outlets.

Prime Quarterly
111 Veterans Boulevard, Metairie
(504) 832-3555
www.primequarterly.com
Since its founding in 1989, this free quarterly publication has targeted local active
readers age 55 and older with local and
national aging news and lifestyle features
on retirement, health, finance, food, leisure,
travel, and relationships, as well as profiles
on active older adults. An estimated
18,000 copies of the only mature-market
publication in the New Orleans area are
mailed at the first of the month each quarter. Prime is also distributed through retail
grocers, coffee shops, and other outlets.

St. Charles Avenue
111 Veterans Boulevard, New Orleans
(504) 832-3555
www.saintcharlesavenue.com
This upstart, upscale monthly news-
magazine targets the Uptown, Old
Metairie, and north shore country club set
"who have children in private schools and
who are making a positive contribution to
the community," says executive editor
Beverly Church. Regular columns in this
12,000- to 15,000-circulation publication,
which averages 48 pages, cover the
gamut of high society from weddings and
debutante Sweet Sixteen parties to fund-
raisers, who's-who profiles, gardening, and
nostalgia. Enjoying the finer things in life?
St. Charles Avenue is distributed at newsstands and more than 70 other locations.

MAGAZINES

Louisiana Life
111 Veterans Boulevard, Metairie
(504) 832-3555
www.louisianalife.com

This magazine was established 24 years ago and offers Dream State residents and visitors a quarterly read on travel, food, and cultural goings-on throughout Louisiana, with a special emphasis on what makes the state tick. Subscriptions to this award-winning, 40,000-circulation magazine cost $6.95 per year.

New Orleans City Life
111 Veterans Boulevard, Metairie
(504) 834–9292
www.neworleanscitybusiness.com/citylife

Finally, a slick urban zine that truly skates a cool business and lifestyle edge without tripping over the same dead weight that can often wind up filling the pages of periodicals of this genre. In fact, the stylish graphics and overall hip, insider vibe of this "sassier, sister publication to *New Orleans CityBusiness*" offers the closest encounter with bona fide cosmopolitanism kind this city has seen in quite a while. From keeping a finger on the pulse of the movers and shakers who are generating local business buzz to upscale travel destinations featured in New Orleans travel writer Patti Nickell's "Great Escapes" column, *City Life* is a smart read. Equally important, the magazine keeps its ear to the ground for those groove makers and risk takers who make New Orleans a dynamic and vibrant environment in which to live. Take an issue for a test drive—you'll find it handles the local terrain with finesse.

New Orleans Magazine
111 Veterans Boulevard, Metairie
(504) 832–3555
www.neworleansmagazine.com

Slick city magazines come and go, but this one has been a local staple for more than 36 years, thanks in part to its entertaining and informative coverage of local culture, politics, lifestyle, history, and consumer-related issues by a masthead of award-winning local writers such as Errol Laborde and Liz Scott Monaghan. "Table Talk" covers the local culinary scene, while occasional features rank and profile the

city's top lawyers, doctors, and up-and-coming New Orleanians to keep an eye on. This 40,000-circulation magazine is distributed during the fourth week of each month and includes a program guide for local Public Broadcasting Station WYES–TV, a calendar of events, hotel and restaurant listings, and a visitor map. Readers can subscribe for $16.95 per year. Some of the city's "select" hotels furnish copies in rooms.

RADIO

Radio in New Orleans got off to an inconspicuous but promising start in 1922 when the city's first station, WWL 870 AM, conducted its first broadcast from cramped quarters at the Loyola University campus. In 2002 the perennially popular radio station, which has long since moved to bigger and better digs, celebrated its 80th anniversary as one of the most successful stations in the city, due in part to its talk/news format and nationally popular talk show personality Rush Limbaugh.

Variety is the spice of life in New Orleans, and radio is certainly no exception, considering the city can count 5 Christian stations, 3 with a community-cultural format, 19 tailored to the rock-contemporary-oldies crowd, 4 with country and 7 talk/news formats, 2 in Spanish, and even a station devoted solely to gospel music, just to name a few.

As the 40th largest market in the United States out of 212 (New York City is the largest), locals watched—or, rather, heard—New Orleans radio expand dramatically in the 1980s and early 1990s with the addition of several stations such as the new frequency KMEZ 102.9 FM, with its oldies format, and KKND 106.7 FM, whose alternative format targets a young demographic tuned into Smash Mouth and REM.

Listeners looking to keep up with national and world events can tune in to CNN at WGSO 990 AM, while WWL's morning host Bob Delgiorno keeps fans ℹ️ *Stuck in commuter traffic but anxious to keep up with what's going on in the world? Tune to WWNO 89.9 FM for National Public Radio's morning and afternoon drive-time broadcasts of world news and in-depth features designed to keep you in the know while stuck in the slow lane.*

abreast of local news. Those who prefer a witty, contemporary edge during drive-times tune in to WKZN 105 FM's Bo Walker and Beth Harris 5:30 to 10:00 A.M., and C. J. Morgan on WQUE 93.3 FM.

WRNO 99.5 FM's John Walton and Steve Johnson, arguably one of the most popular duos in local radio history, also host one of the city's most popular call-in programs, best known for its irreverence and willingness to poke fun at the local establishment.

For a national industry in a cosmopolitan city, local radio earns high marks from listeners for keeping the airwaves full of local flavor and with firm ties to the community. An excellent example is WWOZ 90.7 FM's eclectic and attentive program roster, which reflects the city's multicultural roots and features everything from New Orleans brass band and traditional jazz music to contemporary funk and blues as well as interviews with up-and-coming local artists looking to break new ground.

Two of the most popular urban-contemporary stations are WYLD 98.5 FM and WQUE 93.3 FM. WWNO 89.9 FM wraps its morning-, noon-, and late-afternoon National Public Radio news programs snugly—but never smugly—around its classical music format.

New Orleans is worthy of a good listen.

CHRISTIAN

KKNO 750 AM
WVOG 600 AM
WSHO 800 AM

WLNO 1060 AM
WBSN 89.1 FM

NATIONAL PUBLIC RADIO/ CULTURAL/CLASSICAL

WWNO 89.9 FM
KTLN 90.5 FM

COMMUNITY

WWOZ 90.7 FM

CONTEMPORARY

WEZB 97.1 FM (Top-40 contemporary)
WYLD 98.5 FM (urban adult contemporary)
WLMG 101.9 FM (adult contemporary)
WKZN 105.3 FM (adult contemporary)
WKSY 106.1 (adult contemporary)
KSTE 104.1 FM (Top-40 contemporary)

COUNTRY

KLEB 1600 AM (Cajun)
KLRZ 100.3 FM (Cajun)
WNOE 101.1 FM
KCIL 107.5 FM

GOSPEL/CONTEMPORARY JAZZ/BLUES

KKNO 750 AM
WCKW 1010 AM
WYLD 940 AM
WBOK 1230 AM
WXXF 94.7 FM
KAGY 1519 AM
WXXM 94.9 FM

ROCK/RHYTHM/SOUL

WTUL 91.5 FM (progressive)
WCKW 92.3 FM (lite rock)
WQUE 93.3 FM (urban)
WTIX 94.3 FM (oldies)
WTKL 95.7 FM (oldies)
WRNO 99.5 FM (classic rock)
KMEZ 102.9 FM (oldies)
KNOU 104.5 FM (hip-hop)
WJSH 104.7 FM (oldies)
KBZE 105.9 FM (urban)
KKND 106.7 FM (modern rock)
KXOR 106.3 FM (rock hits)

SPANISH NEWS AND MUSIC

WFNO 830 AM
KGLA 1540 AM

SPECIAL

WRBH 88.3 FM (radio reading service)
WBYU 1510 AM (Disney radio)

TALK AND NEWS/SPORTS

WTIX 690 AM
WASO 730 AM
WWL 870 AM
WGSO 990 AM (business radio)
WSMB 1350 AM
WSLA 1560 AM (ESPN Sports Radio)
WODT 1280 AM (sports)

TELEVISION

On December 18, 1949, a lowly 5,000-watt RCA transmitter helped the city's first television station, WDSU-TV, send its first flickering broadcast into New Orleans homes from a tiny studio on the 14th floor of the Hibernia Bank Building. In 1999 the station celebrated its 50th anniversary. Old-timers can recall how cameras had to be pulled back into the hallway for wide shots of the studio and how even the best live programs and grainy kinescopes at the time left a lot of room for improvement.

And improve it did. A surge in the popularity of this powerful new medium in 1950s New Orleans was fueled by rapid advancements in broadcasting technology, bigger and better TV sets, the arrival of color, and new kids on the block such as WWL-TV and WVUE-TV. Before long people such as Terry Flettrich, the late Mel Levitt, and Wayne Mack, to name just a few of the city's earliest TV personalities, were household names—and faces.

Today eight economically healthy commercial TV stations—WWL-TV Channel 4 (CBS), WDSU-TV Channel 6 (NBC), WVUE-TV Channel 8 (Fox), WGNO-TV Channel 26 (ABC), WUPL-TV Channel 54 (UPN), WNOL-TV Channel 38 (Warner Bros.), WHNO-TV Channel 20 (independ-

Want to add some hot Latin and Brazilian rhythms while tooling around town during a Saturday shopfest? WWOZ 90.7 FM kicks out the Latin jam on Saturday mornings, followed by the cool samba groove of Brazil in the afternoons.

ent), and WPXL-TV Channel 49 (Pax)—enjoy a loyal viewership, while nonprofit Public Broadcasting Stations WYES-TV Channel 12 and WLAE-TV Channel 32 provide essential noncommercial and educational programs, often with a New Orleans slant.

Some of the popular local television personalities include Angela Hill and Jim Henderson, evening anchor and sportscaster, respectively, at WWL-TV and WVUE-TV weatherman Bob Breck.

Weekday morning newscasts start at 5:00 A.M. for WWL-TV, whose local program is one of the most successful morning shows in the country, and WDSU, which airs *The Today Show*. Evening news is broadcast at 5:00, 6:00, and 10:00 P.M. on all the major networks (plus 9:00 P.M. on WVUE-TV only).

Cable started in the late 1970s and has made dramatic inroads since that time in providing a wide variety of programming to meet almost any taste. A partnership between WWL-TV and Cox Cable provides Cox Cable Channel 15 viewers with repeat broadcasts every half hour, round the clock, of WWL's most recent news broadcast.

LOCAL STATIONS

WWL Channel 4 (CBS)
WDSU Channel 6 (NBC)
WVUE Channel 8 (Fox)
WYES Channel 12 (PBS)
WHNO-TV Channel 20 (Independent)
WGNO Channel 26 (ABC)
WLAE Channel 32 (PBS, educational)
WNOL Channel 38 (WB)
WPXL-TV Channel 49 (Pax)
WUPL Channel 54 (UPN)

WORSHIP

From that moment in 1602 when LaSalle planted a cross in the ground claiming this Louisiana territory for God and king, Catholicism has reigned supreme. Along with the more than 470,000 of the faithful who can be found attending Mass all across the metropolitan area every Sunday, Catholicism has been woven into the fabric of everyday life here. The city's most famous party, Carnival, finds its roots in the Mother Church. Mardi Gras, or Fat Tuesday, is the final day of fleshly revelry before the 40 penitent days of Lent begin on Ash Wednesday. Also, the seafood industry may owe much of its livelihood to hungry tourists, but don't discount the Catholics, who fill every seafood house on Friday during Lent—the traditional day of abstention from eating meat. And don't forget our football team, the New Orleans Saints, who were so named as a nod to the city's strong religious ties as well as the fact that the National Football League franchise was awarded to the Big Easy on All Saints' Day, another important holiday here.

Of course, this being New Orleans, the city has developed its own unique form of the faith.

Take St. Expedite. There are many stories to explain how New Orleanians developed the tradition of praying to this completely fictional character, so much so that there is an old mortuary chapel

exhibiting his statue. The best tale is told by historian Buddy Stall in his book *Buddy Stall's New Orleans*. Apparently, as Stall tells it, a group of local French nuns received a large shipment of religious items for their chapel from Italy. One of the boxes containing a statue was marked "*Espedito*"—"send off" in Italian. Stall writes, "Thinking this was a statue of a saint named Expedite—a French word—the statue and a small chapel were dedicated to St. Expedite."

For years afterward New Orleanians prayed to St. Expedite in that chapel. Holy candles with his likeness could be found in religious paraphernalia shops. Even after the mistake was uncovered, nobody really seemed to be bothered by St. Expedite's lack of authenticity. And in a city that takes care of its own, a few New Orleanians still display his likeness in their homes right next to their Mary candles and St. Jude prayer cards—if for no other reason than the fact that it makes them smile to know that they live in a place where people have the imagination to create their own "in" in Heaven.

MASS APPEAL

Until 1803 and the signing of the Louisiana Purchase, New Orleans was populated by French and Spanish colonists who (by royal decree) were Catholic, giving the Mother Church a giant head start on any other faith. Even voodoo, practiced by the city's early slaves, combined aspects of Catholicism—mostly in the form of iconography—with traditional African and West Indian rituals. Immigration in the 19th century brought mostly Irish and Italians who further bolstered Catholicism's stronghold. The early 1800s did see the arrival of a few Protestants, such as the Episcopals and Lutherans, and by the turn

Experience two of New Orleans's most dominant influences, jazz and Catholicism, during Our Lady of the Rosary's jazz Mass, most Sundays at 6:00 P.M. Holy Rosary, as locals call it, is one of the city's most beautiful old churches. It's located near City Park at 3368 Esplanade Avenue; (504) 488-1816.

of the 20th century, New Orleans's federation of religions had grown to include the Disciples of Christ, the Mormons, the city's first Jewish congregation, and the Greek Orthodox. (The city's only Greek Orthodox church, The Cathedral of the Holy Trinity, is known for its beautiful Byzantine-style iconography.) Tours of the Lakefront church, at 1200 Robert E. Lee Boulevard, are available by appointment. Call (504)282-0259. (Donations are accepted.)

In the 1900s the Big Easy diversified even more by welcoming the Southern Baptists, Quakers, Muslims, and Buddhists. Today, the Catholics, with nearly half a million members in the metropolitan area, still far outnumber any other denomination. The second largest group is the Baptists, who since their arrival in 1914 have seen their numbers grow to an estimated 54,000, due in part to the area's large African-American population.

Many local churches offer celebrations that are distinctly New Orleans. Christ Church Cathedral, established in 1805 as the first Protestant church in the Louisiana territory, offers a series of free Sunday afternoon musical concerts encompassing a wide variety of styles

Interested in attending a traditional Latin Mass? Visit St. Patrick's Catholic Church, 724 Camp Street in the Central Business District, Sundays at 9:30 A.M.

including baroque, classical, jazz, and contemporary, performed by local musicians. This Episcopal church is at 2919 St. Charles Avenue, Uptown. Call (504) 895-6602. Donations are welcome. Want to experience two of the city's biggest influences at once? Our Lady of the Rosary Catholic church, or Holy Rosary to locals, offers a jazz Mass most Sunday evenings at 6:00 P.M. One of the city's most beautiful old churches, Holy Rosary is located at 3368 Esplanade Avenue in the historic Esplanade Ridge District. Call (504) 488-1816.

For more information about local congregations, contact the Greater New Orleans Federation of Churches at (504) 488-8788 or check the Yellow Pages under "Churches." Also, check out "Religion News" every Saturday in the Times-Picayune newspaper's "Metro" section for the latest church happenings and service schedules.

Time for Church

Catholicism has played a large part not only in the spiritual lives of locals but also in the city's history. Here are a couple of churches worth seeing. Along with being beautiful monuments to God, they tell the stories of the people who passed through them.

St. Louis Cathedral
615 Pere Antoine Alley, New Orleans
(on Jackson Square)
(504) 525-9585
This Jackson Square landmark has been a French Quarter beacon since the original cathedral, designed by architect Don Gilberto Guillemard, was built in 1794. After a devastating fire destroyed most of the Vieux Carre, the church was reconstructed and enlarged with J.N.B. DePouilly flourishes and today is the oldest active cathedral in the United States and one of only 15 minor basilicas nationwide. It was the site of Pope John Paul II's clergy prayer service during his visit to New Orleans in 1987.

With its 16-foot-wide center aisle, huge chandeliers hanging over the pews, and flags of various countries, it's easy to understand why this awesome church is a favorite among local brides. The church's large altar mural, painted in 1872 by Alsatian artist Erasme Humbrecht, depicts Louis, the saint-king of France, announcing the Seventh Crusade, which he was to lead.

The colorful garden at the back of the church on Royal Street serves as a memorial to the Capuchin priest and devoted humanitarian Father Antonio de Sedella, who arrived here in 1779 and spent the next half-century serving the poorest citizens of this budding territory. Known locally as St. Anthony's Garden, this tranquil spot, ironically, was occasionally the site of bloody duels. If you visit, look for the statue of the Sacred Heart of Jesus and the marble monument commemorating the death of 30 French sailors who died in the city's 1857 yellow fever epidemic.

Free tours are held Monday through Saturday 9:00 A.M. to 5:00 P.M. and Sunday 1:30 to 5:00 P.M., unless there's a wedding scheduled. Donations are accepted.

St. Patrick's Church
724 Camp Street, New Orleans
(504) 525-4413
www.oldstpatricks.org
This Central Business District church, located a couple of blocks off Poydras Street on the Uptown side, tells another important chapter in local history, the early days of the 19th century. It was then that New Orleans began taking its first tentative steps outside of the city's original settlement (now the French Quarter). New American settlers who started arriving following the 1803 Louisiana Purchase began building what would be known as the American sector. Up went homes and businesses and a way of life very different from those of the original Creole inhabitants.

It's no coincidence that the church's construction in 1840 coincided with the growth of the city's Irish immigrant population, tired of squirming in the back pews of St. Louis Cathedral where God seemed to speak only French (and Latin, of course). It is understandable that the Hibernians, many of whom were lured here to build the growing city's transportation canal, wanted their own place of worship.

The impressive Gothic-style church features splendid murals including a depiction of St. Patrick baptizing the daughters of Ireland's King Laoghaire. The murals, painted in 1841 by French-born artist Leon Pomarede, were quite pricey, costing $1,000 each. And even the Creoles had to admit that they were good. A local French newspaper suggested that if Pomarede had been creating similar works for a European church, the event would have attracted daily crowds of onlookers. "The name 'Pomarede' would have been on every lip and everyone would have wished to know him," it read. Later, the Creole neighbors had ample time to study the artist's work when St. Patrick's became the city's main house of worship while St. Louis Cathedral was being rebuilt.

Various restoration projects were undertaken over the years, and today the church and its magnificent vaulted ceilings and arches are pristine reminders of one of the city's turning points—when the Irish built a house where God spoke English. Ironically, it is also now the only place in town where you can attend Mass in Latin. Call for schedule.

INDEX

ABOUT THE AUTHORS

BECKY RETZ

Becky Retz is a native New Orleanian whose other work includes writing about health, education, and entertainment, as well as a weekly automotive column in her staff position with the *Times-Picayune* newspaper. Her early career also included acting stints on stage and in television commercials, as well as stand-up comedy. Becky lives in New Orleans with her son, Chris, and canine pal, Curie.

JAMES GAFFNEY

Veteran travel journalist James Gaffney has been a book, magazine, and newspaper writer and editor since 1985. A cultural explorer at heart, he has traveled the world writing about diverse topics ranging from the aboriginals of Far North Queensland and Mayan burial caves in Honduras's storied Mosquito Jungle to the Byzantine legacy of modern-day Istanbul. Since 1989 he has served as national affairs editor for a syndicated news service covering international travel and aging issues. Television credits include co-writing the 13-episode series "Quest for Adventure" for the Travel Channel. he is the author of *Keys to Understanding Medicare,* published by Barron's, and *Day Trips from New Orleans,* published by The Globe Pequot Press, and co-author of *The National Geographic Traveler New Orleans,* published by The National Geographic Traveler. His award-winning travel photography has been exhibited at local galleries. Recent projects include writing the pilot for a TV documentary series on Congressional Medal of Honor recipients, *In the Company of Heroes.*

Fear and loathing on the lecture circuit—author Becky Retz is seen attending a talk and book signing by one of her favorite writers, Hunter S. Thompson.

While on recent assignment in Prague, James Gaffney, pictured here on the city's historic Charles Bridge, found himself on the other end of the camera.